SOLUTIONS MANUAL

FINANCIAL REPORTING & ANALYSIS

REVSINE · COLLINS · JOHNSON

Prentice Hall, Upper Saddle River, New Jersey 07458

Acquisitions editor: P.J. Boardman
Associate editor: Natacha St. Hill Moore
Senior editorial assistant: Jane Avery
Manufacturer: Victor Graphics, Inc.

Printed in the United States of America

10 9 8 7 6 5 4 3 2

ISBN 0-13-921966-8

Prentice-Hall International (UK) Limited, *London*
Prentice-Hall of Australia Pty. Limited, *Sydney*
Prentice-Hall Canada Inc., *Toronto*
Prentice-Hall Hispanoamericana, S.A., *Mexico*
Prentice-Hall of India Private Limited, *New Delhi*
Prentice-Hall of Japan, Inc., *Tokyo*
Simon & Schuster Asia Pte. Ltd., *Singapore*
Editora Prentice-Hall do Brasil, Ltda., *Rio de Janeiro*

CONTENTS

NOTE TO INSTRUCTORS

Much care and attention has gone into the preparation of this Solutions Manual. Despite these efforts, some minor errors may have escaped our notice. We would appreciate your apprising us of any errors you encounter. Please e-mail us at **rcj@kellogg.nwu.edu**. We will periodically be posting an errata listing on our Website. Please visit us at **www.prenhall.com/phlip/revsine**.

We welcome the opportunity to hear about your experiences in using <u>Financial Reporting & Analysis</u>.

Problems
P1-1. Demand for accounting information

Requirement 1:
a) **Existing shareholders** use financial accounting information as part of their ongoing investment decisions—should more shares of common or preferred stock be purchased, should some shares be sold, or should current holdings be maintained? Financial statements help investors assess the expected risk and return from owning a company's common and preferred stock. They are especially useful for investors who adopt a "fundamental analysis" approach.

Shareholders also use financial accounting information to decide how to vote on corporate matters like who should be elected to the board of directors, whether a particular management compensation plan should be approved, and if the company should merge with or acquire another company. Acting on behalf of shareholders, the Board of Directors hires and fires the company's top executives. Financial statement information helps shareholders and the Board assess the performance of company executives. Dismissals of top executives often occur following a period of deteriorating financial performance.

b) Financial statement information helps **potential (prospective) investors** identify stocks consistent with their preferences for risk, return, dividend yield, and liquidity. Here too, financial statements are especially useful for those investors that adopt a "fundamental approach."

c) **Financial analysts** demand accounting information because it is essential for their jobs. Buy-side and sell-side analysts provide a wide range of services ranging from producing summary reports and recommendations about companies and their securities to actively managing portfolios for investors that prefer to delegate buying and selling decisions to professionals. Analysts rely on information about the economy, individual industries, and particular companies when providing their services. As a group, analysts constitute probably the largest single source of demand for financial accounting information—without it, their jobs would be difficult, if not impossible, to do effectively.

d) **Managers** demand financial accounting information to help them carry out their responsibilities and because their compensation often depends on financial statement numbers like earnings per share, return on equity, return on capital employed, sales growth, and so on. Managers often use a competitor's financial statements to benchmark profit performance, cost structures, financial health, capabilities, and strategies.

e) **Current employees** demand financial accounting information to monitor payouts from profit-sharing plans and employee stock ownership plans (ESOPs). Employees also demand financial accounting information to gauge a company's long-term viability and the likelihood of continued employment, as well as payouts under company-sponsored pension and health-care programs. Unionized employees have other reasons to demand financial statements, and those are described in Requirement 2 which follows.

f) **Lenders** use financial accounting information to help determine the principal amount, interest rate, term, and collateral required on loans they make. Loan agreements often contain covenants that require a company to maintain minimum levels of various accounting ratios. Because these covenants contain accounting ratios, lenders demand financial accounting information to monitor the borrower's compliance with loan terms.

g) **Suppliers** demand financial accounting information about current and potential customers to determine whether to grant credit, and on what terms. The incentive to monitor a customer's financial condition and operating performance does not end after the initial credit decision. Suppliers monitor the financial condition of their customers to ensure that they are paid for the products, materials, and services they sell.

h) **Debt-rating agencies** help lenders and investors assess the default risk of debt securities offered for sale. Rating agencies need financial accounting information to evaluate the level and volatility of the company's expected future cash flows.

i) **Taxing authorities** (one type of government regulatory agency) use financial accounting information as a basis for establishing tax policies. Companies or industries that appear to be earning "excessive" profits may be targeted for special taxes or higher tax rates. Keep in mind, however, that taxing authorities in the United States and many other countries are allowed to set their own accounting rules. These rules, and not GAAP, determine a company's taxable income.

Other government agencies are often the customer. In this setting, financial information can serve to help resolve contractual disputes between the company and its customer (the agency) including claims that the company is earning excessive profits. Financial accounting information can also be used to determine if the company is financially strong enough to deliver the ordered goods and services.

Financial accounting information is also used in rate-making deliberations and rate monitoring of regulated monopolies such as public utilities.

Requirement 2:
Student responses will vary, but examples are shareholder activist groups (CalPERS), labor unions, and customers.

- Shareholder activist groups demand financial accounting information to help determine how well the company's current management team is doing, and whether the managers are being paid appropriately.

- Labor unions demand financial accounting information to help formulate or improve their bargaining positions with employer companies. Union negotiators may use financial statements showing sustained or improved profitability as evidence that employee wages and benefits should be increased.

P1-2. Incentives for voluntary disclosure

Requirement 1:
a) Companies compete with one another for financial capital in debt and equity markets. The want to obtain financing at the lowest possible cost. If investors are unsure about the "quality" of a company's debt and equity securities—the risks and returns of investment—they will demand a lower price (higher rate of return) than would otherwise be the case. Companies have incentives to voluntarily provide information that allows investors and lenders to assess the expected risk and return of each security. Failing to do so means lenders will charge a higher rate of interest, and stock investors will give the company less cash for its common or preferred stock.

b) Companies compete with one another for talented managers and employees. Information about a company's past financial performance, its current health, and its prospects is useful to current and potential employees who are interested in knowing about long-term employment opportunities, present and future salary and benefit levels, and advancement opportunities at the company. To attract the best talent, companies have incentives to provide financial information that allows prospective managers and employees to assess the risk and potential rewards of employment.

c) Companies and their managers also compete with one another in the "market for corporate control." Here companies make offers to buy or merge with other companies. Managers of companies that are the target of a *friendly* merger or tender offer—a deal they want done—have incentives to disclose information that raises the bid price. Examples include forecasts of increased sales and earnings growth. Managers of companies that are the target of *unfriendly* (hostile) offers—deals they don't want done—have incentives to disclose information that shows the company is best left in the hands of current management. Hostile bidders often put a different spin on the same financial information, arguing that it shows just how poorly current management has run the company.

Requirement 2:
- Competitive forces from within the industry (i.e., other firms in the industry are voluntarily disclosing certain information).

- Demands by financial analysts for expanded or increased disclosure by the firm.

- Demands by shareholder activist groups such as CalPERS.

- Demands by debt rating agencies such and Moody's and Standard and Poor's.

- Pressure from governmental regulatory agencies such as the Securities and Exchange Commission. Firms may believe that disclosing certain information voluntarily may prevent the Securities and Exchange Commission from mandating more detailed disclosures at a later date.

- Demands from institutional investors (e.g., mutual funds, pension funds, insurance companies, etc.) that hold the company's securities.

Requirement 3:
The following examples are press release items that could be disclosed voluntarily: forecasts of current quarter or annual earnings; forecasts of current quarter or annual sales; forecasts of earnings growth for the next 3 to 5 years; forecasts of sales growth for the next 3 to 5 years; capital expenditure plans or budgets; research and development plans or budgets; new product developments; patent applications and awards; changes in top management; details of corporate restructurings, spin-offs, reorganizations, plans to discontinue various divisions and/or lines-of-business; announcements of corporate acquisitions and/or divestitures; announcements of new debt and/or equity offerings; and announcements of short-term financing arrangements such as lines of credit. Other student responses are possible.

The advantage of these press releases is that the information is made available to external parties on a far more timely basis than if disclosure occurred in quarterly or annual financial statements.

P1-3. Costs of disclosure

Requirement 1:
a) These include costs to obtain, gather, collate, maintain, summarize, and communicate financial statement data to external users. Examples are the cost of computer hardware and software, fees paid to audit financial statement data, salaries and wages paid to corporate accounting staff in charge of the firm's financial accounting system, and costs to print and mail annual reports to shareholders.

b) These costs occur when competitors are able to use the information in ways detrimental to the company. Examples include highlighting highly profitable markets or geographical areas, technological innovations, new markets or product development plans, and pricing or advertising strategies.

c) These are costs to defend the company against actions brought by shareholder and creditor lawsuits. These suits claim that information about the company's operating performance and heath was misleading, false, or not disclosed in a timely manner. Examples include the direct costs paid to lawyers to defend against the suits, loss of reputation, the productive time lost by managers and employees as they prepare to defend themselves and the company against the suit.

d) Political costs arise when, for example, regulators and politicians use profit levels to argue that a company is earning excessive profits. Regulators and politicians advance their own interests by proposing taxes on the company or industry in an attempt to reduce the level of "excessive" profitability. These taxes represent a wealth transfer from the company's shareholders to other sectors of the economy. Managers of companies in politically sensitive industries sometimes adopt financial reporting practices that reduce the level of reported profitability to avoid potential political costs.

Requirement 2:
Student responses to this question may vary. One possible cost is when disclosure commits managers to a course of action that is not optimal for the company. For example, suppose a company discloses earnings and sales growth rate goals for a new product or market. If these projections become unreachable, managers may drop selling prices, offer "easy" credit terms, or overspend on advertising in an attempt to achieve the sales and earnings growth goals.

P1-4. Proxy statement disclosures

The financial analyst might use the information contained in proxy statements in the following ways:

1) To determine how many members of the board of directors are "outside" versus "inside" directors. Outside directors are people that are not also employees of the company. Knowing how many board members are outside directors tells the analyst something about board independence. Company executives are more accountable to an independent board, and the board itself is more effective at monitoring the performance and decisions of top managers.

2) Information about the background of each board member helps the analyst determine how knowledgeable and effective the board is likely to be in monitoring the decisions and strategies of management. Do board members have business experience, or are they celebrities and politicians who know little about the company and its industry?

3) Proxy statements report the share ownership of company executives. As their share ownership increases, managers' personal wealth becomes more closely tied to the success of the company. As a result, they are more like owners when it comes to strategic decisions and operating tactics. Managers with little (or no) stock in the company don't have the same incentives to make sound business decisions.

4) Proxy statements help analysts understand management compensation (salary, bonus, stock options, and other pay components), and how much of that compensation is performance-based or guaranteed (salary). If a large portion of managerial compensation is in the form of salary, managers have little incentive to work hard or create value for shareholders because pay doesn't depend on performance. On the other hand, if a large portion of compensation is in the form of bonuses or stock options, managers have stronger incentives to work hard and create value for shareholders because pay and performance are linked.

5) The proxy statement also describes any changes that year in executive compensation. Knowing how and why compensation has changed alerts analysts to possible changes in managerial decisions.

6) Other student responses are possible.

P1-5. Your position on the issues

1) Accounting is **not** an exact science. One reason this is the case is that many financial statement numbers are based on estimates of future conditions (e.g., future bad debts and warranty claims). Another reason is that there is no single accounting method that is best for all companies and situations. Thus, different companies use different methods to account for similar transactions (e.g., depreciation of property and the valuation of inventory).

2) While some managers may select accounting methods that produce the most accurate picture of a company's performance and condition, other managers may be strategic when they make financial reporting decisions. Consider the following examples:

- Managers who receive a bonus based on reported earnings or return on equity may make financial reporting decisions that accelerate revenue recognition and delay expense recognition in order to maximize the present value of their bonus payments.

- Managers who must adhere to limits on financial accounting ratios in debt covenants may make reporting decisions designed to avoid violation of these contracts.

- More generally, managers are likely to make financial reporting decisions that portray them in a good light.

The moral is that financial analysts should approach financial statements with some skepticism because management has tremendous influence over the reported numbers.

3) This is probably true. Financial accounting is a slave to many masters. Many different constituencies have a stake in financial statement—existing shareholders, prospective shareholders, financial analysts, managers, employees, lenders, suppliers, customers, unions, government agencies, shareholder activist groups, and politicians. The amount and type of information that each group demands is likely to be different. As a result, accounting standards in the United States reflect the outcome of a process where each constituency tries to advance its interests.

4) This is false. Even without mandatory disclosure rules by the FASB and SEC, companies have incentives to voluntarily disclose information that helps them obtain debt and equity financing at the lowest possible cost. Failure to do so results in higher costs of debt and equity capital.

5) This is true. If the information is value-relevant there is no obvious reason not to disclose except when doing so places the company at a competitive disadvantage.

6) The best response is that the statement is false because:

- Managers have incentives to develop and maintain a good relationship with financial analysts. Failing to disclose value-relevant information (good or bad) on a timely basis may damage this relationship.

- Under the U.S. securities laws, shareholders can sue managers for failing to disclose material financial information on a timely basis. To reduce potential legal liability under shareholder lawsuits, managers have incentives to disclose even bad news in a timely manner.

7) This is false. Fundamental analysis is the detailed study of financial accounting information for purposes of identifying over- and under-priced securities. Thus, financial statement information is essential to fundamental analysis.

8) This is false. Financial accounting information has value in an efficient market to the extent that it aids investors in the prediction of a firm's systematic risk (i.e., beta).

9) This may be true or false. If a company discloses so little information that investors and lenders cannot adequately assess the expected return and risks of its securities, then its cost of capital will be high. In this case, managers are doing shareholders a disservice by not disclosing more information to financial markets. If, on the other hand, increased disclosure harms the company's competitive advantage, managers have helped shareholders.

10) This is true. Other sources include: industry-wide reports; analyst reports about the firm or its industry; governmental reports about macroeconomic trends and conditions; and the financial statements of other firms in the industry.

P1-6. How managers and professional investors rate information

The following is a ranking by the various company performance measures based on a 1996 survey done by Ernst & Young.
(Source: Ernst & Young Center for Business Innovation)

	Importance Ranking	
	<u>Corporate Managers</u>	<u>Professional Investors</u>
Business Segment Results	4	7
Capital Expenditures	14	6
Cash Flow	2	2
Cost Control	5	4
Customer Satisfaction	3	11
Earnings	1	2
Market Growth	10	1
Market Share	13	5
Measures of Strategic Achievement	9	12
New Product Development	6	3
Product and Process Quality	7	13
R&D Productivity	12	9
Research & Development	11	8
Strategic Goals	8	10

Cases
C1-1. AST Research: Restating quarterly results

Let's agree that the two situations—AST and Chambers Development—have several things in common: (a) the dollar amounts involved were "large" in absolute amount and relative to reported sales and earnings; (b) the accounting change had no direct cash flow impact; and (c) both accounting changes involved the SEC.

So, why did investors penalize the share price at Chambers Development but not at AST? One explanation is that AST investors did penalize the share price, but they did so prior to the company's formal announcement of the accounting change on June 8, 1995. If investors correctly **anticipated** the AST accounting change and thought that it was bad news, the company's share price would have fallen **before** the June 8 announcement date.

In point of fact, AST's stock price had not declined during the weeks before its accounting change was announced. Other possible explanations include:

- Chambers Development was using a method that few other companies in the industry used. Investors may have mistakenly failed to adjust for the accounting difference when valuing the company.

- Concerns were raised about Chambers' ability to finance its continued expansion, and investors lowered the stock price to reflect less optimistic forecasts of growth.

- News articles at the time described Chambers' use of capitalization as an attempt to manage its reported earnings. The accounting change may have caused investors to question the quality of the firm's financial statements and management's commitment to shareholder value.

- The AST accounting change seems, on the surface, to have resulted from a simple difference of opinion regarding acquisition accounting rules. There is nothing to suggest lower growth opportunities or questionable behavior on the part of company managers.

Some instructors may want to use this case to explore notions of market efficiency.

How is the company doing today (May 1998)? AST Research reported operating losses in both 1995 and 1996. In April 1997, the company was acquired by Samsung Electronics for $5.40 per share.

C1-2. Henley Manufacturing Inc. (CW): Announcing sales and earnings goals

Requirement A:

1) Potential **costs** of announcing earnings and sales goals include: (a) possible shareholder lawsuits if goals are not met; (b) loss of reputation if goals are not met; (c) disclosure may convey information to competitors about the profitability of products or market territories; (d) managers may make dysfunctional decisions—ease credit terms, increase advertising expenditures, reduce R&D expenditures—near the end of the accounting period if it looks like the goals will not be met.

2) Potential **benefits** include: (a) investors can better understand the risks and rewards of stock ownership because they know more about the company's plans; (b) disclosure may improve relationships with lead investors and analysts, especially if it's part of an ongoing communications strategy and not just a one-time event; (c) investor and creditor uncertainty may be reduced, thus lowering the company's cost of debt and equity financing.

3) Should management disclose its earnings and sales goals? It depends on whether the benefits outweigh the costs, and on how confident management is that the goals can be achieved.

4) Easily achievable goals are likely to be disclosed without much reservation. Difficult goals are less likely to be disclosed because management may not want to risk disappointing investors if results fall short of target. One way to avoid disappointment is to make the goals less specific—for example, "sales are expected to increase by as much as 15%" or "sales are expected to be up substantially next year."

5) In all likelihood, the recommendation would change. Consideration would now have to be given to the fact that, as the planning horizon increases, it becomes more and more difficult to forecast accurately. For example, major changes in market-wide and industry-wide competitive conditions over the next two or three years could have a dramatic impact on whether or not the goals can be achieved.

Requirement B:

In this case, the nature of the goals is quite varied. In all likelihood, investors and financial analysts are going to be more interested in profitability and cash flow forecasts than in other financial aspects of the company. As a result, it seems reasonable to recommend disclosure of the following goals—subject to the cost and benefit considerations mentioned earlier: annual sales growth of 15%; annual earnings growth of 20%; a return on net tangible assets of 16%; a return on common equity of 20%; a minimum profit margin of 5%.

C1-3. Whirlpool Corporation (CW): Disclosing major customers

1) The SEC requires firms to alert financial statement readers about major customers that contribute 10% or more to annual sales. This information helps investors and analysts assess sales volatility and the potential impact on profitability of the loss of a major customer. The information is especially important for companies operating in industries where competition for customers is intense.

2) Financial analysts might use these disclosures in the following ways:

- To assess customer risk. The more revenue a company derives from a single customer or small group of customers, the greater the adverse impact on profitability if one or more of these customers is lost to a competitor or simply goes out of business.

- By studying a firm's major customers (i.e., the products they sell, expected future demand for such products, untapped markets in other countries or geographical areas), an analyst can determine the likelihood of increased future sales to that customer and, hence, profits to the company.

3) The primary reason Sears monitors Whirlpool's financial health is to ensure that Whirlpool can be relied upon as a supplier of durable goods (refrigerators, air conditioners, washers, and dryers, etc.) to be sold at Sears. The buyer (Sears) wants to make certain that goods will be produced, delivered, and available in Sears' stores when consumers want them.

Sears is likely to monitor the following aspects of Whirlpool's operations: inventory levels, expenditures for research and development, overall profitability (i.e., the income statement), financial health and the mix of debt and equity financing (i.e., the balance sheet), and cash flow generating ability (i.e., the cash flow statement).

Whirlpool probably provides Sears with financial information beyond that contained in the company's shareholder financial statements. This additional information might well include inventory levels for individual products, production lead times for various products, new products in development, features being considered for new products, and product improvements being considered.

4) Whirlpool monitors the financial health of Sears to ensure that Sears will be a continuing source of demand for its products in the future. Whirlpool is likely to monitor the following aspects of Sears' operations: inventory levels, sales, advertising expenditures, overall profitability, financial health and debt levels, and cash flow generating ability.

Sears may provide Whirlpool with information beyond that reported in its shareholder financial statements. For example, additional information could include days' sales in inventory for Whirlpool products, market surveys results about features consumers want to see in new products, and special promotions that will feature Whirlpool products.

C1-4. The gap in GAAP (CW)

1) Advantages of allowing managers some flexibility in the choice of financial reporting methods include:

- Accounting must serve as a slave to many masters. Stated differently, financial accounting information is used for many purposes including valuation, credit analysis, and contracting, and there is no reason to believe that a single set of financial reporting methods would serve each of these purposes equally well. By allowing managers some latitude in the choice of financial reporting methods, they can weigh the trade-offs implicit in making the firm's financial reporting data informative for each of these potential uses.

- If managers have some latitude in their choice of financial reporting methods, they can adapt the firm's financial reporting practices to changes in the firm's economic characteristics and/or environment over time. For example, a change in the rate of technological advance in a firm's industry may mean that new long-term assets should be written off at a faster rate than was previously the case. Assuming the firm had been using straight-line, a change to an accelerated depreciation method might be optimal, assuming that managers want the numbers reported in the income statement and balance sheet to present the most accurate picture of the firm's economic environment.

2) The current financial reporting system in the United States is really a combination of the two approaches.

On the one hand, firms have latitude in the selection of accounting methods to summarize various transactions and events. Examples include inventory valuation where firms may select from LIFO, FIFO, or weighted average; depreciation policy where they may select from straight-line or accelerated methods such as sum-of-the-years'-digits or declining-balance methods; and accounting for oil and gas exploration costs where firms may apply the full-cost or the successful-efforts method.

13

On the other hand, there are numerous cases where the FASB (or SEC) has mandated a single accounting method or treatment for various transactions or events. Examples include research and development expenditures which must be expensed in the year incurred; leases which must be capitalized and reported as liabilities on the balance sheet if certain criteria are met; accounting for foreign currency translation; and accounting for pension benefits and other postemployment benefits other than pensions.

3) The **advantages** of a single set of accounting methods include:

- Facilitates comparability of financial information across firms at a point in time and over time. This may be appealing to financial analysts because it potentially makes their work easier.

- Ease of verification by the auditing profession. Might lead to fewer shareholder lawsuits and suits against auditors for aggressive financial reporting decisions made by managers. External auditors may find the ease of verification beneficial to them.

The **disadvantages** of a single set of accounting methods include:

- Assumes that the financial performance and condition of all firms can adequately be captured by a single set of accounting methods. Implicitly assumes that firms are homogeneous. Moreover, that all firms have identical economic features and characteristics and face identical economic environments.

- Assumes that a single set of accounting methods serves all the potential uses of financial statement information (e.g., valuation, credit analysis, and contracting).

4) The **advantages** of allowing some flexibility in the choice of financial reporting methods include:

- Firms can tailor their choice of financial reporting methods to the specific aspects of their economic environment and circumstances. For example, depending on whether the prices of its input products is increasing or decreasing, FIFO may be a more realistic choice of inventory valuation method for income determination purposes when compared to LIFO (or vice versa). As another example, in industries where long-term aspects are subject to a rapid rate of technological advance and change, accelerated depreciation methods may be superior for income determination purposes when compared to straight-line (or vice versa).

The **disadvantages** of allowing some flexibility in the choice of financial reporting methods include:

- May detract from making comparisons across firms at a point in time and over time.

- Managers may use their discretion over reporting methods to distort the firm's performance. They might adopt financial reporting practices that create the appearance of profitability in an attempt to hide or cover up poor operating performance. They might also adopt financial reporting practices that accelerate the recognition of revenues and delay the recognition of expenses in an attempt to maximize the present value of payouts from bonus plans tied to reported profitability.

C1-5. IES Industries: Voting on a merger

Requirement 1:
As an employee-stockholder, two issues would seem to be of most concern: Which deal—the three-way merger or the takeover—will have the most favorable impact on share value and on my continued employment with the company? Because only 100 shares are owned, most of the employee's concerns are likely to focus on job issues.

- What plans do the merger partners have for reducing the workforce at the three companies? What jobs are likely to be affected, and what severance benefits will be offered? How will positions in the merged company be filled?

- Why didn't the IES share price increase following announcement of the three-way merger? Does this mean that there are no benefits to IES shareholders or employees?

- What will happen to my job if MidAmerican buys IES? The extra $500 I will receive from a MidAmerican buyout (100 shares × $5 per share) seems small in proportion to my employment risk.

IES financial statements are not likely to be of much help in answering these questions. The merger prospectus probably identifies key areas of duplication and, thus, may shed some light on where cost savings are likely to be found— but the prospectus will not say much about specific jobs. Nor will MidAmerican say much about possible job reductions at IES because to do so would lessen its chance of receiving a favorable vote from IES shareholders (some of whom are employees).

Requirement 2:
Most institutional investors own stocks for the long term. Historically, utility stocks are held because they have little risk (regulated monopoly) and

predictable dividends. This implies that the institutional investor will be concerned about long-term value (share price appreciation) and dividends in an increasingly competitive environment. Questions might include:

- How will the combined companies position themselves for an increasingly competitive energy environment? What specific plans does management have, are they realistic, and will the combined companies have the capabilities to execute those plans?

- How will the three-way merger affect dividends? Are the three companies generating excess operating cash now, what are they doing with that cash, and how will that change as competition increases?

- Why didn't the share price of IES increase when the three-way merger was announced? What is the market saying about merger benefits to IES shareholders?

- How would MidAmerican position itself for an increasingly competitive energy environment? Which strategy seems to hold the most promise?

- What will MidAmerican do about dividends? Is it generating excess operating cash now? If so, what's being done with the money?

- What specific cost reductions and redundancies have been identified? Are the estimated cost savings realistic? What is the timetable for capturing those cost reductions?

Company financial statements will prove to be of some help in answering these questions, particularly with respect to excess operating cash flows and future dividends. It will also be the case that an institutional investor with 5% ownership will be the target of proxy solicitation attempts by both sides—the merger partners and MidAmerican.

C1-6. Trans World Airlines' (TWA) (CW) Earnings announcement

For discussion purposes, here are some useful comparisons between 1992 and 1993.

	1993	1992
Net income (loss)	$623.8 Million	($317.7 Million)
Gain on debt retirement	1.08 Billion	0
"Pre-gain" loss[1]	(451.8 Million)	(317.7 Million)

[1] (623.8 - 1,080.0) = -456.2 is not equal to the -451.8 million TWA reports in the article. The difference probably reflects some additional credits that TWA does not separately break out in the article.

	1993	1992
Operating income before taxes, misc. credits, and charges	($281.3 Million)	($404.6 Million)
Revenue (decline of 13%)	3.16 Billion	3.63 Billion
Load factor	63.5%	64.7%

There are several things that you might tell your father, almost all of which are bad news.

The bad news:
- TWA was not really profitable in 1993. The one-time gain from debt retirement increased reported income by $1.08 billion, but had no impact on TWA's cash flow. Perhaps more importantly, this income is not a recurring source of sustainable earnings that TWA will earn year in and year out.

The gain arose because TWA exchanged debt whose face amount exceeded the equity shares that were issued. The transaction was part of TWA's bankruptcy process and its negotiations with creditors.

To see the effect of this transaction more clearly, consider the following journal entry:

DR Various bonds/LTD	$XXX	
Various notes	XXX	
CR Stockholders' equity		$XXX
Gain on retirement of debt		1.08 Billion

- TWA's "pre-gain" loss for 1993 was much larger than in 1992 (i.e., 451.8 million versus 317.7 million). This means that, before considering the debt retirement gain, TWA was even more unprofitable in 1993 than it was in 1992.

- Revenues fell by 13%, although part of the reason for the drop is that it appears that TWA reduced airline service in some markets.

- TWA's load factor (percentage of seats filled on a given flight) fell by over 1%.

The good news:
- The loss before taxes, misc. credits and charges decreased from $404.6 million in 1992 to $281.3 million in 1993. Of the numbers reported in the article, this item probably comes closest to a measure of TWA's ongoing (sustainable) income. The fact that it is negative is not good, but the fact that it improved from the prior year means there's hope. It would be important for an analyst to investigate the nature of the misc. credits and charges that were made in 1992 and 1993. This would enable the analyst to make a more meaningful comparison of the numbers TWA reports for loss before taxes, misc. credits and charges.

The bottom line:
"Not all earnings are created equal!" The large gain TWA reported in 1993 creates the illusion of profitability, when, in fact, the company is still operating at a loss.

What should you tell your father? It seems clear that based on current year results, your father should not expect TWA to begin paying dividends, restore any pilots' wage concessions, or to purchase any new aircraft.

C1-7. Landfil's accounting change

- "It's consistent with GAAP and fully disclosed." While true, this approach may not be comforting to analysts and investors concerned about whether capitalization makes the company look more profitable than it really is. Given the steep price decline at Chambers Development, analysts and investors will be scanning their radar screens for other capitalization companies, and they will surely discover Landfil's accounting. Unless capitalization can be strongly defended, the company's share price is likely to fall.

- "We capitalize, and we're proud of it!" The heart of this strategy is the notion that the company has already made the "correct" accounting decision—one that fairly portrays the profit performance and asset base of Landfil. If investors and analysts can be convinced, continued use of capitalization should not result in a share price decline...but can they be convinced?

- "We can afford to change." Even if capitalization is the "best" (most appropriate) accounting method for Landfil, it still might be advantageous to change. First, a change to immediate expensing will dispel any remaining skepticism on the part of investors and analysts. Second, it demonstrates management's confidence in the company's prospects and its ability to absorb the dollar impact of the change. But this strategy is risky—investors and analysts may incorrectly presume that capitalization was being used to "manage" reported earnings. This may cause them to question the company's other accounting methods and the quality of its financial reports.

C1-8. AstroText Company: Questions for the stockholders' meeting

Requirement 1:
An employee shareholder might be interested in the following sorts of questions:

- Why is AstroText willing to pay a $7 per share ($21 million) premium for TextTool?

- How will the premium be financed—operating cash flows, debt, stock, or the sale of TextTool assets?

- What impact will the premium and form of financing have on the value of my AstroText shares and stock options?

- How will the acquisition premium affect our ability to maintain or increase our new product R&D?

- How will my job be affected by the merger/acquisition?

The financial statements of both companies could shed light on some of these questions. For example, we could learn if cash balances and operating cash flows are sufficient to finance the transaction. We might also uncover significant non-operating assets that could be sold to raise cash. R&D spending patterns might suggest financing concerns or indicate redundancies that could be eliminated. SG&A cost comparisons might also identify redundancies that could be eliminated.

The employee-shareholder has two concerns: What will happen to the value of my shares and options, and will I still have a job? Neither question can be fully answered by analyzing company financial reports but the reports will shed some light on the questions.

Requirement 2:
The lead banker for AstroText will have two concerns: How does the proposed transaction affect the risk of loans currently placed with the company, and what are the long-term prospects for the combined companies? Specific questions might include:

- How will AstroText finance its acquisition of TextTool, and will the transaction increase the credit risk of loans we now have with AstroText?

- Does the acquisition require lender approval, and, if so, should we approve the transaction?

- How has TextTool been financing its activities? Who is the lead bank, and do we have an opportunity to increase our business as a result of the acquisition?

- What financing needs will the combined companies have going forward, and how can we help structure credit facilities consistent with those needs?

- Will either company be selling assets as part of the transactions? If so, which assets and for how much? How will the proceeds be used?

Company financial statements will prove to be quite helpful to the lender. TextTool's report will outline its current lending agreements and may even identify its lead banker. This will help identify the competition for future business. The combined cash flow statements will help the lender determine if credit risk has changed. This analysis, coupled with information from management about future plans, can also help uncover new business opportunities.

Exercises

E2-1. Determining accrual and cash basis revenue
(AICPA adapted)

Since the subscription begins with the first issue of 1999, no revenue can be recognized in 1998 on an accrual basis. No product or service has been exchanged between Gee Company and its customers. Therefore, no subscription revenue has been earned.

On a cash basis, Gee would recognize the full amount of cash received of $36,000 as revenue in 1998.

E2-2. Determining unearned subscription revenue
(AICPA adapted)

Since subscription revenue is not earned until the customer has received the video, unearned subscription revenue should be equal to the amount of subscriptions sold but not yet expired.

Sold in 1998/Expiring in 1999	$200,000
Sold in 1998/Expiring in 2000	140,000
Sold in 1997*/Expiring in 1999	125,000
Unearned subscription revenue	**$465,000**

*(The subscriptions sold in 1997 that did not expire in 1997 or in 1998 must be carried over to 1999 where they will be earned and recognized.)

E2-3. Converting from accrual to cash basis revenue
(AICPA adapted)

Under the cash basis of income determination, the company would not regard its accounts receivable as revenue. To find cash basis revenue, we have to subtract the increase in accounts receivable from the revenue figure:

Accrual basis revenue	$1,750,000
+ Beginning accounts receivable balance	375,000
- Ending accounts receivable balance	(505,000)
- Write-offs of accounts receivable	(20,000)
Cash basis revenue (cash collections on accounts receivable)	**$1,600,000**

Alternate Solution:

Accounts Receivable

Beginning balance	$375,000		
Sales on account	1,750,000		
(Accrual basis revenue)			
		$20,000	Accounts receivable write-off
		$1,600,000	Solve for: **Cash collections**
Ending balance	$505,000		

$375,000 + $1,750,000 - $20,000 - X = $505,000
X = $1,600,000

E2-4. Converting from accrual to cash basis revenue
(AICPA adapted)

To convert Tara's 1998 revenue from an accrual basis to a cash basis, we need to subtract the change in accounts receivable from the accrual basis revenue figure. Since no accounts were written off, we need not add back the allowance for doubtful accounts to the accounts receivable amounts.

Accrual basis revenue	$1,980,000
Beginning accounts receivable	415,000
Ending accounts receivable	(550,000)
Cash basis revenue	**$1,845,000**

Accounts Receivable

Beginning balance	$415,000		
Sales on account	1,980,000		
(Accrual basis revenue)			
		$1,845,000	Solve for: **Cash collections**
Ending balance	$550,000		

$550,000 = $415,000 + $1,980,000 - X
X = $1,845,000

E2-5. Converting from cash to accrual basis revenue
(AICPA adapted)

To change Dr. Tracey's revenue from cash basis to an accrual basis, we have to add the earned but uncollected accounts receivable and subtract the beginning accounts receivable collected in 1998 but earned in 1997. We also need to subtract fees collected in 1998 but not earned until 1999 (unearned fees on 12/31/98):

Cash basis revenue	$150,000
Beginning accounts receivable (12/31/97)	(20,000)
Ending accounts receivable (12/31/98)	35,000
Unearned fees on 12/31/98	(5,000)
Accrual basis revenue	**$160,000**

E2-6. Converting from cash to accrual basis revenue
(AICPA adapted)

To transform Marr's 1998 cash basis revenue to an accrual basis, we need to <u>subtract</u> beginning rents receivable collected in the current year (1998) but earned in the previous year (1997) and <u>add</u> ending rents receivable (adjusted for write-offs) representing revenue earned in the current year that will not be collected until the next year(1998).

Cash basis revenue	$2,210,000
Beginning rents receivable	(800,000)
Ending rents receivable	1,060,000
Add back: Uncollectible rents written off in 1998	30,000
Accrual basis revenue	**$2,500,000**

Below is an alternate solution to E2-6 using T-account analysis.

Rents Receivable			
Beginning rents receivable	$800,000		
Solve for:			
Rentals on account	**$2,500,000**		
(Accrual basis revenue)			
		$30,000	Uncollectible rents written off
		2,210,000	Rents collected (Cash basis revenue)
Ending Rents Receivable	$1,060,000		

$800,000 + X - $2,210,000 - $30,000 = $1,060,000
X = $2,500,000

E2-7. Converting from accrual to cash basis expense
(AICPA adapted)

The total amount of insurance premiums paid in 1998 is equal to the insurance expense for 1998 less the beginning balance in prepaid insurance.

1998 Insurance expense	$875,000
Plus: Increase in prepaid insurance ($245,000 - $210,000)	35,000
Insurance premiums paid in 1998	**$910,000**

Alternate Solution:

The amount of premiums paid can be determined from a T-account analysis of prepaid insurance.

Prepaid Insurance			
Beginning balance	$210,000		
Premiums paid	**X**	$875,000	Estimated amounts charged to insurance expense
Ending balance	$245,000		

$210,000 + X - $875,000 = $245,000
X = $875,000 + $245,000 - $210,000
X = $910,000

E2-8. Determining accrued liabilities
(AICPA adapted)

a) Store lease was paid at the beginning of each month so there is nothing to accrue for the 1998 lease.
b) Net sales for 1998 were $450,000. $450,000, less the $250,000 of sales exempt from additional rent, is $200,000: $200,000 × 6% = $12,000
c) The portion of the electric bill that should be accrued for the 1998 balance sheet is 12/16/98–12/31/98 or half of the 30-day period: $850/2 = $425
d) The portion of the telephone bill that should be part of the 1998 balance sheet is only the December service portion, $250.

Total accrued liabilities at December 31, 1998, are:

Accrued rent payable	$12,000
Accrued electrical bill obligation	+425
Accrued telephone bill obligation	+250
Total accrued liabilities	**$12,675**

E2-9. Determining gain (loss) from discontinued operations
(AICPA adapted)

The amount of gain/loss from discontinued operations to be reported on the income statement is computed as follows:

	Munn Corp. Net Gain/Loss from Discontinued Operations			
		1999		1998
Gain on sale of division		$450,000		
Division's loss		(320,000)		($250,000)
Net gain (loss) for division		130,000		(250,000)
Income tax (savings)	$130,000 × 30% =	(39,000)	($250,000) × 30% =	75,000
Net gain (loss) reported		$91,000		($175,000)

E2-10. Determining cumulative effect of accounting change
(AICPA adapted)

The net charge against income in the 1998 income statement would be the $500,000 of prepaid expense less the tax effect of the asset (40% of $500,000), $200,000. So the net charge against income due to the change in accounting principle is $300,000.

E2-11. Determining cumulative effect of accounting change
(AICPA adapted)

The cumulative effect of the accounting change on the 1998 income statement is the increase in inventory due to the change ($500,000) less the tax effect of this increase ($500,000 × 30% = $150,000). The cumulative effect is $350,000.

E2-12. Determining period vs. product costs

	Period	Product	
		Matched with sale as inventory cost	Matched with sale directly
Depreciation on office building	Y		
Insurance expense for factory building		Y	
Product liability insurance premium	Y		
Transportation charges for raw materials		Y	
Factory repairs and maintenance		Y	
Rent for inventory warehouse	Y		
Cost of raw materials		Y	
Factory wages		Y	
Salary to chief executive officer	Y		
Depreciation on factory		Y	
Bonus to factory workers		Y	
Salary to marketing staff	Y		
Administrative expenses	Y		
Bad debt expense			Y
Advertising expense	Y		
Research and development	Y		
Warranty expense			Y
Electricity of plant		Y	

The answers to most items are straightforward. However, there are some subjective calls. For instance, rent for inventory warehousing can be argued to be product costs and included as part of inventory costs. However, many companies expense this cost as a period expense because of materiality considerations.

Some of the product costs are expensed as part of the inventory costs (e.g., cost of raw materials, factory wages, and transportation and transit insurance for inventory purchased), while others are expensed directly in the period in which the products are sold (e.g., bad debt expense and warranty expense).

E2-13. Determining installment accounts receivable

The installment sales receivable balance is computed below.

	1998	1999
Installment sales	($300,000/.3) = **$1,000,000**	($440,000/.4) = **$1,100,000**
Percentage of gross profit recognized	0%	($300,000 - $120,000)/$300,000 = **60%**
Decrease in installment accounts receivable		60% × $1,000,000 = **$600,000**
Remaining 1998 installment sales receivable		$1,000,000 - $600,000 = **$400,000**
1999 Ending installment sales receivable balance	**$1,000,000**	$1,100,000 + 400,000 **$1,500,000**

E2-14. Determining realized gross profit on installment sales
(AICPA adapted)

The cash collections and realized gross profit amounts are computed below.

Installment sales	$280,000/.4 = **$700,000**
Cash collections	$700,000 - $400,000 = **$300,000**
Percentage of installment sales collected	$300,000/$700,000 = **42.86%**
Amount of gross profit to be recognized	42.86% × $280,000 = **$120,000**

E2-15. Determining effect of omitting year-end adjusting entries

OS = overstated
US = understated
NE = no effect

	Assets	Liabilities	Net Income
Supplies Inventory			
Direction of effect	OS	NE	OS
Dollar amount of effect	$9,000		$9,000
Expense not recorded = $12,000 - $3,000			
Unearned Revenue			
Direction of effect	NE	OS	US
Dollar amount of effect		$6,000	$6,000
Revenue not recorded = $6,000 from July 1, 1999 to December 31, 1999			
Gasoline Expense			
Direction of effect	NE	US	OS
Dollar amount of effect		$2,500	$2,500
Gasoline expense not recorded = $2,500			
Interest Expense			
Direction of effect	NE	US	OS
Dollar amount of effect		$4,500	$4,500
Interest expense for 9 months not accrued = $50,000 $\times$ 0.12 x 9/12 = $4,500			
Depreciation Expense			
Direction of effect	OS	NE	OS
Dollar amount of effect	$10,000		$10,000
Depreciation expense not recorded = $30,000/3 = $10,000			

Problems
P2-1. Journal entries and statement preparation

Requirement 1: Journal Entries

1/1/98: To record entry for cash contributed by owners
DR Cash $200,000
    CR Contributed capital $200,000

1/1/98: To record entry for rent paid in advance
DR Prepaid rent $24,000
    CR Cash $24,000

7/1/98: To record entry for purchase of office equipment
DR Equipment $100,000
    CR Cash $100,000

11/30/98: To record entry for salary paid to employees
DR Salaries expense $66,000
    CR Cash $66,000

12/31/98: To record entry for advance consulting fees received from Norbert
        Corp. which are unearned at year-end.
DR Cash $20,000
    CR Advances from customer $20,000

Requirement 2: Adjusting Entries

DR Rent expense $12,000
    CR Prepaid rent $12,000
Only one year's rent is expensed in the income statement for 1998. The balance
will be expensed in next year's income statement.

DR Accounts receivable $150,000
    CR Revenue from services rendered $150,000
The income was earned this year because Frances Corp. has completed its
obligation.

DR Depreciation expense $10,000
    CR Accumulated depreciation $10,000

Annual depreciation is $100,000/5 = $20,000. Since the equipment was used for only 6 months, the depreciation charge for this year is only $20,000/2 = $10,000.

DR Salaries expense $6,000
    CR Salaries payable $6,000
To accrue salaries expense for December 1998.

Requirement 3: Income statement

Frances Corporation Income Statement For Year Ended December 31, 1998		
Revenue from services rendered		$150,000
Less: Expenses		
Salaries	($72,000)	
Rent	(12,000)	
Depreciation	(10,000)	(94,000)
Net income		$56,000

Requirement 4: Balance sheet

Frances Corporation Balance Sheet December 31, 1998		
Assets		
Cash		$30,000
Accounts receivable		150,000
Prepaid rent		12,000
Equipment	$100,000	
Less: Accumulated depreciation	(10,000)	
Net equipment		90,000
Total assets		$282,000
Liabilities		
Salaries payable		$6,000
Advances from customers		20,000
Stockholders' Equity		
Capital stock		200,000
Retained earnings		56,000
Total liabilities and stockholders' equity		$282,000

P2-2. Converting accounting records from cash basis to accrual basis
(AICPA adapted)

Requirement 1:

Baron Flowers
Conversion from Cash basis to Accrual basis
December 31, 1998

	Cash basis Dr.	Cash basis Cr.	Adjustments Dr.	Adjustments Cr.	Accrual basis Dr.	Accrual basis Cr.
Cash	$25,600				$25,600	
Accounts receivable	16,200		$15,800 (1)		32,000	
Inventory	62,000		10,800 (4)		72,800	
Furniture and fixtures	118,200				118,200	
Land improvements	45,000				45,000	
Accumulated depreciation and amortization		$32,400		$14,250 (6)		$46,650
Accounts payable		17,000		13,500 (3)		30,500
Baron, drawings			61,000 (9)		61,000	
Baron, capital		124,600	2,000 (7)	2,600 (5)		125,200
Allowance for uncollectibles				3,800 (2)		3,800
Prepaid insurance			2,900 (5)		2,900	
Contingent liability				50,000 (8)		50,000
Utilities payable				1,500 (7)		1,500
Payroll taxes payable				1,600 (7)		1,600
Sales		653,000		15,800 (1)		668,800
Purchases	305,100		13,500 (3)		318,600	
Salaries	174,000			48,000 (9)	126,000	
Payroll taxes	12,400		500 (7)		12,900	
Insurance expense	8,700		2,600 (5)	2,900 (5)	8,400	
Rent expense	34,200				34,200	
Utilities expense	12,600		600 (7)		13,200	
Living expense	13,000			13,000 (9)		
Bad debt expense			3,800 (2)		3,800	
Amortization and land improvement			2,250 (6)		2,250	
Depreciation expense			12,000 (6)		12,000	
Loss pending litigation			50,000 (8)		50,000	
Cost of goods sold				10,800 (4)		10,800
	$827,000	$827,000	$177,750	$177,750	$938,850	$938,850

Journal entries:

1) **DR** Accounts receivable $15,800
   CR Sales $15,800
   To adjust accounts receivable to $32,000

2) **DR** Bad debt expense $3,800
   CR Allowance for uncollectibles $3,800
   To establish accounts receivable allowance

3) **DR** Purchases $13,500
   CR Accounts payable $13,500
   To adjust accounts payable to $30,500

31

4) **DR** Inventory $10,800
    CR Cost of goods sold $10,800
To adjust inventory to $72,800

5) **DR** Prepaid insurance[1] ($8,700 × 4/12) $2,900
    DR Insurance expense[2] 2,600
    CR Insurance expense $2,900
    CR Baron, capital   2,600

[1] To allocate $8,700 insurance between this year and next.
[2] To record the first 4 months of expense for 1998 ($7,800/12 mos. = $650/mo. × 4 = $2,600).

6) **DR** Amortization of land improvements $2,250
    DR Depreciation expense 12,000
    CR Accumulated depreciation and amortization $14,250
To record depreciation and amortization expense

7) **DR** Baron, capital $2,000
    DR Payroll taxes 500
    DR Utilities 600
    CR Utilities payable $1,500
    CR Payroll taxes payable   1,600
To record year-end accrual expenses and adjust expenses and capital at the beginning of the year

8) **DR** Loss from pending litigation $50,000
    CR Contingent liability $50,000
To accrue a contingent liability

9) **DR** Baron, drawings $61,000
    CR Salaries $48,000
    CR Living expenses   13,000
To adjust drawings account for personal expenses

Requirement 2:

To: Baron Flowers
Re: Reconciliation from cash to accrual basis

When acquiring information about a potential debtor, a lending bank will often request financial statements prepared under the accrual basis. In comparison with cash-basis financial statements, accrual-basis financial statements provide a bank with more relevant information about a potential debtor's ability to meet its obligations as they become due. The accrual basis of accounting attempts to match revenues with their related expenses. Thus, revenues and expenses are recognized when earned or incurred rather than when cash is received or paid. Financial statements based on the accrual basis of accounting provide a better indication of a company's performance. In addition, the accrual basis of accounting provides information that allows more reliable comparisons to be made from period to period.

Accrual-basis financial statements also provide information that would not be recognized under the cash basis, such as noncash expenses or accrued liabilities. The contingent liability arising from the pending litigation against Baron is relevant information that would not have been reflected in cash-basis financial statements. The accrual of this contingency alerts the bank to a future cash outflow that may affect your ability to meet principal or interest payments in the future.

P2-3. Adjusting entries and statement preparation

Requirement 1:

DR Advance to employee	$10,000	
CR Salaries expense		$10,000
DR Prepaid insurance	$6,000	
CR Insurance expense		$6,000
DR Bad debt expense	$24,500	
CR Allowance for doubtful accounts		$24,500
DR Dividends	$10,000	
CR Dividends payable		$10,000

Note: It is customary for companies to record dividends declared after the fiscal year end. This is typically the case with fourth quarter dividends, i.e., the fourth quarter dividends are declared in the 1st quarter of the following year.

Before preparing the financial statements, let us re-construct the trial balance after incorporating all the adjusting entries:

	Debit	Credit
Antonia Retailers, Inc.		
Adjusted Trial Balance		
As of December 31, 1999		
Cash	$42,000	
Accounts receivable	67,500	
Prepaid rent	15,000	
Inventory	100,000	
Equipment	60,000	
Building	90,000	
Allowance for doubtful accounts		$29,500
Accumulated depreciation—equipment		30,000
Accumulated depreciation—building		9,000
Advance from customers		25,000
Accounts payable		18,000
Salaries payable		4,000
Capital stock		70,000
Retained earnings 1/1/99		187,500
Sales revenue		350,000
Cost of goods sold	185,000	
Salaries expense	40,000	
Bad debt expense	35,000	
Rent expense	30,000	
Insurance expense	12,000	
Depreciation expense—building	5,000	
Depreciation expense—equipment	2,000	
Dividends	33,500	
Advance to employee	10,000	
Prepaid insurance	6,000	
Dividends payable		10,000
	$733,000	$733,000

Requirement 2:

Antonia Retailers, Inc. Income Statement For Year Ended December 31, 1999		
Sales revenue		$350,000
Less: Cost of goods sold		185,000
Gross margin		165,000
Less: Operating expenses		
Salaries expense	$40,000	
Bad debt expense	35,000	
Rent expense	30,000	
Insurance expense	12,000	
Depreciation expense—building	5,000	
Depreciation expense—equipment	2,000	
		124,000
Net income		$41,000

Requirement 3:

Antonia Retailers. Inc. Balance Sheet December 31, 1999		
Assets		
Cash		$42,000
Accounts receivable	$67,500	
Less: Allowance for doubtful accounts	(29,500)	
Net accounts receivable		38,000
Prepaid rent		15,000
Prepaid insurance		6,000
Advance to employees		10,000
Inventory		100,000
Equipment	60,000	
Less: Accumulated depreciation	(30,000)	
Net equipment		30,000
Building	90,000	
Less: Accumulated depreciation	(9,000)	
Net building		81,000
Total assets		$322,000

```
Liabilities
Advance from customers                                    $25,000
Accounts payable                                           18,000
Salaries payable                                            4,000
Dividends payable                                          10,000
   Total liabilities                                       57,000
Shareholders' equity
Common stock                                              70,000
Retained earnings                                        195,000
Total liabilities and stockholders' equity             $322,000
```

P2-4. Income measurement under alternative revenue recognition rules

Computation of net income under production basis

1998: 20,000 bu. × ($16.00 - $12.00) $80,000
1999: 4,000 bu. × ($13.00 - $16.00)[1]   -12,000
Total income $68,000

[1] Revision in expected revenue from liquidation sale.

Computation of net income under sales or delivery basis

1998: 16,000 bu. × ($16.00 - $12.00) $64,000
1999: 4,000 bu. × ($13.00 - $12.00)   4,000
Total income $68,000

Computation of net income under cash collection basis

1998: 14,000 bu. × ($16.00 - $12.00) $56,000
1999: 2,000 bu. × ($16.00 - $12.00)   = $8,000
          4,000 bu. × ($13.00 - $12.00)   =   4,000   12,000
Total income $68,000

Requirement 1: Income on a production basis

Agri Pro
Income Statement
Production Basis

Revenues:

Wheat sold: 10,000 bu. @ $2.40 =	$24,000
Wheat produced and in inventory: 5,000 bu. @ ($3.00 - $.10) [1] =	14,500
Total revenues	$38,500

Cost of goods produced:

Depreciation on equipment	$3,000	
Other production costs: 15,000 bu. @ $.50 =	7,500	(10,500)
Gross profit		28,000

Selling and delivery expense: 10,000 bu. @ $.10 =	$1,000	
Miscellaneous administrative expense	4,000	
Interest expense	5,000	(10,000)
Net income		$18,000

Alternate Solution
Production Basis

Sales revenue: 10,000 bu. @ $2.40 =	$24,000

Cost of goods sold:

Depreciation: 10,000 bu. @ $.20 [2] =	$2,000	
Other production costs: 10,000 bu. @ $.50 =	5,000	7,000
Gross profit		$17,000

Selling and delivery expense: 10,000 bu. @ $.10 =	1,000	
Miscellaneous administrative expense	4,000	
Interest expense	5,000	(10,000)
Operating income		7,000

Unrealized holding gain on inventory: 5,000 bu. × ($3.00 - $.10 - $.70) [3]		11,000
Net income		$18,000

[1] Revenues should be recorded at net realizable value which is equal to the current selling price of $3.00 per bushel less selling and delivery costs of $.10 per bushel.

[2] Depreciation per bushel produced $= \dfrac{\$3,000}{15,000} =$ $.20/bu

[3] Other production costs = .50/bu
  Production costs/bushel $.70/bu

Inventory carrying (book) value: 5,000 bu. @ $3.00 = $15,000
Accounts receivable: 10,000 bu. @ $2.40 × 1/4 = $6,000

Requirement 2: Income on sales basis

Agri Pro
Income Statement
Sales Basis

Revenues: 10,000 bu. @ $2.40 =		$24,000
Cost of goods sold:		
Depreciation on equipment: $\frac{\$3,000}{15,000} = \$.20/bu. \times 10,000 =$		2,000
Other production costs: 10,000 bu. @ $.50 =		5,000
Gross profit		$17,000
Selling and delivery expense: 10,000 bu. @ $.10 =	1,000	
Miscellaneous administrative expense	4,000	
Interest expense	5,000	(10,000)
Net income		$7,000

Inventory carrying (book) value: 5,000 bu. @ $.70 = $3,500
Accounts receivable: 10,000 bu. @ $2.40 × 1/4 = $6,000

Requirement 3: Cash collection basis

Agri Pro
Income Statement
Cash Collections Basis

Revenues:		
10,000 bu. @ $2.40 =		$24,000
Less:		
2,500 bu. sold but not collected on (2,500) @ $2.40 =		(6,000)
Revenue from bushels sold and collected		$18,000
Cost of goods sold and collected:		
Depreciation on equipment: $\frac{\$3,000}{15,000} = \$.20 \times 7,500$ bu. =		(1,500)
Other production costs: 7,500 bu. × $.50 =		(3,750)
Gross profit		$12,750
Selling and delivery expense: 10,000 bu. × $.10 =	$1,000	
Miscellaneous administrative expense	4,000	
Interest expense	5,000	(10,000)
Net income		$2,750

Inventory carrying (book) value: 5,000 bu. @ $.70 = $3,500
Accounts receivable: 10,000 bu. @ $2.40 × 1/4 = $6,000
  Less: Deferred gross profit: 10,000 x 1/4 × ($2.40 - $.70) =   (4,250)
Accounts receivable net of deferred gross profit $1,750

P2-6. Percentage-of-completion accounting
(AICPA adapted)

1. Contract billings in 1998 $47,000
   Accounts receivable: construction contracts (15,000)
   Cash collected $32,000

2. Construction in progress $50,000
   Less: Profit included in above (10,000)
   Costs incurred to date $40,000

   Let X = Total costs on project (in $000)
   $$\frac{\$40}{X}(\$800 - X) = \$10$$

   $32,000 - $40X = $10X
   50X = $32,000
   X = $640

3. Contract price $800,000
   Total estimated expenses (640,000)
   Estimated total income $160,000

P2-7. Long-term construction contract accounting

Completed Contract Method

<u>Year 1998</u>

DR Construction in progress $290,000
    CR Cash, payables, materials, etc. $290,000

DR Accounts receivable $260,000
    CR Billings on contract $260,000

DR Cash $240,000
    CR Accounts receivable $240,000

Since the project is incomplete, no revenue is recognized for the year 1998.

Balance Sheet Presentation at the End of 1998	
Completed Contract Method	
Current Assets:	
Construction in progress	$290,000
Less: Billings on contract	(260,000)
Unbilled costs of construction	$30,000
Accounts receivable	$20,000

Year 1999

DR Construction in progress	$150,000	
CR Cash, payables, materials, etc.		$150,000
DR Accounts receivable	$265,000	
CR Billings on contract		$265,000
DR Cash	$285,000	
CR Accounts receivable		$285,000
DR Billings on contract	$525,000	
CR Construction in progress		$440,000
CR Income on long-term construction contracts		85,000

Alternate entry:

DR Construction expense	$440,000	
DR Billings on contract	525,000	
CR Construction in progress		$440,000
CR Construction revenue		525,000

Percentage of Completion Method

Year 1998

DR Construction in progress	$290,000	
CR Cash, payables, materials, etc.		$290,000
DR Accounts receivable	$260,000	
CR Billings on contract		$260,000
DR Cash	$240,000	
CR Accounts receivable		$240,000

DR Construction in progress [1] $60,000
    CR Income on long-term
         construction contracts $60,000

Alternate entry:
DR Construction in progress [1] $ 60,000
DR Construction expense   290,000
    CR Construction revenue $350,000

[1] Contract price		$525,000
- Actual costs to date	($290,000)	
- Estimated costs to complete	($145,000)	
Total estimated costs of project		($435,000)
Estimated total gross margin		$90,000

Revenue earned during the period: ($290,000/$435,000) × $525,000 = $350,000

Gross margin earned during the period: ($290,000/$435,000) × $90,000 = $60,000

Balance Sheet Presentation at the End of 1998
Percentage of Completion Method

Current Assets:

Construction in progress	$350,000
Less: Billings on contract	(260,000)
Unbilled costs of construction	$90,000
Accounts receivable	$20,000

Year 1999
DR Construction in progress $150,000
    CR Cash, payables, materials, etc. $150,000

DR Accounts receivable $265,000
    CR Billings on contract $265,000

DR Cash $285,000
    CR Accounts receivable $285,000

DR Construction in progress $25,000
    CR Income on long-term
         construction contracts $25,000

Alternate Entry:

DR Construction in progress	$25,000	
DR Construction expense	150,000	
CR Construction revenue		$175,000

	Total	1998	1999
Construction revenue	$525,000	$350,000	$175,000
Construction expense	440,000	290,000	150,000
Gross margin	$85,000	$60,000	$25,000

P2-8. Long-term construction contract accounting

Completed Contract Method

Year 1998

DR Construction in progress	$290,000	
CR Cash, payables, materials, etc.		$290,000
DR Accounts receivable	$260,000	
CR Billings on contract		$260,000
DR Cash	$240,000	
CR Accounts receivable		$240,000
DR Anticipated loss on construction contract	$100,000	
CR Construction in progress		$100,000
($525,000 - $290,000 - $335,000)		

Balance Sheet Presentation at the End of 1998 Completed Contract Method	
Current Assets:	
Accounts receivable	$20,000
Current Liabilities:	
Billings on contract in excess of costs & recognized losses ($260,000 - $190,000)	$70,000

Year 1999

DR Construction in progress	$350,000	
CR Cash, payables, materials, etc.		$350,000
DR Accounts receivable	$265,000	
CR Billings on contract		$265,000
DR Cash	$285,000	
CR Accounts receivable		$285,000
DR Billings on contract	$525,000	
DR Loss on long-term construction contracts	15,000	
CR Construction in progress		$540,000

Alternate entry:

DR Construction expense	$540,000	
DR Billings on contract	525,000	
CR Construction in progress		$540,000
CR Construction revenue		525,000

Percentage of Completion Method

Year 1998

DR Construction in progress	$290,000	
CR Cash, payables, materials, etc.		$290,000
DR Accounts receivable	$260,000	
CR Billings on contract		$260,000
DR Cash	$240,000	
CR Accounts receivable		$240,000

DR Loss on construction project[1] $46,400
    CR Construction in progress $46,400

Alternate entry:

DR Cost of earned construction revenue $290,000
    CR Construction revenue $243,600
    CR Construction in progress   46,400

DR Anticipated loss on construction project $53,600
    CR Construction in progress $53,600
        ($100,000 - $46,400)

Percentage of Completion Method Income Statement Presentation for the Year 1998	
Construction revenue	$243,600
- Construction expense	(290,000)
- Anticipated loss on portion yet to be completed	(53,600)
Gross margin	**($100,000)**

Balance Sheet Presentation at the End of 1998 Percentage of Completion Method	
Current Assets:	
Accounts receivable	$20,000
Current Liabilities:	
Billings on contract in excess of costs & recognized profits [$260,000 - ($290,000 - $46,000 - $53,600)]	$70,000

---

[1]Contract price $525,000
 - Actual costs to date $290,000
 - Estimated cost to complete   335,000
Total estimated cost to complete   (625,000)
Estimated total loss   ($100,000)

    Percentage of the project completed: ($290,000/$625,000) × 100   =   46.4%
    Revenue earned during the period: 0.464 × $525,000   = $243,600
    Gross loss on the proportion completed during the period: 0.464 × $100,000   = $ 46,400

Year 1999

DR Construction in progress	$350,000	
CR Cash, payables, materials, etc.		$350,000
DR Accounts receivable	$265,000	
CR Billings on contract		$265,000
DR Cash	$285,000	
CR Accounts receivable		$285,000
DR Loss on long-term construction contracts[1]	$15,000	
CR Construction in progress		$15,000

Alternate entry:

DR Cost of earned construction revenue	$296,400	
CR Construction revenue		$281,400
CR Construction in progress		15,000
DR Billings on contract	$525,000	
CR Construction in progress		$525,000

P2-9. Determining income under installment sales method
(AICPA adapted)

Income before income taxes on installment sale contract:

Sales	$556,000
Cost of sales	417,000
Gross profit	139,000
Interest income (from following calculations)	27,360
Income before income taxes	$166,360

Calculations to determine interest income on installment sale contract:

Cash selling price	$556,000
Less: July 1, 1998, payment	100,000
	456,000
Interest rate	12%
Annual interest	$ 54,720
Interest July 1, 1998, to December 31, 1998 ($54,720 × 1/2)	$ 27,360

---

[1]Construction revenue ($525,000 - $243,600) $281,400
Less:
  Cost incurred on construction contract   ($296,400)
  Loss on long-term construction contract   ($15,000)

P2-10. Determining missing amounts on income statement

International Business Machines Corporation and Subsidiary Companies Consolidated Statement of Earnings For the Year Ended December 31, 19XX	
(Dollars in millions)	19XX
Revenue	
Sales	$33,755
Software	11,103
Maintenance	7,635
Services	7,352
Rentals and financing	4,678
	64,523
Costs	
Sales	19,698
Software	3,924
Maintenance	3,430
Services	6,051
Rentals and financing	1,966
	35,069
Gross profit	29,454
Operating expenses	
Selling, general, and administrative	19,526
Research, development, and engineering	6,522
Restructuring charges	11,645
	37,693
Operating income	(8,239)
Other income, principally interest	573
Interest expense	1,360
Earnings before income taxes	(9,026)
Provision for income taxes	(2,161)
Net earnings before changes in accounting principles	(6,865)
Effect of changes in accounting principles	1,900
Net earnings	($4,965)

Requirement 1:
Recasting the 19XX income statement. Following are the steps needed to calculate the unknowns. The correct income statement appears above.

46

a) Software revenue:
Total revenues are given ($64,523) as are its components, sales ($33,755), maintenance ($7,635), services ($7,352), and rentals and financing ($4,678). Software revenue is just the total of $64,523 minus the sum of all of the other components ($53,420), which leaves $11,103 for software revenue.

b) Costs of rentals and financing:
Total costs of sales and services are given ($35,069) as are its components, sales ($19,698), software ($3,924), maintenance ($3,430), and services ($6,051). Costs of rentals and financing is just the total of $35,069 minus the sum of all of the other components ($33,103), which leaves $1,966 for the costs of rentals and financing.

c) Gross profit is simply total revenues minus total costs of sales and services or:
$$\$64,523 - \$35,069 = \$29,454.$$

d) Selling, general, and administrative expenses:
Total operating expenses are given ($37,693) as are its components, research, development, and engineering ($6,522) and restructuring charges ($11,645). Selling, general, and administrative expenses is just the total operating expenses of $37,693 minus the sum of all of the two other components of operating expenses ($18,167). This leaves $19,526 for selling, general, and administrative expenses.

e) Operating income:
Operating income is calculated by simply subtracting total operating expenses of $37,693 from gross profit of $29,454. Doing so produces the unknown of -$8,239 for operating income.

f) Earnings before taxes:
Since operating income is known from (e), earnings before taxes is arrived at by just subtracting from it interest expense of $1,360 and adding other income, principally interest of $573. This yields earnings before taxes of -$9,026.

g) Net earnings before changes in accounting principles:
To arrive at this figure, the credit for income taxes of $2,161 (given) needs to be added to earnings before income taxes. This yields net earnings before changes in accounting principles of:
$$-\$9,026 + \$2,161 = -\$6,865.$$
or
$$-\$9,026 - (\$2,161) = -\$6,865.$$

h) Net earnings:
To obtain net earnings, just add the $1,900 effect of changes in accounting principles to net earnings before changes in accounting principles of -$6,865:
        -$6,865 + $1,900 = $4,965.

Requirement 2:
The gross profit rates (gross profit/sales) for the various revenue sources are:

Sales: ($33,755 - $19,698) / $33,755 = 41.6%
Software: ($11,103 - $3,924) / $11,103 = 64.7%
Maintenance: ($7,635 - $3,430) / $7,635 = 55.1%
Services: ($7,352 - $6,051) / $7,352 = 17.7%
Rentals and financing: ($4,678 - $1,966) / $4,678 = 58.0%

IBM generates the most gross profit from software sales, followed by rentals and financing, and maintenance. This ordering is not unsurprising because sales from these sources of revenue are not production oriented; thus they do not require much in the way of direct materials.

Requirement 3:
While it may not be immediately obvious to students, this item had no direct impact on IBM's 19XX cash flows. This item represents the accrual of various expenses that IBM expects to incur in the future. Examples include severance pay and health-care benefits for employees that left the firm as part of the restructuring, plant closing costs, etc.

A copy of IBM's 19XX cash flow statement is included as part of the solution so that students can see that the restructuring charge had no impact on its cash flows.

Requirement 4:
Agree: If you agree, you might suggest that R&D costs be carried on the balance sheet as an asset and be charged (i.e., expensed or written off) in future periods as the new products they produce are brought to market. The idea behind this approach is the matching principle. Moreover, since these expenditures are made to benefit future operations and sales, they should be charged to the future periods that benefit.

Disagree: If you disagree, you might argue that many R&D projects fail, while only a small number succeed. If all R&D costs were carried on the balance sheet as an asset, then assets would likely be overstated because some of the projects will fail, and the projected increase in future sales once expected because of them may never materialize. The idea behind this approach is that future benefits to current R&D expenditures are so uncertain, they cannot be reliably measured and reported on the balance sheet.

Requirement 5:

To answer this question, an assumption needs to be made about what revenues and expenses were received or paid in cash during the year. Justification for the inclusion or exclusion of various items rests on whether it is reasonable or not to assume they were paid or received in cash. One possible solution to this question is the following:

a) Assume all revenues were received in cash during the year (total $64,523).

b) Assume that all costs of sales and revenues were paid in cash during the year (total $35,069).

c) Assume that all selling, general, and administrative and research, development, and engineering costs were paid in cash during the year (total $26,048).

d) Assume that the restructuring charge is a non-cash expense.

e) Assume that all other income ($573) is received in cash during the year and that all interest expense ($1360) is paid in cash during the year.

f) Assume that taxes are paid in cash.

Estimated Cash Flow from Operations for 19XX (in millions):	
Inflows from revenues	$64,523
Outflows for expenses:	
Cost of sales	(35,069)
Cash gross profit	29,454
Other operating expenses (excluding restructuring charge)	(26,048)
Cash flows from primary operations	3,406
Other income (assumed all cash)	573
Interest expense (assumed paid in cash)	(1,360)
Estimated pre-tax cash flow	2,619
Less: Income taxes (assumed all cash)	(2,161)
Estimated after-tax cash flow from operations	$ 458

This estimate of $2,619 million cash flow from operations contrasts with the rather large net loss of ($4,965) that IBM reported in its income statement for the year. Thus, the two measures provide very different pictures about the results of IBM's operations. Of course, the difference can be traced to the rather large restructuring charge of $11,645 which reduced Income, but did not reduce cash flow.

International Business Machines Corporation and Subsidiary Companies
Consolidated Statement of Cash Flows
For the Year Ended December 31, 19XX

(Dollars in millions)

Cash Flow from Operating Activities

Net earnings	($4,965)
Adjustments to reconcile net earnings to cash provided from operating activities:	
Effect of changes in accounting principles	(1,900)
Effect of restructuring charges	8,312
Depreciation	4,793
Amortization of software	1,466
(gain) loss on disposition of investment assets	54
Other changes that provided (used) cash:	
Receivables	1,052
Inventories	704
Other assets	(3,396)
Accounts payable	(311)
Other liabilities	465
Net cash provided from operating activities	6,274

Cash Flow from Investing Activities

Payments for plant, rental machines, and other property	(4,751)
Proceeds from disposition of plant, rental machines, and other property	633
Investment in software	(1,752)
Purchases of marketable securities and other investments	(3,284)
Proceeds from marketable securities and other investments	3,276
Net cash used in investing activities	(5,878)

Continued on next page

Cash Flow from Financing Activities

Proceeds from new debt	10,045
Payments to settle debt	(10,735)
Short-term borrowing less than 90 days—net	4,199
Proceeds from (payments to) employee stock plan—net	(90)
Payments to purchase and retire capital stock	-
Cash dividends paid	(2,765)
Net cash provided from (used in) financing activities	654
Effects of exchange rate changes on cash and cash equivalents	(549)
Net change in cash and cash equivalents	501
Cash and cash equivalents at January 1	3,945
Cash and cash equivalents at December 31	$4,446
Supplemental data:	
Cash paid during the year for:	
Income taxes	$1,297
Interest	$3,132

P2-11. Determining income from continuing operations and gain (loss) from discontinued operations
(AICPA adapted)

Requirement 1:
The amounts to be reported for Income from continuing operations after taxes can be computed as follows.

	1999	1998
Loss from division	($640,000)	($500,000)
Gain on sale of division	900,000	
Income from division before taxes	260,000	(500,000)
Taxes (expense) benefit	(130,000)	250,000
Income (loss) from discontinued operations	$ 130,000	($250,000)
Income from continuing operations (as reported)	$1,250,000	$600,000
Adjustments for (income) loss from discontinued operations	(130,000)	250,000[1]
Net income from continuing operations	$1,120,000	$850,000

[1] Since division contributed an after-tax loss in 1998, this loss must be <u>added</u> to reported net income number of $600,000 to arrive at income from continuing operation in 1998 which *excludes* divisional results.

Requirement 2:

	1999	1998
Income (loss) from discontinued operations (net of tax)	$130,000	($250,000)

P2-12. Determining sustainable earnings

Requirement 1:

Income Statements for the Years Ended December 31		
	19X7	19X6
Operating income before taxes (as given)	$161,136	$160,945
Restructuring loss		(23,000)
Gain on sale (nonrecurring item)		33,694
Write-off of investment		(17,305)
Income from continuing operations before taxes	161,136	154,334
Less: Income tax expense (40%)	(64,454)	(61,734)
Income from continuing operations	96,682	92,600
Early extinguishment of debt (net of tax)		(6,660)
Cumulative effect of accounting change (net of tax)	9,756	
Net income	$106,438	$ 85,940

Requirement 2:

Income Statements for the Years Ended December 31		
	19X7	19X6
Operating income before taxes (as given)	$161,136	$160,945
Less: Effect of new accounting method		(890)
Sustainable income from continuing operations before taxes	161,136	160,055
Less: Income tax expense (40%)	64,454	64,022
Sustainable income from continuing operations	$ 96,682	$96,033

Growth rate in sustainable income = ($96,682/$96,033) - 1 = 0.676%
Forecasted sustainable earnings for 19X8 = $96,682 × 1.00676 = $97,335

P2-13. Preparing multiple-step income statement

Requirement 1:

Murphy Oil Corporation Income Statement For Year Ended December 31, 1995	
Sales	$1,646,053
Other operating revenues	45,189
Total operating revenue	1,691,242
Crude oil, products, and other expenses	1,274,780
Exploration expenses	65,755
Selling and general expenses	67,461
Depreciation, depletion, and amortization	225,924
Impairment of long-lived assets	198,988
Provision for reduction in work force	6,610
Interest expense	5,722
Total costs and expenses	1,845,240
Operating Income	(153,998)
Nonoperating revenue (interest income, etc.)	19,971
Income (loss) before income taxes	(134,027)
Income tax benefit	15,415
Net income (loss)	($118,612)

Provision for reduction in work force and impairment of long-lived assets are considered as infrequent, but usual, items that require separate disclosure.

Requirement 2:
First of all, let us reconstruct the income statement of Murphy Oil after excluding the revenues and expenses of the farm, timber, and real estate segment:

53

Murphy Oil Corporation
Income Statement
For Year Ended December 31, 1995

	(1) Total	(2) Deltic Farm & Timber	(1) - (2) Remainder
Sales	$1,646,053	$74,124	$1,571,929
Other operating revenues	45,189	4,618	40,571
Total operating revenue	1,691,242	78,742	1,612,500
Crude oil, products, and other expenses	1,274,780	56,697	1,218,083
Exploration expenses	65,755	-	65,755
Selling and general expenses	67,461	3,673	63,788
Depreciation, depletion, and amortization	225,924	4,053	221,871
Impairment of long-lived assets	198,988	-	198,988
Provision for reduction in work force	6,610	-	6,610
Interest expense	5,722	309	5,413
Total costs and expenses	1,845,240	64,732	1,780,508
Operating income	(153,998)	14,010	(168,008)
Nonoperating revenue (interest income, etc.)	19,971	691	19,280
Income (loss) before income taxes	(134,027)	14,701	(148,728)
Income tax benefit (expense)	15,415	(5,394)	20,809
Net income (loss)	($118,612)	$9,307	($127,919)

The income statement of Murphy Oil can be re-constructed by adding the net income of Deltic Farm & Timber as a single line item under discontinued operations to the income statement of the rest of the company.

Murphy Oil Corporation
Income Statement
For Year Ended December 31, 1995

Sales	$1,571,929
Other operating revenues	40,571
Total operating revenue	1,612,500
Less: Operating expenses	
Crude oil, products, and other expenses	1,218,083
Exploration expenses	65,755
Selling and general expenses	63,788
Depreciation, depletion, and amortization	221,871
Impairment of long-lived assets	198,988
Provision for reduction in work force	6,610
Interest expense	5,413
Total costs and expenses	(1,780,508)
Operating income	(168,008)
Nonoperating revenue (interest income, etc.)	19,280
Income (loss) before income taxes	(148,728)
Income tax benefit	20,809
Loss from continuing operations	(127,919)
Income from discontinued operations (Net of taxes)	
	9,307
Net income (loss)	($118,612)

Cases
C2-1. Smith's Farm: Alternate bases of income determination

Requirement 1:

	Production	Sales	Collection
Realized revenue	$108,000	$108,000	$72,000
Cost of goods sold	(21,000)	(21,000)	(14,000)
Gross profit	$87,000	$87,000	$58,000
Other expenses	(25,000)	(25,000)	(25,000)
Value added to unsold production [($3.60 - $.20) - $.50]	29,000	—	—
Net income	$91,000	$62,000	$33,000

Requirement 2:

	Production	Sales	Collection
Ending inventory ($3.60 - $.20) × 10,000 bu.	$ 34,000		
$.50 × 10,000 bu.		$5,000	$5,000
Accounts receivable	$36,000	$36,000	$36,000
Less: Deferred profit on sale ($3.60 - $.70) × 10,000 bu.	—	—	($29,000)
	$36,000	$36,000	$7,000

Requirement 3:

	Production	Sales
Realized revenues	$ 28,000	$28,000
Less: Carrying value of inventory at 12/31/98	(34,000)	(5,000)
Less: Delivery costs	(2,000)	(2,000)
Net income (loss)	($8,000)	$21,000

The $8,000 loss on the production basis is straightforward. It represents the speculative loss of $.80 per bushel (i.e., $3.40 - $2.60) [1] which occurred during 1999 times the 10,000 bushels that were held in inventory.

[1] $3.40 and $2.60 represent the net realizable values at the start of the year and the time of sale, respectively.

The $21,000 profit on the sales basis is more difficult to explain. It can't be attributable to 1999 farming profit since Smith didn't farm in 1999. Similarly, it can't be considered speculative profit since Smith incurred a 1999 <u>loss</u> of $8,000 on speculation. The $21,000 figure is really a mixture of $29,000 of unrecognized 1998 farming profit and the 1999 speculative loss of $8,000. Thus, the sales basis does not provide a clear delineation of profit by source.

To generalize beyond farm settings, just as Smith was in two "businesses" (farming and speculation) so too most manufacturing concerns—albeit reluctantly—are in two businesses (operations and holding assets). Continuing the analogy, just as the sales basis "mixes" the profit source in a farm setting, so too the sales basis "mixes" the profit source in manufacturing settings. Insofar as these two profit sources (operations and holding assets) entail different risks and patterns of repeatability, then the sales basis provides a precarious basis for risk evaluation and cash flow forecasting.

C2-2. Fuentes Corporation: Preparation of multiple-step income statement

	1995	1994
Net sales	$5,002	$4,350*
Costs and expenses		
Cost of goods sold	(3,927)	(3,288)
Selling, general and administrative	(350)	(328)
Special cost: Corporate restructuring	(91)	
Income from continuing operations before taxes	634	734
Income tax expense	(230)**	(265)
Income from continuing operations	404	469
Income from discontinued ops. (net of tax)	143	93
Loss on disposal of disc. ops. (net of tax)	(53)	
Cumulative effect of accounting principle change (net of tax)	56	
Net income	$550	$562
Pro-forma amounts:		
Income from continuing operations	$404	$477

*Note: $4,350 is computed as follows:

Reported 1994 total sales	$7,475
Reported 1994 sales of discontinued operations	(3,125)
	$4,350

      Cost of goods sold and S,G & A are computed analogously

**Note: ($230) is computed as follows:

Partial income tax expense (part 4 of problem)	($261)
Restructuring tax benefit	31
	($230)

57

C2-3. The Quaker Oats Company: Classification of gains vs. losses

This case shows students how the gray areas of GAAP can be used to alter reported year-to-year comparisons. Analysts who have a shallow understanding of financial reporting might be misled by the numbers which result from this latitude.

Requirements 1 and 2:

The 1991 divestiture appears to have been reported in conformity with a literal interpretation of GAAP. Fisher-Price represented a segment that was far removed from Quaker's primary food-related businesses. It, therefore, seems appropriate to treat the severance of this activity as a discontinued operation.

The issue becomes more murky with the 1995 transactions. In fiscal 1995, Quaker's profits were being eroded by the lackluster performance of the Snapple® brand acquisition in 1994. The company was widely criticized for the price it paid for Snapple® as well as for the drag on earnings it created.

The large gain that resulted from disposition of the pet food businesses was *not* treated as a discontinued operation. Instead, this gain ($1,000.2 million) comprised the bulk of the "above the line" gains on divestitures and restructuring of $1,094.3 reported on the 1995 income statement. (The other components of the $1,094.3 "above the line" figure are appropriate "above the line items".) If the $1,000.2 million pre-tax gains had been included "below the line" as a discontinued item, the 1994 versus 1995 pre-tax operating income comparison would have been dramatically altered:

	1995	1994	% change
Pre-tax operating income as reported	$1,359.9	$ 378.7	+359%
Pre-tax operating income adjusted to exclude $1,000.2 from 1995	359.7	378.7	-5%

Obviously, the "as reported" numbers convey a much more positive change and could—for the inattentive—offset some of the criticism Quaker was receiving.

Requirement 3:

As stated above, the reporting at the 1991 divestiture of Fisher-Price was non-controversial. The 1995 divestiture is another matter.

Quaker probably justified the "above the line" 1995 treatment by contending that it was in the food business in general. Some of its customers were two legged and some four legged. Thus, selling the pet food business simply eliminated a (four-legged) product line. Eliminating a product line, in general, doesn't qualify as a discontinued operation.

On the other hand, one could argue that the pet food division was fundamentally different. All of Quaker's other products were for human consumption. Targeting products for human consumption requires a different set of production, marketing, and quality standards. (Can your dog really tell you that she *slightly* prefers the taste of Brand X over Brand Y?)

The APB Opinion 30 rules do not use a materiality criterion. Even if they did, materiality cannot explain the 1991 versus 1995 differences.

Fisher-Price represented 10.9% (i.e., $601.0/$5,491.2) of Quaker's 1991 sales and was treated as a discontinued operation. By contrast, proportionate 1995 sales of the divested operations were much larger at 20.6% (i.e., $1,315.0/$6,365.2). While no separate sales figure for the pet foods operation was provided in the footnote, the bulk of the reported sales revenue is presumably from the pet foods divisions since the gains on sale of the other divisions represent only 14.6% of the total gain on divested operations.[1]

C2-4. Stewart & Stevenson Services Inc. (KR): Understanding accounts used for long-term construction contract accounting

Requirement 1:

Stewart and Stevenson Services, Inc.

Construction in Progress Inventory

Beginning balance	$80,623	$689,362	Projects completed **(plug number)**
Costs added	685,879		
Profit added	126,647		
Ending balance	$203,787		

Billings on Contract (Progress Payments)

		$55,258	Beginning balance
Projects completed (from above)	$689,362		
		798,182	Progress billings **(plug number)**
		$164,078	Ending balance

Accounts Receivable

Beginning balance	$121,030	$776,046	Cash collected **(plug number)**
Progress billings (from above)	798,182		
Ending balance	$143,166		

---

[1]Total gains on divested pet food operations are $513.0 + $487.2 = $1,000.2. Gains on other divested operations are $4.9 + $74.5 + $91.2 = $170.6. Thus, $170.6/($1,000.2 + $170.6) = 14.57%.

Requirement 2:
Gross margin under the completed contract method:

Beginning accrued profits + Gross margin under the percentage of completion method - Ending accrued profits

$$= \$9,857 + \$126,647 - \$13,117 = \$123,387$$

Sales revenue = $689,362 (See T-account for construction in progress)

Cost of goods sold = Sales revenue - Gross margin = $565,975

Gross margin rate = 17.9%

Requirement 3:
Effects on the accounting equation:

Decrease in construction in progress (Accrued profits recorded under percentage of completion method as per balance sheet)	=	$13,117
Decrease in deferred tax liability ($13,117 × .40)	=	$5,247
Decrease in retained earnings ($13,117 - $5,247)	=	$7,870

The effect on deferred tax liability can be skipped for now.

Requirement 4:
Stewart & Stevenson is one of a few long-term construction contract companies that explicitly provide information on the magnitude of accrued profits that is included in the inventory account. Consequently, in (2), we were able to precisely estimate their gross margin under the completed contract approach. This part considers a more realistic scenario when such information is not available.

Estimation of gross margin under the completed contract method:

Using the 1992 gross margin rate: $689,362 (sales) × 15.6% = $107,540

Using the 1991 gross margin rate: $689,362 (sales) × 17.0% = $117,192

Requirement 5:
Obviously, the answer to part (2) provides the most accurate estimate of the profits under the completed contract method. Of the two estimates provided in (4), the one obtained using the 1991 gross margin rate is closer to the gross margin in (2). This is consistent with the intuition that the higher gross margin contracts that were started in 1991 are being completed during 1992.

Requirement 6:
Estimation of gross margin under the cash collection basis:

Using the 1992 gross margin rate: $776,046 (collections) $\times$ 15.6% = $121,063

Using the 1991 gross margin rate: $776,046 (collections) $\times$ 17.0% = $131,928

C2-5. Baldwin Piano I (KR): Identifying "critical events" for revenue recognition

Requirement 1:

1. For the electronic contracting business, revenue is recognized *at the time of shipment to its customers*–Most Conservative.

2. For keyboard instruments and clocks shipped to its dealer network on a consignment basis, revenue is recognized *at the time the dealer sells the instrument to a third party*.

3. For Wurlitzer, revenue is recognized *at the time of shipment to its dealers*–Least Conservative.

One important caveat is that this ranking does not suggest that Baldwin's Wurlitzer division is prematurely booking its revenue. What it suggests is that, although Wurlitzer recognizes the revenue at the earliest time among all business segments, Baldwin believes that the critical event and measurability criteria have been met. However, it is imperative for a financial analyst to examine the validity of management's assumptions based on available information and further inquiry with management.

Since Baldwin does not wait until the sale to the ultimate customers, method (3) listed above appears to be the least conservative revenue recognition policy. Although the legal title to the goods is transferred to the dealers at the time of shipment, it appears that Baldwin is contingently liable to the dealers' bankers if the dealers default on their bank loan. While the dealers do not appear to have a direct right of return, they have a constructive right in case they default on the loans. Before revenue is recognized, GAAP requires that "the seller does not have significant obligations for future performance to directly bring about the resale of the product by the buyer." (See SFAS 48.) In the case of Wurlitzer, it appears that Baldwin may have some significant future obligations. Although we cannot categorically say that Baldwin has not met the critical event and measurability criteria for its Wurlitzer business, at the same time we also do not have enough information to conclude that it has. To form a clear judgment on this, we must obtain information on the historical loan default rates among its dealers as well as the ability of Wurlitzer to estimate the magnitude of cash outflows from such defaults. One possibility is that, since Wurlitzer was acquired only recently, Baldwin might have decided to continue its existing accounting practices for the moment. Epilogue: Beginning Sept. 1, 1995, Baldwin began shipping all Wurlitzer products under its consignment program. Under this program, sales are reported when the company receives payment from a dealer rather than, as Wurlitzer did, when the instruments were shipped to a dealer. The result was a reduction in the sales reported in the third quarter of 1995 compared to the same quarter in the previous year.

The choice between whether method (1) or method (2) is the most conservative policy is a judgment call. In terms of the critical event, the company recognizes revenue at the same time (sale to ultimate customers) for both the keyboard and electronic contracting segments. While the keyboards are sent to the dealers on a consignment basis, the company records revenue only after the dealers sell the keyboards to the end users.

The measurability criterion raises some interesting issues. The primary customers for the electronic contracting business appear to be original equipment manufacturers. Moreover, unlike the installment contract receivables, the receivables from the sale of printed circuit boards are likely to be short-term. Taken together, this suggests that Baldwin probably has a good estimate on the expected bad debts in the electronic contracting business.

However, the company probably faces greater uncertainties in estimating the bad debts on its installment contract receivables. The revenue from the installment contracts will be realized over a 3- to 5-year period. The important issue is whether Baldwin can reasonably estimate the ability of its customers to fulfill their contractual obligations over this period. Given that the duration of the installment contracts ranges from 3 to 5 years, Baldwin might be liable for substantial amounts of unanticipated bad debts long after the gross margin from the contracts are recognized. However, since Baldwin has been engaged in financing the installment purchases over 80 years, it is quite likely that it has built up a good statistical database for estimating expected bad debts. Overall, the revenue recognition on the installment contract transactions appears to be less conservative than the revenue recognition for the electronic contracting business.

One might wonder, by "selling" its installment contracts to an independent financial institution, whether Baldwin has reduced any of the uncertainties. Although Baldwin has "sold" its receivables, it appears to retain most of the bad debt or credit risk. Note that Baldwin is required to repurchase from the financial institution those installment receivables that are more than 120 days past due or accounts that are deemed uncollectible. This explains why Baldwin is retaining a substantial portion of the interest income. While the customers pay 12% to 16% on the installment contracts, Baldwin pays only 5% interest to the independent financial institution. Thus, a substantial portion of this "spread" (the difference between interest earned and interest paid) is compensation to Baldwin for bearing the credit risk. Consequently, the "sale" of the installment receivables is purely a borrowing vehicle by which Baldwin is financing its investment in receivables. See Chapter 7 problems on the specific accounting issues on sale or transfer of receivables.

Requirement 2:

Over the lives of the contracts, the difference between the original interest earned on the contracts and the interest paid to the independent financial institution is recognized as "Income on the sale of installment receivables." This suggests that Baldwin is using "passage of time" as the critical event for recording the net interest income. Note that the total income from the sale of installment contracts consists of gross margin and interest income. Baldwin recognizes the gross margin at the time of sale of inventory, whereas the interest income is recognized gradually over the life of the contracts. The critical event for recognizing interest revenue or interest expense is typically "passage of time" since interest represents the "time" value of money.

The measurability criterion appears to have been satisfied also. One may be concerned whether Baldwin will be able to collect all of the promised cash flows on the installment contracts. If Baldwin is very uncertain about its ability to estimate expected defaults, then it wouldn't have recognized the gross margin in the first place. In such a case, it would use the installment or cost recovery methods to record the gross margin and interest income.

C2-6. Baldwin Piano II (KR): Analysis and interpretation of income statement

To analyze the change in Baldwin's profitability, we compute the year-to-year change in several of the income statement items.

	1992 to 1993
Net sales	9.61%
Gross profit	0.81%
Income on the sale of installment	9.31%
Interest income on installment	43.87%
Other operating income, net	-7.16%
Operating expenses:	0.00%
Selling, general, and administrative	4.26%
Provision for doubtful accounts	-17.09%
Operating profit	-0.94%
Interest expense	-14.49%
Income from before income taxes	2.59%
Income taxes	0.73%
Income before cumulative effects of changes in accounting principles	3.86%
Cumulative effect of changes in postretirement and postemployment	NA
Net income	-23.16%

Although Baldwin's net sales increased by 9.6%, its net income decreased by about 23%. One of the main reasons for this decline is due to the cumulative effect of adopting the new accounting standard for postretirement benefits. However, even earnings before income taxes and change in accounting principles increased by only about 2.6%.

Several factors have contributed to the less than proportionate increase in profits.

1. It is straightforward to show that the gross margin rate has decreased from 27.7% to 25.4%. Given the 1993 net sales of $120,657,455, this drop translates into more than $2.6 million of lower operating profits. The decrease in GM rate, if it is not transitory, is likely to severely impact the future performance of Baldwin.

2. Other operating income (net) has decreased by 7.2% from 1992 to 1993. However, the case identifies two nonrecurring items that are included in the 1993 "other operating income, net." We first eliminate these two nonrecurring items as follows:

64

Other operating income, net	$ 3,530,761
- Eliminate gain on insurance settlement	(1,412,000)
+ Eliminate expenses relating to peridot	1,105,000
Revised operating income, net	3,223,761
Additional decrease in other income	($307,000)

The elimination of the nonrecurring items further magnifies the drop in other operating income. To understand the reason for this decrease, let us focus on the main component of other operating income. From **Baldwin Piano I**, it seems that the display fees paid by the dealers on the consigned inventory comprise the majority of other operating income. Consequently, the decline in this component of income is likely due to the decrease in the level of consigned inventory. Although we cannot be certain about this, the evidence is consistent with this possibility. As provided in the case, the level of finished goods inventory has decreased by more than 8%. This decrease may be an indication of reduced demand for consigned inventory from the dealers, and consequently, has resulted in lower display fees during 1993. This is, once again, likely to impact future profitability.

However, the following positive "factors" have had a mitigating effect on the income statement.

1. SG&A expenses increased by only 4.3%. This could be due to scale economies. In 1992, the SG&A expenses were 22.82% of sales revenue. By controlling the level of the SG&A expenses, Baldwin has been able to improve its pre-tax profits by about $1.3 million (see below).

Selling, general, and administrative	($26,187,629)
Selling, general, and administrative at 22.82% of sales	(27,532,842)
Additional profit due to lower SG&A	$ 1,345,213

2. Provision for doubtful accounts decreased by 17% from 1992 to 1993; i.e., it has decreased from 1.87% of net sales to about 1.41%. This decrease is consistent with a change in management's estimate. There is very little information in the case to help us understand the reasons for the revision in the management's estimate. Has Baldwin changed its credit evaluation and extension policies? Have the past bad debt expenses been consistently higher than the historical write-offs? There is some evidence to indicate that the composition of Baldwin's sales revenue has changed from 1992 to 1993. While musical products' share of the total revenue has decreased from 81.5% to 72.6%, that of electronic contracting has increased substantially from 13.3% to 22.2%. One possibility is that the electronic contracting business has lower bad debt expense compared to the other business segments, thereby explaining the lower overall bad debt expense. Without a convincing explanation, the

decrease in the bad debt expense needs further scrutiny. Note that if the management had maintained the same level of bad debt expense in 1993 as it had in 1992, then the operating income of Baldwin would have decreased by about $555,000 [i.e., $120,657,455 × (0.0187 - 0.0141)].

3. Interest expense decreased by 14.5%. The statement of cash flows indicates that Baldwin has repaid more than $8.6 million of long-term debt during 1993, which could explain the decrease in the interest expense.

4. As discussed earlier, there are significant differences in the inter-segment growth rates in revenues. The musical products segment now accounts for only 72.7% revenue as opposed to 81.5% in 1992. In addition, the operating profitability of this segment has decreased substantially from 7.6% to 5.0%. However, the electronic contracting segment, whose revenue has been growing at a greater rate, has a higher operating margin. Given that the musical products segment is slowing down and that the electronic contracting business is likely to face severe competition (Baldwin may not have any unique technical advantage here), Baldwin's ability to maintain growth and operating margin in the electronic contracting segment may be a key factor for its future prospects.

Comment on inventory liquidation:
In addition to the above items, Baldwin's income statements were favorably impacted from realization of inventory holding gains (or inflationary profits). The following paragraph is excerpted from the company's financial statements:

During the past three years, certain inventories were reduced, resulting in the liquidation of LIFO inventory layers carried at lower costs prevailing in prior years as compared with the current cost of inventories. The effect of these inventory liquidations was to increase net earnings for 1993, 1992, and 1991 by approximately $694,000 ($ .20 per share), $519,000 ($ .15 per share), and $265,000 ($ .08 per share), respectively.

Chapter 8 discusses some of the implications of LIFO liquidations for financial analysis.

Exercises
E3-1. Determining collections on account
(AICPA adapted)

Cash receipts from sales include cash sales plus collections on account computed as follows:

Cash sales	$200,000
Beginning accounts receivable	400,000
Credit sales	3,000,000
Less: Ending accounts receivable	(485,000)
Total Cash receipts from sales	**$3,115,000**

Alternative Solution: T-account analysis of accounts receivable

Accounts Receivable			
Beginning balance	$ 400,000		
		X	Collections on account
Sales on account	3,000,000		
Ending balance	$ 485,000		

$485,000 = $400,000 + $3,000,000 − X
X = $2,915,000
Total cash receipts from sales:

Cash sales	$200,000
Collections on accounts receivable	2,915,000
Total cash collected on sales	**$3,115,000**

E3-2. Determining cash from operations
(AICPA adapted)

Cash Flows from operations:

Cash received from customers	$870,000
Rent received	10,000
Taxes paid	(110,000)
Cash paid to employees and suppliers	(510,000)
Cash flows from operations	**$260,000**

Notice that cash dividends paid arises from the issuance of stock, a financing activity, and thus is not included in cash flows from operations.

E3-3. Determining cash collections on account
(AICPA adapted)

The provision for bad debts and write-off for uncollectible credit sales are non-cash expenses so they do not enter into the computation of cash receipts. To compute cash receipts, we need only sum the cash collected in May, as follows:

Collections of May credit sales (est.) 20% of $200,000 =	$ 40,000
Collections of April credit sales (est.) 70% of $150,000 =	105,000
Collections of pre-April credit sales	12,000
Total cash receipts from accounts receivable in may	**$157,000**

E3-4. Determining ending accounts receivable
(AICPA adapted)

This problem tests students' understanding of the interrelationships between various balance sheet and income statement accounts.

To solve for the ending accounts receivable (A/R) balance, one needs to determine both sales on account (debit to A/R) and total purchases from an analysis of accounts payable. Once these two accounts are determined, one can conduct an analysis of the A/R T-account to deduce the ending A/R balance.

Step 1: To determine sales on account, one must first determine cost of goods sold as follows:

Beginning inventory (given)	-0-
+Purchases[1]	240,000
=Total cost of goods available for sale	240,000
- Ending inventory (given)	(60,000)
=Cost of goods sold	$180,000

[1]Total purchases is determined from T-account analysis of accounts payable.

Accounts Payable

		-0-	Beginning balance
Payments on account (given)	$200,000		
		X	**Solve for: Purchases on account**
		$40,000	Ending balance

X = $240,000 for purchases

Step 2: Sales on account = 130% of cost of goods sold
$234,000 = 1.3 × $180,000

68

Step 3: T-account analysis of accounts receivable to deduce ending balance:

Accounts Receivable

Beginning balance	$0		
		$170,000	Collections on account (given)
Sales on account (step 2)	234,000		
Solve for: Ending balance	**X**		

X = $234,000 - $170,000
= $64,000

E3-5. Determining cash disbursements
(AICPA adapted)

To answer this question, one needs to first determine the accrual basis expenses and then (1) subtract from this figure expenses not paid in cash; and (2) add amounts paid out in cash not recorded as accrual expenses.

Total accrual basis expenses:
Cost of goods sold = 70% of sales	
= 70% × $700,000	$490,000
Selling, general, & administrative expense	
Fixed portion	71,000
Variable portion = 15% of sales	
= 15% × $700,000	105,000
Total accrual basis expenses	**$666,000**

Subtract: Noncash expenses	
Depreciation expense	(40,000)
Charge for uncollectible accounts (1% x $700,000)	(7,000)
Add: Increase in inventory which represents a net noncash deduction in determining cost of goods sold (see below)	10,000
Total cash disbursements for June	**$629,000**

Cost of Goods Sold

$$\left.\begin{array}{l} \text{Beginning Inventory} \\ \text{+ Purchases} \\ \text{- Ending Inventory} \\ \text{= Cost of Goods Sold} \end{array}\right\} \text{ increase by } \$10,000$$

If inventory increases by $10,000, this means that the non-cash subtraction from cost of goods sold was bigger than the non-cash addition. Therefore, we need to add this inventory increase to the accrual basis expenses to get cash basis expenses.

69

E3-6. Determining cash collections on account
(AICPA adapted)

Cash collected from customers can be determined by finding the change in accounts receivable.

Beginning accounts receivable	$21,600
Sales	438,000
Ending accounts receivable	(30,400)
Cash collections from customers for 1998	**$429,200**

Notice that no accounts were written off during the year so there was no credit to accounts receivable for the $1,000 uncollectible accounts.

E3-7. Determining cash received from customers
(AICPA adapted)

Collections from customers equal sales revenue minus the increase in accounts receivable, or $70,000 ($75,000 - $5,000).

E3-8. Determining cash from operations and reconciling with accrual net income (CW)

Requirement 1:
Cash provided by operating activities:

Net income	$100,000
Noncash expenses:	
Depreciation	30,000
	130,000
Changes in working capital accounts:	
Increase in accounts receivable	(110,000)
Decrease in inventories	50,000
Increase in prepaid expenses	(15,000)
Decrease in accounts payable	(150,000)
Increase in salaries payable	15,000
Decrease in other current liabilities	(70,000)
	(280,000)
Cash provided by operating activities	($150,000)

Requirement 2:
Net income is $100,000, yet cash provided by operating activities is ($150,000). There are several reasons for the difference. Accounts receivable increased by $110,000 (i.e., not all of the sales reported in the 1997 income statement were collected in cash in 1997). Inventories decreased by $50,000 (i.e., part of the cost of goods sold appearing in the 1997 income statement consists of

inventory that was paid for in an earlier year (i.e., 1996). Accounts payable decreased by $150,000 (i.e., the firm paid cash for all of its 1997 purchases of merchandise from suppliers, as well as $150,000 for purchases made in 1996). Other current liabilities decreased by $70,000 (i.e., the firm paid cash for the various operating expenses it incurred in 1997 as well as $70,000 of operating expenses that were incurred, but not paid in cash in 1996). The changes in the prepaid expenses and the salaries payable accounts, along with the depreciation expense, explain the remaining difference between the firm's net Income and its cash flow from operating activities.

Note: This case demonstrates that a firm be profitable under the accrual basis even though it does not generate positive cash flow from operating activities.

E3-9. Determining cash from operations and reconciling with accrual net income (CW)

Requirement 1:
Cash provided by operating activities:

Net income (loss)	($200,000)
Noncash expenses:	
Depreciation	50,000
	(150,000)
Changes in working capital accounts:	
Decrease in accounts receivable	140,000
Increase in inventories	(25,000)
Increase in other current assets	(10,000)
Increase in accounts payable	120,000
Decrease in accrued payables	(25,000)
Increase in interest payable	50,000
	250,000
Cash provided by operating activities	$100,000

Requirement 2:
Net income (loss) is ($200,000), yet cash provided by operating activities is a positive $100,000. There are several reasons for the difference. Accounts receivable decreased by $140,000 (i.e., the firm collected all of 1997's sales in cash as well as some of the sales made in 1996, but not collected in 1996). Inventories increased by $25,000 (i.e., the acquisition of merchandise inventory in 1997 exceeded the amount reported in the income statement for cost of goods sold). Accounts payable increased by $120,000 (i.e., the firm did not pay for all of the merchandise purchases made from suppliers during 1997, thus the amount reported in the income statement for cost of goods sold is an overstatement of cash payments for purchases in 1997). Interest payable increased by $50,000 (i.e., the amount of interest paid in cash in 1997 is less than the amount of interest expense reported in the firm's 1997 income statement). The changes in the other current assets and accrued payables

accounts, along with the depreciation expense explain the remaining difference between the firm's net income and its cash flow from operating activities.

Note: This case demonstrates that a firm can be unprofitable under the accrual basis even though it generates positive cash flow from operating activities.

E3-10. Determining amounts shown on statement of cash flows

	Treatment in Statement of Cash Flows
Cost of goods sold	Not part of the cash flow statement
Acquisitions of property, plant, and equipment	Cash flows from **investing** activities
Decrease in inventories	Cash flows from **operating** activities
Repayments of obligations under long-term lease obligations	Cash flows from **financing** activities
Decrease in salaries payable	Cash flows from **operating** activities
Gain on sale of land	Cash flows from **operating** activities
Increase in receivables	Cash flows from **operating** activities
Purchases of long-term investment securities	Cash flows from **investing** activities
Repayments of long-term borrowings	Cash flows from **financing** activities
Increase in accrued payables	Cash flows from **operating** activities
Proceeds from short-term borrowings	Cash flows from **financing** activities
Decrease in accounts payable	Cash flows from **operating** activities
Sales of property, plant, and equipment	Cash flows from **investing** activities
Proceeds from the sale of long-term borrowings	Cash flows from **financing** activities
Proceeds from sales of long-term investment securities	Cash flows from **investing** activities
Decrease in other current assets	Cash flows from **operating** activities
Purchases of common stock for treasury	Cash flows from **financing** activities
Increase in prepaid expenses	Cash flows from **operating** activities
Dividends paid	Cash flows from **financing** activities
Sales	Not part of the cash flow statement
Depreciation and amortization	Cash flows from **operating** activities
Repayments of shorter-term borrowings	Cash flows from **financing** activities
Increase in current assets	Cash flows from **operating** activities
Proceeds from the exercise of executive stock options	Cash flows from **financing** activities

Problems
P3-1. Preparing income statement and statement of cash flows

Requirement 1:

Accrual Accounting		Cash Flow Accounting	
Sales revenue	$115,000	Cash collected from customers	$115,000
- Cost of goods sold	-90,000	- Cash paid to suppliers	-85,000
Net income	$25,000	Cash flow from operations	$30,000

Computation of cash flow from operations under the indirect method:

Net income (sales - cost of goods sold)	$25,000
- Increase in inventory	(10,000)
+ Increase in accounts payable	15,000
Cash flow from operations (sales - cash paid to suppliers)	$30,000

Requirement 2:
Since all sales are cash sales, sales revenue equals cash collected from customers. Consequently, the adjustments made for changes in inventory and accounts payable must convert the accrual accounting expense of cost of goods sold to its cash flow counterpart, i.e., cash paid to suppliers. The following table illustrates that adjusting for change in inventory converts cost of goods sold to cost of purchases, and further adjusting for change in accounts payable converts the cost of purchases to cash paid to suppliers.

Computation of Cash Flow from Operations under the Direct Method		
Sales (= cash from customers)		**$115,000**
Cost of goods sold	-$90,000	
- Increase in inventory	-10,000	
Cost of purchases	**-100,000**	
+ Increase in accounts payable	+15,000	
Cash paid to suppliers		**-85,000**
Cash flow from operations		**$ 30,000**

P3-2. Explaining differences between cash flow from operations and accrual net income
(CFA adapted)

Requirement 1:
Net income reflects (1) accrual accounting, (2) estimates of certain expenses, (3) and management discretion in certain items.

Net income is not necessarily correlated to cash flows from operations because of accrual accounting. The recording of revenues when earned, and not received in the form of cash, and the recording of expenses in one period, but actually paid in another, are examples of how accrual accounting can result in net income figures that have no correlation to cash flows from operations. Charges for noncash items (depreciation expense and amortization of goodwill) will affect net income but have no effect on cash flows from operations.

Estimates for items such as bad debts expense, depreciation expense and the amortization of intangible assets are largely up to management to determine. These items all lower net income but have no effect on cash flows from operations. Examples include: restructuring of debt, gains, and losses on the sale assets, discontinued operations, extraordinary items and changes in accounting principles. All of these items affect net income, but not cash flows from operations.

Requirement 2:
The cash flow from operations (CFO) focuses on the liquidity aspect of operations and not on measuring the profitability. If used as a measure of performance, the CFO is less subject to distortion than the net income figure. Analysts use the CFO as a check on the quality of earnings. The CFO then is acting as a check on the reported net earnings figure but not as a substitute for

net earnings. Firms with high net earnings and low CFO may be using income recognition techniques that are suspect. The ability for a firm to generate CFO on a consistent basis is an indication of the financial health of the firm. For most firms, CFO is the "lifeblood" of the firm. Analysts search for trends in CFO to indicate future cash conditions and the potential for cash flow troubles.

P3-3. Measurement conventions for balance sheet accounts

Requirement 1:
a) **Fair/current market value:** This valuation corresponds to the amount that would be paid to or received from an independent party in an arm's length transaction. For example, the fair market value of an equity security (i.e., the stock of a publicly held company like Microsoft®) is the price that one party (the seller) would be willing to accept and that another party (the buyer) would be willing to offer for the security. Another example pertains to inventory. Fair market value here is the price that a buyer would be willing to pay and that a seller would be willing to accept for the inventory.

While fair market values for some assets and liabilities may be easy to obtain (e.g., marketable securities), for others they may not (e.g., specialized long-term assets).

b) **Historical cost:** This valuation corresponds to an item's original acquisition cost. For example, the cash paid to acquire a machine in 1988 is its historical cost as is the cash paid to acquire a piece of equipment in 1996. The appeal of historical cost is that it is easy to verify (i.e., just refer to the invoice price paid). A disadvantage is that, as time goes on, historical amounts become more and more outdated (i.e., less and less useful to external users). Further, the historical costs of different periods (e.g., 1983) get commingled with those of other years (e.g., 1997), which may further reduce the informativeness of balance sheet disclosures.

c) **Amortized cost:** This valuation corresponds to original acquisition price (i.e., historical cost) adjusted for any discount or premium. This valuation applies primarily to investments in debt securities expected to be held to maturity. As discussed more fully in Chapter 13, a discount (premium) arises when the price paid is less than (exceeds) the face value of the security. As the discount or premium is amortized over the life of the security, its balance sheet value is adjusted, hence the title amortized cost.

d) **Net realizable value:** This valuation corresponds to historical cost adjusted for various costs expected to be incurred as part of a firm's normal operations. For example, when applied to accounts receivable, net realizable value is the gross amount of accounts receivables (i.e., their historical value) minus expected/estimated costs associated with their collection (i.e., uncollectible accounts/bad debts). In simple terms, net realizable value in this case corresponds to the amount of its accounts receivable that a firm ultimately expects to be able to collect in cash.

e) **Lower of cost or market:** As its title suggests, this valuation is based on either the lower of an item's historical acquisition cost or its current market value. This basis is applied primarily to inventory valuation where firms apply an inventory valuation method like LIFO, FIFO, or weighted average, subject to the constraint that the reported value must be the lower of the inventory's historical cost (based on one of these methods) or its current market price, whichever is lower.

This valuation is also applied in certain instances to long-term assets. In cases where the value of a long-term asset has become impaired (i.e., where the asset's future value is less than its carrying value), a writedown of the asset to its fair market value is required.

f) **Discounted present value:** This valuation corresponds to the present value of the future cash inflows (in the case of an asset) or future cash outflows (in the case of a liability) that are associated with a specific item. For example, long-term debt is reported on the balance sheet at the present value of the principal repayment and future interest payments discounted at the market rate of interest at the time the debt was issued. In addition, long-term obligations under certain leases are reported on the balance sheet at the present value of the future leases' payments.

Requirement 2:
Historical cost is probably the most commonly used measurement basis in the balance sheets of publicly-held companies. In part, this reflects the ease of verifying historical costs, when compared to a basis such as current or fair market value.

Requirement 3:
The biggest advantage to using fair market value is that all the amounts reported would be based on current up-to-date valuations. Presumably, external users would find these the most informative. In addition, this basis would also serve to enhance the comparability of the numbers within the balance sheet over time as well as at a point in time.

The biggest advantage to using historical costs is that these values are objective and verifiable [i.e., they are based on actual (although past) transactions]. Thus, they are easy to obtain and verify.

Requirement 4:
The biggest problem associated with using fair market value as a reporting basis is that readily available objective and verifiable market valuations are not available for many balance sheet items. For example, while current market valuations for various items in inventories and of investments in marketable

debt and/or equity securities are readily available, in other cases such as plant, property, and equipment, and long-term investments in companies whose stock is not traded on a national exchange, readily available market valuations are not available.

Perhaps the major disadvantage associated with historical cost is that as time goes by, historical amounts become more and more outdated (i.e., less and less useful to external users). An additional problem that arises from the use of historical costs is that, as time goes by, historical costs from different periods are combined together, potentially inhibiting the usefulness of the information reported in the balance sheet.

P3-4. Measurement conventions for balance sheet accounts

<u>Measurement basis</u>

Cash:	By its nature, cash is reported at its current market value.
Accounts receivable, net of allowances:	Net realizable value (i.e., gross accounts receivable less an estimate of doubtful accounts).
Inventories:	The lower of historical cost or current market value.
Prepaid expenses:	Historical cost which, since they are current assets, should closely approximate current market value.
Short-term investments in debt securities:	If the intent is to hold these securities to their maturity, the measurement basis is amortized cost; otherwise, the measurement basis is current market value.
Short-term investments in equity securities:	Current market value.
Property, plant, and equipment, net:	Historical cost, less depreciation. In some cases, current/fair market value will be used (i.e., when the value of an asset has become impaired).
Goodwill:	Goodwill is the excess of the purchase price over the fair value of assets acquired when one company purchases another company. The measurement basis is historical cost, less amortization.
Patents:	Historical cost, less amortization.

Notes payable: Historical cost which, since they are current liabilities, should closely approximate current market value. If the notes payable were long-term, the measurement basis would be discounted present value.

Accounts payable: Historical cost which, since they are current liabilities, should closely approximate current market value.

Accrued liabilities: Historical cost which, since they are current liabilities, should closely approximate current market value.

Income taxes payable: Historical cost which, since they are current liabilities, should closely approximate current market value.

Other current liabilities: Historical cost which, since they are current liabilities, should closely approximate current market value.

Long-term debt: Discounted present value.

Non-current deferred income taxes payable: Historical cost (undiscounted).

Long-term obligations under capital leases: Discounted present value.

Common stock: Par value of each share (e.g., $1.00) times the number of shares issued.

Capital in excess of par: Historical cost. Capital in excess of par represents the amount by which the market price of shares sold to the public exceeded their par value at the time the shares were sold. Thus, while this amount reflects a current or fair value at the time of sale, as time goes by and as other equity offers are made, the amount is better thought of in terms of an historical amount. Moreover, as time goes by, and assuming the firm is successful, in all likelihood, the market value of the outstanding shares of stock will exceed the combined balance in the common stock and capital in excess of par accounts.

Retained earnings: Historical cost. Retained earnings is equal to the cumulative net income of all prior years, less dividends paid to stockholders. Since net income itself is a mixture of current/fair values (e.g., sales) and historical costs (e.g., cost of goods sold and depreciation expense), it is perhaps best to think of

78

the measurement basis of retained earnings as historical cost.

Treasury stock: Historical cost which, at the time of acquisition, would have been the current market value of the shares. However, since this account reflects purchases of treasury stock that are likely to have been made at varying points of time in the past, it is better to think of the measurement basis here as historical cost.

P3-5. Determining cash flows from operating and investing activities
(AICPA adapted)

Requirements 1 and 2:
Cash flow from operations and investing activities are computed below.

Karr Inc. Partial Statement of Cash Flows	
Operations	
Net income	$300,000
Depreciation	52,000
Decrease in inventory	20,000
Increase in accounts receivable	(15,000)
Decrease in accounts payable	(5,000)
Gain on sale of equipment	(5,000)
Cash flows from operations	**$347,000**
Investing activities	
Sales of equipment	18,000
Purchase of equipment	(20,000)
Cash flows from investing	**($2,000)**

Notice that the $30,000 increase in notes payable is not included in cash flows from investing activities. It is not a cash transaction if issued in exchange for asset purchases. In the actual cash flows statement, it may be included in the notes as a significant noncash transaction. If the note was issued in exchange for cash, then it would be shown as a source of cash in the financing activities section of the cash flow statement.

P3-6. Determining operating cash flow components
(AICPA adapted)

Requirement 1:
Cash collected during 1999 can be shown by a T-account analysis:

Accounts Receivable

Beginning balance	$ 84,000		
Sales on account in 1999	1,200,000		
		$5,000	Accounts written off
		X	**Cash collections on account**
Ending balance	$ 78,000		

$78,000 = $84,000 + $1,200,000 - $5,000 – X
X = $1,201,000

Requirement 2:
Cash disbursed for purchases of merchandise can be derived by using two T-accounts, inventory and accounts payable.

Inventory

Beginning inventory	$150,000		
		$840,000	Cost of goods sold
Purchases (plug to balance)	**830,000**		
Ending inventory	$140,000		

Using the purchases on account we can analyze accounts payable to determine cash disbursed for merchandise purchases.

Accounts Payable

		$95,000	Beginning balance
		830,000	Purchase account
Solve for: Payments	X		
		$98,000	Ending balance

$98,000 = $95,000 + $830,000 – X
X = $827,000
So cash disbursed for the purchase of merchandise is $827,000.

Requirement 3:

Cash Disbursed for general and administrative expenses is 1999 is computed below.

1999 Variable (G&A)	$120,000	50% paid in 1999	=	$60,000
1998 Variable (G&A)	110,000	50% paid in 1999	=	55,000
1999 Fixed (G&A)	100,000	less: $35,000 (depr.) and $5000 (bad debt) × 80%	=	48,000
1998 Fixed (G&A)	100,000	less: $35,000 (depr.) and $5000 (bad debt) × 20%	=	12,000
Cash disbursement for (G&A)				$175,000

P3-7. Understanding the relation between income statement, cash flow statement, and changes in balance sheet accounts

Requirement 1:
Income statement

Sales:		
Cash collections from customers	$16,670	
+ Increase in accounts receivable	+3,630	$20,300
Cost of goods sold:		
Cash payments to suppliers	$19,428	
- Increase in inventory	(3,250)	
- Decrease in accounts payable	(3,998)	(12,180)
Gross Profit		**$8,120**
Operating expenses:		
Cash payments for operating expenses	$7,148	
- Decrease in accrued operating expenses	(2,788)	(4,360)
Depreciation of equipment		(2,256)
Amortization of patents		(399)
Loss on sale of equipment		(169)
Income before taxes		936
Income tax expense:		
Cash payments for current income taxes	$200	
+ Increase in deferred taxes payable	+127	(327)
Net income		**$609**

Requirement 2:
Cash provided by operating activities:

Net income		$609
Plus/minus noncash items:		
+ Depreciation of equipment	$2,256	
+ Amortization of patents	399	
+ Loss on sales of equipment	169	
+ Increase in deferred taxes payable	127	
		2,951

Plus/minus changes in current asset and liability accounts:		
- Increase in accounts receivable	(3,630)	
- Increase in inventory	(3,250)	
- Decrease in accounts payable	(3,998)	
- Decrease in accrued operating expenses	(2,788)	(13,666)
Cash provided by operating activities		**($10,106)**

Requirement 3:
Explanation for differences between accrual earnings and operating cash flows:

Net income is $609, yet cash provided by operating activities is ($10,106). There are several causes of the difference. Accounts receivable increased during the year (i.e., not all 1997 sales were collected in cash in 1997), inventories increased in 1997 (i.e., more inventory was purchased than is reported as cost of goods sold in the income statement), accounts payable decreased in 1997 (i.e., Cash paid to suppliers covered 1997 purchases as well as some purchases that were made, but not paid for, in 1996), and accrued operating expenses decreased in 1997 (i.e., cash paid for operating expenses in 1997 included all the expenses incurred in 1997 as well as some that were incurred, but not paid, in 1996).

P3-8. Understanding the relation between income statement, cash flow statements, and changes in balance sheet accounts

Requirement 1:
Income statement.

Sales:		
Cash collections from customers	$72,481	
- Decrease in accounts receivable	(4,603)	$67,878
Cost of goods sold:		
Cash payments to suppliers	51,768	
- Increase in inventory	(7,400)	
+ Increase in accounts payable	3,146	47,514
Gross profit		$20,364
Selling and administrative expenses:		
Cash payments for selling and		
administrative expenses	9,409	
+ Increase in the accrued selling		
and administrative expenses account	772	10,181
Depreciation of equipment		7,380
Interest expense:		
Cash payments for interest	1,344	
+ Increase in accrued interest payable	117	1,461
Gain on sale of equipment		327
Income before taxes		$1,669
Income tax expense:		
Cash payments for current income taxes	671	
- Decrease in deferred taxes payable	87	584
Net income (given)		$1,085

Requirement 2:
Cash provided by operating activities:

Net income	$1,085
Plus/minus noncash items:	
+ Depreciation of equipment	7,380
- Gain on sale of equipment	(327)
- Decrease in deferred taxes payable	(87)
	$8,051
Plus/minus changes in current asset and liability accounts:	
+ Decrease in accounts receivable	4,603
- Increase in inventory	(7,400)
+ Increase in accounts payable	3,146
+ Increase in accrued selling and administrative expenses	72
+ Increase in accrued interest payable	117
	$1,238
Cash provided by operating activities	$9,289

Requirement 3:
Explanation for difference between accrual and cash flow from operations:

Net income is $1,085, while cash provided by operating activities is much larger $9,289. There are several causes of the difference. First, $7,380 of depreciation expense reduced income, but it did not reduce cash flow, so it is added back to net income to obtain cash from operations. Accounts receivable decreased during the year (i.e., all 1997 sales were collected in cash in 1997 as well as some sales made in 1996, but not collected in 1996), accounts payable increased in 1997 (i.e., cash paid to suppliers in 1997 was less than the cost of merchandise purchased and sold in 1997). These three items are more than enough to offset the increase in the inventory account of $7,400 (i.e., more inventory was acquired in 1997 than was sold to customers).

P3-9. Understanding the relation between operating cash flows and accrual earnings

Requirement 1:

Sales ($28,000 + $3,000)	$31,000
Less:	
Cost of goods sold ($13,000 + $2,000 - $3,000)	(12,000)
Operating expenses ($9,000 - $2,000)	(7,000)
Depreciation expense	(4,000)
Income tax expense ($4,000 + $1,000)	(5,000)
Amortization expense	(1,000)
Gain on sale of equipment	2,000
Net income	$ 4,000

Requirement 2:

Net income	$4,000
Plus/minus adjustments to reach cash flows	
Operating activities:	
(+) Depreciation	4,000
(+) Amortization of goodwill	1,000
(–) Gain on sale of equipment	(2,000)
(–) Increase in inventory	(3,000)
(+) Increase in accounts payable	2,000
(–) Increase in accounts receivable	(3,000)
(–) Decrease in accrued payables	(2,000)
(+) Increase in deferred income taxes payable	1,000
Cash flows from operating activities	$2,000

P3-10. Finding missing values on a classified balance sheet and analyzing balance sheet changes

Requirement 1:
Microsoft's 19X2 balance sheet appears below. The 19X1 balance sheet is also included to facilitate responding to the remaining parts of the question.

The unknowns in the 19X2 balance sheet are:
- Cash and short-term investments
- Other assets, total assets
- Income taxes payable
- Total stockholders' equity
- Retained earnings.

They may be solved for as follows.

a) **Total Assets:** since total liabilities and stockholders' equity is given ($2,639,903), total assets is just this number, $2,639,903.

b) **Cash and short-term investments:** Total current assets is given as $1,769,704 as are all of its components except cash and short-term investments. The sum of the given components is $424,803 (accounts receivable (net) is $270,215, inventories is $85,873 and other current assets are $68,715). Subtracting the sum of these components from total current assets leaves $1,344,901 for cash and short-term investments.

Total current assets = Cash and short-term investments + Accounts receivable + Inventory + Other current assets

$$\$1,769,704 = X + \$270,215 + \$85,873 + \$68,715$$
$$X = \$1,344,901 = \text{Cash and short-term investments}$$

c) **Other assets (long-term):** To obtain other assets, subtract total current assets of $1,769,704 and property, plant, and equipment of $766,630 from total assets of $2,639,903. This yields $103,569 for other assets.

d) **Income taxes payable:** Total current liabilities is given as $446,945 as all are of its components except income taxes payable. The sum of the given components is $373,912 (accounts payable is $187,519, customer deposits $14,217, accrued compensation is $62,083, notes payable is $8,324, and other current liabilities are $101,769). Subtracting the sum of these components from total current liabilities leaves $73,033 for income taxes payable.

Total current liabilities = Accounts payable + Customer deposits + Accrued compensation + Notes payable + Income taxes payable + Other current liabilities

$$\$446,945 = \$187,519 + \$14,217 + \$62,083 + \$8,324 + X + \$101,769$$
$$X = \$73,033 = \text{Income taxes payable}$$

e) **Total stockholders' equity:** Since Microsoft has no long-term debt, total stockholders' equity is just total liabilities and stockholders' equity of $2,639,903 minus total current liabilities of $446,945. Doing the subtraction yields $2,192,958 for total stockholders' equity.

f) **Retained Earnings:** It can be derived by subtracting common stock and paid-in-capital of $656,855 from total stockholders' equity of $2,192,958. Doing so yields $1,536,103 for retained earnings.

Having derived the unknowns, all that remains is assembling the balance sheet in good form. The correct balance sheet appears below.

MICROSOFT CORPORATION CONSOLIDATED BALANCE SHEET		
	June 30,	
	19X2	**19X1**
(in thousands)		
ASSETS		
Current assets		
Cash and short-term investments	$1,344,901	$686,314
Accounts receivable, net allowances of		
$56,715 and $36,283	270,215	243,304
Inventories	85,873	47,106
Other	68,715	51,779
Total current assets	$1,769,704	$1,028,503
Property, plant, and equipment, net	766,630	530,191
Other assets	103,569	85,490
Total assets	$2,639,903	$1,644,184
LIABILITIES AND STOCKHOLDERS' EQUITY		
Current liabilities		
Accounts Payable	187,519	85,923
Customer deposits	14,217	25,680
Accrued compensation	62,083	41,643
Notes payable	8,324	19,456
Income taxes payable	73,033	44,445
Other	101,769	76,206
Total current liabilities	446,945	293,353
Commitments and contingencies	-	-
Stockholders' equity		
Common stock and paid-in capital		
500,000 shares authorized;		
272,139 issued, 261,351 outstanding	656,855	394,542
Retained earnings	1,536,103	956,289
Total stockholders' equity	$2,192,958	$1,350,831
Total liabilities and stockholders' equity	$2,639,903	$1,644,184

Requirement 2:
The firm appears to be in quite good financial health. Here are a couple of reasons why.

a) The firm's current assets of $1,769,704 are about 4 times its current liabilities of $446,945 (i.e., the firm's current ratio is almost 4.0). Thus, the firm is unlikely to face any type of liquidity crisis.

b) Related to (a), the firm's cash and short-term investments of $1,344,901 far exceed its total current liabilities of $446,945. This is further evidence that the firm has very good short-term liquidity.

Requirement 3:
In general, the changes in Microsoft's balance sheet from 19X1 to 19X2 are favorable. Several notable changes include:

a) Cash and short-term investments increased by about 96%.
($1,344,901/$ 686,314)

b) Current assets increased by about 72%.
($1,769,704/$1,028,503)

c) Microsoft appears to have made some substantial investments in property, plant, and equipment as evidenced by a (net) increase in this account of about $235 million.

d) Retained earnings increased by about $580 million. This suggests that the firm was quite profitable in 19X2 (the income statement could be examined to verify this).

e) Microsoft had no long-term debt in 19X1 or 19X2. One might suspect that Microsoft's operations generate more than enough cash flow for the firm (the cash flow statement could be examined to verify this).

Requirement 4:
Perhaps, the best answer to this question is to say that Microsoft's solid balance sheets provide no obvious reason not to invest in the firm. However, it would be unwise to base an investment recommendation solely on balance sheet information. Moreover, other information about Microsoft should be gathered and analyzed (see the next question).

Requirement 5:
At a minimum, the following information should be obtained:

a) The firm's income statements for the past 4 to 5 years. These data would be used to assess Microsoft's recent profitability and potential future profitability.

b) The firm's cash flow statements for the past 4 to 5 years. These data would be used to assess Microsoft's recent cash-flow generating ability and what the cash flows were used for, as well as to help project the firm's potential future cash flow generating ability.

c) Other information that the analyst might seek to obtain includes:

- Projections of future earnings and/or sales made by Microsoft management.

- Projections about future demand for Microsoft's products from the firm or from industry trade publication, or other independent sources.

- Information about new products that Microsoft has in development and the projected introduction dates for these products.

- Other student responses are possible.

P3-11. Finding missing values on a classified balance sheet and analyzing balance sheet accounts

Requirement 1:

HEWLETT-PACKARD COMPANY
Consolidated Balance Sheet October 31, 19X1

(In millions)	19X1
Assets	
Current assets	
Cash and cash equivalents	$625
Short-term investments	495
Accounts and notes receivable	2,976
Inventories:	
Finished goods	1,100
Purchased parts and fabricated assemblies	1,173
Other current assets	347
Total current assets	6,716
Property, plant, and equipment	
Land	390
Buildings and leasehold improvements	2,779
Machinery and equipment	2,792
	5,961
Less	
Accumulated depreciation	(2,616)
	3,345
Long-term receivables and other assets	1,912
Total assets	$11,973
Liabilities and shareholders' equity	
Current liabilities	
Notes payable and short-term borrowings	$1,201
Accounts payable	686
Employee compensation and benefits payable	837
Taxes payable	381
Deferred revenues	375
Other accrued liabilities	583
Total current liabilities	4,063
Long-term debt	188
Other liabilities	210
Deferred taxes payable	243
Total liabilities	4,704
Shareholders' equity	
Common stock and capital in excess of $ 1 par value (authorized: 600,000,000 shares; issued and outstanding: 251,547,000 in19x1)	1,010
Retained earnings	6,259
Total shareholders' equity	7,269
Total liabilities and shareholders' equity	$11,973

The unknowns in the 19X2 balance sheet are:

- Total liabilities and shareholders' equity
- Land
- Long-term debt
- Notes payable and short-term borrowings
- Retained earnings
- Accounts and notes receivable

They may be solved for as follows.

a) Total liabilities + Shareholders' equity = Total assets (given) = $11,973

b) Land: $390 million

The following amounts, which are given in the problem, are needed to derive the balance in the land account: Total assets of $11,973, total current assets of $6,716, and the balances of all long-term asset accounts except land (buildings and leasehold improvements $2,779, machinery and equipment $2,792, accumulated depreciation ($2,616), and long-term receivables and other Assets $1,912). Thus, the balance in the land account is:

Total assets = Current assets + Land + Buildings and leasehold improvements + Machinery and equipment - Accumulated depreciation + Long-term receivables and other assets

$$\$11,973 = \$6,716 + \text{land} + \$2,779 + \$2,792 - \$2,616 + \$1,912.$$
$$\text{Land} = \$390.$$

c) Long-term debt: $188 million

The following information ($ in millions) in the problem can be used to derive the long-term debt: Total liabilities and shareholders' equity (i.e., total assets) of $11,973, total current liabilities of $4,063, total shareholders' equity of $7,269, other liabilities of $210, and deferred taxes payable of $243.

Long-term debt = Total liabilities and shareholders' equity - Total shareholders' equity - Other liabilities - Deferred taxes payable - Total current liabilities

$$\text{Long-term debt} = \$11,973 - \$7,269 - \$210 - \$243 - \$4,063.$$
$$\text{Long-term debt} = \$188.$$

d) Notes payable and short-term borrowings: $1,201 million.

The given information includes total current liabilities as well as all of its underlying components except for notes payable and short-term borrowings. To solve for notes payable and short-term borrowings simply subtract all of the given current liability components from total current liabilities. Specifically:

Notes payable and short-term borrowings = Total current liabilities - Accounts payable - Employee compensation and benefits payable - Taxes payable - Deferred revenues - Other accrued liabilities

Notes payable and short-term borrowings =
$4,063 - $686 - $837 - $381 - $375 - $583.

Notes payable and short-term borrowings = $1,201 million .

e) Retained Earnings: $6,259 million

The following information given in the case can be used to derive the retained earnings balance: Total shareholders' equity of $7,269 and common stock and capital in excess of $1 par value of $1,010. The balance in the retained earnings account is just the difference between these two figures:

Retained earnings = $7,269 - $1,010

Retained earnings = $6,259.

f) Accounts and notes receivable: $2,976 million

The given information includes total current assets as well as all of its underlying components except for accounts and notes receivable. To solve for accounts and notes receivable, simply subtract all of the given current asset components from total current assets. Specifically:

Accounts and notes receivable = Total current assets - Cash and cash equivalents - Short-term investments - Finished goods - Purchased parts and fabricated assemblies - Other current assets

Accounts and notes receivable = $6,716 - $625 - $495 - $1,100 - $1,173 - $347.
Accounts and notes receivable = $2,976.

2) One way to answer this question is to calculate the ratio of total Stockholders' equity to total assets. Specifically:

$7,269/$11,973 = 60.7%.

This suggests that Hewlett-Packard finances itself by relying slightly more on investment by shareholders rather than creditors.

Of note is that what financing that is provided by creditors is primarily short-term. Moreover, current liabilities are $4,063, while long-term liabilities are only $641.

3) Hewlett-Packard's largest current asset is accounts and notes receivable of $2,976.

4) Hewlett-Packard's largest current liability is notes and short-term borrowings of $1,201.

5) Current ratio = Current assets/Current liabilities.

  = $6,716/$4,063

  = 1.65.

This means that Hewlett-Packard has $1.65 of current assets for each $1.00 of current liabilities. A simple rule of thumb for the current ratio is that it should be greater than one. Thus, Hewlett-Packard appears to have adequate short-term liquidity.

A better way to gauge the adequacy of a firm's current ratio is to compare it to prior years' values for the firm, as well as with the values for other firms in the industry.

6) Other current assets may consist of items such as prepaid expenses like insurance, rent, advertising, etc.

P3-12. Analyzing the difference between operating cash flows and accrual earnings

Item:	(a) Accrual Income	(b) Non-cash Accruals Revenue Earned or Expenses Incurred	(c) Prepayments/ Buildups/Other Adjustments	(d) (a+b+c) Cash Received (+) or Paid (-)
Operating Activities				
Sales	$6,438,507 [1]	- $20,145 [2]		+ $6,418,362 [3]
Cost of goods sold	- 5,102,977 [4]		- $170,933 [5] + 53,099 [6]	- 5,220,811 [7]
Selling and admin. expenses	- 855,809 [8]	+ 45,096 [9]	+ 7,283 [10]	- 803,430 [11]
Interest expense	- 34,436 [12]	- 2,327 [13]		- 36,763 [14]
Depreciation expense	- 104,614 [15]	+ 104,614		- -
Provision for income taxes	- 135,500 [16]	- 5,568 [17]		- 141,068 [18]
Net income	205,171 [19]			
Operating cash flow				+ 216,290 [20]
Investing activities				
Capital expenditures				- 352,092 [21]
Net investing cash flows				- 352,092
Financing activities				
Sale of stock				+ 100,857 [22]
Issuance of long-term debt				+ 89,352 [23]
Dividends				- 48,031 [24]
Net financing cash flows				+142,178
Net cash flow				$6,376
Beginning cash				$428
Ending cash				6,804
Change in cash				$6,376

Notes:

1. Sales from the income statement.

2. The increase in the accounts receivable account (i.e., sales not collected in cash during the year), $97,106 - $76,961.

3. Cash collected during the year.

4. Cost of goods sold from the income statement.

5. The increase in the inventory account (i.e., $844,539 - $673,606).

6. The increase in the accounts payable account for the year (i.e., $343,163 - $290,064).

7. Payments for inventory during the year.

8. Selling and administrative expenses from the income statement.

9. The increase in the accrued expenses account (i.e., $184,017 - $138,921).

10. The decrease in the prepaid expenses account for the year (i.e., $16,684 - $9,401).

11. Selling and administrative expenses paid in cash during the year.

12. Interest expense from the income statement.

13. The decrease in the accrued interest payable account for the year (i.e., $1,067 - $3,394).

14. Interest paid in cash during the year.

15. Depreciation expense from the income statement. Depreciation is a non-cash expense.

16. Accrual accounting income tax expense from the income statement.

17. The decrease in the income tax payable account, (i.e., $37,390 - $42,958).

18. Cash paid for income taxes during the year.

19. From the income statement.

20. By calculation.

21. The change in the property account.

22. The change in the common stock account.

23. The change in the long-term debt account.

24. Given.

Food Tiger Statement of Cash Flows For the Year Ended December 31, 1998		
Operating cash flows		
Net income		$205,171
Plus		
Depreciation		104,614
Increase in accounts payable	53,099	
Increase in accrued expenses	45,096	
Decrease in prepaid expenses	7,283	105,478
Minus		
Increase in accounts receivable	20,145	
Increase in inventory	170,933	
Decrease in accrued interest payable	2,327	
Decrease in income taxes payable	5,568	(198,973)
Net operating cash flows		$216,290
Investing cash flows		
Capital expenditures	(352,092)	
Net investing cash flows		(352,092)
Financing cash flows		
Sale of stock	100,857	
Issuance of long-term debt	89,352	
Dividends	(48,031)	
Net financing cash flows		142,178
Net cash flow		$6,376
Beginning cash balance		$428
Ending cash balance		6,804
Change in cash		$6,376

P3-13 Preparing balance sheet and income statement
(AICPA adapted)

Requirement 1:

Vanguard Corporation Balance Sheet December 31, 1999		
ASSETS		
Cash		$4,386,040
Balance at December 31, 1998		
Add		
1999 net sales	$15,650,000	
Less 12/31/99 accounts receivable	(3,350,000)	12,300,000
Accounts receivable at 12/31/98	3,150,000	
Less: Accounts charged off in 1999	(50,000)	3,100,000
		19,786,040
Less		
Purchases and freight-in	10,905,000	
Other administrative, selling, and general expenses	2,403,250	
	13,308,250	
Less 12/31/99 accounts payable and accrued liabilities	2,221,000	
	11,087,250	
12/31/98 current liabilities	3,391,500	
Interest expense (see income statement)	231,250	
Fixed assets purchased in 1999 ($4,000,000 (fixed asset total		
12/31/99, see below) less $3,300,000 given)	700,000	
Dividends paid (see statement of retained earnings)	410,000	
Installment of 1999 tax paid prior to 12/31/99	400,000	16,220,000
Cash balance at 12/31/99		3,566,040
Accounts receivable (given)		3,350,000
Allowance for doubtful accounts (3% of $3,350,000)		(100,500)
Inventories (obtained from cost of sales section of		
the income statement)		2,750,000
Fixed assets		
Depreciation expense in 1999 (given)	$474,500	
Depreciation on 12/31/98 fixed assets (13% of $3,300,000)	429,000	
Depreciation on fixed asset additions in 1999	$45,500	
One-half year's depreciation taken in year fixed assets		
acquired. Full year's depreciation = $45,500 × 2	$91,000	
Depreciation rate 13% - 1999 fixed asset additions ($91,000/.13)	700,000	
12/31/98 fixed assets	3,300,000	
12/31/99 fixed assets		4,000,000
Accumulated depreciation		
Balance 12/31/98	$1,300,000	
Depreciation expense in 1999 (given)	$474,500	
Accumulated depreciation balance 12/31/99		($1,774,500)
TOTAL ASSETS		$11,791,040

Vanguard Corporation
Balance Sheet
(continued)

LIABILITIES AND STOCKHOLDERS' EQUITY

Notes payable		
Due in twenty equal quarterly installments ($5,000,000/20 = $250,000)		
Four installments each due in 2000		$1,000,000
Accounts payable and accrued liabilities (information given)		2,221,000
Provision for federal income taxes		
Provision for taxes on 1999 earnings per income statement	$530,000	
Less: 1999 estimated tax payment	(400,000)	
Balance 12/31/99		130,000
Notes payable due after one year		
Balance 12/31/98	$4,000,000	
Less: Amount due within one year at 12/31/99		
	(1,000,000)	
Balance 12/31/99		3,000,000
Capital stock		
Balance 12/31/98	$1,000,000	
Stock dividend of 5%	50,000	
Balance 12/31/99		1,050,000
Additional paid-in capital		
$[50,000\,sh. \times \$7 = \$350,000 - (50,000\,sh. \times \$1) = \$300,000\ increase]$		1,800,000
Retained earnings (per statement of retained earnings)		2,590,040
TOTAL LIABILITIES AND STOCKHOLDERS' EQUITY		$11,791,040

Requirement 2:

Vanguard Corporation
Income Statement
Year Ended December 31, 1999

Net sales (given)		$15,650,000
Cost of sales		
Beginning inventory (given)	$2,800,000	
Purchases & freight (given)	10,905,000	
Less	13,705,000	
Ending inventory (plug figure necessary for 30% gross profit)	(2,750,000)	10,955,000
Gross profit (30% of $15,650,000)		4,695,000
Operating and other expenses		
Interest (5% per year on notes adjusted for		
four 1999 quarterly payments of $250,000)		
($62,500 + $59,375 + $56,250 + $53,125)	231,250	
Depreciation and amortization (given)	474,500	
Provision for doubtful accounts:	56,000	
Balance 12/31/99 (3% of $3,350,000)	$100,500	
Balance 12/31/98 (given)	$94,500	
Amounts written off (given)	(50,000)	44,500
Amount required	56,000	
Other administrative, selling, and general expenses (given)	2,403,250	
		3,165,000
Net income before income taxes		1,530,000
Income tax expense (given)		530,000
Net income		$1,000,000

Vanguard Corporation
Statement of Retained Earnings
Year Ended December 31, 1999

Beginning retained earnings (given)		$2,350,040
Net earnings for the year (from income statement)		1,000,000
		$3,350,040
Less cash dividends paid:		
1st quarter 1,000,000 shares @.10	100,000	
2nd quarter 1,000,000 shares @.10	100,000	
3rd quarter 1,050,000 shares @.10	105,000	
4th quarter 1,050,000 shares @.10	105,000	
Total cash dividends paid	$410,000	
Fair value of 50,000 shares of common stock issued		
as stock dividend (50,000 shares @ $7)	350,000	
		760,000
Ending retained earnings		$2,590,040

Cases

C3-1. Debbie Dress Shops: Determining cash flow amounts from comparative balance sheets and income statement
(AICPA adapted)

Requirement 1:
Cash collected during 1998 from accounts receivable is calculated below.

Beginning accounts receivable	$580,000
Net credit sales	6,400,000
Ending accounts receivable	(840,000)
Cash collected during 1998	**$6,140,000**

Requirement 2:
To find cash payments during 1998 on accounts payable to suppliers, we first must compute purchases.

Beginning inventory	$420,000
+ Purchases **(plug figure)**	**5,240,000**
- Ending inventory	(660,000)
= Cost of goods sold (given)	$5,000,000

We then use the purchases amount to compute cash payments made to suppliers.

Ending accounts payable	(530,000)
Purchases	5,240,000
Beginning accounts payable	440,000
Cash payments to suppliers	**$5,150,000**

Requirement 3:

Cash provided by operations can be seen by looking at the 1998 statement of cash flows for Debbie Dress Shops.

Debbie Dress Shops Statement of Cash Flows	
Net income	$400,000
Depreciation ($110,000 - $50,000)	60,000
Increase in accounts payable	90,000
Increase in accrued expenses	10,000
Increase in accounts receivable	(260,000)
Increase in inventory	(240,000)
Increase in prepaid expenses	(50,000)
Cash flows from operating activities	**$10,000**
Purchase of land, buildings, and fixtures	(530,000)
Purchase of long-term investment	(80,000)
Cash flows from investing activities	**($610,000)**
Issuance of common stock	300,000
Issuance of long-term debt	500,000
Payment of cash dividends**	(100,000)
Cash flows from financing activities	**$700,000**
Net cash flows for 1998	**$100,000**

** The amount listed for payment of cash dividends can be computed using T-account analysis.

Retained Earnings

		$330,000	Beginning balance
		400,000	Net income
Dividends declared	$170,000		
		$560,000	Ending balance

Using the dividends declared amount we found in the above, we can find the actual cash paid out for dividends by looking at the dividends payable account.

Dividends payable

		–	Beginning balance
		$170,000	Dividends declared
Cash paid out in dividends	$100,000		
		$70,000	Ending balance

Requirement 4: see above

Requirement 5: see above

C3-2. Snap-on-Tools Corp. (CW): Determining missing amounts on cash flow statement

Required:
Snap-on-Tool's 19X2 cash flow statement appears below. The unknowns are: net cash provided by operating activities, net cash used in investing activities, net cash provided by (used in) financing activities, increase in cash and cash equivalents, and cash and cash equivalents at end of year.

These amounts may be solved for as follows (all in thousands).

a) **Net cash provided by operating activities:**

Cash provided by operating activities = Net earnings + Depreciation + Amortization - Decrease in deferred income taxes - Gain on sale of assets - Increase in receivables + Decrease in inventories - Increase in prepaid expenses - Decrease in accounts payable + Increase in accruals, deposits, and Other Liabilities.

Cash provided by operating activities = $65,975 + $25,484 + $3,973 - $ 6,005 - $250 - $5,458 + $5,928 - $4,829 - $8,202 + $23,330

Cash provided by operating activities = $99,946.

b) Net cash used in investing activities:

Cash used by investing activities = Capital expenditures + Acquisition of Sun Electric, net of cash acquired + Increase in other noncurrent assets - Disposal of property and equipment.

Cash used by investing activities = $21,081 + $110,719 + $3,609 - $3,379.

Cash used by investing activities = $132,030.

c) Net cash provided by (used in) financing activities:

Cash provided by financing activities = Increase in notes payable - Payment of long-term debt + Increase in long-term debt + Proceeds from stock option plans - Cash dividends paid.

Cash provided by financing activities = $52,503 - $8,332 + $78,650 + $4,940 - $45,718

Cash provided by financing activities = $82,043.

d) Increase in cash and cash equivalents:

Increase in cash and cash equivalents = Cash provided by operating activities - Cash used by investing activities + Cash provided by financing activities - Effect of exchange rate changes.

Increase in cash and cash equivalents = $99,946 - $132,030+$82,043 - $1,916.

Increase in cash and cash equivalents = $48,043.

e) Cash and cash equivalents at end of year:

Cash and cash equivalents at end of year = Cash and cash equivalents at beginning of year + Increase in cash and cash equivalents.

Cash and cash equivalents at end of year = $10,930 + $48,043

Cash and cash equivalents at end of year = $58,973.

Snap-on Tools Corporation
Consolidated Statement of Cash Flows

(Amount in thousands)	19X2
Operating Activities	
Net earnings	$65,975
Adjustments to reconcile net earnings to net	
Cash provided by operating activities:	
Depreciation	25,484
Amortization	3,973
Deferred income taxes	(6,005)
Gain on sale of assets	(250)
Changes in operating assets and liabilities:	
(Increase) decrease in receivables	(5,458)
(Increase) decrease in inventories	5,928
Increase in prepaid expenses	(4,829)
Decrease in accounts payable	(8,202)
Increase in accruals, deposits, and other	
long-term liabilities	23,330
Net cash provided by operating activities	99,946
Investing Activities	
Capital expenditures	(21,081)
Acquisition of Sun Electric, net of cash acquired	(110,719)
Disposal of property and equipment	3,379
(Increase) decrease in other noncurrent assets	(3,609)
Net cash used in investing activities	(132,030)
Financing Activities	
Payment of long-term debt	(8,332)
Increase in long-term debt	78,650
Increase (decrease) in notes payable	52,503
Proceeds from stock option plans	4,940
Cash dividends paid	(45,718)
Net cash provided by (used in) financing activities	82,043
Effect of exchange rate changes	(1,916)
Increase in cash and cash equivalents	48,043
Cash and cash equivalents at beginning of year	10,930
Cash and cash equivalents at end of year	$58,973

C3-3. Drop Zone Corp. (CW): Understanding the relation between successive balance sheets and cash flow statement

Drop Zone Corporation **Balance Sheet** **For the Year Ended December 31, 1997**		
	1996 Amount Plus/Minus Change	1997 Amount
Assets		
Current assets		
Cash	($7,410 + $2,565)	$9,975
Accounts receivable, net	($6,270 + $3,990)	10,260
Inventory	($13,395 - $1,425)	11,970
Prepaid assets	($1,995 - $855)	1,140
Total current assets	$29,070	$33,345
Land	($27,930 - $8,550)	19,380
Buildings and equipment	($194,655 + $39,615)	234,270
Less: Accumulated depreciation, buildings and equipment	($40,185 + $5,415)	45,600
Total assets	$211,470	$241,395
Liabilities and stockholders' equity		
Current liabilities		
Accounts payable	($11,400 - $2,850)	$8,550
Accrued payables	($3,135 + $1,140)	4,275
Total current liabilities	$14,535	$12,825
Long-term debt	($19,950 + $16,245)	36,195
Stockholders' equity		
Common stock $10.00 par value	($18,525 + $5,000)	23,525
Paid-in capital	($31,920 + $12,825 - $5,000)	39,745
Retained earnings	($144,780 + $11,400 - $6,270)	149,910
Less: Treasury stock	($18,240 + $2,565)	$20,805
Total liabilities and stockholders' equity	$211,470	$241,395

The details underlying the calculation of the 1997 amounts are as follows:

a) The ending cash account balance of $9,975 is equal to the beginning balance of $7,410 plus the increase in cash of $2,565 reported in the cash flow statement.

b) The ending accounts receivable, net account balance of $10,260 is equal to beginning balance of $6,270 plus the increase in the account's balance of $3,990 reported in the cash flow statement.

c) The ending inventory account balance of $11,970 is equal to the beginning balance of $13,395 minus the decrease in the account balance of $1,425 reported in the cash flow statement.

d) The ending balance in the prepaid assets account of $1,140 is equal to the beginning balance of $1,995 minus the decrease in the account balance of $855 reported in the cash flow statement.

e) The ending balance in the land account of $19,380 is equal to the beginning balance of $27,930 minus the cost of the land that was sold of $8,550.

f) The ending balance in the buildings and equipment account of $234,270 is equal to the beginning balance of $194,655 plus the acquisitions of $39,615.

g) The ending balance in the accumulated depreciation, buildings and equipment account of $45,600 is the beginning balance of $40,185 plus the depreciation of $5,415 for the current year.

h) The ending balance in the accounts payables account of $8,550 is equal to the beginning balance of $11,400 minus the decrease in the account balance of $2,850.

i) The ending balance in the accrued payables account of $4,275 is equal to the beginning balance of $3,135 plus the increase in the account balance of $1,140 reported in the cash flow statement.

j) The ending balance in long-term debt account of $36,195 is the beginning balance of $19,950 plus the amount of long-term debt issued during the year of $16,245.

k) The ending balance in the common stock account of $23,525 is equal to the beginning balance of $18,525 plus the par value of the shares issued during the year of $5,000.

l) The ending balance in the paid-in capital account of $39,745 is equal to the beginning balance of $31,920 plus the proceeds from the common stock issue of $12,825, net of the $5,000 that went to the common stock account (i.e., $7,825).

m) The ending balance of retained earnings of $149,910 is equal to the beginning balance of $144,780 plus net income of $11,400 minus dividends of $6,270.

n) The ending balance in the treasury stock account of $20,805 is the beginning balance of $18,240 plus the cost of the additional shares acquired during 1997 of $2,565.

C3-4. Long Distance Runner Corporation (CW): Understanding the relation between successive balance sheets and cash flow statement

Long Distance Runner Corporation Balance Sheet For the Year Ended December 31, 1996		
	1997 Amount Plus/Minus Change	1996 Amount
Assets		
Current assets		
Cash	($39,825 + $14,175)	$54,000
Accounts receivable, net	($147,825 - $73,575)	74,250
Inventory	($27,000 - $6,750)	20,250
Prepaid expenses	($6,750 + $6,750)	13.500
Total current assets	$ 221,400	$162.000
Land	($202,500 - $67,500)	135,000
Buildings	($202,500 - $202,500)	0.0
Equipment	($40,500 + $13,500)	54,000
Less: Accumulated depreciation, buildings and equipment	($27,000 - $16,875 + $3,375)	13,500
Patents, net	($40,500 + $13,500)	54.000
Total assets	$680,400	$391,500
Liabilities and stockholders' equity		
Current liabilities		
Accounts payable	($62,100 + $22,275)	$84,375
Accrued salaries payable	($20,250 - $13,500)	6,750
Accrued interest payable	($20,250 + $10,125)	30.375
Total current liabilities	$102,600	$121.500
Notes payable—long term	($148,500 + $6,750)	155,250
Long-term debt	($158,625 - $158,625)	0.0
Stockholders' equity		
Common stock $1.00 par value	($23,500 - $7,500)	16,000
Paid-in capital	($233,000 - $168,000)	65,000
Retained earnings	($14,175 - $20,925 + $47,250)	40,500
Less: Treasury stock	($0.0 + $6,750)	6.750
Total liabilities and stockholders' equity	$680,400	$391,500

The details underlying the calculation of the 1996 amounts are as follows (all amounts are obtained by simply working backwards from the ending balances):

a) The beginning balance in the cash account of $54,000 is equal to the ending balance of $39,825 plus the decrease in cash reported in the cash flow statement of $14,175.

b) The beginning balance in the accounts receivable, net account of $74,250 is equal to the ending balance $147,825 minus the increase in the account balance of $73,575 during 1997.

c) The beginning balance in the inventory account of $20,250 is equal to the ending balance of $27,000 minus the increase in the account balance of $6,750.

d) The beginning balance in the prepaid expenses account of $13,500 is equal to the ending balance of $6,750 plus the decrease in the account balance during the year of $6,750.

e) The beginning balance in the land account of $135,000 is equal to the ending balance of $202,500 minus the cash paid to acquire land during 1997 of $67,500.

f) The beginning balance in the buildings account of $0.0 is equal to the ending balance of $202,500 minus the cost of the buildings acquired during the year of $202,500.

g) The beginning balance in the equipment account of $54,000 is equal to the ending balance of $40,500 plus the cost of the equipment sold during the year of $13,500.

h) The beginning balance in the accumulated depreciation, buildings and equipment account of $13,500 is equal to the ending balance of $27,000 the depreciation expense for the year of $16,875, plus the accumulated depreciation on the equipment that was sold in 1997 of $3,375.

i) The beginning balance in the patents, net account of $54,000 is equal to the ending balance of $40,500 plus the amortization expense taken in 1997 of $13,500.

j) The beginning balance in the accounts payable account of $84,375 is equal to the ending balance of $62,100 plus the decrease in the account balance of $22,275.

k) The beginning balance in the accrued salaries payable account of $6,750 is equal to the ending balance of $20,250 minus the increase in the account balance of $13,500 during 1997.

l) The beginning balance in the accrued interest payable account of $30,375 is equal to the ending balance of $20,250 plus the decrease in the account balance of $10,125.

m) The beginning balance in the notes payable—long-term account of $155,250 is equal to the ending balance of $148,500 plus the cash paid to reduce notes payable during 1997 of $6,750.

n) The beginning balance in the long-term debt account of $0.0 is equal to the ending balance of $158,625 minus the long-term debt issued during 1997 of $158,625.

o) The beginning balance in the common stock account of $16,000 is equal to the ending balance of $23,500 minus the par value of the shares issued during 1997 of $7,500.0.

p) The beginning balance in the paid-in capital account of $65,000 is equal to the ending balance of $233,000 minus the proceeds from the stock issued during 1997, net of the increase in the common stock account (i.e., $175,500 - $7,500 = $168,000).

q) The beginning balance in the retained earnings account of $40,500 is equal to the ending balance of $14,175 minus 1997 net income of $20,925 and plus cash dividends paid in 1997 of $47,250.

r) The beginning balance in the treasury stock account of $6,750 is equal to the ending balance of $0.0 plus the cost of the treasury stock that was resold during 1997 of $6,750.

C3-5. Kellogg Company (CW): Determining missing amounts on cash flow statement and explaining causes for change in cash

Requirement 1:
Kellogg's 19X1 cash flow statement appears below.

The unknowns are: additions to properties, cash and temporary investments at end of year, cash dividends, cash used by financing activities, and net earnings.

These amounts may be solved for as follows.

a) Additions to properties:

Cash used by investing activities of ($319.9) is given as are its components (except additions to properties). Property disposals generated $25.2 while other acquisitions used $11.6 of cash. Working backwards from the total investing outflow of $319.9 yields a figure of $333.5 for additions to properties. Specifically:

Total investing outflows = Additions to properties - Property disposals + Other acquisitions.

$$(\$319.9) = X + \$25.2 - \$11.6$$
$$X = \$333.5 = \text{Additions to properties.}$$

b) Cash and temporary investments at end of year:

Cash and temporary investments at the beginning of the year is given as $100.5 as is the increase in cash and temporary investments for the year of $77.5. Cash and temporary investments at end of year is just the sum of the two, or $178.0.

c) Cash used by financing activities:

The following given information is used to solve for this unknown:

Cash provided by operations is $934.4,
Cash used by investing activities is ($319.9).
Effect of exchange rate changes on cash $0.7, and
Increase in cash and temporary investments is $77.5.

To find cash used by financing activities:

Increase in cash = Cash provided by operations - Cash used by investing activities - Cash used by financing activities + the Effect of exchange rate change on cash.

$$\$77.5 = \$934.4 - \$319.9 - X + \$0.7$$
$$X = -\$537.7 = \text{Cash used by financing activities.}$$

d) Cash dividends:

Cash used by financing activities of ($537.7) is obtained from (c). Its components (except cash dividends) are all given in the case: Issuance of common stock $17.7, purchase of treasury stock $83.6, borrowings of notes payable $182.1, issuance of long-term debt $4.3, other financing activities $1.1, reduction of long-term debt $126.0, and reduction of notes payable $274.0. Cash dividends may be derived as follows:

Cash used by financing activities = Issuance of common stock - Purchase of treasury stock + Borrowings of notes payable + Issuance of long-term debt + Other financing activities - Reduction of long-term debt - Reduction of notes payable - Cash dividends.

$$-\$537.7 = \$17.7 - \$83.6 + \$182.1 + \$4.3 + \$1.1 - \$126.0 - \$274.0 - X$$
$$= \$259.3 = \text{Cash Dividends.}$$

e) **Net earnings:**

Net earnings may be derived by taking cash provided by operations of $934.4 and working backwards through the adjustments to net income that are required to arrive at cash provided by operations.

The necessary adjustments (are given as):
Other noncash expenses $16.8, decrease in accounts receivable $10.2, depreciation $222.8, increase in prepaid expenses $22.9, decrease in deferred income taxes $5.4, increase in accounts payable $42.7, Increase in inventories $41.4, and increase in accrued liabilities $105.6.

Net earnings may be derived as follows:

Cash provided by operations = Net earnings + Other noncash expenses + Decrease in accounts receivable + Depreciation - Increase in prepaid expenses - Decrease in deferred income taxes + Increase in accounts payable - Increase in inventories + Increase in accrued liabilities.

$934.4 = X + $16.8 + $10.2 + $222.8 - $22.9 - $5.4 + $42.7 - $41.4 + $105.6.
X = net earnings = $606.0.

Having derived the unknowns, all that remains is assembling the cash flow statement in good form. The correct cash flow statement appears on the next page.

Requirement 2:
Kellogg's cash provided by operations of $934.4 was more than enough to cover the firm's investing outflows of $319.9.

Requirement 3:
This is a trick question. Depreciation is not a source of cash (i.e., reporting more depreciation does not increase cash flow). Depreciation is a noncash expense which needs to be added back to net income to derive Cash Provided by Operations when a firm uses the indirect method to report operating cash flows in its cash statement.

Requirement 4:
There are two primary reasons for the difference. They are that Kellogg's financing activities (e.g., cash dividends, reduction of notes payable, etc.) used $537.7 million of cash and that the firm's investing activities (e.g., additions to properties) used $319.9 million of cash. Together these outflows total $857.6 which, when subtracted from the $934.4 cash inflow from operations, leaves an increase in cash of about $77.5.

Kellogg Company and Subsidiaries
Consolidated Statement of Cash Flows
Year Ended December 31,

(millions of $)	19X1
Operating Activities	
Net earnings	$606.0
Items in net earnings not requiring (providing) cash	
Depreciation	222.8
Deferred income taxes	(5.4)
Other noncash expenses	16.8
Change in operating assets and liabilities	
Accounts receivable	10.2
Inventories	(41.4)
Prepaid expenses	(22.9)
Accounts payable	42.7
Accrued liabilities	105.6
Cash provided by operations	934.4
Investing Activities	
Additions to properties	(333.5)
Property disposals	25.2
Other acquisitions	(11.6)
Cash used by investing activities	(319.9)
Financing Activities	
Borrowings of notes payable	182.1
Reduction of notes payable	(274.0)
Issuance of long-term debt	4.3
Reduction of long-term debt	(126.0)
Issuance of common stock	17.7
Purchase of treasury stock	(83.6)
Cash dividends	(259.3)
Other	1.1
Cash used by financing activities	(537.7)
Effect of exchange rate changes on cash	0.7
Increase (decrease) in cash and temporary investments	77.5
Cash and temporary investments at beginning of year	100.5
Cash and temporary investments at end of year	$178.0

Exercises

E4-1. Inventory turnover
(AICPA adapted)

$$\text{Inventory turnover} = \frac{\text{Cost of goods sold}}{\text{Average inventory}} = \frac{\$2,200,000}{\$550,000} = 4.0$$

$$\$550,000 = \frac{\$500,000 + \$600,000}{2}$$

E4-2. Receivable and inventory turnover
(AICPA adapted)

Accounts receivable turnover

$$= \frac{\text{Net credit sales}}{\text{Average trade receivables}} = \frac{\$2,500,000}{\$462,500} = 5.41$$

$$\$462,000 = \frac{\$475,000 + \$450,000}{2}$$

$$\text{Inventory turnover} = \frac{\text{Cost of goods gold}}{\text{Average inventory}} = \frac{\$2,000,000}{\$575,000} = 3.48$$

$$\$575,000 = \frac{\$600,000 + \$550,000}{2}$$

E4-3. Inventory turnover
(AICPA adapted)

$$\text{Inventory turnover} = \frac{\text{Cost of goods sold}}{\text{Average inventory}} = \frac{\$1,800,000}{\$450,000} = 4.0$$

$$\$1,800,000 = \$400,000 + \$1,900,000 - \$500,000$$

$$\$450,000 = \frac{\$400,000 + \$500,000}{2}$$

E4-4. Receivable turnover
(AICPA adapted)

Total net sales equals total credit sales plus total cash sales. The accounts receivable turnover ratio is used to find total credit sales:

$$\text{Accounts receivable turnover} = \frac{\text{Total credit sales}}{\text{Average receivables}}$$

$$5.0 = \frac{\text{Total credit sales}}{\$275,000} \qquad \$275,000 = \frac{\$250,000 + \$300,000}{2}$$

Total credit sales = $\$275,000 \times 5.0$ = \$1,375,000
Total net sales   = $\$1,375,000 + \$100,000$ = \$1,475,000

E4-5. Current and quick ratios
(AICPA adapted)

The write-off of obsolete inventory would decrease Todd Corporation's current assets, thus decreasing the current ratio. The quick ratio would be unaffected by the inventory write-off because it takes only the most liquid assets (cash, marketable securities, and receivables) into account.

E4-6. Current ratio
(AICPA adapted)

1) The refinancing of a $30,000 long-term mortgage with a short-term note would increase Gil's current liabilities, decreasing the current ratio to .43.

2) Purchasing $50,000 of inventory with a short-term account payable would increase Gil's current assets to $140,000, and increase the current liabilities to $230,000, making the current ratio .61.

3) Paying $20,000 of short-term accounts payable decreases both the current assets and liabilities by $20,000, making the current ratio .44.

4) Collection of $10,000 of short-term accounts receivable has no effect on Gil's current ratio.

E4-7. Interest coverage
(AICPA adapted)

The number of times that bond interest was earned can be calculated by using the following ratio:

$$\text{Times interest earned} = \frac{\text{Income before interest charges \& taxes}}{\text{Interest charges}}$$

$$= \frac{\$800,000 + \$600,000 + \$120,000}{\$120,000} = 12.67 \text{ times}$$

E4-8. Why inventory turnover increased
(AICPA adapted)

The gross profit margin (4) decreased. Sales were unchanged, so the gross profit margin decline would be due to increased cost of goods sold. If inventory were also unchanged, the higher cost of goods sold would result in greater inventory turnover.

E4-9. Days sales outstanding
(AICPA adapted)

Requirement 1:
Gross margin equals net sales minus cost of goods sold. Net sales can be found by using the accounts receivable turnover ratio:

$$\text{Accounts receivable turnover} = \frac{\text{Net sales}}{\text{Average receivables}}$$

$$5 = \frac{\text{Net sales}}{\$950,000} \qquad \$950,000 = \frac{\$900,000 + \$1,000,000}{2}$$

Net sales = $950,000 \times 5 = \$4,750,000$

Cost of goods sold can be found by using the inventory turnover ratio:

$$\text{Inventory turnover} = \frac{\text{Cost of goods sold}}{\text{Average inventory}}$$

$$4 = \frac{\text{Cost of goods sold}}{\$1,150,000} \qquad \$1,150,000 = \frac{\$1,100,000 + \$1,200,000}{2}$$

Cost of goods sold $= 1,150,000 \times 4 \qquad\qquad = \$4,600,000$
Gross margin $\qquad = \$4,750,000 - \$4,600,000 = \$150,000$

Requirement 2:

Days' sales in average receivables $= \dfrac{360}{5} = 72$ days

Days' sales in average inventories $= \dfrac{360}{4} = 90$ days

Problems

P4-1. Ratio Analysis: Alpine Chemical
(CFA adapted)

Requirement 1:

a) EBIT/interest expense = $\dfrac{1,629 + 318}{318} = 6.12x$

b) Long-term debt/total capitalization = $\dfrac{1,491}{(1,491 + 3,075)} = 33\%$

c) Funds from operations/total debt:
(Net income + Depreciation expense)/(Long-term debt + Notes payable)

$= \dfrac{(1,479 + 511)}{(1,900 + 1,491)} = 59\%$

d) Operating income/sales = $\dfrac{2,458}{19,460} = 12.6\%$

Note: Some students may include the $1,900 note payable as part of long-term debt and total capitalization.

Requirement 2:
a) EBIT/interest expense measures Alpine Chemical's ability to make its interest payments from pre-tax earnings. A ratio of less than 1 would indicate that Alpine must sell assets or seek financing to make its interest payments.

b) Long-term debt/total capitalization measures Alpine's financial leverage. A highly leveraged company can find issuing new debt difficult or expensive. Also, a highly leveraged company is more sensitive to a business downturn.

c) Funds from operations/total debt measures Alpine's ability to generate enough working capital from continuing operations to meet its debt obligations and future growth needs.

d) Operating income/sales measures Alpine's profitability. Deterioration in this ratio would indicate that sales volume must be increased, or costs reduced, to generate the same level of operating income. If Alpine cannot raise sales volume or reduce costs, then its ability to issue new debt without adversely affecting current debt holders is limited.

Requirement 3:

a) *EBIT/interest expense.* With the exception of 1994, interest coverage has been consistently above 4X. The year 1998 shows the best (highest) interest coverage of the past six years and is consistent with a rating of an A–AA rated bond.

b) *Long-term debt/total capitalization.* The trend in this leverage measure has been stable in the past three years. During the six-year period, leverage has declined erratically from 44% to 33%. At a leverage ratio of 33%, based on the 1998 financial statements, Alpine would appear to be a weak-A-rated company.

c) *Funds from operations/total debt.* The cash flow ratio has been relatively steady during the past three years and, at 59% in 1998, would reflect a rating between A and AA.

d) *Operating income/sales.* Operating margins remain stable but low. At 12.6%, this ratio would indicate that Alpine should be a strong-BBB-rated company.

In summary, these four credit ratios appear stable or improving. Despite a low operating margin, the four ratios indicate that Alpine should be rated A, based on a comparison with the data in Table 2.

P4-2. Financial statement analysis
(AICPA adapted)

1) $39,000   This value can be derived from the equation that total assets (prior to the restatement) equals total liabilities and stockholders' equity, which is $140,000 (computation follows). Total stockholders' equity is $80,000 ($66,000 + $13,000 + $16,000 - $6,000 - $9,000). The given ratio indicates that total stockholders' equity divided by total liabilities is 4 to 3, making total liabilities equal to $60,000 ($80,000 ÷ 4/3). Now that we know the total liabilities and stockholders' equity equals $140,000, the balance for land can be calculated as follows: $140,000 - $12,000 + $25,000 - $92,000 - $22,000 = $39,000.

2) $5,500   Current liabilities = Current assets - Beginning working capital, or ($22,000 - $16,500).

3) $50,000   The face value of the bonds is equal to the stated interest divided by the interest rate. The stated interest is equal to bond interest expense plus bond premium amortization ($3,500 + $500). Thus, the face value of the bonds is equal to $4,000/.08 = $50,000.

4) $1,900   Deferred income taxes can be found by summing the closing balance on the balance sheet and the debit to the deferred income taxes account during the year (from the statement of cash flows).
($1,700 + $200 = $1,900)

5) **$26,100** Year-end working capital is $17,400, or $16,500 beginning working capital plus $700 increase in noncash working capital + $200 cash increase. Working capital is equal to current assets minus current liabilities. At year end, current assets are 3 times current liabilities (current ratio of 3:1). We can substitute "current assets = 3 × current liabilities" into the working capital equation so that "3 × current liabilities" minus "current liabilities" equals $17,400. Current liabilities must be $8,700 and current assets must be $26,100.

6) **$77,000** The balance for buildings and equipment is equal to the opening balance in this account minus the cost of equipment sold during the year ($92,000 - $15,000). The $15,000 is equal to 3/2 the $10,000 book value of the equipment ($10,000 ÷ 2/3 = $15,000). If the equipment cost $15,000 and had a book value of $10,000, then its accumulated depreciation must have been $5,000.

7) **($23,000)** See (6). The accumulated depreciation is equal to the opening balance plus depreciation expense, less $5,000 accumulated depreciation on equipment sold. ($25,000 + $3,000 - $5,000)

8) **$53,715** The balance in the land account is equal to the opening balance plus the acquisition cost of new land. ($39,000 from balance sheet + $14,715 from statement of cash flows)

9) **$8,000** The ending balance of goodwill is equal to the opening balance (prior to restatement) minus goodwill amortization for 1997 and 1998. ($12,000 - $2,000 - $2,000)

10) **$8,700** See (5)

11) **$42,800** The closing balance of bonds payable is equal to the opening balance—derived in (3)—less the current maturity of long-term debt (from the statement of cash flows). ($50,000 - $7,200)

12) **$2,100** The bond premium can be calculated by subtracting the bond premium amortization (statement of cash flows) from the opening balance ($2,600 - $500).

13) **$73,500** The balance of common stock at year end is equal to the opening balance plus the par value of common stock issued to reacquire preferred stock (statement of cash flows), ($66,000 + $7,500).

14) **$15,400** The ending balance of paid-in capital is equal to the opening balance plus the excess of proceeds from reissue of treasury stock ($13,000 + $2,400). The excess of proceeds from reissue of treasury stock is equal to the proceeds from the reissue less the opening balance of treasury stock from the balance sheet ($11,400 - $9,000).

15) **$8,500** The balance of preferred stock is equal to the opening amount on the balance sheet less the par value of preferred stock reacquired by the issue of common stock ($16,000 - $7,500).

16) **($10,885)** The retained earnings balance is equal to the opening balance as shown on the balance sheet prior to the restatement plus the 1998 net loss (after tax) adjustment plus the prior period adjustment. ($6,000 + $2,885 + $2,000)

The current ratio on January 1, 1998 was 4-to-1, and the total stockholders' equity divided by total liabilities ratio at year end was 1.564 (rounded). Here is a correct comparative balance sheet for the company:

Woods Company Balance Sheet		
	1-Jan-98	31-Dec-98
Current assets	$22,000	$26,100
Building and equipment	92,000	77,000
Accumulated depreciation	(25,000)	(23,000)
Land	39,000	53,715
Goodwill	12,000	8,000
Total assets	$140,000	$141,815
Current liabilities	$5,500	$8,700
Bonds payable (8%)	50,000	42,800
Bond premium	2,600	2,100
Deferred income taxes	1,900	1,700
Common stock	66,000	73,500
Paid-in capital	13,000	15,400
Preferred stock	16,000	8,500
Retained earnings (deficit)	(6,000)	(10,885)
Treasury stock (at cost)	(9,000)	-
Total liabilities and stockholders' equity	$140,000	$141,815

P4-3. Explaining changes in financial ratios
(AICPA adapted)

1) a,b,d Inventory turnover is defined as the cost of goods sold divided by average inventory. A lower inventory would cause the inventory turnover ratio to increase, as would a higher cost of goods sold. Consignment items should still be included in inventory, but in this case were mistakenly recorded as sales and removed from inventory. Credit memos were not

recorded for returned merchandise, understating ending inventory and overstating cost of goods sold. Also, year-end purchases were not recorded, understating ending inventory.

2) a,b,e   Accounts receivable turnover is net credit sales divided by average accounts receivable. Recording goods shipped on consignment before they are actually sold overstates accounts receivable and net credit sales. Failing to record credit memos also overstates accounts receivable and net credit sales. When an unusually large percentage of annual credit sales occur in the last month of the year, the year-end balance in accounts receivable will be unusually high. All three situations produce a decrease in the accounts receivable turnover ratio.

3) a,b,e   If the allowance for doubtful accounts increased in dollars, but the allowance decreased as a percentage of accounts receivable, then accounts receivable must have increased by a greater degree than the allowance decreased. Accounts receivable would increase if items shipped on consignment were mistakenly recorded as sales, if significant credits for returned goods were not recorded, or if a larger percentage of sales occurred during the month compared to the prior year.

4) p   The refinancing of short-term debt as long-term debt at a higher interest rate would cause the long-term debt to increase, but not as significantly as interest expense. This is caused by the increased rate being applied to a greater amount of long-term debt.

5) l,p   Net income for the year can be found from operating income less interest expenses and federal income taxes. If operating income increased but net income decreased, it must be that interest expense and/or federal income taxes increased. This could result from an increase in the effective income tax rate, or from refinancing short-term debt as long-term debt with a higher interest rate.

6) h   Gross margin percentage is defined as gross margin divided by sales. If the gross margin percentage remained constant while the gross margin increased, then sales must have increased by the same proportionate amount. Since gross margin is Sales less cost of goods sold, then cost of goods sold must have also increased by the same proportionate amount.

P4-4. Current asset ratios
(AICPA adapted)

1) Alpha's quick ratio is $\dfrac{\$10,000 + \$50,000 + \$30,000}{\$70,000 + \$20,000} = \dfrac{\$90,000}{\$90,000} = 1.0$

2) The accounts receivable turnover is $\dfrac{\$500,000}{\$100,000} = 5.0$

$$\$100,000 = \dfrac{\$150,000 + \$50,000}{2}$$

3) Alpha's merchandise inventory turnover is $\dfrac{\$1,000,000}{\$120,000} = 8.3$

$$\$120,000 = \dfrac{\$150,000 + \$90,000}{2}$$

4) Alpha's current ratio at December 31, 1999, is

$$\dfrac{\$10,000 + \$50,000 + \$90,000 + \$30,000}{\$70,000 + \$20,000} = \dfrac{\$180,000}{\$90,000} = 2.0$$

P4-5. Financial ratios and the balance sheet

<table>
<tr><th colspan="3">Clapton Corporation
Consolidated Balance Sheet</th></tr>
<tr><th></th><th colspan="2">December 31,</th></tr>
<tr><th></th><th>2000</th><th>1999</th></tr>
<tr><td>Assets:</td><td></td><td></td></tr>
<tr><td>Current assets</td><td></td><td></td></tr>
<tr><td>Cash</td><td>$800,000</td><td>$500,000</td></tr>
<tr><td>Marketable securities</td><td>3,200,000</td><td>2,500,000</td></tr>
<tr><td>Accounts receivable</td><td>2,200,000</td><td>1,800,000</td></tr>
<tr><td>Inventories</td><td>3,250,000</td><td>1,750,000</td></tr>
<tr><td>Prepaid expenses</td><td>550,000</td><td>450,000</td></tr>
<tr><td>Total current assets</td><td>10,000,000</td><td>7,000,000</td></tr>
<tr><td>Property, plant, and equipment,
less accumulated depreciation</td><td>25,000,000</td><td>18,000,000</td></tr>
<tr><td>Non-current assets</td><td></td><td></td></tr>
<tr><td>Long-term receivables</td><td>2,500,000</td><td>2,000,000</td></tr>
<tr><td>Investments</td><td>1,500,000</td><td>1,000,000</td></tr>
<tr><td>Other</td><td>1,000,000</td><td>2,000,000</td></tr>
<tr><td>Total assets</td><td>$40,000,000</td><td>$30,000,000</td></tr>
<tr><td>Liabilities and Stockholders' Equity:</td><td></td><td></td></tr>
<tr><td>Current liabilities</td><td></td><td></td></tr>
<tr><td>Accounts payable</td><td>$2,625,000</td><td>$1,500,000</td></tr>
<tr><td>Wages and employee benefits payable</td><td>775,000</td><td>650,000</td></tr>
<tr><td>Income taxes</td><td>300,000</td><td>750,000</td></tr>
<tr><td>Advances and deposits</td><td>100,000</td><td>200,000</td></tr>
<tr><td>Other current liabilities</td><td>200,000</td><td>400,000</td></tr>
<tr><td>Total current liabilities</td><td>4,000,000</td><td>3,500,000</td></tr>
<tr><td>Long-term liabilities</td><td></td><td></td></tr>
<tr><td>Long-term debt</td><td>16,000,000</td><td>9,000,000</td></tr>
<tr><td>Deferred income taxes</td><td>3,000,000</td><td>2,000,000</td></tr>
<tr><td>other</td><td>1,000,000</td><td>500,000</td></tr>
<tr><td>Total liabilities</td><td>24,000,000</td><td>15,000,000</td></tr>
<tr><td>Stockholders' equity</td><td></td><td></td></tr>
<tr><td>Preferred stock</td><td>1,000,000</td><td>1,000,000</td></tr>
<tr><td>Common stock</td><td>2,000,000</td><td>2,000,000</td></tr>
<tr><td>Paid-in capital</td><td>9,000,000</td><td>9,000,000</td></tr>
<tr><td>Retained earnings</td><td>4,000,000</td><td>3,000,000</td></tr>
<tr><td>Total stockholders' equity</td><td>16,000,000</td><td>15,000,000</td></tr>
<tr><td>Total liabilities and stockholders' equity</td><td>$ 40,000,000</td><td>$ 30,000,000</td></tr>
</table>

1) Some givens from #5 under additional information:

   $s = 1,000,000.$ $t = 2,000,000.$ $u = 9,000,000.$

2) Total assets (j) at the end of 1999 using #9 under additional information:

   LTD/total assets = 0.30 = 9,000,000/j = 0.30. So, j = 30,000,000.

   Total assets must equal total liabilities and stockholders' equity, so, zz also equals 30,000,000.

3) Total assets at the end of 2000 (i) using #6 and #13 under additional information:

   ROA for 2000 = 5% and NOPAT = $1,750,000.
   ROA = NOPAT/Avg. total assets

   $$0.05 = \frac{\$1,750,000}{(30,000,000 + i)/2}$$

   $$i = \frac{(\$1,750,000 \times 2)}{0.05} - \$30,000,000 = \$40,000,000$$

   Total assets must equal total liabilities and stockholders' equity, so, z also equals 40,000,000.

4) LTD (p) at the end of 2000 using #9 under additional information:

   p/40,000,000 = 0.40 which means p = 16,000,000.

5) Current liabilities (o) in 1999:

   From the balance sheet, total liabilities at the end of 1999 are 15,000,000 and total long-term liabilities are 11,500,00. Therefore, current liabilities equal $15,000,000 - $11,500,000 = $3,500,000.

6) Current assets (f) in 1999 using #2 under additional information:

   Since the current ratio at the end of 1999 is 2.0, current assets must be 7,000,000 or (2 × $3,500,000).

7) Other assets (h) in 1999:

   Using "f" and the information about assets in the balance sheet:
   h = 30,000,000 - 7,000,000 - 18,000,000 - 3,000,000 = 2,000,000.

8) Plant, property, and equipment (g) in 2000:

Using the information about assets in the balance sheet:
$g = 40,000,000 - 10,000,000 - 5,000,000 = 25,000,000$.

9) Current liabilities (n) in 2000 using #2 under additional information:

The current ratio at the end of 2000 is 2.5, and current assets at the end of 2000 are 10,000,000 (see the balance sheet).

Current ratio = Current assets/current liabilities
$2.5 = 10,000,000/n$ which means $n = 4,000,000$.

10) Accounts payable (k) in 2000:

Using "n" and the information about current liabilities in the balance sheet:
$k = 4,000,000 - 775,000 - 300,000 - 100,000 - 200,000 = 2,625,000$.

11) Accounts receivable (c) in 2000 using #8 and #12 under additional information:

Days receivable outstanding in 2000 is 36.5. This implies the A/R turnover ratio is 10.

Days AR outstanding = 365/AR turnover
36.5 = 365/AR turnover.
AR turnover = Sales/Avg. AR so that means $10 = 20,000,000/$Avg. AR
Avg. AR = 2,000,000.

Since A/R at the end of 1999 is 1,800,000 (see the balance sheet), for average A/R to be 2,000,000, A/R at the end of 2000 must be 2,200,000. $c = 2,200,000$.

12) Inventories (e) in 1999 using #10 under additional information:

The 1999 quick ratio is 1.5.
quick ratio= (Current assets - Inventories)/Current liabilities
Therefore, $1.5 = (7,000,000 - e)/3,500,000$, and $e = 1,750,000$.

13) Inventories (d) in 2000 using #3, #11, and #12 under additional information:

Days inventory held = 60.8 in 2000. This implies an inventory turnover of 6.0 because:

Days inventory held = 365/Inventory turnover = 60.8
Inventory turnover = 365/60.8 = 6

Next, Inventory turnover = CGS/Average inventory. With a gross profit rate of 25%, CGS as a percentage of sales is 75%. This means CGS in 2000 is $0.75 \times 20,000,000 = 15,000,000$.
Thus, 6 = 15,000,000/Average inventory, and average inventory must be 2,500,000.

With a 1999 inventory of 1,750,000, for the average inventory to be 2,500,000, 2000 ending inventory (d) must be 3,250,000.

14) Marketable securities (b) in 1999:

Using "f" and "e" and the numbers in the balance sheet,
b = 7,000,000 - 4,500,000 = 2,500,000

15) Cash (a) in 2000:

Using "c" and "d" and the numbers in the balance sheet,
a = 10,000,000 - 9,200,000 = 800,000

16) Accounts payable (l) in 1999 using #1 under additional information:

Days' payable outstanding was 45.6, which implies an A/P turnover ratio of 8.
Days' payable outstanding = 365/AP turnover = 45.6
AP turnover = 365/45.6 = 8.
AP turnover = Inventory purchases/Avg. accts payable
  8 = (CGS + Change in inventory)/Avg. accts payable
  8 = (15,000,000 + 1,500,000)/Avg. accts payable
Avg. accts payable = 2,062,500.
Since accts payable at the end of 2000 was 2,625,000, for the average A/P to be 2,062,500, A/P at the end of 1999 must have been 1,500,000.

17) Wages and employee benefits payable (m) for 1999:

Using earlier calculations and existing numbers in the balance sheet:
m = 3,500,000 - 2,850,000 = 650,000.

18) Total stockholders' equity (y) at the end of 1999:

Using earlier calculations and existing numbers in the balance sheet:
y = 30,000,000 - 15,000,000 = 15,000,000.

19) Retained earnings (w) at the end of 1999:

Using earlier calculations and existing numbers in the balance sheet:
w = 15,000,000 - 12,000,000 = 3,000,000.

20) Retained earnings (v) at the end of 2000:

Using earlier calculations, existing numbers in the balance sheet,
and #4 and #7 under additional information:
v = 3,000,000 + 1,250,000 (NI) - 250,000 (dividends) = 4,000,000.

21) Total stockholders' equity (x) at the end of 2000:

Using earlier calculations and existing numbers in the balance sheet:
x = 1,000,000 + 2,000,000 + 9,000,000 + 4,000,000 = 16,000,000.

22) Total liabilities (r) at the end of 2000:

Using earlier calculations and existing numbers in the balance sheet:
r = 40,000,000 - 16,000,000 = 24,000,000.

23) Other long-term liabilities (q) at the end of 2000:

Using earlier calculations and existing numbers in the balance sheet:
q = 24,000,000 - 4,000,000 - 16,000,000 - 3,000,000 = 1,000,000

P4-6. Why financial ratios change
(AICPA adapted)

1) This transaction would decrease the current ratio, have no effect on the inventory turnover ratio, and increase the total debt/total asset ratio. Daley's current liabilities are increased by the declaration of a cash dividend.

2) If customers returned invoiced goods for which they had not paid, Daley's current ratio and inventory turnover would decrease, and the total debt/total asset ratio would increase.

3) The payment of accounts payable would increase the current ratio, have no effect on inventory turnover ratio, and decrease the total debt/total asset ratio.

4) This transaction would increase the current ratio and the total debt/total asset ratio, and have no effect on inventory turnover.

5) The increase in selling price would increase the current ratio, have no effect on inventory turnover, and decrease the total debt/total asset ratio.

P4-7. **Working backward to the statements**
(AICPA adapted)

Requirement 1:
The balance in trade accounts payable can be found from the current ratio. The amount of current assets is equal to total assets minus noncurrent assets ($432,000 - 294,000 = $138,000).

The current ratio is $\dfrac{\text{Current assets}}{\text{Current liabilities}}$; or $1.5 = \dfrac{\$138,000}{\text{Current liabilities}}$

Current liabilities are $\dfrac{\$138,000}{1.5} = \$92,000$

Thus, trade accounts payable is equal to $92,000 - $25,000 = $67,000

Requirement 2:
The balance in retained earnings can be found by examining the following equations, setting X = the balance in long-term debt, and Y = the balance in retained earnings:

a) Total assets = Total liabilities + Total stockholders' equity, and

b) $0.8 = \dfrac{\text{Total liabilities}}{\text{Total stockholders' equity}}$ (given in the problem)

From equation a):

Total liabilities = $92,000 + X, and total stockholders' equity = $300,000 + Y. Therefore, $92,000 + X + $300,000 + Y = $432,000, which yields X = $40,000 - Y.

From equation b):

$0.8 = \dfrac{\$92,000 + X}{\$300,000 + Y}$, which yields ($300,000 + Y)(0.8) = $92,000 + X.

Substituting the relationship we obtained from equation a) for the X in equation b): ($300,000 + Y)(0.8) = $92,000 + $40,000 − Y. Solving for Y yields ($60,000), the balance in retained earnings.

Requirement 3:

The balance in the inventory account can be calculated from three relationships given in the problem:

$$10.5 = \frac{\text{Cost of goods sold}}{\text{Ending inventory}}, \text{ which yields cost of goods sold}$$

= (10.5)(Ending inventory),

$$15 = \frac{\text{Sales}}{\text{Ending inventory}}, \text{ and } \$315,000 = \text{Sales - Cost of goods sold, which yields}$$

Sales = $315,000 + Cost of goods sold.

Beginning with the relationship $15 = \dfrac{\text{Sales}}{\text{Ending inventory}}$, substitute the derived

relationship for Sales, so that $15 = \dfrac{\$315,000 + \text{Cost of goods sold}}{\text{Ending inventory}}$.

Then, substitute the relationship we derived for cost of goods sold, leaving

$$15 = \frac{\$315,000 + (10.5)(\text{Ending inventory})}{\text{Ending inventory}}$$

So ending inventory $= \dfrac{\$315,000}{4.5}$.

Solving for ending inventory yields a balance of $70,000

P4-8. Profitability analysis: Maytag

Step 1

Average total liabilities for 1994:	$1,827,666
Average total equity for 1994:	$659,247
Average total assets for 1994:	$2,486,913

Step 2

Return on assets (ROA)	1994	1993	1992
N.I. (before acct. change)	$151,137	$51,270	($8,354)
+ Interest expense	74,077	75,364	75,004
× (1 - tax rate)	× .65	× .65	× .65
	48,150	48,987	48,753
Adjusted net income	199,287	100,257	40,399
÷ Average total assets	÷2,486,913	÷2,485,494	÷2,518,279
ROA	8.01%	4.03%	1.60%

Decomposition of ROA: Profit margin ratio × total asset turnover ratio

N.I. adjusted for Int. (net of tax)	$199,287	$100,257	$40,399
÷ Sales (net)	÷3,372,515	÷2,987,054	÷3,041,223
Profit margin ratio	5.91%	3.36%	1.33%

	1994	**1993**	**1992**
Sales (net)	$3,372,515	$2,987,054	$3,041,223
÷ Avg. total assets	÷2,486,913	÷2,485,494	÷2,518,279
Total asset turnover ratio	1.36	1.20	1.21

Total asset turnover ratio	1.36	1.20	1.21
× Profit margin ratio	× 5.91%	× 3.36%	× 1.33%
= ROA	8.01%	4.04%	1.61%

Common Size Income Statements:

	1994	**1993**	**1992**
Sales (net)	100.00%	100.00%	100.00%
Cost of goods sold	74.01%	75.76%	76.92%
Selling, general & admin. exp.	16.42%	17.25%	17.37%
Special charges	0.00%	1.67%	3.12%
Nonoperating exp. (income)	0.22%	(0.21)%	(0.13)%
Interest expense	2.20%	2.52%	2.47%
Tax expense	2.67%	1.29%	0.52%
N.I. before cum. effect of acct. changes	4.48%	1.72%	(0.27)%

Note: Net operating expense (income) is the sum of two items on the income statement: loss on business dispositions and other—net.

Comment: The analysis demonstrates that asset turnover was relatively stable over 1992 and 1993 and increased substantially in 1994. Differences in year-to-year profit margins have contributed to earnings variability at Maytag. Increased profit margins from 1992 to 1994 were due primarily to decreased cost of goods sold, which fell from 76.92% of net sales in 1992 to 75.76% of net sales in 1993 and 74.01% of net sales in 1994. With $3.3 billion of sales in 1994, the 1.75% difference in cost of goods sold from 1993 amounts to roughly $59 million. Special charges in 1992 and 1993 also resulted in lower profit margins. Management's discussion and analysis in the 1994 annual report indicates that the company took a $95 million pre-tax charge to income in the third quarter of 1992 for reorganization of its U.S. and European operations, and a $50 million pre-tax charge in the first quarter of 1993 for promotional programs in Europe.

Step 3

Some students might properly focus only on interest-pay debt (notes payable and long-term debt) for purposes of this section. The solution that follows uses "total liabilities" in keeping with the ROE-ROA decomposition. Also, note that some interest charges might not appear on the income statement if Maytag capitalizes interest during construction. The solution presumes that capitalized interest is inconsequential.

Return to debtholders:	1994	1993	1992
Interest expense	$74,077	$75,364	$75,004
× (1 - tax rate)	× (1 - .35)	× (1 - .35)	× (1 - .35)
Interest expense (net of tax)	$48,150	$48,987	$48,753
÷ Average total liabilities	÷1,827,666	÷1,892,491	÷1,713,374
After-tax % return paid to debt	2.63%	2.59%	2.85%

Percent of assets financed with debt:

	1994	1993	1992
Avg. total liab.	$1,827,666	$1,892,491	$1,713,374
÷ Avg. total assets	÷ 2,486,913	÷ 2,485,494	÷ 2,518,279
%Assets financed with debt	73.49%	76.14%	68.04%

These data suggest that the company is becoming more highly leveraged—debt is financing a greater proportion of assets in 1994 than it was in 1992. Also, notice that debt is a rather cheap source of financial capital at Maytag.

Step 4

Return on equity (ROE)	1994	1993	1992
Net income (before acct. change)	$151,137	$51,270	($8,354)
÷ Average stockholders' equity	÷ 659,247	÷ 593,003	÷ 804,905
ROE	22.93%	8.65%	(1.04)%

Decomposition of ROE

	1994	1993	1992
Net income (after interest)	$151,137	$51,270	$(8,354)
÷ Sales (net)	÷3,372,515	÷$2,987,054	÷$3,041,223
Profit margin percent	4.48%	1.72%	(0.27)%
Total asset turnover (see above)	1.36	1.20	1.21
Avg. total assets	$2,486,913	$2,485,494	$2,518,279
÷ Avg. stockholders' equity	÷ 659,247	÷ 593,003	÷ 804,905
Leverage ratio	3.77	4.19	3.13

Profit margin	4.48%	1.72%	-0.27%
× Total asset turnover	× 1.36	× 1.20	× 1.21
× Leverage ratio	×3.77	×4.19	×3.13
ROE	22.97%	8.65%	(1.02)%

Comparison of ROE and ROA

	1994	1993	1992
ROA	8.01%	4.04%	1.61%
ROE	22.97%	8.65%	(1.02)%

The differences between ROA and ROE across the three years are due primarily to the effects of **financial leverage**. As shown above in Step 3, Maytag's average after-tax return paid to debtholders ranged from 2.85% in 1992 to 2.59% in 1993. In 1993 and 1994, when the return on assets was *greater* than the after-tax cost of debt, leverage worked to the benefit of shareholders and increased ROE relative to ROA. In 1992, however, when the return on assets was 1.61% which was *below* the after-tax cost of debt of 2.85%, leverage *decreased* the return to shareholders (ROE = -1.02%) relative to the overall return on assets of 1.61%.

Demonstration of how leverage affected return to common shareholders:

Excess return on assets financed with debt:

	ROA	After-Tax Int. Cost for Debt		Amt. of Assets Financed with Debt (Avg. Total Liab.)		Excess (Reduction) Return to Shareholders
1994	(8.01% - 2.63%) =	5.38%	×	$1,827,666	=	$98,328
1993	(4.04% - 2.59%) =	1.45%	×	$1,892,491	=	$27,441
1992	(1.61% - 2.85%) =	(1.24)%	×	$1,713,374	=	($21,417)

Return on assets financed with common equity:

	ROA		Amt. of Assets Financed with Equity (Avg. Total Equity)		Return to Shareholders
1994	8.01%	×	$659,247	=	$52,806
1993	4.04%	×	$593,003	=	$23,957
1992	1.61%	×	$804,905	=	$12,959

132

Step 5
Student response should summarize key points made above.

Dollar return to shareholders:

	1994	1993	1992
Excess return on assets financed with debt	$98,328	$27,441	($21,417)
Return on assets financed with equity	52,806	23,957	12,959
Total dollar return to shareholders	$151,134	$51,398	($ 8,458)
÷ Average stockholders' equity	÷ 659,247	÷593,003	÷804,905
ROE	22.93%	8.67%	(1.05)%

Leverage benefited shareholders in 1994 and 1993 but reduced their return in 1992 when the after-tax cost of debt was greater than ROA.

P4-9. Comparative analysis of footwear manufacturers (CW)

1) The following table summarizes the key financial ratios for these two companies.

	1994		1993	
	Nike	Reebok	Nike	Reebok
Current ratio	3.15	2.65	3.58	2.84
Quick ratio	2.31	1.41	2.26	1.55
Accounts receivable turnover	5.53	6.63	6.22	6.61
Days receivables outstanding	66.0	55.0	58.7	55.2
Inventory turnover	4.33	3.45	4.49	3.63
Days inventory held	84.3	105.8	81.3	100.6
Accounts payable turnover	12.6	13.5	18.6	12.69
Days accounts payable outstanding	29.0	27.0	19.6	28.8
Return on assets	13.5	17.5	18.8	17.9
ROA decomposition:				
Profit margin	8.1	8.1	9.7	8.5
Asset turnover	1.66	2.16	1.94	2.11
Long-term debt to total assets	0.5	8.0	0.7	9.6
Long-term debt to tangible assets	0.6	8.5	0.7	10.3
Interest coverage ratio	33.1	25.7	24.1	15.5
Operating cash flows/total liabilities	91.1	26.2	48.8	26.1

2) Assessment of profitability, liquidity, and long-term solvency.

Profitability:

- In general, both firms have been reasonably profitable over the 1993–1994 period.

- Nike had a higher ROA in 1993 (18.8% versus 17.9%) but not in 1994 (13.5% versus 17.5%). Nike's NOPAT operating margin fell from 9.7% to 8.1% from 1993 to 1994 while Reebok's fell from 8.5% to 8.1%. In addition, Reebok's asset turnover ratio improved from 2.11 in 1993 to 2.16 in 1994 while Nike's asset turnover ratio fell from 1.94 to 1.66.

Liquidity:

- Nike was more liquid than Reebok in 1993 based on both the current and quick ratios. However, Nike's liquidity deteriorated slightly from 1993 to 1994 (the current ratio declined from 3.58 to 3.15, and the quick ratio increased from 2.26 to 2.31). Nike is more liquid at the end of 1994.

- Nike's accounts receivable turnover tends to be a bit slower than Reebok's (e.g., in 1994 5.53 vs. 6.63) which means Nike's average receivable is outstanding for slightly longer than Reebok's in 1994 (66.0 days vs. 55.0 days).

- Nike's inventory turnover tends to be a bit higher than Reebok's (e.g., in 1994 4.33 vs. 3.45) which means that Nike holds inventory for fewer days (84.3 days vs. 105.8 days in 1994).

- The relatively high accounts payable turnover rates of both firms may be an indication that both pay their A/P rather quickly in order to take advantage of various cash discounts on purchases offered by the suppliers of their raw materials.

Long-Term Solvency:

- Nike uses virtually no long-term debt (long-term debt is 0.05% of total assets at the end of 1994), while Reebok uses a moderate amount of long-term debt (about 8.0% of total assets at the end of 1994). It seems reasonable to conclude that both firms have some unused debt capacity that could be used to fund future expansion of PP&E or for acquisitions.

- Given their relatively modest use of long-term debt, both companies have very high interest coverage ratios. Nike's is 33.1 in 1994 while Reebok's is 25.7. By any standard, these coverage ratios are comfortable.

- The operating cash flow to total liabilities ratio for Nike reveals that its 1993 operating cash flow was large enough to pay off almost half of the firm's liabilities (i.e., a ratio of 48.8%). By the end of 1994, operating cash flow was enough to pay off almost all of the firm's liabilities (i.e., the ratio had increased to 91.1%).

- For Reebok, its 1993 and 1994 operating cash flows were large enough to pay off about 1/4 of the firm's total liabilities in both years (ratios of about 25% in both years).

- In summary, both firms use more equity than debt financing, and Nike uses more equity financing than Reebok.

Based on the ratio analysis above, the analyst might do several things: gather information about the industry to help interpret the ratios and their changes from 1993 to 1994; or contact the companies to obtain additional clarifying information about why the ratios changed over time.

3) Possible non-financial information that might be useful includes:

- Pending lawsuits or other major litigation.
- New product developments or introductions. Patent expiration dates.
- The nature of any restrictive covenants in debt contracts.
- The features of executive compensation and bonus plans and how they may use accounting numbers.
- Expected (future) costs for the firms' raw material inputs. Recent trends in raw material prices.
- Expected (future) labor costs. Recent trends in labor costs.
- Plant capacity and plant utilization rates.
- Expected future demand for various footwear products.
- Athletes under contract for each firm and when these contracts expire.
- Market share in various market segments (e.g., men's footwear, women's footwear, kid's footwear), and penetration into various markets worldwide (i.e., share of U.S. markets, share of European markets, etc.). Potential new markets (e.g., China).
- Recent management earnings and/or sales forecasts for the next "n" quarters or years. Other public disclosures by management (e.g., future R&D expenditures or capital expenditure budgets).
- Reports by various research/brokerage houses.

- Population growth rates and changes in population demographics as they pertain to the demand for the firms' products.
- Managerial quality/skill and managerial reputation in the capital markets.
- Availability (and size) of short-term bank lines of credit.

P4-10. Understanding common-size statements of cash flows

Requirement 1:
Common-size financial statements provide a convenient and effective means to organize and summarize financial information about a company. These statements help analysts identify major trends and relationships among statement items. Comparisons among companies are also made easier by the preparation of common-size statements.

Requirement 2:
The common-size cash flow statement follows.

TOYS 'R US, INC. AND SUBSIDIARIES
CONSOLIDATED STATEMENTS OF CASH FLOWS
(as % of sales)

	Year Ended		
	1993	1992	1991
CASH FLOWS FROM OPERATING ACTIVITIES			
Net earnings	6.1%	5.5%	5.9%
Adjustments to reconcile net earnings to net cash provided by operating activities:			
Depreciation and amortization	1.7%	1.6%	1.4%
Deferred income taxes	0.2	0.3	0.3
Changes in operating assets and liabilities:			
Accounts and other receivables	0.0	0.1	(0.4)
Merchandise inventories	(1.5)	(1.9)	(0.8)
Prepaid expenses and other operating assets	(0.5)	(0.3)	(0.2)
Accounts payable, accrued expenses, and other liabilities	1.6	7.5	(0.7)
Income taxes payable	0.6	0.1	(0.2)
Total adjustments	1.9	7.6	(0.6)
Net cash provided by operating activities	8.0%	13.1%	5.3%
CASH FLOWS FROM INVESTING ACTIVITIES			
Capital expenditures, net	(5.9)%	(9.0)%	(8.8)%
Other assets	(0.3)	(0.2)	0.0
Net cash used in investing activities	(6.2)%	(9.2)%	(8.8)%
CASH FLOWS FROM FINANCING ACTIVITIES			
Short-term borrowings, net	(2.4)%	(1.5)%	3.3%
Long-term borrowings	4.4	3.2	0.6
Long-term debt repayments	(0.1)	0.0	(0.2)
Exercise of stock options	1.2	0.5	0.6
Share repurchase program	(0.4)	0.0	(0.6)
Net cash provided by financing activities	2.8%	2.2%	3.7%
Effect of exchange rate changes on cash and cash equivalents	(0.1)	0.6	(0.3)
CASH AND CASH EQUIVALENTS			
Increase (decrease) during year	4.5%	6.7%	(0.1)%
Beginning of year	6.2	0.6	0.7
End of year	10.7%	7.3%	0.6%

Requirement 3:
The common-size cash flow statements reveal that:

- Except for 1992, net income has been about 6.0% of sales.

- Depreciation and amortization have increased from 1.4% to 1.7% of sales. These expenses have no cash flow impact, but analysts will want to know why they are increasing.

- Cash from operating activities increased from 5.3% to 13.1% of sales. However, cash from operating activities decreased from 13.1% to 8.0% of sales. The decline can be traced to the decrease in accounts payable, accrued expenses, and other liabilities.

- Capital expenditures fell to 5.9% of sales from 9.0%. The analyst should determine if the decline is due to sales increases, reduced capital expenditures, or a combination of both.

- The company does not distribute much cash to shareholders through dividends or share repurchases.

- Long-term borrowings have increased the last three years; however, the amounts do not appear large (0.6%, 3.2%, and 4.4%, respectively) in relation to sales or operating cash flows.

- On balance, cash inflows from financing activities have averaged about 2.9% of sales over the past three years.

Cases
C4-1. J.C. Penney (A): Common-size and trend income statements

Requirement 1:

J.C. Penney Company, Inc. and Subsidiaries			
Consolidated Statements of Income			
(as % of total revenue)			
For the Year	1992	1991	1990
Revenue			
Retail sales	94.4%	93.7%	94.0%
Finance charge revenue	3.0	3.7	3.9
Other revenue	2.7	2.6	2.1
Total revenue	100.0%	100.0%	100.0%
Costs and expenses			
Cost of goods sold, occupancy, buying, and warehousing costs	63.1%	62.7%	63.0%
Selling, general, and administrative expenses	27.0	28.5	28.7
Costs and expenses of other businesses	1.9	2.1	1.8
Interest expense, net	1.4	1.8	1.7
Nonrecurring items	0	2.3	0
Total costs and expenses	93.4%	97.3%	95.2%
Income before income taxes and cumulative effect of accounting change	6.6%	2.7%	4.8%
Income taxes	2.5	1.2	1.5
Income before cumulative effect of accounting change	4.1%	1.5%	3.3%
Cumulative effect of accounting change for postretirement health care benefits, net of income taxes of $116	0	(1.1%)	0
Net income	4.1%	0.5%	3.3%

Requirement 2:
The common-size statements show that:

- Retail sales consistently represent about 94.0% of Total revenues.

- Cost of goods sold, occupancy, buying, and warehousing costs is about 63.0% of total revenues. This means that the gross profit rate has been very stable at 37% of Sales.

- Finance charge revenue has fallen over recent years suggesting that more customers are paying cash—or using bank cards (a cash equivalent)—rather than using Penney's credit cards.

- Selling, general, and administrative expenses run about 27.0% of sales. This percentage has declined from 28.7% in 1990 to 27.0% in 1992, suggesting that management has focused on cost reductions in these areas.

- Interest is not a major expense item for the company. It was only 1.4% of sales in 1992, down from 1.7% in 1990. This may indicate that Penney's lease obligations are structured as operating leases rather than as capital leases. As discussed more fully in Chapter 11, capital leases result in the recognition of interest expense but operating leases do not.

- The net profit margin was 4.1% in 1992—four cents of every sales dollar remained after all expenses. This is an increase of almost one percentage point from 1990. The profit margin for 1991 is not directly comparable to 1990 and 1992 because of the nonrecurring items (2.3% of sales) and the accounting method change (1.1% of sales).

- On balance, the common-size analysis suggests a mature and profitable company whose income statement items are a stable proportion of sales.

Note: It would be instructive to compare the common-size income statements of J.C. Penney with other companies in the industry. This would more clearly identify Penney's strengths and weaknesses relative to competitors.

Requirement 3:
The trend statements are:

J.C. Penney Company, Inc. and Subsidiaries Trend Statements			
For the Year	1992	1991	1990
Revenue:			
Retail sales	110.1	99.0	100
Finance charge revenue	84.6	96.0	100
Other revenue	136.4	120.5	100
Total revenue	109.6	99.3	100
Costs and expenses:			
Cost of goods sold, occupancy, buying, and warehousing costs	109.8	98.8	100
Selling, general, and administrative expenses	103.2	98.5	100
Costs and expenses of other businesses	119.1	116.2	100
Interest expense, net	85.7	102.3	100
Nonrecurring items	-	-	-
Total costs and expenses	107.5	101.5	100
Income before income taxes and cumulative effect of accounting change	151.3	56.3	100
Income taxes	189.0	80.0	100
Income before cumulative effect of accounting change	134.7	45.8	100
Cumulative effect of accounting change for postretirement health care benefits, net of income taxes of $116	-	-	-
Net income	134.7	13.9	100

141

Requirement 4:
The trend analysis reveals that:

- Revenue growth is quite modest. Retail sales grew by only 10% over the period, an average annual increase of about 5.0%.

- Revenue from finance charges is declining. This may indicate that more people are buying with cash rather than credit. It might also mean that the company's credit policies are too strict.

- Cost of goods sold, occupancy, buying, and warehousing grew about 10%, the same increase noted for retail sales revenue.

- Selling, general, and administrative expenses grew by only 3.0%. On the other hand, costs and expenses of other businesses increased about 20% over the period. Interest expense declined about 7.0% per year.

- Income before income taxes and cumulative effect of accounting change grew about 51.0% over the 1990–92 period, an average annual rate of increase of about 25%. Income taxes also increased about 45%, about 90.0% per year.

- Collectively, these revenue and expense trends resulted in a 35% increase in net income over the 1990–92 period.

- On balance, the trend analysis is consistent with the results of the common-size statements and indicates that J.C. Penney is a stable, mature, and profitable company.

The common-size statements and trend statements allow the analyst to look at the same underlying data through two different lenses. The two approaches should be viewed as complements rather than as substitutes for one another.

Requirement 5:
Both common-size and trend statements can reveal important changes in a company's revenues and expenses.

C4-2. J.C. Penney (B): Earnings forecast

Requirement 1:
The projected income statement of J.C. Penney Company for 1993 is as follows (In millions):

<table>
<tr><td colspan="3">J.C. Penney Company, Inc. and Subsidiaries
1993 Projected Income Statement</td></tr>
<tr><td colspan="3">(in millions)</td></tr>
<tr><td colspan="3">Revenue</td></tr>
<tr><td>Retail sales</td><td>$18,891</td><td></td></tr>
<tr><td>Finance charge revenue</td><td>718</td><td></td></tr>
<tr><td>Other revenue</td><td>591</td><td></td></tr>
<tr><td>Total revenue</td><td></td><td>$20,200</td></tr>
<tr><td colspan="3">Costs and expenses</td></tr>
<tr><td>Cost of goods sold, occupancy,
    buying, and warehousing costs</td><td>$12,342</td><td></td></tr>
<tr><td>Selling, general, and
    administrative expenses</td><td>6,060</td><td></td></tr>
<tr><td>Costs and expenses of other
    businesses</td><td>401</td><td></td></tr>
<tr><td>Interest expense, net</td><td>258</td><td></td></tr>
<tr><td>Nonrecurring items</td><td>0</td><td></td></tr>
<tr><td>Total costs and expenses</td><td></td><td>$19,061</td></tr>
<tr><td>Income before income taxes</td><td></td><td>$1,139</td></tr>
<tr><td>Income taxes</td><td></td><td>($364)</td></tr>
<tr><td>Net income</td><td></td><td>$775</td></tr>
</table>

The forecasting steps are:

1993 Retail sales:
    Growth rate 1990–92 $= (18,009/16,365)^{0.5} = 1.049.$
        $18,009 \times 1.049 = 18,891.$

1993 Finance charge revenue:
    $(570/18,009 + 647/16,201 + 674/16,365)/3 = 0.03759 = 0.038.$
           $18,891 \times 0.038 = 718.$

1993 Other revenue:

Growth rate 1990-92 = $(506/371)^{0.5}$ = 1.16785 = 1.168.

506 × 1.168 = 591.

Cost of goods sold:

1992 Gross profit = (19,085 - 12,040)/19,085 = 36.9%

36.9% + 2.0% increase = 38.9%.

This implies that CGS/Sales in 1993 is expected to be 1 - 0.389) = 0.611. Thus, 20,200 (total revenue) × 0.611 = 12,342 (1993 CGS).

Costs and expenses of other businesses :

Growth rate 1990–92 = $(368/309)^{0.5}$ = 1.0913 = 1.091.

368 × 1.091 = 401.

Selling, general, and administrative expenses/Sales in 1992 equals:

5,160/19,085 = 27.0%.

27.0% + 3.0% increase = 30.0%.

20,200 × 30% = 6,060.

Requirement 2:
1993 Compared to 1992

A comparison of the actual 1992 income statement with the projected 1993 income statement reveals that projected net earnings for 1993 of $775 is similar to the actual 1992 net earnings of $777. Penney is not expected to have a better year in 1993 compared to 1992.

The reason is that retail sales are predicted to increase only 5.0%. The expected two percentage point improvement in the gross profit rate is offset by increases in advertising expenditures. Selling, general, and administrative expenses increase from about 27% of total revenue in 1992 to about 30% in 1993 and hold down net earnings growth.

C4-3. Iomega Corporation: Attendance at a financial analysts meeting

There are a number of issues students may want to raise with the CEO and CFO. The following list presents some possibilities.

Income statement:

- Sales fell in 1994 after increasing in 1993. Are sales expected to increase or decrease in 1995?

- The company reported net losses and operating losses in 1993 and 1994 after being profitable in 1992. Will the company be profitable in 1995?

- Explain the restructuring cost "reversal" of $2,491,000 reported in 1994.

- Are further restructurings needed?

- The gross margin decreased from 37.1% of sales in 1993 to 34.6% in 1994. Explain why this drop occurred.

- R&D spending fell from 12.9% of sales in 1993 to 10.9% in 1994. Is the reduction temporary, or have R&D expenditures been permanently reduced?

- What inventory turnover ratio is ideal for the company? How has this model compared with actual results for recent periods?

- In what quarter of the year are most sales recorded?

Balance sheet:

- Comment on the company's short-term liquidity.

- Are there target levels for the current and quick ratios, and, if so, what are they?

- The ratio of accumulated depreciation to the original cost of equipment seems quite high (43,917/59,193 = 74.2%). Please comment.

- The balance sheet reports a liability called "accrued warranty." What are the company's warranty policies?

- Why has the "accrued warranty" liability increased from $2,497 in 1993 to $3,943 in 1994, while sales declined?

- The company has no long-term debt outstanding. Why is this the case?

- Does management expect to raise capital in the near future by issuing long-term notes or bonds? If so, when and how much?

- Series A convertible preferred stock has been issued. Does management expect these shares to be converted into common stock in the near future? If so, what impact will this have on the value of existing common stock?

- Series C participating preferred stock has been authorized, but none issued. Does management expect to sell shares of the Series C preferred stock in the near future? If so, when and how much?

- Does management expect to sell common stock in the near future? If so, when, why, and how much?

- Explain the "note receivable from shareholder"—when is it due, what are the terms, and why was the note issued?

Statement of cash flows:

- Over the last three years, the firm's cash flows from operations have not been large enough to cover the cash outflows for investing activities. Does management see this trend reversing soon; if so, how soon?

- Explain the item proceeds from sale of research and development assets. Is this a one-time cash inflow, or is it a recurring source of cash?

- Why doesn't the company pay dividends?

Other Some students may develop questions that are beyond the scope of the financial statements. Possibilities include:

- Is Iomega a party to any pending lawsuits or major litigation?

- What new products is the company working on, and when might they be introduced?

- What are the patent expiration dates on the company's products?

- Please discuss expected future raw material costs, labor costs, and current plant utilization rates.

- What are your sales projections for current and new products?

- What product markets (e.g., home, educational, governmental, corporate, etc.) have the greatest potential for growth?

- What new worldwide markets are you planning to enter?

- Who are the company's major competitors, and how do their products compare to yours?

C4-4. Nike and Reebok: Examine a management discussion and analysis

Requirement 1:
The annual reports for this case may be obtained from the SEC's EDGAR site, through a related site www.freeedgar.com, or in electronic form from the textbook support site www.prenhall.com/phlip/revsine.

Requirement 2:
Some positives for Nike are:

- Fiscal year 1994 began with record first-quarter revenues and ended with record fourth-quarter revenues. For the first time in the company's history, two $1 billion revenue quarters were achieved in the same fiscal year.

- Fiscal 1994 was the second-best revenue year and third-best net income year in the company's history.

- Momentum slowed after the record first quarter, but was regained in the fourth quarter, and a 10% increase in future orders indicates renewed growth heading into the first six months of fiscal 1995.

- Despite a sluggish economy in the United States and abroad, the company has been able to sustain its worldwide market share.

- The company's international markets are less mature and offer more potential for future growth.

- Gross margin remained level at 39.3% for fiscal 1994 and fiscal 1993, and increased from 38.7 % in fiscal 1992. Steady gross margin performance reflects a solid U.S. inventory position resulting from strong inventory management and the company's innovative advance order futures program.

- Worldwide orders for athletic footwear and apparel scheduled for delivery between June and November 1994 are approximately $1.8 billion, 10% higher than such orders in the comparable period of the prior year.

- Management believes that funds generated by operations, together with currently available resources, will adequately finance anticipated fiscal 1995 expenditures, with the potential exception of the stock repurchase program.

- The company's financial position remains extremely strong at May 31, 1994. Cash and equivalents increased $228 million (78%) as a result of a record $576 million in cash provided by operations.

- Dividends per share of common stock for fiscal 1994 rose $.05 over fiscal 1993 to $.80 per share. Dividend declaration in all four quarters has been consistent since February 1984. Based upon current projected earnings and cash flow requirements, the company anticipates continuing a dividend and reviewing the amount during the second-quarter board meeting.

Some negatives for Nike are:

- In fiscal 1994, revenues decreased for the first time in seven years, slipping 4% from the record $3.93 billion for fiscal 1993.

- Net income also decreased for the first time in seven years, declining 18% to $298.8 million (or $3.96 per share), from the record $365.0 million (or $4.74 per share) earned in fiscal 1993.

- The company faces a mature market in the United States, where industry sources expect growth rates to range between 3 and 5%.

- The results of consolidated operations were negatively affected by strengthening of the U.S. dollar in comparison to foreign currencies. Generally, a stronger U.S. dollar will result in lower translation of operating results in these consolidated statements than would a weaker U.S. dollar.

- Total selling and administrative expenses as a percentage of revenues were 25.7% in 1994 compared to 23.5% in 1993 and 22.4% in 1992. The company expects to continue to invest in growth opportunities and, therefore, expects selling and administrative expenses during fiscal 1995 to increase slightly as a percentage of revenue.

- The company has learned that the EU Commission, at the request of the European footwear manufacturers, might initiate an anti-dumping investigation covering footwear imported from the PRC, Indonesia, and Thailand. The company believes that it is prepared to deal effectively with any such duties that may arise and that any adverse impact would be of a short-term nature.

Some positives for Reebok are:

- Net sales for the year increased by 13.4%, or $386.5 million, to $3.280 billion in 1994 from $2.894 billion in 1993. The increase was due to growth in Reebok U.S. footwear and apparel sales as well as international sales.

- Rockport sales reached a record level of $314.5 million in 1994, a 11.3% increase from $282.7 million in 1993. This increase was due to an increase in the number of pairs shipped both in the United States and internationally.

- The effective tax rate decreased from 38.5% in 1993 to 37.7% in 1994 due primarily to a geographic change in the mix of worldwide income.

- The company's backlog of customer orders at December 31, 1994, was approximately 10.1% higher than the prior-year levels. The backlog position is not necessarily indicative of future sales because the ratio of future orders to "at-once" shipments may vary from year to year.

- The company's financial position remains strong. Working capital increased by $101.1 million, or 13.8% from the same period a year ago.

- Net cash provided by operating activities during 1994 was $172.6 million, compared to $142.5 million and $187.6 million for the years ended December 31, 1993 and 1992, respectively.

- Cash generated from operations, together with the company's existing credit lines and other financing sources, is expected to adequately finance all of the company's current and planned cash requirements.

Some negatives for Reebok are:

- The decrease in gross margin from 40.6% in 1993 to 40.1% in 1994 was due to lower margins in the Reebok division's international business as a result of the poor economic conditions in certain countries. The decrease was partially offset by slightly increased margins in the Reebok division's U.S. footwear business.

- Selling, general, and administrative expenses increased as a percentage of sales from 26.6% in 1993 to 27.1% in 1994, due in part to the continuing increased investments in information systems as well as higher distribution costs mainly associated with the opening of a new apparel distribution facility in Memphis, Tennessee. The increased investments in information systems are expected to continue over the next few years.

Requirement 3:
Overall, the MD&A disclosures tend to complement rather than contradict the results of the earlier financial ratio analysis. In particular, the MD&A disclosures provide an in-depth narrative discussion of the various reasons that caused the observed changes in the numbers reported in the firms' financial statements. In addition, these disclosures contain information that is not and cannot be summarized numerically in the financial statements (e.g., current and expected future product demand, competition, and descriptions of new products).

Requirement 4:
Examples of items the analyst might have wanted the company to disclose: quantitative forecasts of future earnings; quantitative forecasts of future sales; quantitative estimates of trends in the expected future cost of input/raw materials; a discussion of the competitive advantages and disadvantages the firm faces with regard to competitors.

Requirement 5:
No solution provided because it depends on which MD&As are examined by students.

C4-5. Sun Microsystems and Micron Electronics: Comparative financial statement analysis

Requirement 1:
Analysis of common-size income statements for Micron Electronics reveals that:

- The company's largest expense is its cost of goods sold, which represents about 80% of sales (i.e., the gross margin on sales has been about 20% over the past few years).

- The next largest expense is selling, general, and administrative expenses which amounts to about 7% of sales.

- Micron spends very little on R&D. This is consistent with the fact that the company just assembles and sells personal computers, it does not design and develop personal computers.

- Micron's net profit margin was above 8% in 1994, but fell to 2.5% by 1996. The reason for the decline is an increase in cost of goods sold, as well as in selling, general, and administrative expenses. The increase in these expenses as a percent of sales also explains why Micron's operating profit as a percent of sales declined from 14.5% in 1994 to 5.9% in 1996.

Sun Microsystems common-size income statements show:

- Sun's largest expense is also cost of goods sold, which represents about 57% of sales (i.e., the gross margin on sales has been about 43% over the past few years).

- The next largest expense is selling, general, and administrative expenses which have been accounting for about 25% of sales.

- Sun spends significant amounts on R&D. While these expenditures have been declining as a percent of sales over the 1994–1996 period, the company has been spending upwards of 9% of sales on R&D. This is consistent with the fact that Sun puts considerable emphasis on developing new computer hardware and software technology.

- Sun's net profit margin has been increasing over the 1994–1996 period (from 4.1% in 1993 to 6.7% in 1996). The improvement has come primarily from reduced cost of goods sold as a percent of sales, and to a lesser extent, a reduction in R&D expenditures as a percent of sales.

Analysis of the common-size balance sheets for Micron Electronics shows that:

- The majority of Micron's assets are current assets (about 80% of the total). Further, in 1995 and 1996, 51.7% and 55.2% of the firm's assets were either cash or accounts receivable (i.e., highly liquid assets).

- On the liability side, Micron has virtually no long-term debt (less than 2.0% of total assets in 1995 and 4.6% in 1996).

- Micron's largest liability is its accounts payable and accrued expenses, about 46% of sales in each year. Given the firm's liquidity (noted above), this should not be a problem for the firm.

- The firm's shareholders' equity constitutes about 45% of total assets, and the majority is in the form of retained earnings.

- On balance, the common-size analysis of Micron's balance sheets indicates that the firm is in reasonably good financial health.

Sun Microsystems' common-size balance sheets show that:

- Like Micron, the majority of Sun's assets are current assets (about 80% of the total). A substantial portion of these assets are in the form of cash and accounts receivable (41.1% in 1995 and 45.6% in 1996).

- Sun's investment in property, plant, and equipment (net) as a percent of total assets is about 12.0%, which is comparable to Micron's 15.2% prior to 1996. In that year, Micron purchased Zeos International and its fixed assets increased to 24.4% of total assets compared to 14.1% for Sun Microsystems.

- Like Micron, Sun has virtually no long-term debt (less than 3.0% of total assets in 1995).

- Sun's current liabilities constitute about 39% of total assets, which is not alarming, given that most of its assets are highly liquid assets like cash, accounts receivable, and inventory. Given that Sun's inventories and receivables are large current assets, it would be important for the analyst to continually monitor how quickly Sun is able to convert inventory into cash.

- The firm's shareholders' equity constitutes about 60% of total assets and is about evenly split between paid-in capital and earnings that have been retained in the business.

- On balance, the common-size analysis of Sun's balance sheets indicates that the firm is in reasonably good financial health.

151

Comparison of Micron and Sun:

- While Micron has a higher profit margin than Sun in 1994 and 1995, Sun's profit margin has been increasing, whereas Micron's profit margin is on a downward trend. In 1996, Micron's profit margin is only 2.5% compared to 6.7% at Sun. It may be that Micron is feeling the effects of price competition, or other competitive pressures to a greater extent than Sun. Alternatively, the low profit margin for 1996 could have been the result of special expenses related to its acquisition of Zeos International.

- Related to the previous point, Sun has a much higher gross profit rate when compared to Micron, and Sun spends more on selling, general, and administrative expenses as a percent of sales when compared to Micron.

- Refer to balance sheet comments for Sun Microsystems.

Trend analysis of Micron Electronics' income statements:

- Micron has experienced substantial growth over the 1994 to 1996 period. From 1994 to 1995, all income statement items more than doubled (e.g., sales increased by 242% and net income by 176%).

- When 1996 is factored in, Micron's growth is even more astounding. From 1994 to 1996, sales increased by 427% and net income by 121%.

- While not described specifically in the case, Micron acquired Zeos International in 1995. Like Micron, Zeos assembled and sold personal computers via direct mail. Micron's reported 1995 results reflect the merged operations of both firms since April 7, 1995. This explains a portion of the dramatic growth by Micron from 1994 to 1995.

- Even when the acquisition of Zeos International has been factored in, Micron's growth over the 1994 to 1996 period is still impressive and accords with the growth in demand for personal computers by home, educational, corporate, and governmental users.

Trend analysis of Sun Microsystems' income statements:

- While not as dramatic as Micron, Sun also experienced growth over the 1994 to 1996 period. For example, from 1994 to 1995, sales increased by about 25.8%, while net income increased by 81.7%.

- When 1996 is factored in, Sun's growth is even better than the growth from 1994 to 1995. For example, sales increased by 51% (an average annual rate of about 25.6%) and net income by 143% (an average annual rate of about 71.6%) from 1994 to 1996.

Comparison of Micron and Sun:

Micron grew more dramatically than Sun over the 1994 to 1996 period. However, at least four points are to be stressed. First, Micron's growth was aided by the acquisition of Zeos International. Second, the analyst needs to be concerned with whether, and for how long, Micron can sustain the growth observed over the 1994 to 1996 period. Third, while Sun's growth rate over the 1994 to 1996 period is not as dramatic as Micron's, Sun did exhibit a reasonable rate of growth in sales and income. Finally, Micron may not be the appropriate or the only benchmark to evaluate Sun's performance. The analyst might consider gathering similar information about other firms in the industry before drawing any final conclusions about Sun or Micron.

Trend analysis of Micron Electronics' balance sheets:

- Micron's total assets more than doubled from 1994 to 1996. This, of course, is due in part to the acquisition of Zeos.

- Notable changes in Micron's balance sheet assets are that cash increased by about 100%, receivables increased by about 154%, and inventories increased by about 200% from 1994 to 1995. By 1996, cash increased 230.5%, receivables 247.6%, and inventories 124.6%. These changes are not surprising for a growth company like Micron, but they do point to several things an analyst should monitor. These include whether receivables are growing more rapidly than sales, and how quickly inventory turns over.

- A notable change on the liability side of Micron's balance sheet is that total current liabilities increased by about 170% from 1994 to 1995. By 1996, total current liabilities had increased 270%. This increase is not an immediate concern, but the analyst should monitor the firm's liquidity position carefully in the future to ensure that the firm does not grow too fast (i.e., expand receivables and inventories in such a way as to potentially encounter a liquidity problem).

- For 1994 to 1995, notable changes with regard to Micron's shareholders' equity include a 300% increase in additional paid-in capital (related to the merger with Zeos) and a 115% increase in retained earnings (due to the firm's profitability in 1995). By 1996, additional paid-in capital increased 373% and retained earnings 200%.

Trend analysis of Sun Microsystems' balance sheets:

- From 1994 to 1995, Sun's total assets increased by about 22%, far less than Micron's increase of about 150% (again, part of Micron's increase can be explained by its acquisition of Zeos). When 1996 is factored in, the two-year increase in total assets is 31%.

- Notable changes on the asset side of Sun's balance sheet are that cash decreased by about 4%, but short-term investments increased by more than 80%. It appears that Sun made a change to its cash management practices during 1995—but this trend reverses in 1996. Other changes include that Sun's accounts receivable increased by about 22% which is in line with the firm's sales increase from 1994 to 1995, and that inventories increased by only about 8%. By 1996, accounts receivable growth was 41.4% and inventory growth was 56%.

- A notable change on the liability side of Sun's balance sheet is that total current liabilities increased by about 16% which is less than the 27% growth in current assets. This suggests a slight improvement in the firm's short-term liquidity position from the end of 1994 to the end of 1995. Current liabilities growth was 30% by 1996.

- With regard to Sun's shareholders' equity, the overall increases of 30% by 1995 and 38% by 1996 are due primarily to the increase in retained earnings (i.e., the firm's profitability in 1995).

Requirement 2:

Questions an equity research analyst might ask of management include:

- Are there any pending lawsuits or other major litigation facing the firm?

- What new products are under development, and when might they be brought to market?

- What are the recent trends in the prices of the company's raw material and component parts?

- Is the company operating at capacity (i.e., what are the plant utilization rates)?

- Please comment on the expected future demand for various computer products in general, and Micron's products in specific.

- What is the company's market share in each major market segment (e.g., home, educational, governmental, corporate, etc.)?

- Is the company trying to penetrate worldwide markets (e.g., European markets or China)? If not, why not?

- What is management's forecast of earnings and/or sales for the next quarter or year?

- Who are the company's major competitors, and how does management plan to compete with these firms?

C4-6. Sun Microsystems vs. Micron Electronics: Management's discussion and analysis

Requirement 1:
The annual reports for this case may be obtained from the SEC's EDGAR site, through a related site www.freeedgar.com, or in electronic form from the textbook support site www.prenhall.com/phlip/revsine.

Requirement 2:
Some positives for Sun are:

- Net revenue increased $1,193 million, or 20%, to $7,095 million in fiscal 1996 compared to an increase of $1,212 million, or 26%, in fiscal 1995. The net revenue increase in fiscal 1996 was due in part to strong demand for its richly configured servers and high-performance desktop systems.

- In fiscal 1996 and 1995, domestic net revenues grew 19% and 25%, respectively. European net revenues increased by 19% and Japanese net revenues increased 14% in fiscal 1996. Revenues from international operations represented 51% of total net revenues in fiscal 1996 and 1995.

- Gross margin was 44.0% for fiscal 1996, compared with 42.4% and 41.3% for fiscal 1995 and 1994, respectively.

- Research and development (R&D) expenses increased $94.2 million, or 16.7%, in fiscal 1996 to $657 million, compared with an increase of $63.1 million, or 14%, in fiscal 1995.

- R&D spending continued at a substantial level throughout the three-year period ended June 30, 1996, as the company invested in specific projects in support of new software and hardware products. About half the dollar increase in R&D expenses for 1996 reflects increased compensation expense associated with increased staffing.

- Sun's cash portfolio (cash, cash equivalents, and short-term investments) was $990 million at June 30, 1996.

- During fiscal 1996, operating activities generated $688 million cash, compared with $637 million in fiscal 1995.

- The company believes that the liquidity provided by existing cash and short-term investment balances and $812 million in available borrowing will be sufficient to meet the company's capital requirements for fiscal 1997.

- New technologies were introduced in fiscal 1996.

Some negatives for Sun are:

- Because Sun operates in a highly competitive industry characterized by increasingly aggressive pricing, systems repricing actions may be initiated in the future, which would result in downward pressure on gross margin.

- Sun operates in an industry characterized by increasing competition, rapidly changing technology, and increasingly aggressive pricing. As a result, the company's future operating results will depend to a considerable extent on its ability to rapidly and continuously develop, introduce, and deliver in quantity new systems, software, and service products, as well as new microprocessor technologies, that offer its customers enhanced performance at competitive prices.

- Competition in the firm's markets will continue to intensify as Sun and its competitors, principally Hewlett-Packard, International Business Machines, Digital Equipment Corporation, and Silicon Graphics, aggressively position themselves to benefit from changing customer buying patterns and demand.

- The timing of introductions of new desktop and server products by Sun's competitors may negatively impact the future operating results of the company, particularly when occurring in periods leading up to the company's introductions of its own new or enhanced products.

- The company's operating results will also be affected by the volume, mix, and timing of orders received during a period and by conditions in the computer industry and in the general economy, such as recessionary periods, political instability, changes in trade policies, and fluctuations in interest or currency exchange rates.

Some positives for Micron are:

- Net sales for the year ended August 29, 1996, were $1,764.9 million or 48% higher than pro forma net sales for the comparable period in 1995.

- Unit sales of PC systems in 1996 increased approximately 60% compared to 1995.

- Average selling prices for PC systems increased in 1996 as a result of completion of the transition in product mix toward higher priced systems.

- As of August 29, 1996, the company had cash and equivalents of $115.8 million, representing an increase of $46.4 million compared to August 31, 1995.

- The company discontinued the manufacturing and sale of Zeos brand PC systems and closed the related manufacturing facilities.

Some negatives for Micron are:

- The company expects that its working capital requirements will continue to increase. The company believes that currently available cash and equivalents, funds generated from operations and further expansion of terms with trade creditors, will be sufficient to fund its operations through fiscal 1997. However, maintaining an adequate level of working capital through the end of 1996 and thereafter will depend in part on the success of the company's products in the marketplace.

- The success of the company will depend to a large extent on its continuing relationship with MTI, including the continuation of various favorable business arrangements between MTI and the company. MTI owns approximately 80% of the outstanding common stock of the company. In addition, four of the eight directors of the company are directors of MTI, including Steven R. Appleton, Chairman and Chief Executive Officer of MTI. MTI has the power to control the outcome of substantially all matters requiring shareholder approval, including the election of directors, and has the ability to control the management and affairs of the company. MTI's equity ownership has the effect of making certain corporate actions impossible without its support.

- Competition in the PC industry is based primarily upon performance, price, quality, service, and support. The PC industry is highly competitive and has been characterized by intense pricing pressure, rapid technological advances in hardware and software, frequent introduction of new products and low gross margin percentages and declining product prices. The company must, therefore, introduce many new products each year and continue to price its products competitively. Failure by the company to make specific product transitions or to accurately forecast its market demand for product mix may adversely affect the company's results of operations.

Requirement 3:
On balance, the MD&A section of the annual reports tends to complement rather than contradict the results of the financial ratio analysis. Moreover, the MD&A discusses the underlying causal factors that gave rise to the observed changes in the numbers reported by the firms in their financial statements. Furthermore, the MD&A disclose information that is not available in the financial statements (e.g., current and expected future product demand, competition, and descriptions of new products).

Requirement 4:
Additional information about the following would aid the analyst: quantitative forecasts of future earnings and sales; quantitative estimates of trends in the future cost of raw materials and components; a discussion of the company's competitive advantage and disadvantage in markets and by customer segment.

C4-7. Argenti Corporation: Evaluating credit risk

Requirement 1:
Why did the company need to increase its note payable borrowing during the year? An analysis of cash flows provides the answer.

Operating cash flows for 1996	($356) million
Long-term debt repayment	($336) million
Other various cash uses	($176) million
Expansion of note payable	$868 million

The company's operating cash flows are described in the case exhibit. The long-term debt repayment is the account balance decrease (from $423 million to $87 million).

Property, plant, and equipment, and investments declined during 1996, which suggests that these items provided cash rather than consumed it. There does not appear to have been a net expansion in the company's size during the year. Other assets increased $271 million, but much of this increase is likely to be deferred tax-related. Other liabilities decreased $73 million, and there was a net purchase of $17 million in stock plus $9 million in dividends.

Thus, two factors seem responsible for the increased short-term borrowing: repayment of the company's existing long-term debt and the negative cash flow from operations. The company's operating cash flow problems are particularly troublesome because a "mature and established" business should be generating solid earnings and strong operating cash flows.

There are several aspects of the financial statements that point to a company in its decline: falling sales, declining earnings and recent losses, and negative operating cash flows coupled with the absence of any plant expansion.

Requirement 2:

What recommendation would you make regarding the company's request for a $1.5 billion refinancing package?

By almost any measure, Argenti's credit risk has increased substantially since 1994: sales have declined, losses are being recorded, operating cash flows are negative, and the company has already violated its existing loan covenants. In addition, the company recorded a $141 million loss for the first quarter of 1997, and this suggests even greater erosion of profits and operating cash flows are likely this coming year.

Under normal circumstances, this would not be the time for a lender to expand its credit position with the company from $165 million to $1.5 billion. Such a high concentration of credit risk with a single borrower would probably not be considered prudent.

But circumstances are not normal since GE Capital is also Argenti's largest stockholder. In this case, it may be advisable to keep the company afloat by providing the refinancing package, thereby protecting GE Capital's equity investment.

What happened?

This case is drawn from the experience of Montgomery Ward & Company, which was taken private in a $3.8 billion leveraged buyout by GE Capital and the then CEO, Bernard Brennan, in 1988. Shortly after releasing its first-quarter results for 1997, Wards filed for Chapter 11 bankruptcy because lenders failed to agree on a rescue plan. At the time, Wards was the nation's ninth-largest department-store chain and employed 60,000 people. A copy of an article appearing in the *Chicago Tribune* follows:

Wards Files Chapter 11 Bankruptcy—Some Closings, Cuts Expected

Montgomery Ward & Company, the venerable but struggling Chicago retailer, filed for Chapter 11 bankruptcy protection late Monday after lenders failed to agree on a rescue plan. The move is sure to mean significant store closings and layoffs at the nation's ninth-largest department-store chain, which employs 60,000 people, consultants said.

The 400-store, $6.6 billion chain had been desperately negotiating with lenders to delay a $1.4 billion payment due in August and to secure fresh cash to pay suppliers, but talks fell apart late in the day, Wards said. Wards' petition, filed in Delaware, is the largest retail Chapter 11 bankruptcy since the 1990 filing by Federated and Allied Department Stores. "This is no surprise at all," said George Whalin, president of Retail Management Consultants in San Marcos, California. "They owe everybody money, and no one is shipping them merchandise."

159

The filing comes nine years after the dowdy chain known for its polyester pants and cheap mattresses was taken private in a $3.8 billion leveraged buyout by GE Capital Corp. and then-Wards chief executive officer Bernard Brennan.

Bankruptcy protection is "the best way for the company to conclude a quick and effective restructuring," said Edward Stewart, executive vice president of GE Capital, which is Wards' largest shareholder, with a 50% stake.

Wards' stores around the country will be open as usual Tuesday. And shipments of everything from back-to-school apparel to appliances should resume because Wards has lined up $1 billion in so-called debtor-in-possession financing from GE. Many of Wards' anxious suppliers stopped shipping merchandise two weeks ago, raising the prospect that Wards would enter the important back-to-school selling season with empty shelves.

Some of the biggest losers, besides Brennan and GE Capital, include Wards' managers, who own 20% of the privately held company. Under bankruptcy reorganization, shareholders' equity is wiped out before creditors' claims are paid.

Monday's drastic action was taken by Wards CEO Roger Goddu, the former Toys 'R Us executive brought in by GE Capital last January to lead Wards. Goddu had hoped to avoid a bankruptcy filing by selling Wards' highly profitable Signature Group direct-marketing unit and using the $800 million-plus proceeds to satisfy bank and insurance lenders. But the sale was held up when some insurance companies refused to budge on the debt-restructuring plan. Signature, which peddles everything from dental insurance to car-towing services to Wards' database of credit-card customers, isn't included in the bankruptcy filing, Wards said.

The retailer said it is close to selling Signature to HFS Inc., the Parsippany, N.J.-based hotel and real estate brokerage company, but cautioned that a deal requires quick approval of Wards' reorganization plan.

Getting some financial breathing room is key to Goddu's plan to turn around Wards' disheveled retail operation. To slow the financial bleeding, Goddu fired 400 corporate staffers—20% of the headquarters work force—last month. Goddu last week announced plans to upgrade apparel offerings to attract slightly older female customers with household incomes of $25,000-$50,000. But that strategy will have to be put on hold, consultants say, because companies with strong brands such as Nike and Levi won't sell to a company under bankruptcy protection.

Wards' recent decline has been swift and comes despite a healthy economic environment. After earning $109 million in 1994, it lost $9 million in 1995 and $237 million in 1996 on $6.6 billion in revenue as shoppers rejected its offerings of consumer electronics, cheap apparel, and gold jewelry. The retailer has estimated it will lose another $250 million in the first half of 1997.

This isn't the first crisis Wards has faced since it was founded in 1872 by Aaron Montgomery Ward, a retail innovator who stopped selling goods out of his buggy in favor of marketing them through mail-order catalogs. But as would happen repeatedly in Wards' long history, competitors quickly followed suit, creating their own catalogs. By 1985, when Wards was an underperforming unit of Mobil Corp., it was forced to close its catalog, then the nation's third largest, laying off 5,000 people, including 1,000 in Chicago.

Ward's fortunes began looking up in 1988, when veteran retail executive and Wards' CEO Brennan persuaded GE Capital to finance the leveraged buyout of the lackluster chain. The plan was to spiff up Wards' offerings and take the company public again in five years. Brennan, who paid only $3 million for a 30% stake in Wards, moved quickly to turn its stores into a collection of retail boutiques. His Electric Avenue department for consumer electronics soon was doing bangup business. By 1993, Wards had paid down much of its original debt, and sales had grown to $6 billion from $4.8 billion in 1988.

But as consumer electronics played a bigger role in Wards' sales, profit margins began to shrink. New competitors, led by Best Buy and Circuit City Stores, entered the field, slashing prices and stealing Wards' customers.

Meanwhile, Wards was never able to devise a successful strategy to sell apparel, where profit margins are fatter. Top-level executives brought in by Brennan to upgrade apparel offerings in the 1990s were fired when improvements were slow to arrive. Finally, Brennan, already known for micromanaging, tried to run the apparel business himself with disastrous results.

GE Capital, which received ownership of Wards' highly profitable credit-card operation in the buyout in addition to 50% of the equity, ran out of patience with Brennan last fall, forcing him to step down and move out of the retailer's Near North Side headquarters on Chicago Avenue.

But Wards' problems were bigger than one man. Its niche as a value-oriented department store was being squeezed by fast-growing discounters, such as Wal-Mart and Target Stores at one end and a revitalized Sears, Roebuck and Co. and J.C. Penney at the other. "It's been a long time since anyone had an idea who Montgomery Ward was," said Whalin, the consultant. "The strategy hasn't worked for three years, and that's way too long."

Susan Chandler, Tribune Staff Writer
Chicago Tribune July 8, 1997.

C4-8. Southwest Airlines: Management discussion and analysis

Important Items: **Available seat miles (ASM)**—The number of seats available times the number of miles those seats are flown, a measure of overall capacity; **Revenue passenger miles (RPM)**—The number of miles flown by paying passengers, a measure of overall demand or traffic; **Passenger yield**—The average amount one passenger pays to fly one mile; **Load factor**—Percent of seats filled on the average flight, a measure of capacity utilization.

Requirement 1:
Items that a financial analyst could not have learned from the financial statements:

From the company's *Year in Review*

- Southwest posted its highest profits ever in 1995.

- Competitive pressures eased in 1995 . . . the United Shuttle reduced head-to-head competition with Southwest by approximately 50%.

- Southwest continued to expand, adding service to Omaha, Nebraska, and increasing service in many underserved markets, particularly those experiencing reductions in service by other carriers.

- In 1995, capacity and traffic for the domestic airline industry grew approximately 3% and 4%, respectively. Southwest, however, grew capacity aggressively at 12.6%.

- For most of 1995 and in January 1996, Southwest's monthly load factors were below year-ago levels. While it is too early to determine if this trend will continue in 1996, thus far these lower load factors have been offset by strong passenger revenue yield performances.

- The early results of our 1996 expansion into Florida look promising as our load factors for our initial two markets, Tampa and Ft. Lauderdale, have exceeded our systemwide averages. We will begin service to Orlando in April 1996.

- For the second consecutive year, our operating expenses per ASM (available seat mile) also declined year-over-year, down .1% in 1995 primarily due to the significant reduction in the company's distribution costs.

- While our goal is to continue this overall cost trend, recent increases in jet fuel prices and the October 1, 1995 implementation of a 4.3 cents per gallon transportation fuel tax for commercial aviation make near-term reductions in total operating expenses on a per-ASM basis much more difficult.

- During 1996, we plan to add a net of seventeen aircraft to our fleet, which will be used primarily in our Florida expansion and to strengthen our existing route system.

From the company's *Results Of Operations*

- Revenue passenger miles (RPMs) increased 7.9% in 1995, compared to a 12.6% increase in available seat miles (ASMs), resulting in a decrease in load factor from 67.3% in 1994 to 64.5% in 1995. The 1995 ASM growth resulted from the addition of 25 aircraft during the year.

- For the second consecutive year, operating expenses on a per-ASM basis decreased year-over-year, down .1% in 1995. The following table provides a breakdown of expenses on a per ASM basis ("c" denotes cents):

Operating Expenses per ASM (amounts in cents)				
	1995	1994	Increase (Decrease)	Percent Change
Salaries, wages, and benefits	2.17	2.13	.04	1.9%
Employee profit-sharing and savings plans	.23	.22	.01	4.5
Fuel and oil	1.01	1.00	.01	1.0
Maintenance materials and repairs	.60	.59	.01	1.7
Agency commissions	.34	.41	(.07)	(17.1)
Aircraft rentals	.47	.42	.05	11.9
Landing fees and other rentals	.44	.46	(.02)	(4.3)
Depreciation	.43	.43	-	-
Other	1.38	1.42	(.04)	(2.8)
Total	7.07	7.08	(.01)	(0.1)

- Salaries, wages, and benefits per ASM increased 1.9% in 1995. This increase resulted from a 17.8% increase in 1995 average headcount, which outpaced the 1995 capacity (ASM) increase of 12.6%, and offset a 2.6% decrease in average salary and benefits cost per employee.

- Employee profit-sharing and savings plans expense per ASM increased 4.5% in 1995. The increase is the result of increased matching contributions to employee savings plans resulting from increased employee participation and higher matching rates in 1995 for non-contract employees and certain employee groups covered by collective bargaining agreements.

- Fuel and oil expenses per ASM increased 1.0% in 1995, primarily due to a 2.4% increase in the average jet fuel cost per gallon from 1994. Jet fuel prices were relatively stable throughout most of 1995, with quarterly averages through the first three quarters ranging from $.53 to $.55 per gallon. During fourth quarter 1995, the average cost per gallon increased to $.59 and, in January 1996, has averaged approximately $.62 per gallon.

- Maintenance materials and repairs per ASM increased 1.7% in 1995 compared to 1994, primarily as a result of performing more engine overhauls during 1995.

- Agency commissions per ASM decreased 17.1% in 1995 compared to 1994, due to a lower mix of travel agency sales in 1995. The lower travel agency sales mix resulted from 1994 enhancements to Southwest's ticket delivery systems for direct customers.

- Aircraft rentals per ASM increased 11.9% in 1995. The increase primarily resulted from second and third quarter 1995 sale/leaseback transactions involving ten new 737-300 aircraft and a higher percentage of the fleet consisting of leased aircraft.

- Other operating expenses per ASM decreased 2.8% in 1995 compared to 1994. This decrease was primarily due to operating efficiencies.

- Fleet service employees are subject to an agreement with the Ramp, Operations and Provisioning Association (ROPA), which became amendable in December 1994. The company reached an agreement with ROPA which was ratified by its membership in November 1995.

- Southwest's mechanics are subject to an agreement with the International Brotherhood of Teamsters, Chauffeurs, Warehousemen, and Helpers of America (the Teamsters), which became amendable August 16, 1995. Southwest is currently in negotiations with the Teamsters for a new contract.

- In response to actions taken by our competitor-owned reservations systems in 1994, we reduced our operating costs and enhanced our ticket delivery systems by developing our own Southwest Airlines Air Travel (SWAT) system allowing high-volume travel agents direct access to reservations; introduced overnight ticket delivery for travel agents; reduced to three the number of advance days reservations required for overnight delivery of tickets to consumers (Ticket By Mail); developed our own Ticketless system, which was rolled out system-wide on January 31, 1995.

- In August 1993, the Revenue Reconciliation Act of 1993 was enacted, which, among other things, included an assessment of 4.3 cents per gallon in federal jet fuel tax, which became effective September 30, 1995, for aviation. This additional fuel tax increased 1995 other operating expenses by $7.4 million.

From the company's *Liquidity And Capital Resources*

- The 1995 capital expenditures of $728.6 million primarily were for the purchase of 23 new 737-300 aircraft, one used 737-300 aircraft previously leased by Morris, and progress payments for future aircraft deliveries.

- As of January 1996, Southwest had one hundred 737s on firm order, including 20 to be delivered in 1996, with options to purchase another 67. Aggregate funding required for firm commitments approximated $2,614.0 million through the year 2001 of which $461.5 million related to 1996.

- As of December 31, 1995, and since 1990, the company had authority from its board of directors to purchase 3,750,000 shares of its common stock from time to time on the open market. No shares have been purchased since 1990.

- The company has a revolving credit line with a group of banks of up to $460 million (none of which had been drawn at December 31, 1995).

- The company currently has outstanding shelf registrations for the issuance of $260.6 million public debt securities.

Requirement 2:
Here are some candidates for the three most important pieces of information:

- Southwest continued to expand operations in 1995 by entering new markets.

- In 1995, capacity and traffic for the domestic airline industry grew approximately 3% and 4%, respectively. Southwest, however, grew capacity aggressively at 12.6%.

- For most of 1995 and in January 1996, Southwest's monthly load factors were below year-ago levels. While it is too early to determine if this trend will continue in 1996, thus far these lower load factors have been offset by strong passenger revenue yield performances.

- The early results of our 1996 expansion into Florida look promising, as our load factors for our initial two markets, Tampa and Ft. Lauderdale, have exceeded our systemwide averages.

- For the second consecutive year, our operating expenses per ASM (available seat mile) also declined year-over-year, down .1% in 1995.

- The 4.3 cent per-gallon increase in federal jet fuel tax.

Requirement 3:
Here are some candidates for the five questions for Southwest's management to answer:

- What is the company's breakeven load factor?

- What impact will the 4.3 cents per gallon increase in federal jet fuel tax have on the company's operating profits?

- As noted in the MD&A discussion, Southwest has been growing by expanding operations into new markets. Given the highly competitive nature of the airline industry, isn't this a very risky strategy for a small company like Southwest?

- What are the biggest risks faced in implementing this growth strategy?

- What factors will have the greatest impact on profitability over the next five years?

- As other airline companies begin to reduce their costs, how will the company's strategy change?

- Does management expect growth to come from internal expansion, or through acquisitions or mergers with other companies?

Requirement 4:
The percentage increase in Southwest's net income from 1993 to 1994 was 5.8%, however the increase from 1994 to 1995 was only 1.8%. Based on these data, Southwest's 1996 income might be a little higher than in 1995.

On the revenue side, the MD&A discussion notes that "for most of 1995 and in January 1996, Southwest's monthly load factors were below year-ago levels. While it is too early to determine if this trend will continue in 1996, thus far these lower load factors have been offset by strong passenger revenue yield performances." This disclosure is both cautious *and* optimistic about growth in revenue in 1996.

On the cost side, the MD&A discussion notes that "for the second consecutive year, operating expenses on a per-ASM basis decreased . . . while our goal is to continue this overall cost trend, recent increases in jet fuel prices, and the October 1, 1995 implementation of a 4.3 cents per gallon transportation fuel tax for commercial aviation, make near-term reductions in total operating expenses on a per-ASM basis much more difficult." This disclosure has both a cautious and an optimistic tone.

Southwest reported net income of $207,337 in 1996, an increase of 13.5% over 1995 net income.

Problems

P5-1. Quality of earnings essay

Requirement 1:

Quality of earnings relates to how well accrual accounting earnings capture the underlying economic performance of an enterprise for a particular period of time. One important dimension of earnings quality is how sustainable or persistent the reported earnings number is. Poor earnings quality occurs when there are transitory components embedded in earnings that are not sustainable, rendering the current earnings number a poor indicator of future performance.

Requirement 2:

Management can improve earnings in the short run by:

- Changing accounting methods.
- Adjusting expense estimates (e.g., increasing estimated useful lives of fixed assets or reducing bad debt expense estimates).
- Altering timing of revenue or expense recognition (i.e., shifting revenues or expenses from one period to the next).

Requirement 3:

Examples of low quality earning items include:

- One-time gains and losses from sales of assets.
- Liberal accounting choices that increase profits in the short run.
- Reduction in discretionary expenditures for R&D, advertising, and maintenance.
- Illusory profits from LIFO liquidations.

A variety of other examples could be listed here. See articles on earnings quality referenced in the chapter.

P5-2. Explaining differences in P/E ratios

In general, price-earnings (P/E) ratios are inversely related to risk, positively related to growth opportunities, and positively related to the quality of earnings.

Requirement 1:

Group A:

These firms are all from different industries. Chrysler is an automobile manufacturer, Merck is a drug company, and Microsoft is in the computer software industry. Here are some reasons for the observed differences in their P/E ratios:

Chrysler probably has the worst set of growth options. Merck, undoubtedly, has some growth options and probably far more so than Chrysler, but probably not as many or ones as valuable as Microsoft. Thus, the ordering of their P/E ratios appears to roughly correspond to their apparent growth opportunities. In fact, this seems like the most compelling reason for the observed differences in the firms' P/E ratios.

Turning to risk, it seems unreasonable to suspect that Chrysler, being from a cyclical industry, is likely to be riskier than either Merck or Microsoft. On the surface, it also seems reasonable to presume that Merck and Microsoft are unlikely to differ significantly in terms of risk. Thus, the ordering of the firms' P/E ratios also appears to roughly correspond to their apparent risk.

(The Value Line Investment Survey reports a beta of 1.20 for Chrysler and 1.10 for both Merck and Microsoft).

Without a detailed study of the accounting methods used by the three firms, it is difficult to draw any conclusions about the extent to which the observed differences might also be related to differences in the quality of their reported earnings. Given the ordering of the P/E ratios of the firms, one would be led to suspect that Microsoft's earnings are the highest quality, followed by Merck and Chrysler, respectively.

As noted above, in all likelihood, most of the variation in the P/E ratios of these firms is due to differences in their growth opportunities.

Requirement 2:

Group B:

These firms are all from the same industry, personal computer manufacturing. Consistent with this, there is far less variation among their P/E ratios when compared to the firms in Group A. In addition, the P/E ratios of Compaq

Computer and Gateway 2000 are not that far apart. The primary difference among the firms is that Dell's P/E ratio is much larger than that of the other two. Some possible reasons for this might be:

1) Investors perceive that Dell has more valuable growth opportunities, or is better prepared to exploit its existing growth opportunities, when compared to Compaq and Gateway 2000.

2) Investors assign a lower level of risk (i.e., discount rate) to Dell when compared to Compaq and Gateway 2000. In actuality, this appears to be only partly true; *The Value Line Investment Survey* reports a beta of 1.35 for Compaq and 1.05 for both Dell and Gateway 2000.

3) Finally, it might be that investors perceive that Compaq and Gateway 2000's earnings are of similar quality, but that both are inferior to the quality of Dell's reported earnings.

Of the three explanations above, (1) seems to be the most compelling. With regard to the quality of earnings issue in (3), we often find that firms in the same industry tend to use the same accounting methods. Thus, **within an industry**, quality of earnings issues may be of less importance in explaining differences in P/E ratios when compared to when **comparisons across industries** are made (i.e., as in Group A).

P5-3. Abnormal earnings: Some simple examples

Abnormal earnings (AE) = $NOPAT - (r \times BV_{t-1})$.

Requirement 1:

$$AE = \$5,000 - (0.15 \times \$50,000)$$
$$= \$5,000 - \$7,500$$
$$= -\$2,500$$

Requirement 2:

$$AE = \$25,000 - (0.18 \times \$125,000)$$
$$= \$25,000 - \$22,500$$
$$= \$2,500$$

Requirement 3:

$$AE = \$30,000 - (0.18 \times \$125,000)$$
$$= \$30,000 - \$22,500$$
$$= \$7,500$$

NOTE: Higher NOPAT without additional investment (i.e., the same BV_{t-1}) is good.

Requirement 4:

$$AE = \$23,000 - (0.18 \times \$100,000)$$
$$= \$23,000 - \$18,000$$
$$= \$5,000$$

NOTE: Eliminating unproductive assets that do not earn as high a rate of return as other assets increases AE. In this case, the unproductive assets were earning a return of only 8% ($2,000/$25,000).

Requirement 5:

$$AE = \$32,600 - (0.18 \times \$165,000)$$
$$= \$32,600 - \$29,700$$
$$= \$2,900$$

AE increases by $400 (from $2,500 to $2,900). Adding the division makes sense. The new division earns a return of 19% ($7,600/$40,000), which is more than the firm's 18% required rate of return, so value is added, and the change in AE is positive.

Requirement 6:

$$AE = \$8,500 - (0.15 \times \$75,000)$$
$$= \$8,500 - \$11,250$$
$$= -\$2,750$$

AE falls by $250. Adding the new division does not make sense. In essence, the new division does not earn a high enough rate of return to justify investment. The new division earns a return of 14% ($3,500/$25,000) which is less than the firm's 15% required rate of return, so value is lost, and the change in AE is negative.

P5-4. Value creation by two companies

Requirement 1:
The abnormal earnings of the two firms for 1993-1997 appears below.

	__1993__	__1994__	__1995__	__1996__	__1997__
Company A					
NOPAT	$66,920	$79,632	$83,314	$89,920	$92,690
BV_{t-1}	478,000	504,000	541,000	562,000	598,000
Cost of equity capital	0.152	0.167	0.159	0.172	0.166
Return on capital	0.140	0.158	0.154	0.160	0.155
Abnormal earnings	($5,736)	($4,536)	($2,705)	($6,744)	($6,578)
Company B					
NOPAT	$192,940	$176,341	$227,700	$198,900	$282,964
BV_{t-1}	877,000	943,000	989,999	1,020,000	1,199,000
Cost of equity capital	0.188	0.179	0.183	0.175	0.186
Return on capital	0.220	0.187	0.230	0.195	0.236
Abnormal earnings	$28,064	$7,544	$46,530.95	$20,400	$59,950

Requirement 2:
Company B was a better investment than Company A. Company B created value each year via positive abnormal earnings, while Company A actually destroyed value each year by earning negative abnormal earnings.

P5-5 Determinants of P/E ratios

Requirement A:
Present value of growth opportunities:

Price-earnings ratios are positively related to the present value of a firm's growth opportunities. The reason is that the value of the stock is a function of the expected return earned on the assets in place as well as the firm's growth opportunities. Thus, firms with little or no current earnings may still have very high P/E ratios because they have an incredible array of growth options to take advantage of in the future. Some examples are bio-technology and high-technology computer software and hardware companies.

Requirement B:
Risk:

Price-earnings ratios are inversely related to a firm's risk. This is because the discount rate, r, increases as the risk of the firm increases. As the discount rate increases, the P/E ratio declines because investors assign a higher (lower) price [hence, a higher (lower) P/E ratio] *to a given level of earnings*, the lower (higher) the level of risk that is associated with those earnings.

Requirement C:
Accounting methods:

Firms that use conservative accounting methods (i.e., those that tend to recognize expenses sooner rather than later and revenues later rather than sooner) will report lower earnings than would otherwise be the case. The lower earnings means that these firms will tend to have higher P/E ratios than might otherwise be the case. Conversely, firms that use aggressive accounting methods (i.e., those that tend to recognize expenses later rather than sooner and revenues sooner rather than later) tend to report higher earnings than would otherwise be the case. The higher earnings means that these firms will tend to have lower P/E ratios than might otherwise be the case. An interesting issue is the extent to which investors in the market adjust for such accounting method differences when setting the market prices of otherwise similar firms.

P5-6 Interpreting stock price changes

Requirement 1:
A stock price change would be expected, i.e., the stock price is likely to fall. This is because the market was expecting the company to earn $5.00 per share and now managers are reporting that the firm will earn only $4.50. Since the stock price just prior to the announcement is based on expected earnings of $5.00, it will fall to reflect the "bad news" that earnings will only be $4.50.

Requirement 2:
The magnitude of the stock price drop is likely to be greater in case (b) than in (a). This is because the drop in earnings in (a) is due to a transitory event (i.e., the labor strike), while the earnings decline in (b) is due to an event that is likely to have an impact on the firm's permanent earnings.

However, one cannot rule out the possibility that the magnitude of the stock price drop might be greater in (a) than in (b). Such might be the case if the market actually thought that leaving the market for sport-utility vehicles would be good for the firm because the company's operations in that market have led to low profits or even losses.

P5-7 Components of earnings

Requirement 1:
a) Permanent earnings refers to that component of a firm's reported earnings that is value-relevant. Moreover, permanent earnings are those earnings expected to continue into the future. This component roughly corresponds to income from continuing operations as reported in a firm's income statement.

b) Transitory earnings refers to that component of a firm's reported earnings that is value-relevant, but not expected to persist into the future. This component roughly corresponds to income from discontinued operations and extraordinary gains and losses as reported in a firm's income statement.

c) Value-irrelevant earnings is the "noise" component of a firm's reported earnings. This component is unrelated to a firm's future profitability or future cash flows, and thus irrelevant when it comes to valuation of the firm's stock. This component roughly corresponds to the item "cumulative effect of changes in accounting methods" as reported in a firm's income statement.

Requirement 2:
A. Consider an airline company:

An example of permanent earnings would be the earnings that arise from the firm's ongoing/recurring passenger and cargo operations.

An example of transitory earnings would be the one-time earnings effect of a special contract to handle all of the charter flights for an outside travel company for one year only. Another example of transitory earnings is the earnings effect of the retirement of some long-term debt (an extraordinary item).

An example of value-irrelevant earnings would be the increase in earnings due to a change in the useful lives and/or salvage values of the firm's aircraft.

B. Consider an automobile manufacturer:

An example of permanent earnings would be the earnings that arise from the firm's ongoing/recurring sales and leasing of passenger cars, trucks, etc. An example of an increase in the firm's permanent earnings would be a contract to supply all of the new vehicles every year in the future to one of the nation's rental car companies.

An example of transitory earnings would be the one-time earnings effect of a special purchase of cars by one of the nation's rental car companies. Another example of transitory earnings is the earnings effect of a labor strike by one of the firm's unions.

An example of value-irrelevant earnings would be the increase in earnings due to a change in the method used to depreciate the firm's long-term assets.

Numerous other student responses to this question are possible.

P5-8 Stock price assimilation of earnings information

Requirement 1:
The "good news" firms are those that report earnings better than expected when they eventually announce their earnings on "day 0." In other words, these are firms that are performing well during the quarter leading up to the earnings announcement date. The reason for the upward drift during the quarter is that accounting earnings and its announcement at the end of the quarter is not the sole source of value-relevant information about firms. Moreover, during the quarter, other pieces of information will come to the market indicating that these firms are doing better than expected as of the beginning of the quarter (e.g., analyst reports, management forecasts, etc.), and, as a result, their stock prices will increase. The outcome of this process is a plot like the one illustrated in the chapter where the stock prices of these good news firms will tend to drift upward during the quarter as they reflect more and more information confirming the firms' better than expected performance during the period. This good performance is confirmed at the end of the period when, on average, the firms report earnings greater than expected at the beginning of the quarter.

Requirement 2:
The "bad news" firms are those that report earnings worse than expected when they eventually announce their earnings on "day 0." In other words, these are firms that are performing poorly during the quarter leading up to the earnings announcement date. The reason for the downward drift during the quarter is that accounting earnings and its announcement at the end of the quarter is not the sole source of value-relevant information about firms. Moreover, during the quarter, other pieces of information will come to the market indicating that these firms are doing worse than expected as of the beginning of the quarter (e.g., analyst reports, management forecasts, etc.), and, as a result, their stock prices will decrease. The outcome of this process is a plot like the one illustrated in the chapter where the stock prices of these bad news firms will tend to drift downward during the quarter as they reflect more and more information confirming the firms' worse than expected performance during the period. This poor performance is confirmed at the end of the period when, on average, the firms report earnings lower than expected at the beginning of the quarter.

Requirement 3:
The "no news" firms are those that report earnings "equal" to those expected when they eventually announce their earnings on "day 0." In other words, these are firms that are performing as the market expected during the quarter leading up to the earnings announcement date. The reason for the near flat price plot during the quarter is that the information the market receives about these firms during the quarter just confirms that these firms are performing as expected as of the beginning of the quarter. As a result, their stock prices will not change much. This expected performance is confirmed at the end of the period when, on average, the firms report earnings approximate those expected at the beginning of the quarter.

Requirement 4:

A. On "day 0," the good news firms report earnings that are higher than expected. This positive earnings surprise causes the stock prices of these firms to increase, on average.

B. On "day 0," the bad news firms report earnings that are lower than expected. This negative earnings surprise causes the stock prices of these firms to decrease, on average.

C. On "day 0," the no news firms report earnings that are equal to those expected. Since there is no earnings surprise, the stock prices of these firms do not change, on average.

Requirement 5:

One possibility is that the market does not completely react to the information contained in reported earnings; thus, the plot of the good (bad) news group continues on an upward (downward) trend after the earnings announcement date. This suggests that the market is not efficient in processing earnings-related information.

Other student responses are possible.

Requirement 6:

If we assume that more information is produced by external parties (e.g., financial analysts, etc.) about large firms when compared to small firms prior to their earnings announcements, the plots may look something like the following. The good and bad news plots of large firms would begin drifting upward and downward earlier in the quarter when compared to those of small firms as a result of more information being produced and released sooner about large firms vis-à-vis small firms. Stated differently, the plots of small firms would begin to drift upward and downward later in the quarter because less information is produced about them prior to their earnings announcements when compared to larger firms.

Turning to the stock price behavior at the time of the actual earnings announcements of large versus small firms, if we assume that more information is produced by external parties (e.g., financial analysts, etc.) about large firms when compared to small firms prior to their earnings announcements, then the stock price effects of the earnings announcements of small firms should be larger in magnitude than those for large firms because there is more information left to be communicated by the accounting earnings of small firms.

There is some empirical evidence that supports the stock price behavior noted above. (See R. Freeman, "The Association Between Accounting Earnings and Security Returns for Large and Small Firms," *Journal of Accounting and Economics* (July 1987), pp. 195–227, and D. Collins, S. P. Kothari and

J. Rayburn, "Firm Size and the Information Content of Prices with Respect to Earnings," *Journal of Accounting and Economics* (July 1987), pp. 111–138.)

P5-9. Applying P/E multiples to earnings components

Requirement 1:

1) ABC Corp.

Reported EPS: $5.00

EPS decomposition:

Valuation multiple for permanent earnings (1/0.15)	= 6.67
Valuation multiple for transitory earnings	= 1.0
Valuation multiple for value-irrelevant earnings	= 0.0

			Implied valuation
Permanent	75%	($5.00 × 0.75) × 6.67	= $25.00
Transitory	20%	($5.00 × 0.20) × 1	= 1.00
Value-irrelevant	5%	($5.00 × 0.05) × 0	= 0.00

Implied share price:	$26.00
Implied earnings multiple (share price/reported EPS):	5.2

XYZ Corp.

Reported EPS: $5.00

EPS decomposition:

Valuation multiple for permanent earnings (1/.015)	= 6.67
Valuation multiple for transitory earnings	= 1.0
Valuation multiple for value-irrelevant earnings	= 0.0

			Implied valuation
Permanent	55%	($5.00 × 0.55) × 6.67	= $18.33
Transitory	25%	($5.00 × 0.25) × 1	= 1.25
Value-irrelevant	20%	($5.00 × 0.25) × 0	= 0.00

Implied share price:	$19.58
Implied earnings multiple (share price/reported EPS):	3.9

The implied share price and earnings multiple of ABC Corp. is higher than that of XYZ Corp. because the reported earnings of ABC Corp. are higher quality than those of XYZ Corp. Moreover, XYZ Corp.'s reported earnings has both a higher permanent earnings component and a lower value-irrelevant component.

Requirement 2:

ABC Corp.

Reported EPS: $5.00

EPS decomposition:

Valuation multiple for permanent earnings (1/0.08)	=	12.5
Valuation multiple for transitory earnings	=	1.0
Valuation multiple for value-irrelevant earnings	=	0.0

				Implied valuation
Permanent	75%	($5.00 × 0.75) × 12.5	=	$46.875
Transitory	20%	($5.00 × 0.20) × 1	=	1.00
Value-irrelevant	5%	($5.00 × 0.05) × 0	=	0.00

Implied share price:	$47.875
Implied earnings multiple (share price/reported EPS):	9.6

XYZ Corp.

Reported EPS: $5.00

EPS decomposition:

Valuation multiple for permanent earnings (1/0.08)	=	12.5
Valuation multiple for transitory earnings	=	1.0
Valuation multiple for value-irrelevant earnings	=	0.0

				Implied valuation
Permanent	55%	($5.00 × 0.55) × 12.5	=	$34.375
Transitory	25%	($5.00 × 0.25) × 1	=	1.25
Value-irrelevant	20%	($5.00 × 0.25) × 0	=	0.00

Implied share price:	$35.625
Implied earnings multiple (share price/reported EPS):	7.1

As before, the implied share price and earnings multiple of ABC Corp. is higher than that of XYZ because the reported earnings of ABC Corp. are higher quality than those of XYZ Corp. Moreover, XYZ Corp.'s reported earnings has both a higher permanent earnings component and a lower value-irrelevant component.

P5-10. Abnormal earnings valuation: Compaq Computer

Requirement 1:
The abnormal earnings valuation leads to an estimated stock price of $47.24 which is $25.14 less than the actual stock price of $72.375. The abnormal earnings valuation is illustrated in the following worksheet.

Compaq Computer Abnormal Earnings Valuation
at January 1, 1997
Question #1.

| | Actual Results | | | Forecasted Results | | | | | |
| | December 31, | | | | | | | | Beyond |
	1994	1995	1996	1997	1998	1999	2000	2001	2001
Panel A: Earnings Forecasts:									
As reported earnings per share	$3.23	$2.88	$4.72						
Last year's earnings per share				$4.72	$5.62	$6.68	$7.95	$9.47	
× (1 + forecasted growth)				1.19	1.19	1.19	1.19	1.19	
= Forecasted earnings per share				5.62	6.68	7.95	9.47	11.26	
Panel B: Book Value of Equity and Dividends									
Equity book value, beginning of year	10.49	14.07	17.28	22.46	28.58	35.76	44.21	54.18	
+ Earnings per share	3.23	2.88	4.72	5.62	6.68	7.95	9.47	11.26	
+ Stock issued (repurchased)	0.35	0.33	0.46	0.5	0.5	0.5	0.5	0.5	
- Dividends per share	0	0	0	0	0	0	0	0	
= Equity book value, end of year	14.07	17.28	22.46	28.58	35.76	44.21	54.18	65.94	
ROE = EPS/Equity Book Value (beginning)	0.3079	0.2047	0.2731	0.2500	0.2339	0.2224	0.2141	0.2079	
Panel C: Abnormal Earnings									
Equity book value, beginning of year	10.49	14.07	17.28	22.46	28.58	35.76	44.21	54.18	
× Equity cost of capital	0.1575	0.1575	0.1575	0.1575	0.1575	0.1575	0.1575	0.1575	
= Normal earnings	1.65	2.22	2.72	3.54	4.50	5.63	6.96	8.53	
Actual or forecasted earnings per share	3.23	2.88	4.72	5.62	6.68	7.95	9.47	11.26	
- Normal earnings per share	1.65	2.22	2.72	3.54	4.50	5.63	6.96	8.53	
= Abnormal earnings per share	1.58	0.66	2.00	2.08	2.18	2.32	2.50	2.73	

Panel D: Valuation

	Forecasted Results					
	1997	1998	1999	2000	2001	Beyond 2001
Future abnormal earnings per share	$2.08	$2.18	$2.32	$2.50	$2.73	2.94
× discount factor	0.8639	0.7464	0.6448	0.5571	0.4813	
Abnormal earnings in Year 2001						
Assumed growth rate beyond 2001						0.075
Perpetuity factor for Year 2001 [1/(.1575 − .075)]						12.1212
P.V. of abnormal earnings at 1/1/2001						35.64
Discount factor						0.4813
Abnormal earnings discounted to present	$1.80	$1.63	$1.50	$1.39	$1.31	$17.15

Sum of discounted abnormal earnings		$24.78
+ Current equity book value		22.46
= Estimated current stock price on January 1, 1997		**47.24**
Actual stock price on January 1, 1997		72.375
Amount by which the actual price exceeds		
(is less than) the abnormal earnings valuation:		$25.14

Forecasted growth:		0.19
Beta:		1.3
Risk-free rate:		0.06
Market risk premium:		0.075
Cost of equity capital		0.1575
Abnormal earnings growth		0.17 0.075
High EPS growth		0.26
Low EPS growth		0.14
Mean EPS growth		0.19

Requirement 2:
The abnormal earnings valuation leads to an estimated stock price of $69.79 which is $2.59 less than the actual stock price of $72.375. This is much closer to the actual price than the estimate in (1). The abnormal earnings valuation is illustrated in the following worksheet.

Compaq Computer Abnormal Earnings Valuation
at January 1,1997
Question #2.

| | Actual Results | | | Forecasted Results | | | | | |
| | December 31, | | | | | | | | |
	1994	1995	1996	1997	1998	1999	2000	2001	Beyond 2001
Panel A: Earnings Forecasts:									
As reported earnings per share	$3.23	$2.88	$4.72						
Last year's earnings per share				$4.72	$5.95	$7.50	$9.45	$11.90	
× (1 + forecasted growth)				1.26	1.26	1.26	1.26	1.26	
= Forecasted earnings per share				5.95	7.50	9.45	11.90	14.99	
Panel B: Book Value of Equity and Dividends									
Equity book value, beginning of year	10.49	14.07	17.28	22.46	28.91	36.90	46.84	59.24	
+ Earnings per share	3.23	2.88	4.72	5.95	7.49	9.44	11.90	14.99	
+ Stock issued (repurchased)	0.35	0.33	0.46	0.5	0.5	0.5	0.5	0.5	
- Dividends per share	0	0	0	0	0	0	0	0	
= Equity book value, end of year	14.07	17.28	22.46	28.91	36.90	46.84	59.24	74.73	
ROE = EPS/Equity Book Value (beginning)	0.3079	0.2047	0.2731	0.2648	0.2592	0.2559	0.2540	0.2530	
Panel C: Abnormal Earnings									
Equity book value, beginning of year	10.49	14.07	17.28	22.46	28.91	36.90	46.84	59.24	
× Equity cost of capital	0.1575	0.1575	0.1575	0.1575	0.1575	0.1575	0.1575	0.1575	
= Normal earnings	1.65	2.22	2.72	3.54	4.55	5.81	7.38	9.33	
Actual or forecasted earnings per share	3.23	2.88	4.72	5.95	7.50	9.45	11.90	14.99	
- Normal earnings per share	1.65	2.22	2.72	3.54	4.55	5.81	7.38	9.33	
= Abnormal earnings per share	1.58	0.67	2.00	2.41	2.95	3.64	4.52	5.66	

		Forecasted Results					
		1997	1998	1999	2000	2001	Beyond 2001
Panel D: Valuation							
Future abnormal earnings per share		$2.41	$2.95	$3.64	$4.52	$5.66	
× Discount factor		0.8639	0.7464	0.6448	0.5571	0.4813	
Abnormal earnings in Year 2001							6.08
Assumed growth rate beyond 2001							0.075
Perpetuity factor for Year 2001 [1/(.1575 - .075)]							12.1212
P.V. of abnormal earnings at 1/1/2001							73.70
Discount factor							0.4813
Abnormal earnings discounted to present		$2.08	$2.20	$2.34	$2.52	$2.72	$35.47
Sum of discounted abnormal earnings	$47.33						
+ Current equity book value	22.46						
= Estimated current stock price on January 1, 1997	**69.79**						
Actual stock price on January 1, 1997	72.375						
Amount by which the actual price exceeds							
(is less than) the abnormal earnings valuation:	$2.59						

Forecasted growth:	0.26
Beta:	1.3
Risk-free rate:	0.06
Market risk premium:	0.075
Cost of equity capital	0.1575
Abnormal earnings growth	0.075
High EPS growth	0.26
Low EPS growth	0.14
Mean EPS growth	0.19

183

Requirement 3:

Since the only difference between (1) and (2) is the assumed rate of growth in earnings per share (EPS), the answer to this question hinges on which of the EPS growth rates is more realistic. If 19% is more realistic, perhaps the stock is overvalued in the market. If 26% is more realistic, perhaps the current price in the market is about right.

When discussing this problem in class, students should be encouraged to identify ways to determine which of the two growth rates might be more appropriate. For example, a financial analyst might try to obtain a forecast from management as to the expected rate of growth in EPS.

P5-11. Abnormal earnings valuation: Dell Computer

Requirement 1:

The abnormal earnings valuation leads to an estimated stock price of $61.59 which is only $4.54 less than the actual stock price of $66.125. The abnormal earnings valuation is illustrated in the following worksheet.

Dell Computer Abnormal Earnings Valuation
at February 1, 1997
Question #1.

| | Actual Results | | | Forecasted Results | | | | | |
| | Fiscal Year Ended January 31, | | | | | | | | Beyond |
	1995	1996	1997	1998	1999	2000	2001	2002	2002
Panel A: Earnings Forecasts:									
As reported earnings per share	$0.85	$1.34	$2.77	$2.77	$3.46	$4.33	$5.41	$6.76	
Last year's earnings per share									
× (1 + forecasted growth)				1.25	1.25	1.25	1.25	1.25	
= Forecasted earnings per share				3.46	4.33	5.41	6.76	8.45	
Panel B: Book Value of Equity and Dividends									
Equity book value, beginning of year	3.08	4.08	5.20	4.66	8.12	12.45	17.86	24.62	
+ Earnings per share	0.85	1.34	2.77	3.46	4.33	5.41	6.76	8.45	
+ Stock issued (repurchased)	0.15	-0.22	-3.31	0	0	0	0	0	
- Dividends per share	0	0	0	0	0	0	0	0	
= Equity book value, end of year	4.08	5.20	4.66	8.12	12.45	17.86	24.62	33.08	
ROE = EPS/Equity Book Value (beginning)	0.2760	0.3284	0.5327	0.7430	0.5329	0.4345	0.3786	0.3433	
Panel C: Abnormal Earnings									
Equity book value, beginning of year	3.08	4.08	5.20	4.66	8.12	12.45	17.86	24.62	
× Equity cost of capital	0.13875	0.13875	0.13875	0.13875	0.13875	0.13875	0.13875	0.13875	
= Normal earnings	0.43	0.57	0.72	0.65	1.13	1.73	2.48	3.42	
Actual or forecasted earnings per share	0.85	1.34	2.77	3.46	4.33	5.41	6.76	8.45	
- Normal earnings per share	0.43	0.57	0.72	0.65	1.13	1.73	2.48	3.42	
= Abnormal earnings per share	0.42	0.77	2.05	2.82	3.20	3.68	4.28	5.04	

Forecasted Results

	1998	1999	2000	2001	2002	Beyond 2002
Panel D: Valuation						
Future abnormal earnings per share	$2.82	$3.20	$3.68	$4.28	$5.04	
× Discount factor	0.8782	0.7712	0.6772	0.5947	0.5222	
Abnormal earnings in Year 2001						5.41
Assumed growth rate beyond 2001						0.075
Perpetuity factor for Year 2001 [1/(.13875 − .075)]						15.6863
P.V. of abnormal earnings at 2/1/2002						84.86
Discount factor						0.5222
Abnormal earnings discounted to present	$2.47	$2.47	$2.49	$2.55	$2.63	$44.32

Sum of discounted abnormal earnings $56.93
+ Current equity book value   4.66
= Estimated current stock price on February 1, 1997   **61.59**

Actual stock price on February 1, 1997   66.125

Amount by which the actual price exceeds
(is less than) the abnormal earnings valuation: $4.54

Forecasted growth:	0.25
Beta:	1.05
Risk-free rate:	0.06
Market risk premium:	0.075
Cost of capital:	0.13875
Rounded discount rate	0.17
Abnormal earnings growth	0.075
High EPS growth	0.45
Low EPS growth	0.15
Mean EPS growth	0.2525

Requirement 2:
The abnormal earnings valuation leads to an estimated stock price of $141.00 which is $74.88 more than the actual stock price of $66.125. The abnormal earnings valuation is illustrated in the following worksheet.

Dell Computer Abnormal Earnings Valuation
at February 1, 1997
Question #2

	Actual Results			Forecasted Results					
	Fiscal Year Ended January 31,								Beyond
	1995	1996	1997	1998	1999	2000	2001	2002	2002
Panel A: Earnings Forecasts:									
As reported earnings per share	$0.85	$1.34	$2.77						
Last year's earnings per share				$2.77	$4.02	$5.82	$8.44	$12.24	
× (1 + forecasted growth)				1.45	1.45	1.45	1.45	1.45	
= Forecasted earnings per share				4.02	5.82	8.44	12.24	17.75	
Panel B: Book Value of Equity and Dividends									
Equity book value, beginning of year	3.08	4.08	5.20	4.66	8.68	14.50	22.95	35.19	
+ Earnings per share	0.85	1.34	2.77	4.02	5.82	8.44	12.24	17.75	
+ Stock issued (repurchased)	0.15	-0.22	-3.31	0	0	0	0	0	
- Dividends per share	0	0	0	0	0	0	0	0	
= Equity book value, end of year	4.08	5.20	4.66	8.68	14.50	22.95	35.19	52.94	
ROE = EPS/Equity Book Value (beginning)	0.2760	0.3284	0.5327	0.8619	0.6712	0.5824	0.5337	0.5045	
Panel C: Abnormal Earnings									
Equity book value, beginning of year	3.08	4.08	5.20	4.66	8.68	14.50	22.95	35.19	
× Equity cost of capital	0.13875	0.13875	0.13875	0.13875	0.13875	0.13875	0.13875	0.13875	
= Normal earnings	0.43	0.57	0.72	0.65	1.20	2.01	3.18	4.88	
Actual or forecasted earnings per share	0.85	1.34	2.77	4.02	5.82	8.44	12.24	17.75	
- Normal earnings per share	0.43	0.57	0.72	0.65	1.20	2.01	3.18	4.88	
= Abnormal earnings per share	0.42	0.77	2.05	3.37	4.62	6.43	9.06	12.87	

188

| | Forecasted Results | | | | | |
	1998	1999	2000	2001	2002	Beyond 2002
Panel D: Valuation						
Future abnormal earnings per share	$3.37	$4.62	$6.43	$9.06	$12.87	13.84
× Discount factor	0.8782	0.7712	0.6772	0.5947	0.5222	0.075
Abnormal earnings in Year 2001						13.84
Assumed growth rate beyond 2001						0.075
Perpetuity factor for Year 2001 [1/(.13875 − .075)]						15.6863
P.V. of abnormal earnings at 2/1/2002						217.10
Discount factor						0.5222
Abnormal earnings discounted to present	$2.96	$3.56	$4.36	$5.39	$6.72	$113.37

Sum of discounted abnormal earnings $136.36
+ Current equity book value 4.66
= Estimated current stock price on February 1, 1997 **141.02**

Actual stock price on February 1, 1997 66.125

Amount by which the actual price exceeds
(is less than) the abnormal earnings valuation: -$74.90

Forecasted growth: 0.45
Beta: 1.05
Risk-free rate: 0.06
Market risk premium: 0.075
Cost of capital: 0.13875

Abnormal earnings growth 0.075
High EPS growth 0.45
Low EPS growth 0.15
Mean EPS growth 0.2525

Requirement 3:
Since the only difference between (1) and (2) is the assumed rate of growth in earnings per share (EPS), the answer to this question hinges on which of the EPS growth rates is more realistic. The assumed rate of 25% leads to a valuation very similar to that observed in the market while the rate of 45% seems to suggest that Dell's stock is grossly undervalued. Since, on average, the consensus of analysts' estimates will consistently be more accurate from period to period than any one analyst's estimate, the average growth rate of 25% is easier to defend. It might be that the analyst predicting a 45% growth rate is using an overly optimistic set of assumptions about the economic conditions he/she expects Dell to face in the future.

Requirement 4:
The higher (lower) the growth rate in earnings per share, the higher (lower) will be the abnormal earnings valuation.

The higher (lower) the cost of equity capital, the lower (higher) will be the abnormal earnings valuation.

The higher (lower) the growth in abnormal earnings after the initial five-year horizon, the higher (lower) will be the abnormal earnings valuation.

P5-12. Discussion questions on the role of accounting numbers in valuation

Requirement 1:
The role of accounting numbers in corporate valuation:

Corporate valuation involves estimating the worth or price of a company, one of its operating units, or its ownership shares. Some equity valuation approaches are based on discounting a firm's future earnings or operating cash flows. In such settings, the role of accounting numbers (i.e., the information in financial statements) is to aid in the development of projections of the firm's future earnings or operating cash flows. These projections are then discounted at the firm's risk-adjusted cost of equity capital to arrive at an estimate of the equity's value.

Requirement 2:
The role of accounting numbers in cash flow assessment:

Cash flow assessment is important to assessing the credit risk of a company. Banks and other lenders use accounting numbers (as well as other information) to estimate a firm's future cash flows. These estimates are then compared to projected future debt-service requirements. Companies with projected operating cash flows in excess of debt principal and interest payments are classified as good credit risks, while those with less favorable operating cash flow prospects are classified as high credit risks and may be denied credit, charged higher interest rates, or have stringent conditions placed on their loans. Simply stated, accounting numbers play a key role in lending decisions by providing information that is used to assess the amount, timing, and uncertainty (i.e., risk) of a firm's future cash flows.

Requirement 3:
Sustainable earnings:

Sustainable or permanent earnings is that component of earnings that is valuation-relevant and is expected to persist into the future. Earnings generated from repeat customers or from a high quality product that enjoys steady customer demand is an example of sustainable earnings. Examples of unsustainable earnings items include gains or losses resulting from debt retirement, write-off of assets from corporate restructuring and plant closings, or a reduction in discretionary expenditures for advertising, or research and development.

Requirement 4:
The process of valuation:

The process of valuation involves the following steps:
1) Forecasting the future values of the financial attributes deemed to drive the value of a firm (i.e., value-relevant attributes). Examples of commonly used value-relevant attributes include distributable or free cash flows, accounting earnings, and balance sheet book values.

2) Determining the risk or uncertainty associated with the value-relevant attribute(s).

3) Determining the discounted present value of the expected future values of the value-relevant attribute(s). The discount rate will reflect the risk or uncertainty inherent in the value attribute(s) of interest.

Requirement 5:
The free cash flow approach to valuation:

Free cash flow is operating cash flow minus cash outlays for the replacement of existing operating capacity like buildings, equipment, and furnishings. A company's free cash flow thus represents the amount available to finance planned expansion of operating capacity, reduce debt, pay dividends, or repurchase stock.

Under the free cash flow approach to valuation, the price of the stock at time = 0, P_0, is equal to the sum of the future stream of expected free cash flow per share discounted back to the present at the firm's cost of equity capital. Multiplying the estimated stock price, P_0, by the number of common shares outstanding produces an estimate of the total common equity value of the company. Simply put, the free cash flow model expresses today's market value of each common share as a function of investors' current expectations of the firm's future economic prospects as measured by its expected future free cash flows.

Requirement 6:
The abnormal earnings approach to valuation:

Abnormal earnings is the difference between actual earnings for period t (X_t) and stockholders' required dollar return on invested capital at the beginning of the period ($r \times BV_{t-1}$). More specifically:

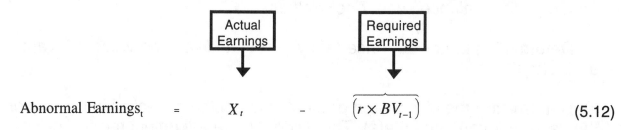

$$\text{Abnormal Earnings}_t \quad = \quad X_t \quad - \quad \overbrace{\left(r \times BV_{t-1}\right)} \tag{5.12}$$

Perhaps the most important aspect of the abnormal earnings model is that investors will pay a premium only for the stocks of firms that earn more than their cost of equity capital (i.e., firms that earn positive abnormal earnings). Conversely, investors will pay less than book value for firms that earn negative abnormal earnings. As described in the text, the abnormal earnings valuation model is:

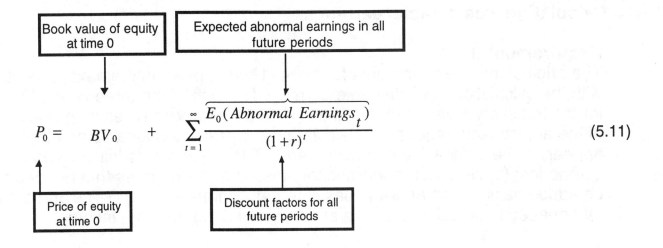

$$P_0 = BV_0 + \sum_{t=1}^{\infty} \frac{E_0(Abnormal\ Earnings_t)}{(1+r)^t} \tag{5.11}$$

where–

- *BV* denotes equity book value (assets minus liabilities) shareholders have invested in the firm;

- E_0 denotes the expectation about future abnormal earnings formed at time 0; and

- *r* is the cost of equity capital.

The cost of equity capital, *r*, also corresponds to the risk-adjusted return stockholders *require* from their investment. Therefore, $r \times BV_{t-1}$ —or stockholders' required rate of return multiplied by beginning of period invested capital—is the earnings level the company must generate in period *t* to satisfy stockholders. Any difference between actual earnings for period t (X_t) and stockholders' required dollar return on invested capital at the beginning of the period ($r \times BV_{t-1}$) represents **abnormal earnings**.

Requirement 7:
Earnings surprise:

An earnings surprise represents new information that is conveyed to investors at the time of a firm's quarterly or annual earnings announcement. An earnings surprise occurs when the earnings that a firm reports is different from what the market was expecting the firm to report. Investors use earnings surprises to revise their expectations of the firm's future earnings and cash flow prospects. The stock price change will be positive when the earnings surprise is *"good news"* (i.e., reported earnings exceeded what the market had expected. The stock price change will be negative when the earnings surprise is *"bad news"* (i.e., reported earnings was less than what the market had expected).

P5-13. Calculating sustainable earnings

Requirement 1:
The original income statements for 1994–1996 appear on the next page along with the calculation of sustainable earnings for each of the three years. Except for the transitory revenue of $1 billion in 1996, which was given in the case, all of the adjustments required to calculate each year's sustainable earnings appear on the original income statements. The adjustments fall into two categories: (1) Non-recurring/transitory losses and expenses that needed to be added back (on an after-tax basis) to net income; and (2) Gains and credits that needed to be subtracted (on an after-tax basis) from net income.

Colonel Electric Inc.
(in millions of $)

For Years Ended December 31,	As Reported Earnings			Sustainable Earnings Calculation		
	1996	1995	1994	1996	1995	1994
Revenues						
Sales of goods	$54,196	$53,177	$52,767	$54,196	$53,177	$52,767
Sales of services	11,923	10,836	8,863	11,923	10,836	8,863
Royalties and fees	1629	753	783	629	753	783
Total revenues	67,748	64,766	62,413	66,748	64,766	62,413
Costs and Expenses:						
Cost of goods sold	(24,594)	(24,308)	(22,775)	(24,594)	(24,308)	(22,775)
Cost of services sold	(8,425)	(6,785)	(6,274)	(8,425)	(6,785)	(6,274)
Restructuring charges (+ reversals)	1,000	0	(2,500)	0	0	0
Interest charges	(595)	(649)	(410)	(595)	(649)	(410)
Other costs and expenses	(6,274)	(5,743)	(5,211)	(6,274)	(5,743)	(5,211)
Litigation charges (+ income)	550	0	(250)	0	0	0
Losses (+ gains) on sales of investments	(75)	0	25	0	0	0
Losses (+ gains) on sales of misc. assets	0	55	0	0	0	0
Losses (+ gains) on sales of fixed assets	25	0	(35)	0	0	0
Inventory write-offs	0	(18)	0	0	0	0
Asset impairments	0	0	(24)	0	0	0
Special item charges	(34)	0	(8)	0	0	0
Loss from labor strike	0	(20)	0	0	0	0
Total costs and expenses	(38,422)	(37,468)	(37,462)	(39,888)	(37,485)	(34,670)
Earnings from continuing operations before income taxes	29,326	27,298	24,951	26,860	27,281	27,743
Provision for income taxes (34%)	(9,971)	(9,281)	(8,483)	(9,132)	(9,276)	(9,433)
Earnings from continuing operations	19,355	18,017	16,468	17,728	18,005	18,310
Loss (+ income) from discontinued operations (net of tax)	0	(250)	1,100	0	0	0
Loss (+ gain) on sale of discontinued operations (net of tax)	750	0	0	0	0	0
Extraordinary loss (+ gain) on early debt retirement (net of tax)	(50)	0	10	0	0	0
Cumulative loss (+ gain) from change in accounting methods (net of tax)	(110)	0	55	0	0	0
Net Earnings	$19,945	$17,767	$17,633	$17,728	$18,005	$18,310

195

Requirement 2:

An interesting conclusion emerges when reported earnings is compared with sustainable earnings. While the firm's reported earnings increased each year from 1994–1996, its sustainable earnings fell each year from 1994–1996. This points to the importance of paying attention to and adjusting for the presence of non-recurring and other transitory Items in the income statement when attempting to gauge a firm's potential long-run earnings generating ability.

P5-14. Net accruals and discretionary accruals

Requirement 1:

Total accruals are the difference between operating cash flow and net income:

Total accruals = Operating cash flow   - Net income
$$= \quad (\$38,460) \qquad - \ \$12,540$$
$$= (\$51,000)$$

Requirement 2:
The individual components are:

Adjustments to net income:

Add to net income:

Depreciation expense	$14,000
Decrease in prepaid expenses	5,000
Increase in accounts payable	65,000
Increase in interest payable	12,000
Net additions	$96,000

Subtract from net income:

Increase in accounts receivable	20,000
Increase in inventories	30,000
Decrease in accrued payables	80,000
Decrease in income tax payable	17,000
Net subtractions	$147,000

Net accruals   ($51,000)

Requirement 3:
a) Depreciation policy because the manager selects the depreciation methods, useful lives, and salvage values.

b) The change in accounts receivable is also subject to managerial discretion through the provision for bad debts.

c) The change in the inventories account also is subject to some managerial discretion as the manager has control over the level of the firm's inventory (i.e., purchasing policy) and makes decisions about the timing of the write-off of obsolete inventory.

d) Managers also have control over prepaid expenses as they decide what items, if any, to prepay during or at the end of the accounting period.

e) The change in the accounts payable and accrued payables accounts also give managers discretion over the firm's net accruals. This is because management has influence over when payment is made to suppliers. Payments can be accelerated or delayed at the end of the accounting period, and this will affect the firm's total accruals.

Requirement 4:
Reasons to manipulate accruals include the following:

The manager may have a bonus plan that is a function of the firm's reported earnings. In most cases, a bonus is paid if net income exceeds a minimum level (the floor) and increases until a maximum level of earnings is reached (the ceiling). In cases where net income is above the floor but below the ceiling, a manager may try to increase income (e.g., via adjustments to depreciation policy and the bad debt allowance) to increase his bonus. In cases where net income is well below the floor or above the ceiling, the manager may try to decrease income via various accruals because there is no advantage to higher income in these two settings. Doing this is likely to increase the probability of receiving a bonus in a future year.

P5-15. Earnings-based equity valuations

With no growth in earnings and dividends, and a 100% payout ratio, the following valuation formula applies to the value of a share of equity:

Price = Expected earnings/Cost of equity

Requirement 1:
Dennison's required rate of return:
$28.00 = $7.00/r
r = 25.0%

Requirement 2:
Sampson's current price:
Price = $5.00/0.22
= $22.73

Requirement 3:
Johnson's expected earnings:
= Expected earnings/0.15
Expected earnings = $6.00

P5-16. Earnings-based equity valuations

With no growth in earnings and dividends, and a 100% payout ratio, the following valuation formula applies to the value of a share of equity:

Price = [k × (earnings × (1 + g)]/(r - g),
where k is the dividend payout ratio, r is the cost of equity, and g is the firm's growth rate.

Requirement 1:
Growth rate of earnings:
g = r (the rate of return on new investment) × (1 - k)
g = 0.15 × 0.50
= 0.075 = 7.5%

Requirement 2:
Jackson's required rate of return on equity:
$40.00 = [0.50 × ($5.00 × (1.075)]/(r - 0.075)
= $2.6875/(r - 0.075)
r = 14.2% rounded

Requirement 3:
Wilson's current stock price:
Price = [0.50 × ($9.00 × (1.075)]/(0.225 - 0.075)
= $32.25

P5-17. Common stock valuations

Requirement 1:
Stock price with no investment:

In this case, the price of the firm is simply its EPS divided by the required rate of return.

EPS = $75,000/15,000 shares = $5.00/share
P = $5.00/0.12
= $41.67

Requirement 2:
Stock price with investment in one year:

In this case, the price of the firm is equal to the value without the growth option of $41.67 (see part 1), plus the present value of the growth opportunity (PVGO).

The present value of the investment option at time 1 is:
($50,000/0.12) - $90,000
= $326,667

At time 0, this has a present value of:
$326,667/(1.12) = $291,667

On a per-share basis, this is:
$291,667/15,000 shares = $19.44/share

Thus, the stock price in this case is:
P = $41.67 + $19.44
= $61.11

P5-18. Common stock valuations

Requirement 1:
Analysis of buy decision when Frances is selling at $29.00:

Step 1: Calculate the growth rate in earnings:

g = (1 - Dividend payout) × Return on new investment
= 0.80 × .14
= 0.112 or 1.2%

Step 2: Calculate the stock price:

$P = [k \times E_0(1 + g)]/(r - g)$, where k is the dividend payout ratio, E_0 is earnings for the most recent year, g is the growth rate of earnings, and r is the investor's required rate of return.

P = [0.20 × $10.00 (1 + 0.112)]/(0.18 - 0.112)
= $32.71

Since this price is more than what the stock is presently selling for ($29.00), you would buy the stock.

Valuation of Frances when all earnings are paid out as dividends:

In this case, the price of the firm is simply its EPS divided by the required rate of return.

EPS = $125,000/50,000 shares = $2.50/share
P = $2.50/0.20
= $12.50

Requirement 2:
Valuation of Frances with investment in $100,000 project one year from now:

In this case, the price of the firm is equal to the value without the growth option of $12.50 (see part 2), plus the present value of the growth opportunity (PVGO).

The present value of the investment option at time 1 is:
($15,000/0.20) - $100,000 = -$25,000.

At time 0, this has a present value of:
-$25,000/(1.20) = -$20,833.

On a per-share basis, this is:
-$20,833/50,000 shares = -$0.42/share

Thus, the stock price in this case is:
P =$12.50 - $ 0.42
    =$12.08

Requirement 3:
Analysis of differences in (1) and (2):

The stock price is lower in (2) because the investment actually destroys value rather than creating value [i.e., return on new investment (15%) is *less* than cost of capital].

P5-19. The usefulness of management earnings forecasts to financial analysts and investors

Requirement 1:
Since managers are inside the firm, they have access to information that external users (e.g., analysts) do not have. Thus, disclosures by managers have the potential to convey new information to external users, where new information is taken to mean information that is not publicly available. To the extent that the new information is value-relevant, it has the potential to be useful to external parties in their decision-making, for example, the valuation of a firm's common stock by an analyst or investor.

Requirement 2:
Managers often claim that the stock market excessively punishes firms when they report earnings that are lower than expected, where punishing means bidding the price of the firms' stock downward. Thus, managers might issue conservative forecasts so that when actual earnings is announced, the deviation from expectations is positive, and the perception is that the firm did even better than expected (where the amount expected was the amount forecast by the manager).

In addition, it may be costly for a manager in terms of lost reputation (his and the firm's) to issue forecasts that are overly optimistic and not always achieved by the firm. The bottom line to this line of reasoning is that, for whatever reason, managers perceive that it is better to do a bit better than expected than to do a bit worse.

Requirement 3:
One thing that an analyst could do is estimate the amount or percent by which management has been consistently understating its forecasts in the past, and use this amount to adjust subsequent forecasts upward to eliminate the downward bias built into the manager's forecast.

Requirement 4:
One potential disadvantage is that external parties may start paying less attention to the manager's forecasts. Another disadvantage is that analysts may tire of management's actions and devote their time to following other firms (i.e., the firm's reputation with analysts may suffer, and its following in the investment community may be affected). Finally, issuing forecasts that are known to be overly conservative means that the price of the firm's stock might be lower than it would otherwise be because of the value-relevant information not being disclosed in the form of a more accurate forecast.

Requirement 5:
For the reason discussed in (3), it seems unlikely that external users would consistently be fooled over and over again by managers who consistently issue conservative earnings forecasts. What seems more likely is that external users (i.e., "the market") would begin to make adjustments to the forecasts issued by such firms so as to correct for any built-in understatement. The result of such adjustments would be that the firms' expected earnings would be more accurate estimates of the actual earnings that firms would subsequently report, and there would be no reason to expect any stock price increases (changes) at the time of the actual earnings announcements of firms that attempt to continually "low ball" analysts with conservative forecasts.

P5-20. Information disclosure by retail firms

Requirement 1:
Assuming that a firm's net profit margin is relatively stable from quarter to quarter and year to year, as each month's sales are reported by the firm, the analyst would be able to update his forecast for the upcoming quarter and year with one additional month of actual results. This should result in the forecast becoming more and more accurate.

Consider the following example. Assume that a given retail firm's net profit rate is 5.0% and that this rate has been quite stable in the past. If an analyst expected the firm's sales to be $1,200, $1,000, and $1,500, respectively, in each month of the upcoming quarter, the analyst would be forecasting earnings of $185.00 ($3,700 × 0.05). Now assume that the firm reports sales of $1,300 for the first month of the fiscal quarter.

Assuming the analyst still expects sales of $1,000 and $1,500 in each of the next two months, he/she would issue a revised earnings forecast of $190.00 ($3,800 × 0.05). Thus, the retailer's monthly sales announcement has allowed the analyst to update his/her forecast with more current information. In the absence of the monthly sales announcement, the updated forecast might not be possible.

Requirement 2:
The most likely reason is that the firm's sales are highly seasonal. Thus, it makes more sense to compare the sales of April 1997 with April 1996 (Easter shopping season) and December 1997 with December 1996 (Christmas shopping season) and so on, rather than to compare sales on a month-to-month basis (e.g., April 1997 with March 1997, and March 1997 with February 1997, etc.). Controlling for these known seasonal variations in the sales of retailing firms allows more meaningful inferences to be drawn about the level of, and changes in, their sales over time.

Requirement 3:
Some possibilities include:
   a) monthly earnings,
   b) expected sales in coming months,
   c) gross and/or net profit margins on a monthly basis along with the sales data, and
   d) sales by geographic region.

Other student responses are possible.

Requirement 4:
The most likely reason that firms might not want to voluntarily release such additional information is that they may feel that doing so would put them at a competitive disadvantage. To the extent that such additional disclosures by a firm point out sources (i.e., markets) of high or increasing profitability, the attention of competitors might be attracted to these markets, thereby reducing the firm's profitability as a result.

Requirement 5:
It seems likely that most analysts would object to the discontinuance of these disclosures. This is because these monthly sales data are not available from any other source. Thus, there would be a loss of potentially valuable information if the disclosures were discontinued.

Also see the discussion above under Requirement 1.
Other student responses are possible.

P5-21. Valuation of growth opportunities

Requirement 1:
GHI P/E ratio with no additional investment:

P/E ratio = Price per share/EPS
Price per share = EPS/r
= ($450,000/175,000)/0.15
= $17.14

P/E ratio = $17.14/$2.57
= $6.67

Requirement 2:
Maximum amount GHI would be willing to pay to add the new division:

The maximum amount that the firm would pay to make the investment is that amount where the present value of the future cash flows generated by the investment just equals the initial cost of the investment (i.e., where the investment's net present value is $0). Paying more would reduce firm value (i.e., produce a negative net present value) while paying less would increase firm value (i.e., produce a positive net present value). Since the investment generates $200,000 forever, the present value of the future cash inflows is simply the present value of a perpetuity of $200,000. Therefore:

Maximum investment   = $200,000/0.15
  = $1,333,333

Requirement 3:
GHI's P/E with investment of $1,000,000:

> P/E ratio = 1/r + Present value of growth per share/EPS
> = 1/0.15 + ($333,333/175,000)/$2.57
> = $6.67 + $0.74
> = $7.41

P5-22. Restructuring charges (and reversals) and the quality of earnings

Requirement 1:

Analysts claim the earnings and book values are the cleanest in many years because the write-offs explicitly recognized events that had previously not been recognized on the balance sheet or income statement. The effect of this recognition is to decrease earnings and book values in the year of recognition. The decrease in book values can occur by a write down of assets, a "write-up" of liabilities or a non-recurring charge to earnings. Each of the three previous events results in a decrease in owners' equity. Thus, analysts feel the earnings and book values are "clean" because assets, liabilities, and owners' equity are now expressed closer to their fair values.

Consequently, analysts feel conservative accounting produces high quality book values because assets that were over-valued are written down to market value, liabilities are more explicitly recognized, and, thus, owners' equity is adjusted to account for these transactions. Conservative earnings are higher quality because charges are included to account for the transactions noted above. Note, that conservatism implies "that possible errors in measurement be in the direction of understatement rather than overstatement of net income and net assets." This distinction is an important one because of GAAP's tendency to understate assets, net income, and owners' equity while overstating liabilities.

Thus, a profitable firm with conservative earnings must have really earned a profit because the accountants have been conservative and, when in doubt, have "understated" income. Similarly, the balance sheet is strong because, when in doubt, owners' equity is understated because assets are "understated" and liabilities are "overstated."

Agree:

The basis for agreement is outlined in the above answer. Essentially, conservatism allows financial statement users to know that management manipulation of the balance sheet and income statement is limited. Thus, financial statement users have some confidence that management has not excessively manipulated the financial statements to make the firm look better.

Disagree:

The basis for disagreement could focus on the notion that management manipulation is still possible. This manipulation may be to overstate net assets and net income or, alternatively, to understate net assets and net income. Thus, financial statement users are not receiving the "true" picture.

Requirement 2:

For one thing, accruals and subsequent reversals of restructuring charges induce volatility into earnings. This is because when the charge is recognized earnings is lower while the reversal increases earnings. Thus, a case can be made that earnings quality decreases because of this induced volatility. On the other hand, an argument for an increase in quality of earnings can be based on the idea that when the charge was recognized, it was an appropriate estimate and the reversal was subsequently made when the estimate was determined to be incorrect. Again, conservatism plays a role in this situation. Namely, GAAP recognizes the charge against earnings at a time when it is reasonably estimated. The reversal, which increases income, is allowed only after the charge is found to be too high. This issue is why analysts' main focus is on net income before non-recurring charges. The focus should be on sustainable earnings and, thus, non-recurring charges are less important because they are not likely to occur again.

Requirement 3:

Perhaps the most obvious reason to over-accrue restructuring charges is that the over-accrual provides a "bank" of earnings that is available to manipulate the reported earnings of a future year(s). By definition, an over-accrual means that the firm took too large of a charge in the current period (i.e., current year's income was reduced by more than it should have been). As a result, at some point in the future, the over-accrual will have to be corrected. The correction will entail an increase to the reported earnings of one or more future years. As a result, managers have the opportunity to increase the reported earnings of a future year, perhaps a year when the firm has not performed well. Thus, the over-accrual creates a "bank" of earnings that managers will be able to draw upon when "they need a little help" in the future.

Requirement 4:

To the extent that firms do not report a "write-on" as a separate line item on the income statement in the year it is taken, there is reason for analysts to be concerned. This is because, in the absence of being clearly labeled as a "reversal" of a previous year's write-off, in all likelihood the amount of the "write-on" would implicitly be considered to be a part of the firm's sustainable earnings, when, in fact, it is not sustainable. To the extent that "write-ons" are netted against an expense account, or included as part of other income or other credits to income on the income statement, the analyst has no way of backing this number out when calculating the firm's sustainable earnings.

Requirement 5:
As noted in Requirement 4, the biggest problem is likely to be knowing when the firm is taking a "write-on" or making a reversal in its income statement.

Requirement 6:
As reported on the firm's 1993 income statement, the amount of the restructuring charge was $14,131,000. While the restructuring charge reduced Iomega's 1993 earnings, it is an example of a charge that is transitory and non-recurring. Thus, it reduced the quality of Iomega's 1993 earnings because it is not a permanent reduction to the firm's earnings that will occur every year. The important point here is that when calculating Iomega's 1993 NOPAT or 1993 sustainable earnings, the tax-adjusted amount of the charge [i.e., $14,131,000 \times (1.0 - \text{tax rate})$] should be added back. This will make 1993 NOPAT and sustainable earnings more comparable with past and future years.

Requirement 7:
As reported on the firm's 1994 income statement, the amount of the restructuring reversal was $2,492,000. While the restructuring reversal increased Iomega's 1993 earnings, it is an example of a gain or credit that is a one-time adjustment to earnings (i.e., it is transitory /non-recurring). Thus, it reduced the quality of Iomega's 1993 earnings because it does not reflect a permanent increase in the firm's earnings that will occur every year. When calculating Iomega's 1994 NOPAT or 1994 sustainable earnings, the tax-adjusted amount of the reversal [i.e., $2,492,000 \times (1.0 - \text{tax rate})$] should be subtracted from net income. This will make 1994 NOPAT and sustainable earnings more comparable with past and future years.

Cases
C5-1. Allied Signal (JB): Abnormal earnings valuation

Requirement 1:

```
Allied Signal - 1994 (Valuation)
(Assumes persistent ROE)
($ in Millions except per share amounts)
```

Cost of capital			0.14								
Initial book value - 12/31/94		$	2,982								
Dividend payout			0.25								

	YR. 1	YR. 2	YR. 3	YR. 4	YR. 5	YR. 6	YR. 7	YR. 8	YR. 9	YR. 10
Year ahead										
Predicted net income	$ 954 [(1)]	1,183	1,467	1,819	2,256	2,797	3,469	4,301	5,334	6,614
End-of-year book value	3,698 [(2)]	4,585	5,686	7,050	8,742	10,840	13,442	16,668	20,668	25,629
Predicted abnormal net income	537 [(3)]	666	825	1,023	1,269	1,574	1,951	2,420	3,000	3,720
Discount factor	0.8772	0.7695	0.6750	0.5921	0.5194	0.4556	0.3996	0.3506	0.3075	0.2697
PV of abnormal net income	471 [(4)]	512	557	606	659	717	780	848	923	1,004

Initial book value	$ 2,982
PV of abnormal net income	7,076
Estimated value	10,058
Shares (millions)	283
Predicted price	**35.54**
Actual high	$ 36.00
Actual low	$ 30.00

[1] $2,982 (12/31/94 equity book value) × 32% (ROE) = $954

[2]
Beginning equity book value	$2,982
+ Estimated net income	954
- Estimated dividend payment (25% × $954)	(238)
Ending equity book value	$3,699

[3]
Predicted net income	$954
- "Normal" earnings (14% × $2,982)	(417)
Predicted abnormal earnings	$537

[4]
Abnormal earnings at end of Year 1	$537
× PV of sum for 1 period @ 14%	x .8772
PV of abnormal earnings at 12/31/94	$471

Allied Signal - 1993 (Valuation)
(Assumes persistent ROE)
($ in Millions except per share amounts)

Cost of capital		0.14								
Initial book value - 12/31/93	$	2,390								
Dividend payout		0.25								

	YR. 1	YR. 2	YR. 3	YR. 4	YR. 5	YR. 6	YR. 7	YR. 8	YR. 9	YR. 10
Year ahead										
Predicted net income	$ 430 (1)	488	554	629	714	810	920	1,044	1,185	1,345
End-of-year book value	2,713 (2)	3,079	3,495	3,966	4,502	5,109	5,799	6,582	7,471	8,479
Predicted abnormal net income	95 (3)	109	123	140	159	180	204	232	263	299
Discount factor	0.8772	0.7695	0.6750	0.5921	0.5194	0.4556	0.3996	0.3506	0.3075	0.2697
PV of abnormal net income	83 (4)	83	83	83	82	82	82	81	81	81

Initial book value	$	2,390
PV of abnormal net income		821
Estimated value		3,211
Shares (millions)		283
Predicted price		**11.35**
Actual high	$	40.00
Actual low	$	35.00

[1] $2,390 (12/31/93 equity book value) × 18% (ROE) = $430

[2]
Beginning equity book value (12/31/93) $2,390
+ Estimated net income   430
- Estimated dividend payment (25% × $430)   (108)
Ending equity book value $2,712

[3]
Predicted net income $430
- "Normal" earnings (14% × $2,390)   (335)
Predicted abnormal earnings $95

[4]
Abnormal earnings at end of Year 1 $95
× PV of sum for 1 period @ 14%   x .8772
PV of abnormal earnings at 12/31/93 $83

C5-2. General Motors (CW): Income statement discussion

Optional Note to Instructors:

Included as part of the solution are edited (i.e., shortened versions) of General Motors' balance sheets, income statements, and cash flow statements for the period covered by the case. When covering the case, you might consider handing these out in advance of covering the case in class or, alternatively, handing them out on the day you cover the case in class.

1) Some points made in the article that are worth mentioning include:

		4th Quarter	Annual
a)	Net loss	($651.8 M)	($23.5 B)
b)	Revenue	$35.76 B	$132.43 B
	(year-ago fourth quarter)	$33.60 B	$123.08 B
	Increase	6.4%	7.6%
c)	"Pre-charge income"	$273.8 M	
	(year-ago fourth quarter)	($519.8 M)	

		1992	1991	
d)	Income before various charges	$92 M	($3.45 B)	
e)	North American Operations	($3.5 B)	($6.89 B)	$3.5 B improvement
f)	Cash	$7.2 B	$3.32 B	(Increase of $3.98 B)
g)	Unfunded pension liability	$14 B	$8.4 B	

While the primary theme of the article is the huge annual loss due to the accounting change for retiree medical benefits of $22.2 billion, the positive aspects of the article tend to outnumber the negative aspects. Moreover:

Requirement 1:
Positives:

a) Revenue for the fourth quarter increased by 6.4% compared to the year-earlier quarter. Revenue for the year increased by 7.6% compared to the previous year.

b) Income before write-offs and charges for the fourth quarter of the current year was $273.8 million, compared to a loss of $519.8 in the same period of the previous year.

c) Income before various charges for the current year was $92 million, compared to a loss of $3.45 billion for the prior year.

d) The firm's cash position improved from $3.32 billion at the end of 1991 to $7.2 billion at the end of 1992.

e) The firm's loss on North American Operations narrowed to $3.5 billion in the current year from $6.89 billion in the prior year.

Negatives:

The firm's unfunded pension liability increased from $8.4 billion at the end of last year to $14 billion in the current year. It is important to note, however, that this amount represents a liability to be paid over a period of years in the future, not a liability that all comes due in a single year.

Requirement 2:
Possible responses to issues (1)–(10).

1) The article states that the losses reported for the fourth quarter and for the year are primarily attributable to one-time charges for restructuring charges of $1.5 billion and $22.2 billion for an accounting change related to retiree medical benefits. The key feature to appreciate about these items is that they are non-cash charges. In other words, they reduced income in the current year or quarter, but did not reduce cash (i.e., did not require a cash outflow in the current period). Moreover, the Liability for retiree medical benefits constitutes a claim against the firm's future cash flows, not its current cash flows. Thus, these charges themselves do not reduce the ability of the firm to pay dividends. In fact, as noted in the article, the firm ended the year with $3.98 billion more in cash on hand than at the beginning of the year.

2) As noted in (1), the one-time charges have no immediate impact on the firm's cash flow in the current year. These charges represent claims to future cash flows. Thus, the real issue is whether the firm will generate sufficient cash flows in the future to pay its retirees' medical benefits and the payouts related to the restructuring of its operations (e.g., employee buyouts).

3) One rationale is commonly referred to as the "big bath." A big bath occurs when a firm is already doing poorly in a particular period and, because of this, it decides to take a host of income-reducing write-offs and/or charges that would otherwise need to be taken in a future year. Given that their firm is already doing poorly, it is often alleged that managers feel that this is the ideal time to "bite the bullet" and take whatever additional charges are on the horizon (i.e., "we're already going to report a loss so what's the difference if we make the loss bigger by taken some additional charges?"). The perceived benefit is that such write-offs obviate the need to reduce the income of a future year (i.e., taking a big bath clears the deck for reporting improved profitability in the future).

4) Conservative accounting means income that is unlikely to be overstated and/or book values that are unlikely to be overstated. By reducing its book value by the entire amount of its retiree medical benefit liability in the current year; by lowering the expected rate of return on its pension assets; and by increasing the amount of expense related to product warranties, the company's accounting became more conservative. Moreover, current and future years' income is less likely to be overstated, and the book value of the firm is much lower (i.e., less likely to be overstated).

5) The turnaround the CFO is referring to is that GM earned $273.3 million before one-time charges in the fourth quarter of the current year compared to a loss of $519.8 in the fourth quarter of the prior year.

6) The stock price increase is likely a reflection of the fact that the huge "reported" loss was heavily influenced by one-time charges, while, before such charges, the firm's performance actually improved from the prior period. Furthermore, in spite of the huge "reported" loss, the firm's cash position actually improved by about $3.5 billion during the current period.

7) Based on reported balance sheet numbers, GM may appear to be more highly leveraged. However, this ignores the fact that external parties were aware of GM's retiree medical benefit liabilities long before the FASB required the firm to bring this liability onto its balance sheet. Because bond-rating agencies like Moody's and Standard and Poor's will have previously incorporated this information into their bond-rating process, it seems unlikely that GM's credit rating would be affected.

8) Perhaps, the best earnings number is GM's sustainable earnings. This would be measured as the firm's Income from continuing operations adjusted for any non-recurring gains and/or losses.

9) As discussed above under (1) and (2), much of the loss was attributable to one-time charges that did not require a cash outlay in the current year.

10) As discussed under (7), the firm's credit rating is unlikely to be impacted; thus, the firm's ability to secure financing is unlikely to be adversely affected.

Requirement 3:
Frankly, this is a difficult question to answer in a precise manner based solely on the information contained in the article. An argument in favor of maintaining the club's current holdings could be based on the fact that the stock market responded favorably to the announcement (the stock price increased $1.25). In other words, the market did not interpret the information in the article as a negative signal about GM's future opportunities and profitability. On the other hand, given the ongoing uncertainty associated with GM's North American Operations, an argument could be made that now might be a good time to

sell-off some of the club's equity in GM, especially, since the announcement bumped the stock price up $1.25 a share.

Additional information that might be useful:

1) GM's financial statements for the current year (i.e., income statement, balance sheet, statement of cash flows).

2) Reports by financial analysts that follow GM.

3) The results reported by GM's competitors (Ford and Chrysler) for the current period.

General Motors Corporation Consolidated Balance Sheet		
	December 31	
(Dollars in millions except per-share amounts)	**1992**	**1991**
Assets		
Cash and cash equivalents	$7,789.9	$4,281.9
Other marketable securities	7,485.3	5,910.5
Total cash and marketable securities	15,275.2	10,192.4
Finance receivables—net	67,032.7	81,373.8
Accounts and notes receivable (less allowances)	6,476.7	6,498.5
Inventories (less allowances)	9,343.6	10,066.0
Contracts in process	2,456.4	2,283.1
Net equipment on operating leases	11,427.1	8,653.0
Deferred income taxes	18,394.6	4,265.2
Prepaid expenses and other deferred charges	5,686.2	5,027.7
Other investments and miscellaneous assets	10,055.1	9,425.3
Property		
Net real estate, plants, and equipment	27,371.1	27,939.8
Special tools—at cost	7,979.1	8,419.5
Total property	35,350.2	36,359.3
Intangible assets	9,515.0	10,181.2
Total assets	$191,012.8	$184,325.5

(continued on next page)

Liabilities and Stockholders' Equity		
Accounts payable (principally trade)	$9,678.4	$10,061.3
Notes and loans payable	82,592.3	94,022.1
Income taxes–deferred and payable	3,140.1	4,491.2
Postretirement benefits other than pensions	35,550.7	-
Other liabilities	51,506.1	45,602.2
Deferred credits	1,554.6	1,531.5
Total liabilities	$184,022.2	$155,708.3
Stocks subject to repurchase	765.0	1,289.6
Stockholders' equity		
Preferred stocks	234.4	234.4
Preference stocks	4.5	3.9
Common stocks		
$ 1-2/3 Par value	1,178.1	1,034.9
Class E	24.2	10.4
Class H (issued)	7.0	3.8
Capital surplus	10,971.2	4,710.4
Net income retained for use in the business (accumulated deficit)	(3,354.2)	21,525.2
Subtotal	$9,065.2	$27,523.0
Minimum pension liability adjustment	(2,925.3)	(936.8)
Accumulated foreign currency translation Adjustments and net unrealized gains (losses) on marketable equity securities	85.7	741.4
Total stockholders' equity	$6,225.6	$27,327.6
Total liabilities and stockholders' equity	$191,012.8	$184,325.5

General Motors Corporation
Consolidated Financial Statements Of Consolidated Income

(Dollars in millions except per-share amounts)	Years Ended December 31		
	1992	**1991**	**1990**
Net sales and revenues			
Manufactured products	$113,323.9	$105,025.9	$107,477.0
Financial services	10,402.1	11,144.2	11,785.0
Computer systems services	4,806.7	3,666.3	2,787.5
Other income	3,896.7	3,219.6	2,655.6
Total net sales and revenues	$132,429.4	$123,056.0	$124,705.1
Costs and expenses			
Cost of sales	105,063.9	97,550.0	96,155.7
Selling, general, and administrative expenses	11,621.8	10,817.4	10,030.9
Interest expense	7,305.4	8,296.6	8,771.7
Depreciation	6,144.8	5,684.9	5,104.1
Amortization of special tools	2,504.0	1,819.5	1,805.8
Amortization of intangible assets	310.2	411.4	451.7
Other deductions	1,575.4	1,547.0	1,288.3
Special provision for scheduled plant closings and other restructurings	1,237.0	2,820.8	3,314.0
Total costs and expenses	$135,762.5	$128,948.3	$126,922.2
Loss before income taxes	(3,333.1)	(5,892.3)	(2,217.1)
Income tax credit	(712.5)	(900.3)	(231.4)
Loss before cumulative effect of accounting changes	(2,620.6)	(4,992.0)	(1,985.7)
Cumulative effect of accounting changes	(20,877.7)	539.2	-
Net loss	($23,498.3)	($4,452.8)	($1,985.7)

General Motors Corporation
Statement Of Consolidated Cash Flows

(Dollars in Millions)	Years Ended December 31 1992	1991	1990
Cash flows from operating activities			
Loss before cumulative effect of accounting changes	($2,620.6)	($4,992.0)	($1,985.7)
Adjustments			
Depreciation	3,646.3	3,719.8	3,662.9
Depreciation of leased assets	2,498.5	1,965.1	1,441.2
Amortization of special tools	2,504.0	1,819.5	1,805.8
Amortization of intangible assets	310.2	411.4	451.7
Amortization of discount and issuance costs on debt issues	118.1	194.4	291.7
Provision for financing losses	144.5	947.1	814.5
Special provision for scheduled plant closings and other restructurings	1,237.0	2,820.8	2,848.0
Provision for inventory allowances	28.5	40.1	92.2
Pension expense, net of cash contributions	273.4	1,167.7	364.9
Gain on the sale of Daewoo Motor Co.	(162.8)	-	-
Net gain on sale of building	-	(610.3)	-
Write-down of investment in National Car Rental	813.2	-	-
Provision for ongoing Postretirement benefits other than pensions, net of cash payments	2,198.8	-	-

(continued on next page)

Change in other investments, miscellaneous assets, deferred credits	(298.7)	(1,034.8)	246.5
Proceeds from sale of receivables	-	349.3	-
Net change in other operating assets and liabilities:			
(Details omitted)			
Accounts receivable	34.7	(1,067.6)	(285.2)
Inventories (*)	886.4	(310.4)	(1,431.8)
Prepaid expenses and other deferred charges	(399.3)	129.0	(516.5)
Deferred taxes and income taxes payable (*)	(1,956.6)	(3,874.9)	(1,711.8)
Other liabilities (*)	1,560.8	3,390.4	1,701.9
Other (*)	(469.8)	1,192.4	(1,008.7)
Net cash provided by operating activities	10,346.6	6,257.0	6,781.6
Cash flows from investing activities			
(Details omitted)			
Net Cash Provided by (used in) investing activities	1,245.8	(4,609.3)	(8,354.4)
Cash Flows from Financing Activities			
Net decrease in short-term loans payable	(12,072.2)	(4,670.7)	(2,133.7)
Increase in long-term debt	18,884.8	15,830.4	14,406.5
Decrease in long-term debt	(18,588.0)	(12,665.1)	(10,355.8)
Redemption of preference stocks	(243.9)	(225.1)	(207.2)
Redemption of put options	(300.0)	(600.0)	-
Repurchases of common stocks	(7.2)	(10.4)	(362.3)
Proceeds from issuing common and preference stocks	5,555.7	2,506.6	375.7

(continued on next page)

Cash dividends paid to stockholders	(1,376.8)	(1,162.3)	(1,956.5)
Net cash used in financing activities	(8,147.6)	(996.6)	(233.3)
Effect of exchange rate changes on cash	63.2	(57.7)	(130.8)
Net increase (decrease) in cash	3,508.0	593.4	(1,936.9)
Cash and cash equivalents at beginning of the year	4,281.9	3,688.5	5,625.4
Cash and cash equivalents at end of the year	$7,789.9	$4,281.9	$3,688.5

Accounting Changes

Effective January 1, 1992, the corporation adopted SFAS No. 106, "Employers' Accounting for Postretirement Benefits Other Than Pensions." This Statement requires that the cost of such benefits be recognized in the financial statements during the period employees provide service to the Corporation. The corporation's previous practice was to recognize the cost of such postretirement benefits when incurred (i.e., pay-as-you-go method). The cumulative effect of this accounting change as of January 1, 1992 was $33,116.1 million, or $20,837.7 million after-tax ($33.38 per share).

C5-3. Financial variables/ratios and the prediction of bankruptcy and loan default (CW)

Requirements 1 and 2:
Numerous empirical studies have examined the ability of various financial variables/ratios to discriminate between firms that are likely to experience financial difficulty (i.e., go bankrupt or into loan default). Some of the variables/ratios typically studied are discussed below. Students are likely to suggest others. In such cases, students should be asked to discuss how the variable/ratio is likely to be an indication of a firm's risk of default or of changes in the likelihood of a firm's default.

Some variables/ratios typically used to capture the probability of bankruptcy/loan default:

a) *Current ratio:* The lower the current ratio, the more likely a firm will potentially face a liquidity crisis and not be able to repay its debt or interest on its debt in a timely manner; thus, the greater the risk of default/bankruptcy.

b) *Earnings variability:* As measured by the standard deviation of earnings, percentage change in earnings, or the return on asset ratio. Assuming a firm's accounting earnings tracks its true underlying economic profitability in a meaningful way, as earnings becomes more variable, the firm's future earnings are more uncertain. Since future profitability is an important determinant of a firm's long-term viability, the greater the variance of a firm's earnings stream, the more likely it may encounter financial difficulty in the future; thus, the greater the risk of default/bankruptcy.

c) *Interest coverage ratio:* The lower this ratio, the more likely a firm will be unable to make the interest payments on its outstanding obligations; thus, the greater the risk of default/bankruptcy.

d) *Size:* As measured by total assets or the market value of the firm. It is generally believed that large firms are better equipped to weather periods of financial difficulty (i.e., economic downturns) more easily than small firms. One reason is because larger firms typically have more resources within the firm as well as greater financial flexibility outside the firm (i.e., larger lines-of-credit and easier access to capital markets). Thus, the risk of default/bankruptcy decreases as the size of the firm increases.

e) *Capital structure* (i.e., the mix of debt and equity): As measured by the ratio of long-term debt to stockholders' equity; long-term debt to total assets; total debt to total assets; or similar long-term solvency ratios. The intuition here is fairly clear. As the amount of debt in a firm's capital structure increases, the firm's default risk increases because more of the firm's operating cash flows (and earnings) are committed to interest payments on the debt. In such cases, the firm becomes more sensitive to economic downturns which may make it harder for the firm to service its long-term debt.

f) *Variability of the firm's operating cash flows:* As measured by the standard deviation of operating cash flow or the percentage change in operating cash flow. Since servicing of a firm's long-term payables requires fixed interest payments, the greater the variability of a firm's operating cash flow, the more likely it may encounter financial difficulty in the future; thus, the greater the risk of default/bankruptcy.

Requirement 3:

While students are unlikely to be able to articulate the specific statistical techniques that might be used to develop and test a model of bankruptcy prediction, they should be able to discuss in general terms how this process is likely to work.

In general terms, the process would begin by identifying samples of firms that went bankrupt and those that did not during a given period of time. The next step would be to see if the variables discussed above can distinguish between the two samples. Assuming that such variables are able to distinguish between the two samples, the next step of the process would be to develop a model that employs them in an attempt to predict future bankruptcies in a new sample of firms (i.e., in a future time period).

The above explanation is purposely very general. After such a general discussion, the instructor might go on to briefly mention to students that statistical methods like discriminant analysis and logistic and probit models are often used to develop and test bankruptcy prediction models in the real world.

C5-4. Microsoft Corporation (CW): Unearned revenues and earnings management

Requirement 1:

The net profit margin is equal to net income divided by sales. For Microsoft, the rates are:

Fourth quarter of 1996:
Net profit margin = $559/$2,255 = 24.8%

Fourth quarter of 1997:
Net profit margin = $1,057/$3,175 = 33.3%

Year 1996:
Net profit margin = $2,195/$8,671 = 25.3%

Year 1997:
Net profit margin = $3,454/$11,358 = 30.4%

By any standard, Microsoft's net profit margin is very high, and it improved from 1996 to 1997.

Requirement 2:

Working capital is the difference between current assets and current liabilities, and the current ratio is the ratio of current assets to current liabilities. For Microsoft, the values are:

Year 1996:
Working capital = $7,839 - $2,425 = $5,414

Year 1997:
Working capital = $10,373 - $3,610 = $6,763

Year 1996:
Current ratio   = $7,839/$2,425 = 3.23

Year 1997:
Current ratio   = $10,373/$3,610 = 2.87

Microsoft is unlikely to face a short-term liquidity crisis. It had more than $5 billion of working capital in 1996 and more than $6 billion in 1997. Its current ratio is high by any standard, and even though it fell from 3.23 in 1996 to 2.87 in 1997, short-term liquidity will not be a problem for the firm.

Requirement 3:

Microsoft just exceeded analysts' expectations in the fourth quarter. The firm earned 80 cents per share, and analysts were expecting 79 cents per share.

Requirement 4:

Ending balance = Beginning balance + additions - reductions
 $1,418 = $1,285 + additions - 0; additions = $133.0

Requirement 5:

Income effect per share = increase in income/shares used to calculate fourth quarter EPS
 = $133.0/1,327 = 0.10 or 10 cents

Requirement 6:

Ending balance = Beginning balance + additions - reductions
$1,418 = $560 + additions - $188.0; additions = $1,046.0

Requirement 7:

Income effect per share = increase in income/shares used to calculate fourth quarter EPS

 = $1046.0/1,312
 = $0.80 or 80 cents

Requirement 8:
This answer is the balance in the account of $1,418 divided by the number of shares used to calculate 1997 annual earnings.

= $1,418/1,312 = $1.08

Requirement 9:
In periods when the firm's earnings are less than management would like to report, the balance in the Unearned revenues account could be drawn down in order to increase earnings to a level that management would like to report (subject, of course, to the available balance in the account).

In periods when the firm is doing very well, management could try to "bank" some future earnings by increasing the amount reported in the Unearned revenues account.

Requirement 10:
This is a tough task for the analyst. One thing that the analyst might do is monitor the firm's balance sheets on a quarter-to-quarter basis, paying special attention to the Unearned revenues account. What the analyst could watch for are large increases in the account balance in periods when the firm is doing very well, and perhaps, more importantly, declines in the account balance in periods when the firm has done poorly, or periods where the market expects the firm to do poorly. In either case, since the analyst will get to observe only the net change in the account balance from period-to-period, detecting with any degree of reliability that the account is being used to manage the firm's earnings will be a very difficult task.

Requirement 11:
No. It might very well be that the firm's managers believe that the proper matching of revenues and expenses requires that some of the revenues collected from customers in a given year be deferred and recognized in a later period when product upgrades are delivered and/or various types of services are provided.

C5-5. M&W Retailing & Corp. (CW): Cash flow assessments and credit analysis

Requirement 1:
This case is based on Montgomery Ward & Co. This firm filed for bankruptcy protection on July 7, 1997. Using this firm provides an opportunity to illustrate how well and how far in advance financial statement numbers and ratios begin to signal information about impending financial difficulty.

a) Income statement analysis:

On balance, the information revealed by the trend and common-size income statements is not favorable:

1) While M&W's Sales grew each year from 1991 to 1995, so did its cost of goods sold. In fact, the increase in cost of goods sold tended to outstrip the increase in sales over the total period (125.74% versus 125.29%).

2) The firm's selling, general, and administrative expenses increased dramatically in the last two years for which data are reported. The rate of increase of 37.25% far exceeded the total growth in the firm's sales of 25.29% over the entire period.

3) The common-size income statements reveal that the drop in the firm's Income from continuing operations as a percent of sales from 2.38% in 1991 to 0.15% in 1995 is primarily due to the increase in selling and administrative expenses over this period.

b) Balance sheet analysis:

As with the income statement information, the information revealed by the balance sheet analysis does not put M&W in a very favorable light:

1) The firm's cash fell dramatically from 1991 to 1992 (by about 80%). From 1992 to 1993, the firm's cash increased slightly, but then fell sharply in 1994.

2) Over the 1991–1995 period, the firm's receivables and inventories grew substantially. Receivables grew a total of 157.53% while Inventories grew by a total of 77.0%. Part of the latter increase appears to have been funded by an increase in accounts payable which increased by 47.03% over the period.

3) Given the decline in the firm's cash position over the 1991–1995 period, it also appears that part of the increase in inventory was financed by paying cash (perhaps suppliers began to demand cash rather than granting credit to M&W). The growth in receivables also explains the lower cash level later in the 1991–1995 period.

4) The common-size balance sheets reveal that, as a percent of total assets, cash declined over the 1991–1995 period, while receivables and inventories tended to increase. These observations are consistent with the results of the trend analysis previously discussed.

c) Cash flow statement analysis:

Consistent with the analysis of the other financial statements, the information revealed by the cash flow statements provides further evidence of a firm in some financial difficulty:

1) Except for 1993, the firm's cash flow from operations declined from year to year. In fact, in the most recent year (1995), operations **used** cash flow of $182 million.

2) In 1995, the firm cut back on the amount of cash used in investing activities, as cash flows used by investing activities declined from -$304.0 million in 1994 to -$109.0 million in 1995. The decrease was accomplished by reducing capital expenditures by $62.0 million, cash from the sale of PP&E of $39.0 million, and by reducing acquisitions from $120.0 million in 1994 to $0.0 in 1995.

3) In recent years, M&W has begun to use financing activities to raise cash. While cash flows from financing activities were negative in 1991 and 1992, they have been increasingly positive over the 1993–1995 period. For example, over the 1993–1995 period, the firm issued an increasing amount of common and preferred stock to raise cash. In addition, while the firm reduced long-term debt by $137.0, $403.0, and $107.0 million in 1991, 1992, and 1994 respectively, it increased long-term debt by $82.0 and $188.0 million in 1993 and 1995, respectively.

4) Overall, in three of the five years during the 1991–1995 period, M&W reported a net negative cash flow. Further, in the two years when a positive net cash flow was reported, the amounts were only $17,000 (1993) and $4,000 (1995). This compares with net negative cash flow of $446.0 million reported in total for 1991, 1992, and 1994.

d) Analysis of select financial ratios:

The analysis of various financial ratios does not paint a very good picture about M&W:

1) Cash flow per share declined by about 42% from 1994 to 1995.

2) The firm's inventory turnover ratio has been declining over the past five years. This could be an indication that M&W doesn't have the products and merchandise that consumers are demanding in the prevailing retail market.

3) Consistent with (2), the days to sell inventory has increased each year from 1991. As a result, the firm's operating cycle also increased each year during this period.

4) Over the 1991–1995 period, the firm's profitability has declined annually. For example, the firm's pre-tax profit margin fell from 3.09% in 1991 to 0.14% in 1995. In addition, the firm reports a dismal return on assets ratio of 3.48% in 1991, which worsened to an even more abysmal 0.23% in 1995.

5) The firm's interest coverage ratio, which had been above 3.0 prior to 1995, fell to the dangerously low level of 1.11 in 1995.

6) The remaining ratios reported in the case reveal that the firm has become more highly levered in recent years.

e) Analysis of preliminary results for 1996:

The preliminary results for 1996 all bode poorly for M&W.

1) The firm earned a loss of $237 million versus a small profit of $11 million in the prior year.

2) Revenues fell by about 7% from the prior year ($6,620 million in 1996 versus $7,085 in 1995).

3) The firm's operating activities generated a negative cash flow of $356 million. That is, the firm's operations were a net user rather than a net provider of cash flow during 1996. This negative cash flow from operations of $356 in 1996 is on top of a negative $182 in cash flow from operations in the prior year.

4) While the firm's overall cash flow for 1996 was only a -$5.0 million, this was accomplished by issuing about $500 million in short-term debt. A firm in M&W's situation cannot expect to survive by relying on short-term borrowings as a means to generate the necessary funds to operate.

f) The decision as whether to grant the increase in the firm's line of credit.

The above analysis does not present a strong case for granting the desired increase in M&W's line of credit. Perhaps the only reason to do so would be if the firm's inventory (or some other asset) were put up as collateral.

Summary:

Overall, the information reported in M&W's financial statements in the past few years did a reasonably good job of signaling to external users that the firm was heading toward financial difficulty.

Requirement 2:
Other information that might be considered before making a final decision includes:

a) Management's strategic plan as to how the company will be turned around.

b) The finalized financial statements for 1996.

c) The opinion of M&W's independent accounting firm as to the viability of M&W as a going concern.

d) Reports by financial analysts in the retail industry.

e) The financial statements of other retail firms could be used to see if M&W's financial woes are specific to the firm, or whether the industry in general is going through difficult times.

C5-6. Monsanto Corporation (CW): Economic value added (EVA™)

Requirement 1:
To calculate Monsanto's EVA™ for 1993–1995, we need NOPAT and the capital charge each year.

The capital charge each year is 16% of Monsanto's total debt and stockholders' equity. Moreover,

Capital for 1993 = $0.16 \times \$9,085 = \$1,454$
Capital for 1994 = $0.16 \times \$8,640 = \$1,382$
Capital for 1995 = $0.16 \times \$8,891 = \$1,423$

To calculate Monsanto's NOPAT, first notice that the firm reports a restructuring charge each year and gain from the disposal of a line of business in 1995. To calculate NOPAT, the tax-adjusted amount of the restructuring charges needs to be added back to net income while the tax-adjusted amount of the gain on the disposal of the line of business needs to be subtracted. The presumption here is that these items are transitory and are not part of the firm's sustainable income and should be excluded from NOPAT. (One might argue that since some restructuring charges were incurred each year, they are not transitory). The view taken here is that a firm may go through a period of years during which various aspects of its operations are restructured. Thus, from a long-run view, these charges are viewed as transitory.

Monsanto's NOPAT is:

1993:
NOPAT = $494 + [$5 × (1.0 - 0.34)]
      = $497.3

1994:
NOPAT = $622 + [$40 × (1.0 - 0.34)]
      = $648.4

1995:
NOPAT = $739 + [$156 × (1.0 - 0.34)] - [$189 × (1.0 - 0.34)]
      = $717.2

EVA™ is:

1993:
EVA™ = $497.3 - $1,454
     = - $956.7

1994:
EVA™ = $648.4 - $1,382
     = - $733.6

1995:
EVA™ = $717.2 - $1.423
     = - $705.8

The results indicate that Monsanto destroyed some shareholder value each year from 1993–1995.

NOTE to the Instructor:

Stern Stewart reports the following calculations for Monsanto (The Stern Stewart Performance 1000, Stern Stewart Management Services, 1996, New York, NY).

	1995	1994	1993
Beginning Capital	$10,345	$10,076	$10,235
Cost of Capital	12.75%	12.40%	12.01%
EVA™	-$475	-$440	-$632

226

Requirement 2:
Perhaps the simplest way to use EVA™ to compensate top mangers is to tie their annual bonuses to EVA™. For example, when EVA™ is positive, managers could be paid an annual bonus that is an increasing function of EVA™. When EVA™ is negative (i.e., when the managers don't earn the firm's cost of capital), they do not receive a bonus.

C5-7. IBM Corporation (CW): Firm-specific information releases and large stock price changes

a) IBM.

Requirement 1:
Since the stock price fell as a result of the article, on average, investors interpreted the information in the article as bad news. Some of the individual items that could be cited as bad news include:

1) "...IBM will break even on an operating basis in the fourth quarter... and there's no sign of improvement in early 1993."

2) "...the company is reevaluating its long-standing goal to show an 18% return on equity by the mid 1990s."

3) "IBM's weakness over the past few months, particularly in the crucial markets of Japan and Germany, caught the company off guard."

4) "IBM said it will slash development spending next year by $1 billion..."

5) "It said it will keep cutting its capital spending, which fell by $1 billion in 1992."

6) "...Moody's Investors Service Inc., which said it is considering downgrading the ratings of $18 billion in debt of Big Blue and its subsidiaries."

7) "...warning that its once-sacrosanct dividend is in danger."

8) "...declaring that it expects to make its first layoffs in a half century..."

9) "IBM will take a $6 billion pre-tax charge for the fourth quarter..."

All of the above items convey some bad news about IBM's current and future opportunities.

Requirement 2:
This is a tough question to answer. If an analyst could always answer questions like this correctly, he/she would own an island somewhere in the South Pacific.

Given the tone of the article, it appears that management feels that the worst is not yet over. Thus, one might suggest that his/her clients sell their shares or maintain their holdings, but be cautious about buying any additional shares.

On the other hand, since the article states that IBM is now trading well below its book value of $62.00, this may be a good reason to buy the stock.

Before making a recommendation, an analyst could prepare an abnormal earnings valuation of IBM's stock using the techniques discussed in the chapter, and then based on the outcome make a recommendation as to whether to buy or sell IBM's shares.

Other student responses are possible.

Requirement 3:
At a minimum, one would want to examine IBM's financial statements (income statement, balance sheet, and statement of cash flows) for the last 4–5 years. Other information to consider would be data on forecasted demand for the types of hardware and software marketed by IBM and new products in development by IBM. Information about the current products (and products in development) by competitors would also be relevant.

Other student responses are possible.

Requirement 4:
One response is that capital markets are efficient and that, on average, they do over- or underreact to information such as that disclosed by IBM. In this case, you would tell your client that it is unlikely that the market overreacted to the announcement. Of course, another response is to say that if the client feels quite strongly (for whatever reasons) that the market has overreacted, perhaps he/she should buy more shares of IBM.

Other student responses are possible.

b) IBM.

Requirement 1:
Since the stock price increased as a result of the article, on average, investors interpreted the information in the article as good news. Some of the individual items that could be cited as good news include:

1) "…boosted its dividend by 14%, the second such rise in a year…" This is good news because firms usually do not increase dividends unless they feel they can maintain them.

2) "…announced a $3.5 billion stock-repurchase plan…" An oft-cited reason for firms to buy back some of their own stock in the market is that they feel it is undervalued.

Requirement 2:
As noted in "IBM A," one response is that capital markets are efficient and that, on average, they do over- or underreact to information such as that disclosed by IBM. Thus, you might tell your client that it is not unlikely that the stock is overvalued in light of the information that is currently publicly available. Of course, another response is to say that if the client feels quite strongly (for whatever reasons) that the stock is overvalued, he/she should sell some or all of his shares.

c) Nike.

Requirement 1:
Since the stock price fell as a result of the article, on average, investors interpreted the information in the article as bad news. Some of the individual items that could be cited as bad news include

1) "…shifts in order patterns and other factors would drag fiscal fourth-quarter earnings below Wall Street forecasts."

2) "Nike said that it expects earnings of between 51 and 56 cents a share for the fourth quarter, … Wall Street had been expecting 69 cents a share."

3) "…Nike said that retailers are making fewer at-once orders in the current quarter. That implies that retailers' sales are lower than they expected."

4) "…it had $30 million of canceled orders in the quarter, slightly more than it has typically had in recent quarters."

5) "Analysts said the domestic market for Nike is mature, and suggested that Nike may have priced shoes at a point where competitors can cut into Nike sales."

Requirement 2:

The answer to this question depends on whether an analyst feels that Nike's earnings downturn in the current quarter is transitory or permanent. If transitory, the analyst might reduce the earnings projection for 1998, but not the ensuing five years, or the analyst might not reduce any of his/her earnings forecasts for future years. On the other hand, if the analyst feels that Nike's earnings change is permanent, due perhaps to competitive changes in the industry, then the earnings forecasts of future years would likely be reduced.

Requirement 3:

It is quite possible that the stock prices of Nike's competitors would change on the same day Nike made this announcement. Whether the stock prices of these other firms would increase or decrease would depend on how the market interpreted information in the article. For example, if the market interpreted Nike's earnings downturn as information that other firms in the industry were taking market share away from Nike, then it's likely that the stock prices of these firms would have increased. On the other hand, if the market interpreted the article has information that sales across the industry were flattening or slowing, perhaps because the market is reaching maturity or saturation, then the stock prices of these other firms may have decreased.

d) General questions

Requirement 1:

a) Some firms adopt the strategy of releasing bad news after the market close because of the naïve and mistaken belief that investors will not become aware of the disclosure and, thus, the price of the firm's stock will not fall (especially when the announcement is released after the market closes on Friday). In essence, firms think that they can hide the information from investors by reporting it after the market closes. A potential cost of this type of strategy is that the firm's and/or its management's reputation with investors and analysts may suffer.

b) A plausible rationale to delay the report of bad news until after the market closes is to give investors time to interpret and assess the impact of the information on the value of the firm. Here, management may be trying to reduce the volatility in its stock price by delaying the announcement until after the market closes. By doing so, investors process the information overnight, and when the firm's stock opens for trading on the following day, the price impounds the effect of the information very quickly.

Requirement 2:
Some examples include:

Earnings announcements, announcements of dividend changes (increases or decreases), management forecasts of earnings, announcements of mergers or tender offers, product recalls, major restructurings of the firm's operations, new product announcements, etc.

How large the stock price effects will be in any single case will be a function of how big a revision in investors' expectations of the firm's future cash flows the announcement results in.

Other student responses are possible.

Exercises
E6-1. Conflicts of interest and agency costs

Requirement:

An *agency relationship:* whenever someone hires another person (the agent) to act on his or her behalf. Jensen and Meckling (p. 308) define an agency relationship as "a contract under which one or more individuals (principals) engage another person (the agent) to perform some service on their behalf which involves delgating some decision-making authority to the agent." *Agency costs* are what the principals pay (in reduced wealth or utility) when they delegate decisions to the agent. An example: expected value of profits lost to the BookWorm owner when the manager closes the shop to join an old friend for lunch.

In the oil and gas drilling partnership, the general partner—Huge Gamble—makes all the operating decisions. Huge Gamble is the agent for the investor group (you and your friend). Is there any *agency conflict* here? Yes, because Huge Gamble gets paid whether oil and gas are discovered or not, but investors win only if petroleum deposits are uncovered. According to the management contract, Huge Gamble is reimbursed for all "operating costs" and receives a share of the profits if oil and gas are found. This contract structure encourages Huge Gamble to *overspend* by taking risky bets on exploration. After all, Huge Gamble has little downside risk (all costs are reimbursed) and big upside potential if oil and gas are discovered. This tendency to overspend is a *cost of the agency relationship*.

See: M.C. Jensen and W.H. Meckling, "Theory of the Firm: Managerial Behavior, Agency Costs and Ownership Structure," Journal of Financial Economics (October 1976), pp. 305–360; and M.A. Wolfson "Empirical Evidence of Incentive Problems and Their Mitigation in Oil and Gas Tax Shelter Programs," in *Principals and Agents: The Structure of Business* (Boston, MA: Harvard Business School Press, 1985), pp. 101–125.

E6-2. Understanding debt covenants

Requirement:

Debt covenants are restrictive provisions written into loan agreements by the lender. Covenants are designed to reduce potential conflicts of interest between the lender and borrower. Typical restrictions include limits on additional debt, dividend payments, mergers, asset sales, as well as the various accounting-based covenants described in the chapter.

Lenders include covenants as a form of protection against managerial actions that might unfairly reduce the likelihood of debt repayment. Borrowers agree to these restrictions because it reduces the cost of borrowing. Without covenants, lenders would charge more for the loan (a higher interest rate) as compensation for the added risks of lending. Debt covenants make both borrowers and lenders better off.

E6-3. Affirmative and negative debt covenants

Requirement:
Affirmative covenants describe actions that the borrower *must* take. Examples include: using the loan for the agreed-upon purpose (i.e., not substituting a more risky investment in place of the original investment the loan was sought for); having the company's financial statements audited by an independent accounting firm; providing those statements to the lender on a timely basis, complying with all laws (e.g., environmental regulations); allowing the lender to inspect the borrower's financial records or physical assets; and maintaining insurance on assets and key employees.

Negative covenants describe actions that the borrower may not take. Examples include: limits on total debt, capital expenditures, loans and advances to affiliated companies, cash dividends, share repurchases, mergers, and asset sales.

E6-4. Debt covenants and accounting methods

Requirement:
There are several reasons lenders may not want to require borrowers to use specific accounting methods. One important consideration is just the cost associated with keeping multiple sets of accounting records. Suppose a company had five loans, each from a different bank, and each bank required the company to prepare financial statements using a "fixed" set of accounting methods. Five loans, five banks, and five sets of books! This could prove to be very costly, especially if the loans required attestation by an independent accounting firm (five audits?).

Allowing some discretion also benefits lenders because managers can then adapt their accounting methods to the company's changing economic circumstances. Example: changing to LIFO inventory accounting when raw material price increases are expected. LIFO accounting can save tax dollars, and this cash flow improvement makes the debt less risky.

Another reason lenders may not want to require "fixed" accounting methods is that GAAP has a built-in tendency for conservatism (i.e., to understate assets and income, and to overstate liabilities).

Despite these reasons, some lenders do stipulate the accounting method(s) to be used in preparing financial data for loan covenant compliance purposes.

E6-5. Contracts and accounting numbers

Advantages:

- **Low cost**: Since the borrower (company) must produce financial statements anyway, there is no added out-of-pocket cost to using these same statements as a basis for loan agreements.

- **Accounting numbers are audited**: Since the financial statements are audited by independent accounting firms, lenders can be assured that the reported numbers are relatively free from error and material misstatements.

Disadvantages:

- **Management manipulation**: Even though the financial statements are audited, management still has some discretion over the reported numbers statements. Opportunistic reporting can never be completely ruled out. Examples include voluntary accounting method changes and changes in accounting estimates.

- **Mandatory accounting changes**: Accounting-based loan covenants can be influenced by mandatory accounting changes imposed by the FASB or other regulatory group. Lenders may feel that such changes detract from the ability of accounting numbers to accurately portray changes in a borrower's credit risk. And, mandatory accounting changes may cause borrowers to be in technical violation of debt covenants even though there has been no real change in underlying default risk.

E6-6. Regulatory costs

Requirement:
Taxes and regulations can transfer wealth from companies and their stockholders to other groups or individuals. Consider, for example, local property taxes paid by a company. These taxes represent a wealth transfer from the company (and its stockholders) to the beneficiaries—often local school districts, their employees, students, and their parents.

Electricity rate regulation provides another example. State utility regulators set the price of electricity so that stockholders can earn a "fair" rate of return on their investment. If they earn too small a return, the company is allowed to raise its prices, transferring wealth from customers to stockholders. On the other hand, if stockholders earn too high a return, regulators force the company to lower its prices, transferring wealth back to customers.

234

Regulatory costs are important for understanding a company's financial reporting choices because financial statement data are used by regulators to justify taxes and to set rates charged by utility companies. Consequently, companies have an incentive to "manage" their financial statements in ways that will influence regulators favorably. Local companies do not want to appear too profitable for fear that property taxes might be raised. Electric utility companies also do not want to appear too profitable for fear that their rates might be reduced.

E6-7. Regulatory accounting principles

Requirement:
When "construction in progress" costs are included in the rate base, regulators are allowing the company and its shareholders to earn a *return* on those costs *before* the construction project is completed. Other things equal, this should benefit shareholders at the expense of customers. Here's an example:

($ in millions)	CIP included	CIP excluded
Allowed operating costs	$1,120	$1,120
Assets in service	$3,200	$3,200
Construction in progress	500	0
Allowed assets	$3,700	$3,200
Allowed return on assets (8%)	$296	$256
Revenue requirement	$1,416	$1,376
Estimated demand (millions of KWH)	14,000	14,000
Rate allowed per KWH	$0.1011	$0.0983

In this case, including CIP in the rate base allows the company to set electricity prices so that it receives $1,416 million in revenue rather than only $1,376 million. What's the source of the added revenue? Customers pay 10.11 cents per KWH instead of 9.83 cents per KWH. Once the project has been completed, however, the CIP costs are transfered to "operating assets" and the allowed revenue number then becomes the same.

Notice also that including CIP costs in the rate base may actually benefit customers if it results in earlier construction of additional and more efficient generating facilities, transmission systems, and distribution systems. That's because the new facilities and systems might well result in lower future customer costs per KWH.

E6-8. Equipment repairs and rate regulation

Requirement:

The answer depends on *when* rates will be adjusted as well as *how* the tornado loss is classified for rate-making purposes. Let's compare two different situations: rates set in the year of the loss *versus* rates set one year later.

($ in millions)	Rates Set in Loss Year		Rates Set One Year Later	
	Expense	Capitalize	Expense	Capitalize
Allowed operating costs (before loss)	$600.00	$600.00	$600.00	$600.00
Tornado damage	5.00	–	–	–
	$605.00	$600.00	$600.00	$600.00
Assets in service	$1,600.00	$1,600.00	$1,600.00	$1,600.00
Capitalized tornado damage	–	5.00	–	4.00
Allowed assets	$1,600.00	$1,605.00	$1,600.00	$1,604.00
Allowed return on assets (8%)	$128.00	$128.40	$128.00	$128.32
Revenue requirement	$733.00	$728.40	$728.00	$729.32
Estimated demand (millions of KWH)	14,000	14,000	14,000	14,000
Rate allowed per KWH	$0.05236	$0.05203	$0.05200	$0.05201

If electricity rates are set in the loss year, it is better for shareholders to have the company treat the repairs as an *expense*. That's because doing so produces the highest allowed revenue—$733 million. But this also means that **customers** pay the full cost of the tornado repairs (through higher rates) in the first year and in each year thereafter until rates are set again.

If electricity rates are set in the loss year and the repairs are *capitalized*, customers may still pay the full cost of the repairs—but over an extended period of time. The exact amount paid and the timing depends on when rates are set again.

If rates are to be set the year after the tornado loss (but not the loss year), it is better for customers (but worse for shareholders) if the repairs are expensed in the loss year. That is because the repairs will then *not* be recovered in higher electricity rates—shareholders, not customers, bear the cost of the tornado.

If the repairs are capitalized, and rates are set in the year after the loss, customers pay for some (but not all) of the tornado damage. Notice that allowed operating costs in the example are $601 million—the extra $1 million represents depreciation of the capitalized repair costs (over a 5-year period). Capitalization produces the highest allowed revenue—$728.32 million.

Notice that if rates are set both years, it is still better for shareholders (but worse for customers) to expense the repairs immediately because the entire cost of the repairs is recovered the first year. As a practical matter, some state utility commissions allow unusual losses such as this to qualify for special rate relief.

E6-9. Capital adequacy

Requirement:
Banks and insurance companies are required to maintain minimum levels of investor capital for two reasons. First, it provides a cushion to ensure that funds are available to pay depositors and beneficiaries. Second, investors who are also managers will make less risky business decisions when some of their own money is at stake. See the discussion in E6-1.

Minimum capital requirements affect the financial statements which banks and insurance companies prepare for shareholders in several ways:

- There's expanded disclosure regarding a company's capital structure and its compliance with regulatory capital requirements.

- Certain "exotic" financial instruments that count as investor capital for regulatory purposes (and are shown as capital in the financial statements) may in fact be debt and should be so regarded by analysts. Example: manditorily redeemable preferred stock.

E6-10. Incentive design

	Advantages	Disadvantages
After-Tax Operating Profits	Pays for accounting performance of core business; doesn't reward or penalize managers for one-time gains or losses.	Neglects asset utilization and, thus, it's one-dimensional. Can be influenced by "earnings management."
Return on Assets (ROA)	Incorporates profitability and asset utilization.	Ignores the cost of capital; ROA is increased when assets are depreciated. Can be influenced by "earnings" and "balance sheet" management (operating leases).
ROA or Earnings Peer Group	Pays for performance relative to competition; doesn't reward or penalize managers when the whole industry improves or declines.	Unclear how the peer group should be identified.

All three changes may cause managers to adopt a short-term focus and devote attention to managing the performance measure rather than managing the business.

E6-11. Medical malprofits

Requirement:

When doctors own the hospitals where they work, they may be tempted to *overprescribe* or *overdiagnose* medical treatments and procedures. That's because hospital profits flow to the doctors who make decisions about the scope and level of treatment and diagnosis. Third-party reimbursement and trusting patients may not be effective impediments to this behavior. (Note: At the time of publication, the criminal investigation of Columbia/HCA was not resolved.)

E6-12. Bonus tied to EPS performance

Requirement :

Most shareholders would not feel very comfortable if managers had this type of compensation package. Consider, for example, the incentive bonus. It is based on annual increases in EPS, and the larger the EPS increase, the larger the bonus payment. But there are ways of increasing EPS that do not increase the value of the company's common shares. LIFO liquidations and stock buybacks are just two examples. Notice also that Mr. Brincat's stock options vest only if EPS grows by 20% or more in each of the next five years.

The combination of annual bonuses and stock options tied to EPS growth sends a clear signal to management: EPS is all that matters. Shareholders, on the other hand, want to make certain that EPS growth translates into higher dividends or greater share price appreciation.

Problems
P6-1. Managerial incentives and stock ownership

Requirement 1:

By the end of 1994, Mr. Johnson must hold stock worth $757,500 \times 3 =$ $2,272,5000$. Since his current holdings are worth $1,600,000, he must acquire an additional $672,500 worth of common stock by the end of the year.

Johnson's after-tax salary for 1994 is $800,000 \times (1 - 0.35) = $520,000$. This means that he must invest 129% of this amount in the company's stock. Johnson must put some of his personal financial resources into the stock.

Requirement 2:
Advantages:

Requiring managers to purchase an equity stake in the company increases the likelihood that they will act in the best interests of the shareholders. In other words, equity ownership by managers reduces potential shareholder-manager conflicts of interest. Managers will be less inclined to waste corporate resources because doing so reduces their personal wealth. When managers own stock in the companies they run, they have a strong incentive to seek out investment opportunities that add the greatest value to the business. That is because they share in any value increase.

Disadvantages:

It is possible for too much of a manager's wealth to be invested in the company's stock. If this occurs, managers may become more risk-averse than shareholders would like. That is because managers lack diversification opportunities that are available to investors. The company's other shareholders, who can diversify their investment risk, will prefer the business to undertake riskier projects than management would like.

Note: Some students will also consider the perspectives of creditors and employees when discussing the advantages and disadvantages of the stock ownership plan.

Requirement 3:

Institutional investors should favor the plan because it is designed to make managers act like "owners" (including those owners who are institutional investors). But, too much ownership by management can be bad for institutional investors. For example, managers with a controlling interest in the company may be inclined to pay higher dividends rather than reinvest in the company. Or they may spend lavishly on corporate offices. There is little institutional investors (or other shareholders) can do about it because the usual corporate governance mechanisms—proxy contests for board seats—do not work when management owns a controlling interest in the company.

P6-2. Managerial incentives and pay

Based solely on the information appearing in *The Wall Street Journal* article, Hudgens appears to have the upper hand.

Requirement 1:

Among the points that Hudgens should make are:

- *ConAgra's earnings-per-share growth should be evaluated relative to the performance of competitors.* This approach is called "relative performance evaluation" and is used by many companies today. It rewards the CEO only when company performance exceeds the performance of the industry (or a group of designated peer companies). The idea is to diminish the influence of industry-wide business cycles (both good times and bad) on executive pay. Hudgens believes that some (much?) of the ConAgra's earnings-per-share growth has been driven by favorable economic conditions throughout the industry rather than good management at the company.

- *The performance targets in the compensation plan are too low, and so it is too easy to earn the bonus.* Mr. Hudgens points out that ConAgra's "earnings have grown at a 15.4% compounded annual rate" over the last five years. Thus, the CEO will not have a difficult time achieving the performance goals required by the compensation plan. The share award is almost a sure thing.

- *ConAgra's internal goal is to achieve earnings-per-share growth of more than 14% a year.* This stated performance goal suggests that the minimum 10% growth rate specified in the incentive contract might not be very difficult to achieve.

- *Measured EPS growth should be based on Income from Continuing Operations.* Hudgens' point here is that nonoperating items—like discontinued operations, extraordinary gains and losses, and the cumulative effect of accounting method changes—should be excluded

240

from EPS growth calculations for compensation purposes. This recommendation has considerable merit.

Requirement 2:
Based only on the information in the case, ConAgra's Vice President for Human Resources has a more difficult task than does Hudgens. The news article provides no real guidance on the issues to be addressed by the VP, but here are two possibilities:

- ConAgra's Board of Directors believes that the EPS-growth target used in the compensation contract is a reasonable basis on which to evaluate and reward the performance of the CEO.

- The company's earnings have grown at an annually compounded rate of 15.4% in the last five years. The current incentive plan, with its minimum EPS-growth rate of 10%, is designed to motivate and reward the CEO for continuing to generate this superior level of earnings performance in a more challenging competitive marketplace.

Requirement 3:
Institutional investors are likely to approve incentive pay plans that provide managers with stronger incentives to increase firm value and shareholder wealth. In this particular case, Mr. Hudgens' proposals attempt to "raise the bar" by requiring the CEO to achieve an even higher level of performance. These proposed changes are consistent with what other companies are doing, and the performance goal seems attainable. It is quite likely that institutional investors will also favor adoption of these changes.

Requirement 4:
The company's 1995 proxy statement (dated September 28, 1995) shows that Hudgens was not entirely successful in his attempt to change the company's compensation practices. Mr. Fletcher's special long-term incentive plan (described in the news article) was continued. A long-term senior management incentive plan tied to EPS growth was also continued in 1995, but the award target was raised to 14% growth in earnings per share. The company did not adopt Hudgens' recommendation that incentive compensation be based on performance relative to 13 other food companies.

P6-3. Corporate governance

Requirement 1:
The separation of company ownership (shareholders) from control of company resources (management) leads to potential conflicts of interest between shareholders and managers. For example, managers have incentives to divert corporate resources away from profitable investment projects toward such things as corporate jets, lavishly decorated offices, and other expenditures that

do not add value to the company. This resource diversion makes managers better off, but shareholders are worse off because they (not the managers) pay the bills.

The Board of Directors hires company officers (the CEO and other top executives). Then the Board monitors the behavior and performance of those officers to help ensure that they always act in the best interests of shareholders. Directors are elected by shareholders. They advise top management, approve major company decisions—like proposed mergers, divestitures, and major acquisitions—and ensure that the resources entrusted to management are properly maintained.

Requirement 2:
Long-time *personal friends of the CEO* who serve as directors may weaken the company's corporate governance structure if their personal friendship prevents them from exercising their responsibility to advise and monitor managerial performance. Close personal friends may find it difficult to vote to fire a poorly performing CEO even when doing so is in the best interests of shareholders.

Board members who own little or no common stock in the company have no real economic stake in the business. With nothing to lose, such directors may be less inclined to scrutinize management's performance or oppose management's decisions. Only the director's reputation suffers when decision outcomes are bad and performance is poor.

Board members that *serve on ten or more boards* weaken the corporate governance structure for the simple reason that they are spread too thin. With board responsibilities at several companies, it becomes difficult to effectively monitor and advise management at any one company.

Company-funded *retirement plans* weaken corporate governance when the plans are overly generous. In such cases, board members may be less inclined to monitor and advise management out of concern for their pension benefits.

Requirement 3:
The Calper's proposals:

#1: By toughening the *definition of an independent director*, this proposal presumably improves corporate governance by ensuring that board members are free to scrutinize and oppose management's decisions. Less independent directors may be less effective in this capacity because they fear reprisal—termination of lucrative personal service contracts or loss of corporate contributions to nonprofit organizations.

#2: Requiring the board to have a majority of independent directors gives outsiders (shareholders and their representatives) a stronger voice in the company. When insiders—the CEO and other corporate officers—dominate the board, it is more difficult to monitor management performance and conduct.

#3: The board chairman is usually the company's CEO. Picking an independent lead director to serve as co-chair lessens the CEO's power and influence over board matters, including when meetings are held and what is on the agenda.

#4: This proposal is aimed at encouraging board members to reduce competing time commitments by making those commitments public. A board member who seems overextended is less likely to be re-elected by shareholders.

#5: This proposal is not likely to enhance corporate governance. It presumes that older directors are less able to provide oversight and advice than are younger directors. We do not find this argument particularly compelling. At the same time, by encouraging board turnover, the proposal does provide a way of bringing contemporary thinking and new perspectives to a board.

Requirement 4:

The anecdotal evidence suggests that the answer is: Yes. Recent changes in the corporate governance practices of companies like IBM and General Motors were followed by improved financial performance. A substantial amount of research on corporate governance issues has been produced in the last 10 years, but few clear conclusions have yet emerged. The results of one study are described in the following *Wall Street Journal* article:

HEARD ON THE STREET: WHARTON STUDY CONNECTS STRENGTHS AND FLAWS OF DIRECTORS TO COMPANIES' FINANCIAL RETURNS.

If a chief executive names his friends to his company's board, some might say that raises ethical issues. Now a study by three professors at the University of Pennsylvania business school, the Wharton School, suggests that it also raises questions about the company's future performance.

What the study found is that domineering, 'entrenched' chief executive officers with weak boards tend to get higher pay than other CEOs, and that the companies' returns on assets and stock performance tend to be weaker than others'.

Wharton Profs. John Core, Robert Holthausen, and David Larcker found six different board characteristics linked to both higher CEO pay and weaker performance: the same person serving as CEO and chairman; a large board; outside directors directly appointed by the CEO; outside directors who receive income from an association with the company; 'busy' outside directors who sit on several other boards; and outside directors aged 70 or older.

'The conclusion,' says Prof. Holthausen, 'is that any of these factors is going to tend to cause poor governance systems and ultimately lead to poorer financial performance by the firm.'

Some money managers say they already look at such corporate-governance issues in identifying stocks to buy or to avoid. 'It is a very important factor for us,' says Anthony Kreisel, co-manager of the $24 billion Fund for Growth & Income at Putnam Investments in Boston. 'The strong, confident, and mature CEO really looks for people on his board who will challenge and help him. He welcomes someone looking at his performance.'

Mr. Kriesel says the decision by International Business Machines' CEO Louis Gerstner to add Emerson Electric Chairman Charles Knight to the board a couple of years ago helped him decide that depressed IBM stock was worth buying. And the presence on Eastman Kodak's board of strong members, such as Coca-Cola Chairman Roberto Goizueta, suggested to him that weakening Kodak was due for a management shake-up—which occurred in 1993 and helped the stock.

The Wharton study was based on data collected on 205 large companies in 1982, 1983, and 1984 by an unidentified compensation-consulting firm. The authors identified negative board characteristics, correlated them with the chairman's compensation and, through that relationship, related them to stock performance and return on assets over five years.

If a company's board structure indicated a 30% excess in CEO compensation, for example, that correlated with a 2.3 percentage-point deficit in annual stock return. In a year when the average company gained 15%, that company would be expected to gain just 12.7%.

The authors identified a 'busy' outside director as one who sits on three or more other boards—or six or more for retirees. Their study didn't point to an optimal size for boards; it simply indicated that the average size at the time was 13, and smaller was better.

One surprise: Although shareholder activists today favor outside directors, the authors found that companies generally did better with more inside directors. That could be because, in practice, outside directors often are handpicked by the CEO.

The study also noted that if someone other than the CEO owned 5% or more of the stock, that signaled better performance, as did the amount of the CEO's stock ownership.

A representative of Fidelity Investments indicated that fund managers at the Boston mutual-fund complex aren't convinced that separating a board chairman from a CEO is always a good idea. But Fidelity does look at whether the chief executive owns 'a substantial amount of stock' in the company as one factor among many.

The study's findings are useful, but not foolproof. Prof. Holthausen says that H. J. Heinz and NationsBank are two companies that today have some board warning signs. Heinz's 18-member board is larger than average, he says. Of its nine outside directors, six are older than 69 and four are 'busy.' Its chairman is CEO. NationsBank, he says, has a 'huge,' 26-member board, with eight of the 24 outsiders busy.

Heinz responds that its 12% profit growth last year and 24% stock-price gain in the past year are more important than corporate-governance debates. NationsBank notes that its stock has outperformed the market for most periods since the 1980s.

NationsBank also has outperformed most other big banks. But Heinz's stock price has generally trailed those of other food companies and the market over the past five years.

Board Warnings:

Characteristics of boards of directors that can be danger signs for a stock, according to a study by three professors at the Wharton School:

- Chairman and chief executive are the same person
- Large board
- Chief executive himself appoints outside directors
- Outside directors who have business dealings with company
- Outside directors age 70 or over
- 'Busy' outside directors who serve on many other boards

Source: *The Wall Street Journal*, April 25, 1997

P6-4. Compensation of outside directors

Requirement 1:
Two advantages of the plan are:

- Making directors stakeholders in the company provides them stronger incentives to more carefully monitor management decisions. This is because, as investors, they will share in any gains from good management, and they will suffer from poor management, just like other stockholders.

- It is often alleged that managers are too focused on short-term results rather than on the company's long-term success. Linking director compensation to stock value (or return) may encourage directors to adopt a long-term perspective when evaluating management's plans and performance.

Potential disadvantages of the plan are:

- Stock-based compensation is risky and may cause directors to become too risk-averse. Stock prices are influenced by a variety of factors that are outside the control of management and the board. The added risk may cause directors to prefer safe investment projects and to reject risky, positive, net-present-value investment opportunities. As a result, stock-based compensation may be less effective than a fixed cash payment. One way overcome this problem is to pay directors for the added risk of a stock-based compensation plan by using an expected payoff higher than the fixed cash payment.

- The value of the stock may be a very small portion of a director's overall wealth, and, thus, provide little incentive for increased monitoring of top management. (Of course, the same could be said about the amount of any director's fees paid entirely in cash.)

Requirement 2:
Managers and directors should not be rewarded (or punished) for performance outcomes that are beyond their control. Doing so introduces unwanted variation (or "noise") into the performance evaluation process and adds performance risk that managers and directors cannot influence. Companies in cyclical industries (e.g., construction) are a case in point. A company's stock price will suffer during a business downturn no matter how well management has positioned the business to weather that downturn. Some compensation plans address this issue by indexing stock-based compensation to changes in the value of a market-wide or an industry-wide share price index. This approach has gained popularity in recent years and is known as ***relative performance evaluation***.

Requirement 3:
Shareholders receive a return on their investment in two ways: cash dividends and share price appreciation. Other things equal, eliminating cash dividends will result in a higher stock price. To see this, consider a company whose stock is now selling for $10 per share with a $1 per-share annual dividend. Suppose investors require (demand) a 12% return on the company's stock and that management delivers this level of performance by earning $1.20 per share. If $1 is paid out as dividends, the stock will be worth $10.20, but if no dividends are paid out, the stock will be worth $11.20.

Stock options, however, have a fixed exercise price that does not rise or fall with changes in the company's dividend policy. This means that, other things equal, Times Warner directors would favor the elimination of cash dividends any time they are holding options that cannot be exercised. Eliminating the dividend would cause the company's share price to rise more quickly in the future, and thereby increase the value of directors' stock options.

P6-5. Earnings quality and pay

Requirement 1:
The first thing to note about the suggested adjustments is that none of the nonoperating income items and gains are mentioned. The list provided by company managers is one-sided: It identifies nonoperating and extraordinary items that **decreased** reported earnings for the year, but it does not point to any of those items that **increased** earnings. Of course, without access to the complete financial statement, the compensation committee would not be aware of this intentional oversight.

Requirement 2:
Let us start with the three income-reducing special items:

a) Restructuring and other nonrecurring charges
b) Income (loss) from discontinued operations prior to sale (net of tax)
c) Extraordinary charge, early retirement of debt (net of tax effect)

The compensation committee could agree that the bonus should be paid solely on the basis of reported net income and that no adjustment is necessary. One justification for this view is that income-reducing items such as these are offset by income-increasing items not contained on the adjustment list.

On the other hand, a reasonable argument can be made to exclude (a) and (b) from the bonus calculation. Changes in the company's economic environment may have contributed to the need for a restructuring and the discontinued operations. Managers should not be penalized for making good business decisions. And, if annual bonuses are influenced by such nonrecurring items, managers will be less inclined to make these tough decisions in the future.

A similar argument can be made for excluding (c) from the bonus calculation. Here, changes in the company's optimal financial structure (best mix of debt and equity) may have prompted the early debt retirement. Don't penalize managers for making good business decisions.

d) Cumulative effect on prior years of changes in accounting principles for:

- Postretirement benefits other than pensions (net of tax effect).

Although management could determine the timing of this accounting, the change itself was not voluntary. The FASB required all companies to adopt a new approach to accounting for postretirement benefits. For this reason, it seems reasonable to exclude the loss from the bonus calculation.

- Postemployment benefits (net of tax effect).

The same comment made above for "postretirement benefits other than pensions" applies here as well.

- Warehouse and catalog costs (net of tax effect).

This accounting change was initiated by management and not required by the FASB or some other regulatory body. As such, no adjustment to the bonus calculation should be made because managers presumably understood how the action would affect their compensation. A counterargument is that managers should not be penalized (or rewarded) for accounting decisions that have no real economic impact on the company.

Three possibilities for the appropriate net income figure come to mind:

(a) Income from continuing operations. The rationale here is to exclude items that have no direct bearing on the company's sustainable income for the year.

(b) Income from continuing operations, adjusted for all nonrecurring items. The idea to exclude nonrecurring losses so that managers have an incentive to restructure operations when needed, and without harming their annual bonus. Nonrecurring gains are excluded so that managers are not rewarded for temporary income increases.

(c) Income from continuing operations, adjusted for nonrecurring losses only. As in (b), the rationale here is to provide managers with an incentive to restructure operations when needed and to reward them for any realized gains (even those gains that are not sustainable).

For most companies, the best choice is (b).

P6-6. Avoiding debt covenant violations

Requirement 1:
For most companies, the **fixed charges ratio** is just a variation of the interest coverage ratio. With only two weeks until the books are closed, the company needs to "find some income" that can increase the numerator of this ratio. Possible sources of income are:

- Accelerate the recognition of revenue from the first few days of next year into the last few days of this year (i.e., leave the books open past the fiscal year end).

- Delay the recognition of expenses from the last few days of this year until the first few days of next year (i.e., close the books early for expenses).

- Postpone discretionary expenses like maintenance, research and development, or advertising.

- Sell assets that have market values substantially in excess of their book values.

- Change one or more accounting methods to increase reported earnings. For instance: expand straight-line depreciation to all long-lived assets, eliminate LIFO accounting.

- Change one or more accounting estimates. For instance, increase the estimated useful lives of long-term assets, decrease salvage value estimates or bad debt allowances.

Requirements 2 and 3:
Some actions that could be taken are:

- Any of the actions outlined in (1) also apply here.

- Issue common stock before the end of the year.

- Reissue treasury stock before the end of the year.

- To reduce the ratio of consolidated debt to total capitalization (i.e., to total assets), the company could retire some debt before the end of the year. If the debt could be retired for a price close to its carrying amount, net worth would not change much.

- The last three items could be combined into a stock-for-debt exchange offer, although most transactions of this sort require more than two weeks' time.

Requirement 4:
Answers to this question will vary from student to student. The dilemma confronting the banker involves a trade-off between (a) using covenants to restrict management's action and thereby reduce credit risk and (b) inhibiting management from taking prudent actions that enhance cash flows and the likelihood of debt repayment. Students should be encouraged to see both sides of this situation.

P6-7. Investment projects and stockholder-bondholder conflict

Requirement 1:
The expected value of project A is:

$$= (\$250,000 \times 0.50) + (\$500,000 \times 0.50)$$
$$= \quad \$125,000 \quad + \quad \$250,000 \quad = \$375,000$$

The expected value of project B is:

$$= (\$100,000 \times 0.50) + (\$650,000 \times 0.50)$$
$$= \quad \$50,000 \quad + \quad \$325,000 \quad = \$375,000$$

If the company has no debt, risk-neutral shareholders are indifferent between the two projects because they have the same expected value. However, if the project is financed with debt, shareholders will prefer project B because of its greater payoff dispersion. This increases the likelihood of a higher payoff for shareholders. Here is how: Project A generates either just enough to pay bondholders ($250,000) or enough to pay the debt and to put $250,000 in the pockets of shareholders. Project B will generate either $100,000 (stockholders walk away and bondholders lose $150,000) or enough to pay bondholders in full and put $400,000 in the pockets of shareholders. The greater dispersion of project B relative to project A is why shareholders prefer project B.

Why are shareholders risk-neutral? The usual explanation is that they can diversify their risk across many investments, and, thus, care little about the risk of any individual investment.

Requirement 2:
The bondholders clearly prefer project A because regardless of which outcome occurs, this project always generates enough cash to repay the full $250,000 of debt. Project B has only a 50% chance of generating enough cash to repay the debt in full, and there is a 50% chance that bondholders will lose $150,000.

Requirement 3:
The availability of project B creates a problem for bondholders if they price the debt assuming that project A will be selected. If project B is chosen instead, the value of the debt will fall because of the increased likelihood of default (non-payment). The decline in the value of the debt would be mirrored by an increase in share value.

On the other hand, if bondholders realize other investment projects may be available, they will protect themselves from asset substitution. One way to achieve this protection is to price the debt so that it reflects the possibility that a project riskier than A will be selected. But rational managers know that bondholders "price-protect" so they willingly agree to use the loan proceeds only for project A. The debt gets priced accordingly, and the company gets a lower cost of capital.

P6-8. Executive pay when the CEO nears retirement

Requirement 1:
As a CEO approaches retirement, his/her decision horizon naturally becomes shorter. For example, suppose a CEO is paid an annual bonus based on the reported earnings. The CEO may be reluctant to invest in long-term projects if retirement is one or two years away. Nearing retirement also creates an incentive to manage the company's financial reporting decisions (accounting method choices and accruals) so that revenue recognition is accelerated and expense recognition is delayed. Doing so can increase the last couple of bonus payments.

In addition, reported earnings can also be increased in the short run by reducing outlays for research and development, advertising, or other discretionary items. Such actions are likely to be detrimental in the long run, however.

Because annual bonuses may not be an effective way to motivate CEOs approaching retirement, it makes sense to change the incentive pay package. Common adjustments include eliminating or reducing earnings-based bonuses or deferring stock awards beyond the retirement date. These changes reduce the incentive to adopt a short-term decision horizon.

Requirement 2:
Some advantages are:

- The plan provides Mr. Stiritz with an incentive to focus on the long term because the value of his stock grant depends on how well the company performs after he retires. This seems to provide a strong incentive for him to select the best person as his successor.

- The options become exercisable in three tiers (or tranches) that become exercisable on September 26, 1998, 2001, and 2004, respectively. These staggered vesting dates mean that Stiritz cannot exercise the options all at once shortly after he retires. The fact that some options cannot be exercised until 2004 provides added incentive for Stiritz to adopt a long-term perspective as he selects a successor.

- Unless certain minimum levels of stock price performance are met, Stiritz will not be allowed to exercise the options. For example, the options scheduled to vest on 9/26/98 cannot be exercised unless the company's stock price has increased to at least $74.14. If the share price is below this amount on 9/26/98, the options do not vest until the $74.14 price is subsequently reached. These minimum stock price requirements provide Stiritz with an added incentive to choose a successor who can create the most value for shareholders.

Some disadvantages are:

- As noted in the case, "all of the shares become exercisable, in any event, on the ninth anniversary of the date of grant." Thus, regardless of how well or poorly the company's stock performs over the nine-year period, Stiritz can exercise the options after nine years.

- The options are not indexed to the performance of the overall stock market or to the performance of Ralston's industry. This means that part of any increase in the price of Ralston's stock could reflect favorable market conditions or industry-wide conditions, rather than superior performance on the new CEO.

Requirement 3:
Some suggestions are:

- Set the exercise price at a level higher than the market price of the stock on the date the options were granted. This would require a higher level of performance by the new CEO and diminish the impact of favorable market-wide or industry-wide share price increases.

- Index the vesting date and exercise price to the company's stock price performance relative to the industry or a peer group of similar companies.

- In addition to freezing Striritz's salary for the last couple of years before his retirement, require that a significant portion of his compensation be used to purchase Ralston's common stock.

Requirement 4:
Many shareholders are likely to be disappointed by this outcome. The board's stated rationale for changing its approach to compensating Stiritz was to get him to focus on "locating the right successor so that the company will do well after his retirement." One interpretation of the appointment of two existing executives as co-chief executives is that Stiritz was unable to decide who should run the company after his retirement.

P6-9. CEO compensation at Walt Disney Company

Requirement 1:

In a corporation, shareholders delegate to professional managers control over the company's resources and day-to-day operating decisions. However, shareholders are unable to directly observe the effort level put forth by the managers they hire. They cannot know whether managers are working hard to enhance the value of the firm, or whether they are just shirking. If top managers are paid a fixed salary, they have an incentive to shirk because they receive the same pay without regard to how well or how poorly the company does. Earnings-based bonus plans overcome this problem and allow the managers to share in the company's success. Mangers then have an incentive to put forth more effort because their pay increases with profits, and profits increase when they put forth greater effort running the company.

The plan requires Disney to earn a minimum rate of return of 11% before Eisner begins to receive a bonus. Is this a reasonable threshold?

- One way to answer this question would be to look at the rate of return that Disney was earning prior to the adoption of the plan in 1989. If the company had been earning a higher rate of return, then one might conclude that the performance level required by the plan is too low.

- You might also look at the rate of return earned by Disney's competitors. If the required rate of return is at or above the industry average, one might conclude that the performance level required by the plan is reasonable. Alternatively, if the required rate of return is below the industry average, one might conclude that the performance level required by the plan is too easy.

Requirement 2:

In addition to paying Eisner an annual cash bonus, Disney also awards stock options that provide a further incentive for Eisner to work hard to create value for shareholders. One problem with annual bonus plans is that managers can manipulate accounting income in the short term. Stock option grants get managers to take a long-term perspective.

Requirement 3:

The reason the exercise price of some options is set at a level above the current market price of Disney stock is that it provides Eisner with an added incentive to further increase the share value. Notice that these options are not "in the money" (have no value to Eisner) until Disney's shareholders are all made better off by at least $10 per share. Setting the exercise price above the market price on the grant date also serves to reduce the impact of stock price run-ups that are due to general economic conditions (i.e., a bull market).

Requirement 4:

The table shows the value of $100 invested in Disney common stock, the S&P 500 market index, and the industry peer group (with dividend reinvestment). For example, $100 invested in Disney stock in September 1991 would be worth $229 in September 1996. Similar investments in the S&P 500 and the peer group would be worth $203 and $226, respectively. Investors in Disney common stock earned a return of 129% over the five-year period, compared to a market and peer group return of 103% and 126%, respectively.

This means that the Disney investment would be worth only $3 more than an investment in the peer group, and only $26 more than the market index. In percentage terms, Disney outperformed the market by an annual average of 5.2%, but by only about 0.6% over the peer group.

On the surface, the fact that Disney performed about the same as the peer group over the 1991-1996 period might suggest that Eisner was paid handsomely to match, but not outperform, peer companies.

However, before concluding that his compensation was excessive in relation to performance, the compensation strategies of the peer groups should be examined. One possibility is that peer group companies performed as well as Disney (on average) even though they had less expensive CEO pay plans. This would add credence to the claim that Disney's shareholders overpaid Eisner for the level of stock price performance he delivered over the 1991-1996 period. On the other hand, peer group firms may have had even richer CEO pay packages.

Requirement 5:

The fact that Disney's management selects peer group firms is problematic. Management may be tempted to select a peer group that it knows it will out-perform. This complicates any analysis of pay-for-performance because you cannot be certain if Disney's superior performance was due to have a better (more motivating) pay plan or because the peer group consists of relatively weak companies. One way analysts and investors can overcome this problem is to construct their own peer group for use in gauging Disney's performance.

P6-10. A new employment agreement at Disney

Requirement 1:

To receive a bonus under the new plan, Eisner must increase Disney's earnings-per-share (EPS) by more than 7.5% from the 1996 level. For example, if EPS was $1.00 in 1996, it would have to exceed $1.075 in 1997 (i.e., exceed $1.00 × 1.075) before Eisner receives a bonus.

The old bonus plan required Disney to earn an 11% return on stockholders' equity (ROE). The new plan calls for EPS *growth* of 7.5%. Despite this difference, the two plans are alike in many ways. For example, they both pay for earnings performance, and the dollar earnings hurdle increases each year (as long as Disney's dividend payout ratio is less than 1.0).

Stock options are granted under both plans. Under the old plan, 75% of the options had an exercise price equal to the market price of the stock on the grant date. Under the new plan, this percentage falls to 62.5% with the remaining 37.5% having higher exercise prices. These staggered exercise prices range from 25% above the market price to 100% above the market price. This feature of the new plan should provide a stronger incentive for Eisner to increase the value of Disney shares.

Requirement 2:
Are the new performance goals reasonable? There is no correct answer to this question, but here are some points to consider:

- How does the new performance goal compare to the company's past record of EPS growth? If EPS has been growing at a rate substantially above 7.5%, the new performance goal should be easily achieved and, thus, might be too low.

- In addition to Disney's historical performance, how does the goal compare to the EPS growth rates of the company's competitors? Again, if competitor EPS growth has been substantially above 7.5%, the new performance goal might be too low to provide an incentive for superior performance.

- One issue that does arise with regard to the new bonus plan is the impact that share repurchases can have on EPS growth. If Disney aggressively repurchases common shares each year, the number of shares outstanding will decline, and EPS will increase over time even though earnings itself stays level. The new bonus plan creates an incentive to repurchase shares instead of paying cash dividends to stockholders because doing so makes it easier to achieve the EPS growth target.

Requirement 3:
There is no "correct" answer to this question. On the one hand, the agreement continues to tie compensation to accounting performance, not shareholder value, and that is a reason to vote against the contract. On the other hand, the staggered exercise price on the options does provide an incentive to increase the company's share price, and that is a reason to vote for the contract. In the end, the question is simply: Does the new contract better align Eisner's incentives with those of shareholders?

Given the (hypothetical) value of Eisner's options as reported in the problem (in excess of $190 million), some students may be tempted to respond to this question by saying that they would vote against the plan because the level of compensation seems so excessive. The following points should also be considered:

- How does Eisner's compensation package compare with that of other CEOs in the industry?

- How successful has Disney been under Eisner's leadership? How much value has been created for shareholders, and how does this compare to other companies in the industry and to the level of compensation paid to Eisner?

- What other employment opportunities does Eisner have? If he is an exceptional CEO with a national reputation, his pay package might have to be rich just to keep him at Disney. Skilled executive talent is a scarce resource, and the most talented CEOs should be the most richly rewarded.

P6-11. Understanding rate regulation and accounting choices

Requirement 1:
The following table shows the impact of the proposed accounting changes on 1998's revenue requirement and rate per kilowatt hour:

($ in millions)	Base Case	Extend Plant Life	Increase Bad Debts	Amortize Takeover Costs	Write-Up Inventories
		Proposed accounting changes			
Allowed operating costs	$1,120.0	$1,120.0	$1,120.0	$1,120.0	$1,120.0
Accounting change adjustment	–	(5.0)	7.0	1.5	–
	$1,120.0	$1,115.0	$1,127.0	$1,121.5	$1,120.0
Assets in service	$3,200.0	$3,200.0	$3,200.0	$3,200.0	$3,200.0
	–	175.0	(7.0)	3.0	60.0
	$3,200.0	$3,375.0	$3,193.0	$3203.0	$3,260.0
Allowed return at 8.75%	$280.0	$295.3	$279.4	$280.3	$285.3
Revenue requirement	$1,400.0	$1,410.3	$1,406.4	$1,401.8	$1,405.3
Estimated demand (millions of KWH)	14,000	14,000	14,000	14,000	14,000
Rate per KWH allowed	$0.10000	$0.10074	$0.10046	$0.10013	$0.10038

Alternate solution format:

($ in millions)		Estimated Demand	Rate per KWH Allowed
Current allowed operating costs	$1,120.0	14,000	$0.08000
Effects of proposed accounting changes:			
Extend plant depreciation life	($5.0)	14,000	($0.00036)
Increase bad debts	$7.0	14,000	$0.00050
Amortize hostile takeover costs	$1.5	14,000	$0.00011
Write-up fuel and materials inventories	$0.0	14,000	$0.00000
Subtotal	$1,123.5	14,000	$0.08025
Current assets in service × 8.75%	$280.00	14,000	$0.02000
Effects of proposed accounting charges:			
Extend plant depreciation life ($175 million × 8.75%)	$15.31	14,000	$0.00109
Increase bad debts ($7 million decrease × 8.75%)	($0.61)	14,000	($0.00004)
Amortize hostile takeover costs ($3 million × 8.75%)	$0.26	14,000	$0.00002
Write-up fuel and materials inventories			
($60 million × 8.75%)	$5.25	14,000	$0.00038
Subtotal	$300.2	14,000	$0.02144

Requirement 2:

The **bad debt increase** seems quite plausible as long as the revised estimate (1.5% of sales) conforms to the company's actual experience. This change would probably be allowed.

The **inventory write-up** to current replacement value makes good economic sense. Investors should be allowed to earn a fair return (8.75%) on their current investment in the company, not on an outdated historical measure of that investment. If LIFO inventory accounting were used, for example, the inventory cost numbers could be several decades old. Unfortunately, regulators have so far rejected this line of argument and required utilities to maintain their balance sheet at historical cost.

The **plant life extension** would be allowed, but not the $400 million increase in asset book value.

Regulators would disallow **amortization of the hostile takeover cost** incurred last year. This is nothing more than a bold attempt to get one of last year's expenditures into this year's rate base. The company may initiate a request for a special rate surcharge to cover this unusual expenditure, but that too is likely to be rejected because the outlay was of little benefit to customers.

Cases

C6-1. Genesco Inc., Worthington Industries, Inc., and Symantec Corporation (CW): A tale of three dividend constraints

Requirement 1:

Symantec's inventory of payable funds (IPF) for 1996 is equal to $10.0 million plus 25% of the company's net income since 1993, minus the sum of all cash dividends and share repurchases since 1993. The financial statement excerpt does not indicate how proceeds from stock sales are to be handled in the IPF calculation, so two alternative IPF numbers are shown below.

Excluding the proceeds from stock sales:

IPF = $10,000,000 + 0.25 × (-$44,421,000 + $33,409,000 - $39,783,000)

  = $10,000,000 - $12,698,750 = -$2,698,750

Based on this calculation, Symantec has a negative IPF and cannot pay cash dividends or repurchase stock.

Including the proceeds from stock sales:

IPF = $10,000,000 + 0.25 × (-$44,421,000 + $33,409,000 - $39,783,000)
    + ($47,969,000 + $21,395,000 + $20,770,000)

  = $10,000,000 - $12,698,750 + $90,134,000 = $87,435,250

Based on this calculation, Symantec can pay cash dividends or repurchase stock up to the amount of $87,435,250.

Requirement 2:

The percentages are: Genesco 50%, Worthington 75%, and Symantec 25%.

Why does this percentage vary across companies and industries? By limiting a company's ability to pay cash dividends, bondholders are implicitly imposing a *minimum reinvestment constraint* on the business. Limiting cash distributions to shareholders means that more cash is retained in the business and available to fund new investments—new product development, capital projects, advertising, and so on. Bondholders benefit from these investments if they enhance future cash flows of the firm, because this increases the likelihood of debt repayment.

Thus, one reason the IPF net income percentage might be set low is that bondholders want the company to reinvest a larger portion of its earnings. This might be true for small companies, companies that have recently gone public, or companies in highly competitive industries.

Requirement 3:
Cash dividends and share repurchases are treated the same for IPF purposes because they both reduce the cash available to repay debt. In addition, since the cash leaves the company, dividends and share repurchases also reduce the cash available for investment in positive NPV projects inside the company. This reduces the future cash flows available for debt repayment.

Requirement 4:
Bondholders limit cash distributions to shareholders to prevent managers from just giving the money away to owners and increasing the default risk of the business. Cash dividends paid out of debt proceeds or funded by asset sales increase default risk. That is why the IPF is not increased when the company issues more debt.

Cash dividends paid from the stock sale proceeds do not increase the company's default risk—managers are merely taking money in from new stockholders and paying it out to old stockholders.

Requirement 5:
In the *very* near term, the deficit could be eliminated by issuing common stock, making an income-increasing accounting method change, or reducing discretionary expenditures like advertising or R&D. Of course, the best way to eliminate the deficit would be to improve the company's real profitability. Generate higher sales, reduce costs, and grow earnings.

Requirement 6:
Why do companies like Worthington maintain large IPF balances? One reason is that managers are reluctant to cut cash dividends when earnings performance slackens. This is because the stock market reacts negatively to most dividend cuts. Thus, a company that maintains a small or negligible IPF runs the risk of having to cut dividends in any year that earnings are small or negative (loss). Earnings volatility thus plays an important role in managers' decisions about optimal IPF balances. Companies that maintain a sizable IPF balance do not find it necessary to reduce dividends as quickly.

C6-2. Huffy Corporation, Caesars World, and Lands' End (CW):
Accounting-based incentive bonus plans

Requirement 1:
In a corporation, shareholders delegate control over the company's resources and day-to-day operating decisions to professional managers. However, shareholders are unable to directly observe the effort level put forth by the managers they hire. They cannot know whether managers are working hard to enhance the value of the firm, or whether they are just shirking. If top managers are paid a fixed salary, they have an incentive to shirk because they receive the same pay without regard to how well or how poorly the company does. Earnings-based bonus plans overcome this problem and allow the managers to share in the company's success. Managers then have an incentive to put forth more effort because their pay increases with profits, and profits increase when managers put forth greater effort running the company.

Requirement 2:
Huffy reported net income of $4,215,000 and income before the cumulative effect of accounting changes of $11,843,000. Average net assets are $121,342,000 [($124,997,000 + $117,687,000)/2]. Whether or not managers achieved a RONA greater than 8.5% depends on whether the income effect of the accounting method change is included or excluded from the RONA calculation:

RONA (including the accounting change) = $4,215,000/$121,342,000

= 3.47%

RONA (excluding the accounting change) = $11,843,000/$121,342,000

= 9.76%

Without the bonus plan details, we cannot tell if Huffy's managers are entitled to a bonus. A reasonable presumption is that the RONA calculation used by the board of directors excludes the income effect of the accounting change, especially if the change is one mandated by the FASB. In fact, one way to avoid this kind of problem is to have the bonus based on Income from continuing operations rather than net income.

Requirement 3:
Calculations for both years appear below. Two calculations for each year are presented, with and without the adjustment for stock sales and repurchases.

For 1993:

Pre-tax income = $133,976

Beginning equity = $384,648 (i.e., the ending equity of 1992)

Beginning equity adjusted for
stock sales and repurchases = $384,648 + $1,369 (stock sales in 1993)
- $1,338 (stock repurchased in 1993)

= $384,679

Minimum required rate of return for 1993:

= $384,648 × 0.12 = $46,157.76
or
= $384,679 × 0.12 = $46,161.48

In either case, the minimum required rate of return is met because pre-tax income is $133,976.

For 1994:

Pre-tax income = $128,555

Beginning equity = $472,890 (i.e., the ending equity of 1993)

Beginning equity adjusted for
stock sales and repurchases = $472,890 + $2,111 (stock sales in 1994)
- $2,337 (stock repurchased in 1994)

= $472,664

Minimum required rate of return for 1994:

= $472,890 × 0.12 = $56,746.80
or
= $472,664 × 0.12 = $56,719.68

In either case, the minimum required rate of return is met because pre-tax income is $128,555.

Requirement 4:
To receive the annual bonus, pre-tax income must exceed 6% of sales:

	Sales	× 0.06	=	Threshold	Pre-tax Income
1991:	$601,991	× 0.06	=	$36,119.46	$29,943
1992:	$683,427	× 0.06	=	$41,005.62	$47,492
1993:	$733,623	× 0.06	=	$44,017.38	$54,033
1994:	$869,975	× 0.06	=	$52,198.50	$69,870
1995:	$992,106	× 0.06	=	$59,526.36	$59,663

The threshold rate of return was not earned in 1991, but was earned in 1992–1995.

Requirement 5:
Perhaps the most reasonable response to this question is that different companies (and different industries) are likely to have different *value drivers* (i.e., key factors that enhance shareholder wealth). For example, asset utilization is often a key value driver in capital-intensive industries, whereas cost containment and margins are important in retail. Different economic circumstances require managers to be focused on different financial performance measures.

Requirement 6:
All three compensation plans are based on accounting earnings. As a result, managers have an incentive to make financial reporting decisions that accelerate revenues and delay expenses because doing so can increase the present value of their bonuses. Examples of financial reporting decisions that might be worth monitoring include:

- Changes in accounting methods (e.g., accelerated to straight-line depreciation),
- Increases in the useful lives of long-term assets,
- Accruals for future obligations under warranties,
- Accruals for future bad debts,
- Decisions about the classification of marketable equity securities as trading securities versus securities available for sale, and
- Expenditures for research and development activities and advertising expenditures.

Requirement 7:

Are the performance targets in these plans reasonable? The answer to this question is highly subjective when based solely on the information contained in the case. However, one way to answer this question is to see how often the company achieved the minimum performance level in the past and by how much. If the performance target was exceeded each year and by a substantial amount, the target is probably too low.

Some instructors may find it helpful to focus student attention on the second question: What information do you need in order to determine if the performance targets are reasonable? Here's some information that might be useful:

- Past values of the performance measure (i.e., return on assets, return on stockholders' equity, the ratio of pre-tax income to sales) for the company. These values provide a natural starting point for assessing reasonableness.

- Past values of the performance measure for other companies in the industry. If the company has underperformed others in the industry, it may make sense to tie a portion of the bonus to absolute performance and the rest to performance relative to the industry. For instance, managers could receive some bonus when RONA exceeds a minimum level (say 8%) and another bonus determined by how much RONA exceeds the industry average.

C6-3. Sunshine-Jr. Stores Inc. (CW): Debt covenants and financial distress

Note to instructors: This is a challenging case. As a result, some find that it is best suited for class discussion of the issues surrounding loan renegotiations than as a graded homework assignment. A useful feature of the case is that the revised loan terms are included in the solution. This allows students to see what lenders actually did.

Requirement 1:

With regard to the **amount of collateral**, given that Sunshine-Jr. violated its earlier lending agreements, lenders are likely to demand collateral in an amount equal to face value of the debt.

With regard to the **type of collateral**, lenders prefer assets that are extremely marketable and, thus, can be sold quickly if Sunshine-Jr. defaults. Receivables and Inventories are usually good candidates. Less desirable, but still useful are company-owned stores, furnishing, and fixtures.

The revised lending agreement stated that: *The Company will pledge as collateral its interest in approximately 95 stores which are located outside of its primary market areas and which it is planning to offer for sale.*

264

Requirement 2:
The fact that Sunshine-Jr. defaulted on the earlier lending agreement is a clear indication that the company's credit risk has increased. To compensate for the added risk, lenders often require a higher interest rate.

The actual revised lending agreement stated the following: *The interest rates on the loan agreements will be increased to 9.43% and prime plus 1.5% for Prudential and First Florida, respectively.*

Requirement 3:
As stated in the revised lending agreement, lenders could require the company to use the proceeds from any asset sale to reduce outstanding debt. In addition to limitations on cash dividends, this requirement prevents the management from selling valuable assets and distributing the proceeds to shareholders, an action that would make the lenders worse off.

The actual revised lending agreement stated the following: *Additional principal reductions in the amount of $1,000,000 are required on both the note payable to Prudential and the revolving note payable to First Florida on April 1, 1993.*

The proceeds from any sales of assets (20% through September 30, 1992; 30% through March 31, 1993; 40% from April 1, 1993 through June 30, 1993; and 75% thereafter) must be applied toward additional principal reductions.

Requirement 4:
This will be a difficult question for students to answer in a precise fashion. We recommend making the following point before sharing the actual revisions with them. Lenders are likely to ask for future profit and cash flow projections as part of the renegotiations. These projections provide a natural starting point for determining revised covenant limits. Students should also recognize that the final outcome here is **negotiated.**

The actual revised lending agreement stated the following: *The new financial covenants, all calculated based on inventories accounted for on a FIFO basis, are as follows:*

Period ending	Net Worth	Minimum FIFO Working Capital (deficit)	Fixed Coverage Ratio, as defined
March 1992	$20,000,000	($5,500,000)	1.30:1.0
June 1992	$20,500,000	($6.000,000)	1.25:1.0
September 1992	$21,000,000	($5,500,000)	1.35:1.0
December 1992	$21,000,000	($5,500,000)	1.40:1.0
March 1993	$20,500,000	($5,000,000)	1.40:1.0
June 1993	$21,500,000	($4,000,000)	1.20:1.0
September 1993	$22.500,000	($4,000,000)	1.30:1.0
December 1993	$22,500,000	($3,500,000)	1.40:1.0
March 1994 and thereafter	$22,500,000	($3,000,000)	1.40:1.0

Note that the revised covenants are based on FIFO inventory values even though Sunshine-Jr. uses LIFO for financial reporting purposes (see the balance sheet). One interpretation of this feature is that lenders believe that FIFO values provide a more accurate indication of the company's credit risk than do LIFO values.

Requirement 5:
Sunshine-Jr. defaulted on the earlier loan and is clearly experiencing some financial difficulty. Allowing the company to pay dividends gives management an opportunity to reorder the claims of bondholders and shareholders. Payment of cash dividends decreases the likelihood of debt repayment because there is less cash in the company. The company should not be allowed to resume the dividend.

The actual revised lending agreement stated the following: *Negative covenants in the Company's debt agreements prohibit the payment of dividends.*

C6-4. Maxcor Manufacturing: Compensation and earnings quality

Requirement:
There are several reasons why Ms. Magee should feel uneasy about Maxcor's computation of 1993 operating profits:

- Some research and development (R&D) expenses are shown above the operating profit line (in cost of goods sold) and some are below the line (as research and development expense). The classification decision may allow considerable discretion. For example, about 72% of total R&D was charged to cost of goods sold in 1992 when operating profits were still above the level required to earn a 200% bonus. But in 1993, only about 34% of total R&D was charged to cost of goods sold. Operating profits that year were barely above the bonus threshold of $4.0 million.

- Plant closing costs lowered net income for the year. The issue here is whether management should be penalized (or rewarded) for this business decision. As a practical matter, many companies excluded such costs from the bonus calculation.

Should the 100% bonus payout for 1993 be approved? Probably not! Sales are down nearly 12%. Operating costs fell by a similar percentage, but much of that decrease can be traced to the smaller R&D charge to cost of goods sold. The degree to which management should be held accountable for the sales decline, and the extent to which R&D classification is discretionary would also influence the committee's decision.

Here are some possible changes to the bonus formula:

- Eliminate discretion in R&D classification but encourage productive investment of R&D dollars.

- Set performance goals relative to competitor performance.

- Eliminate the step-up feature of the bonus hurdles in favor of a smooth payout function.

- Use a "bonus bank" that spans several years to guard against the tendency to shift earnings from one year to another. The bank would accumulate bonuses over a three-year period, paying out one-third of the bank balance each year.

- Charge for the capital used in the company so that bonus payments reflect value creation, not just earnings performance.

- Use stock options, phantom shares, or stock purchases to make managers into owners.

Exercises

E7-1. Account analysis
(AICPA adapted)

To find the amount of gross sales, start by determining credit sales. We can do this with the accounts receivable T-account below.

Accounts Receivable

Beginning AR	$80,000		
		$1,000	Accounts written off
Credit sales	X		
		35,000	Cash collected
Ending AR	$74,000		

$80,000 + X - $1,000 - $35,000 = $74,000
X = $30,000 = credit sales

Now that we know the amount of credit sales, we can add cash sales to this amount to find gross sales.

Credit sales	$30,000
Cash sales	30,000
Gross sales	**$60,000**

E7-2. Account analysis
(AICPA adapted)

(Note to instructor: Students should be aware that the account titles allowance for uncollectibles and allowance for doubtful accounts are used interchangeably in practice.

To find the amount of accounts receivable before the allowance, we need to recreate the journal entries that affected accounts receivable and the allowance for doubtful accounts to record bad debt expense. Since we know that $10,000 was written off as uncollectible from accounts receivable, the first journal entry is:

DR Allowance for doubtful accounts	$10,000	
CR Accounts receivable		$10,000

The entry for $40,000 of bad debt expense would be:

DR Bad debt expense $40,000
  CR Allowance for doubtful accounts $40,000

Based on the two entries above, the balance in the allowance for doubtful accounts at the end of the year was $30,000. The amount of accounts receivable *before* the allowance for doubtful accounts that should appear on the balance sheet is calculated as:

Net accounts receivable	$250,000
Allowance for doubtful accounts	30,000
Gross accounts receivable	**$280,000**

E7-3. Ratio effects of write-offs
(AICPA adapted)

1. The current ratio does not change as a result of the write-off to the allowance account. Accounts receivable and its contra account, allowance for doubtful accounts are reduced by the same amount. Thus, accounts receivable (net), which is the number used in computing the current ratio, does not change.
b. X equals Y

2. The accounts receivable (net) balance does not change as a result of the write-off to the allowance account. When the $100 account is written off, accounts receivable and allowance for doubtful accounts are reduced by the same amount. Thus *net* receivables is the same before and after the write-off. Further write-offs to the allowance account will increase the allowance account and decrease accounts receivable (net).
b. X equals Y

3. Gross accounts receivable will be lower after the write-off than before the write-off because accounts receivable is credited for the $100 uncollectible account that is written-off. Gross accounts receivable is the amount of receivables before subtracting the allowance so there is no change.
a. X greater than Y

E7-4. Bad debt expense
(AICPA adapted)

We can determine the amount of bad debt expense in 1998 by first examining the allowance for doubtful accounts.

Exhibit II
COMPUTER SUPERSTORES, INC.
Las Vegas Store
Exhibit 2: Budgeted Statement of Cash Receipts and Disbursements
For the Three Months Ending August 31, 19X6

	June	July	August
Cash balance, beginning	$ 29,000	$ 25,000	$ 25,470
Cash receipts, collections & cash sales (schedule b)	376,000	607,000	454,000
(a) Total cash available before financing	$ 405,000	$ 632,000	$479,470
Cash disbursements:			
Merchandise (schedule d)	$ 420,000	$ 240,000	$240,000
Fixtures	55,000	-	-
Salaries, wages, commissions, @ 20% x sales	140,000	80,000	80,000
Other variable expenses, @ 4% x sales	28,000	16,000	16,000
Fixed expenses	55,000	55,000	55,000
(b) Total disbursements	$ 698,000	$ 391,000	$391,000
Minimum cash balance desired	25,000	25,000	25,000
Total cash needed	$ 723,000	$ 416,000	$416,000
Excess (deficiency)	$(318,000)	$ 216,000	$ 63,470
Financing:			
Borrowing, at beginning of period	$ 318,000	$ -	$ -
Repayment, at end of period.	-	(212,000)	(61,000)
Interest, 10% per annum	-	(3,530)*	(1,530)**
(c) Total effects of financing	$ 318,000	$(215,530)	$ (62,530)
(d) Cash balance (a + c - b)	$ 25,000	$ 25,470	$ 25,940

*10% x $212,000 x 2/12 = $3,530
**10% x $ 61,000 x 3/12 = $1,525, rounded to $1,530.

E7-7. Note receivable carrying amount
(AICPA adapted)

Requirement 1:

DR Cash	$5,000	
DR Note receivable	3,100	
CR Interest revenue		$8,100

Requirement 2:
The account increases the carrying amount of the note receivable which will ultimately total $100,000.

Problems

P7-1. Allowance for uncollectibles

Requirement 1:

Based on the aging schedule, the ending balance in the allowance for doubtful accounts is calculated as follows:

Age of Receivables	Amount	Expected Bad Debt	Dollar Amount
Zero to 30 days old	$30,000	5%	$1,500
31 days to 90 days old	10,000	11%	1,100
Over 90 days old	5,000	30%	1,500
			$4,100

The company needs to record an additional bad debt expense of $600 ($4,100 - $3,500) to increase the allowance balance to $4,100.

December 31, 1998

DR Bad debt expense $600

CR Allowance for uncollectibles $600

	Assets	Liabilities	Net Income	Cash Flow from Operations
Direction of effect	-	NE	-	NE
Dollar amount of effect	600		600	

The journal entries for the other transactions are provided below:

January 1, 1999

No journal entry is recorded since the ultimate resolution of the account receivable is still uncertain.

March 1, 1999

DR Allowance for uncollectibles $800

CR Accounts receivable $800

40% of $2,000 is written-off as uncollectible.

	Assets	Liabilities	Net Income	Cash Flow from Operations
Direction of effect	NE	NE	NE	NE
Dollar amount of effect				

Since write-offs are typically realizations of events that have already been anticipated (through the bad debt provision), they do not affect the assets or the net income.

May 7, 1999
    DR Cash $1,200
        CR Accounts receivable $1,200

	Assets	Liabilities	Net Income	Cash Flow from Operations
Direction of effect	NE	NE	NE	+
Dollar amount of effect				1,200

Requirement 2:
Based on the aging schedule, the ending balance in the allowance for doubtful accounts is calculated as follows:

Age of Receivables	Amount	Expected Bad Debt	Dollar Amount
Zero to 30 days old	$30,000	3%	$ 900
31 days to 90 days old	10,000	8%	800
Over 90 days old	5,000	22%	1,100
			$2,800

Since the company has a larger balance than what is required by the aging schedule, the company should decrease its bad debt expense by $700 ($3,500 - $2,800).

December 31, 1998
    DR Allowance for uncollectibles $700
        CR Bad debt expense $700

	Assets	Liabilities	Net Income	Cash Flow from Operations
Direction of effect	+	NE	+	NE
Dollar amount of effect	700		700	

The other journal entries do not change from Requirement 1.

P7-2. Account analysis
(AICPA adapted)

Start with the 1999 allowance for doubtful accounts:

1999
Allowance for Doubtful Accounts

		$	Beginning balance
Accounts written-off	$50		
		X	Bad debt expense
		$	Ending balance

Solving for X:
$47 - $50 + X = $30
X = $33

Now divide bad debt expense by charge sales.
$33/$1,100
Bad debt expense = 3% of charge sales

Since we know that there has been no change in method during the three years shown, we can apply this ratio to 1998.

1998
Allowance for Doubtful Accounts

		Y	Beginning balance
Accounts written-off	$2		
		X	Bad debt expense
		$	Ending balance

We can find X because we know that it is 3% of charge sales.
$900 X .03 = $27

Now plug bad debt expense into the equation:
Y + $27 - $2 = $47
Y = $22

The 1998 beginning balance in the allowance for doubtful accounts is **$22,000.**

P7-3. Comprehensive receivables and allowance analysis

Requirement 1:

To record the credit sales for the year.

DR Accounts receivable	$100,000	
CR Sales revenue		$100,000

To record the collections for the year.

DR Cash	$92,000	
CR Accounts receivable		$92,000

Bad debts written off during the year.

DR Allowance for uncollectibles	$9,000	
CR Accounts receivable		$9,000

Accounts receivable	**DR**	**CR**
Beginning balance	$20,000	
Credit sales	100,000	
Cash collections		$92,000
Bad debts written-off		9,000
Ending balance	$19,000	

		Expected Bad Debts	
Aging Information	Book Value	%	$
> 90 days past due	$2,000	30%	600
31–90 days past due	7,000	20%	1,400
Current **(plug number)**	10,000	10%	1,000
Total from gross A/R T-account	**$19,000**		$3,000

Allowance for uncollectibles	**DR**	**CR**
Beginning balance		$2,000
Bad debt expense **(plug number)**		10,000
Bad debts written-off	$9,000	
Ending balance **(from aging schedule)**		$3,000

To record entry for bad debt expense (from the allowance account)

DR Bad debt expense	$10,000	
CR Allowance for uncollectibles		$10,000

Requirement 2:
Balance sheet presentation

Accounts receivable (gross)	$19,000
Less: allowance for uncollectibles	(3,000)
Accounts receivable (net)	$16,000

Requirement 3:

The bad debt expense for 1998 can be broken down into the following three components:

Breakdown of bad debt expense

Current year's actual bad debts	$ 5,000
(bad debts written off from this year's sales)	
Current year's expected bad debts	
(ending balance in the allowance account)	3,000
Excess of 1997's actual over expected bad debts	
($4,000 minus $2,000)	2,000
	$10,000

The learning objective for this requirement is to enable students to understand how and when expected and realized bad debts affect the bad debt expense. One component arises from sales made *and* settled during the current year. Another component comprises the expected bad debts due to sales made during the current year that are yet to be settled. The final component is the result of an error made in the previous year's estimate of bad debts on outstanding accounts receivable.

A second aspect of the problem is to highlight how much of the information is publicly available in the financial statements. This problem is specifically constructed with breakdowns provided on collections and bad debts grouped by the year of sale. However, in a typical annual report, it will not be possible to see these components without additional disclosures in the management discussion and analysis section.

P7-4. Interest schedule

Year Ending December 31	(a) Beginning A/R (given)	(b) = (a)x 11.12% Interest Revenue	(c) Receivable Collected (given)	(d) = (b) + (c) Cash Received	(e) = (a) - (c) Ending A/R
1996	$63,930	$7,109	$20,724	$27,833	$43,206
1997	43,206	4,805	15,896	20,701	27,310
1998	27,310	3,037	11,559	14,596	15,751
1999	15,751	1,752	7,179	8,931	8,572
2000	8,572	953	8,559	9,512	13
2001	13	1	13	14	0

12/31/96:
   DR Cash $27,833
      CR Accounts receivable $20,724
      CR Interest revenue   7,109

12/31/97:
   DR Cash $20,701
      CR Accounts receivable $15,896
      CR Interest revenue   4,805

12/31/98:
   DR Cash $14,596
      CR Accounts receivable $11,559
      CR Interest revenue   3,037

12/31/99:
   DR Cash $8,931
      CR Accounts receivable $7,179
      CR Interest revenue   1,752

12/31/00:
   DR Cash $9,512
      CR Accounts receivable $8,559
      CR Interest revenue   953

2/31/01:
   DR Cash $14
      CR Accounts receivable $13
      CR Interest revenue   1

P7-5. Account analysis

Requirement 1:
Journal Entries for 1995

	DR	CR
Allowance for doubtful accounts		
Beginning balance 1995		$ 35,000
Provision for doubtful accounts		150,631
Bad debts written off **(plug number)**	**$105,771**	
Ending balance 1995		$ 79,860

	DR	CR
Gross accounts receivable		
Beginning balance 1995	$ 210,758	
Revenues	2,218,139	
Bad debts written off (from ADA)		$105,771
Cash collected **(plug number)**		**1,997,897**
Ending balance 1995	$ 325,229	

	DR	CR
DR Accounts receivable	$2,218,139	
CR Revenues		$2,218,139
DR Provision for doubtful accounts	$150,631	
CR Allowance for doubtful accounts		$150,631
DR Allowance for doubtful accounts	$105,771	
CR Accounts receivable		$105,771
DR Cash	$1,997,897	
CR Accounts receivable		$1,997,897

Journal Entries for 1996

	DR	CR
Allowance for doubtful accounts		
Beginning balance 1996		$ 79,860
Provision for doubtful accounts		20,585
Bad debts written off **(plug number)**	0	
Ending balance 1996		$100,445

	DR	CR
Gross accounts receivable		
Beginning balance 1996	$ 325,229	
Revenues	2,175,475	
Bad debts written off (from ADA)	0	
Cash collected **(plug number)**		**$2,146,981**
Ending balance 1996	$ 353,723	

DR Accounts receivable	$2,175,475	
CR Revenues		$2,175,475

DR Provision for doubtful accounts	$20,585	
CR Allowance for doubtful accounts		$20,585

DR Allowance for doubtful accounts	0	
CR Accounts receivable		0

DR Cash	$2,146,981	
CR Accounts receivable		$2,146,981

Requirement 2:

The answer provided below discusses a set of plausible events that is consistent with the allowance and write-off activity reported over the period 1994 to 1996. The management's actual explanation for the changes in provision for doubtful accounts is also provided below.

	1996	1995	1994
Provision for doubtful accounts/revenue	0.95%	6.79%	4.32%
Allowance for doubtful accounts/			
Gross accounts receivable	28.40%	24.56%	16.61%

1994 to 1995

Provision for doubtful accounts has increased probably due to higher than expected customer defaults. This is reflected in the higher ratio of allowance for doubtful accounts to gross accounts receivable at the end of 1995 when compared to 1994.

1995 to 1996

Provision for doubtful accounts for 1996 is at a historically low figure as a percentage of revenues. However, the allowance for doubtful accounts as a percentage of gross accounts receivable has increased further to 28.4% in 1996 from 24.56% in 1995. Note that the provision for doubtful accounts for 1996 equals the change in allowance for doubtful accounts over this period indicating that no accounts receivable were written off during the year. It appears that provision for doubtful accounts entirely represents anticipated or expected bad debts for revenues not yet collected. In addition, during 1996, it seems that the company may be continuing to pursue claims against its customers for whom it has already reported provision for doubtful accounts during 1995. In such cases, the company will not yet write off these accounts until a final resolution of the claims. This appears to have resulted in a higher percentage of allowance for doubtful accounts as a percentage of gross accounts receivable.

In the management discussion and analysis section of the 10-K report, the management of Buck Hills Falls Company provided the following explanations for the changes in provision for doubtful accounts:

1994 to 1995

"General and administrative expenses increased 11.2% in 1995 as compared to 1994, principally resulting from increases in legal and accounting fees, **bad debt expense** and depreciation expense...**Bad debt expense increased...because of increased provision for uncollectible receivables."** (emphasis added)

1995 to 1996

"Bad debt expense decreased...due to uncollectible accounts relating to the Buck Hill Inn and other accounts receivable being written off in 1995."

Consistent with the conjecture, it appears that, during 1995, the company experienced higher bad debts in one of its operations (Buck Hill Inn). However, we have no direct evidence to corroborate our conjecture on the higher allowance for doubtful accounts as a percentage of gross accounts receivable.

P7-6. Cash discounts and returns

Note to instructor: This problem covers cash discount/credit terms not discussed in the chapter and, thereby, provides an opportunity to introduce these issues.

Requirement 1:
1/1/98:
To record sale of beer :

DR Accounts receivable	$45,000	
CR Sales revenue		$45,000

To record expected sales returns:

DR Sales returns	$2,250	
CR Allowance for sales returns		$2,250

Note: Allowance for sales returns is a contra asset account for accounts receivable. Similar to the allowance for doubtful accounts, it is subtracted from Gross accounts receivable in the balance sheet. It is calculated at 5% of $45,000.

1/9/98:
To record receipt of payment:
    DR Cash $21,825
    DR Cash discount   675
      CR Accounts receivable $22,500

Note: The credit terms "3/10, n/30" means that the customer gets a 3% cash discount for payment made within 10 days. However, the entire amount is due within 30 days. Since the customers settled half of the receivables within 10 days, they are entitled to a 3% cash discount ($45,000 × 0.50 × 0.03 = $675).

1/15/98:
To record return of beer from customers:
    DR Allowance for sales returns $2,000
      CR Accounts receivable $2,000

Note: This reflects the actual return of goods that was anticipated earlier.

1/28/98:
To record receipt of payment:
    DR Cash $20,500
      CR Accounts receivable $20,500

Note: Balance due is $22,500 ($45,000 × 0.50) minus $2,000 of sales return. Since the payment was received after the 10th day, no cash discount is given to the customers.

    DR Allowance for sales returns $250
      CR Sales returns $250

Note: Recall that *expected* sales returns of $2,250 were recorded on January 1, 1998. However, since the actual sales returns were only $2,000, we reverse the 1/1/98 journal entry to the extent of $250.

Requirement 2:
Journal entries prior to January 15, 1998 are unaffected.

1/15/98:
To record return of beer from customers:
    DR Allowance for sales returns $2,250
    DR Sales returns   750
      CR Accounts receivable $3,000

Note: This reflects the actual return of goods to the extent it was anticipated earlier ($2,250). For goods returned in excess of expected sales returns ($3,000 - $2,250), we decrease the net revenue by debiting sales returns and decreasing accounts receivable further by $750.

1/28/98:
To record receipt of payment:
DR Cash	$19,500	
CR Accounts receivable		$19,500

Note: Balance due is $22,500 ($45,000 × 0.50) minus $3,000 of sales returns. Since the payment was received after the 10th day, no cash discount is given to the customers.

Requirement 3:

1/1/98:
To record sale of beer:
DR Accounts receivable	$45,000	
CR Sales revenue		$45,000

1/9/98:
To record receipt of payment:
DR Cash	$21,825	
DR Cash discount	675	
CR Accounts receivable		$22,500

Note: The credit terms "3/10, n/30" mean that the customer gets a 3% cash discount for payment made within 10 days. However, the entire amount is due within 30 days. Since customers settled half of the receivables within 10 days, they are entitled to a 3% cash discount ($45,000 × 0.50 × 0.03 = $675).

1/15/98:
To record return of beer from the customers:
DR Sales returns	$2,000	
CR Accounts receivable		$2,000

Note: Since expected sales returns were not recorded, actual returns decrease net revenue by a debit to sales returns.

1/28/98:
To record receipt of payment:
DR Cash	$20,500	
CR Accounts receivable		$20,500

Note: Balance due is $22,500 ($45,000 × 0.50) minus $2,000 of sales returns. Since the payment was received after the 10th day, no cash discount is given to the customers.

Requirement 4:

Assuming the company uses the calendar year as its fiscal year, all transactions pertaining to the sale of beer took place within one accounting period (sale of goods, return of goods, and collection of cash). However, if sales revenue is recorded in one accounting period and actual sales returns are recorded in the following period, then the matching principle is likely to be violated. This problem is mitigated by recording expected sales returns in the same period as when sales revenue is recorded. A second advantage is that the users of the financial statements might receive more information under the expected sales return approach since material deviations from expectations will affect future financial statements (See Requirement 3). If disclosed, this might provide evidence of the manager's ability to forecast sales returns. However, in some companies, estimated sales returns may not be materially different from actual sales returns, in which case, firms might minimize their bookkeeping costs by recording sales returns when goods are actually returned.

Requirement 5:

If the customer decides to take advantage of the cash discount, the optimal time to do this is on the tenth day (i.e., the customer does not obtain any benefit by paying any sooner). If the customer decides not to take the cash discount, the full amount is due on the 30th day. (Once again, the customer does not obtain any benefit by paying any sooner.) Consequently, to take advantage of the cash discount, the customer pays 20 days sooner than it would otherwise.

Given that its incremental borrowing rate is 18%, the customer could borrow $21,825 and pay interest for 20 days (i.e., $21,825 × 18% × 20/365 = $215) —i.e., it has to pay $22,040 ($21,825 + $215) on the borrowing. However, if it had waited for the entire credit period of 30 days, then it would have to pay $22,500 to Hillock Brewing. Consequently, by taking advantage of the cash discount through borrowing, the customer is better off to the extent of $460 ($22,500 minus $22,040). The $460 also represents the difference between the cash discount ($675) and the interest cost on the borrowing ($215). In summary, the customer is better off taking advantage of the cash discount.

Another way to answer the question is to view the cash discount ($675) as the return on investment in accounts receivable ($21,825) for 20 days. This converts into an annualized rate of return of 56.4% ($675/$21,825 × 365/20 × 100) when compared to the incremental borrowing rate of 18%.

P7-7. Factoring receivables

Note to the instructor: When receivables are transferred with recourse, the cash received from the factor is treated as an operating or a financing cash inflow depending on whether the transfer of receivables receive the sale or loan treatment under the GAAP. To highlight this aspect, the solution also indicates the effects of each cash transaction on the statement of cash flows for all parts of the problem.

Requirement 1:

a) To record the sale of receivables to the factor:

Calculation of the proceeds from the factor

Gross accounts receivable factored	$200,000
(-) Interest for one month	
(200,000 × 0.12 × 1/12)	(2,000)
(-) Factoring fee (6% of $200,000)	(12,000)
(-) Holdback for returns (5% of $200,000)	(10,000)
Net proceeds	$176,000

DR	Allowance for uncollectibles	$4,000
DR	Cash	176,000
DR	Loss on sale of receivables	10,000
DR	Receivable from factor—holdback of 5%	10,000
	CR Accounts receivable	$200,000

Since the factor is responsible for all the bad debts on the factored receivables, the allowance for uncollectibles with respect to these receivables should be eliminated (by debiting the allowance account). The loss on sale of receivables can be broken down into three components as follows:

Interest expense	$2,000
Factoring fee	12,000
(-) Elimination of allowance	(4,000)
Loss on sale of receivables	$10,000

- In essence, the loss on sale of receivables represents several different income statement items. While there is loss of information from combining these items into a single loss account, the above journal entry is one of the most common approaches to record sale of receivables.

- Note that the entire Interest expense has been recorded at the time of sale as part of the loss amount. However, for long-term receivables, the financing cost (Interest expense) will be recorded (and probably paid) over the duration of the receivables' life.

Effect on statement of cash flows: The $176,000 received from the factor will also show up as part of operating cash flows. Since the risk of credit loss (bad debts) is borne by the factor, the cash received is treated as part of operating cash flows (i.e., it is equivalent to collecting cash from the customers). The fact that the customers have not yet paid is irrelevant.

An alternative approach is to separately show the three components included in the loss on sale of receivables as follows:

DR	Allowance for uncollectibles	$4,000	
DR	Cash	176,000	
DR	Interest expense	2,000	
DR	Factoring fee	12,000	
DR	Receivable from factor—holdback of 5%	10,000	
	CR Bad debt expense		$4,000
	CR Accounts receivable		200,000

- The debit to the allowance for uncollectibles and the credit to the bad debt expense represent the reversal of the journal entry for bad debt expense on the $200,000 of the factored receivables. The intuition behind this is that the factoring fee is expected to include a compensation for the credit risk (bad debts) borne by the factor. Consequently, by not reversing the bad debt expense, we will be double counting.

- The loss on sale of receivables in the original journal entry is now decomposed into two debits (to interest expense and factoring fee) and a credit (bad debt expense reversal). However, the net effect on the income statement ($2,000 + $12,000 - $4,000 = $10,000) is identical.

b) To record return of $3,000 of merchandise:

DR	Sales returns	$3,000	
	CR Receivable from factor		$3,000

c) To record receipt of payment from the factor:

DR	Cash	$7,000	
	CR Receivable from factor		$7,000

Effect on statement of cash flows: The $7,000 cash is an operating cash flow.

d) The actual bad debts incurred by the factor were $7,500.

Atherton will not record a journal entry to record this event. Recall that the receivables were sold without recourse for bad debts, in which case, the factor is responsible for all the bad debts. In the given scenario, the actual bad debts of $7,500 were more than the expected bad debts of $4,000 (2% of 200,000). Consequently, the factor might have suffered an unexpected loss. On the other hand, if the actual bad debts had been only $1,000, the factor would have reaped some benefits. In any case, Atherton is paying a fixed sum (the factoring fee) so the factor is bearing the risk of credit loss.

General Comments:

Before answering parts 2 and 3, it is instructive to compare the information provided in part 1 with that of parts 2 and 3. First, note that the factoring fee charged is substantially lower for parts 2 and 3 (2.5%) compared to the "without recourse" scenario (6%). The extra 3.5% paid to the factor is to cover the expected bad debts and the additional administrative costs of pursuing the delinquent accounts. Second, the hold back for parts 2 and 3 (7%) is higher than the 5% holdback in the "without recourse" scenario. In part 1, the factor was not responsible for sales returns and, consequently, held back 5%, being the expected sales returns from the receivables. In parts 2 and 3, the factor is also not responsible for bad debts, and therefore, is holding back an additional 2%. Third, unlike part (a), the receivables are transferred in parts 2 and 3 **without notification**. Given Atherton is responsible for all bad debts, it has stronger incentives to follow up on the delinquent customers. Hence, transferring **without notification** may be a more efficient approach to collecting the receivables.

It is important to remember that a company might be able to treat a transfer of receivables **with recourse** as a "sale" as long as it satisfies the three conditions listed in SFAS No. 125. The purpose of parts 2 and 3 is to demonstrate the differential financial statement effects depending on whether the transfer of receivables is treated as a sale or a borrowing under GAAP. In addition, many of the financial reporting and analysis issues that are discussed here are also very relevant in securitization transactions.

Requirement 2:
a) To record the sale of receivables to the factor:

Calculation of the proceeds from the factor

Gross accounts receivable factored	$200,000
(-) Interest for one month	
$(200,000 \times 0.12 \times 1/12)$	(2,000)
(-) Factoring fee (2.5% of $200,000)	(5,000)
(-) Holdback (7% of $200,000)	(14,000)
Net proceeds	$179,000

DR Loss on sale of receivables	$ 7,000	
DR Cash	179,000	
CR Accounts receivable		$186,000

Note, in effect, the factor is "financing" $186,000 worth of receivables (i.e., net proceeds + interest cost + factoring fee), i.e., the factor is providing $179,000 cash today with the expectation of receiving $186,000 later.

Effect on statement of cash flows: Since the receivables are eliminated from the books, the $179,000 received from the factor will show up as part of the operating cash flows.

Since Atherton continues to be responsible for all the bad debts on the factored receivables, the allowance for uncollectibles with respect to these receivables should *not* be eliminated. The loss on sale of receivables can be broken down into two components as follows:

Interest expense	$2,000
Factoring fee	5,000
Loss on sale of receivables	$7,000

b) To record return of $3,000 of merchandise:

DR Sales returns	$3,000	
CR Accounts receivable		$3,000

c) To record bad debts written off on the transferred receivables. Recall that Atherton had anticipated only $4,000 of bad debts, and, consequently, the excess write-offs increase bad debt expense.

DR Bad debt expense	$1,500	
DR Allowance for doubtful accounts	4,000	
CR Accounts receivable		$5,500

d) To record the collection from the customers and pay off to the factor. Since the transfer was treated as a sale, only the net proceeds (i.e., the difference between the collections and the payoff) is recorded in the books.

Face value of receivables	$200,000
(-) Sales returns	(3,000)
(-) Bad debts written off	(5,500)
Cash collected from customers	$191,500
(-) Due to the factor	(186,000)
= Net proceeds	$5,500

DR Cash	$5,500	
CR Accounts receivable		$5,500

Effect on statement of cash flows: The $5,500 cash is an operating cash flow.

Requirement 3:

a. To record the transfer of receivables to the factor:

Calculation of the proceeds from the factor

Gross accounts receivable factored	$200,000
(-) Interest for one month	
($200,000 × 0.12 × 1/12)	(2,000)
(-) Factoring fee (2.5% of $200,000)	(5,000)
(-) Holdback (7% of $200,000)	(14,000)
Net proceeds	$179,000

DR Cash	$179,000	
DR Interest expense	2,000	
DR Factoring fee	5,000	
CR Loans payable		$186,000

Effect on statement of cash flows: The $186,000 borrowing will show up as part of financing inflow, whereas the $7,000 will show up as operating outflow. Alternatively, the company might show the net cash inflow of $179,000 as a financing flow.

b) To record return of $3,000 of merchandise:

DR Sales returns	$3,000	
CR Accounts receivable		$3,000

c) To record bad debts written off on the transferred receivables. Recall that Atherton had anticipated only $4,000 of bad debts, and consequently, the excess write-offs increase bad debt expense.

DR Bad debt expense	$1,500	
DR Allowance for doubtful accounts	4,000	
CR Accounts receivable		$5,500

d) To record receipt of payments from customers:

Face value of receivables	$200,000
(-) Sales returns	(3,000)
(-) Bad debts written-off	(5,500)
Cash collected from customers	$191,500

DR Cash	$191,500	
CR Accounts receivable		$191,500

Effect on statement of cash flows: $191,500 is an operating inflow.

e) To record the payment to the factor:
    DR Loans payable $186,000
           CR Cash $186,000

Effect on statement of cash flows: $186,000 is a financing outflow.

P7-8. Reconstructing T-accounts

Requirement 1:

Journal Entries

	DR	CR
Allowance for doubtful accounts		
Beginning balance		$4,955,000
Provision for doubtful accounts (income statement)		5,846,000
Bad debts written-off **(plug number)**	$6,876,000	
Ending balance		$3,925,000
Gross accounts receivable		
Beginning balance	$31,651,000	
Revenue (from income statement)	137,002,000	
Bad debts written-off **(from ADA)**		$6,876,000
Cash collected **(plug number)**		134,833,000
Ending balance	$26,944,000	

    DR Gross accounts receivable $137,002,00
        CR Revenue $137,002,000

    DR Provision for doubtful accounts $5,846,000
        CR Allowance for doubtful accounts $5,846,000

    DR Allowance for doubtful accounts $6,876,000
        CR Gross accounts receivable $6,876,000

    DR Cash $134,833,00
        CR Gross accounts receivable $134,833,000

Requirement 2:

	1994	1993	1992
Provision for doubtful accounts as % of revenue	4.27%	5.98%	6.30%

Revised provision for 1994 using the 1993
percentage ($137,002,000 × 5.98%) $8,192,720

	DR	CR
Allowance for doubtful accounts		
Beginning balance		$4,955,000
Provision for doubtful accounts (from above)		8,192,720
Bad debts written-off	$6,876,000	
Ending balance **(plug number)**		**$6,271,720**

Balance sheet presentation of receivables (1994)
Gross accounts receivable	$26,944,000
Less: Allowance for doubtful accounts	6,271,720
Net accounts receivable	$20,672,280

Note: Altering the 1994 provision for doubtful accounts does not change gross accounts receivable.

The revised operating income is calculated below:

	1994
Operating income before taxes (as reported)	$6,900,000
(+) Provision for doubtful accounts (as reported)	5,846,000
(-) Provision for doubtful accounts (revised)	8,192,720
Operating income before taxes (revised)	$4,553,280
Decrease in operating income	-34.01%

Note that the operating income would have decreased by 34% if Ramsay had reported the 1994 bad debts at the same percentage of revenue as it did in 1993. Although Ramsay probably has good reasons for the lower provision for doubtful accounts, it is important for an analyst to follow up with Ramsay's management for information regarding this decline.

Requirement 3:

	1994	1993
Allowance for doubtful accounts as a % of gross A/R	14.57%	15.66%

Revised balance in allowance account
($26,944,000 × 15.66%) $4,218,114

	DR	CR
Allowance for doubtful accounts		
Beginning balance		$4,955,000
Provision for doubtful accounts **(plug number)**		**6,139,114**
Bad debts written off	$6,876,000	
Ending balance (from above)		$4,218,114

The revised operating income is calculated below:

	1994
Operating income before taxes (as reported)	$6,900,000
(+) Provision for doubtful accounts (as reported)	5,846,000
(-) Provision for doubtful accounts (revised)	(6,139,114)
Operating income before taxes (revised)	$6,606,886
Decrease in operating income	-4.25%

Operating income would have decreased only by about 4% if Ramsay had reported the 1994 allowance for doubtful accounts at the same percentage of gross receivables as it did in 1993.

Requirement 4:
Requirements 2 and 3 lead to substantially different estimates for bad debt expense (provision for doubtful accounts). Recall that a bad debt expense calculation based on the sales revenue approach would have decreased Ramsay's operating income by 34%. However, the decline would have been much smaller under the gross receivables approach. To better understand this difference, let us first calculate the gross accounts receivable as a percentage of revenue:

	1994	1993
Gross accounts receivable	$26,944,000	$31,651,000
Revenue	137,002,000	136,354,000
Year-end gross A/R as a % of revenue	19.67%	23.21%

It appears that Ramsay has apparently improved its accounts receivable collections. At the end of 1994, the receivables are less than 20% of revenue compared to a figure of more than 23% at the end of 1993. If Ramsay had maintained the same percentage of receivables (23.21%) at the end of 1994 also, then what would have been the balance in gross accounts receivable?

	1994
Gross accounts receivable (as reported)	$26,944,000
Gross accounts receivable (23.21% of revenue)	31,798,164
Difference	($4,854,164)

The above table suggests that Ramsay would have reported almost $5 million of additional receivables at the end of 1994 if the receivables balance continued to be 23.21% of revenue. This suggests that the substantial difference in the answers to Requirements 2 and 3 appears to be due to substantial improvement in the quality of Ramsay's accounts receivable, i.e., improved collections and lower write-offs.

The intertemporal pattern of the bad debt expense is also consistent with this intuition:

	1994	1993	1992
Provision for doubtful accounts as % of Revenue	4.27%	5.98%	6.30%

The bad debt expense as a percentage of revenue has monotonically decreased from 6.3% to about 4.3% over a three-year period.

However, an analyst should obtain corroborating information from the management to further substantiate this inference. This is because the observed trend in the provision for doubtful accounts is also consistent with under-provision for expenses. For instance, although the receivables balance is lower at the end of 1994, they might consist primarily of lower quality (or substantially aged) receivables.

P7-9. Restructured note receivable

Requirement 1:

Warren Companies
To record the fully depreciated asset at its fair market value:

DR Equipment	$14,000	
CR Gain on disposal of asset		$14,000

To record the settlement:

DR Note payable	$48,000	
DR Interest payable	2,400	
CR Cash		$20,000
CR Equipment		14,000
CR Extraordinary gain on debt		16,400

General Equipment Manufacturers

To record the settlement:

DR Cash	$20,000	
DR Equipment	14,000	
DR Loss on receivable restructuring	16,400	
CR Note receivable		$48,000
CR Interest receivable		2,400

Requirement 2:
Warren Companies

1/1/97: To record the modified sum:

DR Note payable	$48,000	
DR Interest payable	2,400	
CR Restructured note payable		$50,400

<u>Calculation of Discount Rate:</u>

Present value = future value × present value factor (3 years, ?? interest rate)
i.e., $50,400 = $57,600 × present value factor (3 years, ?? interest rate)

Dividing both sides by $57,600, we have

Present value factor (3 years, ?? interest rate) = $50,400/$57,600 = 0.8750

i.e., $1/(1 + r)^3 = 0.8750$

$\rightarrow (1 + r)^3 = 1/0.8750 = 1.1429$

$\rightarrow (1 + r) = (1.1429)^{1/3} = 1.0455$

$\rightarrow r = 1.0455 - 1 = 0.0455$ or 4.55%

Alternately, this can also be obtained by interpolation.

Present value of future flows @ 4%	Restructured note amount	Present value of future flows @ 5%
$57,600		$57,600
× .889		× .86384
$51,206.4	$50,400.0	$49,757.0

$806.4

$1,449.4

Then, $\dfrac{\$\ 806.4}{\$1,449.4} = .556$

So the interpolated rate is 4% + .556% or 4.556%.

12/31/97: To record interest payable:
  DR Interest expense $2,296
    CR Restructured note payable $2,296
[$50,400 × 4.556% = $2,296]

Interest expense is calculated at 4.556% of the book value of the notes payable as of January 1, 1997.

12/31/98: To record interest payable:
  DR Interest expense $2,401
    CR Restructured note payable $2,401
[($50,400 + $2,296) × 4.556% = $2,401]

12/31/99: To record interest payable:
  DR Interest expense $2,503
    CR Restructured note payable $2,503
[($50,400 + $2,296 + $2401) × 4.556% = $2,503[‡]]
  [‡]rounded

12/31/99: To record payment of amount due:
  DR Restructured note payable $57,600
    CR Cash $57,600

General Equipment Manufacturers
1/1/97: To record the modified sum:
  DR Restructured note receivable $49,757
  DR Loss on receivable restructuring   643
    CR Note receivable $48,000
    CR Interest receivable   2,400

Note: The restructured note is valued at $49,757, being the present value of $57,600 to be received in three years discounted at 5%. The factor is .86384.

12/31/97: To record interest receivable:
  DR Restructured note receivable $2,488
    CR Interest income $2,488
($49,757 × 5% = $2,488)

12/31/98: To record interest receivable:
    DR Restructured note receivable $2,612
        CR Interest income $2,612
[($49,757 + $2,488) × 5% = $2,612]

12/31/99: To record interest receivable:
    DR Restructured note receivable $2,743
        CR Interest income $2,743
[($49,757 + $2,488 + $2,612) × 5% = $2,743]

12/31/99: To record receipt of amount due:
    DR Cash $57,600
        CR Restructured note receivable $57,600

Requirement 3:
Warren Companies
1/1/97: To record the modified sum:
    DR Note payable $48,000
    DR Interest payable   2,400
        CR Restructured note payable $48,000
        CR Extraordinary gain on debt   2,400

12/31/99: To record payment of amount due:
    DR Restructured note payable $48,000
        CR Cash $48,000

General Equipment Manufacturers
1/1/97: To record the modified sum:
    DR Restructured note receivable $41,464
    DR Loss on receivable restructuring   8,936
        CR Note receivable $48,000
        CR Interest receivable   2,400

Note: The restructured note is valued at $41,464, being the present value of $48,000 to be received in three years discounted at 5%. The factor is .86384.

12/31/97: To record interest receivable:
    DR Restructured note receivable $2,073
        CR Interest income $2,073
($41,464 × 5% = $2,073)

12/31/98: To record interest receivable:
    DR Restructured note receivable $2,177
        CR Interest income $2,177
[($41,464 + $2,073) × 5% = $2,177]

12/31/99: To record interest receivable:
    DR Restructured note receivable $2,286
        CR Interest income $2,286
    [($41,464 + $2,073 + $2,177) × 5% = $2,286]

12/31/99: To record receipt of amount due:
    DR Cash $48,000
        CR Restructured note receivable $48,000

P7-10. Accounting for transfer of receivables

It seems that Ricoh Company is treating the discounting of receivables as a sale. Note that Ricoh indicates that "trade notes receivable discounted are contingent liabilities." If Ricoh had treated the discounting of receivables as a borrowing, then there is no need for reporting the contingent liability since the borrowing would have been included in the balance sheet as a liability.

Crown Crafts appear to use a similar accounting treatment, i.e., the money received from the factor is considered as a liquidation of the receivables.

The following passage from Foxmeyer's footnote indicates that it is also using the sale treatment for the transfer of receivables: "Such accounts receivable sold are not included in the accompanying consolidated balance sheet at March 31, 1994."

There are substantial differences in the economics of the transactions. Crown Craft transfers the receivable without recourse as to credit losses, i.e., in effect, the factor becomes the "true" owner of the receivables by bearing the credit risk. Whereas, Ricoh is still responsible for all the credit risk since the transfers are with full recourse, i.e., Ricoh retains the economic risk (i.e., risk of credit losses) of owning the receivables. However, Foxmeyer falls somewhere in between since the investors in the company's receivables have only *limited recourse* against the company. Consequently, it is imperative for an analyst to carefully examine the details of the factoring or securitization transactions to find out who is really bearing the risks of receivables ownership. If the ownership risks (and the corresponding rewards) are retained by the company, then the transaction is more like a borrowing where the lender does not directly bear the risk of owning the security (i.e., the receivable). On the other hand, if the ownership risks are borne by the factor, then the company has, in effect, sold the receivables, and, therefore, their removal from the balance sheet is consistent with economic reality. In essence, companies facing different economic realities might chose similar accounting treatment because they "satisfy" the requirements under the GAAP.

Cases
C7-1. Ralston Purina Co. (CW): Comprehensive receivables

Requirement 1:

Allowance for Doubtful Accounts (1988)		Allowance for Doubtful Accounts (1989)	
	$8.0 Beginning balance		"B" Beginning balance
	5.2 Current year bad debt provision		7.0 Current year bad debt provision
Write-offs "A"		Write-offs $3.9	
	$8.3 Ending balance		"C" Ending balance

1988:
End. balance = beg. balance + current year bad debt provision - write-offs

$8.3 = $8.0 + $5.2 - A

A = $4.9

1989:
B = Beginning balance in 1989 = ending balance in 1988 = $8.3

End. balance = beg. balance + current year bad debt provision - write-offs

C = $8.3 + $7.0 - 3.9

C = $11.4

Allowance for Doubtful Accounts (1990)

	"D" Beginning balance
	17.1 Current year bad debt provision
Write-offs $7.2	
	"E" Ending balance

Allowance for Doubtful Accounts (1991)

	"F" Beginning balance
	9.5 Current year bad debt provision
Write-offs "G"	
	"H" Ending balance

Allowance for Doubtful Accounts (1992)

	$19.5 Beginning balance
	"J" Current year bad debt provision
Write-Offs 8.4	
	$26.4 Ending balance

1990:

D = Beginning balance in 1990 = ending balance in 1989 = $11.4

End. balance = beg. balance + current year bad debt provision - write-offs

E = $11.4 + $17.1 - 7.2

E = $21.3

1991:

F = Beginning balance in 1991 = ending balance in 1990 = $21.3

H = Ending balance in 1991 = beginning balance in 1992 = $19.5

End. balance = beg. balance + current year bad debt provision - write-offs

$19.5 = $21.3 + $9.5 - G

G = $11.3

End. balance = beg. balance + current year bad debt provision - write-offs

$26.4 = $19.5 + J - $8.4

J = $15.3

Requirements 2 & 3:

	Allowance method			**Direct write-off**		
1988	DR Allowance for doubtful accounts	$4.9		DR Bad debt exp.	$4.9	
	CR Accounts receivable		$4.9	CR Accounts receivable		$4.9
	DR Bad debt exp.	$5.2		NO ENTRY		
	CR Allowance for doubtful accounts		$5.2			
1989	DR Allowance for doubtful accounts	$3.9		DR Bad debt exp.	$3.9	
	CR Accounts receivable		$3.9	CR Accounts receivable		$3.9
	DR Bad debt exp.	$7.0		NO ENTRY		
	CR Allowance for doubtful accounts		$7.0			
1990	DR Allowance for doubtful accounts	$7.2		DR Bad debt exp.	$7.2	
	CR Accounts receivable		$7.2	CR Accounts receivable		$7.2
	DR Bad debt exp.	$17.1		NO ENTRY		
	CR Allowance for doubtful accounts		$17.1			
1991	DR Allowance for doubtful accounts	$11.3		DR Bad debt exp.	$11.3	
	CR Accounts receivable		$11.3	CR Accounts receivable		$11.3
	DR Bad debt exp.	$9.5		NO ENTRY		
	CR Allowance for doubtful accounts		$9.5			
1992	DR Allowance for doubtful accounts	$8.4		DR Bad debt exp.	$8.4	
	CR Accounts receivable		$8.4	CR Accounts receivable		$8.4
	DR Bad debt exp.	$15.3		NO ENTRY		
	CR Allowance for doubtful accounts		$15.3			

Requirement 4:
The allowance method is consistent with the matching principle underlying the accrual accounting model, whereas the direct write-off method is not.

Requirement 5:
The cumulative income difference is equal to the change in the balance of the allowance account from 1988 to 1992.

Allow. for doubtful accounts end.	1992:	$26.4
Allow. for doubtful accounts beg.	1988:	8.0
Income difference (cumulative)		$18.4

The proof is to check the sum of the yearly income differences:

Year	Income Difference
1988	($.3)
1989	(3.1)
1990	(9.9)
1991	1.8
1992	(6.9)
Total	($18.4)

Calculate the same numbers by subtracting the "expense" that would be reported under the allowance method from what would be reported under the direct write-off method.

Year	Income Difference
1988	($4.9 - $5.2)
1989	(3.9 - 7.0)
1990	(7.2 - 17.1)
1991	(11.3 - 9.5)
1992	(8.4 - 15.3)
Total	($18.4)

Requirement 6:

If the firm wanted to be conservative, the initial provision could be increased by the entire $10.0 million. If the firm wanted to be optimistic, the initial provision would not be increased at all. Perhaps, the best recommendation to make is to take a middle ground and accrue a portion of the $10.0. For example, management could be asked to make an estimate of the probability that the customer will go bankrupt (e.g., 35.0%), and then the initial provision could be increased by this probability times the $10.0 (i.e., $3.5 million). Management's estimate of the probability might be based on how often customers with similar financial problems in the past eventually went bankrupt and did not pay their account balance.

Requirement 7:

a) Here, management might want to take the entire $10.0 million as an additional provision because earnings before income taxes of $65.0 million is well below the bonus plan minimum of $100.0 million. In other words, by taking the entire $10.0 million as an additional bad debt provision, management doesn't lose any bonus money. In fact, by taking the additional provision this year, managers may enhance their bonus in the future (e.g., next year) by not having to take an extra provision in a year when they are "in the bonus range."

b) Here, management might not want to take any additional bad debt provision because earnings before income taxes of $110.0 million is above the bonus plan minimum of $100.0 million. Every dollar of extra bad debt provision taken reduces the bonus by 1%. For example, taking an additional provision of $5.0 million costs management $50,000 in bonus money.

c) Here, management might want to take the entire $10 million as an additional bad debt provision because earnings before income taxes of $225.0 million exceeds the ceiling of the bonus plan ($200.0 million). Here, management doesn't lose any bonus money by taking any or all of the $10 million as an additional bad debt provision. In fact (as in part a), by taking the additional provision this year, managers may enhance their bonus in the future (e.g., next year) by not having to take an extra provision in a year when they are "in the bonus range."

d) Here, management might want to take an additional provision of $5.0 million because earnings before income taxes of $205.0 million exceeds the ceiling of the bonus plan ($200.0 million) by $5.0 million. Here, as long as the extra provision doesn't exceed $5.0 million, management doesn't lose any bonus money. Any amount above $5.0 million, of course, begins to reduce the bonus.

The moral of the story is that management's financial reporting decisions are not going to be made in isolation of other factors.

Requirement 8:
a) Managers might use the provision for bad debts to help avoid violation of debt covenant restrictions that are written in terms of accounting numbers. Some debt contracts contain minimum (or maximum) levels that various financial ratios must adhere to or the firm will be declared in technical default on the debt. These ratios are often a function of reported earnings and, thus, can be improved by postponing the recognition of expenses into future years or by accelerating the recognition of revenue. Ratios/accounting numbers often seen in debt contracts include interest coverage, net worth, current ratio, debt to equity, debt to total assets, among others.

Requirement 9:
"Managing" a financial statement item suggests the ability to influence net income and the pattern of net income growth from year to year. Smoothing income and taking "big-bath" charge-offs are examples.

Other items that can potentially be managed include:

a) Depreciation method choice.

b) Useful lives for tangible and intangible assets.

c) Estimates of future warranty expense by firms that offer product warranties (e.g., car makers like GM and Ford).

d) The timing and amounts for special charges/write-downs, restructurings, asset sales, etc.

e) Inventory method choice.

f) Write-offs or write-downs of obsolete inventory.

g) Related to (b), changes in the useful lives or salvage values of depreciable assets.

C7-2. Great Southwest Corporation (KR): Valuing notes and recording interest (Adapted from In the Matter of Reports of Great Southwest Corporation, Securities Exchange Act of 1934, Section 15(c)(4), Release No. 9934, January 15, 1973)

Requirement 1:
The journal entries are not consistent with GAAP because they do not reflect the *present value* of consideration given for the amusement park. Despite the various numbers and terms (e.g., stated interest and principal payments) used in the problem with respect to the note, what GSC has actually received as consideration is $5,412,500 (down payment + prepaid interest) cash up front and the promise of a future cash flow stream of $2,137,500 per year over 35 years, starting three years from signing of the contract. Assuming (for the monent) that the interest rate stated in the contract is appropriate, the future cash flows should be discounted at an interest rate of 6.5%.

The 35 payments of $2,137,500 beginning on 1/1/72 and ending on 1/1/06 can be viewed as a 35-year ordinary annuity from 1/1/71. The lump sum present value of all those payments discounted at 6.5% on 1/1/71 is ($2,137,500 × 13.68695673 = $29,255,868). This lump sum amount on 1/1/71 can then be discounted back 2 years at 6.5% to get the value of the note on 1/1/69 which is ($29,255,868 × .881659283 = $25,793,709).

Some students may feel more comfortable seeing the solution in amortization table form. The following table provides details of the present value calculation as well as the amortization of the notes receivable:

Payment	Beginning of Year	Interest Revenue	Cash Received	Change in Receivable	Balance of Notes Receivable	Present Value at 1/1/69	Discount Factor	Discounting Time
	1969				$25,793,709			0
	1970	$1,676,591[1]	-	$1,676,591	27,470,300			1
	1971	1,785,570	-	1,785,570	29,255,870			2
1	1972	1,901,632	$2,137,500	(235,868)	29,020,002	$1,769,527	0.8278	3
2	1973	1,886,300	2,137,500	(251,200)	28,768,802	1,661,528	0.7773	4
3	1974	1,869,972	2,137,500	(267,528)	28,501,274	1,560,120	0.7299	5
4	1975	1,852,583	2,137,500	(284,917)	28,216,357	1,464,902	0.6853	6
5	1976	1,834,063	2,137,500	(303,437)	27,912,920	1,375,495	0.6435	7
6	1977	1,814,340	2,137,500	(323,160)	27,589,760	1,291,544	0.6042	8
7	1978	1,793,334	2,137,500	(344,166)	27,245,594	1,212,718	0.5674	9
8	1979	1,770,964	2,137,500	(366,536)	26,879,058	1,138,702	0.5327	10
9	1980	1,747,139	2,137,500	(390,361)	26,488,696	1,069,204	0.5002	11
10	1981	1,721,765	2,137,500	(415,735)	26,072,961	1,003,947	0.4697	12
11	1982	1,694,742	2,137,500	(442,758)	25,630,204	942,673	0.4410	13
12	1983	1,665,963	2,137,500	(471,537)	25,158,667	885,139	0.4141	14
13	1984	1,635,313	2,137,500	(502,187)	24,656,481	831,117	0.3888	15
14	1985	1,602,671	2,137,500	(534,829)	24,121,652	780,391	0.3651	16
15	1986	1,567,907	2,137,500	(569,593)	23,552,059	732,762	0.3428	17
16	1987	1,530,884	2,137,500	(606,616)	22,945,443	688,039	0.3219	18
17	1988	1,491,454	2,137,500	(646,046)	22,299,397	646,046	0.3022	19
18	1989	1,449,461	2,137,500	(688,039)	21,611,358	606,616	0.2838	20
19	1990	1,404,738	2,137,500	(732,762)	20,878,596	569,593	0.2665	21
20	1991	1,357,109	2,137,500	(780,391)	20,098,205	534,829	0.2502	22
21	1992	1,306,383	2,137,500	(831,117)	19,267,088	502,187	0.2349	23
22	1993	1,252,361	2,137,500	(885,139)	18,381,949	471,537	0.2206	24
23	1994	1,194,827	2,137,500	(942,673)	17,439,275	442,758	0.2071	25
24	1995	1,133,553	2,137,500	(1,003,947)	16,435,328	415,735	0.1945	26
25	1996	1,068,296	2,137,500	(1,069,204)	15,366,125	390,361	0.1826	27
26	1997	998,798	2,137,500	(1,138,702)	14,227,423	366,536	0.1715	28
27	1998	924,782	2,137,500	(1,212,718)	13,014,705	344,166	0.1610	29
28	1999	845,956	2,137,500	(1,291,544)	11,723,161	323,160	0.1512	30
29	2000	762,005	2,137,500	(1,375,495)	10,347,666	303,437	0.1420	31
30	2001	672,598	2,137,500	(1,464,902)	8,882,765	284,917	0.1333	32
31	2002	577,380	2,137,500	(1,560,120)	7,322,645	267,528	0.1252	33
32	2003	475,972	2,137,500	(1,661,528)	5,661,116	251,200	0.1175	34
33	2004	367,973	2,137,500	(1,769,527)	3,891,589	235,868	0.1103	35
34	2005	252,953	2,137,500	(1,884,547)	2,007,042	221,473	0.1036	36
35	2006	130,458	2,137,500	(2,007,042)	0	207,956	0.0973	37
		$49,018,791	$74,812,500	$(25,793,709)		$25,793,709	= Total PV	

---

[1] Interest revenue of $1,676,591 is calculated by multiplying the 1969 beginning of year balance in notes receivable ($25,793,709) by 6.5%.

The consideration received is calculated as follows:

Down payment	$2,000,000
Prepaid interest	3,412,500
Present value of note receivable	25,793,709
Total consideration	$31,206,209

1/1/69: To record sale of amusement park for cash and a note:

Even though $3,412,500 is called prepaid interest, the relevant factor for measuring the gain is the present value of current and future cash flows. Consequently, the breakdown between down payment and stated interest is not necessary when recording the sale of the amusement park.

DR Cash	$5,412,500	
DR Note receivable	25,793,709	
CR Amusement park		$22,000,000
CR Gain on sale		9,206,209

Requirement 2:
This requirement illustrates the effects of a difference between the stated rate and the prevailing market interest rate. Contracts might specify different stated rates to manage the contracting parties' cash flow streams. For example, zero-coupon bonds have no periodic interest payments even though the effective interest rate is positive. However, for valuation purposes, what matters is the present value of current and future cash flows discounted at a rate commensurate with the riskiness of the future cash flows (referred to as the effective interest rate).

The 35 payments of $2,137,500 viewed as an ordinary annuity from 1/1/71 are:

$2,137,500 \times 9.644158973 = $20,614,389

Discounted back to 1/1/69:

$20,614,389 \times .82644628 = $17,036,686

Thus, the present value of the note at January 1, 1969 at 10% would be $17,036,686.

The following table provides details of the present value calculation as well as the amortization of the note receivable using a discount rate of 10%:

Payment	Beginning of Year	Interest Revenue	Cash Received	Change in Receivable	Balance of Notes Receivable	Present Value at 1/1/69	Discount Factor	Discounting Time
	1969				$17,036,686			0
	1970	$1,703,669	-	$1,703,669	18,740,354			1
	1971	1,874,035	-	1,874,035	20,614,390			2
1	1972	2,061,439	$2,137,500	(76,061)	20,538,329	$1,605,935	0.7513	3
2	1973	2,053,833	2,137,500	(83,667)	20,454,662	1,459,941	0.6830	4
3	1974	2,045,466	2,137,500	(92,034)	20,362,628	1,327,219	0.6209	5
4	1975	2,036,263	2,137,500	(101,237)	20,261,391	1,206,563	0.5645	6
5	1976	2,026,139	2,137,500	(111,361)	20,150,030	1,096,875	0.5132	7
6	1977	2,015,003	2,137,500	(122,497)	20,027,533	997,160	0.4665	8
7	1978	2,002,753	2,137,500	(134,747)	19,892,786	906,509	0.4241	9
8	1979	1,989,279	2,137,500	(148,221)	19,744,564	824,099	0.3855	10
9	1980	1,974,456	2,137,500	(163,044)	19,581,521	749,181	0.3505	11
10	1981	1,958,152	2,137,500	(179,348)	19,402,173	681,073	0.3186	12
11	1982	1,940,217	2,137,500	(197,283)	19,204,890	619,158	0.2897	13
12	1983	1,920,489	2,137,500	(217,011)	18,987,879	562,871	0.2633	14
13	1984	1,898,788	2,137,500	(238,712)	18,749,167	511,701	0.2394	15
14	1985	1,874,917	2,137,500	(262,583)	18,486,584	465,182	0.2176	16
15	1986	1,848,658	2,137,500	(288,842)	18,197,742	422,893	0.1978	17
16	1987	1,819,774	2,137,500	(317,726)	17,880,017	384,448	0.1799	18
17	1988	1,788,002	2,137,500	(349,498)	17,530,518	349,498	0.1635	19
18	1989	1,753,052	2,137,500	(384,448)	17,146,070	317,726	0.1486	20
19	1990	1,714,607	2,137,500	(422,893)	16,723,177	288,842	0.1351	21
20	1991	1,672,318	2,137,500	(465,182)	16,257,995	262,583	0.1228	22
21	1992	1,625,799	2,137,500	(511,701)	15,746,294	238,712	0.1117	23
22	1993	1,574,629	2,137,500	(562,871)	15,183,424	217,011	0.1015	24
23	1994	1,518,342	2,137,500	(619,158)	14,564,266	197,283	0.0923	25
24	1995	1,456,427	2,137,500	(681,073)	13,883,193	179,348	0.0839	26
25	1996	1,388,319	2,137,500	(749,181)	13,134,012	163,044	0.0763	27
26	1997	1,313,401	2,137,500	(824,099)	12,309,913	148,221	0.0693	28
27	1998	1,230,991	2,137,500	(906,509)	11,403,405	134,747	0.0630	29
28	1999	1,140,340	2,137,500	(997,160)	10,406,245	122,497	0.0573	30
29	2000	1,040,625	2,137,500	(1,096,875)	9,309,370	111,361	0.0521	31
30	2001	930,937	2,137,500	(1,206,563)	8,102,807	101,237	0.0474	32
31	2002	810,281	2,137,500	(1,327,219)	6,775,587	92,034	0.0431	33
32	2003	677,559	2,137,500	(1,459,941)	5,315,646	83,667	0.0391	34
33	2004	531,565	2,137,500	(1,605,935)	3,709,711	76,061	0.0356	35
34	2005	370,971	2,137,500	(1,766,529)	1,943,182	69,146	0.0323	36
35	2006	194,318	2,137,500	(1,943,182)	0	62,860	0.0294	37
		$57,775,814	$74,812,500	$(17,036,66)		$17,036,686	= Total PV	

The consideration received is now recalculated as follows:

Down payment	$ 2,000,000
Prepaid interest	3,412,500
Present value of note receivable	17,036,686
Total consideration	$22,449,186

1/1/69: To record sale of amusement park for cash and a note:
    DR Cash $ 5,412,500
    DR Note receivable   17,036,686
        CR Amusement park $22,000,000
        CR Gain on sale   449,186

12/31/69: To record 10% interest on 1/1/69 book value of $17,036,686:
    DR Note receivable $1,703,669
        CR Interest revenue $1,703,669

12/31/70: To record 10% interest on 1/1/70 book value of $18,740,354:
    DR Note receivable $1,874,035
        CR Interest revenue $1,874,035

12/31/71: To record 10% interest on 1/1/71 book value of $20,614,390:
    DR Note receivable $2,061,439
        CR Interest revenue $2,061,439

1/1/72: To record receipt of cash payment:
    DR Cash $2,137,500
        CR Note receivable $2,137,500

12/31/72: To record 10% interest on 1/1/72 book value of $20,538,329:
    DR Note receivable $2,053,833
        CR Interest revenue $2,053,833

C7-3. Spiegel Inc. (KR): Analyzing receivables growth

Dear Ms. Kang:

I have had a chance to review the information on Spiegel's accounts receivable. Before I discuss the results of my analysis, let me first compute more precisely some of the ratios you had mentioned in your letter:

	1995	1994
% Change in net sales	6.63%	15.81%
% Change in net receivables	-34.04%	12.74%
% Change in receivables owned	-31.77%	12.09%

I am not sure whether you used gross or net receivables in your calculations. However, the inferences are very similar either way. Consequently, unless it impacts my analysis, I will use gross and net receivables interchangeably.

I have also been able to verify your receivables turnover calculations:

	1995	1994	1993
Net sales	$2,886,225	$2,706,791	$2,337,235
Receivables, net (from bal. sheet)	742,480	1,125,728	998,525
Average receivables	934,104	1,062,127	
Receivables turnover ratio	3.09	2.55	
Collection period (days)	118	143	

The collection period has indeed decreased from 143 days to less than 120 days. However, the decline appears to be primarily due to increased usage of factored receivables rather than faster payments by customers. One approach to examining the effect of factoring is to estimate the receivables turnover assuming that Spiegel does not factor any of the receivables. This would give us a better estimate of how fast Spiegel's customers are paying off their debt.

To perform this analysis, we first have to figure out what the receivables balance would have been without any factoring. These numbers are provided under receivables generated from operations, which Spiegel calls receivables serviced. Note that receivables owned represents those receivables that are included in Spiegel's balance sheet under net receivables. Over the last 3 years, the proportion of the factored receivables (receivables sold) has continuously increased:

	1995	1994	1993
Receivables sold	$1,180,000	$ 480,000	$ 330,000
Receivables owned	821,081	1,203,444	1,073,618
Total receivables generated from operations	$2,001,081	$1,683,444	$1,403,618

	1995	1994	1993
Receivables sold	58.97%	28.51%	23.51%
Receivables owned	41.03%	71.49%	76.49%
Total receivables generated from operations	100.00%	100.00%	100.00%

Note that the factored receivables as a percentage of total receivables has more than doubled from 1994 to 1995. To better understand the effect of this on receivables turnover, let us recalculate Spiegel's receivables turnover using the total receivables rather than just the receivables owned:

	1995	1994	1993
Net sales	$2,886,225	$2,706,791	$2,337,235
Receivables generated from operations	2,001,081	1,683,444	1,403,618
Average receivables	1,842,263	1,543,531	
Receivables turnover ratio	1.57	1.75	
Collection period (days)	233	208	

307

These calculations suggest that the customers are, in fact, taking a longer time to pay off their debt (233 days in 1995 versus 208 days in 1994). *However, Spiegel's receivables turnover "improved" because a substantial portion of its receivables are off the balance sheet due to increased factoring.*

One consideration we have to keep in mind is that Spiegel has sold its receivables *without recourse* for bad debt risk. Consequently, whether the cash is received from the factor or directly from the customer may not be of much concern to an analyst. *However, the long-run implications of the factoring are not clear.* Can Spiegel continue to factor almost 60% of receivables in the near future? Since the "true" collection period has indeed deteriorated, it might have implications for future factoring agreements. For instance, the factors might demand a larger factoring fee due to the extended collection time. Alternatively, the factors might accept only transfers of receivables *with recourse* to avoid bearing any increased bad debt risk from slower collection.

The second issue relates to the accounting for sale of receivables. To get better intuition on this, let us first try to understand the journal entry recorded by Spiegel when it factors its receivables. Recall that Spiegel is still responsible for sales returns although the investors in the securitized receivables bear the bad debt risk. Consequently, while an allowance for *returns* on the factored receivables must continue to be maintained in Spiegel's books, the allowance for *uncollectibles* on those receivables is eliminated. Let me draw your attention to the following information that you provided to me earlier:

Allowance for doubtful accounts

	1995	1994	1993
Beginning balance	$49,954	$46,855	$37,231
Increase due to CR to allowance acct.	91,612	79,183	69,160
Reduction for receivables sold	(33,600)	(6,300)	(1,609)
Other			695
Accounts written off	(67,134)	(69,784)	(58,622)
Ending balance	$40,832	$49,954	$46,855

"Other" represents the beginning balance of Newport News which was acquired in 1993.

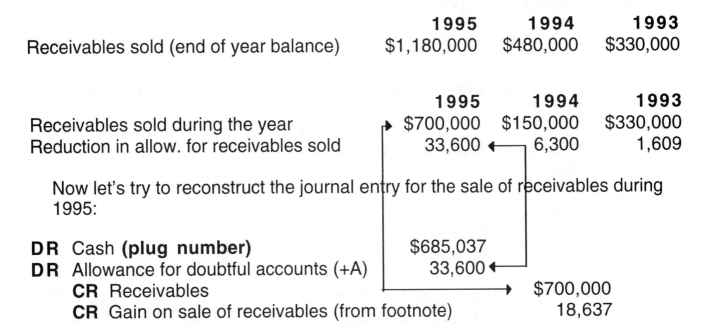

	1995	1994	1993
Receivables sold (end of year balance)	$1,180,000	$480,000	$330,000

	1995	1994	1993
Receivables sold during the year	$700,000	$150,000	$330,000
Reduction in allow. for receivables sold	33,600	6,300	1,609

Now let's try to reconstruct the journal entry for the sale of receivables during 1995:

DR Cash **(plug number)**	$685,037	
DR Allowance for doubtful accounts (+A)	33,600	
CR Receivables		$700,000
CR Gain on sale of receivables (from footnote)		18,637

Note that the gain on sale of receivables is included under other revenue.

Since $700,000 of receivables have been removed from the books, Spiegel cannot continue to show the corresponding allowance for returns as a contra asset account (Note: It appears that the investors in the factored receivables are not holding back any funds for expected sales returns). Instead, Spiegel seems to reclassify the allowance for returns on the factored receivables as a liability. **This explains why a portion of the allowance for sales returns is disclosed under accrued liabilities**. Recall that Spiegel continues to be responsible for sales returns, so the allowance for returns cannot be eliminated altogether.

If Spiegel is selling receivables with a present value of expected net cash flows of only $666,400 ($700,000 minus $33,600), why are the investors paying $685,037 for these receivables? Why the $18,637 disparity exists is not readily apparent. One possibility is that the interest rate on the customer receivables is higher than the rate of return earned by the investors on the receivables. If so, the gain on sale represents a "brokerage fee" retained by Spiegel for obtaining financing for its customers; i.e., it is too costly for the customers to obtain outside financing and too costly for the investors in receivables to independently evaluate the quality of receivables. Consequently, Spiegel earns a "brokerage fee" for acting as an intermediary. A second possibility is that market interest rates have decreased from the time the receivables were first created to the time the receivables were sold to the investors. If this is true, the higher cash received represents the lower prevailing discount rate at the time of the sale of receivables. In any case, it is important to understand the reasons for the gain on sale of receivables to evaluate the quality of Spiegel's earnings.

C7-4. Thompson Traders (KR): Bad-debt analysis

Tony Barclay's calculation:

The following table provides the necessary calculations to support Tony Barclay's analysis.

Year	Revenue	Bad Debts Written-off	%
1993	$30,000	$ 600	2.00%
1994	40,000	1,000	2.50%
1995	60,000	1,500	2.50%
1996	80,000	2,400	3.00%
1997	90,000	3,000	3.33%

However, Tony's analysis suffers from an important limitation. By expressing bad debts **written off** as a percentage of revenues, Tony is comparing apples and oranges. Note that the bad debts written off in a given year pertains to sales made during that year as well as the previous year. This could lead to biased estimates for bad debt expense since the matching principle requires matching the revenue of a given year with all the bad debts relating to that year's sale whether written off in the same period or not. This takes us to Ian Spencer's analysis.

Ian Spencer's calculation:

The following table provides the necessary calculations to support Ian Spencer's analysis:

Year	Revenue	Written-off	Bad Debts Pertaining to Sales Made During 1993	1994	1995	1996	1997
1993	$30,000	$ 600	$600				
1994	40,000	1,000	300	$ 700			
1995	60,000	1,500	-	500	$1,000		
1996	80,000	2,400	-	-	800	$1,600	
1997	90,000	3,000	-	-	-	800	$2,200
			$900	$1,200	$1,800	$2,400	$2,200
% of revenue			3.00%	3.00%	3.00%	3.00%	2.44%

As correctly pointed out by Ian, bad debts as a percentage of a given year's sales has remained constant. (Note that the 1997 figure (2.44%) is incomplete since some of the 1997 receivables might be written off only in 1998.) Ian was able do this analysis by keeping track of all the bad debts pertaining to a given year's sale. However, Ian's conclusion to retain the current formula is misguided since the actual bad debts are 0.25% higher than the bad debt expense recorded under the current formula (i.e., 2.75% bad debt expense versus 3.00% "true" bad debts). Consequently, since the trend in bad debts is expected to remain at historical levels, the company should revise the formula to 3% of revenue.

Brian Joshi:

As pointed out by Brian Joshi, we have to not only revise the bad debt expense formula beginning 1997, but also adjust the balance in the allowance account to correct for the underestimation. However, the adjustment for the under-estimation must be treated as a change in an accounting estimate rather than a change in accounting principle. Moreover, there is no need to adjust the past financial statements to rectify the estimation error. On the contrary, the understatement in the allowance for doubtful accounts as of the end of 1996 must be corrected by increasing the bad debt expense for the year 1997.

The following table summarizes the actual transactions in the allowance for uncollectibles account:

	Allowance Account (Actual = 2.75% of sales)			
	1993	1994	1995	1996
Beginning balance	-	$ 225	$ 325	$ 475
(+) Bad debt expense	$825	1,100	1,650	2,200
(-) Bad debts written-off	(600)	(1,000)	(1,500)	(2,400)
Ending balance	$225	$ 325	$ 475	$ 275

To calculate the underestimation error, the following table estimates the balance in the allowance account **assuming the company had reported bad debts at 3% of revenue for all prior years**:

	Allowance account (revised internal calculations = 3.00% of sales)			
	1993	1994	1995	1996
Beginning balance	-	$ 300	$ 500	$ 800
(+) Bad debt expense	$900	1,200	1,800	2,400
(-) Bad debts written-off	(600)	(1,000)	(1,500)	(2,400)
Ending balance	$300	$ 500	$ 800	$ 800

	1996
ADA balance (using 3% formula)	$800
(-) ADA balance (using 2.75% formula)	(275)
Past underestimation error	$525

The bad debt expense for 1997 is calculated as follows:

Bad debts based on 3% of $90,000	$2,700
Correction of past estimation error	525
Bad debt expense for 1997	$3,225

311

In essence, the company can use its accumulated historical experience to examine the accuracy of its bad debt estimation method. The historical data suggests that the company had consistently underestimated its bad debt provision. Consequently, the bad debt expense for 1997 includes a component to reflect the current year's estimated bad debts using the revised formula plus a component reflecting the past underprovision.

The following table summarizes the actual transactions in the allowance for uncollectibles account through 1997:

Allowance for uncollectibles	1993	1994	1995	1996	1997
Beginning balance	-	$ 225	$ 325	$ 475	$ 275
(+) Bad debt expense	$825	1,100	1,650	2,200	3,225
(-) Bad debts written off	(600)	(1,000)	(1,500)	(2,400)	(3,000)
Ending balance	$225	$ 325	$ 475	$ 275	$ 500

Journal Entry:

DR Bad debt expense $3,225
        CR Allowance for uncollectibles $3,225

Note that the change in the bad debt formula will impact the bad debt expense of the future years also. Therefore, under GAAP, the company should disclose the impact of the change in this accounting estimate on its income statement for 1997 (i.e., $90,000 \times 0.25\% = \$225$). Notice that 0.25% is simply 3% minus 2.75%.

C7-5. The Software Toolworks, Inc. (KR): Account reconciliation and analysis

Requirement 1:

	DR	CR
Allowance for returns		
Beginning balance		$6,363,000
Provision for returns		10,942,000
Actual returns **(plug number)**	$12,041,000	
Ending balance		$5,264,000
Allowance for doubtful accounts		
Beginning balance		$4,151,000
Provision for doubtful accounts		946,000
Bad debts written off **(plug number)**	$1,527,000	
Ending balance		$3,570,000

	DR	CR
Accounts receivable (gross)		
Beginning balance	$ 34,754,000	
Revenues **(see below)**	130,540,000	
Actual returns (from allowance for returns a/c)		$12,041,000
Bad debts written-off (from allowance for da)		1,527,000
Cash collected **(plug number)**		12,831,000
Ending balance	$ 38,895,000	

Revenues are calculated after adding back the provision for returns to the revenues reported in the financial statements.

	1993	1992
Revenues (net of provision for returns)	$119,598,000	$102,646,000
Provision for returns	10,942,000	8,863,000
Gross revenues	$130,540,000	$111,509,000

While provision for returns is contra to the revenue account, provision for doubtful accounts is an expense account.

The company actually includes sales returns and allowances as well as allowance to distributors for advertising in the T-account allowance for returns. Consequently, a portion of the provision for returns is treated as a contra sales account, and the remainder is treated as an expense. This fine distinction is ignored in the case to keep it simple.

Requirement 2
The receivables are analyzed using the following approaches:

- Examining the trend in provision for doubtful accounts as a percentage of revenues

- Comparing the growth in revenues to the growth in receivables

- Comparing allowance for doubtful accounts as a percentage of gross accounts receivable with the provision for doubtful accounts as a percentage of revenues

First, let us focus on the provision for doubtful accounts as a percentage of revenues.

	1993	1992
Revenues (net of provision for returns)	$119,598,000	$102,646,000
Provision for doubtful accounts	946,000	3,673,000
Provision for DA as % of revenues	0.79%	3.58%

Note that the revenue figure used is net of provision for returns. This is because bad debts are likely to be related only to inventory sales that are not expected to be returned by the customers. If gross revenue figures are used, then variations in Provision for doubtful accounts as a percentage of revenue could be due to variations in expected sales returns rather than changes in expected bad debts.

The company's provision for doubtful accounts has decreased substantially from about 3.6% of Revenue to less than 1%. In general, changes in this ratio can indicate changes either in the quality of receivables or earnings management. In this case, it appears that the 1992 higher provision is more likely due to temporarily higher bad debts. Note that the company experienced higher than expected bad debts in 1992 due to a customer bankruptcy and an arbitration case. This information provided in the case was obtained from the management discussion and analysis section. Let us recalculate the ratios after excluding these potentially "transitory" items:

	1993	1992
Provision for doubtful accounts	$946,000	$3,673,000
(-) Chapter 11 customer		(2,167,000)
(-) Receivable in arbitration		(583,000)
Provision for doubtful accounts (adjusted)	$946,000	$ 923,000
Provision for da (adj.) as % of revenues	0.79%	0.90%

Notice that the current year provision is much more comparable to that of last year's after excluding the two specific bad debts. Without any further information, it appears that the company has not substantially revised its bad debt provision during the year. One caveat here is that the change from 0.90% to 0.79% may have a material impact on the bottom line of the company. If profit figures were available, we could calculate the impact on the 1993 net income if the company had maintained the provision at 0.90% as in 1992.

Similar to provision for doubtful accounts, we can also examine the trend in provision for returns:

	1993	1992
Revenues (net of provision for returns)	$119,598,000	$102,646,000
Provision for returns	10,942,000	8,863,000
Gross revenues	$130,540,000	$111,509,000
Prov. for returns as % of gross revenues	8.38%	7.95%

For provision for returns, the appropriate benchmark is a comparison with gross revenues. Once again, the figures indicate only a minor variation from 1992 to 1993.

A second approach involves comparing percentage of growth in sales with percentage of growth in receivables. If the growth in sales has occurred gradually over the year, then we would expected the two growth rates to be comparable. While disproportionate growth in receivables may indicate potential collection problems, decrease in receivables may suggest declining demand.

Percentage Change from 1992 to 1993

% Change in receivables (gross)	11.92%
% Change in A/R (-) returns	18.46%
% Change in net receivables	24.01%
% Change in gross revenues	17.07%
% Change in revenues (net of returns)	16.52%
% Change in revenue (-) provision for DA	19.88%

Given so many alternatives, we have to decide whether to compare percentage change in net or gross receivables with percentage change in net or gross revenues. If we use the percentage change in **gross** receivables as a benchmark for comparison, it appears that the company has efficiently managed its receivables. However, note that while **provisions** for returns and doubtful accounts immediately decrease the net receivables value, they decrease the gross receivables only when the customers actually return the goods and/or when the bad debts are finally written off. Consequently, when there are large write-offs taking place in a year, you would notice a less than proportionate growth in gross receivables. This is actually what happened for the company.

Write-offs as % of allowance for DA	161.42
($1,527,000/$946,000)	
Actual returns as % of allowance for returns	110.04
($12,041,000/$10,942,000)	

Since write-offs were 60% more than the provision for doubtful accounts, the growth in gross receivables appears to be much lower than the growth in sales. However, the change in net receivables (24%) is higher than the growth in gross or net sales. As an analyst, one should conduct further analysis or follow up with the management. Before investigating further, it may be fruitful to get a handle on the materiality of any build-up in receivables, i.e., we should estimate the level of "abnormal" accounts receivable.

| | Balances as of March 31 | |
	1993	1992
Net accounts receivable	$30,061,000	$24,240,000
Projected net accounts receivable (118%)	28,603,200	
Abnormal receivable	$ 1,457,800	

For instance, based on the growth in sales, we might project that the receivables should have grown by around 18%, which is a rough average of the three percentages changes computed above: 17.07%, 16.52%, and 19.88%. Using this assumption, the estimated "abnormal receivable" is $1,457,800. Depending on whether this amount is material or not, additional follow-up action may be taken.

A third approach is to compare the provision for doubtful accounts as a percentage of revenue with the allowance for doubtful accounts as a percentage of receivables.

	1993	1992
Provision for da (Adj.) as % of revenues	0.79%	0.90%
Allowance for da as % of (A/R - returns)	10.62%	14.62%

Obviously, one would expect the allowance percentage to be higher than the provision percentage since more of the delinquent customers are likely to be included in the year-end receivables. The evidence is quite consistent with this conjecture. Moreover, we see a drop in the allowance balance as a percentage of receivables, which is consistent with the larger write-offs experienced during 1993 as a result of higher than usual bad debt provision in 1992.

The following table provides a similar comparison for sales returns:

	1993	1992
Prov. for returns as % of gross revenues	8.38%	7.95%
Allowance for returns as % of A/R	13.53%	18.31%

Unlike bad debts, there is no reason why we should expect larger sales returns on year-end receivables unless the fourth quarter sales have different return privileges compared to the other period sales. Consequently, the larger allowance percentage compared to the provision percentage needs further scrutiny.

Exercises

E8-1. Account analysis
(AICPA adapted)

To find merchandise inventory, we first need to find cost of goods sold. This figure can be computed by using the gross margin percentage given. If profit is 20% of sales, then cost of goods sold must be (1-20%) or 80% of sales. So 80% of $2,000,000 is $1,600,000—cost of goods sold. Now we can look at the T-account for the answer.

Inventory

Beginning balance	$300,000		
Purchases	1,900,000		
		$1,600,00	Cost of goods sold
Ending balance	X		

Now we can solve for X.
$300,000 + $1,900,000 - $1,600,000 = X
X = $600,000

E8-2. Cost flow computations
(AICPA adapted)

Requirement 1:
Below we have computed the cost of goods sold and the cost of ending inventory under the FIFO method.

FIFO

FIFO

January 12	150 @ $18		$2,700
January 30	50 @ $18		900
	50 @ $20		1,000
Units sold	250	Cost of goods sold	$4,600

Now we know how many units are no longer in inventory, and we can compute the ending balance from the units remaining.

Remaining in ending inventory:
FIFO

	50 @ $20	$1,000
	100 @ $22	2,200
	150 units	**$3,200**

The cost of ending inventory under FIFO is $3,200. We can use the same method to find the cost of ending inventory under LIFO.

Requirement 2:
LIFO

January 12	100 @ $22		$2,200
	50 @ $20		1,000
January 30	50 @ $20		1,000
	50 @ $18		900
Units sold	250	Cost of goods sold	$5,100

Since City Stationers, Inc., does not use perpetual inventory records, we do not need to worry about the dates of the purchases and sales.

LIFO ending inventory: 150 @ $18 = $2,700

Under LIFO, ending inventory is $500 less than it is under FIFO, or $2,700.

E8-3. Account analysis
(AICPA adapted)

We can find cost of goods sold for 1998 by analyzing the inventory account.

Inventory

Beginning balance	$X		
Purchases	$315,000		
(Cash + increase in accounts payable)			
		??	Cost of goods sold (solve for)
Ending balance	$X - 10,000		

Purchases can be found by adding together the disbursements for purchases of merchandise ($290,000) and the increase in trade accounts payable ($25,000).

We know that the ending balance in inventory is $10,000 less than the beginning balance. If we began with $X, and purchased $315,000, and ended with $X - 10,000, we must have sold all $315,000 that was purchased plus $10,000 of beginning inventory. Cost of goods sold is $325,000—total purchases plus the decrease in merchandise inventory.

E8-4. Account analysis
(AICPA adapted)

To find Dumas' sales for 1998, we need to first look at the inventory T-account.

Finished Goods Inventory

Beginning balance	$45,000		
Cost of goods manufactured	340,000		
		X	Solve for: Cost of goods sold
Ending balance	$52,000		

Since we already know cost of goods manufactured, we do not need to analyze work in process inventory.

We can solve for cost of goods sold:
$45,000 + $340,000 - X = $52,000
X = $333,000

Now that we know cost of goods sold, we can solve for sales using this figure and the gross profit amount given. Gross profit is the difference between sales revenue and cost of goods sold. So to find sales, we need only add cost of goods sold to gross profit. Sales in 1998 would be:

$$\$333,000 + \$96,000 = \underline{\$429,000}$$

E8-5. Account analysis
(AICPA adapted)

In this problem, we need to determine the accuracy of the inventory account. We know that cost of goods sold is 70% of sales [70% of $3,000,000 = $2,100,000]. Now let's examine the T-account to see if our estimate is matched.

Inventory

Beginning balance	$550,000		
Purchases	2,250,000		
		X	Cost of goods sold
Ending balance	$600,000		

Solve for X as you would if you did not know the answer.

$550,000 + $2,250,000 - $600,000 = X
X = **$2,200,000**

The amount we solved for is $100,000 more than cost of goods sold found using the gross margin percentage ($2,200,000 - $2,100,000). We would estimate the cost of missing inventory at $100,000.

E8-6. Account analysis
(AICPA adapted)

To solve for ending work in process inventory (WIP), we need to analyze the other two inventory accounts to find the missing numbers. First, we will look at raw materials (RM).

Raw Materials			
Beginning RM	$30,000		
Purchases	115,000		
		X	RM transferred to WIP (direct materials)
Ending RM	$62,000		

We can now solve for X (direct materials).
$30,000 + $115,000 - $62,000 = X
X = **$83,000**

Now we have direct materials of $83,000 to plug into WIP. But we also need to know cost of goods manufactured, so we must analyze finished goods (FG).

Finished Goods			
Beginning FG	$140,000		
Cost of goods manufactured	X		
		$255,000	Cost of goods sold
Ending FG	$119,000		

(Cost of goods sold is 75% of sales of $340,000 or $255,000.)

Once again we can solve for X:
- $140,000 + $119,000 + $255,000 = X
X = **$234,000**

Now that we have direct materials and cost of goods manufactured, we can solve for the ending balance of WIP inventory.

320

Work In Process

Beginning WIP	$100,000		
Direct materials	83,000		
Direct labor	80,000		
Manufacturing overhead	40,000		
		$234,000	Cost of goods manufactured
Ending WIP	X		

Finally, we can now solve for ending WIP.
$100,000 + $83,000 + $80,000 + $40,000 - $234,000 = X
X = $69,000

Ending work in process inventory is $69,000.

E8-7. Cost flow computations
(AICPA adapted)

To find ending inventory under these methods, we need some information that is not given directly. We need to know how many units have been sold. To find this number, we can sum the purchases (4,200 units) and beginning inventory (800 units) to find the units available for sale (5,000). Next, we subtract the units on hand (1,600) from the units available. This figure (3,400) is the number of units that have been sold. Now that we know the number of units sold, we first compute the cost of goods sold under each method.

Requirement 1:
FIFO

Sold:

800	@ $9		$7,200
1,500	@ $10		15,000
1,100	@ $10.50		11,550
3,400		Cost of goods sold	$33,750

Since we now know cost of goods sold, and beginning inventory and purchases were given, we can compute ending inventory from an analysis of the inventory T-account.

Inventory

Beginning balance	$7,200		
Purchases	44,550		
		$33,750	Cost of goods sold
Ending inventory	X		

$7,200 + $44,550 - $33,750 = X
X = $18,000

We can use the same procedure for LIFO and weighted average.

Requirement 2:
LIFO

Sold:

900	@ $11.50		$10,350
600	@ $11		6,600
1,200	@ $10.50		12,600
700	@ $10		7,000
3,400		Cost of goods sold	$36,550

Inventory

Beginning balance	$7,200		
Purchases	44,550		
		$36,550	Cost of goods sold
Ending balance	X		

$7,200 + $44,550 - $36,550 = X
X = $15,200

Requirement 3:
Weighted average

Sold:

3,400 @ $10.35[1] **Cost of goods sold $35,190**

[1] The computation of the weighted average unit price is as follows:

800	@ $9		$7,200
1,500	@ $10		15,000
1,200	@ $10.50		12,600
600	@ $11		6,600
900	@ $11.50		10,350
Total inventory cost			$51,750
Total inventory units			5,000
Weighted average cost per unit			**$10.35**

Inventory

Beginning balance	$7,200		
Purchases	44,550		
		$35,190	Cost of goods sold
Ending balance	X		

$7,200 + $44,550 - $35,190 = X
X = $16,560

E8-8. Absorption versus variable costing
(AICPA adapted)

Requirement 1:
Finished goods inventory under variable (direct) costing.

Finished Goods Inventory

Beginning balance	0		
Cost of goods manufactured	$630,000		
		?	Cost of goods sold
Ending balance	**X**		

To begin, we know cost of goods manufactured and the beginning balance. We need to find cost of goods sold in order to find ending inventory. To do this, we must identify the cost to make one unit. We can obtain this number by dividing the variable cost of goods manufactured ($630,000) by the number of units manufactured, which is given as 70,000. From this calculation, we get $9 per item as the variable cost. With this number, we can find cost of goods sold. Cost of goods sold is equal to the cost to produce each unit multiplied by the number of units sold, 60,000. So cost of goods sold is $9 × 60,000 = $540,000. With cost of goods sold, we can solve for ending inventory in the following schedule:

Beginning inventory	$0
+ Cost of goods manufactured	630,000
Total goods available for sale	630,000
− Ending inventory (solve for)	X = $90,000
Cost of goods sold	$540,000

Peterson's ending inventory under the variable costing method would be $90,000.

Requirement 2:
Operating income under absorption costing is computed below.

Net sales		$1,400,000
Cost of goods sold:		
Variable	540,000	
Fixed	270,000	(810,000)
Gross margin		590,000
Operating expenses:		
Variable	98,000	
Fixed	140,000	(238,000)
Operating income		$352,000

Absorption costing includes fixed manufacturing costs in inventory. To find the fixed manufacturing cost portion of cost of goods sold, we take:

$315,000/70,000 units produced = $4.50 × 60,000 units sold = $270,000

Under absorption costing, operating (SG&A) expenses are treated as period costs, and, therefore, the entire amount ($238,000) is expensed.

E8-9. Absorption versus variable costing
(AICPA adapted)

Requirement 1:
To find the cost of finished goods inventory at December 31, 1998, we first need to find cost of goods sold for the year; then we will use a T-account analysis to obtain a figure for ending inventory. To find cost of goods sold under the direct costing method, we have to allocate all variable manufacturing costs to the number of units produced and determine direct cost for the 10,000 units produced.

Direct materials	$40,000
Direct labor	20,000
Variable factory overhead	12,000
Variable manufacturing cost	$72,000

Variable manufacturing cost per unit = $72,000/10,000 = $7.20
Cost of goods sold = $7.20 × 9,000 = $64,800

Now that we know cost of goods sold, we can analyze at the finished goods inventory T-account.

Finished Goods Inventory			
Beginning balance	0		
Variable cost of goods manufactured	$72,000		
		$64,800	Cost of goods sold
Ending balance	**X**		

$72,000 - $64,800 = X
X = $7,200

Requirement 2:

Cost of goods manufactured under absorption costing is computed as follows:

Direct materials	$40,000
Direct labor	20,000
Variable factory overhead	12,000
Fixed factory overhead	25,000
Full manufacturing cost	$97,000

Full manufacturing cost per unit = $97,000/10,000 = $9.70
Cost of goods sold = $9.70 × 9,000 = $87,300

Therefore, comparative total expense would be:

	Variable Costing	Absorption Costing
Cost of goods sold	$64,800	$87,300
Variable selling and administrative	4,500	4,500
Fixed factory overhead (100%)	25,000	
	$94,300	$91,800

Operating Income under absorption costing would be $2,500 higher than under variable costing since absorption expenses are $2,500 lower (i.e., $94,300 - $91,800).

E8-10. Change to LIFO method
(AICPA adapted)

	1999
Final inventory	
FIFO	$270,000
LIFO	210,000
Difference in ending inventory	$60,000
Net Income	
FIFO	$170,000
LIFO ($170,000 - $60,000)	$110,000

When LIFO is adopted, it is generally very difficult to determine what the LIFO inventory costs would have been in prior years. Therefore, in the year of the change, the base inventory is taken to be the beginning inventory under the "old" inventory method (in this case, the FIFO inventory value of $240,000).

Therefore, the effect of the inventory change on the current period's net income is simply the difference between ending inventory under LIFO ($210,000) and ending inventory under FIFO ($270,000) or $60,000. Because LIFO ending inventory is *lower*, this means that LIFO cost of goods sold would be *higher* than under FIFO, and net income would be correspondingly

$60,000 lower under LIFO. (The instructor should point out that this computation ignores taxes.)

E8-11. Inventory errors
(CMA adapted)

The easiest way for students to visualize inventory error adjustment is to use the cost of goods sold formula and analyze the errors one at a time. Starting with the 1997 error and assuming beginning 1997 inventory was correctly stated:

	1997 Error
Beginning inventory	None
Plus: Purchases	None
Equals: Goods available	None
Minus: Ending inventory	overstated by $23,000
Equals: Cost of goods sold	understated by $23,000

Since cost of goods sold is understated due to the ending inventory overstatement, 1997's income is overstated by $23,000. Corrected 1997 income is:

$138,000 - $23,000 = $115,000.

Moving on to 1998, the December 31, 1997 ending inventory becomes the beginning 1998 inventory. Therefore, two adjustments must be made to 1998 income—one for the feedforward effect of the 1997 error and another for the $61,000 1998 understatement.

	1997 Error	**1998 Error**
Beginning inventory	overstated by $23,000	None
Plus: Purchases	None	None
Equals: Goods available	overstated by $23,000	None
Minus: Ending inventory	None	understated by $61,000
Equals: Cost of goods sold	overstated by $23,000	overstated by $61,000

Therefore, 1998 cost of goods sold is overstated by $84,000, and income is understated by this amount. The corrected 1998 income is $254,000 + $84,000 = $338,000.

The 1999 computation is:

	1998 Error	**1999 Error**
Beginning inventory	understated by $61,000	None
Plus: Purchases	None	None
Equals: Goods available	understated by $61,000	None
Minus: Ending inventory	None	understated by $17,000
Equals: Cost of goods sold	understated by $61,000	overstated by $17,000

Therefore, 1999 cost of goods sold is understated by $44,000.
1999 corrected income is $168,000 - $44,000 = $124,000.

E8-12. Lower of cost or market
(AICPA adapted)

Moore should use the historical cost of $45 in pricing product #2 ending inventory. The rule is the lower of cost or market. The replacement cost of $46 is between the ceiling ($74) and floor ($44) and is higher than historical cost.

Ending inventory for product #1 is priced at $16 per unit ($25 NRV less $9 profit), which is the floor.

E8-13. Dollar-value LIFO
(AICPA adapted)

To compute ending inventory at base year prices, we need to divide the year-end prices of each year by the respective price index, then separate the layers to compute ending inventory at LIFO Cost. Here are the computations:

Year Ended December 31,	Inventory at Respective Year-End Prices	External Price Index (Base Year 1996)	Inventory at Base Year (1996) Price
1997	$363,000	1.10	$330,000
1998	$420,000	1.20	$350,000
1999	$430,000	1.25	$344,000

<u>December 31, 1997</u>
Base $300,000
1997 layer at 1997 cost: ($330,000 - $300,000 = $30,000 × 1.10)   <u>33,000</u>
$333,000

<u>December 31, 1998</u>
Base $300,000
1997 layer at 1997 cost 33,000
1998 layer at 1998 cost: ($350,000 - $330,000 = $20,000 × 1.20)   <u>24,000</u>
$357,000

<u>December 31, 1999</u>
Base $300,000
1997 layer at 1997 cost 33,000
1998 layer at 1998 cost: ($344,000 - $350,0000) = ($6,000);
($6,000) + $20,000= $14,000 × 1.20)   <u>16,800</u>
$349,800

E8-14. Dollar-value LIFO
(AICPA adapted)

The computation of dollar value LIFO can be seen below. The first step is to find the base-year price of ending inventory. We can do this by dividing ending inventory at year-end prices by the price index. The next step is to separate the layers at base-year prices and use the price indices to find ending inventory at LIFO Cost as is done below.

Ending inventory	Price Index	Base-Year Price
$780,000	1.2	$650,000

Layers at Base-Year Price	Price Index	Ending Inventory at LIFO Cost
$600,000	1.0	$600,000
<u>$50,000</u>	1.2	<u>60,000</u>
<u>$650,000</u>		<u>$660,000</u>

E8-15. Inventory costing concepts
(AICPA adapted)

Requirement 1:
Description of fundamental cost flow assumption:

a) It is difficult, if not impossible, to measure the physical flow of goods and, therefore, to cost items on an average price basis provides a better representation. Average cost is usually justified on the basis of practicality. It is simple to apply and not as susceptible to income manipulation as other methods.

b) The first-in-first-out (FIFO) method assumes that goods are used or sold in the order they were purchased, and, therefore, the remaining inventory represents the most recent purchases. One objective of FIFO is to approximate the physical flow of inventory.

c) Last-in-first-out (LIFO) matches the cost of the most recent goods purchased with revenue—a measure of the existing margin at the time of sale.

Requirement 2:
Reasons for using LIFO in an inflationary environment:

In an inflationary economy, LIFO is a useful tool. When using LIFO, as prices rise, the company's cost of goods sold expense also rises because it is assumed the sale is always the most recent inventory purchase. So, as prices go up, cost of goods sold goes up, and net income is decreased. The company will pay less in income tax, because reported income is lower.

Requirement 3:
Proper accounting treatment when utility of goods is below cost:

The prevailing accounting treatment in this case is to value the inventory at the *lower of cost or market.* Lower of cost or market can be justified by the convention of conservatism. Accountants tend to prefer conservative asset measures. Relevance can also be used to defend the lower of cost or market convention. Accountants generally believe that, in asset impairment situations, historical cost is no longer a relevant measure of carrying value. As discussed in the text, however, there are many conceptual and pragmatic problems with the lower of cost or market method.

Problems
P8-1. Account analysis

Requirement 1:
Computation of cost of raw materials used:

Cost of raw materials used = Beginning balance in raw material inventory + Purchases of raw materials - Ending balance in raw material inventory

= $34,000 + $116,000 - $38,000
= $112,000

Requirement 2:
Computation of cost of goods manufactured/completed:

Cost of goods manufactured = Beginning balance in work in process inventory + Raw materials used + Wages to factory workers + Salaries to factory supervisors + Depreciation on factory building + Utilities for factory building - Ending balance in work in process inventory

= $126,000 + $112,000 + $55,000 + $25,000 + $10,000 + $5,000 - $145,000
= $188,000

Requirement 3:
Computation of cost of goods sold:

Cost of goods sold = Beginning balance in finished goods inventory + Cost of goods manufactured - Ending balance in finished goods inventory

= $76,000 + $188,000 - $68,000 = $196,000

Requirement 4:
Computation of gross margin:

Gross margin = Sales - Cost of goods sold

= $300,000 - $196,000 = $104,000

Requirement 5:
Computation of net income:

Net income = Gross margin - Salary to selling and administration staff - Depreciation on office building - Utilities for office building - Provision for income tax

$$= \$104,000 - \$40,000 - \$12,000 - \$7,500 - \$17,800 = \underline{\$26,700}$$

P8-2. Inventory accounting—comprehensive

Requirement 1:
Ending inventory and cost of goods sold under FIFO, weighted average, and LIFO

	Cost of Ending Inventory	Cost of Goods Sold
FIFO	5,500 × $4.75 = $26,125 6,500 × $5.00 = 32,500 $58,625	$40,000 + $32,800 + $51,600 + $33,375 + $2,375 = $160,150 or $218,775 - $58,625 = $160,150
Weighted Average	Unit Cost: 218,775/50,000 = $4.3755 Ending inventory: 12,000 × 4.3755 = $52,506	38,000 × $4.3755 = $166,269
LIFO	10,000 × $4.00 = $40,000 2,000 × $4.10 = 8,200 $48,200	$32,500 + $28,500 + $33,375 + $51,600 + $24,600 = $170,575 or $218,775 - $48,200 = $170,575

Requirement 2:
Replacement cost of ending inventory and LIFO reserve.

a) Replacement cost of the ending inventory = 12,000 × $5.00 $60,000
    Less: book value of LIFO inventory   (48,200)
    LIFO reserve at the end of the year $11,800

b) Cost of goods sold under FIFO (periodic).

FIFO COGS = LIFO COGS + Beginning LIFO reserve - Ending LIFO reserve

= $170,575 + 0 - $11,800
= $158,775

As discussed in the text, the reconciliation procedure is an approximation. Adding the LIFO reserve to the LIFO inventory equals replacement cost. If the inventory turns quickly, then inventory replacement cost *approximates* FIFO inventory. But the adjustment will seldom be exact. This explains the difference between the FIFO cost of goods sold number in Requirement 1 and the FIFO number in this requirement.

c) Pros and cons of the accountant's suggestions.

Pros:
Under periodic LIFO, COGS is computed at 12/31/98, i.e., year-end. Therefore, the 10,000 units acquired on 12/31/98 would be included in the COGS for the year 1998. This increases the COGS for the year and reduces the net income which results in a tax savings.

COGS with the 10,000 units: $(10,000 \times \$5) + (6,500 \times \$5) + (6,000 \times \$4.75) + (7,500 \times \$4.45) + (8,000 \times \$4.30)$
=$178,775

Increase in COGS = $178,775 - $170,575 = $8,200

Tax savings = $8,200 \times 0.40 = \$3,280$.

Cons:
Inventory carrying cost is higher, and the company is exposed to the risk of an unexpected fall in demand.

Requirement 3:
This will be the same as the periodic FIFO method.

Proof:

Cost of Goods Sold under Perpetual FIFO

Date of Sale	Units	Cost/Unit	Total Cost
March 1	7,000	$4.00	$28,000
Sept. 1	3,000	4.00	12,000
	8,000	4.10	32,800
	9,000	4.30	38,700
	20,000		
Dec. 1	3,000	4.30	12,900
	7,500	4.45	33,375
	500	4.75	2,375
	11,000		
			$160,150

Total COGS under Perpetual FIFO = \$160,150 = COGS under Periodic FIFO

Regardless of whether periodic or perpetual inventory procedure is used, the cost of goods sold and ending inventory values will be the same under FIFO cost flow assumption. However, the answers will typically be different under LIFO. Under FIFO, the units purchased on January 1 will be assigned to cost of goods sold first, irrespective of when cost of goods sold is calculated. On the other hand, identifying the most *recent* units purchased depends on when the calculations are performed. For instance, if LIFO cost of goods sold is calculated on September 1, the units purchased on April 12 will be the first assigned to the cost of goods sold. If the calculation is performed on December 31, then the units purchased on December 29 will be the first assigned to the cost of goods sold. Under perpetual LIFO, the cost of goods sold is calculated every time a new sale is made. On the other hand, the cost of goods sold under periodic LIFO is calculated only once at the end of the accounting period. Consequently, they usually result in different values under perpetual and periodic procedures.

P8-3. LIFO liquidation

Requirement 1:
Effect on cost of goods sold (COGS)

COGS effect = pre-tax effect on income of LIFO liquidation

$$\text{Pre-tax effect} = \frac{\text{After-tax effect}}{1 - \text{tax rate}} = \frac{\$36,000}{1 - .40} = \$60,000$$

Requirement 2:
Effect on 1998 taxes

Taxes were \$24,000 *higher* because income was higher as a result of the liquidation.

$$\begin{array}{r} \$60,000 \\ \times\ .40 \\ \hline \$24,000 \\ \hline \end{array}$$

Requirement 3:
The average cost per unit of the 10,000 units removed from the January 1, 1998 LIFO inventory was:

Let X = historical cost of units liquidated

Pre-tax effect of liquidation = (replacement cost - historical cost) × units liquidated

$60,000 = ($22 - X)10,000$
$60,000 = 220,000 - 10,000X$
$-160,000 = -10,000X$
$X = $16/unit$

Requirement 4:
The January 1, 1998 LIFO cost of inventory was:

$$
\begin{array}{lll}
20,000 \text{ units @ } \$13 & = & \$260,000 \\
10,000 \text{ units @ } \$16 & = & \underline{\$160,000} \\
& & \$420,000
\end{array}
$$

Requirement 5:
The reported 1998 cost of goods sold for Ruedy Company was:

Beginning inventory	$420,000
+ Purchases (20,000 units @ $22)	440,000
Total cost of goods available for sale	860,000
- Ending inventory	(260,000)
= Cost of goods sold	$600,000

P8-4. Criteria for choosing a cost flow assumption

Responses to each of the issues raised follow.

1. Use of FIFO will produce both higher income and higher working capital and, thus, help satisfy the covenants.

2. FIFO would lead to higher income and, hence, higher bonuses.

3. This is not possible due to the LIFO conformity rule.

4. If firms dip into the LIFO layers when inventory levels are falling, then they may have to pay taxes on LIFO liquidations (i.e., cumulative holding gains from inflation). FIFO cannot solve the problem, since we would have paid the taxes earlier under FIFO. In terms of present value, therefore, we are much better off under LIFO which defers tax payments until liquidation occurs.

5. This is not possible. LIFO ensures better matching, but FIFO generates a more current inventory value in the balance sheet.

6. Not necessarily. If securities markets are "efficient," then higher income due to a different accounting method does not ensure a higher stock price, especially when sophisticated investors can estimate the amount of realized holding gains in reported FIFO income.

P8-5. Inventory alternatives

Requirement 1:
Units in ending inventory = units purchased - units sold = 72,000 - 62,000
= 10,000.

Cost of Goods Sold under Periodic FIFO

	Units	Cost/Unit	Total
January 1, 1998	20,000	$7.00	$140,000
March 1, 1998	16,000	9.00	144,000
June 1, 1998	14,000	11.00	154,000
September 1, 1998	10,000	13.00	130,000
December 1, 1998	2,000	15.00	30,000
	62,000		$598,000

Ending Inventory under Periodic FIFO

	Units	Cost/Unit	Total
December 1, 1998	10,000	$15.00	$150,000
	10,000		$150,000

Gross Margin = $984,000 - $598,000 = $386,000

Requirement 2:

Cost of Goods Sold under Periodic LIFO

	Units	Cost/Unit	Total
January 1, 1998	10,000	$7.00	$70,000
March 1, 1998	16,000	9.00	144,000
June 1, 1998	14,000	11.00	154,000
September 1, 1998	10,000	13.00	130,000
December 1, 1998	12,000	15.00	180,000
	62,000		$678,000

Ending Inventory under Periodic LIFO

	Units	Cost/Unit	Total
January 1, 1998	10,000	$7.00	$70,000
	10,000		$70,000

Gross Margin = $984,000 - $678,000 = $306,000

The company has to disclose the ending LIFO reserve under the LIFO method.

Replacement cost of ending inventory (10,000 × 15)	=	$150,000
Less: LIFO cost of ending inventory	=	(70,000)
Ending LIFO reserve	=	$80,000

Since the company started doing business only during 1998, there is no beginning LIFO reserve.

FIFO COGS = LIFO COGS + Beginning LIFO reserve - Ending LIFO reserve

= $678,000 + 0 - $80,000
= $598,000

Requirement 3:

Date	Units Sold	Current Output Price	Current Input Price	True Operating Margin
March 2, 1998	24,000	$14/unit	$9/unit	$120,000
Sept. 2, 1998	18,000	16/unit	13/unit	54,000
Dec. 2, 1998	20,000	18/unit	15/unit	60,000
				$234,000

Requirement 4:
a) The LIFO inventory accounting method does a good job of matching revenues and expenses during both inflationary and deflationary times. The one major exception to this is when a company experiences declining inventory levels (LIFO liquidation).

b) The specific identification method matches the physical flow of goods with revenue. However this is not the objective of the matching principle. The objective is to match the revenue flow with the cost flow. The specific identification method is appropriate only for larger valued items with high variance in their prices/costs and/or inventories that are customized (e.g., jewelry, construction projects, car dealerships, etc.). Also, managers have discretion to manipulate earnings under the specific identification method of inventory accounting because they can "choose" which items to sell.

c) Given the inflationary situation faced by the company, the FIFO inventory accounting method can be used to maximize current profits. However, the specific identification method of inventory accounting can be used to achieve a high profit too.

d) Given the inflationary situation faced by the company, the LIFO inventory accounting method can be used to minimize current profits and, hence, minimize the present value of future income tax outflows. However, the specific identification method of inventory accounting can be "tailored" to show the lowest profit in a given year and, hence, could also be used to "minimize" the present value of future income tax outflows.

e) This is not allowed. Under the LIFO conformity rule, if a company uses LIFO for tax purposes, it must choose LIFO for financial reporting purposes also. Consequently, B.T. Kang's suggestion cannot be implemented.

P8-6. Inventory turnover

Requirement 1:
FIFO COGS = LIFO COGS + Beginning LIFO reserve - Ending LIFO reserve

= $89,970,702 + $6,828,615 - $8,085,250
= $88,714,067

Cost of Goods Manufactured

Finished goods beginning balance	$39,328,177
FIFO cost of goods manufactured **(plug number)**	85,535,699
FIFO COGS (from above)	(88,714,067)
Finished goods ending balance	$36,149,809

Requirement 2:

	FIFO
Cost of goods sold	$88,714,067
Average finished goods inventory	37,738,993
Finished goods inventory turnover ratio	2.35
Number of days to sell finished goods	155
Cost of goods manufactured	$85,535,699
Average WIP inventory	6,512,778
WIP inventory turnover	13.13
Number of days for manufacture	28

It takes Baldwin, on average, 28 days to manufacture pianos and another 155 days to sell them. WIP turnover (in days) appears consistent (or at least not inconsistent) with the production process for piano manufacture. More importantly, the finished goods turnover (in days) is quite consistent with its consignment sales approach. Consider the following statement from its annual report:

The Company charges a monthly display fee on all consigned inventory held by dealers longer than ninety days. This display fee, on an annual basis, ranges from 12% to 16% of the selling price of such inventory to the dealer. Display fee income comprises the majority of the amount reported in the consolidated statements of earnings as "other operating income, net."

The finished goods turnover suggests that, on average, Baldwin Piano earned a 14% (mean of 12% and 16%) display fee for 65 days (155 - 90) based on its selling price. The expected display fee can be approximated using the total sales revenue as follows (which assumes that all sales are consignment sales); i.e., expected display fee = $120,657,455 × 14% × 65/365 = $3,008,172, which is 85% of other operating income.

One interesting question relates as to why we are calculating FIFO inventory component turnover ratios for a LIFO company. The answer is that we have no choice in the case of Baldwin Piano. Instead of reporting LIFO values of inventory *components* (and then adding the LIFO reserve), Baldwin is disclosing the FIFO values of the inventory components and then subtracting the aggregate LIFO reserve from it. The most likely explanation for this type of disclosure is that Baldwin is probably using FIFO for internal management purposes and converts these numbers to LIFO before financial statements are prepared.

P8-7. Gross margins and cash flow sustainability

Requirement 1:
FIFO income for 1997 is:

Sales revenues:

	Pounds		
lst Qtr:	700,000 @ $8.20 =	$5,740,000	
2nd Qtr:	600,000 @ $8.40 =	5,040,000	
3rd Qtr:	700,000 @ $8.80 =	6,160,000	
4th Qtr:	650,000 @ $9.10 =	5,915,000	
			$22,855,000

Cost of goods sold:

	Pounds		
Beg. Inv.	300,000 @ $7.00 =	$2,100,000	
Purchases:			
1st Qtr:	600,000 @ $7.20 =	4,320,000	
2nd Qtr:	700,000 @ $7.40 =	5,180,000	
3rd Qtr:	800,000 @ $7.80 =	6,240,000	
4th Qtr:	600,000 @ $8.10 =	4,860,000	
Goods available for sale		$22,700,000	
Minus:			
End. Inv.	350,000 @ $8.10	(2,835,000)	
			(19,865,000)
Gross margin			2,990,000
Operating costs			(2,800,000)
Net income			$190,000

338

Requirement 2:

McDowell Corporation did not earn a profit from its operating activities in 1997. This becomes evident after computing the amount of realized holding gains that are automatically included in the $190,000 FIFO net income figure in part 1. The computation is:

Date of Yelpin Cost Change	Amount of Cost Change	Pounds in Inventory	Realizable Holding Gain
Jan. 1, 1997	+20¢	300,000	$60,000
Apr. 1, 1997	+20¢	200,000*	40,000
Jul. 1, 1997	+40¢	300,000**	120,000
Oct. 1, 1997	+30¢	400,000***	120,000
Total			$340,000

	B.I.	+ Purch.	- Sales	
*	300,000	+600,000	- 700,000	= 200,000
**	200,000	+700,000	- 600,000	= 300,000
***	300,000	+800,000	- 700,000	= 400,000

Realizable holding gains (i.e., the holding gains that arose during 1997) totaled $340,000. On a FIFO basis, all of these gains were realized in 1997 and included in income. (Since 4th-quarter sales of 650,000 lbs. exceeded the 10/1/97 inventory of 400,000, FIFO considers all of the 10/1/97 inventory to have been sold in the 4th quarter, and the holding gain was realized.) Using this information, we can dichotomize reported FIFO Income as follows:

1997 FIFO Income
$190,000

1997 Realized Holding
Gains
$340,000

1997 Operating Profit
(Loss)
($150,000)

Thus, it is evident that McDowell reported profits only because yelpin costs were rising in 1997.

Requirement 3:

With current sales volume of 2,650,000 pounds and cash operating costs of $2,800,000, the $1 per pound markup is too low to generate profitable operating performance. This condition was masked by historical cost FIFO accounting since the operating loss of $150,000 was more than offset by the realized holding gains of $340,000 that are automatically included (undisclosed) in FIFO income.

Under these conditions, McDowell's ability to repay the loan from operating profits (which are identical to operating cash flows in this instance) is problematic. Given the company's average quarter-end inventory levels, if yelpin costs start declining, FIFO losses would ensue, *certeris paribus*.

P8-8. Evaluating inventory cost-flow changes

Requirement 1:
"Better matching of revenues and expenses . . ."
- Matching does not refer to the physical flow of goods, but rather to cost-flow assumptions.
- LIFO better matches current costs to current sales.
- Unless customers have a choice of which particular unit to buy (as in the case of, say, used cars), management may be able to manipulate cost recognition to produce desired earnings and balance sheet presentations.

"Better correlation of accounting and financial information . . ."
- This is a very ambiguous statement. Without additional explanation of "the method by which the company in managed," it is difficult to gauge its validity.
- Overall, it is difficult to believe that a product line for which LIFO was deemed applicable in the past would be better served now by specific identification.

"Better presentation of inventories . . ."
- LIFO provides more information because of the requirement to disclose LIFO reserve.
- Under specific identification, financial statement users will not know whether the inventory balance contains new costs, old costs, or a mixture.
- As noted under point 1), the opportunity for managerial manipulation exists. If customers are able to choose which unit(s) they buy, why was LIFO used in the past?

Requirement 2:
"Conform all inventories . . . to the same method of valuation."
- This would simplify the analyst's task.

"Reflects more recent costs in the balance sheet . . ."
- If input costs are changing, the average cost method will reflect more recent costs than LIFO would.
- However, if the objective is to reflect more recent costs on the balance sheet, then FIFO is superior to the average cost method.

"Better matching of current costs with current revenues . . ."
- If the company expects to reduce its inventory levels, LIFO liquidation would distort margins, so the average cost method would be preferable.
- In "an economic environment of low inflation," the average cost method would presumably lead to minimal margin distortion.

340

P8-9. Inter-firm comparisons

Requirement 1:

	Fraser	KAS
Gross margin rate (Gross margin/sales)	40.0%	49%
Return on sales (Net income/sales)	17.5%	21%
Inventory turnover COGS/average inventory	3.4	1.8

The above figures indicate why the CEO was concerned about the performance of Fraser. A mechanical comparison of the ratios suggests that Fraser has lower gross margin and return on sales, whereas it appears to have better inventory turnover. However, the comparisons are substantially affected by the choice of inventory accounting methods. Regardless of whether prices are increasing or decreasing, LIFO typically provides a better job of matching current period revenues with current cost of goods sold except when there is LIFO liquidation. In this problem, since the book value of inventory has increased more than 30% over the year, it appears that LIFO liquidation is not an issue here.

In addition, it appears the company is facing rising input costs. The table below shows that the LIFO reserve of the company has increased from 33% of LIFO inventory value to 75%. This is consistent with the increase in input costs over the year.

	Ending	Beginning
LIFO inventory	$200,000	$150,000
LIFO reserve	$150,000	$ 50,000
LIFO reserve as % of LIFO inventory	75.0%	33.3%

During periods of increasing costs, LIFO will lead to higher values for cost of goods sold, and, *ceteris paribus*, LIFO companies are likely to report lower gross margin rates when compared to FIFO companies. This is an important factor that might potentially explain the lower profit margins.

In contrast, the inventory turnover ratio under LIFO is likely to be biased upwards when prices are increasing. This is because the denominator of the inventory turnover is biased downward. In general, FIFO inventory values reasonably approximate the current value of inventory. The table which follows indicates that LIFO inventories' values are between 57% and 75% of the current value of the inventory. Consequently, the LIFO inventory turnover ratio will be higher during periods of rising prices, and, therefore, Fraser's higher reported turnover does not imply that it has better inventory management.

	Ending	Beginning
FIFO inventory (see Requirement 2)	$350,000	$200,000
LIFO inventory	$200,000	$150,000
LIFO inventory as % of FIFO inventory	57.14%	75.00%

Requirement 2:

Let us first try to re-state the financial statements of Fraser under FIFO accounting:

Sales Revenue		$1,000,000
Less: cost of goods sold		
Beginning inventory	200,000	
Add: purchases	650,000	
Less: ending inventory	(350,000)	
		(500,000)
Gross profit		500,000
Less: selling and administrative expenses		(150,000)
Net income before taxes		350,000
Less: income taxes		(105,000)
Net income		$245,000

Based on the LIFO income statement, it is assumed the tax rate is 30% ($75,000 divided by $250,000). Using the FIFO numbers, we now recalculate the ratios for Fraser and compare them to KAS:

	Fraser	**KAS**	**Difference**
Gross margin rate (Gross margin/sales)	50.0%	49%	+1.0%
Return on sales (Net Income/sales)	24.5%	21%	+3.5%
Inventory turnover COGS/average inventory	1.82	1.80	+0.02

The table suggests that, once we control for differences in the accounting methods, the superiority in the inventory turnover disappears. (The term "superiority" is used loosely because very high inventory turnover may lead to large stockout costs.) Both companies seem to have similar turnover ratios.

On the other hand, the apparent superiority of KAS in terms of gross margin vanishes once we restate Fraser's income statement using FIFO. In fact, Fraser seem to have slightly higher gross margin rate (a difference of 1%).

One interesting comparison is with respect to return on sales. How does Fraser's return on sales become 3.5 percentage points higher than that of KAS when its gross margin rate is only one percent higher? To explain this, note that Fraser's selling and administrative expenses (S&A expenses) are 15% of sales revenue ($150,000/$1,000,000). Let us try to infer the S&A expenses of KAS. For this purpose, we will assume that KAS's tax rate is also 30%. Given that KAS's after-tax return on sales is 21%, its pre-tax return on sales is 30% (i.e., .21/(1 - 0.30)).

	KAS
Gross margin rate (Gross margin/sales)	49%
Pre-tax return on sales	30%
S&A expenses as a % of sales	19%

Given that KAS's gross margin rate is 49% and its pre-tax return on sales is 30%, its S&A expenses must be 19% (assuming it has no other expenses). This suggests that Fraser has better control over its S&A expenses which are only 15% of sales revenue. The following table summarizes the total difference in the performance between the two companies.

Fraser vs. KAS

Difference in gross margin rate	1.0%
Difference in S&A expenses	4.0%
Difference in pre-tax return on sales	5.0%

At a pre-tax level, Fraser is, in fact, earning a return on sales that is five percentage points higher than KAS, which converts to the 3.5% after-tax difference that was noted earlier (24.5% minus 21%).

A final note is that Fraser is probably doing even better than what is indicated by the above table. Note that, by using LIFO, Fraser is paying lower taxes. If Fraser continues to grow in the future, then this tax savings is retained indefinitely. To get some idea of the additional advantage this gives Fraser, we can re-calculate Fraser's income statement by subtracting its LIFO taxes from the FIFO income:

Sales revenue		$1,000,000
Less: cost of goods sold		
Beginning inventory	$200,000	
Add: purchases	650,000	
Less: ending inventory	(350,000)	
		(500,000)
Gross profit		500,000
Less: selling and administrative expenses		(150,000)
Net income before taxes		350,000
Less: income taxes		(75,000)
Net income		$275,000

343

Based on this income statement, we can recalculate return on sales as follows:

	Fraser	KAS
Return on Sales	27.5%	21%
(Net income/sales)		

Once we consider the effect of potential tax savings, then the superiority of Fraser is even more noticeable. Fraser's return on sales is now 6.5% higher than that of KAS.

P8-10. LIFO and ratio effects

Requirement 1:
Cost of goods manufactured:

Finished Goods Inventory			
Beginning inventory	$2,420	$65,374	Cost of goods sold
Cost of goods manufactured	?		
Ending inventory	$2,684		

Therefore, cost of goods manufactured = $2,684 - $2,420 + $65,374 = $65,638

Finished goods inventory turnover:

$$\frac{\text{Cost of goods sold}}{\text{Average finished goods inventory}} = \frac{\$65,374}{0.5(\$2,684 + \$2,420)} = 25.62$$

$$\frac{365}{25.62} = 14.25 \text{ days}$$

Work-in-process inventory turnover:

$$\frac{\text{Cost of goods manufactured}}{\text{Average work-in-process inventory}} = \frac{\$65,638}{0.5(\$40,285 + \$39,921)} = 1.64$$

$$\frac{365}{1.64} = 233 \text{ days}$$

Comments:

Yes. We know that Bacardi ages its rum for 1–3 years, so we would expect work-in-process turnover to be slow. (In fact, 223 days is shorter than the ex-ante expectation.) Conversely, it makes sense that finished goods turnover is much more rapid. Once the rum is ready for sale, it is shipped quickly.

Requirement 2:
FIFO income (estimate):

FIFO net income = LIFO net income + Change in LIFO reserve (1 - tax rate*)

= $45,568 + ($700 - $20,800) (1 - 0.17)

= $28,885

* Tax rate = 17% per information given in the question.

Comments:

The substantial drop in the LIFO reserve indicates that the price of molasses (the major component of raw materials inventory) has declined considerably during 1982. Hence, Bacardi faces a deflationary situation that results in higher net income under LIFO than under FIFO.

Requirement 3:
Inventory turnover ratio (in days):

$$\frac{\text{LIFO cost of goods sold} + \text{Pre-tax liquidation}}{\text{Avg. LIFO inventory} + \text{Avg. LIFO reserve}} = \frac{\$65,374 - \$1,400 * /(1-0.17)}{0.5(\$53,812 + \$20,800 + \$51,892 + \$700)}$$

$$\frac{\$63,687}{\$63,602} = 1.001$$

$$\frac{365}{1.001} = 364.5 \text{ days}$$

* Recall that liquidation caused a *decrease* in net income.

Comments:

This total turnover measure should reflect the entire conversion process from purchase of raw materials through manufacture and aging up to sale of finished product. Yet the estimate computed above is less than the 1- to 3-year aging schedule disclosed in Bacardi's annual report.

One possible reason for this apparent discrepancy is the equal weight given to beginning and ending LIFO reserves in the denominator, which assumes that price declines have been uniform throughout the year.

P8-11. LIFO inventory—comprehensive

Requirement 1:
FIFO income before taxes.

FIFO income before taxes = LIFO income before taxes + Ending LIFO reserve - Beginning LIFO reserve

1995 FIFO income before taxes = $2,032 + $672 - $1,011
= $1,693 million

1994 FIFO income before taxes = $307 + $1,011 - $648
= $670 million

Requirement 2:
Realized holding gains included in 1995, 1994, and 1993 income before taxes:

1995: $167 million/(1 - 0.35) = $257 million (realized holding gain)

1994: $29 million/(1 - 0.35) = $45 million (realized holding gain)

1993: $10 million/(1 - 0.35) = $15 million (realized holding loss)

Requirement 3:
Explanation of why FIFO income differs from LIFO income.

<u>1995:</u>
FIFO income before taxes is lower by $339 million. To help understand why, we will first reconcile the year-to-year change in the LIFO reserve:

1/1/95 LIFO reserve	$1,011
LIFO liquidation	(257)
Decrease in inventory prices (plugged)	(82)
12/31/95 LIFO reserve	$672

So FIFO income is lower because of two factors, 1) LIFO liquidation and 2) falling inventory prices. The $339 million difference is the sum of $257 + $82.

<u>1994:</u>
FIFO income before taxes is higher by $363 million. Here's why:

1/1/94 LIFO reserve	$648
LIFO liquidation	(45)
Increase in inventory prices (plugged)	408
12/31/94 LIFO reserve	$1,011

So FIFO income is higher by $408 - $45 = $363 million.

Requirement 4:
Total amount of income tax saved at the end of 1995 and 1994.

<u>1995:</u> $672 million × 0.35 = $235.2 million

<u>1994:</u> $1,011 million × 0.35 = $353.9 million

Shell paid $118.7 million ($353.9 - $235.2) more taxes under LIFO during 1995.

Requirement 5:
Unadjusted and adjusted inventory turnover.

Unadjusted inventory turnover ratio:

$$\frac{\$18,051}{(\$567 + \$564)/2} = 31.92 = 11.4 \text{ days}$$

Adjusted inventory turnover ratio:

$$\frac{\$18,051 + \$256.9}{[(\$567 + \$672) + (\$564 + \$1,011)]/2} = 13.01 = 28.1 \text{ days}$$

$256.9 is the pre-tax effect of LIFO liquidation on cost of goods sold. This number is derived as follows: We are told that LIFO liquidation improved *net* income by $167. Assuming a 35% effective tax rate, the pre-tax effect is $167 = X - .35X where X is the pre-tax effect. Solving for X yields $256.9.

P8-12. LIFO reporting—comprehensive

Requirement 1:
Operating income on the LIFO basis:

<u>1997</u>			<u>1998</u>		
Sales revenues:			Sales revenues:		
30,000 @ $3.80 =		$114,000	43,000 @ $4.00 =		$172,000
50,000 @ $3.90 =		195,000	43,000 @ $4.30 =		184,900
		309,000			356,900
Cost of goods sold:			Cost of goods sold:		
40,000 @ $2.70 =	$108,000		40,000 @ $3.00 =	$120,000	
40,000 @ $2.50 =	100,000		40,000 @ $2.75 =	110,000	
		(208,000)	2,000 @ $1.30 =	2,600	
			4,000 @ $1.00 =	4,000	
					(236,600)
Other expenses		(60,000)	Other expenses		(66,000)
Operating income		$41,000	Operating income		$54,300

Requirement 2:
Current cost income from continuing operations

1997			**1998**		
Sales revenues		$309,000	Sales revenues		$356,900
Current cost of goods sold:			Current cost of goods sold:		
30,000 @ $2.50 =	$ 75,000		43,000 @ $2.75 =	$118,250	
50,000 @ $2.70 =	135,000		43,000 @ $3.00 =	129,000	
		(210,000)			(247,250)
Other expenses		(60,000)	Other expenses		(66,000)
Current cost income from continuing operations		$39,000	Current cost income from continuing operations		$43,650

Requirement 3:
Total increase in current cost amounts (realizable cost savings)

1997
Opening inventory = 7,000 units

7,000 × ($2.50 − $2.75)   = $ 700
(Jan.–June current cost)   (July–Dec. current cost)

July 1 inventory = 17,000 units

17,000 × ($2.70 − $2.50)   = 3,400
(July–Dec. current cost)   (Jan.–June current cost)

Total holding gains during 1997 $4,100

1998
Opening inventory = 7,000 units

7,000 × ($2.75 − $2.70)   = $350
(Jan.–June current cost)   (July–Dec. current cost)

July 1 inventory = 4,000 units

4,000 × ($3.00 − $2.75)   = 1,000
(July–Dec. current cost)   (Jan.–June current cost)

Total holding gains during 1998 $1,350

Requirement 4:
Realized holding gains ("inventory profits")

1997		**1998**	
Current cost of goods sold	$210,000	Current cost of goods sold	$247,250
LIFO cost of goods sold	(208,000)	LIFO cost of goods sold	(236,600)
Realized holding gains	$2,000	Realized holding gains	$10,650

Requirement 5:
LIFO reserve in 1996, 1997, and 1998

The answer to this question demonstrates the relationship between LIFO, the LIFO reserve, and current cost. The initial LIFO reserve balance at December 31, 1996, consisted of:

December 31, 1996 current cost of inventory (7,000 units @ $2.40)	$16,800
December 31, 1996 LIFO cost of inventory	7,600
December 31, 1996 LIFO reserve	$9,200

The changes in the LIFO reserve arise because of realizable holding gains (Req. 3) and realized holding gains (Req. 4). To illustrate the numbers:

January 1, 1997 LIFO reserve	$9,200
Plus: Realizable holding gains in 1997 (Req. 3)	4,100
Minus: Realized holding gains in 1997 (Req. 4)	(2,000)
December 31, 1997 LIFO reserve	$11,300[1]

Similarly, for 1998:

January 1, 1998 LIFO reserve	$11,300
Plus: Realizable holding gains in 1998 (Req. 3)	1,350
Minus: Realized holding gains in 1998 (Req. 4)	(10,650)
December 31, 1998 LIFO reserve	$2,000[2]

To summarize, current cost increases cause the LIFO reserve to increase. LIFO dipping reduces the reserve. Seeing the relationship between current cost and LIFO reserves enhances understanding.

Requirement 6:
Explanation of why inventory profits are *not* kept out of income in this case.

Although LIFO is designed to keep inventory profits out of income, it must be remembered that LIFO is, in the final analysis, a historical cost accounting technique. Thus, the charge to cost of goods sold can never exceed the historical cost of the last units in.

---

[1] This result can be "proved" as follows. The 12/31/97 inventory at current cost is 7,000 units @ $2.70 = $18,900. LIFO cost is $7,600. The LIFO reserve is the difference, i.e., $18,900 - 7,600 = $11,300.

[2] The 12/31/98 current cost is 1,000 units @ $3.00 = $3,000. LIFO cost is $1,000. Therefore, the LIFO reserve is $3,000 - $1,000 = $2,000.

Notice that during the last half of 1997, 50,000 units were sold. At that time, the current cost per unit was $2.70. However, Maple Company had purchased only 40,000 units at this price. The LIFO charge for the 10,000 "extra" units had to be made at the January–June purchase cost of $2.50 per unit, which was the LIFO (historical cost) for the next newest layer. Therefore, the LIFO cost of goods sold number for these 10,000 units is 20¢ per unit less (i.e., $2.70 - $2.50) than the current cost at the time of sale. This causes $2,000 of realized holding gains to be included in operating income (i.e., 10,000 units times 20¢ per unit). The general point here is that "inventory profits" can exist under LIFO even when no previous years' LIFO layers have been liquidated. This was clearly the case in 1997 since the number of units in the beginning of the year's inventory equalled the number of units in the end of the year's inventory (7,000).

"Inventory profits" exist in 1998 for a different reason. In 1998, LIFO inventory layers that had accumulated in previous years are depleted. The difference between the LIFO carrying cost of these layers and the current cost at the time of sale constitutes the amount of the realized holding gain. The total, $10,650, can be reconciled as follows:

3,000 unit depletion during second half of 1998 when current
   cost was $3.00:
      3,000 units from 1998 first half layer ($3.00 - $2.75) = $ 750

3,000 unit depletion during first half of 1998 when current
   cost was $2.75:
      2,000 units from 1968 layer ($2.75 - $1.30)   =   2,900
      4,000 units from base layer ($2.75 - $1.00)   =   7,000

     Total inventory profit during 1998 $10,650

One final point. Students are often confused about how the realized holding gain during 1998 ($10,650) can exceed the realizable holding gain that arose during 1998 ($1,350 from Requirement 3). There is no mystery here so long as one understands that the $10,650 consists of realizable holding gains that took place in years prior to 1998. In other words, these are the cumulative holding gains that became realizable from 1960 through 1998 as the current cost of the units represented in the LIFO layers increased.

P8-13. LIFO—comprehensive

Requirement 1:

Year	Cost of goods sold		Ending inventory	
1996	12,000 units × $20 =	$240,000	3,000 units × $20 =	$60,000
1997	18,000 units × $25 =	$450,000	2,000 units × $25 =	$50,000
			3,000 units × $20 =	$60,000
				$110,000
1998	5,000 units × $30 =	$150,000		0
	2,000 units × $25 =	$50,000		
	3,000 units × $20 =	$60,000		
		$260,000		

Requirement 2:

Income statements	1996	1997	1998
Sales revenue	$420,000	$720,000	$400,000
COGS	(240,000)	(450,000)	(260,000)
Gross margin	180,000	270,000	140,000
Operating expenses	(60,000)	(90,000)	(65,000)
Pre-tax income	120,000	180,000	75,000
Tax expense	(48,000)	(72,000)	(30,000)
Net income	$ 72,000	$108,000	$ 45,000

Requirement 3:

<u>1996</u> Since the price changes only at the beginning of the year, there is no LIFO reserve at the end of 1996.

<u>1997</u> 1996 layer. 3,000 units @ ($25 - $20) = $15,000

<u>1998</u> Since there is no ending inventory, there is no LIFO reserve.

Requirement 4:

<u>1997</u> Purchases exceed sales; hence, there is no LIFO liquidation.

<u>1998</u> Replacement cost of layers liquidated:

(2,000 + 3,000) × $30 =	$150,000
Less LIFO cost of layers liquidated	110,000
Effect of LIFO liquidation on COGS	$40,000

Effect of LIFO liquidation on net income
= Effect of LIFO liquidation on COGS × (1 - tax rate)
= $40,000 × (1 - .4) = $24,000

Requirement 5:

Inventory turnover for 1997	Inventory turnover for 1998
COGS/Average inventory	COGS/Average inventory
= $450,000/[($60,000 + $110,000)/2] = 5.294	= $260,000/[($110,000 + 0)/2] = 4.727

1997: ending inventory (the denominator) is understated; hence, the inventory turnover ratio is overstated.

1998: COGS (numerator) is also understated due to LIFO liquidation; hence, the net effect of the numerator and the denominator biases is not obvious.

Requirement 6:

Adjusted inventory turnover for 1997

$$= \frac{\text{COGS} + \text{effect of LIFO liquidation on COGS}}{[(\text{Beg. inventory} + \text{Beg. LIFO reserve}) + (\text{End. inventory} + \text{End. LIFO reserve})]/2}$$

$$= \frac{\$450,000 \quad + \quad 0}{[(110,000 + 15,000) + (60,000 + 0)]/2}$$

$$= 4.8648$$

Adjusted inventory turnover for 1998

$$= \frac{\text{COGS} + \text{effect of LIFO liquidation on COGS}}{[(\text{Beg. inventory} + \text{Beg. LIFO reserve}) + (\text{End. inventory} + \text{End. LIFO reserve})]/2}$$

$$= \frac{\$260,000 \quad + \quad \$40,000}{[(\$110,000 + \$15,000) + 0]/2}$$

$$= 4.8$$

Requirement 7:

Gross margin rate for 1997	Gross margin rate for 1998
($270,000/$720,000) = 37.5%	($140,000/$400,000) = 35%

Gross margin on a per-unit basis: ($40 - $25)/$40 = 37.5% in 1997, and ($40 - $30)/$40 = 25% in 1998. The reported LIFO gross margin rate of 35% in 1998 overstates the "true" gross margin rate because of LIFO liquidation.

Requirement 8:

Estimated FIFO COGS = LIFO COGS + Beginning LIFO reserve - Ending LIFO reserve

<u>1996:</u> $240,000 + 0 - 0   = $240,000

<u>1997:</u> $450,000 + 0 - $15,000   = $435,000

<u>1998:</u> $260,000 + $15,000 - 0   = $275,000

Requirement 9:

<u>1996:</u> 0

<u>1997:</u> $15,000 × 0.40   = $6,000

<u>1998:</u> ($15,000) × 0.40   =   ($6,000)

Requirement 10:

= (6,000 × 0.82645) + (-6,000 × 0.75131)   = <u>$450.84</u>

P8-14. Identifying FIFO holding gains

When inventory levels are constant (or nearly so), a good estimate of realized holding gains included in FIFO Income is:

Beginning inventory × % change in input costs for the year.

One way to estimate the percentage change is to use Fischer Confection's change in LIFO reserve (adjusted for dipping) as a percent of starting inventory value. The computation is:

$$7\% = \frac{\$6,000,000 + \$1,000,000}{\$88,000,000 + \$12,000,000}$$

The denominator is the January 1, 1998 replacement cost of inventory, and the numerator is the change in the LIFO reserve *plus* the LIFO dipping. (The realized holding gains from LIFO dipping are added back to the numerator because these gains *reduce* the LIFO reserve.) Thus, the estimated realized holding gain in 1997 FIFO Income is:

$60,000,000 × 7% = $4,200,000

Another way to estimate the percentage change in Input costs is to use a producer price index for the specific SIC code for Caldwell's output. These price indices are prepared by the U.S. Department of Labor, Bureau of Labor Statistics. The 4% increase in the consumer price index given in the problem is unlikely to approximate the specific input cost increase, except by coincidence.

Cases

C8-1. Barbara Trading Company (KR): Understanding LIFO distortions

Requirement 1:

Since units purchased during 1995 equal units sold, the cost of goods sold under periodic LIFO equals the cost of purchases (i.e., 100,000 × $25). This means that the book value of beginning inventory for 1995 will equal the book value of the ending inventory.

Computation of cost of goods sold for 1996:

	Units	Cost Per Unit	Total Cost
Purchases in 1996	90,000	$30.00	$2,700,000
1980 layer	5,000	12.00	60,000
Base layer	5,000	7.00	35,000
Cost of goods sold for 1996			$2,795,000

The ending inventory for 1996 is $35,000 (5,000 units at $7.00 per unit all from the base layer).

Barbara Trading Company Income Statement For the Years Ended December 31,		
	1996	**1995**
Sales revenue	$4,000,000	$3,500,000
Cost of goods sold	(2,795,000)	(2,500,000)
Gross profit	1,205,000	1,000,000
Operating expenses	(600,000)	(600,000)
Income before tax	605,000	400,000
Income tax (40%)	(242,000)	(160,000)
Net income	$363,000	$240,000

Requirement 2:

Inventory Turnover Ratio =

$$\frac{\text{Cost of goods sold}}{(\text{Beginning inventory} + \text{Ending inventory})/2} = \frac{\$2,795,000}{(\$130,000 + \$35,000)/2} = 33.88 \text{ times}$$

"True" inventory turnover = no. of units sold/average units on hand

$$\frac{100,000}{(15,000 + 5,000)/2} = \frac{100,000}{10,000} = 10 \text{ times}$$

Since information on physical units is available, we can estimate the "true" turnover by calculating the physical inventory turnover ratio. This ratio will avoid any potential biases that may arise from the use of dollar figures generated from various inventory cost flow assumptions. *While a single measure of physical turnover can be easily calculated for a single product firm, it may be hard to define such a measure for multiple product firms.* Consequently, the purpose of this exercise is to merely illustrate the potential limitations of the inventory turnover ratio based on LIFO financial statements.

Limitations of the CEO's analysis

a) Some competitors may be using the FIFO method versus the LIFO method used by Barbara. If the competitors are using FIFO, their "true" turnover may actually be better because FIFO typically does a much better job of measuring inventory turnover.

b) Even if the competitors are using the LIFO method, they may not have very old layers of LIFO inventory as Barbara Trading Company does.

Requirement 3:

a) The true reason for the change in net income is the dip into the LIFO layers. For instance, if the company had purchased 10,000 additional units at $30.00 per unit, then LIFO dipping would not have occurred. In which case, the cost of goods sold would have increased by $205,000 ($3,000,000 - $2,795,000) bringing the gross margin to the same level as last year ($1,000,000). It is not suggested that the company should have purchased more units just to avoid LIFO liquidation. The drop in the inventory level appears to be the result of a conscious change in the inventory management policy. However, this has led to a distortion in the income measurement due to the application of LIFO cost flow assumption.

b) Although the selling price has gone up, the gross margin *per unit* has remained the same. This once again suggests that the financial performance of the company has not changed from the previous year's.

356

c) The operating expenses remained unchanged, suggesting that improved inventory management did not reduce Expenses, or if they did reduce the expenses, they were apparently offset by inefficiencies in other areas.

Requirement 4:
As shown in Requirement 3, the COGS was lowered by a LIFO liquidation of $205,000, thereby increasing the current tax liability by $205,000 × 0.40 = $82,000.

On the other hand, had the company used FIFO all along, it would have paid this tax over the past several years. Therefore, the firm is still better off in a present value sense by postponing the payment of taxes.

C8-2. General Electric: Interpreting a LIFO footnote

Requirement 1:
What are the total tax savings as of 12/31/91 that GE has realized as a result of using the LIFO inventory method?

	In millions
LIFO reserve on 12/31/91 =	$2,143
Tax rate	34%
Total tax savings	**$728.62**

Requirement 2:
What would GE's after-tax earnings have been in 1991 if they had been using FIFO?

Change in LIFO Reserve = $2,279 - $2,143 = $136 decrease
Change in LIFO Reserve × (1 - Tax rate)
$136 × (1 - .34) = $89.76 *Lower* under FIFO since LIFO
                             reserve decreased
$2,636 - $89.76 = $2,546.24 FIFO earnings

Requirement 3:
What 12/31/91 balance sheet figures would be different and by how much if GE had used FIFO?

						Difference
Inventory at 12/31/91	=	FIFO cost	-	LIFO cost		
		$8,541	-	$6,398	=	**$2,143.00 (higher)**

Cash at 12/31/91 (or other net assets) = LIFO reserve × (tax rate)

$2,143 × 34%	=	**$728.62 (lower)**

Retained earnings
  at 12/31/91 = RE under LIFO + LIFO reserve (1 - tax rate)

(not given)	$2,143 ×	(1 - .34)	=	**$1,414.38 (higher)**

Requirement 4:
LIFO liquidation profits in 1991.

Before Tax = **$118** (given)

After Tax = $118 × (1 - .34) = **$77.88**

Note: Decrease in LIFO reserve in 1991 = $136
Less: amount due to LIFO liquidation (unit decline)   (118)
Decrease due to decline in RC of inventory $18

Requirement 5:
GE reported Cost of goods sold in 1991 of $24,635 million. Calculate the level of purchases they would have had to make in 1991 to avoid the LIFO liquidation.

	$ millions
B. I.	$6,707
+ Purchases	24,326 ←(plug figure)
- E. I.	(6,398)
= COGS (LIFO)	$24,635

	$ millions
Beginning LIFO inv.	$6,707
Ending LIFO inv.	(6,398)
Cost of LIFO inv. liquidated	309
LIFO liquidation effect (RC - HC)	+ 118
Cost of purchases to avoid liquidation	$427

Purchases (production) needed to avoid liquidation $24,326 + $427 = $24,753

Requirement 6:
a) Total tax savings as of 12/31/97

	$ millions
LIFO reserve on 12/31/97	$1,098
Tax rate	34%
Total tax savings	373.32

b) 1997 After-tax FIFO earnings
Change in LIFO reserve = $1,217 - $1,098 = $119 decrease
Change in LIFO reserve × (1 - tax rate)
$119 × (1 - .34) = $78.54   *Lower* under FIFO
$8,203 - $78.54 = $8,124.46   FIFO earnings

c) 12/31/97 balance sheet differences

						Difference
Inventory at 12/31/97	=	FIFO cost	-	LIFO cost		
		$6,207	-	$5,109	=	**$1,098.00 (higher)**

Cash at 12/31/97 (or other net assets) = LIFO reserve × (tax rate)

$$\$1,098 \times 34\% \quad = \quad \textbf{\$373.32 (lower)}$$

Retained earnings
at 12/31/97 = RE under LIFO + LIFO reserve (1 - tax rate)
      (not given) $1,098 × (1 - .34)   =   **$724.68 (higher)**

d) LIFO liquidation profits in 1997

(Note to instructor. This item was not asked for in Requirement 6 since, as the book went to press, we did not know whether there was a LIFO liquidation in 1997.)

Before tax = $59 (given)

After tax = $59 × (1 - .34) = **$38.94**

Note:		
Decrease in LIFO reserve in 1997	=	$119
Less: amount due to LIFO liquidation		(59)
Decrease due to decline in RC of inventory		$60

C8-3. Harsco Corp.: Interpreting a LIFO footnote

Requirement 1:
Change in LIFO reserve:
    $41,256,000 - $47,219,000   = $5,963,000
                                          × (1 - .34)

FIFO income (after-tax) would be *lower* than
    LIFO by this amount. $3,935,580

Requirement 2:

LIFO reserve as reported at 12/31/90	$41,256,000
+ LIFO Effect = (R.C. - H.C.) of layer liquidated	+ 687,000
Base layer	$41,943,000

Requirement 3:
FIFO would *lower* tax by

Change in LIFO reserve	$5,963,000
	× .34
	$2,027,420

359

Requirement 4:

LIFO inv. at 12/31/89	$98,549,000
LIFO inv. at 12/31/90	91,515,000
Cost basis of LIFO liquidation	7,034,000
R.C. - H.C. of LIFO layer liquidated	+ 687,000
Additional purchases needed to avoid liquidation	$7,721,000

Requirement 5:

FIFO E.I. 12/31/90 + Adjustment for additional purchases to bring inventory level back to beginning of year

$$
\underset{\text{LIFO inv.}}{\$91,515,000} + \underset{\text{LIFO reserve}}{\$41,256,000} + \underset{\substack{\text{Add'l purchases} \\ \text{to avoid liq.}}}{\$7,721,000} = \underline{\$140,492,000}
$$

FIFO E.I. 12/31/89

$$
\underset{\text{LIFO inv.}}{\$98,549,000} + \underset{\text{LIFO reserve}}{\$47,219,000} = \underline{\$145,768,000}
$$

Therefore, the estimated rate of price change for Harsco's inventory in 1990 was:

$$
\frac{\text{FIFO end. inv.}}{\text{FIFO beg. inv.}} = \frac{\$140,492,000}{\$145,768,000} = \underline{-3.62\%}
$$

C8-4. Baines Corporation: Absorption vs. variable costing

Requirement 1:
The mood of the management team undoubtedly changed because of the considerable decline in 1998 pre-tax profit and, thus, in 1998 bonuses. Since sales and costs remained constant at 1997 levels, the profit decline was attributable to the negative earnings impact of absorption costing when inventory levels decreased. The effect exists because the 1998 income statement absorbed an extra amount of fixed costs.

Given the facts in the case, 1998 pre-tax profit was:

Sales revenues	(4,000,000 @ $3.50)	$14,000,000
Cost of goods sold:		
Variable production costs	(4,000,000 @ $1.45)	($5,800,000)
Fixed production costs:		

Fixed production costs:

From 1997 ending inventory	(1,500,000 × $1.50)	2,250,000
From 1998 production sold in 1998	(2,500,000 × $1.875)[1]	4,687,500
		(6,937,500)
Operating profit		1,262,500
Interest expense		(100,000)
Pre-tax profit		$1,162,500

[1]Fixed cost per unit of 1998 production $= \dfrac{\$6,000,000}{3,200,000} = \$1.875$

Notice that total fixed overhead charged as expense in 1997 was $6,000,000, whereas the figure for 1998 was $6,937,500 (i.e., $2,250,000 from 1997 ending inventory plus $4,687,500 from 1998 production sold in 1998).

Requirement 2:
The problem could have been prevented had Mr. Carleton anticipated the artificial decrease in profit that was sure to take place as inventory levels were decreased. Then, this decrease could have been removed from the profit figure used to calculate the bonus. The easiest way to do this would have been to base the computation on variable cost income rather than absorption cost income.

Had Baines Corporation been using variable costing as the computation base, the comparative income figures for 1997 and 1998 would have been:

		1997	1998
Sales revenues	(4,000,000 @ $3.50)	$14,000,000	$14,000,000
Cost of goods sold:			
Variable production costs	(4,000,000 @ $1.45)	(5,800,000)	(5,800,000)
Fixed production costs (period expense)		(6,000,000)	(6,000,000)
Operating profit		2,200,000	2,200,000
Interest expense		(200,000)	(100,000)
Pre-tax profit		$2,000,000)	$2,100,000

On the variable costing basis, notice that the comparative income figures improved due to the reduction in interest cost. Using these figures to compute the bonuses would have reflected the managers' excellent efforts in controlling inventories.

Although earnings are widely used as a basis for incentive compensation plans, there are several problems with earnings-based incentives. One of the more obvious ones is that earnings changes can be illusory when they result from changes in accounting procedures. Furthermore, accounting profit is not sensitive enough to capture situations like those where managers postpone discretionary expenditures in order to artificially raise the current period's profits.

C8-5. Handy & Harman: Comprehensive LIFO analysis

This case asks students to adjust between LIFO pre-tax income and FIFO pre-tax income. The LIFO reserve is so large that the setting also provides a nice vehicle for exploring ratio distortions (and required adjustments) for companies on LIFO. Explanations for the LIFO-FIFO income difference as well as the cumulative tax savings under LIFO are also covered.

We have deliberately set the case in 1980 rather than in the 1990s because the issues that we want to illustrate are much more dramatic and transparent in this earlier period. There are two reasons for this. First, precious metals prices increased significantly in 1979. Second, the Hunt Brothers' attempt to corner the silver market occurred during this period, and their failure led to a steep fall in silver prices in 1980.

We try to use the most up-to-date example we can find. However, our philosophy in this book is to choose illustrations for their instructional value, not just for their recency. If an "old" example helps us make our point better than a newer one, we use the old example. Setting this case in the 1990s (using 1990s data) would significantly reduce its "punch line," in our view.

Requirement 1:
Before addressing the first question in the case, the instructor might begin with a general analysis of the financial distortions that LIFO potentially injects into accounting statements. A good place to begin is with the inventory turnover ratios for 1979 and 1980. Try to steer the discussion so that participants end up computing the ratios "conventionally," that is, without any adjustment whatsoever for LIFO. Using average balance sheet inventories as the denominator, the values are:

$$1979: \frac{\$541,582}{(\$78,253 + \$90,432)/2} = 6.42 \text{ times or every 57 days}$$

$$1980: \frac{\$639,481}{(\$90,432 + \$102,897)/2} = 6.62 \text{ times or every 55 days}$$

Of course, these turnover numbers are not meaningful in light of the enormous LIFO reserves in each year. The "failure" of the conventional turnover computation is best conveyed to the students by using a dimensional analysis of the intent of the ratio, i.e.,

$$\frac{\text{Cost of goods sold}}{\text{Average inventory}}$$

In dimensional terms, the numerator is expressed in dollars per period of time, where the time period is usually one year. Insofar as sales are spread fairly evenly over the year, and new LIFO layer formation is small, the numerator is expressed (approximately) in dollars of mid-year cost. The denominator, average inventory, is also designed to approximate mid-year dollars and will do so insofar as beginning and ending inventories are fairly stable and indeed are representative of typical interim inventory levels. Thus, the intent of the ratio computation as seen in dimensional terms is:

$$\frac{\text{Cost of goods sold}}{\text{Average inventory}} = \frac{\$/\text{time}}{\$} = \frac{\$}{\text{time}} \times \frac{1}{\$}$$

or, after performing the calculation, $\dfrac{\text{a pure number}}{\text{time}}$.

The turnover ratio result, e.g., 6+ times a year in the Handy & Harman case, is dimensionally correct only if the dollar cancellation takes place. But, in this instance, the dollar cancellation conceptually does not take place since the volatile price changes for gold and silver and the LIFO layers mean that the dollars in the numerator and denominator relate to different time periods. To make the computation "work," the dollars in both the numerator and denominator must relate to the same period; this is accomplished by adding the LIFO reserves to the denominator in each year's computation. In addition, the MD&A disclosure indicates that 1979 profit included a pre-tax increase of $10,157,000 resulting from a LIFO liquidation. Therefore, the 1979 numerator must be adjusted as well.

1979: $\dfrac{\$541,582 + \$10,157}{[(\$78,253 + \$151,892) + (\$90,432 + \$646,795)]/2} = $ 1.14 times (every 320 days)

1980: $\dfrac{\$639,481}{[(\$90,432 + \$646,795) + (\$102,897 + \$431,554)]/2} = $ 1.01 times (every 361 days)

The instructor can then use the magnitude of the difference between the two turnover measures as an attention-directing device to explain that conventionally computed turnover ratios always incorporate a similar (but usually much smaller) distortion for all companies on LIFO. Therefore, the turnover ratio must be computed using the LIFO reserve in order for its interpretation to be valid for LIFO firms. If the instructor chooses, this could be a good point at which to explore other ratio distortions which exist under LIFO (e.g., the current ratio, etc.).

With this background established, the instructor can turn to the issue addressed in Requirement 1. Since the LIFO reserve increased by $494,903,000 in 1979, pre-tax income goes from the LIFO figure of $22,506,000 to a FIFO figure of $517,409,000 (a 23-fold increase!). In 1980, the LIFO reserve dropped by $215,241,000, and so, on a FIFO basis, a pre-tax loss of $160,331,000 would exist, instead of a LIFO pre-tax profit of $54,910,000.

The case provides an ideal setting for explaining that the LIFO to FIFO adjustment which often appears in financial statement analysis texts is approximate. For example, the sum of the 1979 ending LIFO inventory and the 1979 ending LIFO Reserve ($90,432,000 + $646,795,000 = $737,227,000) only *approximates* ending FIFO inventory. The slower the real inventory turnover, the less precise the approximation. Since Handy & Harman's inventories turn over only about once a year, and, since price fluctuations have been extreme over the period covered in the case, this $737,227,000 figure probably departs considerably from what the FIFO inventory carrying amount would have been on December 31, 1979. Therefore, the entire LIFO to FIFO income adjustment must be interpreted as an estimate, albeit, a usually fairly accurate estimate.

Requirement 2:

The two potential causes for LIFO/FIFO income differences are:
1) changing prices and
2) dipping into old LIFO layers.

The 1979 income difference is easy to explain. Exhibit 3 of the case shows a virtually continuous increase in monthly average prices for both gold and silver in 1979. Under conditions of rising input costs, the use of LIFO obviously generates a lower income number.

The 1980 income difference is slightly more complicated, but still relatively straightforward. Neither the 10-K nor the annual report disclose any LIFO liquidations during 1980. While GAAP does not mandate such disclosures in the annual report, the SEC does in Staff Accounting Bulletin 11 when the "inventory profits" (or realized holding gains) are material. Since no such disclosure was made, we must conclude that LIFO dipping was *not* the cause for the 1980 LIFO/FIFO income difference. The only other possible explanation for why LIFO pre-tax income is so much higher than FIFO pre-tax income is *falling prices* during 1980.

At first glance, Exhibit 2 seems to indicate that, rather than falling, gold and silver prices *rose* during 1980. For example, management's discussion says:

> The average price for gold [in 1980] was $612.51 per ounce and the average price for silver [in 1980] was $20.63 per ounce, representing increases of 99% and 86%, respectively, over the previous year.

But closer scrutiny of Exhibit 3 reveals that while the overall annual averages for each commodity increased between 1979 and 1980, the price behavior differed between the first and last six months of 1980.

	Gold	Silver
Average price, Jan.–June, 1980	$587.65	2,337.6¢
Average price, July–Dec., 1980	$637.37	1,788.7¢

Silver's average price over the July–December 1980 period fell 23.5% below its average January–June price, while gold's July–December average price rose 8.5% over the 1980 first six months' average. Thus, 1980 FIFO income was so much lower because silver apparently dominates in Handy & Harman's production function; under the FIFO cost flow assumption, the higher early-in-the-year costs are put into cost of goods sold. By contrast, LIFO puts the lower, end-of-year silver costs through the income statement.

One additional point. For this explanation to be correct, not only must silver represent a larger percentage of cost of goods sold than gold but also the inventory turnover across commodities must differ from the approximately once every 326–361 day figure derived in analyzing Requirement 1. If silver inventory, indeed, turned over only about once a year (and if purchases were spread evenly over the year), then FIFO cost of goods sold would approximately represent 1979 purchases, whereas LIFO cost of goods sold would represent 1980 purchases. Quick scrutiny of Exhibit 3 of the case reveals that 1980 LIFO income would be *lower* than 1980 FIFO income under these conditions, not higher. Therefore, in order to reconcile the discussion in Requirement 1 with the income differential observed in Requirement 2, not only must silver predominate in Handy & Harman's production function, but also the turnover of silver must be somewhat quicker than the once a year turnover computed across all commodities. For example, if inventory turnover for silver is, say, every 6 months—and if silver predominates in production—then FIFO cost of goods sold represents purchases from January through June of 1980, and FIFO cost of goods sold would be considerably higher than LIFO cost of goods sold.

Requirement 3:

The answer to this question depends upon the point in time at which the computation is done. Conceptually, the LIFO reserve represents the realized holding gains that would have been included in income under FIFO. Therefore, assuming an effective tax rate of 46%, the use of LIFO saved Handy & Harman $297,525,700 in taxes as of December 31, 1979 (i.e., 46% of the 12/31/79 LIFO reserve of $646,795,000.

Repeating the computation at year-end 1980 generates an estimated tax saving number of $198,514,840 (i.e., 46% of the 12/31/80 LIFO reserve of $431,554,000). The instructor should point out to the students that the decline in the cumulative tax saving number between 1979 and 1980 is perfectly consistent with the answer to Requirement 2 of the case. Since prices dropped towards the latter half of 1980, being on LIFO raised Handy & Harman's taxes and, therefore, dissipated part of the previous years' tax savings.

C8-6. Weldotron Corporation (KR): Strategic choice of accounting methods

	1994	1993	1992
FIFO net loss	(2,211)	(3,121)	(2,221)
Effect of accounting change	0	128	(97)
LIFO net loss	(2,211)	(2,993)	(2,318)

	2/28/1994
Retained earnings as reported under FIFO	($783)
Effect of the accounting change on '94 income	0
Effect of the accounting change on '93 income	128
Effect of the accounting change on '92 income	(97)
Effect of the accounting change on '91 retained earnings	(2,356)
Pro forma retained earnings under LIFO	($3,108)

Reported working capital under FIFO ($15,449 - $7,144) + current portion of borrowing under credit facility ($3,215 - $1,500). This adjustment is typically done for current liabilities arising from the borrowing.	$8,305
	1,715
Working capital under FIFO for covenant purposes	$10,020

Pro forma working capital under LIFO for covenant purposes ($10,020 - $2,325[1])	$7,695

[1]Note: ($2,325) = $128 + ($97) + ($2,356)

Working capital to be maintained as per covenants	$9,500

Notice that under LIFO, Weldotron would be in violation of the working capital covenant.

Note: Due to significant losses during the current period, no tax liability was recorded at the time of switch to FIFO.

Reported stockholders' equity under FIFO	$9,010
- Accumulated undistributed earnings of foreign subsidiary	(352)
Reported tangible **domestic** net worth under FIFO	$8,658

Pro forma tangible domestic net worth under LIFO ($8,658 - $2,325) $6,333

Tangible domestic net worth maintained as per covenants $8,200

Again, the shift to FIFO avoided a covenant violation.

With some foresight, the management would have known that it is likely to violate both net worth and working capital covenants.

It cannot use additional long-term debt to address this problem for two reasons:

1. Debt would increase only working capital levels but would have no direct effect on net worth.

2. Since "substantially all of the assets of the company have been pledged for the existing borrowing under credit facility," it is unlikely that the company will find somebody who is willing to provide it long-term *unsecured* debt.

A second alternative is to issue additional equity which will increase both working capital and net worth. In fact, it did that. It issued almost $1.107 million of equity (see changes in common stock + additional paid-In capital). However, it was not sufficient to bring net worth and working capital to the minimum levels required under the covenants.

A third strategy is to change the inventory method from LIFO to FIFO since both net worth and working capital are typically higher under FIFO compared to LIFO. How about the tax consequences? They appear to be minimal since the company incurred substantial losses during the current period. The working capital and net worth would be increased by the pre-tax difference between LIFO and FIFO inventory values since no additional tax liability needs to be recorded.

Exercises

E9-1. Determining asset cost and depreciation expense
(AICPA adapted)

First determine the depreciable value of the machine.

Purchase price	$150,000
Installation	$4,000
Less: salvage value	($5,000)
Total depreciable value of machine	**$149,000**

We use this as the depreciation base. The machine has a useful life of 10 years, so the computation for straight-line depreciation would be:

$$\$149,000/10 \text{ years} = \$14,900$$

Action should record $14,900 as depreciation expense in 1998.

E9-2. Determining depreciation expense
(AICPA adapted)

The schedule below shows Turtle's depreciation over 5 years. The italicized number is the amount that should appear on Turtle's December 31, 1998 balance sheet as accumulated depreciation.

December 31,	Depreciation Expense	Accumulated Depreciation	Book Value
1997	$20,000 *	$20,000	$30,000
1998	12,000 *	32,000	18,000
1999	6,000	*38,000*	12,000
2000	6,000	44,000	6,000
2001	6,000	50,000	-

*Depreciation under the double-declining balance method.
The straight-line depreciation rate is 1/5, or 20%. Double this is 40%. This percentage is multiplied by the book value of the asset each period. As of 1/1/1999, the book value of the asset is $18,000; we now depreciate this amount on a straight-line basis over the remaining useful life (5 - 2 = 3). $18,000/3 = $6,000 each year until fully depreciated.

E9-3. Depreciation base
(AICPA adapted)

First determine the book value of the machine at the beginning of 1998 as shown in the schedule below.

	Depreciation Expense	Accumulated Depreciation	Book Value of Machine
January 1, 1988	-	-	$30,000
1988	$1,500	$1,500	28,500
1989	1,500	3,000	27,000
1990	1,500	4,500	25,500
1991	1,500	6,000	24,000
1992	1,500	7,500	22,500
1993	1,500	9,000	21,000
1994	1,500	10,500	19,500
1995	1,500	12,000	18,000
1996	1,500	13,500	16,500
1997	1,500	15,000	*15,000*

The italicized number is the book value of the machine at January 1, 1998. The $5,000 overhaul increases the value of the machine by $5,000, so the new book value is $20,000 ($15,000 + $5,000). The overhaul added 5 years onto the life of the machine, so the remaining useful life of the machine at January 1, 1998 is 15 years (10 yrs. + 5 yrs). To find the depreciation expense for 1998, take the new book value ($20,000) divided by the remaining useful life of the machine (15 years).

$20,000/15 years = $1,333

Depreciation expense for 1998 is $1,333.

E9-4. Analysis of various costs
(AICPA adapted)

All of the costs incurred for the printing press can be capitalized.

Purchase price of attachment	$84,000
Installation	36,000
Replacement parts	26,000
Labor and overhead	14,000
Total costs to be capitalized	**$160,000**

E9-5. Deferred payment contract

The plant assets should be recorded at the discounted present value of the payments:

Payment date	Amount	Discount Factor at 10%	Discounted Present Value
January 1, 1998	$10,000	1.00000	$10,000.00
January 1, 1999	10,000	.90909	9,090.90
January 1, 2000	10,000	.82645	8,264.50
January 1, 2001	10,000	.75132	7,513.20
January 1, 2002	10,000	.68301	6,830.10
Total			$41,698.70

DR Plant assets	$41,698.70	
CR Cash		$10,000.00
CR Contract payable		31,698.70

E9-6. Analysis of various costs
(AICPA adapted)

First, we must find the total cost of the machine.

Purchase price	$65,000
Freight-in	500
Installation	2,000
Testing	300
Total cost of machinery	$67,800
Less: salvage value	(5,000)
Depreciation base	**$62,800**

Now we can find depreciation expense for 1996 and 1997:
$62,800/20 years = $3,140

Next, we need to determine the depreciation base of the machine in January 1998. The machine has been depreciated for two years, so:

Depreciation base, January 1, 1996	$62,800
1996 depreciation	(3,140)
1997 depreciation	(3,140)
Depreciation base, January 1, 1998	**$56,520**

The accessories add $3,600 to the machine's value, so the depreciation base at January 1, 1998 is: [$56,520 + $3,600 = $60,120].

The accessories did not add useful life or more salvage value. The remaining useful life of the machine is 18 years (20 - 2). To find straight-line depreciation expense, we divide the depreciation base by the remaining useful life.

$$\$60,120/18 \text{ years} = \$3,340$$

Samson should record $3,340 as depreciation expense for 1998.

E9-7. Classification of costs
(AICPA adapted)

Included in the cost of land are any preparations to ready the land for the intended purpose, and fees paid in connection with finding and purchasing the land. Any salvaged materials sold are subtracted from the total cost of land. The computation for the cost of land is shown below.

Purchase price of land	$50,000
Demolition of old building	4,000
Legal fees	2,000
Less: sale of salvaged materials	(1,000)
Total cost of land	**$55,000**

The cost of the building includes all costs incurred in construction; architect's fees would fall into this category.

Construction costs	$500,000
Architect's fees	10,000
Total cost of building	**$510,000**

E9-8. Classification of costs
(AICPA adapted)

First determine what percentage of the total appraised value the land represents:

Land	$200,000
Total current appraised value	$500,000

$200,000/$500,000 = 40%. The land comprises 40% of the total package value.

Now, we need to apply this ratio to the price Town paid for the warehouse and land.

[40% × $540,000] = $216,000. Town should record the land on the balance sheet at $216,000.

E9-9. Capitalized interest
(AICPA adapted)

The avoidable interest during 1998 is:

Cost incurred evenly over the year	$2,000,000
	× .50
Average cost during the year	$1,000,000
Incremental borrowing rate	× .12
Avoidable interest	$120,000

Since the actual interest incurred ($102,000) was lower than avoidable interest, Clay should report $102,000 as capitalized interest at December 31, 1998.

E9-10. Capitalized interest
(AICPA adapted)

The interest on weighted average accumulated expenditures is the amount of avoidable interest. Since the avoidable interest ($40,000) is less than the interest actually accrued ($70,000), only the avoidable interest is capitalized. The journal entry to record this transaction follows.

DR Building (capitalized interest)	$40,000	
DR Interest expense	$30,000	
CR Cash		$70,000

E9-11. Account analysis
(AICPA adapted)

To determine the amount debited in 1998, we reconstruct the accumulated depreciation T-account:

Accumulated Depreciation		
	$370,000	Beginning balance (1/1/98)
	55,000	Depreciation expense
Accumulated depreciation from retirement of PP&E X		
	$400,000	Ending balance

$370,000 + $55,000 - X = $400,000
X = $25,000

Weir must have debited $25,000 to accumulated depreciation during 1998 because of property, plant, and equipment retirements.

E9-12. Depreciation expense patterns
(AICPA adapted)

Line II corresponds to the sum-of-the-years'-digits method, and Line III corresponds to the double-declining balance method. Sum-of-the-years' digits is a linear pattern, while double-declining balance is more accelerated and non-linear.

E9-13. Intangibles amortization
(AICPA adapted)

First, determine the book value of the trademark at 1/1/98:

December 31,	1994	1995	1996	1997
Amortization amount ($400,000/16)	$25,000	$25,000	$25,000	$25,000
Book value	$375,000	$350,000	$325,000	*$300,000*

The italicized number represents the book value of the asset at December 31, 1997 (or January 1, 1998). The legal fees paid add $60,000 to the cost of the patent that also must be amortized. The book value of the patent at January 1, 1998 is:

$$\$300,000 + \$60,000 = \$360,000$$

The patent has been amortized for four years so it has 12 years of remaining useful life (16 - 4 = 12). To find amortization expense for 1998, divide the book value of the patent by the remaining useful life.

$$\$360,000/12 \text{ years} = \$30,000$$

Vick would record $30,000 of trademark amortization expense for the year ended December 31, 1998.

E9-14. Intangibles
(AICPA adapted)

Find the book value of the patent at 12/31/98. The patent is amortized over its useful life (10 yrs.) instead of its valid legal life (15 yrs.) because the useful life is shorter.

December 31,	1995	1996	1997	1998
Amortization amount				
($90,000/10 years)	$9,000	$9,000	$9,000	$9,000
Book value of patent	$81,000	$72,000	$63,000	*$54,000*

On December 31, 1998, the patent has a book value of $54,000. If the product is permanently withdrawn from the market, then the patent becomes worthless. Lava would incur a loss on impairment for the entire book value of the patent, $54,000. The journal entry to record this impairment is:

DR Loss on impairment $54,000
  CR Patent $54,000

The total charge to income in 1998 is $63,9000, i.e., $54,000 + $9,000.

E9-15. R&D cost treatment
(AICPA adapted)

All of the costs should be expensed as research and development for 1998.

R&D services performed by Key Corp.	$150,000
Design, construction, testing	200,000
Testing for new product/process alternatives	175,000
Total research & development expense	**$525,000**

E9-16. R&D cost treatment
(AICPA adapted)

Costs incurred in Ball Labs that will not be reimbursed by the governmental unit should be expensed as research and development. The computation follows:

Depreciation	$300,000
Salaries	700,000
Indirect costs	200,000
Materials	180,000
Total	**$1,380,000**

Ball should expense $1,380,000 as research and development for 1998.

E9-17. Depletion
(AICPA adapted)

Units of production is not explicitly discussed in the text. This problem gives the instructor an opportunity to introduce it.

To determine the depletion base, we need to add together the costs associated with the mine and subtract any salvage value.

Purchase price of mine	$2,640,000
Development costs	360,000
Restoration costs	180,000
Less: salvage value	(300,000)
Depletion base	**$2,880,000**

Next we need to find the depletion cost per unit, computed below:

$$\frac{\text{Depletion base}}{\text{Total estimated units available}} = \frac{\$2,880,000}{1,200,000} = \$2.40 \text{ per unit removed}$$

Knowing the depletion cost per unit and the number of units (tons) removed, we can solve for depletion expense:

60,000 tons of ore removed × $2.40 per ton = $144,000

Vorst should report $144,000 as depletion expense for 1998.

Problems

P9-1. Depreciation expense computations
(AICPA adapted)

The table below shows the amount of depreciation expense in 1998 under each method. Computations are shown below the schedule.

Straight-line

1997	$90,000
1998	$90,000

Double-declining balance

1997	$216,000
1998	$162,000

Sum-of-years' digits

1997	$160,000
1998	$140,000

Units of production

1997	-
1998	$120,000

Requirement 1:
Straight-line:

$$\frac{\text{Total cost} - \text{Salvage value}}{\text{Estimated useful life}} = \frac{\$864,000 - \$144,000}{8 \text{ years}} = \$90,000 \text{ per year}$$

Requirement 2:
Double-declining balance:

Depreciation in 1997

Straight-line rate = 1/8 or 12.5%. Double this is 25%

$864,000 × 25% = $216,000

Depreciation in 1998

[Book value = total cost - accumulated depreciation]

$648,00 = $864,000 - $216,000

648,000 × 25% = $162,000

Requirement 3:
Sum-of-years' digits:

Depreciation in 1997

$$\frac{\text{Year}}{\text{Sum-of-years' digits}} \times [\text{Total cost} - \text{Salvage value}]$$

$$= \frac{8}{1 + 2 + 3 + 4 + 5 + 6 + 7 + 8} \times [\$864,000 - \$144,000]$$

$$= \frac{8}{36} \times \$720,000$$

$$= \$160,000$$

Depreciation in 1998

$$= \frac{7}{36} \times \$720,000$$

$$= \$140,000$$

Requirement 4:
Units of production:

Units of production is not explicitly discussed in the text. This problem gives the instructor an opportunity to introduce it.

$$\frac{\text{Total cost} - \text{Salvage value}}{\text{Total estimated units produceable}} = \frac{\$864,000 - \$144,000}{1,800,000 \text{ units}}$$

$$= \frac{\$720,000}{1,800,000 \text{ units}}$$

$$= \$0.40 \text{ per unit}$$

Depreciation = depreciation cost per unit x number of units actually produced

$$= \$0.40 \text{ per unit x } 300,000 \text{ units} = \$120,000$$

P9-2. Lump-sum purchases

Requirement 1:
Cost of land and building:

Land:

FMV of land/FMV of land and building

$6,300,000/$17,500,000 = 36%

Cost of land   = $15,000,000 × .36 = $5,400,000

Building:

FMV of building/FMV of land and building

$11,200,000/$17,500,000 = 64%

Cost of building = ($15,000,000 × .64) + cost of modifications to building

= $9,600,000 + 1,000,000

= $10,600,000.

Requirement 2:
Depreciation is not recorded on land. Thus, the higher the amount assigned to the land, the lower will be future years' depreciation expense, and the higher will be the net income of such years.

P9-3. Asset cost under a deferred payment plan

At a discount rate of 10%, the present value of the note is:

$400,000 × $1/(1 + 0.10)^4$

= $400,000 × 0.683

= $273,200.

Since this is more than the cash price of $250,000, Cayman should pay cash.

At a discount rate of 13%, the present value of the note is:

$400,000 × $1/(1 + 0.13)^4$

= $ 400,000 × 0.613

= $245,200.

In this case, since the present value of the note is less than the cash price of $250,000, Cayman should issue the note to the seller rather than paying cash.

P9-4. Allocation of acquisition costs among asset accounts

Relative fair market values of the land and building at the time of purchase:

Land: $105,000,000/$125,000,000 = 84%

Building: $20,000,000/$125,000,000 = 16%

Purchase price of the land and buildings:

Cash	$ 25,000,000
Note payable	5,000,000
Common stock	80,000,000 ($80 × 1,000,000)
Legal fees	25,000
Total	$110,025,000

Initial allocation of cost:

Land: $110,025,000 × 0.84 = $92,421,000

Buildings: $110,025,000 × 0.16 = $17,604,000

Allocation of subsequent costs:

Land:

Initial cost	$92,421,000
Demolish old building	50,000
Grade land	250,000
Total cost assigned to the land account:	$92,721,000

Building:

Initial cost	$ 17,604,000
Cost of new building	100,000,000
Renovate old building	25,000,000
Interest incurred during construction	10,000,000
Total cost assigned to the buildings account:	$152,604,000

Land improvements:

Asphalt parking lot	$450,000
Lighting	200,000
Landscaping	75,000
Total cost assigned to the land improvements account:	$725,000

The $725,000 would be recorded in the land improvements account rather than the land account because the parking lot, lighting, and landscaping have a finite useful life over which the $725,000 would be depreciated. Land, on the other hand, has an infinite useful life and is not depreciated.

The property taxes of $150,000 would be charged against 1998 income.

P9-5. Capitalize or expense various costs

Requirement 1:
These expenditures constitute normal repairs and maintenance and would be charged against 1998's income. Moreover, they do not extend the assets' useful lives, or increase efficiency or capacity.

Requirement 2:
Since the new engines extend the useful lives of the related trucks, they would be capitalized and depreciated over their expected useful life.

Requirement 3:
These expenditures constitute normal repairs and maintenance and would be charged against 1998's income. Moreover, they do not extend the assets' useful lives, or increase efficiency or capacity.

Requirement 4:
Since the rust-proofing extends the useful lives of the trucks, the costs would be capitalized and depreciated over the revised useful life of the trucks.

Requirement 5:
This "opportunity cost" would not be capitalized or expensed. While an economic loss, such costs are not recognized in GAAP financial statements.

While "economic income" reflects the costs of forgone opportunities, accounting income does not. Accounting income is pragmatic because forgone opportunities are infinite and not subject to reliable measurement. Consequently, an opportunity cost notion imbedded in accounting income would not be operational.

P9-6. Capitalize or expense various costs

Requirement 1:
1) Since the new engines increase the future service potential of the aircraft, the amount should be capitalized and depreciated over the engines' useful life.

2) Since there is no increase in useful life, future service potential, or efficiency, the amount should be charged to expense in the current year. Some might argue that this is a bit of a gray area. For example, if the campaign is successful,

future service potential might increase. On the other hand, the expenditure is also a bit like advertising, which is a period expense.

3) Since the repairs are routine (i.e., recurring), the amount should be charged to expense in the current year.

4) The noise abatement equipment is mandated and is, thus, an unavoidable, necessary cost that allows the planes to use runways and airports that could not be utilized otherwise. Therefore, this cost is capitalizable.

5) Since the new systems increase the future service potential of the aircraft, the amount should be capitalized and depreciated over the useful life of the systems.

6) Again, some might argue that this is another gray area. Since the objective of the expenditure is to increase business, it might warrant capitalization. On the other hand, since there is no increase in useful life, future service potential, or efficiency, the amount could be charged to expense in the current year.

7) Since the overhauls increase the efficiency of the engines, the amount should be capitalized and depreciated over the expected useful life of the improvements.

Requirement 2:
Perhaps the easiest way for a firm like Fly-by-Night to use some of the above expenditures to manage earnings upward is to capitalize a portion of those that might otherwise be treated as expenses of the period. Other ways Fly-by-Night could manage earnings is to defer maintenance expenditures while keeping them just above the minimum required by the Federal Aviation Administration. Fly-by-Night might also consider "bunching" expenditures in a given year to achieve a "big bath." This would then improve future years' earnings.

P9-7. Determining an asset's cost

Invoice price	$15,000,000
Trade-in	(150,000)
Cost before discount	14,850,000
2% discount	(297,000)
Shipping	15,000
Insurance	5,000
Wages to set-up machine	20,000
De-icing fluid used during testing	35,000
Cost of the machine	$14,628,000

Additional comments:

1) The new building erected to store the machine would be recorded at a cost of $105,000 and would be recorded in CPS's buildings account.

2) The $250,000 to repair the damage to the cargo plane would be recorded as a loss in CPS's 1998 income statement. The firm would probably classify the loss under a heading such as other expenses. The $750,000 in forgone revenue, while an economic loss to the firm, would not appear directly in CPS's financial statements. (Of course, it does appear indirectly insofar as sales are $750,000 lower than they would otherwise be).

P9-8. Asset impairment

Requirement 1:
Book value:

$$= \$35{,}000{,}000 - (\$35{,}000{,}000/7) \times 4$$
$$= \$35{,}000{,}000 - 20{,}000{,}000$$
$$= \$15{,}000{,}000$$

Requirement 2:
Yes, the asset is impaired.

The book value of $15,000,000 is greater than the undiscounted future cash flows of $11,000,000.

Impairment loss to be reported in the income statement:

$$= \$15{,}000{,}000 - \text{Fair market value of the asset}$$
$$= \$15{,}000{,}000 - 9{,}500{,}000$$
$$= \ \ \$5{,}500{,}000$$

Requirement 3:
The balance sheet amount at the end of year 4 is $9,500,000, the asset's fair market value. Omega would depreciate this amount over the asset's remaining useful life.

P9-9. Accounting for computer software costs

Requirement 1:
Until the technological feasibility of the product is proven, all costs are expensed as R&D. After technological feasibility is proven, the costs are capitalized up to the point the product is made available for sale. These capitalized costs are then amortized over the expected life of the project. If any costs are incurred after the product has been made available for sale, they are expensed.

Requirement 2:
This amount cannot be determined from the information given. While we can determine the costs incurred after technological feasibility has been shown (see Requirement 3), we cannot know how much IBM expended up to the point that technological feasibility was reached on the various projects.

Requirement 3:
$2,419 + $11,276 = $13,695.

Requirement 4:
($2,963 + $10,793) + $2,997 - X = ($2,419 + $11,276)

X = $3,058, where X is the gross amount of software-related costs that were written off in 1995. (We assume that the costs written off in 1995 were fully amortized; therefore, the offsetting DR was to accumulated amortization.) So:

$10,793 - $3,058 + Y = $11,276

Y = $3,541, where Y is the credit to accumulated amortization. The offsetting DR of $3,541 is the estimate of IBM's amortization in 1995.

Requirement 5:
Total capitalized software at the end of 1995/software amortization for 1995:

($2,419 + $11,276)/$3,541 = 3.87 (about 4 years).

(This assumes that a full year's amortization was taken on the amount of software capitalized in 1995.)

Requirement 6:
Earnings can be managed by judicious selection of the point in time when technological feasibility has been reached. For example, a firm that wants to boost income in a given year would declare that technological feasibility has been reached sooner than warranted so that costs could begin to be capitalized rather than expensed. The situation is reversed for firms that want to depress current year earnings.

P9-10. Asset impairment

Requirement 1:
The asset is not impaired, and no loss needs to be recognized. The undiscounted present value of the future cash flows from the Supersweet patent are:

[($58.7 + 64.3 + 70.7 + 77.8 + 85.6) × 0.50] + $25.0 = $203.55

Since $203.55 is greater than the book value of the patent, no impairment of the asset has occurred.

Requirement 2:
The asset is impaired, and a loss needs to be recognized. The undiscounted present value of the future cash flows from the Supersweet patent are:

$$[(\$58.7 + 64.3 + 70.7 + 77.8 + 85.6) \times 0.25] + \$25.0 = \$114.275$$

Since $114.275 is less than the book value of the patent of $125.0, an impairment of the asset has occurred. The amount of the loss to recognize is:

Current book value - current market value

$125.0 - $68.0 = $57.0 million.

The loss would be recognized in National Sweetener's 1998 income statement, and the patent would be reported at $68.0 million in the firm's 1998 ending balance sheet.

P9-11. Interest capitalization

Requirement 1:
$$(\$80,000,000 \times 0.13) + (\$200,000,000 \times 0.115) = \$33,400,000.$$

Requirement 2:
$$(\$80,000,000 \times 0.13) + (\$70,000,000 \times 0.115) = \$18,450,000.$$

This is the avoidable interest. Note that $80,000,000 + $70,000,000 equals the average balance in construction-in-progress.

Requirement 3:
Zero: Firms are not allowed to include the "implicit" cost of equity financing as part of the cost of self-constructed assets. Thus, GAAP implicitly assigns a *zero* cost to equity issued to help finance the construction.

Requirement 4:
The amount of capitalized interest will be added to the firm's construction-in-progress account.

Requirement 5:
$33,400,000 - 18,450,000 = $14,950,000.

Requirement 6:
The amount of capitalized interest will reduce future earnings over the useful life of the facility, as it will be a component of the depreciation expense taken each year of the asset's useful life.

Requirement 7:
Net income after taxes with capitalization of interest:

$50,000,000
-14,950,000 (Interest expense)
 35,050,000
-11,917,000 (Income tax at 34%)
$23,133,000 Net income

NOPAT operating margin = $23,133,000/$450,000,000 = 5.1%

Net income after taxes without capitalization of interest:

$50,000,000
-33,400,000 (Interest expense)
 16,600,000
 -5,644,000 (Income tax at 34%)
$10,956,000 Net income

NOPAT operating margin = $10,956,000/$450,000,000 = 2.4%

With the capitalization of the interest, the NOPAT operating margin is more than twice what it would otherwise be. In industries where some firms are constructing their own assets while other firms are not, the capitalization of interest by some firms may result in their NOPAT operating margins appearing to be higher just due to the accounting treatment of the interest.

Requirement 8:
Interest coverage ratio with interest capitalization:

= $50,000,000/$14,950,000
= 3.34 times.

Interest coverage ratio without interest capitalization:

= $50,000,000/$33,400,000
= 1.50 times.

The interest coverage ratio *without* the interest capitalization would be more helpful to a creditor because it is based on the interest that the firm must actually pay.

P9-12. Accounting for internally developed patents vs. purchased patents

Requirement 1:
Micro Systems Inc. must expense the $10,000,000 each year as R&D. Macro Systems Inc. will capitalize $10,000,000 each year and amortize it over a 5-year period.

Requirement 2:
Micro Systems Inc.

This firm's profit margin increases each year as sales grow faster than the firm's expenses.

Micro Systems Inc. (000 omitted)	1996	1997	1998	1999
Sales	$200,000	$242,000	$290,000	$350,000
Operating expenses	140,000	170,000	205,000	245,000
R&D	10,000	10,000	10,000	10,000
Patent amortization expense	0	0	0	0
Income before tax	50,000	62,000	75,000	95,000
Income taxes	17,000	21,080	25,500	32,300
Net income	$33,000	$40,920	$49,500	$62,700
Profit margin	0.165	0.169	0.171	0.179

Macro Systems Inc.

This firm's profit margin falls over the first 3 years as the patent amortization expense increases each year. In 1999, it increases slightly as the increase in sales is enough to offset the increase in operating expenses and amortization expense. Note that Macro's profit margin is higher than Micro's each year, due to the capitalization and related amortization of its patent acquisitions.

The key aspect of this analysis for the financial analyst is that while the two firms were otherwise identical (i.e., same sales, operating expenses, and tax rate), the fact that one firm performed its own R&D while the other purchased it from other firms led to some important differences in their apparent profitability. In fact, one could argue that the firms were equally profitable over the 1996-1999 period.

Macro Systems Inc. (000 omitted)	1996	1997	1998	1999
Sales	$200,000	$242,000	$290,000	$350,000
Operating expenses	140,000	170,000	205,000	245,000
R&D	0	0	0	0
Patent amortization expense	2,000	4,000	6,000	8,000
Income before tax	58,000	68,000	79,000	97,000
Income taxes	19,720	23,120	26,860	32,980
Net income	$38,280	$44,880	$52,140	$64,020
Profit margin	0.191	0.185	0.180	0.183

Amortization of patent

1996: $2,000 ($10,000/5)
1997: $4,000 ($10,000/5) + ($10,000/5)
1998: $6,000 ($10,000/5) + ($10,000/5) + ($10,000/5)
1999: $8,000 ($10,000/5) + ($10,000/5) + ($10,000/5) + ($10,000/5)

Requirement 3:
In this case, the net income and profit margins of the firms would converge to the same amount because Macro Systems Inc. would hit a steady state of $10,000,000 in patent amortization each year which equals the $10,000,000 spent on R&D by Micro Systems. Thus, the differences noted in Requirement 2 become less important over time if R&D expenditures are stable for the two firms.

P9-13. Earnings effects of changes in useful lives and salvage values

Requirement 1:

Original cost of buildings	$4,694,000,000
Multiplied by (1 - .353)	.647
Estimated book value of buildings	$3,037,018,000

Requirement 2:
Revised depreciation schedule:

Book value after 12 years	$3,037,018,000
Less: Salvage value (10% of Cost)	469,400,000
Amount to depreciate	$2,567,618,000
Annual depreciation ($2,567,618,000/28*)	$91,700,642

*Remaining useful life = 40 - 12 = 28

Increase in income before tax due to the changes:

Old depreciation expense:

Original cost of buildings	$4,694,000,000
Less: salvage value (5% of cost)	234,700,000
Amount to depreciate	$4,459,300,000

Annual depreciation ($4,459,300,000/34)	$131,155,882
Revised depreciation expense:	91,700,642
Increase in income before tax	$39,455,240

Increase in net income:

$39,455,240 × (1 - 0.34) = $26,040,458

P9-14. Straight-line versus accelerated depreciation ratio effects

Requirement 1:
The solution under straight-line depreciation is:

SL Company	1996	1997	1998	1999
Sales	$1,000.00	$1,250.00	$1,562.50	$1,953.13
Cost of goods sold[1]	600.00	811.67	860.04	912.04
Gross profit	400.00	438.33	702.46	1,041.08
Operating expenses[2]	150.00	256.00	262.24	268.73
Income before tax	250.00	182.33	440.22	772.35
Income taxes	85.00	61.99	149.67	262.60
Net income	$165.00	$120.34	$290.55	$509.75
Cost of machine	$500.00			
Cost of new computer	$300.00			
Average total assets	$1,000.00	$1,200.00	$1,440.00	$1,728.00
Gross profit rate (rounded)	0.40	0.35	0.45	0.53
NOPAT margin (rounded)	0.17	0.10	0.19	0.26
Return on assets (rounded)	0.17	0.10	0.20	0.29

[1] *Total cost of goods sold.*

	1996	1997	1998	1999
a) Excluding the depreciation on the new machine, the cost of goods sold is expected to increase at a rate of 7.5%. This amount is:	$600.00	$645.00	$693.38	$745.38
b) The depreciation component is $500/3		166.67	166.66	166.66
Total cost of goods sold		$811.67	$860.04	$912.04

[2] *Total operating expenses.*

	1996	1997	1998	1999
a) Excluding the depreciation on the new computer, operating expenses are expected to increase at a rate of 4.0%. This amount is:	$150.00	$156.00	$162.24	$168.73
b) The depreciation component is ($300/3)		100.00	100.00	100.00
Total operating expenses		$256.00	$262.24	$268.73

Requirement 2:
The solution under sum-of-years' digits is:

SYD Company	1996	1997	1998	1999
Sales	$1,000.00	$1,250.00	$1,562.50	$1,953.13
Cost of goods sold[1]	600.00	895.00	860.04	828.71
Gross profit	400.00	355.00	702.46	1,124.41
Operating expenses[2]	150.00	306.00	262.24	218.73
Income before tax	250.00	49.00	440.22	905.68
Income taxes	85.00	16.66	149.67	307.93
Net income	$165.00	$32.34	$290.55	$597.75
Cost of new machine	$500.00			
Cost of new computer system	$300.00			
Average total assets	$1,000.00	$1,200.00	$1,440.00	$1,728.00
Gross profit rate (rounded)	0.40	0.28	0.45	0.58
NOPAT margin (rounded)	0.17	0.03	0.19	0.31
Return on assets (rounded)	0.17	0.03	0.20	0.35

[1] Total cost of goods sold.

a) Exluding the depreciation on the new machine, the cost of goods sold is expected to increase at a rate of 7.5%. This amount is:	$600.00	$645.00	$693.38	$745.38
b) The depreciation component is:		250.00	166.66	83.33
Total cost of goods sold		$895.00	$860.04	$828.71

[2] Total operating expenses.

a) Excluding the depreciation on the new computer, operating expenses are expected to increase at a rate of 4.0%. This amount is:	$150.00	$156.00	$162.24	$168.73
b) The depreciation component is:		150.00	100.00	50.00
Total operating expenses		$306.00	$262.24	$218.73

Requirement 3:
The ratios are shown in the schedules in Requirements 1 and 2. With regard to the differences between the ratios of the two firms, the following points are worth noting. While the firms are otherwise identical except for the choice of depreciation method (i.e., same sales, cost of goods sold, operating expenses, income tax rate, growth rates in various income statement items), there are some important differences that arise in the ratios due to the choice of depreciation method.

a) In 1997, SL Company's ratios significantly exceed those of SYD Company. For example, a gross profit rate of 35% versus 28%, a NOPAT margin of 9.6% versus 2.6%, and a return on asset ratio of 10.0% versus 2.7%. This is, of course, due to the greater amount of depreciation expense reported by SYD Company relative to SL Company in 1997.

b) In 1998, all ratios are the same because the depreciation expense under both methods is the same.

c) In 1999, SYD Company's ratios exceed those of SL Company. For example, a gross profit rate of 57.6% versus 53.3%, a NOPAT margin of 30.6% versus 26.1%, and a return on asset ratio of 34.6% versus 29.5%. This is, of course, due to the greater amount of depreciation expense reported by SL Company relative to SYD Company in 1999.

d) It is also worth noting that across all years the firms report identical totals for their income statement items (e.g., cost of goods sold, gross profit, etc.). This, of course, is due to the fact that the amount of depreciation recorded under each method is the same over the life of the asset; all that differs between the two methods is the year-to-year pattern in the amount of depreciation recorded.

e) In summary, the behavior of the ratios of the two firms illustrates that depreciation policy choice can introduce "artificial" differences in the apparent profitability of two otherwise identical firms. This means that analysts should pay attention to the depreciation policy choices of firms they intend to compare.

P9-15. Approaches to long-lived asset valuation

Requirement 1:
Expected benefit approaches focus on the estimated value of long-term Assets in an output market, that is, a market where the assets could be sold. This approach assigns a value to an asset based on the expected future cash flows the asset is capable of generating. One valuation measure under this approach is the Discounted Present value of the future cash flows the asset is expected to generate. For example, a Boeing 777 jet owned by United Airlines

might be valued on the basis of the net operating cash flows (i.e., passenger revenues less applicable costs) it is expected to generate over its useful life.

Another valuation measure under this approach is what the asset would bring if it were sold in the marketplace. In this case, the Boeing 777 would be valued at its net realizable value. Problems that arise in implementing the discounted present value approach include determining the appropriate discount rate as well as estimating the future net operating cash flows that the asset will generate. A problem that arises under the net realizable value approach is that not all assets have readily available quoted market prices.

Economic sacrifice approaches focus on an asset's cost in an input market—a market where the asset could be acquired. The most obvious example of this approach is an asset's historical cost, which is what the firm paid for the asset when it was originally acquired. The main advantage of this approach is that an asset's historical cost is easy to measure, is objective, and is verifiable. Historical cost is the dominant approach underlying current GAAP. A second example of an economic sacrifice approach is current replacement cost. This is the amount that would be required to purchase/replace the asset today with an "identical" or "similar" asset. A problem that arises under this approach is that the current replacement cost of existing assets may be difficult to obtain for some assets.

Requirement 2:
From the perspective of a financial analyst, the answer to the question is yes. Since the primary input into financial analysis is information about a firm, analysts would like to have these other valuations in addition to historical cost. After all, if they feel that any of the additional valuations are not as reliable as historical cost in a given setting, they can always choose to ignore them. But having these data would make trend analyses, cross-sectional comparisons, and basic ratio analysis more meaningful since the distortions of historical cost accounting would be reduced.

Requirement 3:
The primary benefit is a more relevant valuation of the company's assets, and, thus, a more relevant valuation of the entire company (i.e., its common stock). The primary cost, which most managers would probably argue exceeds the expected benefit, is that many of these numbers would need to be based on estimates about the future conditions of the firm and appropriate discount rates. Many managers believe that the necessity of these estimates will introduce enough measurement error into these voluntary disclosures so as to make them less than perfect measures of true underlying asset values and diminish their usefulness to outside parties.

Cases
C9-1. Microsoft (CW): Capitalization vs. expensing of R&D

Requirement 1:
Current GAAP requires that R&D costs be expensed in the year incurred. Thus, even though such expenditures may benefit future operations, they are not allowed to be capitalized and amortized against future years' income.

Requirement 2:

($s in millions)	1994	1995	1996
Sales	$4,649	$5,937	$8,671
Net income (NOPAT)	1,146	1,453	2,195
Total assets	5,363	7,210	10,093
Total shareholders' equity	4,450	5,333	6,908
Research and development	$610	$860	$1,432
NOPAT margin	0.247	0.245	0.253
Asset turnover	1.014	0.944	1.002
Return on assets	0.250	0.231	0.254
Return on shareholders' equity	0.298	0.297	0.359

Requirement 3:
The 1994 income statement would reflect 1/3 of the total R&D cost incurred during 1994 and each of the past two years rather than the entire amount of R&D incurred in the current year. The firm's *ending* 1994 balance sheet would record an asset, deferred R&D, which would pick up the capitalized R&D from the current period (2/3 of the R&D incurred during 1994) and the unamortized portion of the prior year's R&D (1/3 of the R&D incurred during the prior year).

Requirement 4:
3-year R&D write-off period
($s in millions)

	1994	1995	1996
Sales	$4,649	$5,937	$8,671
Net income (NOPAT)	1,146	1,453	2,195
Total assets	5,363	7,210	10,093
Total shareholders' equity	4,450	5,333	6,908
Research and development	$610	$860	$1,432
Revised research and development[1]	$ 477.33	$ 646.67	$ 967.33
Revised net income[2]	1,233.56	1,593.80	2,501.68
Revised total assets[3]	5,926.33	7,986.67	11,334.33
Revised stockholders' equity[4]	$4,537.56	$5,473.80	$ 7,214.68
NOPAT margin	0.265	0.268	0.289
Asset turnover	0.915	0.853	0.898
Return on assets	0.243	0.229	0.259
Return on shareholder's equity	0.314	0.318	0.394

[1]Calculation (illustrated for '94): ($352 + 470 + 610)/3 = $477.33
[2]Calculation (illustrated for '94): $1,146 + [($610 - 477.33) × 0.66] = $1,233.56
[3]Calculation (illustrated for '94): $5,363 + ($610 × 2/3) + (470 × 1/3) = $5,926.33
[4]Calculation (illustrated for '94): $4,450 + [($610 - 477.33) × 0.66] = $4,537.56

The differences in the ratios appear to be significant.

a) Net income over the 1994–1996 period is higher with capitalized R&D because the amount of recorded R&D expense is lower and because the firm (and R&D) is growing.

b) As in (a), NOPAT margins over the 1994–1996 period are higher with capitalization because the amount of recorded R&D expense is lower, and net income is higher.

c) Asset turnover rates over the 1994–1996 period are lower because the firm's asset base is larger due to the capitalization of some of the R&D costs.

d) Return on asset ratios over the 1994–1996 period are lower (except 1996) because the firm's asset base is larger due to the capitalization of some of the R&D costs. The increase in net income from capitalization is not enough to offset the Increase in the asset base, so the ratio falls.

e) Finally, return on shareholders' equity ratios over the 1994–1996 period is higher because the firm's net income each year is higher due to the capitalization of some of the R&D costs.

C9-2. Southwest Airlines (CW): Financial statement effects of capitalized interest

Requirement 1:

The rationale for capitalizing interest is the matching principle. If the interest were expensed in the year incurred rather than matched with the future revenues the new assets will help to generate, income during the construction period would be understated and income in the years after the assets are placed in service would be overstated. Another rationale for capitalizing interest is that it is considered to be a legitimate cost of the asset.

Requirement 2:

Income before income taxes:	$341,362	(as reported)
Capitalized interest	-22,267	
Revised Income before income taxes	$319,095	(without capitalization)

Percentage decline   = ($319,095 - $341,362)/$341,362
                = -6.5%

Requirement 3:

Net income	$207,337	(as reported)
Capitalized interest (after-tax)	-14,696	[22,267 × (1-0.34)]
Revised net income	$192,641	

Percentage decline   = ($192,641 - $207,337)/$207,337
                = -7.1%

Requirement 4:

This is possible because the capitalized Interest is related to the total accrual-based interest expense incurred by the firm, not the amount actually paid in cash in a given year.

Requirement 5:

The capitalized interest will reduce future years' reported earnings—in comparison to earnings without capitalization—because it will enter the income statement as part of the depreciation expense on the associated assets.

C9-3. Delta Air Lines (CW): Financial statement effects of depreciation policy changes

Requirement 1:
The bottom line effect of the decrease is $34.0 million times (1 - 0.34), or $22.44 million. Delta reported an actual net earnings effect of $22 million in the footnotes to its financial statements. The difference could be due to rounding or to a slight difference in the tax rate that Delta used.

Requirement 2:
Reported earnings in the future will be higher than they would otherwise have been because depreciation expense will be lower than it would otherwise have been.

Requirement 3:
The analyst might examine the footnotes to the financial statements of other airline companies (with fleets reasonably similar to Delta) to see if they are making similar adjustments, or if they already using similar useful lives to those Delta just changed to.

Requirement 4:
Firms can strategically change the useful lives and salvage values of their long-term assets to manage earnings upward or downward. Firms cannot endlessly use the latitude they have over depreciation policy choices to repeatedly manage earnings because they have only a certain amount of assets to depreciate, and because their outside auditors must sanction/agree with the changes they make.

Requirement 5:
The change increases income. If the company has debt contracts which require the maintenance of certain minimum or maximum levels of various financial ratios/numbers (e.g., interest coverage, debt-to-equity, net worth, etc.), such numbers will be favorably impacted by the change in the firm's depreciation policy. So, too, will be the present value of management compensation that is tied to reported earnings.

Of course, it is entirely possible that Delta made the change because management felt that the revised useful lives better reflected industry conditions and would provide a more realistic measure of the firm's net earnings.

C9-4. Dayton Hudson and Kmart (CW): Depreciation differences and financial statement analysis

Requirement 1:
The estimated average useful life of Dayton Hudson's assets is:

Average useful life = average gross PP&E (excluding construction in progress)/depreciation expense

$$= ([(\$5{,}812 + 2{,}482) + (\$5{,}943 + 2{,}652)]/2)/\$650$$

$$= \$8{,}444.5/\$650$$

$$= 13.0 \text{ years}$$

The estimated average useful life of Kmart's assets is:

Average useful life = average gross PP&E (excluding construction in progress)/depreciation expense

$$= ([(\$440 + 1{,}438 + 5{,}132 + 2{,}875) + (\$995 + 1{,}470 + 5{,}050 + 2{,}820)]/2)/\$654$$

$$= \$10{,}110/\$654$$

$$= 15.5 \text{ years}$$

Requirement 2:
Kmart's revised, estimated 1997 depreciation expense would be:

$$= \$10{,}110/13.0$$

$$= \$777.7$$

Kmart's revised, estimated 1997 depreciation expense is higher because of the shorter average useful life of Dayton Hudson's assets.

Kmart's income before taxes would fall by $777.7 - $654.0, or $123.7 (i.e., the increase in the depreciation expense that would have been recorded). The revised amount of income before tax of $330.0 - $123.7 = $206.3 might be more comparable with Dayton Hudson's reported earnings before tax of $783.0 if the difference in average useful lives is not due to real underlying economic differences in the firms' circumstances.

Kmart's net loss of $220 for 1997 would increase by $81.6 [$123.7 × (1 - .34)] to $301.6, which, again, might be more comparable with Dayton Hudson's reported net income of $463.0 for 1997 if the useful lives' differences do not reflect differences in underlying economic conditions.

Requirement 3:
Dayton Hudson's revised, estimated 1997 depreciation expense would be:

= $8,444.5/15.5

= $544.8

Dayton Hudson's revised, estimated 1997 depreciation expense is lower because of the longer average useful life of Kmart's assets.

The following calculations are simply the flip side of those in Requirement 2 and are included to show the alternative avenue of adjustment.

Dayton Hudson's income before taxes would increase by $650.0 - $544.8, or $105.2 (i.e., the decrease in the depreciation expense that would have been recorded). The revised amount of income before tax of $783.0 + $105.2 = $888.2 might be more comparable with Kmart's reported earnings before tax of $330.0. Again, this answer presumes that the differences in useful lives do not reflect different underlying economic conditions.

Dayton Hudson's net income of $463.0 for 1997 would increase by $69.4 [$105.2 × (1 - .34)] to $532.4, which might be more comparable with Kmart's reported net loss of $220.0 for 1997.

Requirement 4:
The comparability of the financial statements of firms in the same industry, hence, comparisons involving their financial ratios, can be hindered by differences in depreciation policy. The analysis above provides a means to control for differences emanating from differences in useful lives for assets that are expected to be similar in most respects.

Requirement 5:
Some factors that affect the reliability and accuracy of the adjustments made above include:

a) The analysis assumes that the firms have similar proportions of the various assets included in the overall plant and equipment category.

b) The analysis above assumes that the salvage values used by the firms are reasonably similar.

E10-5. Gain or loss at early retirement
(AICPA adapted)

The gain on bond retirement can be computed as follows:

Reacquisition price		($1,020,000)
Face value	1,000,000	
Unamortized premium	78,000	
Book value of bonds 5/1/99		1,078,000
Gain on retirement of debt		$58,000

The reaquisition price is the cash paid out by Davis to reaquire its bonds. Since it is less than the book value of the bonds, the company realizes a gain on the retirement of its debt.

E10-6. Amortizing a premium
(AICPA adapted)

To find the amount of unamortized premium on June 30, 1999, we first need to find the interest expense for 1999 (6% of the June 30, 1998, book value, 6% of $105,000).

Date	Interest Payment	Interest Expense	Premium Amortization	Book Value
6/30/98				105,000
6/30/99	7,000	6,300	700	104,300

The carrying (or book) value of the bond on June 30, 1999, is $104,300. We know that the face value of the bond is $100,000 and the book value is $104,300; the difference between the face value and book value of the bond must be the unamortized premium. So Webb should report $4,300 of unamortized premium in its June 30, 1999, balance sheet.

E10-7. Loss contingencies
(AICPA adapted)

Brower expects to receive $3.2 million as compensation for the expropriation of its manufacturing plant. The plant has a book value of $5.0 million, so the estimated loss is $1.8 million ($5.0 book value - $3.2 million expropriation proceeds). The journal entry to record the intended expropriation is:

DR Estimated loss on expropriation of foreign plant		$1,800,000
CR Allowance for estimated loss on foreign plant		$1,800,000

E10-8. Bonds sold at par

The bonds have a face value of $10 million, mature in 20 periods, pay interest at the rate of 4% per period ($400,000), and are sold at a market yield rate of 4% per period.

Present value of principal ($10 million at 4% for 20 periods	$4,563,869
Present value of interest payment (Annuity of $400,000 for 20 periods at 4%)	5,436,131
Bond market price 1/1/98 (Present value of the bond)	$10,000,000

So, the bonds were issued at par for $10 million. That is easy to see, because the coupon rate and the market yield rate are the same, 4%. And, because the bonds are issued at par, there is no discount or premium to record.

E10-9. Debt-for-equity swap

Requirement 1:
The bonds were originally issued at par for $100 million on January 1, 1998. Because they were issued at par, and no discount or premium was recorded, the book value of the bonds will remain at $100 million until maturity in 10 years.

On January 1, 2001 (three years later), the market yield on the bonds is 14% and their market value is:

Present value of principal ($100 million at 7% for 14 periods)	$38,781,724
Present value of interest payment (Annuity of $5 million for 14 periods at 7%)	43,727,340
Bond market price 1/1/01 (Present value of the bond)	$82,509,064

Requirement 2:
If the company retired all of these bonds in exchange for stock of equal market value, the entry would be (ignoring tax effects):

DR Bonds payable	$100,000,000	
CR Common stock		$82,509,064
CR Gain on retirement of bonds		17,490,936

E10-10. Zero coupon bonds

Requirement 1:
These bonds have a face value of $250 million, a zero coupon rate, a market yield rate of 12%, and mature in 20 years. The issue price is:

Present value of principal ($250 million at 12% for 20 periods)	$25,916,691
Present value of interest payment (Annuity of zero for 20 periods at 12%)	0
Bond market price 1/1/99 (Present value of the bond)	$25,916,691

If the quoted interest rate is really 12% semi-annually (6% each period for 40 periods), then the bond issue price would be $24,305,547.

Requirement 2:
How much interest expense would the company record on the bonds in 1999? Well, the bonds don't **pay** interest, but an expense would still be recorded:

Expense = $25,916,691 × 12% = $3,110,003

E10-11. Floating rate debt

Requirement 1:
The floating interest rate for 1998, set on January 1 of that year, was 12% or the LIBOR rate of 6% plus 6% additional interest. The 1998 interest payment was $24 million ($12 million every 6 months), or the $200 million borrowed multiplied by the 12% floating rate for the year.

For 1999, the floating rate will be 14%, or a LIBOR rate of 8% plus 6% additional interest. So the company will pay out $28 million ($14 million every 6 months) in interest that year, or $200 million borrowed multiplied by the 14% floating rate for the year.

Requirement 2:
The debentures were issued at par for $200 million, so there is no discount or premium to amortize. Interest expense just equals the required cash interest payment: $24 million in 1998 and $28 million in 1999.

E10-12. Incentives for early debt retirement

Requirement 1:
We must first determine the book value of the bonds on December 31, 1997— almost two years after issuance. That would seem easy because the bonds were issued at par, but there is a catch: The interest payment due that day has

not yet been paid, so we must bring the books up to date by first recording accrued interest from July 1 through December 31:

DR Interest expense to December 31 $5,000,000
       CR Interest payable $5,000,000

$5,000,000 = \$125 \text{ million} \times 4\%$

The total book value (including Interest) of the debt on December 31, 1997, is $130 million, the $125 million borrowed plus the $5 million of interest owed for July 1 through December 31.

The market value of the bonds on December 31, 1997, is: $125 million face value, 8% coupon rate paid semi-annually, 13 years to maturity, and yield of 12%:

Present value of principal ($125 million at 6% for 26 periods)	$27,476,254
Present value of interest payment (Annuity of $5 million for 26 periods at 6%)	65,016,831
Bond present value 12/31/98	$92,492,085

Plus the accrued interest of $5 million gives a total market value of the bond equal to $97,492,085.

The entry to record the debt retirement is:

DR Bonds payable $125,000,000
DR Accrued interest payable   5,000,000
       CR Cash $97,492,085
       CR Gain on retirement of debt   32,507,915

DR Tax expense (@ 40%) $13,003,166
       CR Taxes payable $13,003,166

Requirement 2:
There are several reasons a company might want to retire debt early: take advantage of lower interest rates; postpone scheduled principal repayments; eliminate a conversion feature attached to the debt; improve the company's mix of debt and equity capital; or earnings management using the "paper" gains from debt retirement.

E10-13. Off-balance sheet debt

Notice that the joint venture (Woodly Partners) borrowed the $200 million, not the two partner companies. Neither partner (Wood or Willie) owns more than 50% of the joint venture's common stock, so consolidation is not required (see Chapter 15 for the details on this point). The $200 million will show up on the books of the joint venture, but not on the books of Wood or Willie. Both partners will probably provide a footnote description of the joint venture, its borrowing and thus their guarantee of the debt.

E10-14. Noninterest bearing loan

Requirement 1:
The present value of this payment stream, discounted at 9%, is:

Present value of $100,000 at delivery	$100,000
Present value of $200,000 in 1 Year	183,486
Present value of $200,000 in 2 Years	168,336
Total present value of payment stream	$451,822

$183,436 = \$200,000 \times 1/(1.09)$
$168,336 = \$200,000 \times 1/(1.09)^2$

Requirement 2:
The purchase would be recorded at its implied cash price of $451,822 as:

DR Equipment	$451,822	
CR Cash		$100,000
CR Note payable		351,822

Interest expense at 9% per year on the unpaid balance would also be recorded over time.

Requirement 3:
McClelland should purchase from Agri-Products because it has offered the best price.

Problems
P10-1. Bonds issued at a discount

Requirement 1:

The issuance price of the bonds on January 1, 1998, is equal to the present value of the principal repayment plus the present value of the semi-annual interest payments. Since the bonds pay interest semi-annually, the present value calculations are based on a twenty-period horizon using a market interest rate of 5% (i.e., 10%/2).

Present value of the principal repayment:

$$= \$15,000,000 \times \text{Present value of \$1 to be received in 20 periods at 5\%}$$
$$= \$15,000,000 \times 0.3769 = \$5,653,500$$

Present value of the interest payments:

$$= (\$15,000,000 \times 0.04) \times \text{Present value of an ordinary annuity of \$1 to}$$
$$\text{be received for 20 periods at 5\%}$$
$$= \$600,000 \times 12.4622 = \$7,477,320$$

Price of the bonds:

$$= \$5,653,500 + \$7,477,320 = \$13,130,820$$

Requirement 2:

The amortization schedule appears below:

Effective Amortization of Bond Discount for McVay Corp.				
[Market Interest Rate of 5% (semi-annual)]				
Date	(a) Interest Expense (0.05 × e)	(b) Cash Payment (Fixed)	(c) Amortization of Bond Discount (a - b)	(d) Discount on B/P (Beginning Balance minus c)	(e) Carrying Amount ($15,000,000 minus d)
7/1/98				$1,869,180.00	$13,130,820.00
12/31/98	$656,541.00	$600,000.00	$56,541.00	1,812,639.00	13,187,361.00
6/30/99	659,368.05	600,000.00	59,368.05	1,753,270.95	13,246,729.05
12/31/99	662,336.45	600,000.00	62,336.45	1,690,934.50	13,309,065.50
6/30/00	665,453.28	600,000.00	65,453.28	1,625,481.22	13,374,518.78

Requirement 3:
The journal entries for the first four interest payments are:

12/31/98:
    DR Interest expense $656,541.00
        CR Cash $600,000.00
        CR Discount on bonds payable   56,541.00

6/30/99:
    DR Interest expense $659,368.05
        CR Cash $600,000.00
        CR Discount on bonds payable   59,368.05

12/31/99:
    DR Interest expense $662,336.45
        CR Cash $600,000.00
        CR Discount on bonds payable   62,336.45

6/30/00:
    DR Interest expense $665,453.28
        CR Cash $600,000.00
        CR Discount on bonds payable   65,453.28

Requirement 4:
The balance sheet presentation at 12/31/98 would be:

Bonds payable	$15,000,000.00
Less: Discount on bonds payable	1,812,639.00
Carrying amount of bonds payable	$13,187,361.00

The balance sheet presentation at 12/31/99 would be:

Bonds payable	$15,000,000.00
Less: Discount on bonds payable	1,690,934.50
Carrying amount of bonds payable	$13,309,065.50

P10-2. Bonds issued at a premium

Requirement 1:
The issuance price of the bonds on January 1, 1999, is equal to the present value of the principal repayment plus the present value of the semi-annual interest payments. Since the bonds pay interest semi-annually, the present value calculations are based on a twenty-period horizon using a market interest rate of 3% (i.e., 6%/2).

Present value of the principal repayment:

$$= \$25,000,000 \times \text{Present value of } \$1 \text{ to be received in 20 periods at 3\%}$$
$$= \$25,000,000 \times 0.5537 = \$13,842,500$$

Present value of the interest payments:

$$= (\$25,000,000 \times 0.04) \times \text{Present value of an ordinary annuity of } \$1 \text{ to be received for 20 periods at 3\%}$$
$$= \$1,000,000 \times 14.8775 = \$14,877,500$$

Price of the bonds:

$$= \$13,842,500 + \$14,877,500 = \$28,720,000$$

Requirement 2:
The amortization schedule appears below:

Effective Amortization of Bond Premium for Fleetwood Inc. [Market interest rate of 3% (semi-annual)]					
Date	(a) Interest Expense (0.03 × e)	(b) Cash Payment (Fixed)	(c) Amortization of Bond Premium (b - a)	(d) Premium on B/P (Beginning Balance minus c)	(e) Carrying Amount ($25,000,000 plus d)
1/1/99				$3,720,000.00	$28,720,000.00
6/30/99	$861,600.00	$1,000,000.00	$138,400.00	3,581,600.00	28,581,600.00
12/31/99	857,448.00	1,000,000.00	142,552.00	3,439,048.00	28,439,048.00
6/30/00	853,171.44	1,000,000.00	146,828.56	3,292,219.44	28,292,219.44
12/31/00	848,766.58	1,000,000.00	151,233.42	3,140,986.02	28,140,986.02

Requirement 3:
The journal entries for the first four interest payments are:

6/30/99:
DR Interest expense $861,600.00
DR Premium on bonds payable 138,400.00
  CR Cash $1,000,000.00

12/31/99:
DR Interest expense $857,448.00
DR Premium on bonds payable 142,552.00
  CR Cash $1,000,000.00

6/30/00:
DR Interest expense $853,171.44
DR Premium on bonds payable 146,828.56
  CR Cash $1,000,000.00

12/31/00:
DR Interest expense $848,766.58
DR Premium on bonds payable 151,233.42
  CR Cash $1,000,000.00

Requirement 4:
The balance sheet presentation at 12/31/99 would be:

Bonds payable	$25,000,000.00
Plus: Premium on bonds payable	3,439,048.00
Carrying amount of bonds payable	$28,439,048.00

The balance sheet presentation at 12/31/00 would be:

Bonds payable	$25,000,000.00
Plus: Premium on bonds payable	3,140,986.02
Carrying amount of bonds payable	$28,140,986.02

P10-3. Understanding the numbers

The following tables were generated using the bond amortization template.

Alternative A:

Bond Principal	$500,000
Coupon Interest Rate	10.0%
Market Interest Rate	9.0%

Amortization Table

Year	Period	Bond Carrying Amount at Start of Year	Interest Expense	Bond (Premium) Discount Amortization	Premium (Discount) Balance	Bond Carrying Amount at Year End	Cash Interest Payment	Principal Payment
Issue date:		$545,643			$45,643			
1999	1	$545,643	$49,108	($892)	$44,751	$544,751	$50,000	$0
2000	2	544,751	49,028	(972)	43,778	543,778	50,000	0
2001	3	543,778	48,940	(1,060)	42,718	542,718	50,000	0
2002	4	542,718	48,845	(1,155)	41,563	541,563	50,000	0
2003	5	541,563	48,741	(1,259)	40,303	540,303	50,000	0
2004	6	540,303	48,627	(1,373)	38,931	538,931	50,000	0
2005	7	538,931	48,504	(1,496)	37,435	537,435	50,000	0
2006	8	537,435	48,369	(1,631)	35,804	535,804	50,000	0
2007	9	535,804	48,222	(1,778)	34,026	534,026	50,000	0
2008	10	534,026	48,062	(1,938)	32,088	532,088	50,000	0
2009	11	532,088	47,888	(2,112)	29,976	529,976	50,000	0
2010	12	529,976	47,698	(2,302)	27,674	527,674	50,000	0
2011	13	527,674	47,491	(2,509)	25,165	525,165	50,000	0
2012	14	525,165	47,265	(2,735)	22,430	522,430	50,000	0
2013	15	522,430	47,019	(2,981)	19,448	519,448	50,000	0
2014	16	519,448	46,750	(3,250)	16,199	516,199	50,000	0
2015	17	516,199	46,458	(3,542)	12,656	512,656	50,000	0
2016	18	512,656	46,139	(3,861)	8,796	508,796	50,000	0
2017	19	508,796	45,792	(4,208)	4,587	504,587	50,000	0
2018	20	504,587	45,413	(4,587)	(0)	500,000	50,000	500,000

Total Interest Expense	$954,357		Total Interest Paid	$1,000,000
Interest Tax Deduction	$381,743			
Present Value of Tax Savings	$176,023			

Alternative B:

Bond Principal	$700,000
Coupon Interest Rate	6.0%
Market Interest Rate	9.0%

Amortization Table

Year	Period	Bond Carrying Amount at Start of Year	Interest Expense	Bond (Premium) Discount Amortization	Premium (Discount) Balance	Bond Carrying Amount at Year End	Cash Interest Payment	Principal Payment
Issue date:		$508,301			($191,699)			
1999	1	$508,301	$45,747	$3,747	($187,952)	$512,048	$42,000	$0
2000	2	512,048	46,084	4,084	(183,868)	516,132	42,000	0
2001	3	516,132	46,452	4,452	(179,416)	520,584	42,000	0
2002	4	520,584	46,853	4,853	(174,564)	525,436	42,000	0
2003	5	525,436	47,289	5,289	(169,274)	530,726	42,000	0
2004	6	530,726	47,765	5,765	(163,509)	536,491	42,000	0
2005	7	536,491	48,284	6,284	(157,225)	542,775	42,000	0
2006	8	542,775	48,850	6,850	(150,375)	549,625	42,000	0
2007	9	549,625	49,466	7,466	(142,909)	557,091	42,000	0
2008	10	557,091	50,138	8,138	(134,771)	565,229	42,000	0
2009	11	565,229	50,871	8,871	(125,900)	574,100	42,000	0
2010	12	574,100	51,669	9,669	(116,231)	583,769	42,000	0
2011	13	583,769	52,539	10,539	(105,692)	594,308	42,000	0
2012	14	594,308	53,488	11,488	(94,204)	605,796	42,000	0
2013	15	605,796	54,522	12,522	(81,683)	618,317	42,000	0
2014	16	618,317	55,649	13,649	(68,034)	631,966	42,000	0
2015	17	631,966	56,877	14,877	(52,157)	646,843	42,000	0
2016	18	646,843	58,216	16,216	(36,941)	663,059	42,000	0
2017	19	663,059	59,675	17,675	(19,266)	680,734	42,000	0
2018	20	680,734	61,266	19,266	(0)	700,000	42,000	700,000

Total Interest Expense	$1,031,699	Total Interest Paid	$840,000
Interest Tax Deduction	$412,680		
Present Value of Tax Savings	$180,861		

423

Alternative C:

Bond Principal	$400,000
Coupon Interest Rate	12.0%
Market Interest Rate	9.0%

Amortization Table

Year	Period	Bond Carrying Amount at Start of Year	Interest Expense	Bond (Premium) Discount Amortization	Premium (Discount) Balance	Bond Carrying Amount at Year End	Cash Interest Payment	Principal Payment
Issue date:		$509,543			$109,543			
1999	1	$509,543	$45,859	($2,141)	$107,401	$507,401	$48,000	$0
2000	2	507,401	45,666	(2,334)	105,068	505,068	48,000	0
2001	3	505,068	45,456	(2,544)	102,524	502,524	48,000	0
2002	4	502,524	45,227	(2,773)	99,751	499,751	48,000	0
2003	5	499,751	44,978	(3,022)	96,728	496,728	48,000	0
2004	6	496,728	44,706	(3,294)	93,434	493,434	48,000	0
2005	7	493,434	44,409	(3,591)	89,843	489,843	48,000	0
2006	8	489,843	44,086	(3,914)	85,929	485,929	48,000	0
2007	9	485,929	43,734	(4,266)	81,662	481,662	48,000	0
2008	10	481,662	43,350	(4,650)	77,012	477,012	48,000	0
2009	11	477,012	42,931	(5,069)	71,943	471,943	48,000	0
2010	12	471,943	42,475	(5,525)	66,418	466,418	48,000	0
2011	13	466,418	41,978	(6,022)	60,395	460,395	48,000	0
2012	14	460,395	41,436	(6,564)	53,831	453,831	48,000	0
2013	15	453,831	40,845	(7,155)	46,676	446,676	48,000	0
2014	16	446,676	40,201	(7,799)	38,877	438,877	48,000	0
2015	17	438,877	39,499	(8,501)	30,376	430,376	48,000	0
2016	18	430,376	38,734	(9,266)	21,109	421,109	48,000	0
2017	19	421,109	37,900	(10,100)	11,009	411,009	48,000	0
2018	20	411,009	36,991	(11,009)	(0)	400,000	48,000	400,000

Total Interest Expense	$850,457		Total Interest Paid	$960,000
Interest Tax Deduction	$340,183			
Present Value of Tax Savings	$159,553			

424

Requirements 1 through 5:

		Alternative A	Alternative B	Alternative C
1)	Issue price of each bond	$545,643	$508,301	$509,543
2)	Cash paid out in 1999 (first-year interest)	50,000	42,000	48,000
3)	Interest expense recorded in 2000	49,028	46,084	45,666
	Interest expense recorded in 2005	48,504	48,284	44,409
4)	Total interest expense over life of loan	954,357	1,031,699	850,457
5)	Total cash payments to bondholders:			
	Interest payments	1,000,000	840,000	960,000
	Principal payment	500,000	700,000	400,000
6)	Present value of tax savings on interest	176,023	180,861	159,553

Requirement 6:

All three loans raise enough cash to finance the building expansion, and each loan carries the same market yield rate (9%). That means that Cory's pre-tax cost of capital is the same in each case. But the after-tax cost of capital is not the same because the loans differ in terms of dollars assigned to interest expense and dollars assigned to debt principal, and only interest expense dollars are tax-deductible.

The easiest way to see what Cory should do is to consider the **after-tax net present value** of the building expansion: $500,000 minus the present value of interest tax deductions from the loan. Since Alternative B has the highest tax savings, it is the least costly way of financing the expansion. Of course, this also means that Alternative B will produce the lowest reported earnings because it has the highest interest expense.

P10-4. Evaluating loan alternatives

The following tables were generated from the bond amortization template.

Alternative A:

Bond Principal	$1,000,000
Coupon Interest Rate	12.5%
Market Interest Rate	12.0%

Amortization Table

Year	Period	Bond Carrying Amount at Start of Year	Interest Expense	Bond (Premium) Discount Amortization	Premium (Discount) Balance	Bond Carrying Amount at Year End	Cash Interest Payment	Principal Payment
Issue date::		$1,037,347			$37,347			
1999	1	$1,037,347	$124,482	($518)	$36,829	$1,036,829	$125,000	$0
2000	2	1,036,829	124,419	(581)	36,248	1,036,248	125,000	0
2001	3	1,036,248	124,350	(650)	35,598	1,035,598	125,000	0
2002	4	1,035,598	124,272	(728)	34,870	1,034,870	125,000	0
2003	5	1,034,870	124,184	(816)	34,054	1,034,054	125,000	0
2004	6	1,034,054	124,087	(913)	33,141	1,033,141	125,000	0
2005	7	1,033,141	123,977	(1,023)	32,118	1,032,118	125,000	0
2006	8	1,032,118	123,854	(1,146)	30,972	1,030,972	125,000	0
2007	9	1,030,972	123,717	(1,283)	29,688	1,029,688	125,000	0
2008	10	1,029,688	123,563	(1,437)	28,251	1,028,251	125,000	0
2009	11	1,028,251	123,390	(1,610)	26,241	1,026,641	125,000	0
2010	12	1,026,641	123,197	(1,803)	24,838	1,024,838	125,000	0
2011	13	1,024,838	122,981	(2,019)	22,819	1,022,819	125,000	0
2012	14	1,022,819	122,738	(2,262)	20,557	1,020,557	125,000	0
2013	15	1,020,557	122,467	(2,533)	18,024	1,018,024	125,000	0
2014	16	1,018,024	122,163	(2,837)	15,187	1,015,187	125,000	0
2015	17	1,015,187	121,822	(3,178)	12,009	1,012,009	125,000	0
2016	18	1,012,009	121,441	(3,559)	8,450	1,008,450	125,000	0
2017	19	1,008,450	121,014	(3,986)	4,464	1,004,464	125,000	0
2018	20	1,004,464	120,536	(4,464)	(0)	1,000,000	125,000	1,000,000

Total Interest Expense	$2,462,653	Total Interest Paid	$2,500,000
Interest Tax Deduction	$985,061		
Present value of Tax Savings	$369,770		

426

Alternative B:

Bond principal $900,000
Coupon interest rate 14.0%
Market interest rate 12.0%

Amortization Table

Year	Period	Bond Carrying Amount at Start of Year	Interest Expense	Bond (Premium) Discount Amortization	Premium (Discount) Balance	Bond Carrying Amount at Year End	Cash Interest Payment	Principal Payment
Issue date::		$1,034,450			$134,450			
1999	1	$1,034,450	$124,134	($1,866)	$132,584	$1,032,584	$126,000	$0
2000	2	1,032,584	123,910	(2,090)	130,494	1,030,494	126,000	0
2001	3	1,030,494	123,659	(2,341)	128,153	1,028,153	126,000	0
2002	4	1,028,153	123,378	(2,622)	125,532	1,025,532	126,000	0
2003	5	1,025,532	123,064	(2,936)	122,596	1,022,596	126,000	0
2004	6	1,022,596	122,711	(3,289)	119,307	1,019,307	126,000	0
2005	7	1,019,307	122,317	(3,683)	115,624	1,015,624	126,000	0
2006	8	1,015,624	121,875	(4,125)	111,499	1,011,499	126,000	0
2007	9	1,011,499	121,380	(4,620)	106,879	1,006,879	126,000	0
2008	10	1,006,879	120,825	(5,175)	101,704	1,001,704	126,000	0
2009	11	1,001,704	120,204	(5,796)	95,908	995,908	126,000	0
2010	12	995,908	119,509	(6,491)	89,418	989,418	126,000	0
2011	13	989,418	118,730	(7,270)	82,148	982,148	126,000	0
2012	14	982,148	117,858	(8,142)	74,005	974,005	126,000	0
2013	15	974,005	116,881	(9,119)	64,886	964,886	126,000	0
2014	16	964,886	115,786	(10,214)	54,672	954,672	126,000	0
2015	17	954,672	114,561	(11,439)	43,233	943,233	126,000	0
2016	18	943,233	113,188	(12,812)	30,421	930,421	126,000	0
2017	19	930,421	111,651	(14,349)	16,071	916,071	126,000	0
2018	20	916,071	109,929	(16,071)	(0)	900,000	126,000	900,000

Total Interest Expense $2,385,550   **Total Interest Paid** $2,520,000

Interest Tax Deduction $954,220

Present Value of Tax Savings $363,131

Alternative C:

Bond Principal	$1,100,000
Coupon Interest Rate	11.0%
Market Interest Rate	12.0%

Amortization Table

Year	Period	Bond Carrying Amount at Start of Year	Interest Expense	Bond (Premium) Discount Amortization	Premium (Discount) Balance	Bond Carrying Amount at Year End	Cash Interest Payment	Principal Payment
Issue date:		$1,017,836			($82,164)			
1999	1	$1,017,836	$122,140	$1,140	($81,024)	$1,018,976	$121,000	$0
2000	2	1,018,976	122,277	1,277	(79,746)	1,020,254	121,000	0
2001	3	1,020,254	122,430	1,430	(78,316)	1,021,684	121,000	0
2002	4	1,021,684	122,602	1,602	(76,714)	1,023,286	121,000	0
2003	5	1,023,286	122,794	1,794	(74,920)	1,025,080	121,000	0
2004	6	1,025,080	123,010	2,010	(72,910)	1,027,090	121,000	0
2005	7	1,027,090	123,251	2,251	(70,659)	1,029,341	121,000	0
2006	8	1,029,341	123,521	2,521	(68,138)	1,031,862	121,000	0
2007	9	1,031,862	123,823	2,823	(65,315)	1,034,685	121,000	0
2008	10	1,034,685	124,162	3,162	(62,152)	1,037,848	121,000	0
2009	11	1,037,848	124,542	3,542	(58,611)	1,041,389	121,000	0
2010	12	1,041,389	124,967	3,967	(54,644)	1,045,356	121,000	0
2011	13	1,045,356	125,443	4,443	(50,201)	1,049,799	121,000	0
2012	14	1,049,799	125,976	4,976	(45,225)	1,054,775	121,000	0
2013	15	1,054,775	126,573	5,573	(39,653)	1,060,347	121,000	0
2014	16	1,060,347	127,242	6,242	(33,411)	1,066,589	121,000	0
2015	17	1,066,589	127,991	6,991	(26,420)	1,073,580	121,000	0
2016	18	1,073,580	128,830	7,830	(18,591)	1,081,409	121,000	0
2017	19	1,081,409	129,769	8,769	(9,821)	1,090,179	121,000	0
2018	20	1,090,179	130,821	9,821	(0)	1,100,000	121,000	1,100,000

Total Interest Expense	$2,502,164	Total Interest Paid	$2,420,000
Interest Tax Deduction	$1,000,866		
Present Value of Tax Savings	$369,666		

Requirements 1 through 5:

		Alternative A	Alternative B	Alternative C
1)	Issue price of each note	$1,037,347	$1,034,450	$1,017,836
2)	Cash paid out in 1999 (first-year interest)	125,000	126,000	121,000
3)	Interest expense recorded in 2000	124,419	123,910	122,277
	Interest expense recorded in 2005	123,977	122,317	123,251
4)	Total interest expense over life of loan	2,462,653	2,385,550	2,502,164
5)	Total cash payments to bondholders:			
	Interest payments	2,500,000	2,520,000	2,420,000
	Principal payment	1,000,000	900,000	1,100,000
6)	Present value of tax savings on interest	369,770	363,131	369,666

428

Requirement 6:

All three loans raise enough cash to finance the distribution center expansion, and each loan carries the same market yield rate (12%). That means Zelda's pre-tax cost of capital is the same in each case. But the after-tax cost of capital is not the same because the loans differ in terms of dollars assigned to interest expense and dollars assigned to debt principal, and only interest expense dollars are tax-deductible.

The easiest way to see what Cory should do is to consider the *after-tax net present value* of the building expansion: $1,000,000 minus the present value of interest tax deductions from the loan. Since Alternative B has the lowest tax savings, it is the most costly way of financing the expansion. That leaves Alternatives A and C, both producing about the same tax savings. The additional funds generated by Alternative A (almost $20,000 higher issue price) can be invested in a risk-free government security paying about 6% annually, or 3.6% after taxes. The earnings on this investment can be used to offset interest expense on the loan, tilting the scales in favor of Alternative A.

P10-5. Early debt retirement

Requirement 1:

The issuance price of the bonds on January 1, 1998, is equal to the present value of the principal repayment plus the present value of the semi-annual interest payments. Since the bonds pay interest semi-annually, the present value calculations are based on a twenty-period horizon using a market interest rate of 5.5% (i.e., 11%/2).

Present value of the principal repayment:

= $75,000,000 × Present value of $1 to be received in 20 periods at 5.5%

= $75,000,000 × 0.3427 = $25,702,500

Present value of the interest payments:

= ($75,000,000 × 0.045) × Present value of an ordinary annuity of $1
   to be received for 20 periods at 5.5%

= $3,375,000 × 11.9504 = $40,332,600

Price of the bonds: = $25,702,500 + $40,332,600 = **$66,035,100**

429

Requirement 2:

Appearing below is a partial amortization table for these bonds. The book value of the books on January 1, 2000 (i.e., December 31, 1999) is given in the last row of the table.

	(a) Interest Expense (0.055 × e)	(b) Cash Payment (Fixed)	(c) Amortization of Bond Discount (a-b)	(d) Discount on B/P (Beginning Balance minus c)	(e) Carrying Amount ($75,000,000 minus d)
Amortization of Bond Discount for Tango-In-The-Night Inc. [Market Interest Rate of 5.5% (semi-annual)]					
Date					
1/1/98				$8,964,900.00	$66,035,100.00
6/30/98	$3,631,930.50	$3,375,000.00	$256,930.50	8,707,969.50	66,292,030.50
12/31/98	3,646,061.68	3,375,000.00	271,061.68	8,436,907.82	66,563,092.18
6/30/99	3,660,970.07	3,375,000.00	285,970.07	8,150,937.75	66,849,062.25
12/31/99	3,676,698.42	3,375,000.00	301,698.42	7,849,239.33	**67,150,760.67**

The book value of the bonds on January 1, 2000, is $67,150,760.67.

Requirement 3:

The price of the bonds on January 1, 2000, is equal to the present value of the principal repayment to be received in eight years (i.e.,16 periods) plus the present value of the remaining semi-annual interest payments. Since the bonds have been outstanding for two years and pay interest semi-annually, there are sixteen remaining interest payments to be paid. The present value calculations are based on a sixteen-period horizon using a market interest rate of 5% (i.e., 10%/2).

Present value of the principal repayment:

    = $75,000,000 × Present value of $1 to be received in 16 periods at 5%

    = $75,000,000 × 0.4581 = $34,357,500

Present value of the interest payments:

    = $3,375,000 × Present value of an ordinary annuity of $1 to be received in 16 periods at 5%

    = $3,375,000 × 10.8378 = $36,577,575

Price of the bonds on January 1, 2000:

    = $34,357,500 + $36,577,575 = $70,935,075

Requirement 4:

If the bonds were retired on January 1, 2000, the journal entry would be:

DR Bonds payable	$75,000,000	
DR Loss on early extinguishment of debt	3,784,314	
CR Discount on bonds payable		$7,849,239*
CR Cash		70,935,075

*Rounded down by $0.33

P10-6. Partial debt retirement

Requirement 1:

The issuance price of the bonds on July 1, 1999, is equal to the present value of the principal repayment plus the present value of the semi-annual interest payments. Since the bonds pay interest semi-annually, the present value calculations are based on a twenty-period horizon using a market interest rate of 3.5% (i.e., 7%/2).

Present value of the principal repayment:

= $250,000,000 × Present value of $1 to be received in 20 periods at 3.5%

= $250,000,000 × 0.5026 = $125,650,000

Present value of the interest payments:

= ($250,000,000 × 0.0425) × Present value of an ordinary annuity of $1 to be received for 20 periods at 3.5%
= $10,625,000 × 14.2124 = $151,006,750

Price of the bonds: = $125,650,000 + $151,006,750 = $276,656,750

Requirement 2:
Appearing below is a partial amortization table for these bonds.

	(a) Interest Expense (0.035 × e)	(b) Cash Payment (Fixed)	(c) Amortization of Bond Premium (b - a)	(d) Premium on B/P (Beginning balance minus c)	(e) Carrying Amount ($250,000,000 plus d)
Date					
7/1/99				$26,656,750.00	$276,656,750.00
12/31/99	$9,682,986.25	$10,625,000.00	($942,013.75)	25,714,736.25	275,714,736.25
6/30/00	9,650,015.77	10,625,000.00	(974,984.23)	24,739,752.02	274,739,752.02
12/31/00	9,615,891.32	10,625,000.00	(1,009,108.68)	23,730,643.34	273,730,643.34
6/30/01	9,580,572.52	10,625,000.00	(1,044,427.48)	22,686,215.86	272,686,215.86

Effective Amortization of Bond Premium for Mirage Company [Market Interest Rate of 3.5% (semi-annual)]

Requirement 3:
The journal entries for the first four interest payments are:

12/31/99:
```
DR Interest expense                  $9,682,986.25
DR Premium on bonds payable             942,013.75
   CR Cash                                              $10,625,000.00
```

6/30/00:
```
DR Interest expense                  $9,650,015.77
DR Premium on bonds payable             974,984.23
   CR Cash                                              $10,625,000.00
```

12/31/00:
```
DR Interest expense                  $9,615,891.32
DR Premium on bonds payable           1,009,108.68
   CR Cash                                              $10,625,000.00
```

6/30/01:
```
DR Interest expense                  $9,580,572.52
DR Premium on bonds payable           1,044,427.48
   CR Cash                                              $10,625,000.00
```

Requirement 4:
The price of the bonds on July 1, 2001, is equal to the present value of the principal repayment to be received in eight years (i.e.,16 periods) plus the present value of the remaining semi-annual interest payments. Since the bonds have been outstanding for two years and pay interest semi-annually, there are sixteen remaining interest payments to be paid. The present value calculations are based on a sixteen-period horizon using a market interest rate of 4% (i.e., 8%/2).

Present value of the principal repayment:

    = \$250,000,000 × Present value of \$1 to be received in 16 periods at 4%

    = \$250,000,000 × 0.5339 = \$133,475,000.00

Present value of the interest payments:

    = \$10,625,000 × Present value of an ordinary annuity of \$1 to
        be received in 16 periods at 4%

    = \$10,625,000 × 11.6523 = \$123,805,687.50

Price of the bonds on July 1, 2001:

    = \$133,475,000.00 + \$123,805,687.50 = \$257,280,687.50

Requirement 5:
If 50% of the bonds were retired on July 1, 2001, the journal entry would be:

DR Bonds payable	\$125,000,000	
DR Premium on bonds payable	11,343,108*	
CR Cash		\$128,640,344**
CR Gain on early extinguishment		7,702,764

For ease of presentation: *Rounded up by \$0.07; **Rounded up by \$0.25

P10-7. Reading the financials

Requirement 1:
To compute interest expense, we multiply the beginning book value of the debt by its effective interest rate:

    Interest expense = \$182,700,000 × 14.6% = \$26,674,200

Notice that interest expense is different from the cash interest payment, which can be found by multiplying the debt face value by the stated interest rate:

    Interest payment = \$300,000,000 × 7%   = \$21,000,000

The discount amortization is the difference between the expense and cash payment shown above, or **\$5,674,200** = \$26,674,200 - \$21,000,000. The book value change shown on the balance sheet is **\$5,900,000** or \$188.6 million - \$182.7 million. The discount amortization should equal the change in balance sheet book values, but the two numbers differ here because of rounding in the reported effective interest rate or in the reported book values.

Requirement 2:
There are two ways to compute interest expense on the zero coupon bonds:

$$\text{Interest expense} = \$239,200,000 \times 12.0\% = \$28,704,000$$

Or, since the entire expense is amortized (there's no cash payment), it is all added to the debt book value. Consequently, interest expense will equal the increase in carrying value of the bonds, or:

$$\text{Interest expense} = \$267.9 \text{ million} - \$239.2 \text{ million} = \$28.7 \text{ million}$$

Requirement 3:
The following entry would have been made on December 31, 1992, for the participating mortgages:

DR Interest expense	$72.549	
CR Cash		$71.949
CR Discount on mortgage		0.600

$$\$72.549 = \$833.9 \times 8.7\% \quad \text{and} \quad \$0.600 = \$834.5 - \$833.9$$

Requirement 4:
The zero coupon bonds do not pay cash interest. $21 million was paid out on the 7% debentures, i.e., $300 million face value times 7%.

P10-8. Hedging

Requirement 1:
Foreign exchange forward contracts are agreements to exchange a specified amount of one currency (say, $100 million U.S. dollars) for a specified amount of another currency (say, $700 million Mexican pesos) at some specified date in the future (say, January 15, 2003). The contract locks in an exchange rate and insulates the company from exchange rate fluctuations in the future. Suppose Quaker Oats had to make a $700 million peso payment on January 15, 2003, and the cash for this payment was coming from the company's U.S. operations. Signing the forward contract now locks in a "$7 peso equals $1 dollar" exchange rate so that the company's peso payment is no longer subject to exchange rate risk.

Requirement 2:
There are at least two reasons for this difference in hedging strategies. One reason is that the company may feel that there is less volatility in the British pound compared to the Dutch guilder, so that there is less to be gained from a more complete hedge of its British exposure. A second reason is that it may be more costly to hedge the pound than it is to hedge the guilder.

Requirement 3:
The swap allowed the company to insulate its debt from exchange rate fluctuations. Here is how. The U.S. debt was presumably used to finance the company's operations in Germany and was to be repaid from DM operating cash flows. Without the swap, Quaker would have to convert its DM cash flows into U.S. dollars every time it made an interest or principal payment on the debt. By swapping the U.S. debt for DM debt, Quaker avoids the need for currency conversion and, thus, reduces its exposure to foreign exchange rate fluctuations.

Requirement 4:
After the company sold its European pet food operations, it no longer had the DM operating cash flows that were to be used to pay the DM swap debt. Lacking a local currency cash flow, it made sense to undo the swap because retaining the DM debt exposed the company to DM exchange rate risk.

Requirement 5:
Commodity options contracts give Quaker the right (but not the obligation) to buy grains at a specified price and date in the future. Commodity futures contracts *obligate* the company to buy grains at a specified price and date in the future. Both contracts reduce the company's exposure to commodity price fluctuations because the future purchase price is fixed by contract.

Requirement 6:
An interest rate swap allows Quaker to replace its floating-rate interest payment obligation with a fixed-rate interest payment obligation. Doing so reduces the company's exposure to changing interest rates in the future. In Quaker's case, the swap was used to hedge fixed interest rates in anticipation of a new debt issue.

Requirement 7:
Pre-paid interest represents the fee paid by Quaker for the swap. It is amortized over the life of the swap because it is just another cost of the overall borrowing.

Requirement 8:
An interest rate cap is a contract that limits Quaker's exposure to rising interest rates. A counterparty (probably a bank) has agreed to be responsible for any interest payments in excess of a specified maximum floating interest rate. To see how this benefits Quaker, suppose the company had issued debt with a floating rate of "LIBOR plus 2%." If the LIBOR is at 6%, Quaker pays interest at the rate of 8%. If the LIBOR hits 8%, Quaker's interest rate increases to 10%. By "capping" the rate, Quaker pays all interest up to some maximum rate (say, 9%) and the bank pays any excess over that amount (say, the 1% needed for the total to equal 10%). Quaker effectively transforms its floating-rate debt into fixed-rate debt when the floating rate reaches the cap.

P10-9. Callable bonds

Requirement 1:
Computation of issue price of the bond

PV of Interest	= 13.5903 × $100k	= $1,359,030
PV of principal	= 0.4564 × $2 million	= 912,800
Issue price of bonds		= $2,271,830

Requirement 2:
Computation of interest expense for 1999

Interest expense for first 6 months = 4% × $ 2,271,830 = $90,873
Premium on bonds payable $9,127
Cash   (5% × $2 million) $100,000

Carrying value of bonds on 7/1/99 = $2,271,830 - $9,127 = $2,262,703

Interest for second six months   = $2,262.703 × 4%   = $90,508

Total interest expense for 1999   = $90,873 + $90,508 = $181,381

Requirement 3:
Adjustment required on cash flow statement using the indirect method.

Premium amortization—first six months:
  $100,000 - $90,873 = $9,127
Premium amortization—second six months:
  $100,000 - $90,508 = $9,492
Total amount of premium, amortized in 1999 $18,619

$18,619 is the total amount that would be subtracted from the accrual basis net income to get cash flows from operations. Cash interest expense is more than accrual interest expense when bonds are sold at a premium.

Requirement 4:
Savings from exercising the call option rather than an open market purchase:

$P_{18|4.5\%}$	= 12.1600 × $100,000 =		$1,216,000
$P_{18|4.5\%}$	= .4528 × $2 million	=	905,600
Market price of bond on 1/1/00			$2,121,600
Call price = 102% × $2 million			(2,040,000)
Amount saved by exercising call option to retire bonds			$81,600

Requirement 5:
Entry to record bond retirement:

DR	Bonds payable	$2,000,000	
DR	Premium on bonds payable	253,211	
	CR Cash (102% × $2 million)		$2,040,000
	CR Extra gain on bond retirement		213,211

Original premium on bonds issued (see part A)	=	$271,830
Premium amortized in 1999 = $9,127 + $9,492	=	(18,619)
Unamortized premium when bonds are called on 1/1/00		$253,211

P10-10. Working backward from an amortization table

Requirement 1:
Compute:

- Discount or premium on the sale

  Premium = Amount received ($540,554) - Face value ($500,000)
  = $40,554

- Semi-annual stated interest rate: ($25,000/$500,000) × 100 = 5%

- Semi-annual effective interest rate: ($21,622/$540,554) × 100 = 4%

Requirement 2:
At the time of issuance, the bondholders exchanged today's cash flow for tomorrow's, but with the same present value on a risk-adjusted basis. Consequently, neither the borrower nor the lender made a profit (or loss) at the time of the issuance of bonds. Consequently, no gain or loss should be recorded at that time. The discount/premium merely reflects the difference between the face value and the price of the bonds, a difference that arises because the stated interest rate is not equal to the market yield (effective) rate. Amortizing discounts and premiums over time allows interest expense to be properly recorded at the true cost of borrowing.

Requirement 3:
It is the present value of an annuity of $25,000 for the next 5 periods plus the present value of $500,000 to be received at the end of 5 periods, both discounted at the original semi-annual effective rate of 4%.

Requirement 4:

New price of the bonds on January 1, 2002, is:

$$\$478,939 = (\$25,000 \times 4.21236) + (\$500,000 \times 0.74726)$$

The economic gain that results from the interest rate increase is:

Book value of the bond	=	$522,258
Market value (present value) of debt	=	478,939
Economic gain		$43,319

Considering just the debt, the company and its shareholders are better off because of the interest rate increase. The economic gain is the reduced present value of debt payments (principal plus interest) at the new higher interest rate. The cash outflow has a lower present value—indicating bondholders will be receiving a less valuable payment stream.

Of course, things get a bit more complicated when the interest rate increase has a negative impact on the company's other activities. For example, if the company sells products to customers on an installment payment plan, higher interest rates may lead to lower product sales. In addition, we have presumed that interest rates have increased throughout the economy and not just for this company

P10-11. How notes affect cash flows

Requirement 1:
Present value of $5 million to be repaid at the end of 4 periods:
$$= \$5\ m \times 0.76290 = \$3,814,500$$

Present value of $250,000 to be paid at the end of each period:
$$= 3.38721 \times \$250,000 = \$846,803$$

Therefore, total proceeds = $846,803 + $3,814,500 = $4,661,303

Requirement 2:
Bond amortization schedule:

Period	Interest Expense	Semi-Annual Payment	Increase in Liability	Net Liability
0				$4,661,303
1	$326,291	$250,000	$76,291	4,737,594
2	331,632	250,000	81,632	4,819,226
3	337,346	250,000	87,346	4,906,572
4	343,428*	250,000	93,428	5,000,000

*Rounded down from $343,460 (.07 × $4,906,572)

Requirement 3:
Journal entries :

Issuance of notes
DR Cash $4,661,303
DR Discount on notes payable   338,697
     CR Notes payable $5,000,000

Accrual and payment of interest on December 31, 1998
DR Interest expense $326,291
     CR Cash $250,000
     CR Discount on notes payable   76,291

Payment of face value on maturity
DR Notes payable $5,000,000
     CR Cash $5,000,000

Requirement 4:
Effects on cash flow statement:

- Issuance of bonds: Financing inflow $4,661,303

- Payment of interest: Operating outflow $250,000

- Payment of face value on maturity:
     Financing outflow $4,661,303
     Operating outflow $338,697

Requirement 5:
The price of the bond will be $5,000,000. The company will be worse off because it could have borrowed at a lower rate, but now it is committed to 14% unless the notes are callable or otherwise allow for the liquidation of the liability before maturity with no penalty. The interest rate decline may actually help the company if it can refinance the notes at the new lower rate.

P10-12. Serial bonds
(AICPA adapted)

Requirement 1:
Below is a schedule of the bond's future cash flows[1].

1/1/1999	1/1/2000	1/1/2001	1/1/2002	1/1/2003
(200,000)	(200,000)	(200,000)	(200,000)	(200,000)
(50,000)	(40,000)	(30,000)	(20,000)	(10,000)

To find the selling price of the bond, we need to find the present value of its future cash flows. We can start by finding the present value of the principal payments. Using the formula for an ordinary annuity[2], we get:

$200,000 \times$ PV of an annuity for 5 years at 6% $= \$200,000 \times 4.2124 = \$842,480$

Next, we have to find the present value of the interest payments; since the principal is repaid on a yearly basis, interest will also decrease annually. We must find the present value of $1 for each separately.

a) $\$50,000 \times$ PV of $1 at 6% for 1 year $= \$50,000 \times .9434 = \$47,170$

b) $\$40,000 \times$ PV of $1 at 6% for 2 years $= \$40,000 \times .8900 = \$35,600$

c) $\$30,000 \times$ PV of $1 at 6% for 3 years $= \$30,000 \times .8396 = \$25,188$

d) $\$20,000 \times$ PV of $1 at 6% for 4 years $= \$20,000 \times .7921 = \$15,842$

e) $\$10,000 \times$ PV of $1 at 6% for 5 years $= \$10,000 \times .7473 = \$7,473$

---

[1] The interest payments are computed in the following table

	1/1/1998	1/1/1999	1/1/2000	1/1/2001	1/1/2002	1/1/2003
Bond Liability	1,000,000	800,000	600,000	400,000	200,000	0
Interest Payment (5%)		50,000	40,000	30,000	20,000	10,000

The interest payment for the year is equal to 5% of the bond liability for that year. The interest is paid at the end of the period (or the beginning of the next period), while the principal is paid at the beginning of the respective period. Therefore, $50,000 is 5% of $1,000,000 and is the interest accrued in the bonds for 1998, not 1999.

[2] Even though the principal is paid at the first of the year, we can use the ordinary annuity formula because the end of the year and the first of the year fall within one day of each other. There is no material difference between using the annuity due formula and discounting it back one year or using the ordinary annuity formula.

Now that we have found the present value of each interest payment, we need only sum the interest payments and the principal payments to find the price of the bond.

$$\$842,480 + 47,170 + 35,600 + 25,188 + 15,842 + 7,473 = \mathbf{\$973,753}$$

So, the total amount received from issuance of the bonds January 1, 1998, was $973,753.

Requirement 2:
Schedule of amortization

Date	Interest Payment	Interest Expense	Discount Amortization	Decrease in Bond Liability	Book Value
1998					**$973,753**
1999	50,000	58,425	8,425	200,000	782,178
2000	40,000	46,931	6,931	200,000	589,109
2001	30,000	35,347	5,347	200,000	394,455
2002	20,000	23,667	3,667	200,000	198,123
2003	10,000	11,877	1,877	200,000	(0)

P10-13. Discount and premium amortization

Requirement 1:
The carrying values of both bonds in each of the two years presented is simply the present value of the principal and interest payments discounted over the remaining life of the bond.

To illustrate, the December 31, 1998, value of $9,653,550 for the 10% bonds due in 2000 can be derived as follows. Note that these bonds pay semi-annual interest of $500,000 and have four periods until they mature.

Present value of the principal repayment:

= $10,000,000 × Present value of $1 to be received in 4 periods at 6%
= $10,000,000 × 0.7921   = $7,921,000

Present value of the interest payments:

= $500,000 × Present value of an ordinary annuity of $1 to be received in
     4 periods at 6%
= $500,000 × 3.4651   = $1,732,550

Carrying value of the bonds at December 31, 1998:

= $7,921,000 + $1,732,550 = $9,653,550

In a similar fashion, the December 31, 1999, value of $10,362,950 for the 10% bonds due in 2001 can be derived as follows. Note that these bonds pay semi-annual interest of $500,000 and have four periods until they mature.

Present value of the principal repayment:

= $10,000,000 × Present value of $1 to be received in 4 periods at 4%
= $10,000,000 × 0.8548   = $8,548,000

Present value of the interest payments:

= $500,000 × Present value of an ordinary annuity of $1 to be received in 4 periods at 4%
= $500,000 × 3.6299   = $1,814,950

Carrying value of the bonds at December 31, 1999:

= $8,548,000 + $1,814,950 = $10,362,950

The December 31, 1999 carrying value of the 10% bonds due in 2000 is equal to the present value of the principal repayment to be received in 2 periods plus the present value of the 2 remaining interest payments discounted at the original market rate of 6% (i.e., 12%/2).

Present value of the principal repayment:

= $10,000,000 × Present value of $1 to be received in 2 periods at 6%
= $10,000,000 × 0.8900   = $8,900,000

Present value of the interest payments:

= $500,000 × Present value of an ordinary annuity of $1 to be received in 2 periods at 6%
= $500,000 × 1.8334   = $916,700

Carrying value of the bonds at December 31, 1999:

= $8,900,000 + $916,700   = $9,816,700

The December 31, 1998, carrying value of the 10% bonds due in 2001 is equal to the present value of the principal repayment to be received in 6 periods plus the present value of the 6 remaining interest payments discounted at the original market rate of 4% (i.e., 8%/2).

Present value of the principal repayment:

$$= \$10,000,000 \times \text{Present value of \$1 to be received in 6 periods at 4\%}$$
$$= \$10,000,000 \times 0.7903 \qquad = \$7,903,000$$

Present value of the interest payments:

$$= \$500,000 \times \text{Present value of an ordinary annuity of \$1 to be received in 6 periods at 4\%}$$
$$= \$500,000 \times 5.2421 \qquad = \$2,621,050$$

Carrying value of the bonds at December 31, 1998:

$$= \$7,903,000 + \$2,621,050 \qquad = \$10,524,050$$

Requirement 2:
The amount of interest expense recognized in 1999 on the bonds due in 2000 is equal to the cash interest payment of $1 million ($500,000 on both June 30 and December 31) plus the amortization of the bond discount during 1999. This latter amount is the difference between the carrying value of the bonds at December 31, 1998, and December 31, 1999. Based on the calculations in part 1, this amount is:

$$= \$9,816,700 - \$9,653,550 \qquad = \$163,150$$

Total interest expense:

$$= \$1,000,000 + \$163,150 \qquad = \$1,163,150$$

Requirement 3:
The amount of interest expense recognized in 1999 on the bonds due in 2001 is equal to the cash interest payment of $1 million ($500,000 on both June 30 and December 31) minus the amortization of the bond premium during 1999. This latter amount is the difference between the carrying value of the bonds at December 31, 1998, and December 31, 1999. Based on the calculations in part 1, this amount is:

$$= \$10,524,050 - \$10,362,950 = \$161,100$$

Total interest expense:

$$= \$1,000,000 - \$161,100 \qquad = \$838,900$$

P10-14. Loss contingencies

Requirement 1:
A loss contingency is an event that results in the possibility of future loss. A primary example of a loss contingency is litigation. Loss contingencies can be disclosed either by recognizing a charge to income and an associated liability **or** as a footnote disclosure. GAAP provides specific guidelines (SFAS No. 5) about when loss contingencies must be recorded on the books rather than just given footnote disclosure.

Loss contingencies are included in the financial statements because the event will possibly cause future loss. That is, the event has potential economic ramifications for the firm. Conservatism requires that possible liabilities be disclosed in the financial statements while possible gains are not disclosed.

The Exxon illustration is an example of a loss contingency. Apparel America's situation represents a noncontingent, <u>existing</u> liability. A loss contingency meets SFAS No. 5 requirements for recognizing a charge against income and an associated liability when 1) the event represents a **probable** liability, and 2) the amount of the loss can be **reasonably estimated.** However, while the Exxon example represents a probable loss, the amount of the loss cannot be reasonably estimated. Therefore, the loss will be disclosed in a footnote.

Requirement 2:
Present value of Apparel America's settlement as of December 1994:

PV of $150,000		= $150,000
PV of 5 semi-annual payments at 4.5%	= $50,000 × 4.38998	= 219,499
PV of final payment in 6 periods at 4.5%	= $60,000 × 0.767896	= 46,074
Present value of settlement		= $415,573

Present value of Apparel America's settlement as of June 30, 1996:

Payment date	Amount	Factor		
12/31/96	$50,000	.956938	=	$ 47,847
6/30/97	50,000	.915730	=	45,787
12/31/97	60,000	.876296	=	52,578
				$146,212

Present value as of July 31, 1996:

Present value at June 30, 1996	$146,212
Adjustment factor to reflect that <u>each</u> payment is one month closer than shown above:	
$[1 + (.045 / 6 \text{ mos.})] = 1.0075$	x 1.0075
	$147,309

$147,309 would be included in the balance sheet as a liability.

Requirement 3:

There are several reasons why Exxon does not report a dollar amount for the loss contingency. First, while a liability clearly exists, a reasonable estimate of the amount of the liability may not be possible. Second, even if Exxon could reasonably estimate the liability, it may be hesitant to disclose the estimate because doing so could harm the company. For example, suppose Exxon estimates the cost of settling the Valdez oil spill at $50 billion. This disclosure could harm Exxon if plaintiffs are willing to settle for $35 billion because then the plaintiffs would know that Exxon was willing to pay higher damages. Incentives exist for Exxon to either disclose an estimate that is considerably smaller than the company's "true" estimate, or to claim that the loss cannot be reasonably estimated.

Requirement 4:

Stock analysts are unlikely to ignore the loss contingency when valuing Exxon. Analysts realize that a significant loss has occurred even if the company does not place a specific dollar amount on the loss. In this situation, analysts will form their own estimate of the loss contingency. Notice that analysts may come up with different estimates of this liability, and, thus, different analysts may have different valuations for Exxon.

P10-15. Floating-rate debt

Requirement 1:

Journal entry to record the issuance on January 1, 1998:

DR Cash $250,000,000
   CR Bonds payable $250,000,000

If the bonds were issued at par, the effective (or market) interest rate must have been equal to the stated rate of "LIBOR + 5.5%", or 12%, since the LIBOR was 6.5% at the issue date.

Requirement 2:

Interest expense for 1998:

Interest rate   =   LIBOR + 5.5%   = 6.50% + 5.50% = 12.0%
Interest expense = 12.0% × $250,000,000   = $30,000,000

DR Interest expense $30,000,000
   CR Cash $30,000,000

Interest expense for 1999:

Interest rate   =   LIBOR + 5.5%   = 7.00% + 5.50% = 12.5%
Interest expense = 12.5% × $250,000,000   = $31,250,000

| **DR** Interest expense | $31,250,000 | |
| **CR** Cash | | $31,250,000 |

Interest expense for 2000:

| Interest rate | = | LIBOR + 5.5% | = 5.50% + 5.50% | = 11.0% |
| Interest expense | =11.0% × $250,000,000 | | | = $27,500,000 |

| **DR** Interest expense | $27,500,000 | |
| **CR** Cash | | $27,500,000 |

Requirement 3:
If the only factor influencing the market value of these bonds is the LIBOR, the bonds will have a market value of $250 million on 12/31/2001. This is because the interest rate on the bonds is reset annually so that the present value of the principal and remaining interest payments always equals $250 million at the new rate.

P10-16. Unconditional purchase obligations

Requirement 1:
There is no simple way to find the present value of the 10 payments required under the purchase obligation contract except using a spreadsheet or a series of individual calculations. Each payment should be discounted at 9%, and the total present value will equal $208,103,371 (or $217,468,023 when adjusted for mid-year payment).

Here is one such series of calculations:

PV on 12/31/96 of a 6-year deferred annuity of	
$31 million beginning on 12/31/01	$98,516,072
PV on 12/31/96 of:	
$35 million lump sum payment on 12/31/97	32,110,092
$34 million lump sum payment on 12/31/98	28,617,120
$33 million lump sum payment on 12/31/99	25,482,055
$33 million lump sum payment on 12/31/00	<u>23,378,031</u>
Total PV of future payments on 12/31/96	$208,103,370

Requirement 2:
The impact of capitalizing unconditional purchase obligations on the debt-to-equity ratio is shown below:

	$ in millions	
	As reported	**As capitalized**
Long-term debt	$1,194	$1,194
Unconditional purchase obligation		$208
Total	$1,194	$1,402
Divided by shareholder's equity	$431	$431
Debt-to-equity ratio	2.77	3.25

Requirement 3:
Under current GAAP, contracts of this sort are not booked because neither party is viewed as having taken any action—no cash or property has yet been exchanged, there is just a promise to do so in the future. Some companies prefer this approach because it keeps a real economic obligation (true liability) off of the balance sheet. Off-balance sheet debt may also reduce the probability of debt covenant violations.

P10-17. Debt-for-debt swaps

Requirement 1:
Since the bonds were originally sold at par, the carrying amount on December 31, 2000, is equal to $5,000,000. If this bond issued were retired in exchange for a bond issue valued at $3,200,000 there would be a pre-tax gain of $1,800,000. The journal entry to record the exchange would be:

DR Bonds payable (old)	$5,000,000	
CR Bonds payable (new)		$3,200,000
CR Income tax payable (current)*		630,000
CR Gain on debt retirement**		1,170,000

*$630,000 = $1,800,000 × 0.35   **$1,170,000 = $1,800,000 × (1.0 - 0.35)

Requirement 2:
Long-term debt-to-equity ratio after the swap:

= ($7,500,000 - $5,000,000 + $3,200,000)/($410,000,000 + $1,170,000)
= 51.0%

Requirement 3:
The transaction would increase net income by $1,170,000 (see above).

Requirement 4:
Other ways to avoid the covenant's violation include: issue additional common stock, reissue any treasury stock that is being held, make changes to accounting methods (e.g., depreciation of assets, useful lives, salvage values, etc.) that are income increasing, and/or exchange common stock for some outstanding debt.

P10-18. Zero coupon bonds

Requirement 1:
Price of the debentures = Present value factor × Total maturity value

$$\text{Present value factor} = \frac{1}{(1.0375)^{40}} = 0.229337875\ldots$$

Price of the debentures = 0.229337875 . . . × $862.5 million = $197.804 million which is very close to the total issue price of $197.806 million

Requirement 2:
The annualized rate of return $= (1.0375)^2 - 1.00 = 0.0764$ or 7.64%

Requirement 3:
Journal entry at the time of issuance:

DR Cash (financing inflow)	$191,872	
DR Other assets (issuance costs)	$5,934	
CR Zero coupon debentures		$197,806

At the end of 1990

DR Interest expense (from cash flow statement)	$412	
CR Zero coupon debentures		$412

DR Debt issuance expense	$296.70	
CR Other assets ($5,934 amortized over 20 years)		$296.70

During 1991

DR Interest expense (from cash flow statement)	$15,002	
CR Zero coupon debentures		$15,002

DR Debt issuance expense	$296.70	
CR Other assets		$296.70

During 1992

DR Interest expense (from statement)	$15,746	
CR Zero coupon debentures		$15,746

DR Debt issuance expense	$296.70	
CR Other assets		$296.70

During 1993

 DR Interest expense (from statement) $14,912
  CR Zero coupon debentures $14,912

 DR Debt issuance expense $296.70
  CR Other assets $296.70

 DR Zero coupon debentures (from statement) $243,878
  CR Cash (financing outflow) $243,878

 DR Extraordinary item (write-off of debt issuance costs)$1,426.20
  CR Other assets $1,426.20

An alternative classification of cash flows:

- At the time of issuance:
  Financing inflow $ 197,806
  Operating outflow   5,934

- At the time of redemption:
  Financing outflow $197,806
  Operating outflow   46,072

Requirement 4:

Treatment of debt issuance costs: The company did not expense these costs at the time of issuance, but instead capitalized the amount creating an asset. This asset is then being amortized (charged to income) over the life of the debt. The company's approach is consistent with Concept Statement No. 6 in that debt issuance costs are being spread over the life of the debt, just like a discount would be. However, most companies amortize debt issuance costs on a *straight-line basis*, which is inconsistent with the *effective interest* amortization of the discount.

P10-19. Comprehensive problem on premium bond

The following schedule shows the details for most parts of this question.

Amortization table for 20-year bond with semi-annual interest payments

Bond Principal	$20,000,000
Coupon Interest Rate	6.0%
Market Interest Rate	4.0%
Month and Year Issued	July-99

Amortization Table

Month/Year	Period	Bond Carrying Amount at Start of Period	Interest Expense	Bond (Premium) Discount Amortization	Premium (Discount) Balance	Bond Carrying Amount at End of Period	Cost Interest Payment	Principal Payment
Issue date:		$27,917,110			$7,917,110			
January-00	1	$27,917,110	$1,116,684	($83,316)	$7,833,794	$27,833,794	$1,200,000	$0
July-00	2	27,833,794	1,113,352	(86,648)	7,747,146	27,747,146	1,200,000	0
January-01	3	27,747,146	1,109,886	(90,114)	7,657,032	27,657,032	1,200,000	0
July-01	4	27,657,032	1,106,281	(93,719)	7,563,313	27,563,313	1,200,000	0
January-02	5	27,563,313	1,102,533	(97,467)	7,465,845	27,465,845	1,200,000	0
July-02	6	27,465,845	1,098,634	(101,366)	7,364,479	27,364,479	1,200,000	0
January-03	7	27,364,479	1,094,579	(105,421)	7,259,058	27,259,058	1,200,000	0
July-03	8	27,259,058	1,090,362	(109,638)	7,149,421	27,149,421	1,200,000	0
January-04	9	27,149,421	1,085,977	(114,023)	7,035,397	27,035,397	1,200,000	0
July-04	10	27,035,397	1,081,416	(118,584)	6,916,813	26,916,813	1,200,000	0
January-05	11	26,916,813	1,076,673	(123,327)	6,793,486	26,793,486	1,200,000	0
July-05	12	26,793,486	1,071,739	(128,261)	6,665,225	26,665,225	1,200,000	0

Requirement 1:
The January 1, 1999, issue price is $27,917,110.

Requirement 2:
The amortization table is shown above.

Requirement 3:
Interest expense and cash interest payment information is given in the amortization table. The entry for June 30, 2001, is:

DR Interest expense	$1,106,281	
DR Premium on bonds	93,719	
CR Cash		$1,200,000

The entry for December 31, 2001, is:

DR Interest expense	$1,102,533	
DR Premium on bonds	97,467	
CR Cash		$1,200,000

Requirement 4:
Points to be made include: the company received $27.9 million cash in exchange for a promise to repay on $20 million in principal and $2.4 million in interest each year; because more than $20 million was received, the true interest rate is less than 6% each period; some of each year's interest payment is really a payment on the principal; to reflect these facts properly on the books, interest expense is recorded at the true market rate (4% each period) and using the true amount owed—book value of the debt including unamortized premium.

Requirement 5:
Deere will not record the guarantee as a liability on its financial statements but may disclosure its contingent obligation in a footnote to the financials.

Requirement 6:
From the amortization schedule in Requirement 1, we can see that the book value of the entire debt issue is $26,793,486 on January 1, 2005. So, the book value of 40% of the debt would be $10,717,394 (rounded). If the company exercised its call provision and retired 40% of the debt (or $8,000,000 face value) at a price of 105, the following entry would be made:

DR Bonds payable	$8,000,000		
DR Premium on bonds	2,717,394		
CR Cash		$8,400,000	
CR Gain on extinguishment of debt		2,317,394	

Requirement 7:
If the market yield on the debt is 10%, its market price would be $23,074,490 and 40% of the debt would have a market value of $9,229,796. This means that the company paid $1,487,598 less by calling the debt than it would have paid buying the debt on the open market.

Cases

C10-1. Tuesday Morning Corporation (CW): Interpreting long-term debt disclosures

Requirement 1:
$1,402 from the balance sheet

Requirement 2:
$1,298 from the cash flow statement

Requirement 3:
The difference is $104. This appears to suggest that payment on the note payable in Note 5 was not made during 1994, but that it is included in the current maturities amount of $2,747 as of the end of 1994.

From Note 5: $2,747 - $1,794 - $416 - $432 = $105 $\cong$ $104

Rounded, where $416 is (4 × $104) and $432 is (4 × $108).

Requirement 4:
Current portion is $2,747

$1,794	Remaining principal on note
432	4 quarterly installments on industrial development bond
416	4 quarterly installments on note payable
104	see Question #3
1	Rounding
$2,747	

Requirement 5:
Journal entry for March 31:

DR Current installment on mortgage	$108	
DR Interest expense	49	
CR Cash		$157

Simple interest = $1,401 × .14 × 1/4 = $49

Requirement 6:
Journal entry for April 30:

DR Current installment on mortgage		$1,794	
DR Interest expense*		63	
CR Mortgage on property			$1,794
CR Cash			63

* $1,794 × .14 × 1/4 = $63

Requirement 7:
Journal entry for April 30, assuming full payment.

DR Current installment on mortgage	$1,794	
DR Interest expense	63	
CR Cash		$1,857

C10-2. Century bonds and beyond (CW)

Requirement 1:
Coupon payments	= $200,000,000 × .075	=	$15,000,000
Present value of coupon payments	= $15,000,000 × 13.32369	=	199,855,395
Present value of principal	= $200,000,000 × .000723	=	144,605
Issue price of bond	= $199,855,395 + $144,605	=	$200,000,000

Virtually all of the "value" of this 100-year bond lies in the interest payment stream. The principal payment of $200 million is so far into the future that bondholders are willing to pay only $144,605 to receive it. Note: when the stated rate of interest is equal to the market rate of interest, the bond will be issued at par.

Requirement 2:
Tax savings associated with the Century bond

PV of tax savings for 100 years	= $199,855,395 × .40	=	$79,942,158
PV of tax savings for first 40 Years	= $15,000,000 × 12.59441 ×.40	=	75,566,452
PV of lost tax savings	= $79,942,158 – $75,566,452	=	4,375,706

Requirement 3:
Issue price for bonds with stated interest rate of 7.5% and market rate of 8.5%

Present value of coupon payments	= $15,000,000 × 11.76134	=	$176,420,040
Present value of principal	= $200,000,000 ×.000286	=	57,287
Issue price	= $176,240,040 + $57,287	=	176,477,327

Issue price for bonds with stated interest rate of 7.5% and market rate of 6.5%

Present value of coupon payments	= $15,000,000 × 15.35629	=	$230,344,399
Present value of principal	= $200,000,000 ×.00184093	=	368,187
Issue price	= $230,344,399 + $368,187	=	230,712,586

Notice how small fluctuations in the market interest rate (± 1%) produce large changes in the market value of century bonds.

Requirement 4:

Safra Republic's millennium bonds:

Coupon Payments	= $250,000,000 × .07125	=	$17,812,500

Present value of coupon payments	= $17,812,500 × 14.03508772	=	250,000,000
Present value of principal	= $200,000,000 × 1.28578E-30	=	0
Issue price of bond		=	250,000,000

Notice that investors in millennium bonds are not willing to pay even $1 for the $250 million principal payment. The entire value of these bonds lies in the cash interest payment stream.

Requirement 5:

Analysis of tax savings

PV of tax savings for 1,000 years	= $250,000,000 × .40	=	$100,000,000
PV of tax savings for first 40 years	= $17,812,500 × 13.140585 × .40	=	93,626,667
PV of lost tax savings	= $100,000,000 − $93,626,667	=	6,373,333

Requirement 6:

Issue price when the market yield is 8.125%:

Present value of coupon payments	= $17,812,500 × 12.30769	=	$219,230,769
Present value of principal	= $250,000,000 × 1.18544E-34	=	0
Issue price		=	219,230,769

Issue price for bonds with stated interest rate of 7.125% and market rate of 6.125%

Present value of coupon payments	= $17,812,500 × 16.326531	=	$290,816,327
Present value of principal	= $250,000,000 × 1.52159E-26	=	0
Issue price	=		290,816,327

Notice how much more volatile the market price of millenium bonds is to interest rate fluctuations.

Requirement 7:

The U.S. Treasury Department objected to the interest deduction on these securities because the Treasury argued they were a form of permanent investment capital—not debt—and payments to providers of permanent capital—like common stockholders—are not tax deductible in the United States. The Treasury has proposed a middle-ground solution where interest payments would be deductible for the first 40 years only—a period of time that is about 10 years longer than a normal 30-year corporate bond.

Requirement 8:
Issues to be considered in this memo include: tax deductibility of payments made to capital providers (lowers the company's cost of capital); impact on existing debt covenants (limitations on additional debt but not preferred stock); impact on regulatory capital requirements, if any; financial statement cosmetics—interest expense vs. dividends, and debt vs. quasi-equity. At the beginning of 1998, the U.S. Treasury was still formulating its policies regarding the tax treatment of century and millennium bonds.

C10-3. Food Lion, Inc. (CW): Fair value disclosure of long-term debt

Requirement 1:
As disclosed in the footnote, the market value of Food Lion's long-term debt at the end of 1996 is $535.7 million. This is the amount that would be required for Food Lion to retire its long-term debt.

Requirement 2:
Ignoring transactions costs and income taxes, the journal entry would be:

DR Long-term debt (various accounts)	$496,084*	
DR Loss on early extinguishment of debt	39,616	
CR Cash		$535,700

*Total long-term debt from the footnote.

Requirement 3:
The loss would be treated as an extraordinary item (early extinguishment of debt) and would be shown net of tax on the income statement below income from continuing operations.

1997's income statement item income before taxes would be higher than if the debt had not been retired because interest expense will be lower (i.e., if the debt is retired no interest expense would be paid on it in 1997). Moreover, income before taxes would be higher by the entire amount of interest expense that no longer must be paid. Net income would be higher by (1 - tax rate) times the amount of interest expense that no longer needs to be paid.

Requirement 4:
The book value of the long-term debt is $496,084. If the debt could be retired at 98% of par, the cost to the firm would be $486,162 ($496,084 × 0.98). The difference between these two numbers, $9,922, is the extraordinary gain (before tax) that would be recognized in 1996. The gain would be treated as an extraordinary item (early extinguishment of debt) and shown net of tax on the income statement below income from continuing operations.

The 1997 income statement would be affected as described in (3) above.

Requirement 5:
When a company's debt is collateralized, lenders have a claim to company assets as security for loan.

This type of arrangement might be preferable for creditors because it increases the likelihood that the loan will be repaid. For example, if the company goes bankrupt, creditors can take possession of the collateral and sell it to recover all (or a portion of) the amount they are owed.

Management agrees to such arrangements because doing so allows access to financing that might not otherwise be available, or because the financing can be obtained at a lower cost (i.e., a lower interest rate) that would be the case without collateralization.

From the creditors' perspective, collateralized loans make sense only when the collateral assets can be sold quickly and easily. Lenders check to see if there is a readily available secondary market for the assets that are serving as collateral. Examples include airline companies where aircraft are put up as collateral, railroads where boxcars and locomotives serve as collateral, and retail companies where inventory and receivables often serve as collateral.

C10-4. ShopKo Stores Inc. (CW): Comprehensive case on long-term debt

Requirement 1:
Long-term debt issued in 1993: $200,000,000 from Note C.

Requirement 2:
The footnote indicates that proceeds from issuing the debt totaled $197.1 million, but that figure is net of $1.9 million in underwriting and insurance costs. So, the gross cash proceeds from the debt must have been $199.0 million. The journal entry is:

DR Cash	$199.0	
DR Discount on notes	1.0	
CR Nonds payable		$200.0
DR Bond issue costs (an asset)	$1.9	
CR Cash		$1.9

Requirement 3:
The original issue discount was $1.0 million, as shown above. The footnote indicates that the unamortized discount is $0.888 million ($0.332 plus $0.556) at year-end, so amortization for the year must have been $0.112 million.

Requirement 4:
Most of the proceeds ($181.2 million) was used to repay outstanding borrowings under a credit agreement with another company—SUPERVALU; the remainder was used for working capital and general corporate purposes.

Requirement 5:
According to the "fair value" disclosure in footnote H, the 9.25% unsecured notes had a market value of $107.341 million, compared to a book value of $99.444 million. If the company could repurchase the entire debt issue at this market price, the following entry would be made:

DR 9.25% Notes payable	$100.000	
DR Loss on early debt extinguishment	7.897	
CR Cash		$107.341
CR Discount on notes		0.556

C10-5. Coca-Cola Company (CW): Using long-term debt footnotes

Requirement 1:
As reported in the footnote, the current portion of Coke's long-term debt is $9 million. This is the amount that is due in the next year.

Requirement 2:
Also reported in the footnote is the amount of debt maturing in each of the next five years. The amounts and years are:

Year	Dollar Amount (in millions)
1997	$9
1998	$422
1999	$16
2000	$257
2001	$2

Requirement 3:
The schedule of future debt payments is important because the amounts represent contractually obligated cash *outflows* that the company must make. Unless the debt is refinanced, the cash needed for these payments must come from the company's operating cash flows. That means fewer operating cash flow dollars would be available for reinvestment—capital expenditures or R&D—and dividends.

Coke has several options: repayment from operating cash flows, issuing new long-term debt, issuing new equity, or re-issuing treasury stock currently held.

Requirement 4:
Effective interest rate:

= Interest expense for 1996/Average book value of long-term debt
= $100,000,000/[($1,125,000,000 + $1,693,000,000)/2] = 7.1%

Requirement 5:
Estimated 1997 interest expense:

= 7.1% × Book value of long-term debt at December 31, 1996
= 0.071 × $1,125,000,000 = $79,875,000

Requirement 6:
Apparently, Coke has operations in these foreign countries. As a result, the company's foreign business transactions occur in local currencies, not U.S. dollars. To finance these operations, Coke issues long-term debt in the local currency. There are several reasons for doing so. First, Coke avoids currency conversion costs that would be incurred if it borrowed in U.S. dollars and then paid to convert dollars into local currencies for use by its foreign subsidiaries. Second, Coke also avoids exposure to foreign exchange rate risks that would be present if the U.S. borrowing were to be repaid from cash (in local currencies) produced by the foreign businesses. Third, it may simply be the case that foreign-denominated debt is available at more attractive interest rates than is U.S. debt. For example, it is not unusual for a company of Coke's size and reputation to receive economic development incentives in the form of reduced interest rates.

Exerises
E11-1. Lessee and lessor accounting
(AICPA adapted)

Requirement 1:
The amount of gross profit on the sale is the fair market value (FMV) of the equipment less the cost of the equipment to the lessor. We can assume that the present value of the minimum lease payments is the same as the FMV of the equipment and we are given the cost of the equipment. The computation follows:

PV of minimum lease payments	$3,165,000
Cost of equipment	2,675,000
Gross profit on sale of equipment	**$490,000**

Next, we have to compute the amount of interest income for 1998. Keep in mind that the lease has been in effect for only 6 months, so we will need to pro-rate annual interest income so we can show the amount accrued after 6 months. Using the partial lease amortization schedule, we will demonstrate this calculation.

Date	Annual Lease Payments	Interest on Net Investment	Net Investment Recovery	Net Investment: PV of Minimum Lease Payments
7/1/98				$3,165,000
7/1/98	$500,000	$0	$500,000	2,665,000

The first scheduled payment is July 1, 1998, at the inception of the lease. This reduces the net investment of the lessor by $500,000. At year end, we need to know the interest accrued on the remaining investment ($2,665,000). We can find this number as follows:

$$\begin{array}{r} \$2,665,000 \\ \times \quad 12\% \\ \times \quad \underline{0.5 \text{ yrs}} \\ = \mathbf{\$159,900} \end{array}$$

So Fox's interest income for 1998 is $159,900. Interest income for the first 6 months of 1999 is also $159,900. To accrue the interest income, Fox would make the following entry *twice*, once on December 31, 1998, and once on June 30, 1999:

DR Accrued interest receivable $159,900
   CR Interest income $159,900

When the $500,000 cash payment is made on July 1, 1999, the balance in accrued interest receivable will be $319,800 (i.e., $159,900 × 2). Fox would make the following entry:

DR Cash $500,000
   CR Accrued interest receivable $319,800
   CR Net investment in lease   180,200

After making this entry, the net investment in the lease on Fox's books is $2,665,000 - $180,200 or $2,484,800. Interest for the last half of 1999 would be $2,484,800 × 12% × 1/2 or $149,088. Total interest income for 1999 is therefore:

January–June 1999 interest income	$159,900
July–December 1999 interest income	149,088
	$308,988

Requirement 2:

To find Tiger's 1998 depreciation expense, we need to compute depreciation for a full year and then prorate that amount for 6 months.

FMV of the equipment	$3,165,000
Economic life of the equipment	10 years
Straight line depreciation expense for 1 Year	$316,500
Prorated depreciation expense ($316,500/2)	**$158,250**

Next, we must find Tiger's interest expense. Here, we can use the same method for the lessee as we did for the lessor. (Note: The lease obligation is the present value of the minimum lease payments.)

Date	Annual Lease Payments	Interest on Net Investment	Net Investment Recovery	Net Investment: PV of Minimum Lease Payments
7/1/98				$3,165,000
7/1/98	$500,000	$0	$500,000	2,665,000

We can see that since the lessee and lessor use the same discount rate their amortization schedules are identical. We need to again find the amount of interest expense that Tiger has accrued in the 6 months that the lease was in effect during 1998.

$$
\begin{aligned}
&\quad \$2,665,000 \\
\times &\qquad\; 12\% \\
\times &\qquad \underline{0.5 \text{ yrs}} \\
= &\; \mathbf{\$159,900}
\end{aligned}
$$

Tiger's 1998 interest expense is the same as Fox's interest income, $159,900. Its journal entries are:

December 31, 1998, and June 30, 1999:
DR Interest expense	$159,900	
CR Interest payable		$159,900

July 1, 1999
DR Interest payable	$319,800	
DR Lease obligation	180,200	
CR Cash		$500,000

After making the July 1 entry, the lease obligation on Tiger's books is $2,665,000 - $180,200 or $2,484,800. Tiger's interest expense for 1999 mirrors Fox's interest income computed in part 1:

January–June 1999 interest expense	159,900
July–December 1999 interest expense	149,088*
	$308,988

* $2,484,800 × 12% × 1/2

Depreciation expense for 1999 is $316,500.

E11-2. Lessee accounting
(AICPA adapted)

Since Lafayette's lease is structured as an ordinary annuity, there is no reduction of the lease obligation at the inception of the lease as there is if the lease is an annuity due. Interest expense for 1998 is simply 10% of the lease obligation, which is the PV of the minimum lease payments. The computation is shown in the partial amortization schedule that follows.

Date	Lease Payments	Interest on Unpaid Obligation	Reduction of Lease Obligation	Lease Obligation
1/2/98				$92,170
1/1/99	$15,000	$9,217	$5,783	86,387

As we can see from the table, the interest expense for 1998 is:

($92,170 × 10%) = $9,217

Since the lease began at the start of the year, we do not need to prorate these amounts.

Depreciation expense is simply the FMV of the drill press allocated on a straight-line basis over the economic life of the asset. (Note: When title to the asset passes to the lessee in a capital lease, the lessee must accrue depreciation expense over the economic life of the asset, not the lease period.)

FMV of drill press	$92,170
Economic life of drill press	15 years
Depreciation expense for 1998 ($92,170/15) =	**$6,145**

E11-3. Lessee accounting: Purchase option
(AICPA adapted)

Since the purchase option approximates the fair value of the machine in 10 years, it is not a bargain purchase option and is, therefore, not included in our computation.

To find the amount of the capitalized lease, we need to find the present value of the minimum lease payments plus the present value of any guaranteed residual value. There is no guaranteed residual value in this lease, so we need simply to find the PV of the lease payments. The computation is shown below.

Annual rental payments	$40,000
PV of an annuity due at 14% for 10 periods	× 5.95
Present value of the minimum lease payments	**$238,000**

So, the amount of the capitalized lease asset is $238,000.

E11-4. Lessee accounting and classification
(AICPA adapted)

Requirement 1:
To compute the 12/31/99 lease liability amount, we can construct an amortization schedule.

Date	Annual Lease Payments	Interest on Unpaid Obligation	Reduction of Lease Obligation	Lease Obligation
12/31/98				$676,000
12/31/98	$100,000	$0	$100,000	576,000
12/31/99	$100,000	57,600	42,400	533,600

We can see from the amortization table that the reduction of the lease liability in 1998 is the entire $100,000 rental payment. In 1999, interest accrues on only $576,000, so the interest expense for 1999 is 10% of $576,000 ($57,600), and the lease obligation is reduced by $42,400 to **$533,600.**

Requirement 2:
To find out what portion of the lease obligation should be classified as a current liability, we need to look at the next year on the amortization schedule.

Date	Annual Lease Payments	Interest on Unpaid Obligation	Reduction of Lease Obligation	Lease Obligation
12/31/98				$676,000
12/31/98	$100,000	$0	$100,000	576,000
12/31/99	100,000	57,600	42,400	533,600
12/31/00	100,000	53,360	46,640	486,960

We can see that in 2000, the reduction of the lease obligation will be $46,640. The current portion of the lease obligation on December 31, 1999, is equal to the reduction in the lease obligation that will take place in 2000, i.e., **$46,640.**

E11-5. Lessor accounting
(AICPA adapted)

The following are expenses incurred on the machine in 1998.

Depreciation Expense:

Cost of machine	$720,000
Useful life of machine	10 years
Cost / Useful life	$72,000

Depreciation expense is $72,000. Maintenance and executory costs are given as $15,000. So, the sum of these two costs is the total expense resulting from the machine—$87,000. Operating profit on this asset is the rental revenue less the expenses Grady incurred:

Rental revenue				$125,000
Expenses incurred				87,000
Operating profit on leased asset				**$38,000**

E11-6. Lessor accounting: Sales-type lease
(AICPA adapted)

To find the amount of interest income for 1999, we need to look at the lease amortization schedule below. Benedict accrues the interest over the year. For example, the interest revenue associated with the 1/1/99 payment ($292,000) is actually accrued in 1998.

Date	Annual Payment	Interest Revenue	Reduction in Net Investment	Net Investment
Inception				$3,520,000
1/1/98	$600,000	$0	$600,000	2,920,000
1/1/99	600,000	292,000	308,000	2,612,000
1/1/00	600,000	261,200	338,800	2,273,200

We can see from the table that for the second year, ending 12/31/99, the interest revenue that was accrued is **$261,200** (see the 1/1/00 payment).

E11-7. Lessor accounting: Direct financing leases
(AICPA adapted)

To find the amount of interest revenue earned over the life of the lease, we need to first determine the amount of the each lease payment. Let Y = amount of each payment.

Fair value of equipment = PV of annuity due factor × Y

Fair market value of equipment (PV of lease payments)	$323,400
Present value of an annuity due (5 yrs @ 8%)	4.312

$323,400 = 4.312 × Y
Y = $323,400/4.312 = $75,000

Amount of annual lease payment	**$75,000**

Next, we must find the gross investment or lease payments receivable:

$75,000 × 5 yrs = **$375,000**

The interest revenue earned over the life of the lease is equal to the gross investment less the net investment.

Gross investment	$375,000
Net investment (PV of lease payments)	323,400
Total interest revenue	**$51,600**

Total interest revenue that Glade will earn over the life of the lease is $51,600.

E11-8. Lessor accounting: Sales-type lease
(AICPA adapted)

The amount of profit on the sale can be determined by the following computation.

Selling price of equipment	$3,520,000
Cost of equipment to Howe	(2,800,000)
Profit on sale	**$720,000**

To find the interest revenue earned on the lease in 1998, we first look at the partial lease amortization schedule below.

Date	Annual Payment	Interest on Net Investment	Net Investment Recovery	Net Investment
Inception				$3,520,000
7/1/98	$600,000	$0	$600,000	2,920,000
7/1/99	600,000	292,000	308,000	2,612,000
7/1/00	600,000	261,200	338,800	2,273,200

To determine the amount of interest that should be recorded in 1998, we must prorate the interest for the period 7/1/98 to 7/1/99. This interest that was earned between July 1,1998, and July 1,1999, is $292,000. We need to allocate 6 months of this interest, or one-half of $292,000, to 1998.

Interest earned between 7/1/98–7/1/99	$292,000
Portion earned in 1998 (6 mos.)	.5
Amount of interest recorded in 1998	**$146,000**

Thus, Howe should record profit on sales of $720,000 and interest revenue of $146,000.

E11-9. Lessee accounting: Discount rate
(AICPA adapted)

We can determine the amount of Day's lease liability at the beginning of the lease term as follows:

Annual rent payable	$50,000
Present value of an annuity due (6 yrs @ 12%)	×⎯⎯4.61
Total lease liability at the beginning of the lease	**$230,500**

Since Day knows the lessor's implicit rate and the implicit rate is less than Day's incremental borrowing rate, Day must use Parr's implicit discount rate.

E11-10. Lessee accounting: Purchase option
(AICPA adapted)

To find the amount of lease liability that Robbins should record at the inception of the lease, we need to find the present value of the lease payments and the present value of the bargain purchase option. Robbins' incremental borrowing rate (14%) is more than the lessor's 12% implicit rate of return on the lease. Robbins must use 12% in its calculations because it is less than Robbins' own incremental borrowing rate and because Robbins is aware of the lessor's implicit rate since it is specified in the lease contract.

Annual rental payments	$10,000
Present value of an annuity due (10 yrs @ 12%)	×6.328
Present value of minimum lease payments	$63,280
Bargain purchase option	$10,000
Present value of a lump sum (10 yrs @ 12%)	×0.322
Present value of bargain purchase option	$3,220

Present Value of :	
Annual rental payments	$63,280
Bargain purchase option	3,220
Liability at beginning of the lease term	**$66,500**

Robbins would record $66,500 as its lease liability at the beginning of the lease term.

E11-11. Lessee accounting
(AICPA adapted)

Annual lease payment	$13,000
Present value of an annuity due (5 yrs @ 9%)	× 4.24
Present value of minimum lease payments	$55,120
Residual value guarantee	$10,000
Present value of a lump sum (5 yrs @ 9%)	× 0.65
Present value of residual value guarantee	$6,500
Present value of minimum lease payments	$55,120
Present value of residual value guarantee	6,500
Recorded capital lease liability at inception	$61,620

We know that there is no interest accrued when the first payment is made since this is an annuity due. The entire $13,000 payment is a reduction of the lease liability, so after the first payment we have:

Date	Annual Payment	Interest on Unpaid Obligation	Reduction of Lease Obligation	Lease Obligation
Inception				$61,620
1/1/98	$13,000	$0	$13,000	48,620
1/1/99	13,000	$4,376	8,624	39,996

After the first payment, the lease liability is reduced by $13,000 to $48,620.

E11-12. Lessee reporting: Executory costs
(AICPA adapted)

A partial lease amortization table for Roe Company follows. Keep in mind that executory costs are part of the annual payment but they do not reduce the lease obligation. Thus, the $5,000 in executory costs is subtracted from the annual payment in the amortization table.

Date	Annual Payment	Executory Costs	Interest on Unpaid Obligation	Reduction of Lease Obligation	Lease Obligation
					$417,000
12/31/97	$105,000	$5,000	0	$100,000	317,000
12/31/98	105,000	5,000	31,700	68,300	248,700

As shown in the table, Roe would report $248,700 as its lease liability on the December 1998 balance sheet.

E11-13. **Sale and leaseback**
(AICPA adapted)

Requirement 1:

Sales price	$480,000
Carrying amount	(360,000)
Deferred gain on sale of equipment	$120,000

The gain on the sale of equipment in a sale and leaseback is deferred and amortized over the life of the lease. Therefore, no gain is recognized on the sale and leaseback in 1998.

Requirement 2:
Lane should defer the $120,000 gain on the sale of equipment and amortize it over the 12-year lease term.

Problems

P11-1. Lease accounting overview: Lessors and lessees

Requirement 1:
The computation of the annual lease payments is shown below:

Fair market value of the machine	$100,000
Present value of the residual value [.3855 × $10,000]	(3,855)
Amount to be recovered by the lessor	$96,145
Present value factor for an annuity due for 10 Yrs @ 10%	6.75902
Annual lease payments [$96,145/6.75902]	$14,225

Requirement 2:
Since the residual value is not guaranteed, it is not included in the lease obligation. The computation of the lessee's lease obligation at signing is illustrated below.

Annual lease payment	$14,225
Present value factor for an annuity due for 10 Yrs @ 10%	× 6.759
Lease obligation at signing	$96,145*

*Rounded

Requirement 3:
Partial lease amortization schedules appear below for the lessee and lessor, assuming a 10% discount rate. Note that the entire amount of the initial payment goes toward reduction of the lease obligation (receivable). By the end of year 1, the lessee has accrued $8,192 of interest expense based on the present value of the lease obligation of $81,920 following the initial payment.

Lessee Co. Lease Amortization Schedule

Year	Annual Payment	Interest Expense	Reduction of Lease Obligation	Lease Obligation
Inception				$96,145
1	$14,225	$0	$14,225	81,920
2	14,225	8,192	6,033	75,887

The lessor will recover $100,000 because the machine will have residual value at the end of the lease, even though it may be unguaranteed. Thus, by the end of the first year the lessor has earned $8,758 in interest revenue from the lease based on the present value of the net investment of $85,775 following the initial payment.

Lessor Co. Lease Amortization Schedule

Year	Annual Payment	Interest Revenue	Net Investment Recovery	Net Investment
Inception				$100,000
1	$14,225	$0	$14,225	85,775
2	14,225	8,578	5,647	80,128

Requirement 4:

a) If the residual value were guaranteed, it would change the lease obligation as follows:

Annual lease payment	$14,225
Present value factor of an annuity due for 10 Yrs @ 10%	× 6.75902
Present value of 10 annual rental payments (rounded)	$96,145
Guaranteed residual value	$10,000
Present value factor of a lump sum for 10 Yrs @ 10%	× .38554
Present value of guaranteed residual value	$3,855
Lease obligation at signing ($96,145 + $3,855)	$100,000

b) A revised amortization table for Lessee Co. follows:

Year	Annual Payment	Interest Expense	Reduction of Lease Obligation	Lease Obligation
Inception				$100,000
1	$14,225	$0	$14,225	85,775
2	14,225	8,578	5,648	80,128

As shown in the table, the interest expense for Lessee Co. for year 1 is now $8,578 instead of $8,192 under Requirement 3.

The computation for Lessor Co. would not change if the residual value were guaranteed. The reason is that the net investment in the lease ($100,000) is the same irrespective of whether the residual value is guaranteed or unguaranteed.

P11-2. Lessees' accounting for capital leases

Requirement 1:
Given that the leased asset has an expected useful life of 6 years, Seven Wonders must account for the lease as a capital lease since the lease term of 5 years covers more than 75% of the asset's useful life (5/6 = 83.3%).

Requirement 2:
Present value of future lease payments:

= $277,409.44 × the present value of an ordinary annuity at 12% for 5 periods.

= $277,409.44 × 3.60478

= $1,000,000

Appearing below is the amortization schedule for the lease liability:

Amortization of Capital Lease Liability
Seven Wonders Incorporated

(In thousands)

Date	Interest Portion[1]	Cash Payment[2]	Liability Reduction[3]	Lease Liability[4]
1/1/98				$1,000,000.00
12/31/98	$120,000.00	$277,409.44	$157,409.44	842,590.56
12/31/99	101,110.87	277,409.44	176,298.57	666,291.99
12/31/00	79,955.04	277,409.44	197,454.40	468,837.59
12/31/01	56,260.51	277,409.44	221,148.93	247,688.66
12/31/02	29,720.78*	277,409.44	247,688.66	0.00

*Rounded by $1.85

[1] The interest portion is 12% of the carrying amount at the beginning of the period.

[2] The cash payment is fixed by the lease at $277,409.44.

[3] The reduction in the liability is the difference between the cash payment and the interest portion.

[4] The lease liability declines each year by the amount of the liability reduction.

Requirement 3:
The journal entries are:

1/1/98:
    DR Leased assets—capital leases $1,000,000.00
        CR Obligations under capital leases $1,000,000.00

12/31/98:
    DR Interest expense $120,000.00
    DR Obligations under capital leases   157,409.44
        CR Cash $277,409.44

2/31/99:
    DR Interest expense $101,110.87
    DR Obligations under capital leases   176,298.57
        CR Cash $277,409.44

12/31/98–12/31/02:
Annual depreciation expense =
    $1,000,000/5 = $200,000

    DR Depreciation expense $200,000.00
        CR Accumulated depreciation
            —leased assets $200,000.00

Requirement 4:
Under the capital lease method, the total expense recognized in 1998 is the interest expense of $120,000 plus the depreciation of $200,000 for a total of $320,000. Under the operating lease method, the amount of expense would have been $277,409.44. Thus, income before tax will be lower by $42,590.56 in 1998 as a result of classifying the lease as a capital lease because capital lease accounting "front-end loads" lease expense in comparison to the operating lease approach.

P11-3. Lessees' accounting for capital leases

Requirement 1:
Present value of future lease payments:

    = $277,409.44 × the present value of an annuity due
        at 12% for 5 periods.

    = $277,409.44 × 4.03735

    = $1,119,999

Appearing below is the amortization schedule for the lease liability:

Amortization of Capital Lease Liability
Seven Wonders Incorporated

First payment due at the inception of the lease

Date	Interest Portion[1]	Cash Payment[2]	Liability Reduction[3]	Lease Liability[4]
Inception				$1,119,999.00
1/1/98	$0.00	$277,409.44	$277,409.44	842,589.56
1/1/99	101,110.75	277,409.44	176,298.69	666,290.87
1/1/00	79,954.90	277,409.44	197,454.54	468,836.33
1/1/01	56,260.36	277,409.44	221,149.08	247,687.25
1/1/02	29,722.19*	277,409.44	247,687.25	0.00

*Rounded by $0.28

[1] The interest portion is 12% of the carrying amount at the beginning of the period and is accrued over the year preceding the payment.

[2] The cash payment is fixed by the lease at $277,409.44.

[3] The reduction in the liability is the difference between the cash payment and the interest portion.

[4] The lease liability declines each year by the amount of the liability reduction.

Requirement 2:
The journal entries are:

1/1/98:
DR Leased assets—capital leases	$1,119,999.00	
CR Obligations under capital leases		$1,119,999.00

12/31/98:
DR Interest expense	$101,110.75	
CR Interest payable		$101,110.75

1/1/99:
DR Interest payable	$101,110.75	
DR Obligations under capital leases	176,298.69	
CR Cash		$277,409.44

12/31/99:
    DR Interest expense $79,954.90
        CR Interest payable $79,954.90

1/1/00:
    DR Interest payable $79,954.90
    DR Obligations under capital leases   197,454.54
        CR Cash $277,409.44

12/31/98–12/31/02:
Annual depreciation expense =
  $1,119,999/5 = $223,999.80

    DR Depreciation expense $223,999.80
        CR Accumulated depreciation
            —leased assets $223,999.80

NOTE: The total amount expensed in these two cases is the same (adjusted for a rounding error).

In the previous problem, the total amount expensed over the term of the lease would be $1,387,047.20 ($387,047.20 interest expense and $1,000,000 of depreciation expense).

In the present problem, the total amount expensed over the term of the lease would be $1,387,047.20 ($267,048.20 of interest expense and $1,119,999.00 of depreciation expense).

The interest expense is less in Problem 11-3 because the first payment was made on the inception date of the lease.

P11-4. Lessees' accounting for capital leases including executory costs and residual value guarantee

Requirement 1:
This is a capital lease to Bare Trees Company because the lease term of 3 years is equal to 75% of the asset's useful life of 4 years.

With the residual value guarantee of $15,000, the present value of future lease payments is calculated as:

  = ($59,258.09 × the present value of an ordinary annuity at 9% for
     3 Periods) + ($15,000 × the present value of $1 at 9% in 3 periods).

    (The $59,258.09 figure is the $62,258.09 annual lease payment minus the $3,000 annual executory costs).

  = ($59,258.09 × 2.53130) + ($15,000 × 0.77218)

  = $161,583

Appearing below is the amortization schedule for the lease liability:

Amortization of Capital Lease Liability
Bare Trees Company
($15,000 Guaranteed Residual Value)

Date	Interest Portion[1]	Cash Payment[2]	Liability Reduction[3]	Lease Liability[4]
1/1/98				$161,583.00
12/31/98	$14,542.47	$59,258.09	$44,715.62	$116,867.38
12/31/99	$10,518.06	$59,258.09	$48,740.03	$68,127.35
12/31/00	$6,130.74*	$59,258.09	$53,127.35	$15,000.00

*Rounded by $0.73.

[1] The interest portion is 9% of the carrying amount at the beginning of the period.

[2] The cash payment is fixed by the lease at $59,258.09, excluding the $3,000 of annual executory costs.

[3] The reduction in the liability is the difference between the cash payment and the interest portion.

[4] The lease liability declines each year by the amount of the liability reduction.

Requirement 2:
The journal entries are:

1/1/98:
    DR Leased assets—capital leases $161,583.00
        CR Obligations under capital leases $161,583.00

12/31/98:
    DR Interest expense $14,542.47
    DR Obligations under capital leases   44,715.62
    DR Misc. expenses   3,000.00
        CR Cash $62,258.09

12/31/99:
    DR Interest expense $10,518.06
    DR Obligations under capital leases   48,740.03
    DR Misc. expenses   3,000.00
        CR Cash $62,258.09

12/31/98–12/31/00:
Annual depreciation expense =
   ($161,583 - 15,000)/3 = $48,861.00

    DR Depreciation expense $48,861.00
        CR Accumulated depreciation
        —leased assets $48,861.00

Requirement 3:

DR Obligation under capital leases	$15,000.00
CR Assets under capital leases	$15,000.00

Requirement 4:

DR Obligation under capital leases	$15,000.00	
DR Loss on residual value guarantee	3,000.00	
CR Assets under capital leases		$15,000.00
CR Cash		3,000.00

P11-5. Capital lease effects on ratios and income

Requirement 1:
The amortization schedule for the lease is shown below.

Date	Annual Lease Payment	Interest	Reduction of Lease Obligation	Balance of Lease Obligation
12/31/97				$100,000
12/31/98	$41,635	$12,000	$29,635	70,365
12/31/99	41,635	8,444	33,191	37,174
12/31/00	41,635	4,461	37,174	0

Requirement 2:
The adjusted current ratio at December 31, 1997 is:

$$\frac{\text{Current assets} \quad \$500,000}{\text{Current liabilities} \quad \$294,118 \ + \ \$29,635} = 1.554$$

The portion of the December 31, 1998, payment representing principal reduction is a current liability at December 31, 1997.

Requirement 3:
Pre-tax income on a capital lease basis would be:

Income on operating lease basis	$225,000
Less: Excess of capital lease over operating lease expense	3,698*
Capital lease pre-tax income	$221,302

*Computation:

Depreciation: $100,000/33	$33,333
1998 interest expense	12,000
Capital lease expense	45,333
Operating lease expense	41,635
Excess of capital lease expense over operating lease expense	$3,698

P11-6. Lessors' direct financing lease

Requirement 1:
The amount of annual periodic lease payments is:

Present value = $725,000 - PV of unguaranteed residual value
            = $725,000 - $40,835*
            = $684,165

*The discount factor for a payment due in 5 years @ 8% = 0.68058
$60,000 × 0.68058 = $40,835

Annual payments = $684,165/4.31213#	= $158,661

#The discount factor for a five-year annuity due at 8% = 4.31213

Requirement 2:

Gross lease receivable = (5 × $158,661) + $60,000	= $853,305
Unearned interest revenue = $853,305 - $725,000	= $128,305

Requirement 3:

Present value of lease payments = $158,661 × 4.31213	= $684,165

(Since Rakin's implicit rate of return of 8% is lower than
Liska's incremental borrowing rate, Liska must use 8%.)

Depreciation expense = $684,165/5 years	= $136,833
Interest expense = ($684,165 - $158,661) × 8%	= $42,040

P11-7. Lessors' direct financing lease

Requirement 1:

The lease must be accounted for as a direct financing lease because Railcar Leasing Incorporated is not a manufacturer and because both of the Type II characteristics discussed in the chapter are met, and two of the Type I characteristics (only one is required) are met.

The two Type I characteristics that are met are:

a) The lease covers more than 75% as the asset's useful life
(i.e., 8/8 = 100%), and

b) The present value of the future minimum lease payments of $8,345,640 exactly equals the leased asset's fair market value at the inception of the lease (i.e., it exceeds 90% of the leased asset's fair market value at the inception of the lease). The present value of the future minimum lease payments is:

= ($1,500,000 × present value factor of an ordinary annuity for n = 7 periods at r = 12.0%) + $1,500,000 (i.e., the present value of the first payment on January 1, 1998)

= ($1,500,000 × 4.56376) + $1,500,000

= $8,345,640.

Requirement 2:

The amortization schedule for Railcar Leasing Incorporated is as follows:

Amortization Schedule for Railcar Leasing Incorporated

Year	Cash Payment	Interest Income	Principal Reduction	Remaining Principal
Inception				$8,345.640.00
1/1/98	$1,500,000.00	$0.00	$1,500,000.00	6,845,640.00
1/1/99	1,500,000.00	821,476.80	678,523.20	6,167,116.80
1/1/00	1,500,000.00	740,054.02	759,945.98	5,407,170.82
1/1/01	1,500,000.00	648,860.50	851,139.50	4,556,031.31
1/1/02	1,500,000.00	546,723.76	953,276.24	3,602,755.07
1/1/03	1,500,000.00	432,330.61	1,067,669.39	2,535,085.68
1/1/04	1,500,000.00	304,210.28	1,195,789.72	1,339,295.96
1/1/05	1,500,000.00	160,704.04*	1,339,295.96	0.00
		$3,654,360.00		

*Rounded by $11.48.

Requirement 3:
The journal entries are:

The journal entry to record the purchase of the boxcars by Railcar Leasing Incorporated would be:

DR Equipment	$8,345,640.00	
CR Cash		$8,345,640.00

1/1/98:
Gross investment in leased asset = Total lease payments over the lease

= $1,500,000 × 8
= $12,000,000

DR Gross investment in leased assets	$12,000,000.00	
CR Equipment		$8,345,640.00
CR Unearned financing income		
—leases		3,654,360.00

1/1/98:

DR Cash	$1,500,000.00	
CR Gross investment in leased assets		$1,500,000.00

12/31/98:

DR Unearned financing income—leases	$821,476.80	
CR Financing income—leases		$821,476.80

1/1/99:

DR Cash	$1,500,000.00	
CR Gross investment in leased assets		$1,500,000.00

12/31/99:

DR Unearned financing income—leases	$740,054.02	
CR Financing income—leases		$740,054.02

P11-8. Lessor accounting

Requirement 1:
Under the operating lease method, the lessor does not make any entry at the inception of the lease.

The annual lease payment would be recorded as follows:

12/31/98 and 12/31/99:

DR Cash	$1,500,000	
CR Rental income—leases		$1,500,000

479

Under the operating lease method, the lessor also depreciates the assets over 8 years, which is their remaining useful life. The annual depreciation charge would be $8,345,640/8 = $1,043,205. The journal entries would be:

12/31/98 and 12/31/99:
   DR Depreciation expense $1,043,205
         CR Accumulated depreciation $1,043,205

Requirement 2:
Over the life of the lease, the lessor would recognize income before tax of $456,795 ($1,500,000 - $1,043,205) per year for a total of $3,654,360 over the 8-year life of the lease.

Requirement 3:
The amount of income before tax of $3,654,360 is the same as that which was recognized in P11-7 when the lease was treated as a direct financing lease. One difference is that, when the lease was classified as a direct financing lease in P11-7, the income statement reported financing income each year which totaled $3,654,360 over the life of the lease, while under the operating lease method, the income statement reported rental income of $1,500,000 and depreciation expense of $1,043,205 each year, which **net** to a total of $3,654,360 over the life of the lease. Another difference is that treating the lease as a direct financing lease would result in higher (lower) income being reported in the early (later) years of the lease relative to treating it as an operating lease.

P11-9. Lessor accounting for sales-type leases

Requirement 1:
The lease must be accounted for as a sales-type lease because ABC Builders Incorporated is a manufacturer and because both of the Type II characteristics discussed in the chapter are met, and two of the Type I characteristics (only one is required) are met.

The two Type I characteristics that are met are:

a) The lease covers more than 75% as the asset's useful life (i.e., 6/6 = 100.0%), and

b) The present value of the future minimum lease payments of $19,354,730 exactly equals the leased asset's fair market value at the inception of the lease (i.e., it exceeds 90% of the leased asset's fair market value at the inception of the lease.) The present value of the future minimum lease payments is:

= ($5,000,000 × present value factor of an ordinary annuity for
  n = 6 periods at r = 15.0%) + ($1,000,000 × present value factor
  of $1 for n = 6 periods at r = 15.0%)

= ($5,000,000 × 3.78448) + ($1,000,000 × 0.43233)

= $19,354,730.

Requirement 2:

The amortization schedule for ABC Builders Incorporated is as follows:

Year	Cash Payment	Interest Income	Principal Reduction	Remaining Principal
1/1/98				$19,354,730.00
12/31/98	$5,000,000.00	$2,903,209.50	$2,096,790.50	17,257,939.50
12/31/99	5,000,000.00	2,588,690.93	2,411,309.08	14,846,630.43
12/31/00	5,000,000.00	2,226,994.56	2,773,005.44	12,073,624.99
12/31/01	5,000,000.00	1,811,043.75	3,188,956.25	8,884,668.74
12/31/02	5,000,000.00	1,332,700.31	3,667,299.69	5,217,369.05
12/31/03	5,000,000.00	782,630.95	4,217,369.05	1,000,000.00

Requirement 3:

The journal entries are:

1/1/98:
Gross investment in leased asset = Total lease payments over the lease +
Guaranteed residual value

= ($5,000,000 × 6) + $1,000,000

= $31,000,000

DR Gross investment in leased assets	$31,000,000.00		
CR Sales		19,354,730.00	
CR Unearned financing income			
—leases		$11,645,270.00	
DR Cost of goods sold	$15,000,000.00		
CR Inventory		$15,000,000.00	

12/31/98:
    DR Cash $5,000,000.00
          CR Gross investment in leased assets $5,000,000.00

    DR Unearned financing income—leases $2,903,209.50
          CR Financing income—leases $2,903,209.50

12/31/99:
    DR Cash $5,000,000.00
          CR Gross investment in leased assets $5,000,000.00

    DR Unearned financing income—leases $2,588,690.93
          CR Financing income—leases $2,588,690.93

Requirement 4:
The journal entry is:

    DR Cash $1,000,000.00
          CR Gross investment in leased assets $1,000,000.00

Since the lessee guarantees the residual value, if the leased asset is not worth $1,000,000, the lessee makes up the difference in cash.

P11-10. **Financial statement effects for lessees:** Capital versus operating leases

Requirement 1:
Trans Global must account for the lease as a capital lease. While a lease must only meet one of the four criteria specified for capital leases to be classified as a capital lease, this lease actually meets two of the requirements.

a) The lease term covers 80% of the assets' useful life (i.e., is greater than 75%).

b) The present value of the minimum lease payments is $49,676,400 (see below) which is more than 90% of fair market value of the leased assets ($55,000,000 × 0.90 = $49,500,000).

Present value of future lease payments:

= $10,000,000 × the present value of an ordinary annuity, r = 12%,
                          n = 8 periods.

= $10,000,000 × 4.96764

= $49,676,400

Requirement 2:
Appearing below is the amortization schedule for the lease liability:

Amortization of Capital Lease Liability
Trans Global Airlines

Date	Interest Portion[1]	Cash Payment[2]	Liability Reduction[3]	Lease Liability[4]
1/1/98				$49,676,400.00
12/31/98	$5,961,168.00	$10,000,000.00	$4,038,832.00	45,637,568.00
12/31/99	5,476,508.16	10,000,000.00	4,523,491.84	41,114,076.16
12/31/00	4,933,689.14	10,000,000.00	5,066,310.86	36,047,765.30
12/31/01	4,325,731.84	10,000,000.00	5,674,268.16	30,373,497.14
12/31/02	3,644,819.66	10,000,000.00	6,355,180.34	24,018,316.79
12/31/03	2,882,198.01	10,000,000.00	7,117,801.99	16,900,514.81
12/31/04	2,028,061.78	10,000,000.00	7,971,938.22	8,928,576.58
12/31/05	1,071,423.42*	10,000,000.00	8,928,576.58	0.00

* Rounded by $5.77.

[1] The interest portion is 12% of the carrying amount at the beginning of the period.

[2] The cash payment is fixed by the lease at $10,000,000.

[3] The reduction in the liability is the difference between the cash payment and the interest portion.

[4] The lease liability declines each year by the amount of the liability reduction.

The journal entries are:

1/1/98:
    DR Aircraft under capital leases $49,676,400.00
        CR Obligations under capital leases $49,676,400.00

12/31/98:
    DR Interest expense $5,961,168.00
    DR Obligations under capital leases   4,038,832.00
        CR Cash $10,000,000.00

12/31/99:
    DR Interest expense $5,476,508.16
    DR Obligations under capital leases   4,523,491.84
        CR Cash $10,000,000.00

12/31/00:
  DR Interest expense $4,933,689.14
  DR Obligations under capital leases   5,066,310.86
    CR Cash $10,000,000.00

12/31/05:
  DR Interest expense $1,071,423.42
  DR Obligations under capital leases   8,928,576.58
    CR Cash $10,000,000.00

12/31/98–12/31/05:
  Annual depreciation expense =
  $49,676,400/8 = $6,209,550.00

  DR Depreciation expense $6,209,550.00
    CR Accumulated depreciation
        —leased aircraft $6,209,550.00

Requirement 3:
Journal entries for 1998, 1999, 2000, and 2005, assuming the lease is an operating lease:

  DR Rent expense $10,000,000.00
    CR Cash $10,000,000.00

Requirement 4:
Year-to-year expense recognition: capital vs. operating lease.

	Capital Lease			Operating Lease	
Date	Interest Portion	Depreciation	Total		Difference
12/31/98	$5,961,168.00	$6,209,550.00	$12,170,718.00	$10,000,000.00	$2,170,718.00
12/31/99	5,476,508.16	6,209,550.00	11,686,058.16	10,000,000.00	1,686,058.16
12/31/00	4,933,689.14	6,209,550.00	11,143,239.14	10,000,000.00	1,143,239.14
12/31/01	4,325,731.84	6,209,550.00	10,535,281.84	10,000,000.00	535,281.84
12/31/02	3,644,819.66	6,209,550.00	9,854,369.66	10,000,000.00	(145,630.34)
12/31/03	2,882,198.01	6,209,550.00	9,091,748.01	10,000,000.00	(908,251.99)
12/31/04	2,028,061.78	6,209,550.00	8,237,611.78	10,000,000.00	(1,762,388.22)
12/31/05	1,071,423.42	6,209,550.00	7,280,973.42	10,000,000.00	(2,719,026.58)
Total	$30,323,600.00	$49,676,400.00	$80,000,000.00	$80,000,000.00	$0.00

Under the capital lease method, the annual income statement effect is the sum of the interest expense recognized plus depreciation expense. Under the operating lease method, the annual income statement effect is the amount of the annual lease payment.

As can be seen from the above table, income before tax would be lower under the capital lease in 1998–2001, and then higher in 2002–2005 when compared to the operating lease method. Over the term of the lease, both methods end up recognizing the same amount of total expense, thus the net difference in income before tax is $0 at the end of the lease. All that differs under the two approaches is the manner and pattern of the expense recognition over the term of the lease.

Requirement 5:
Trans Global's mangers are likely to prefer the operating lease approach because it allows them to keep the lease liability, as well as the asset, off the balance sheet.

P11-11. Direct financing versus operating leases: Lessors' income statement and balance sheet effects

The present value of the future minimum lease payments of $99,817,750 (see below) exactly equals the leased asset's fair market value at the inception of the lease. Specifically, the present value of the future minimum lease payments is:

= $25,000,000 × present value of an ordinary annuity for
   n = 5 periods at r = 8.0%)
= $25,000,000 × 3.99271
= $99,817,750.

The amortization schedule is as follows:

Year	Cash Payment	Interest Income	Principal Reduction	Remaining Principal
1/1/98				$99,817,750.00
12/31/98	$25,000,000.00	$7,985,420.00	17,014,580.00	82,803,170.00
12/31/99	25,000,000.00	6,624,253.60	18,375,746.40	64,427,423.60
12/31/00	25,000,000.00	5,154,193.89	19,845,806.11	44,581,617.49
12/31/01	25,000,000.00	3,566,529.40	21,433,470.60	23,148,146.89
12/31/02	25,000,000.00	1,851,853.11*	23,148,146.89	0.00
		$25,182,250.00		

*Rounded by $1.36

Under the operating method, the firm would recognize rental income of $25,000,000 each year along with depreciation expense of $19,963,550 (i.e., $99,817,750/5).

Based on these calculations, the year-to-year income statement and balance sheet differences under the two methods appear in the following table:

Operating Method versus Direct Financing Method:
Income Statement and Balance Sheet Comparisons

Year	Lease Payment (a)	Annual Deprec. (b)	Operating Method Income (c)	Direct Financing Income (d)	Income Difference (e)	Operating Method Asset Balance (f)	Direct Financing Method Asset Balance (g)	Asset Balance Difference (h)
12/31/98	$25,000,000.00	$19,963,550.00	$5,036,450.00	$7,985,420.00	($2,948,970.00)	$79,854,200.00	$82,803,170.00	($2,948,970.00)
12/31/99	25,000,000.00	19,963,550.00	5,036,450.00	6,624,253.60	(1,587,803.60)	59,890,650.00	64,427,423.60	(4,536,773.60)
12/31/00	25,000,000.00	19,963,550.00	5,036,450.00	5,154,193.89	(117,743.89)	39,927,100.00	44,581,617.49	(4,654,517.49)
12/31/01	25,000,000.00	19,963,550.00	5,036,450.00	3,566,529.40	1,469,920.60	19,963,550.00	23,148,146.89	(3,184,596.89)
12/3102	25,000,000.00	19,963,550.00	5,036,450.00	1,851,853.11	3,184,596.89	0.00	0.00	0.00
	$125,000,000.00	$99,817,750.00	$25,182,250.00	$25,182,250.00	$0.00			

(a) The annual payment is given as $25,000,000.
(b) Annual depreciation under the operating method is: $99,817,750/5 = $19,963,550.
(c) Income under the operating method is equal to a - b.
(d) Income under the direct financing method was calculated in the table above.
(e) The income difference is c - d. A negative (positive) number means income under the operating (direct financing) method was lower (higher).
(f) The original cost of $99,817,750 minus the accumulated depreciation charges of $19,963,550 per year.
(g) The asset balance under the direct financing method was calculated in the above table.
(h) The difference in asset balances is f - g. A negative (positive) number means the asset balance under the operating (direct financing) method was lower (higher).

P11-12. Asset acquisition: Cash purchase vs. lease vs. note payable

Requirement 1:
The option with the lowest present value to the firm should be selected. The present value of the three options are as follows:

Option I: Non-interest bearing note:

To calculate the present value of this option, discount the note using Corporal Motors' incremental borrowing rate of 8%. Specifically,

Present value $= \$125,000 \times$ Present value of \$1 for $r = 8\%$ and $n = 5$ periods.

$= \$125,000 \times 0.68058 = \$85,073$

Option II: Lease the machine at a cost of \$22,000 per year for 5 years:

To calculate the present value of this option, discount the 5 lease payments using Corporal Motors' incremental borrowing rate of 8%. Specifically,

Present value $= \$22,000 \times$ Present value of an ordinary annuity for $r = 8\%$ and $n = 5$ periods.

$= \$22,000 \times 3.99271 = \$87,840$

Option III: The present value of this option is simply the purchase price of \$90,000.

The firm should choose Option I.

Requirement 2:
Under Option I, the acquisition of the asset would be recorded as follows:

1/1/98:
DR Property, plant, and equipment	$85,073	
DR Discount on note payable	39,927	
CR Note payable		$125,000

The discount on note payable represents interest expense that must be recognized each year over the term of the note. The following table sets forth the amortization of the discount (i.e., recognition of interest expense over the term of the note):

Interest Expense Recognition Under Option I

Date	Interest Expense (a)	Amortization of Discount (b)	Balance in Discount on N/P (c)	Carrying Amount of N/P (d)
1/1/98			$39,927	$85,073
12/31/98	$6,806	$6,806	33,121	91,879
12/31/99	7,350	7,350	25,771	99,229
12/31/00	7,938	7,938	17,833	107,167
12/31/01	8,573	8,573	9,259	115,741
12/31/02	9,259	9,259	0	125,000

(a) = 0.08% times the previous balance in column (d) (i.e., times the carrying amount of the liability).

(b) = Since the note is non-interest bearing, the amount of the discount amortized is equal to the amount of imputed interest expense in column (a).

(c) = The previous balance in the column minus (b) (i.e., the existing discount minus the amount amortized in the current year).

(d) = $125,000 (the face amount of the note), minus the amount of unamortized discount on the note.

In addition to the annual interest expense recognized in accordance with the above table, the firm would also depreciate the asset over its 5-year useful life. The annual depreciation expense would be:

Annual depreciation = $85,073/5 = $17,015.

The total expense for Year 1 under this option would be $6,806 of interest and $17,015 of depreciation expense for a total of $23,821.

Requirement 3:
Over the entire 5-year period, the total expense under Option I would be $125,000. This would consist of $39,927 of interest expense (see the table above) and $85,073 of depreciation expense ($17,015 × 5).

Requirement 4:
If Option II is adopted and the lease were to be accounted for as an operating lease, the total expense recognized in the first year would be the amount of the annual lease payment, $22,000.

Requirement 5:

If Option II is adopted and the lease were to be accounted for as an operating lease, the total expense recognized over the 5-year lease term would be $110,000 (i.e., $22,000 × 5).

Requirement 6:

If Option II is adopted and the lease were to be accounted for as a capital lease, the total expense recognized in the first year would consist of interest expense and depreciation on the leased asset. As shown under question (1), the present value of the lease payments is $87,840. Based on this and the firm's incremental borrowing rate of 8%, the amortization of the lease liability would be as follows:

Amortization of capital lease liability under Option II

Date	Interest Portion[1]	Cash Payment[2]	Liability Reduction[3]	Lease Liability[4]
1/1/98				$87,840
12/31/98	$7,027	$22,000	$14,973	72,867
12/31/99	5,829	22,000	16,171	56,697
12/31/00	4,536	22,000	17,464	39,232
12/31/01	3,139	22,000	18,861	20,371
12/31/02	1,629*	22,000	20,371	0

*Rounded by $1.

[1] The interest portion is 8% of the carrying amount at the beginning of the period.

[2] The cash payment is fixed by the lease at $22,000.

[3] The reduction in the liability is the difference between the cash payment and the interest portion.

[4] The lease liability declines each year by the amount of the liability reduction.

The total expense recognized in the first year would be $24,595, and would consist of $7,027 of interest expense and $17,568 ($87,840/5) of depreciation expense.

Requirement 7:

If Option II is adopted and the lease were to be accounted for as a capital lease, the total expense recognized over the 5-year lease term would be $110,000 (the same as that for the operating lease). This would consist of interest expense of $22,160 and depreciation expense of $87,840.

Requirement 8:
If Option III were adopted, the firm would record an asset with a cost of $90,000. With a 5-year useful life and no salvage value, the annual depreciation expense would be $18,000. Thus, the total expense recognized in the first year would be $18,000 and would consist entirely of depreciation expense.

Requirement 9:
Under Option III, the total expense recognized over the 5-year period would be $90,000 and would consist entirely of depreciation expense.

P11-13. Constructive capitalization of operating leases

Requirement 1:
The implicit interest rate is calculated as follows:

$70 = 77 × Present value of $1 for 1 period at r%

$70/77 = Present value of $1 for 1 period at r%

0.90909 = Present value of $1 for 1 period at r%

To find the rate, examine the table for the present value of $1 for 1 period, and try to find the rate that gives a present value factor that is close to 0.90909. In this case, the exact rate is 10%.

Requirement 2:
The 1996 capital lease payment:

DR Obligations under capital leases	$70	
DR Interest expense	7	
CR Cash		$77

Requirement 3:
First, calculate the amount of the four payments due after 2002. These four payments are:

= $12,979/4
= $3,245 (rounded)

The following table illustrates the calculation of the present value of the operating lease payments:

Year	Payment	Present Value Factor $1 @ 10%	Present Value of Payment
1998	$8,494	0.9091	$7,722
1999	6,835	0.8264	5,649
2000	4,952	0.7513	3,721
2001	4,740	0.6830	3,237
2002	4,023	0.6209	2,498
2003	3,245	0.5645	1,832
2004	3,245	0.5132	1,665
2005	3,245	0.4665	1,514
2006	3,245	0.4241	1,376
		PV of operating leases:	$29,214

Requirement 4:
  DR Leased assets—capital leases $29,214
    CR Obligations under capital leases $29,214

Requirement 5:
The interest portion of the payment would be:

= $29,214 × 0.10

= $2,921

The reduction in the lease liability would be:

= Payment - Interest portion
= $8,494 - $2,921
= $5,573

  The journal entry would be:

  DR Interest expense $2,921
  DR Obligations under capital leases   5,573
    CR Cash $8,494

Requirement 6:
The effect is indeterminable in general, given the information in the problem.
If we assume that the present value of the capitalized operating leases are

depreciated straight-line over 9 years, annual depreciation is $29,214 ÷ 9 =
$3,246. The effect on the interest coverage ratio is:

$$\frac{\text{Income}}{\text{Interest}} = \frac{+\$8,494 - \$3,246}{+\$2,921} = \frac{+\$5,248}{+\$2,921}$$

To know whether this increases or decreases the interest coverage ratio
would require information not provided in the problem regarding the initial
levels of 1) operating income before taxes and interest and 2) interest
expense.

Requirement 7:
All of the firm's leverage ratios would deteriorate. That is, they would
indicate a greater amount of leverage when compared to that based on
reported financial statement numbers that do not give effect to the operating
leases.

Requirement 8:
The payment of $8,494 would impact the cash flow statement in two distinct
ways. The interest portion ($2,921) would be imbedded as part of cash from
operating activities, while the reduction in liability ($5,573) would be
classified as a financing activity.

Requirement 9:
In the case of an operating lease, the entire amount of the payment ($8,494)
would be imbedded as part of cash from operating activities.

Requirement 10:
The basic rationale for treating certain leases as capital leases is that when
they meet any one of the four criteria discussed in the chapter, they transfer
valuable property rights from the lessor to the lessee. As a result, the lease
should be accounted for in a manner more reflective of the acquisition of an
asset. In the case of a capital lease, this entails recognizing the leased asset
as an asset on the balance sheet and the present value of the future
payments to be made as a liability on the balance sheet. When none of the
four criteria is met, then property rights are not considered to have been
transferred, and the operating lease approach must be used.

P11-14. Capital leases: Visualizing the asset-liability relationship over time

Requirement 1:
a) At 8%, the accrual of interest causes the liability at the end of the first
    year to total $103,718.87 (i.e., a beginning balance of $96,035.99 plus
    accrued interest of $7,682.88) which exceeds the asset amount of
    $100,734.19. However, after making the second $10,000 payment, the
    liability drops to $93,718.87. The liability does not permanently exceed
    the asset until early in the fourth year.

b) At 12%, the accrual of interest causes the liability at the end of the first year to total $82,496.70 (i.e., a beginning balance of $73,657.77 plus accrued interest of $8,838.93) which exceeds the asset amount of $79,474,88. However, after making the second $10,000 payment, the liability drops to $72,496.70. Again, the liability does not permanently exceed the asset until early in the fourth year.

c) As in parts 1(a) and (b), the accrual of interest causes the liability to exceed the asset starting at the end of year one. But after making the $10,000 payment, the liability amount is lower than the asset amount through the start of year 5. The liability amount does not permanently overtake the asset amount until early in the year 5.

Requirement 2:
a) With payments at the end of each year, the carrying value of the asset will never exceed the liability when the discount rate is 8% and the lease runs for twenty years.

b) Raising the interest rate and/or shortening the duration of the lease does not change this result. The carrying value of the asset will always be lower than the liability when payments are made at the end of the year.

Cases

C11-1. MCI: Lessee accounting and constructive capitalization

Requirement 1:

Summary journal entries (all amounts in $ millions)

Capital Lease:

DR Interest expense (8.0%* × $867**)	$69.36	
DR Lease obligation (plug)	117.64	
CR Cash (from lease footnote)		$187.00

* Incremental borrowing rate.   ** Present value of capital leases on 12/31/91.

DR Depreciation expense ($1,039/10)	$103.9	
CR Accumulated depreciation		
—leased equipment		$103.9

Operating Lease:

DR Rent expense (from lease footnote)	$186	
CR Cash		$186

Requirement 2: Effect of capitalizing operating leases on various ratios (all amounts in $ millions)

Ratio	Before	After
Working Capital Ratio (CA/CL)	$1,758/\$2,300 = 76.43\%$	$\$1,758/(\$2,300 + \$131.94^{(1)}) = 72.29\%$ [1] $8\% \times \$675.76$ (PV of operating leases on 12/31/91) (see Exhibit A which follows) = 54.06 interest expense component of 1992 lease payment. $\begin{array}{ll}\$186.00 & \text{Operating lease payment in 1992} \\ \underline{-54.06} & \text{Interest component} \\ \$131.94 & \text{Principal component of 1992 lease payment}\end{array}$
Debt-to-Equity Ratio (Debt/Equity)	$\dfrac{\text{Total Debt 12/31/91}}{\text{Total Stk. Equity 12/31/91}}$ $\$5,875/\$2,959 = 1.99$	$\dfrac{(\$5,875 + \$637.92^{(1)})}{(\$2,959 - \$70.28^{(2)})} = \dfrac{\$6,512.92}{\$2,888.72} = 2.25$ [1] Present value of leases on 12/31/91 (see Exhibit A which follows) of 675.76 less tax effect of 37.84 $= 35\% \times$ Cumulative difference in earnings if operating leases had been capitalized at start. (Difference between liability balance and asset balance) $= 35\% \times (\$675.76 - \$567.64) = \$37.84$. [2] Difference between change in assets ($567.64) and change in liabilities ($637.92) from capitalizing operating leases net of tax effects = $108.12 - \$37.84 = \$70.28$.
Interest Coverage (IBIT/Interest Expense)	$\dfrac{(\$848^* + \$212^{**})/212}{\$1060/\$212} = 5.0$ * Income before tax ** Interest expense	$\dfrac{(\$848 + \$192^{(1)} - \$116.51^{(2)} - \$64.28^{(3)} + \$212 + \$64.28^{(3)})}{(\$212 + \$64.28^{(3)})} = \dfrac{\$1135.49}{276.28} = 4.11$ [1] Operating lease payment in 1991 that would *not* be expensed if leases are capitalized. [2] Depreciation expense on capitalized asset value on 12/31/90 (See Exhibit A) (12/31/90 PV $\times$ 87% /6 yrs) = $803.49 \times 87\% = \$699.04/6$ yrs. $= \$116.51$ [3] $8\% \times$ 12/31/90 Present value of operating leases = $803.49 \times .08 = \$64.28$

495

Ratio	Before	After

Return on Assets

$\dfrac{\text{(NI + Interest Expense(1 - tax rate)}}{\text{Average Total Assets}}$

Before:

$$\dfrac{(\$551* + [\$212 \times (1 - .35)]**)}{(\$8,249 + \$8,834)/2} =$$

$$\dfrac{\$551 + \$137.80}{\$8,541.50} = 8.06\%$$

*Net income after taxes
**Interest net of tax

After:

$$\dfrac{(\$551 + \$124.80^{(1)} - \$41.78^{(2)} - \$75.74^{(3)} + (\$212 + \$64.28^{(4)}) \times .65)}{(\$8,249 + \$699.04^{(5)} + \$8,834 + \$567.64^{(6)})/2} = 8.04\%$$

[1] 1991 Operating lease payment net of taxes $192 × .65 = $124.80

[2] Additional interest expense (net of tax) in 1991 if operating leases are capitalized (12/31/90 PV × 8%) = $803.49 × 8% = $64.28 × .65 = $41.78

[3] Depreciation expense (net of tax)
(12/31/90 PV × 87%/6 yrs) = $803.49 × 87% = $699.04/6 yrs. = $116.51 × .65 = $75.74

87% is the ratio of asset carrying value to lease liability carrying value for the combination of interest rate (8%), total lease life and asset life expired (40%) in this case. See Table 3 of Imhoff, Lipe, and Wright, "Operating Leases: Impact of Constructive Capitalization," *Accounting Horizons* (March 1991), pp 51-62.

[4] Interest expense for capitalized operating leases in 1991
= 8% × $803.49 (PV of operating leases on 12/31/90
= $64.28

[5] See Exhibit A for asset book values added on 12/31/90.

[6] See Exhibit A for asset book values added on 12/31/91.

496

Exhibit A
Effect of Capitalizing Operating Lease Commitment
MCI Corporation

Year	Scheduled Cash Flows	8% PV Factor	PV on 12/31/90	8% PV Factor	PV on 12/31/91
1991	$192	0.9259	$177.77		
1992	186	0.8573	159.46	0.9259	$172.22
1993	150	0.7938	119.07	0.8573	128.60
1994	121	0.7351	88.95	0.7938	96.05
1995	114	0.6806	77.59	0.7351	83.80
1996	107	0.6302	67.43	0.6806	72.82
1997-2001	45*	2.5161**	113.22	2.7174***	122.27
Lease obligation			$803.49		$675.76
Ratio of asset book value to lease obligation****			87%		84%
Asset Book Value			$699.04		$567.64

*$225/5 years = $45/year
** PV factor @ 8% for 11 years - PV factor @ 8% for 6 years
***PV factor @ 8% for 10 years - PV factor @ 8% for 5 years

****Asset book values are the approximate ratio of asset to liability balance based on a combination of total lease life, the interest rate used to discount the lease obligation, and the percentage of original lease life expired [see Table 3 of Imhoff, Lipe, and Wright, "Operating Leases: Impact of Constructive Capitalization," *Accounting Horizons* (March 1991), pp. 51-62]. The instructor should consider assigning this article as a reading to accompany this case. Alternatively, the instructor may wish to give the students the 87% and 84% ratios.

```
┌─────────────────────────────────────────────────────────────────────────┐
│                               Exhibit B                                   │
│      Effect of Capitalizing Operating Leases on the 12/31/91 Balance Sheet│
│                             MCI Corporation                               │
│                                                                           │
│  Assets:                         Liabilities:                             │
│  Unrecorded net assets  $567.64  Unrecorded leases              $675.76   │
│                                    (from Exhibit A)                        │
│                                  Tax consequences                         │
│                                    (.35 × $108.12)              ($37.84)   │
│                                  Net liability effect            $637.92   │
│                                                                           │
│                                  Equity:                                  │
│                                  Cumulative effect on retained            │
│                                  earnings (net of tax)          ($70.28)  │
│  Total assets           $567.64  Total liabilities and equity   $567.64   │
└─────────────────────────────────────────────────────────────────────────┘
```

Requirement 3:

Bond ratings would probably go down if constructive capitalization of operating leases was not already factored into the rating since the working capital ratio, debt/equity ratio, times interest earned and ROA all deteriorate after operating leases are treated as capital leases.

C11-2. May Department Stores (CW): Constructive capitalization of operating leases

(all $ amounts in millions)

Requirement 1:
2/1/97:

> **DR** Leased assets—capital leases $242
>   **CR** Obligation under capital leases $242

Requirement 2:
Long-term debt-to-equity ratio based on reported numbers:

> = $3,849/$3,650
> = 1.05

Requirement 3:
Long-term debt-to-equity ratio based on reported numbers after giving effect to operating leases:

> = ($3,849 + $242)/$3,650
> = 1.12

The ratio increases by about 7% as a result of "capitalizing" the firm's operating leases. While the increase is not dramatic, it does illustrate that using reported balance sheet figures to calculate a firm's leverage position has the potential to understate a firm's "true" leverage.

Requirement 4:
To see if the rate implicit in the leases is closer to 10% or 11%, discount the future operating lease payments using the two rates and see which yields the estimate that is closest to the $242,000,000 that May reports in its footnotes. The following table reports these calculations:

Calculation of the approximate interest rate that is implicit in May's operating leases.

Year	Operating Lease Payment	PV Factor 10%	PV of Operating Lease at 10%	PV Factor 11%	PV of Operating Lease at 11%
1997	$44.00	0.909091	$40.00	0.900901	$39.64
1998	40.00	0.826446	33.06	0.811622	32.46
1999	35.00	0.751315	26.30	0.731191	25.59
2000	32.00	0.683013	21.86	0.658731	21.08
2001	29.00	0.620921	18.01	0.593451	17.21
2002	29.70	0.564474	16.76	0.534641	15.88
2003	29.70	0.513158	15.24	0.481658	14.31
2004	29.70	0.466507	13.86	0.433926	12.89
2005	29.70	0.424098	12.60	0.390925	11.61
2006	29.70	0.385543	11.45	0.352184	10.46
2007	29.70	0.350494	10.41	0.317283	9.42
2008	29.70	0.318631	9.46	0.285841	8.49
2009	29.70	0.289664	8.60	0.257514	7.65
2010	29.70	0.263331	7.82	0.231995	6.89
2011	29.70	0.239392	7.11	0.209004	6.21
		Total PV	$252.53	Total PV	$239.79

Based on the calculations in the above table, it appears that the interest rate implicit in the present value of May's operating leases is closer to 11% than to 10%.

Requirement 5:
1997 Lease payment:

Interest portion $= \$242.0 \times 0.11$

$\qquad = \$26.6$

Reduction in lease liability $= \$44.0 - 26.6$

$\qquad = \$17.4$

DR Interest expense	$26.6
DR Obligation under capital leases	17.4
CR Cash	$44.0

C11-3. Tuesday Morning Corporation (CW): Comprehensive leasee reporting

Requirement 1:
No. The 1993 balance sheet lists a zero balance for current installments on capital lease obligation (current liability) and capital lease obligations, excluding current installments (long-term liability).

Requirement 2:
It had a bargain purchase option. See Note 6.

Requirement 3:
$2,642,000. See Note 6.

Requirement 4:
A: Total lease payments is just the sum of the annual payments from 1995-1999.

$= \$933 + 933 + 707 + 255 + 170$

$= \$2,998$

B: Amount representing interest is equal to A - C = $570.

C: Present value of minimum lease payments is equal to $607 + 1,821 = $2,428.

Requirement 5:
The interest portion is:

$= \$2,428 \times 0.125$
$= \$304$

The reduction in the liability is:

= $933 - 304
= $629

DR Interest expense	$304	
DR Obligation under capital leases	629	
CR Cash		$933*

* From Note 6.

Requirement 6:

The following table presents the calculation of the present value of the operating lease payments based on an interest rate of 12%.

Year	Payment	Present Value Factor at 12.00%	Present Value of Payment
1995	$12,437	0.8929	$11,104
1996	10,487	0.7972	8,360
1997	8,211	0.7118	5,845
1998	6,239	0.6355	3,965
1999	3,106	0.5674	1,762
2000	1,985	0.5066	1,006
Total	$42,465		$32,042

Estimated present value of capital lease obligation using a rate of 12%
= $32,042

Requirement 7:

DR Leased assets—capital leases	$32,042	
CR Obligation under capital leases		$32,042

Requirement 8:

The interest portion is:

= $32,042 × 0.12
= $3,845

The reduction in the liability is:

= $12,437 - $3,845
= $8,592

DR Interest expense	$3,845	
DR Obligation under capital leases	8,592	
CR Cash		$12,437*

* From Note 6.

Requirement 9:
Long-term debt to shareholders' equity ratio:

Based on reported balance sheet numbers:

= ($4,952 + $1,821 + $2,920)/$58,630

= 16.5%

Long-term debt to shareholders' equity ratio after adjusting for the constructive capitalization of the operating leases:

= ($4,952 + $1,821 + $2,920 + $32,042)/$58,630

= 71.2%

Requirement 10:
The "reported" leverage of the firm increases by over 400% after giving effect to the present value of the future operating lease payments.

C11-4. Delta Air Lines, Inc. (CW): Constructive capitalization of operating leases

Requirement 1:
Long-term capital lease obligations (E) can be obtained from the balance sheet information provided as part of the case. The amount is $322.

Current obligations under capital leases (D) can be obtained from the balance sheet information provided as part of the case. The amount is $62.

Present value of future minimum capital lease payments (C) is simply the sum of D and E. $322 + $62 = $384.

Total minimum lease payments (A) is simply the sum of the amounts listed in the lease footnote. That is, $101 + $100 + $68 + $57 + $57 + $118 = $501.

Amounts representing interest (B) is the difference between the undiscounted future capital lease payments minus the discounted value of the future capital lease payments (i.e., B = A - C). B = $501 - $384 = $117.

Requirement 2:

The two payments after 2002 are assumed to be the same. The amount of each payment is estimated to be $118/2 = $59.0

Requirement 3:

Using the weighted average interest rate of 9.0%, the present value of the capital lease payments is $374. The calculation appears in the following table.

Calculation of the Present Value of Delta's Capital Lease Obligation Based on an Interest Rate of 9%

Year	Payment	Present Value Factor at 9.0%	Present Value of Payment
1998	$101	0.9174	$93
1999	100	0.8417	84
2000	68	0.7722	53
2001	57	0.7084	40
2002	57	0.6499	37
2003	59	0.5963	35
2004	59	0.5470	32
Total	$501		$374

The estimated present value of the capital lease obligation using a rate of 9.0% is $374.0.

The amount appearing in the footnote for the present value of the capital leases is $384.0. The amounts are not that far apart, indicating that our estimated interest rate of 9.0% is reasonably accurate. The accuracy of our estimated rate is important to know since we will be using it to capitalize Delta's operating leases. Finally, since the present value of $374.0 that we estimate is less than that reported in the footnote ($384.0), the 9% rate is slightly more than the rate implicit in Delta's capital lease obligation.

Requirement 4:

The amount of the capital lease payment is $101.0. Using our 9.0% interest rate, the journal entry would be:

DR Interest expense (0.09 x $374) $33.7
DR Obligation under capital leases ($101.0 - $33.7) 67.3
   CR Cash $101.0

Requirement 5:

The twelve payments after 2002 are assumed to be the same. The amount of each payment is estimated to be $9,780/12 = $815.0.

Requirement 6:

Using the weighted average interest rate of 9.0%, the present value of the operating lease payments is $7,095. The calculation appears in the following table:

Year	Payment	Present Value Factor at 9.0%	Present Value of Payment
1998	$860	0.9174	$789
1999	860	0.8417	724
2000	840	0.7722	649
2001	830	0.7084	588
2002	850	0.6499	552
2003	815	0.5963	486
2004	815	0.5470	446
2005	815	0.5019	409
2006	815	0.4604	375
2007	815	0.4224	344
2008	815	0.3875	316
2009	815	0.3555	290
2010	815	0.3262	266
2011	815	0.2992	244
2012	815	0.2745	224
2013	815	0.2519	205
2014	815	0.2311	188
Total	$14,020		$7,095

Estimated present value of operating leases is: $7,095

Requirement 7:

DR Leased aircraft—capital leases $7,095
   CR Obligation under capital leases $7,095

Requirement 8:

The amount of the payment is $860.0. Using our 9.0% interest rate, the journal entry would be:

DR Interest expense (0.09 × $7,095) $638.6

    CR Obligation under capital leases

        ($860.0 - $638.6) $221.4

    CR Cash   860.0

Requirement 9:

a) Ratios based on reported balance sheet numbers:

Long-term debt to shareholders' equity: (using just "long-term debt")

= $1,475/$3,007
= 49.1%

Long-term debt to shareholders' equity: (using total noncurrent liabilities)

= $4,644/$3,007
= 154.4%

Total liabilities to total assets:

= ($4,083 + $4,644 + $1,007)/$12,741
= 76.4%

These ratios reveal that Delta is very highly leveraged.

b) Ratios adjusted for the present value of Delta's operating lease payments:

Long-term debt to shareholders' equity: (using just long-term debt)

= ($1,475 + $7,095)/$3,007
= 285.0%

Long-term debt to shareholders' equity: (using total noncurrent liabilities)

= ($4,644 + $7,095)/$3,007
= 390.4%

Total liabilities to total assets:

= ($4,083 + $4,644 + $1,007 + $7,095)/($12,741 + $7,095)
= 84.8%

All three ratios increase from those based simply on the reported numbers.

Requirement 10:
The most often cited reason is to keep debt off of the firm's balance sheet. As was shown above, long-term debt-to-equity ratios tend to increase dramatically when operating leases are constructively capitalized. Another reason to prefer operating leases over capital leases is that the interest coverage ratio will tend to be higher when operating leases are used in place of capital leases. Finally, for firms that enter into new leases at a rate faster than with which older leases are terminating, their income will tend to be lower (year in and year out) when the leases are capitalized versus when they are accounted for as operating leases. This is because the combined effect of the interest expense and depreciation expense under the capital lease treatment will tend to exceed the amount of rent expense that would have been recorded under the operating lease method. As a result, income will be lower.

C11-5. Nationsbank (KR): Lease classification and the times interest earned ratio

Requirement 1:
As discussed throughout the book, companies do have some discretion in how they choose to report a given economic transaction. For instance, a company might be able to convert a true "capital" lease into an operating lease by carefully designing the lease agreement. In addition, GAAP financial statements are general purpose financial statements, and, consequently, different users might make different modifications to the GAAP numbers to make them suitable for their own purposes.

Lenders are not bound by the GAAP definition of financial leverage; instead, they are more interested in measuring the "true" financial leverage of their borrowers. Typically, textbooks define the coverage ratio as income before interest and taxes divided by interest expense. The GAAP definition for interest expense also includes interest expense on capital leases. Consequently, the classification of a lease agreement into operating versus capital lease might impact the fixed coverage ratio. This is especially true after a borrower enters into a credit agreement where the thresholds have already been defined.

Assume the company treats its lease as a capital lease for accounting purposes. Based on its current income figures, the company enters into a credit agreement that requires the company to maintain a times interest earned ratio of 1.20 on June 30, 1997, which will increase to 1.50 at the end of September 30, 1997. After entering into the credit agreement, the company "somehow" restructures the lease agreement to satisfy the definition of an operating lease. The effect of this restructuring on the times interest earned ratio is provided below:

	Capital Lease	Operating Lease
Income before interest and taxes	$120,000	$60,000
Interest on capital lease	$ 60,000	
Interest on borrowings	40,000	$40,000
Total interest expense	$100,000	$40,000
Times interest earned	1.20	1.50

Now, the $60,000 interest expense will be part of the lease rent expense, and, therefore, will be subtracted from the income before interest and taxes. This raises the times interest earned ratio to 1.50. The higher ratio provides more flexibility to the borrower. For instance, the company's income before interest and taxes can go down by as much as $12,000 (from $120,000 to $108,000) without violating the covenant for the times interest earned ratio. Consequently, the company may be inclined to take on riskier projects that increase the variance in earnings. Of course, higher earnings variability increases the credit risk, and, therefore, the lender might be worse off. Alternatively, without increasing its "true" performance, the company will have already reached the threshold for September 30, 1997, by treating the capital lease as an operating lease. Once again, this might provide greater flexibility to managers, which may not be in the best interest of the lender.

In order to reduce such managerial opportunism, most lenders provide their own definitions for financial ratios. For instance, Nationsbank of Texas includes rent expenses from operating leases as part of the fixed charges in calculating the coverage ratio. Consequently, a borrower will not be able to increase the coverage ratio by merely restructuring some of the capital leases as operating leases. In fact, the ratio will go down since the rent expense under operating leases is likely to be greater than the interest expense component of the capital lease. To illustrate this point, let us assume that the depreciation on the leased equipment is $30,000. Also assume that if the capital lease were structured as an operating lease, the annual lease expense will equal the sum of the depreciation and interest expense under the capital lease ($30,000 + $60,000). Based on these assumptions, the fixed charges coverage ratio is calculated under the two accounting methods:

	Capital Lease	Operating Lease
Income before deprec., rent, interest and taxes	$150,000	$150,000
(-) Depreciation on leased equipment	30,000	
Income before rent, interest and taxes	$120,000	$150,000
Rent for operating lease		$90,000
Interest on capital lease	$ 60,000	
Interest on borrowings	40,000	40,000
Fixed charges	$100,000	$130,000
Fixed charges coverage ratio	1.20	1.15

While $30,000 is assumed for the illustrative purposes, the fixed charges coverage ratio will decline for any depreciation number. In essence, by providing its own definition for the coverage ratio, Nationsbank of Texas has tried to mitigate the effects of any opportunistic behavior on the part of its borrowers.

Requirement 2:
Note that if the times interest earned ratio is more than 1.00, reclassification of the lease into an operating lease will increase the ratio from 1.20 to 1.50. In contrast, if the ratio is less than 1.00, this reclassification will decrease the ratio. This is illustrated through the following example (assume that income before interest and taxes was $95,000 under the capital lease scenario):

	Capital Lease	Operating Lease
Income before interest and taxes	$95,000	$35,000
Interest on capital lease	60,000	
Interest on borrowings	40,000	40,000
Total interest expense	$100,000	$40,000
Times interest earned	0.95	0.88

In the above case, a company might have incentives to reclassify the operating lease into a capital lease to increase the times-interest-earned ratio. Does the fixed charges coverage ratio used by Nationsbank solve this incentive problem? To examine this, let us recalculate the fixed charges coverage ratio assuming the lower income level:

	Capital Lease	Operating Lease
Income before depreciation, rent, interest and taxes	$125,000	$125,000
(-) Depreciation on leased equipment	30,000	
Income before rent, interest and taxes	$95,000	$125,000
Rent for operating lease		$70,000
Interest on capital lease	$40,000	
Interest on borrowings	60,000	60,000
Fixed charges	$100,000	$130,000
Fixed charges coverage ratio	0.95	0.96

Unlike the times interest earned ratio, the fixed charges coverage ratio actually decreases from 0.96 to 0.95. Consequently, it takes away the incentives to switch from operating to capital leases when the borrower is performing poorly.

Note: In addition to the fixed charges coverage ratio, bankers also typically include a leverage ratio. For instance, Nationsbank had the following leverage covenant in the lending agreement:

Borrower shall not permit the ratio of Total Liabilities to Tangible Net Worth to be greater than as indicated below, (a) as at the end of each fiscal quarter of Borrower, ending during the period indicated or (b) on the date indicated:

Effective Date through December 31, 1996	2.50 to 1.00
March 31, 1997 and thereafter	1.75 to 1.00

"Tangible Net Worth" means, with respect to Borrower, shareholders' equity, as shown on a balance sheet prepared in accordance with GAAP on a consolidated basis, less the aggregate book value of intangible assets shown on such balance sheet.

"Total Liabilities" means all liabilities of Borrower which would be classified as total liabilities on a balance sheet prepared in accordance with GAAP on a consolidated basis.

If a borrower attempts to switch from an operating to a capital lease, it might adversely affect the borrower's compliance with the leverage covenant since capital leases are included under liabilities in GAAP financial statements. In summary, by including multiple financial ratio covenants, lenders try to effectively monitor and control any ex-post opportunistic behavior on the part of borrowers.

C11-6. The Retail Industry (CW): Comparative effects of constructive capitalization

The instructor should point out to students that different assumptions were made regarding the duration of the operating lease payments after 2001 for each of the companies. The specific duration was chosen to reflect the decay function in each firm's five-year payment schedule. That is, the computed 2002 payment (and those of following years) is lower than the 2001 payment by an "appropriate" amount. Similarly, the discount rate for each firm's operating leases was calculated using the approach for Sears in Requirement 1, which immediately follows.

Requirement 1:

The capital lease payments due after 2001 are assumed equal and made over a 15-year period. The amount of the assumed payment is $40 ($600/15).

The following table calculates the present value of the capital lease payments at interest rates of 12% and 13%. Since the present value of $335.75 at 12% is closer to the $333.0 amount reported by the firm, the interest rate implicit in the capital lease obligation is closer to 12% than to 13%.

Calculation of the Present Value of the Capital Lease Payments
Sears Roebuck
(In Millions)

Year	Payment	Present Value Factor @ 12%	Present Value of Payment @ 12%	Present Value Factor @ 13%	Present Value of Payment @ 13%
1997	$56.00	0.8929	$50.00	0.8850	$49.56
1998	52.00	0.7972	41.45	0.7831	40.72
1999	49.00	0.7118	34.88	0.6931	33.96
2000	47.00	0.6355	29.87	0.6133	28.83
2001	44.00	0.5674	24.97	0.5428	23.88
2002	40.00	0.5066	20.27	0.4803	19.21
2003	40.00	0.4523	18.09	0.4251	17.00
2004	40.00	0.4039	16.16	0.3762	15.05
2005	40.00	0.3606	14.42	0.3329	13.32
2006	40.00	0.3220	12.88	0.2946	11.78
2007	40.00	0.2875	11.50	0.2607	10.43
2008	40.00	0.2567	10.27	0.2307	9.23
2009	40.00	0.2292	9.17	0.2042	8.17
2010	40.00	0.2046	8.18	0.1807	7.23
2011	40.00	0.1827	7.31	0.1599	6.40
2012	40.00	0.1631	6.52	0.1415	5.66
2013	40.00	0.1456	5.82	0.1252	5.01
2014	40.00	0.1300	5.20	0.1108	4.43
2015	40.00	0.1161	4.64	0.0981	3.92
2016	40.00	0.1037	4.15	0.0868	3.47
Total present value:			$335.75		$317.25

Requirement 2:
The operating lease payments due after 2001 are assumed equal and made over a 6-year period. The amount of the assumed payment is $175 ($1,050/6). The present value of the operating lease payments of Sears is given in the following table. The amount is $1,267.05 (in millions of $s).

Calculation of the Present Value of the
Operating Lease Payments
Sears Roebuck
(In Millions)

Year	Payment	Present Value Factor @ 12%	Present Value of Payment @ 12%
1997	$279.00	0.8929	$249.11
1998	259.00	0.7972	206.47
1999	231.00	0.7118	164.42
2000	207.00	0.6355	131.55
2001	189.00	0.5674	107.24
2002	175.00	0.5066	88.66
2003	175.00	0.4523	79.15
2004	175.00	0.4039	70.68
2005	175.00	0.3606	63.11
2006	175.00	0.3220	56.35
2007	175.00	0.2875	50.31
Total present value:			$1,267.05

Requirement 3:

The operating lease payments due after 2001 are assumed equal and made over a 7-year period. The amount of the assumed payment is $21,000 ($147,000/7). The present value of the operating lease payments of Dillard's is given in the following table. The amount is $147.49 (in millions of $s).

Calculation of the Present Value of the Operating Lease Payments
Dillard
(In Thousands)

Year	Payment	Present Value Factor @ 12%	Present Value of Payment @ 12%
1997	$29,444.00	0.8929	$26,290.55
1998	26,241.00	0.7972	20,919.32
1999	24,746.00	0.7118	17,614.20
2000	24,093.00	0.6355	15,311.10
2001	22,857.00	0.5674	12,969.06
2002	21,000.00	0.5066	10,638.60
2003	21,000.00	0.4523	9,498.30
2004	21,000.00	0.4039	8,481.90
2005	21,000.00	0.3606	7,572.60
2006	21,000.00	0.3220	6,762.00
2007	21,000.00	0.2875	6,037.50
2008	21,000.00	0.2567	5,390.70
Total present value:			$147,485.83

Requirement 4:

The operating lease payments due after 2001 are assumed equal and made over a 10-year period. The amount of the assumed payment is $125.0 ($1,250/10). The present value of the operating lease payments of Federated is given in the following table. The amount is $982.6 (in millions of $s).

Calculation of the Present Value of the
Operating Lease Payments
Federated
(In Millions)

Year	Payment	Present Value Factor @ 11%	Present Value of Payment @ 11%
1997	$174.60	0.9009	$157.30
1998	151.40	0.8116	122.88
1999	139.00	0.7312	101.64
2000	132.80	0.6587	87.48
2001	128.70	0.5935	76.38
2002	125.00	0.5346	66.83
2003	125.00	0.4817	60.21
2004	125.00	0.4339	54.24
2005	125.00	0.3909	48.86
2006	125.00	0.3522	44.03
2007	125.00	0.3173	39.66
2008	125.00	0.2858	35.73
2009	125.00	0.2575	32.19
2010	125.00	0.2320	29.00
2011	125.00	0.2090	26.13
Total present value:			$982.56

Requirement 5:
Ratios based on reported balance sheet data:

Long-term debt to shareholders' equity:

Sears: $12,170/$4,945 = 246.1%

Dillard: $1,186.7/$2,717.2 = 43.7%

Federated: $4,605.9/$4,669.2 = 98.6%

Long-term debt to total assets:

Sears: $12,170/$36,167 = 33.7%

Dillard: $1,186.7/$5,059.7 = 23.5%

Federated: $4,605.9/$14,264.1 = 32.3%

Requirement 6:
Ratios adjusted for the effect of operating leases:

Long-term debt to shareholders' equity:

Sears: ($12,170 + $1,267.05)/$4,945 = 271.7%

Dillard: ($1,186.7 + $147.49)/$2,717.2 = 49.1%

Federated: ($4,605.9 + $982.6)/$4,669.2 = 119.7%

Long-term debt to total assets:

Sears: ($12,170 + $1,267.05)/($36,167 + $1,267.06) = 35.9%

Dillard: ($1,186.7 + $147.49)/($5,059.7 + $147.49) = 25.6%

Federated: ($4,605.9 + $982.6)/($14,264.1 + $982.6) = 36.7%

Discussion of long-term debt to shareholders' equity:

All of the firms' ratios increase as a result of capitalizing their operating leases. However, only Sears' and Federated's increases seem significant, while that of Dillard is not large. Specifically, Sears' ratio increases by about twenty-five percentage points, Federated's increases by about nineteen percentage points, while Dillard's increases by only about five percentage points.

Discussion of long-term debt to total assets:

All of the firms' ratios increase as a result of capitalizing their operating leases. However, all of the increases are quite modest. Across the three firms, the increase in the ratios range from about two to four percentage points.

C11-7. United Airlines: Capital lease criteria and reporting incentives
(The Case of the Curious Speech)

This case setting encompasses two primary issues. First, there is the technical question of what constitutes a "bargain purchase option." Exploring this issue allows the instructor to discuss the flexibility ("looseness") inherent in both SFAS No. 13 and in financial reporting in general as well as the ambiguity surrounding materiality judgments. Second, the case provides an excellent vehicle for outlining managerial motivations for "off-balance sheet" transactions.

Requirement 1:
Whether the lease with the Export/Import Bank contains a bargain purchase option is open to some interpretation. Clearly, the opportunity to buy the DC-10s at the end of the lease "for the fair market value at that time or for 50 percent of the original amount of financing, *whichever is less*" raises the *possibility* of a bargain acquisition.

SFAS No. 13 defines a bargain purchase option as follows (para. 5.d.):

> A provision allowing the lessee, at his option, to purchase the leased property for a price which is sufficiently lower than the expected fair value of the property at the date the option becomes exercisable, that exercise of the option appears, at the inception of the lease, to be reasonably assured.

The key issue is what is meant by "exercise of the option appears . . . to be reasonably assured."

Let's examine the two possibilities that could exist at lease expiration. First, fair market value could be lower than 50% of the original amount of financing. In this instance, on the surface there would appear to be no special inducement to exercise the option. On the other hand, if United needs the aircraft, there still may be a positive incentive to acquire these specific aircraft. The reasoning is as follows: Prevailing market price incorporates "market for lemons" considerations[1]. However, after 15-1/4 years of use, United will know the operating condition of these three aircraft with virtual certainty. If United knows these aircraft to be of superior quality, then this information asymmetry could make acquisition even at the fair market price a "bargain" nonetheless. Second, if fair market value exceeds 50% of the original amount of financing, a "bargain" exists, and there is an obvious incentive to exercise the option. Under these conditions, the option would be exercised independent of whether United's load factors justify acquisition since the aircraft could be resold immediately to others at a profit.

Considering both possible alternatives at lease expiration, there is a real possibility that the purchase option would be exercised. Indeed, this likelihood increases dramatically if United perceives that it will need the capacity at lease expiration. But does this "likelihood" constitute "reasonable assurance"? Judgments of this sort permeate financial reporting, and this setting provides a good forum for discussing the issue.

---

[1] See G. Akerlof, "The Market for 'Lemons': Qualitative Uncertainty and the Market Mechanism," *Quarterly Journal of Economics*, August, 1970, pp. 488-500).

Although this lease option falls into a gray area, it is evident that classifying this as an operating lease is somewhat aggressive, as Ferris himself points out. If time permits, the instructor might use this as a vehicle for discussing the pressures on auditors to accede to clients' reporting choices in a competitive audit environment. Issues that could be introduced here include the cost structure of repeat engagements (i.e., the slope of the learning curve), auditors' power (i.e., are audits becoming commodity goods), and the prevalence of auditor changes.

Requirement 2:
This is the most intriguing part of the case. What motivated Ferris to advertise to the analyst community that UAL's statements may not reflect the underlying economics of the lease transaction?

One possibility is that he was simply alerting the analysts to the sophistication of UAL's management. The ability to engineer admittedly clever terms in order to circumvent capital lease treatment told the airline analysts that UAL was in financially expert hands and this expertise could lead to extraordinary future performance. While it is possible that this may have been Ferris' motive, it is likely that the real reason for discussing the off-balance sheet financing was more subtle.

Consider the following alternative motivation. By 1984, it was widely recognized that the deregulated environment made airline growth not only feasible, it also made such growth essential in order to be economically competitive in the newly created "hub and spoke" route structure. But United (along with several major competitors) experienced financial difficulties and large operating losses over the several years preceding the speech. It is reasonable to assume that the analysts may have feared that future expansion needs would be stymied by loan covenant restrictions and/or impending covenant violations. If so, then Ferris was probably signaling the analysts that United Airlines had the financial acumen and requisite borrowing capacity to acquire the new aircraft necessary to compete in the deregulated environment.

Notice that this interpretation is consistent with two major themes in the speech: (1) the considerable emphasis on UAL, Inc.'s improved debt-to-equity ratio ("one of the strongest ratios in the industry") and (2) the announced intention of continuing "similar [lease] transactions in the future without putting debt on our balance sheet." In this view, the "curious" element in the speech is understandable in light of the newly deregulated airline environment: Ferris was signaling the analysts that United had the ability to grow and to thereby be in a strong position to compete effectively.

Exercises

E12-1. Determining current taxes payable
(AICPA adapted)

The amount of current income tax liability that would be reported on Ross Co.'s December 31, 1998, balance sheet is determined as follows:

Net income before depreciation expense and income taxes	$100,000
Depreciation expense (for tax purposes)	(20,000)
Taxable income	80,000
Tax rate	30%
Current income tax liability	**$24,000**

E12-2. Determining deferred tax liability
(AICPA adapted)

To determine the deferred income tax liability reported on the December 31, 1999, balance sheet requires a calculation of the *cumulative* temporary (timing) differences that give rise to future taxable amounts as of that date. Gross margin temporary differences are as follows:

Year	(Book purposes) Accrual Method	(Tax purposes) Installment Method	Temporary Differences (Future Taxable Amount)
1998	$800,000	$300,000	$500,000
1999	1,300,000	700,000	600,000
Total temporary differences as of 12/31/99			$1,100,000
Tax rate in effect when differences will reverse			25%
Deferred tax liability on 12/31/99			**$275,000**

E12-3. Determining deferred tax liability
(AICPA adapted)

Tow's deferred tax liability for December 31, 1998, is computed as follows:

Year	Reversal of Excess Tax Deduction	Enacted Tax Rate	Deferred Tax Liability
1999	$50,000	35%	$17,500
2000	40,000	35%	14,000
2001	20,000	25%	5,000
2002	10,000	25%	2,500
	Deferred tax liability on 12/31/98		**$39,000**

E12-4. Deferred tax effects on balance sheet
(AICPA adapted)

If the asset's financial reporting basis exceeds its tax basis, it means that the depreciation for tax purposes has been *higher* than depreciation for book purposes. A taxable temporary difference and a deferred tax liability are the result. Since the difference will reverse in future years when the enacted tax rate is 40%, Noor should record a deferred tax liability of

Temporary depreciation difference	$250,000
Tax rate when difference will reverse	40%
Deferred tax liability on 12/31/98	**$100,000**

E12-5. Deferred tax effects on long-term contracts
(AICPA adapted)

Since income recognized for tax purposes exceeds the income recognized for book purposes, Mill has cumulative temporary differences that result in *future deductible amounts* giving rise to a deferred tax asset computed as follows:

Year	(Tax purposes) Percentage-of-completion	(Book purposes) Completed Contract	Temporary Difference Increase (Decrease) in Future Deductible Amounts
1998	$400,000	$0	$400,000
1999	625,000	375,000	250,000
2000	750,000	850,000	(100,000)
Cumulative temporary difference on 12/31/2000			$550,000
Tax rate			40%
Deferred tax asset on December 31, 2000			**$220,000**

519

E12-6. Determining current portion of tax expense
(AICPA adapted)

Requirement 1:
The current portion of tax expense is the tax payable to the IRS for 1998.

Taxable income	$650,000
Tax rate	30%
Current portion of tax expense	**$195,000**

Requirement 2:
Deferred portion of tax expense is determined by the depreciation timing differences during the year.

Depreciation timing difference in 1998 ($750,000 - $650,000)	$100,000
Tax rate	30%
Deferred portion of tax expense	**$30,000**

Requirement 3:
Journal entry to record tax expense for 1998.

DR Tax expense—current ($650,000 × 30%)	$195,000	
DR Tax expense—deferred ($100,000 × 30%)	30,000	
CR Deferred tax liability		$30,000
CR Prepaid estimated tax payments*		90,000
CR Taxes payable ($195,000 - $90,000)		105,000

*This credit assumes the following entry was made when Tyre made its estimated tax payment during 1998:

DR Prepaid estimated tax payments	$90,000	
CR Cash		$90,000

E12-7. Determining current taxes payable
(AICPA adapted)

The calculation of the current income tax liability of Dunn Co. for the December 31, 1998, balance sheet is as follows:

Pre-tax income (per books)	$90,000
Adjustments for permanent differences:	
- Interest on municipal bonds	(20,000)
Adjustments for temporary differences:	
+ Rent received in advance	16,000
- Excess of tax depreciation over book depreciation	(10,000)
Taxable income	$76,000
Tax rate	30%
Current income tax liability on 12/31/98	**$22,800**

E12-8. Determining deferred tax liability and current portion of tax expense
(AICPA adapted)

Requirement 1:
Deferred tax liability on December 31, 1996

Cumulative temporary difference on 12/31/96	$20,000
Enacted tax rate when temporary differences will reverse	40%
Deferred tax liability on 12/31/96	**$8,000**

Requirement 2:
Current portion of 1996 tax expense

Taxable income for 1996	$129,000
Enacted tax rate	40%
Current portion of tax expense in 1996	**$51,600**

E12-9. Determining deferred tax asset amounts
(AICPA adapted)

Rent revenue for tax purposes (total received in 1998)	$36,000
Rent revenue *earned* in 1998 (1/2 × $36,000)	(18,000)
Temporary difference (future deductible amount)	$18,000
Enacted tax rate when temporary difference will reverse	40%
Deferred tax asset on December 31, 1998	**$7,200**

E12-10. Determining deferred tax asset amounts
(AICPA adapted)

The warranty temporary differences give rise to future deductible amounts and a deferred tax asset for Black Co. on December 31, 1998, computed as follows:

Year	Reversal of Warranty Temporary Difference	Enacted Tax Rate	Deferred Tax Asset
1999	$100,000	30%	$30,000
2000	50,000	30%	15,000
2001	50,000	30%	15,000
2002	100,000	25%	25,000
Deferred tax asset on 12/31/98			**$85,000**

E12-11. Deferred portion of tax expense
(AICPA adapted)

To determine the deferred portion of Quinn's 1999 income tax expense requires the amount of temporary differences created in 1999 ($100,000 given) and the enacted (statutory) tax rate for 1999. Since the only difference between pre-tax (book) income and taxable income is the $100,000 temporary difference, this implies that the statutory (enacted) tax rate is the same as Quinn's effective (book) tax rate (since there are no permanent differences). Thus, the deferred portion of the 1999 tax expense is calculated as follows:

Temporary differences in 1999	$100,000
Enacted (statutory) tax rate	30%
Deferred portion of 1999 tax expense	**$30,000**

E12-12. Temporary and permanent differences
(AICPA adapted)

Tara's equity in Flax's 1998 earnings 40% × $750,000 =	$300,000
- Tara's share of Flax's 1998 dividend distribution 40% × $250,000 =	(100,000)
Tara's share of Flax's *un*distributed earnings	$200,000
Less: 80% that will never be taxed	(160,000)
Undistributed earnings that will be taxed in the future when distributed as dividends (future taxable amount)	40,000
Enacted tax rate in the future	25%
Increase in deferred tax liability for 1998	**$10,000**

E12-13. Loss carrybacks and carryforwards
(AICPA adapted)

Requirement 1:
Tax benefit due to NOL carryback and carryforward is:

Amount of loss carryback	$450,000
Amount of loss carryforward	150,000
	$600,000
Tax rate	40%
Total tax benefit reported on 1999 income statement	**$240,000**

Requirement 2:
Deferred tax asset on December 31, 1999 balance sheet:

Amount of loss carryforward	$150,000
Tax rate	40%
Deferred tax asset	**$60,000**

E12-14. Tax effects of loss carryback and carry forward
(AICPA adapted)

Requirement 1:
Tax benefit reported on 1998 income statement

Loss carried back to 1997	$100,000
Loss carried forward to 1999	100,000
Total	$200,000
Tax rate	40%
Tax benefit recognized in 1998 income statement	**$80,000**

Requirement 2:
Deferred tax asset reported on 12/31/98 balance sheet

Operating loss carryforward	$100,000
Tax rate	40%
Deferred tax asset reported on 12/31/98 balance sheet	**$40,000**

Requirement 3:
Amount reported as current taxes payable in 1999

Taxable income in 1999	$400,000
Less: Operating loss carryforward	(100,000)
Taxable income after adjustment	$300,000
Tax rate	40%
Current taxes payable on 12/31/99 balance sheet	**$120,000**

Entry to record taxes on 12/31/99: (not required)

DR Tax expense (40% × $400,000)	$160,000	
CR Deferred tax asset (40% × $100,000)		$40,000
CR Current taxes payable		120,000

E12-15. Accounting for loss carryforwards
(AICPA adapted)

Requirement 1:
If the loss occurred in 1998, then the tax benefit reported in the 1998 income statement would be $180,000 × 30% = $54,000. If the loss occurred prior to 1998, then no tax benefit would be reported in the 1998 income statement.

Requirement 2:
The additional account that would be debited when the loss carryforward is recognized would be deferred tax assets for $54,000. The entry would be:

DR Deferred tax asset $54,000
      CR Income tax expense (carryforward benefit) $54,000

E12-16. Accounting for loss carrybacks and carryforwards
(AICPA adapted)

Requirement 1:
Calculation of tax benefit and journal entry reported in 1998:

Loss carryback	$300,000
Loss carryforward ($700,000 - $300,000)	400,000
Total	700,000
Tax rate	30%
Tax benefit reported on 1998 income statement	**$210,000**

Journal entry in 1998 to record tax benefit:

DR Deferred tax asset
    (30% × $400,000 loss carry*forward*) $120,000
DR Tax refund receivable
    (30% × $300,000 loss carry*back*)   90,000
      CR Income tax expense
          (carryback and carryforward benefit) $210,000

Requirement 2:
Amount reported as current income tax liability in 1999:

1999 Taxable income before NOL carryforward	$1,200,000
Less: Operating loss carryforward	(400,000)
Taxable income after adjustment	$800,000
Tax rate	30%
Current income tax liability in 1999	**$240,000**

E12-17. Deferred tax asset and valuation allowance
(AICPA adapted)

Future deductible amount from warranty expense temporary difference	$300,000
Tax rate	30%
Deferred tax asset before adjustment	$90,000
Less: Valuation allowance (1/3 of $90,000)	(30,000)
Deferred tax asset net of valuation allowance	**$60,000**

E12-18. Deferred tax asset and valuation allowance
(AICPA adapted)

Taft's equity in Flame's earnings	$180,000
Less: Dividends received from Flame	(30,000)
Taft's equity in Flames' *un*distributed earnings	150,000
Less: 80% that will never be taxed under dividend exclusion rule (80% × $150,000)	(120,000)
Undistributed earnings that will be taxed in future period when distributed as dividends (future taxable amount)	30,000
Tax rate	30%
Deferred tax liability reported on 12/31/98	**$9,000**

E12-19. Determining tax expense, taxes payable, and deferred taxes
(CMA adapted)

Requirements 1 and 2:
Calculation of taxable income and taxes payable for 1998:

Pre-tax book income	$4,000,000
Adjustment for permanent difference: Interest income	(100,000)
Adjustment for temporary difference: Rent revenue	(80,000)
Taxable income	**$3,820,000**
Tax rate	×40%
Taxes payable	**$1,528,000**

Requirement 3:
Change in deferred taxes for 1998:

Temporary difference Rent revenue–future taxable amount	$80,000
Tax rate	×40%
Increase in deferred tax liability	**$32,000**

525

Requirement 4:

Calculation of income tax expense for 1998:

Income tax expense = Taxes payable + Increase in deferred tax liability
                     = $1,528,000 + $32,000
Income tax expense   = $1,560,000

Requirement 5:

Repeat requirements (1)–(4) for 1999
Calculation of taxable income and taxes payable for 1999:

Pre-tax book income	$5,000,000
Adjustment for permanent difference:	
Interest income	(100,000)
Adjustment for temporary difference:	
Rent revenue	80,000
Taxable income	**$4,980,000**
Tax rate	× 40%
Taxes payable	**$1,992,000**

Change in deferred taxes for 1999:

Reversal of temporary difference originating in 1998	
Rent revenue	($80,000)
Tax rate	× 40%
Decrease in deferred tax liability	**($32,000)**

Calculation of income tax expense for 1999:

Income tax expense   = Taxes payable - Decrease in deferred tax liability
                     = $1,992,000   - $32,000
Income tax expense = $1,960,000

Problems

P12-1. Deferred tax amounts with different tax rates
(AICPA adapted)

	Future Taxable Amounts	Enacted Tax Rate	Deferred Tax Liability
1997	$50,000	30%	$15,000
1998	75,000	30%	22,500
1999	100,000	25%	25,000
Deferred tax liability reported in 12/31/96 balance sheet			$62,500

P12-2. Temporary and permanent differences and tax entry

Requirement 1:
Calculation of temporary difference:

Income tax expense	$52,000
- Income taxes payable	(32,000)
Deferred taxes payable	$20,000

$$\text{Amount of temporary difference} = \frac{\text{Deferred taxes}}{\text{Tax rate}}$$

$$\text{Temporary difference due to depreciation} = \frac{\$20,000}{.40} = \$50,000$$

Since tax expense per books is greater than taxes payable per tax return, taxable income is *lower* than book income.

Requirement 2:
Calculation of permanent difference:

Tax expense = Pre-tax book income (excluding permanent difference) × tax rate

Let X = Pre-tax book income (excluding permanent difference)
$52,000 = .40X
$52,000/.40 = $130,000 = Pre-tax book income (excluding permanent difference)

Book income (excluding permanent difference)	$130,000
Book income before taxes (given)	(106,000)
Permanent difference	$24,000

Book income will be *lower* than taxable income because of this permanent difference.

Requirement 3:
Journal entry to record tax expense for year:

DR Tax expense (given)	$52,000	
CR Taxes payable (given)		$32,000
CR Deferred taxes payable (see Req. 1)		20,000

Requirement 4:
Effective tax rate	= Tax expense/Pre-tax book income
	= $52,000/$106,000
Effective tax rate	= 49.1%

The effective tax rate is higher than the statutory tax rate of 40% because the goodwill deduction reported on Ramesh's books is not deductible for tax purposes.

P12-3. Deferred tax amount on income statement
(AICPA adapted)

Beginning balance, unearned royalties, 1/1/97	$400,000
Additional royalties received in 1997	600,000
Less: Unearned royalties on 12/31/97	(350,000)
Royalty income recognized for book purposes	$650,000
Amount recognized for tax purposes:	
Royalty collections in 1997	(600,000)
Temporary differences	50,000
Tax rate	50%
Deferred income tax expense	**$25,000**

Journal entry to record taxes for 1997 (not required):

DR Income tax expense (50% × $650,000)	$325,000	
CR Income taxes payable (50% × $600,000)		$300,000
CR Deferred tax asset (50% × $50,000)		25,000

P12-4. Current and deferred portion of tax expense
(AICPA adapted)

Requirement 1:
Current provision for 1998 income tax expense is the taxes payable to the IRS on 1998 income computed as:

Taxable income	$450,000
Tax rate	34%
Current provision for income taxes	$153,000

Requirement 2:
Determination of deferred income taxes on 1998 income statement:

Construction revenue recorded on tax returns but not on books—future deductible amount	$100,000
Excess of accelerated depreciation for tax over straight-line for books—future taxable amount	(400,000)
Net future taxable amount	(300,000)
	34%
Deferred portion of tax expense (DR)	$102,000

Entry to record 1998 tax provision:

DR Tax expense	$255,000	
CR Taxes payable (current)		$153,000
CR Deferred taxes payable		102,000

P12-5. Tax expense and deferred tax calculations

Requirement 1:
Computation of taxable income and financial reporting income:

	1996		1997	
	Taxable	Financial	Taxable	Financial
Revenue (less other expenses)	$500,000	$500,000	$500,000	$500,000
Less:				
- Depreciation expense	-60,000 [1]	-45,000 [2]	- 30,000 [1]	- 45,000 [2]
- Amortization of goodwill		-50,000		- 50,000
Net income	$440,000	$405,000	$470,000	$405,000

[1] SYD method depreciation
1996 = 2/3 × $90,000 = $60,000
1997 = 1/3 × $90,000 = $30,000

[2] Straight-line depreciation
$90,000/2 years = $45,000

Requirement 2:

A permanent difference item is a revenue or expense that is recognized for book purposes but never for tax purposes or recognized for tax purposes but never for book purposes. That is, GAAP and tax rules permanently differ in how they recognize the revenue or expense item in question.

Goodwill amortization is an example of a permanent difference item for Nelson. (Beginning in 1993, goodwill arising from certain acquisitions can be amortized for tax purposes also.) Other common permanent difference items include Interest on municipal bonds and premiums paid on officers' life insurance.

Temporary differences are revenue or expense items that are recognized in a different period for book purposes than for tax purposes. GAAP and tax rules agree that temporary differences are included in income determination, but differ as to the timing of the recognition.

An example of a temporary difference for Nelson is the excess of sum-of-years'-digits depreciation for tax purposes over straight-line depreciation for book purposes.

Requirement 3:

Year	Ending Balance in Tax Liability	Tax Expense	Ending Balance in Deferred Income Taxes
1996	$440,000 × 0.20 = $88,000	$455,000 × 0.20 = $91,000	$3,000 CR[1]
1997	$470,000 × 0.20 = $94,000	$455,000 × 0.20 = $91,000	0

Note: Ignore amortization of goodwill when computing tax expense:

[1] Temporary depreciation difference = $60,000 - $45,000 = $15,000 × 20% = $3,000

Requirement 4:

Increase/decrease in deferred income taxes:

Change in tax rate × Future taxable amount due to depreciation timing difference

$$(.30 - .20) \times (\$60,000 - \$45,000)$$

= $1,500 increase in deferred tax liability

Journal entry required to accomplish this:

DR Income tax expense $1,500
   CR Deferred tax liability $1,500

Income Tax Liability for 1997:

Taxable income × tax rate =
    $470,000   ×   0.30   = $141,000

Income Tax Expense for 1997:

Pre-tax book income (excluding permanent differences) × tax rate =
$455,000 × 0.30 = $136,500 + $1,500 from change in the tax rate applied to
                    future taxable amount
            = $138,000

P12-6. Determining current and deferred portion of tax expense and reconciling statutory and effective tax rates

Requirement 1:
Determining taxes payable:

	(in $000)
Taxable income (given)	$1,400
Tax rate	35%
Taxes payable	$490

Requirement 2:
Change in deferred tax assets (liabilities):

Temporary differences giving rise to future taxable amounts:

Depreciation	$800
Enacted tax rate	40%
Increase in deferred tax liability	$320

Temporary differences giving rise to future deductible amounts:

Warranty costs	$400
Rent received in advance	600
	$1,000
Enacted tax rate	40%
Increase in deferred tax asset	$400

Requirement 3:
Tax expense for 1998:

Tax expense = Taxes payable + Increase in deferred tax liability - Increase
                in deferred tax asset

$410 = $490 + $320 - $400

531

Requirement 4:
Reconciliation of statutory and effective tax rates (amounts):

$$\text{Effective (book) tax rate} = \frac{\text{Tax expense (Req. 3)}}{\text{Pre - tax income (given)}} = \frac{\$410}{\$1,000} = 41\%$$

	Amount	Percentage of Pre-Tax Income
Expected tax expense at statutory rate (35% × $1,000)	$350	35%
Effect of permanent differences		
Amortization of goodwill (35% × $400)	140	+ 14
Interest on municipal bonds (35% × $200)	(70)	- 7
Effect of higher tax rates on temporary differences		
Depreciation (5% × $800)	40	+ 4
Warranty costs (5% × $400)	(20)	- 2
Rent received in advance (5% × $600)	(30)	- 3
Effective tax rate ($410/$1,000)	$410	41%

P12-7. Entries for loss carrybacks and carryforwards

Requirement 1:
Smith Corporation will offset the 2004 loss against the 2002 income and a portion of the income of year 2003 until the entire loss of $350,000 is fully offset. Note that the income prior to 2002 is beyond the allowable 2-year period.

Using the 2-year carryback rule, Smith Corporation will calculate its income tax refund as follows:

Year	Taxable Income	Tax Rate	Tax Refund	Income Remaining
2002	$250,000	35%	$87,500	-
2003	100,000	32%	32,000	$300,000
	$350,000		$119,500	

The tax refund is calculated using the tax rates prevailing in the respective carryback years. Since the entire 2004 net loss is offset against past income using the carryback provision, the income tax benefit will be identical to income tax refund receivable. Consequently, the following journal entry will be recorded in 2004:

Entry for 12/31/04:
DR Income tax refund receivable $119,500
    CR Income tax expense or benefit $119,500

Note that the effective tax "benefit" rate during 2004 is 34.14% ($119,500/$350,000), which is more than the 2004 statutory tax rate of 30%. This is because the carryback provision allows companies to obtain the tax benefit based on the tax rates prevailing in the carryback years (i.e., 2002 and 2003).

Smith Corporation will offset the entire loss for the year 2005 against the remaining income from 2003. Using the 2-year carryback rule, Smith Corporation will calculate its income tax refund as follows:

Year	Taxable Income	Tax Rate	Tax Refund	Income Remaining
2003	$275,000	32%	$88,000	$25,000
	$275,000		$88,000	

The tax refund is calculated using the tax rate prevailing in the carryback year. Since the entire 2005 net loss is offset against past income using the carryback provision, the income tax benefit will be identical to income tax refund receivable. Consequently, the following journal entry will be recorded in 2005:

Entry for 12/31/05:
  DR Income tax refund receivable $88,000
       CR Income tax expense or benefit $88,000

The effective tax "benefit" rate during 2005 is 32% ($88,000/$275,000), which is more than the 2005 statutory tax rate of 30%. This is because the carryback provision allows companies to obtain the tax benefit based on the tax rates prevailing in the carryback years (i.e., 2003).

Smith Corporation will offset the 2010 net loss of $800,000 against the past two years income beginning from 2008. Based on this carryback, Smith Corporation will be eligible for an income-tax refund, calculated as follows:

Year	Taxable Income	Tax Rate	Tax Refund	Income Remaining
2008	$275,000	30%	$82,500	-
2009	300,000	35%	105,000	-
	$575,000		$187,500	

The following journal entry will be recorded in 2010 to show the income tax refund:

Entry for 12/31/10:
  DR Income tax refund receivable $187,500
       CR Income tax expense or benefit $187,500

Note, however, Smith Corporation had earned only $575,000 during the previous two years. Consequently, the company needs to examine whether a deferred tax asset should be created for the remaining 2010 loss of $225,000 ($800,000 - $575,000). Based on the information in the problem, we create a deferred tax asset assuming the tax benefits of this loss will be fully realized at a rate of 35% ($225,000 × 0.35).

Entry for 12/31/10:
    DR Deferred tax asset $78,750

        CR Income tax expense or benefit $78,750

Recall that by 2011, Smith Corporation has completely exhausted the benefits from the loss carryback provision. However, once again based on the information in the problem, we create a deferred tax asset assuming the tax benefits of this loss will be fully realized at a rate of 35% ($250,000 × 0.35).

Entry for 12/31/11:
    DR Deferred tax asset $87,500

        CR Income tax expense or benefit $87,500

At the end of 2011, the company has loss carryforwards of $475,000 - $225,000 from 2010 and $250,000 from 2011. Consequently, when Smith Corporation earned $150,000 net income during 2012, it was able to offset this income against $150,000 of the 2010 loss carried forward. Without any tax liability during 2012, the journal entry for the expense reflects the realized tax benefit from the deferred tax assets ($150,000 × 0.35):

Entry for 12/31/12:
    DR Income tax expense $52,500

        CR Deferred tax asset $52,500

Requirement 2:
In Requirement 2, it is more likely than not that only 40% of the tax benefits will be realized through loss carryforward. Consequently, we need to create a valuation allowance for 60% of the tax benefits not expected to be realized. We do this in two steps. First, we record the journal entry assuming that all the tax benefits will be realized (as in Requirement 1).

Entry for 12/31/10:
    DR Deferred tax asset $78,750

        CR Income tax expense or benefit $78,750

Next, we create a valuation account to reduce the carrying value of the deferred tax asset account by 60% ($78,750 × 0.60). The purpose of the "Allowance" account is to reduce the carrying value of the deferred tax asset to net realizable value.

DR Income tax expense or benefit	$47,250	
CR Valuation allowance		$47,250

At the end of 2010, the deferred tax asset will be reported in the balance sheet as follows:

Deferred Tax Asset as of the end of 2010

Tax benefit of loss carryforward	$78,750
Less: Valuation allowance	(47,250)
	$31,500

The journal entries for 2011 follow the same two steps:

Entry for 12/31/11:

DR Deferred tax asset	$87,500	
CR Income tax expense or benefit		$87,500

Similar to 2010, we use the valuation account to reduce the carrying value of the deferred tax asset account by 60% ($87,500 × 0.60).

DR Income tax expense or benefit	$52,500	
CR Valuation allowance		$52,500

At the end of 2011, the deferred tax asset will be reported in the balance sheet as follows:

Deferred Tax Asset as of the end of 2011

Tax benefit of loss carryforward	$166,250
Less: Valuation allowance	(99,750)
	$66,500

At the end of 2012, the valuation allowance is eliminated since it is more likely than not that the entire tax benefits will be realized.

Entry for 12/31/12:

DR Valuation allowance	$99,750	
CR Income tax expense or benefit		$99,750

As in Requirement 1, the following journal entry is recorded to show the tax expense on the income of $150,000.

> **DR** Income tax expense $52,500
>   **CR** Deferred tax asset $52,500

Deferred Tax Asset as of the end of 2012

Tax benefit of loss carryforward $113,750

One interesting result is that, although the company reports a positive pre-tax income for 2012, it reports no income tax expense. In fact, the reversal of the valuation allowance results in an income tax benefit in the income statement.

Income Statement for the Year 2012

Pre-tax income	$150,000
+ Income tax benefit ($99,750 - $52,500)	47,250
Net income	$197,250

P12-8. Entries for loss carrybacks and carryforwards

Barron Corporation will offset the 2005 loss against the 2003 and 2004 taxable incomes. Note that income prior to 2003 is beyond the allowable 2-year period.

Using the 2-year carryback rule, Barron Corporation will calculate its income tax refund as follows:

Year	Taxable Income	Tax Rate	Tax Refund	Income Remaining
2003	$90,000	40%	$36,000	-
2004	60,000	40%	24,000	$140,000
	$150,000		$60,000	

Since the entire 2005 net loss is offset against past income using the carryback provision, the income tax benefit will be identical to income tax refund receivable. Consequently, the following journal entry will be recorded in 2005:

Entry on 12/31/05:

> **DR** Income tax refund receivable $60,000
>   **CR** Income tax expense
>   (benefit from loss carryback) $60,000

Barron Corporation will offset the 2006 loss against the remaining income from 2004. Using the carryback rule, Barron Corporation will calculate its income tax refund as follows:

Year	Taxable Income	Tax Rate	Tax Refund	Income Remaining
2004	$140,000	40%	$56,000	-
	$140,000		$56,000	

The following journal entry will be recorded in 2006 to show the income tax refund:

Entry on 12/31/06:
   DR Income tax refund receivable $56,000
      CR Income tax expense
          (benefit from loss carryback) $56,000

Note, however, Barron Corporation had only $140,000 of income available during the carryback period. Consequently, the company needs to examine whether a deferred tax asset should be created for the remaining 2006 loss of $40,000 ($180,000 - $140,000). Based on the information in the problem, we create a deferred tax asset assuming the tax benefits of this loss will be fully realized at a rate of 40% ($40,000 × 0.40).

Entry on 12/31/06:
   DR Deferred tax asset $16,000
      CR Income tax expense
          (benefit from loss carryforward) $16,000

At the end of 2006, the company has a loss carryforward of $40,000 from 2006. Consequently, when Barron Corporation earned $125,000 net income during 2007, it was able to offset this income against $40,000 of the 2006 loss carried forward. The income tax liability for 2007 is calculated as follows:

Calculation of Tax Liability for 2007

2007 Taxable income	$125,000
- 2006 Loss carryforward	(40,000)
Income subject to tax	$85,000
Tax rate	40%
Tax liability at 40%	$34,000

The journal entry to record the 2007 income tax expense reflects the realization of the deferred tax asset from the 2006 loss carryforward:

Entry on 12/31/07:

DR Income tax expense	$50,000	
CR Income tax payable		$34,000
CR Deferred tax asset		16,000

In 2008, the company incurred a net loss of $120,000. Only $85,000 of the loss can be offset against the 2007 income under the carry**back** provision. Recall that $40,000 of the 2007 net income was offset against the 2006 loss under the carry**forward** provision.

The loss carryforward for 2008 is calculated as follows:

Calculation of Loss Carryforward for 2008

2008 Net loss	($120,000)
+ 2007 Income subject to tax	85,000
2008 Loss carryforward	($35,000)

Therefore, the company is entitled to claim a refund of the all the taxes paid for the 2007 income. For the remainder of the loss, we record a deferred tax asset to represent the future benefits from the carryforward provision ($35,000 × 0.40 = $14,000):

Entry on 12/31/08:

DR Income tax refund receivable	$34,000	
DR Deferred tax asset	14,000	
CR Income tax expense or benefit		$48,000

P12-9. Reconciling statutory and effective tax rates

Requirement 1:
Determination of taxable income and taxes payable—

Pre-tax accounting income (loss) per books	($1,500,000)
Less: Permanent difference items:	
+Charge for in-process technology	2,000,000
+Amortization of goodwill ($1,000,000/20 years)	50,000
- Income from municipal bonds	(80,000)
+Management fee for municipal bond investments	10,000
+Insurance premium on executives	15,000
- Insurance proceeds	(250,000)
Pre-tax income adjusted for permanent differences	245,000
Adjustments for temporary differences:	
- Excess of bad debts written off over provision for uncollectibles	(75,000)
- Excess of accelerated depreciation for tax over S/L depreciation for books ($210,000 - $140,000)	(70,000)
Taxable income	100,000
Statutory tax rate	35%
Taxes payable	$35,000

Requirement 2:
Determination of change in deferred tax assets (liabilities):

Reversal of timing difference on bad debts (Decrease in deferred tax asset)–$75,000 × .35 =	$26,250 **CR**
Originating temporary difference for depreciation (Increase in deferred tax liability)–$70,000 × .35 =	$24,500 **CR**

Requirement 3:
Calculation of income tax expense:

Tax expense = Taxes payable + Decrease in deferred tax asset + Increase in deferred tax liability

= $35,000 + $26,250 + $24,500

= $85,750

Alternative calculation, since no change in tax rates:

GAAP income adjusted for permanent differences (see above) $245,000
Statutory tax rate 35%
Tax expense $85,750

Requirement 4:
Effective tax book rate = $85,750/($1,500,000) = 5.72%

Reconciliation of effective and statutory tax rate:

Companies typically provide a table similar to the one shown below to explain the difference between the statutory tax rate and the effective tax rate.

	Tax Expense (Credit)	Tax Rate
Expected tax credit at the statutory rate ($1,500,000 loss × 35%)	($525,000)	-35.00%
Effect of permanent differences:		
+ Charge for in-process R&D (35% × $2 million)	700,000	46.67%
+ Amortization of goodwill (35% × $50,000)	17,500	1.17%
- Income from municipal bonds (35% × $80,000)	(28,000)	-1.87%
+ Management fee for municipal bonds (35% × $10,000)	3,500	0.23%
+ Insurance premium on executives (35% × $15,000)	5,250	0.35%
- Insurance proceeds ($250,000 × 35%)	(87,500)	-5.83%
Effective tax rate [$85,750/($1,500,000)]	$85,750	5.72%

The expected tax credit at the statutory rate is calculated by multiplying the loss before income taxes by 35%. Each item below is calculated by multiplying the corresponding permanent difference by 35%. The tax rate column is obtained by dividing each item in the tax expense column by the loss before income taxes.

Note: The problem is loosely based on the 1996 financial statements of World Com, Inc. The company's effective tax rate was substantially different from its statutory tax rate due to the GAAP write-off of in-process technology.

Requirement 5:
The journal entry to record the tax expense is:

DR Income tax expense	$85,750	
CR Income tax payable		$35,000
CR Deferred tax asset		26,250
CR Deferred tax liability		24,500

Note that the higher bad debts written off indicates a reversing difference. The company would have recorded a deferred tax asset initially when recording the bad debt expense, which is being reversed when the bad debts are written off.

In contrast, given the depreciation methods used by the company, the higher depreciation expense indicates an originating difference. The company is creating a deferred tax liability today when the tax depreciation is higher. This will reverse ultimately when the financial accounting depreciation becomes larger than the tax depreciation.

P12-10. Analytical insights from deferred tax account

Requirement 1:
The following table provide the balances in the deferred tax liability over the equipment life:

Year	Depreciation Expense St. Line (a)	Depreciation Expense SOYD (b)	Annual Difference in Depreciation (c) = (b) - (a)	Cumulative Difference in Depreciation (d)	Balance in Deferred Tax Liability (e) = (d) × 0.35
Year 1	$20,000	$30,000	$10,000	$10,000	$3,500
Year 2	20,000	20,000	-	10,000	3,500
Year 3	20,000	10,000	(10,000)	-	-
	$60,000	$60,000	$ -	$ -	$ -

The following table summarizes the balance in the deferred tax liability of Weber, assuming it buys new equipment for $60,000 every year through the year 2003:

Asset Acquired in	12/31/98	12/31/99	12/31/00	12/31/01	12/31/02	12/31/03
1998	$3,500	$3,500	-			
1999		3,500	$3,500	-		
2000			3,500	$3,500	-	
2001				3,500	$3,500	-
2002					3,500	$3,500
2003						3,500
	$3,500	$7,000	$7,000	$7,000	$7,000	$7,000

Requirement 2:
The following tables provide the balances in the deferred tax liability over the equipment life for each of the assets acquired during 1999 through 2003 [See (1) for the equipment acquired in 1998]:

Equipment acquired in 1999:

Year	Depreciation Expense St. Line (a)	Depreciation Expense SOYD (b)	Annual Difference in Depreciation (c) = (b) - (a)	Cumulative Difference in Depreciation (d)	Balance in Deferred Tax Liability (e) = (d) × 0.35
Year 1	$22,000	$33,000	$11,000	$11,000	$3,850
Year 2	22,000	22,000	-	11,000	3,850
Year 3	22,000	11,000	(11,000)	-	-
	$66,000	$66,000	$ -	$ -	$ -

Equipment acquired in 2000:

Year	Depreciation Expense St. Line (a)	Depreciation Expense SOYD (b)	Annual Difference in Depreciation (c) = (b) - (a)	Cumulative Difference in Depreciation (d)	Balance in Deferred Tax Liability (e) = (d) × 0.35
Year 1	$24,000	$36,000	$12,000	$12,000	$4,200
Year 2	24,000	24,000	-	12,000	4,200
Year 3	24,000	12,000	(12,000)	-	-
	$72,000	$72,000	$ -	$ -	$ -

Equipment acquired in 2001:

Year	Depreciation Expense St. Line (a)	Depreciation Expense SOYD (b)	Annual Difference in Depreciation (c) = (b) - (a)	Cumulative Difference in Depreciation (d)	Balance in Deferred Tax Liability (e) = (d) × 0.35
Year 1	$26,000	$39,000	$13,000	$13,000	$4,550
Year 2	26,000	26,000	-	13,000	4,550
Year 3	26,000	13,000	(13,000)	-	-
	$78,000	$78,000	$ -	$ -	$ -

Equipment acquired in 2002:

Year	Depreciation Expense St. Line (a)	Depreciation Expense SOYD (b)	Annual Difference in Depreciation (c) = (b) - (a)	Cumulative Difference in Depreciation (d)	Balance in Deferred Tax Liability (e) = (d) × 0.35
Year 1	$28,000	$42,000	$14,000	$14,000	$4,900
Year 2	28,000	28,000	-	14,000	4,900
Year 3	28,000	14,000	(14,000)	-	-
	$84,000	$84,000	$ -	$ -	$ -

Equipment acquired in 2003:

Year	Depreciation Expense St. Line (a)	Depreciation Expense SOYD (b)	Annual Difference in Depreciation (c) = (b) - (a)	Cumulative Difference in Depreciation (d)	Balance in Deferred Tax Liability (e) = (d) × 0.35
Year 1	$30,000	$45,000	$15,000	$15,000	$5,250
Year 2	30,000	30,000	-	15,000	5,250
Year 3	30,000	15,000	(15,000)	-	-
	$90,000	$90,000	$ -	$ -	$ -

The following table summarizes the temporary differences and the balance in the deferred tax liability of Weber assuming it buys new equipment every year through the year 2003 (the cost of the equipment increases linearly from $60,000 in 1998 to $90,000 in 2003):

Year	Book Depreciation (a)	Tax Depreciation (b)	Yearly Difference (c)	Cumulative Difference (d) = b - a	Balance in Deferred Tax Liability Account (e) = d × .35
1998	$20,000	$30,000	$10,000	$10,000	$3,500
1999	42,000	53,000	11,000	21,000	7,350
2000	66,000	68,000	2,000	23,000	8,050
2001	72,000	74,000	2,000	25,000	8,750
2002	78,000	80,000	2,000	27,000	9,450
2003	84,000	86,000	2,000	29,000	10,150

Requirement 3:
The answer to this requirement involves extending the last table for two more years without considering any new equipment purchases:

Year	Book Depreciation (a)	Tax Depreciation (b)	Yearly Difference (c)	Cumulative Difference (d) = b - a	Balance in Deferred Tax Liability Account (e) = d × .35
2003	$84,000	$86,000	$2,000	$29,000	$10,150
2004	58,000	44,000	(14,000)	15,000	5,250
2005	30,000	15,000	(15,000)	-	-

Requirement 4:
Several generalizations can be made by examining the answers to the above three requirements. One controversy pertains to whether a deferred tax liability is really an economic liability. As discussed in the chapter, if a company sells its equipment at its accounting book value, then it will end up paying tax equal to the deferred tax liability for that equipment. In that sense, one might consider a deferred tax liability as a "true" liability. For instance, consider the equipment purchased for $60,000 on January 1, 1998. The following table summarizes the change in the deferred tax liability with respect to this asset:

Year	Depreciation Expense St. Line (a)	Depreciation Expense SOYD (b)	Annual Difference in Depreciation (c) = (b) - (a)	Cumulative Difference in Depreciation (d)	Balance in Deferred Tax Liability (e) = (d) × 0.35
Year 1	$20,000	$30,000	$10,000	$10,000	$3,500
Year 2	20,000	20,000	-	10,000	3,500
Year 3	20,000	10,000	(10,000)	-	-
	$60,000	$60,000	$ -	$ -	$ -

Assume that this equipment is sold for its accounting book value on January 1, 1999. At the time of sale, the accounting book value of the asset is $40,000 ($60,000 - $20,000), whereas its tax book value (referred to as tax basis) is only $30,000 ($60,000 - $30,000). The company will report no gain or loss in its financial reporting statements; however, it will report an income of $10,000 in its tax statement. Consequently, it will end up paying tax equal to $3,500 (35% of $10,000) in 1999. This $3,500 is exactly equal to the deferred tax liability reported at the end of 1998.

However, companies typically invest in property, plant, and equipment not with an objective of selling them, but with a view to using them in their operations to generate revenues. Companies in growth or mature stages are likely to continually reinvest in new property and equipment to meet their increasing or continuing customer demands. For these firms, the deferred tax liability might represent the present value of obligation that could be

544

postponed almost indefinitely through growth and expansion; consequently, the present value of the obligation is likely to be substantially smaller than the reported value of the deferred tax liability.

Note that in Requirement 1, when Weber is continuing to buy new equipment at the rate of $60,000, the deferred tax liability remains stable at $7,000 from 1999 to 2003. However, when the cost of the equipment increases over time, the balance in deferred tax liability in fact keeps increasing from $7,000 in 1998 to $10,150 in the year 2003. Many growth companies invest increasingly larger amounts in property and equipment to build capacity. Even mature companies that expect to maintain capacity invest increasingly larger *dollar* amounts due to inflation in equipment prices. In essence, Requirements 2 and 3 indicate that the economic value of the deferred tax liability may be substantially lower than its reported value.

Requirement 4 shows that a continuing decline in deferred tax liability might indicate that a company is shrinking or declining since it is reducing its Investment in new property and equipment.

P12-11. Comprehensive tax allocation problem

Requirement 1:
First, let us calculate the depreciation expense for the computer equipment. Under both the straight-line and SOYD methods, original cost minus the estimated salvage value ($330,000 - $30,000) is depreciated over the useful life. The SOYD depreciation figures will be used for calculating the income tax liability.

Method	Annual Depreciation Expense					
	1998	**1999**	**2000**	**2001**	**2002**	**Total**
St. Line	$60,000	$60,000	$60,000	$60,000	$60,000	$300,000
SOYD	100,000	80,000	60,000	40,000	20,000	300,000

Based on the straight-line method of depreciation, the financial reporting income statements are provided below:

Financial Reporting Income Statements for the Years Ended

	1998	1999
Sales revenue	$1,000,000	$1,200,000
Income from municipal bonds	60,000	75,000
- Cost of goods sold	(400,000)	(504,000)
- Depreciation expense	(60,000)	(60,000)
- Warranty expense	(100,000)	(110,000)
- Provision for uncollectibles (8% of sales)	(80,000)	(96,000)
- Life insurance premium for executives	(30,000)	(30,000)
- Other operating expenses	(300,000)	(350,000)
Income before income taxes	90,000	125,000
- Income tax expense (see below)	(21,000)	(28,000)
Net income	$69,000	$97,000
Effective tax rate (tax expense/pre-tax income)	23.33%	22.40%

After excluding the permanent differences, the income tax expense is calculated as follows:

Calculation of Income Tax Expense

	1998	1999
Income before income taxes	$90,000	$125,000
- Income from municipal bonds	(60,000)	(75,000)
+Life insurance premium for executives	30,000	30,000
Income before permanent differences	$60,000	$80,000
Tax rate	35%	35%
Income tax expense at 35%	$21,000	$28,000

Requirement 2:

To calculate the income tax liability, we need to prepare the income statement for tax purposes. This requires two adjustments to the financial reporting income statement. First, the permanent differences are excluded. Second, the expenses that are subject to timing or temporary differences are recalculated using the tax rules. The depreciation is calculated using the SOYD method (see answer to Requirement 1). The actual warranty expenditures made to correct defective products are shown as an expense. Similarly, the actual bad debts written off are allowed as a deduction for tax purposes.

The actual warranty expenditures are calculated by reconstructing the T-account for warranty liability.

CR

Warranty Liability

Balance as of 1/1/98	-
Warranty expense for 1998 (per income statement)	$100,000
Cash paid for warranty services '98 (plug)	(85,000)
Balance as of 12/31/98 (given)	15,000
Warranty expense for 1999 (per income statement)	110,000
Cash paid for warranty services '99 (plug)	(100,000)
Balance as of 12/31/99	$25,000

The bad debts written off are calculated by reconstructing the T-account for allowance for uncollectibles.

CR

Allowance for Uncollectibles

Balance as of 1/1/98	-
Provision for uncollectibles for 1998 (per Req. 1)	$80,000
Bad debts written off (plug number)	(30,000)
Balance as of 12/31/98 (given)	50,000
Provision for uncollectibles for 1999 (per Req. 1)	96,000
Bad debts written off (plug number)	(125,000)
Balance as of 12/31/99 (given)	$21,000

Based on the above calculations, the taxable income for tax purposes is computed as follows:

Tax Income Statements for the Years Ended

	1998	1999
Book income before tax	$90,000	$125,000
Adjustments for permanent differences:		
Tax-exempt municipal bond interest	(60,000)	(75,000)
Nondeductible life insurance premiums	30,000	30,000
Book income adjusted for permanent differences	60,000	80,000
Adjustments for temporary differences:		
Additional tax depreciation	(40,000)[1]	(20,000)[2]
Warranty expense (accrual to cash basis)	15,000[3]	10,000[4]
Bad debts (accrual to cash basis)	50,000[5]	(29,000)[6]
Taxable income	$85,000	$41,000
Times tax rate	× .35	× .35
Income tax liability	$29,750	$14,350

[1] $100,000 (tax) - $60,000 (book) = $40,000

[2] $80,000 (tax) - $60,000 (book) = $20,000

[3] $100,000 (book) - $85,000 (tax) = $15,000

[4] $110,000 (book) - $100,000 (tax) = $10,000

[5] $80,000 (book) - $30,000 (tax) = $50,000

[6] $96,000 (book) - $125,000 (tax) = ($29,000)

Requirement 3:

Reconciliation of Effective Tax Rate and Statutory Tax Rate

	1998		1999	
Income tax expense at statutory rate	$31,500	35.00%	$43,750	35.00%
- Effect of non-taxable Income	(21,000)	-23.33%	(26,250)	-21.00%
+Effect of nondeductible expense	10,500	11.67%	10,500	8.40%
Income tax expense	$21,000	23.33%	$28,000	22.40%

Requirement 4:

Deferred Tax Accounts as of 12/31/1998	DR Asset	CR Liability
Depreciation expense ($100,000 - $60,000) × 0.35		$14,000
Warranty expense ($100,000 - $85,000) × 0.35	$5,250	
Bad debts ($80,000 - $30,000) × 0.35	17,500	
Total	$22,750	$14,000
Net deferred tax asset	**$8,750**	

548

Deferred Tax Liability for Depreciation Expense

	CR
Balance as of 12/31/98	$14,000
Additional timing difference ($80,000 - $60,000) × 0.35	7,000
Balance as of 12/31/99	$21,000

Deferred Tax Asset for Warranty Expense

	DR
Balance as of 12/31/98	$5,250
Additional timing difference ($110,000 - $100,000) × 0.35	3,500
Balance as of 12/31/99	$8,750

Deferred Tax Asset for Bad Debt Expense

	DR
Balance as of 12/31/98	$17,500
Reversal of timing difference ($125,000 - $96,000) × 0.35	(10,150)
Balance as of 12/31/99	$7,350

Deferred Tax Accounts as of 12/31/1999	DR Asset	CR Liability
Depreciation expense		$21,000
Warranty expense	$8,750	
Bad debts	7,350	
Total	$16,100	$21,000
Net deferred tax liability		**$4,900**

Requirement 5:

Reconciliation of Income Tax Expense and Income Tax Liability

	1998	1999
Income tax expense	$21,000	$28,000
Changes in deferred tax arising from:		
Depreciation expense	(14,000)	(7,000)
Warranty expense	5,250	3,500
Bad debt expense	17,500	(10,150)
Income tax liability	$29,750	$14,350

The tables in the answers to Requirements 3 through 5 are commonly provided in company annual reports.

Requirement 6:

Entry on 12/31/98:

DR Income tax expense	$21,000	
DR Deferred tax asset	22,750	
CR Deferred tax liability		$14,000
CR Income tax payable		29,750

The debit to deferred tax asset is due to warranty expense ($5,250) plus bad debts ($17,500). The credit to deferred tax liability is due to accelerated depreciation for tax purposes.

Entry on 12/31/99:

DR Income tax expense	$28,000	
CR Deferred tax asset		$6,650
CR Deferred tax liability		7,000
CR Income tax payable		14,350

The net credit to deferred tax asset is due to the tax effect of $10,150 from the reversal of the timing difference for bad debts offset by the debit from the tax effect of $3,500 from the additional originating timing difference in warranty expense. The credit to deferred tax liability is due to the additional originating difference in depreciation expense.

P12-12. Determination of taxes payable, deferred taxes and tax expense

Requirement 1:

Reality Corp.
Calculation of Taxable Income and Taxes Payable

Computation of Taxable Income:

Pre-tax accounting income (given)	$200,000
Adjustments for permanent differences:	
- Interest on municipal bonds	(5,000)
+Premium on executive life insurance	3,000
+Amortization of implicit goodwill	10,000
- 80% equity in investee's earnings	(72,000)
Adjustments for permanent differences	(64,000)
Income before adjustment for temporary differences	$136,000

Adjustments for Temporary Differences:

Excess of tax depreciation over book depreciation		(125,000)
Excess of equity in investee earnings over dividends		
Received, less portion considered permanent due to		
80% dividend exclusion rule [(20%) ($90,000 - $30,000)]		(12,000)
Rent income included in book income in 19X1, taxed in 19X0		(4,000)
Rent received in advance, taxable in 19X1		10,000
Temporary difference on sale of land:		
Amount recognized per book	(30,000)	
Amount recognized for tax	10,000	(20,000)
Warranty timing difference:		
Amount recognized per book	50,000	
Amount recognized for tax	(15,000)	35,000
Bad debt timing difference:		
Amount recognized per book	15,000	
Amount recognized for tax	(6,000)	9,000
Operating loss carryforward		(10,000)
Taxable income		**$19,000**
Tax rate		×40%
Taxes payable		**$7,600**

Requirement 2:
Computation of change in deferred tax asset and deferred tax liability accounts:

	Temporary Difference	Deferred Tax Asset	Deferred Tax Liability
(org)	Depreciation		
	($225,000 - $100,000) × 40%		$50,000 **CR**
(org)	Equity in investee earnings		
	40% [20% × ($90,000 - $30,000)]		4,800 **CR**
(rev)	Rental income earned in 19X1, taxed in 19X0		
	40% ($4,000)	($1,600) **CR**	
(org)	Rent received in advance		
	40% ($10,000)	4,000 **DR**	
(org)	Deferred profit on sale of land		
	40% ($20,000)		8,000 **CR**
(org/rev)	Warranty cost timing difference		
	40% ($35,000)	14,000 **DR**	
(org/rev)	Bad debt timing difference		
	40% ($15,000 - $6,000)	3,600 **DR**	
(org/rev)	Tax benefit of loss carryforward		
	40% ($10,000)	(4,000) **CR**	
	Change in deferred tax asset (liability)	$16,000 **DR**	$62,800 **CR**

Requirement 3:
Determination of tax expense for 19X1

Tax expense = Taxes payable + Increase in deferred tax liability - Increase in deferred tax asset (less allowance)

Before allowance:

$$\begin{array}{ll} \$54,400 & = \$7,600 + \$62,800 - \$16,000 \\ -\underline{11,200} & \text{Allowance (see below)} \\ \underline{\underline{\$43,200}} \end{array}$$

Deferred tax asset beginning balance	$40,000
Increase in 19X1 (see Requirement 2)	16,000
	$56,000
	× 20%
Estimated allowance	**$11,200**

P12-13. Leasing and deferred taxes

Requirement 1:

	1998	1999	2000
Income before lease transaction	$100,000	$100,000	$100,000
Lease expense	(10,000)	(10,000)	(10,000)
Taxable income	90,000	90,000	90,000
Income tax liability at 40%	$36,000	$36,000	$36,000

Requirement 2:
Note: Since the company leased the equipment for its entire useful life, it must use capital lease accounting for financial reporting purposes. A schedule showing the interest component (using the implicit interest rate) and reduction of principal for each lease payment is shown below.

Year	Interest Expense	Repayment of Lease Obligation	Balance of Lease Obligation
			$24,869
1998	$2,487	$7,513	17,356
1999	1,736	8,264	9,092
2000	908	9,092	0

	1998	**1999**	**2000**
Income before lease transaction	$100,000	$100,000	$100,000
Interest on capital lease	(2,487)	(1,736)	(908)
Depreciation expense	(8,290)	(8,290)	(8,289)
Income before income tax	89,223	89,974	90,803
Income tax expense at 40%	(35,689)	(35,990)	(36,321)
Net income	$53,534	$53,984	$54,482

Requirement 3:

1998

DR Income tax expense	$35,689	
DR Deferred income tax asset	311	
CR Income taxes payable		$36,000

1999

DR Income tax expense	$35,990	
DR Deferred income tax asset	10	
CR Income taxes payable		$36,000

2000

DR Income tax expense	$36,321	
CR Deferred income tax asset		$321
CR Income tax payable		36,000

Cases

C12-1. Baldwin Piano and Organ Company (KR): Analysis of tax footnote

Requirement 1:

Entry for 12/31/91:

DR Income tax expense	$2,884,000	
CR Income tax payable		$2,598,000
CR Net deferred tax asset/liability		286,000

Entry for 12/31/92:

DR Income tax expense	$4,090,000	
DR Net deferred tax asset/liability	745,000	
CR Income tax payable		$4,835,000

Entry for 12/31/93:

DR Income tax expense	$4,120,000	
CR Income tax payable		$3,390,000
CR Net deferred tax asset/liability		730,000

Requirement 2:

Baldwin Piano specifically identifies four accounting items that cause the income tax expense to be different from the taxes currently payable or income tax liability. These items are accounting for inventory writedowns, allowance for doubtful accounts, nondeductible accruals, and factory closing. Note that all the items are expenses. Recall that when expenses are recorded first in the tax books, and subsequently in the financial statements, then they give rise to deferred tax liabilities (e.g., accelerated depreciation for tax purposes and straight-line depreciation for financial reporting purposes). In contrast, when expenses are recorded initially in the financial reporting books, then they give rise to deferred tax assets (e.g., warranty expenses). Of the four items mentioned above, we find deferred tax assets for three of the items in the balance sheet as of 12/31/1993 (inventory writedowns, allowance for doubtful accounts and nondeductible accruals). This suggests that, with respect to each one of these items, the expense must first be reported in the financial statement, and in a future period, deducted for tax purposes.

First, let us focus on bad debt accounting. While companies use the matching principle to estimate bad debt expense for financial reporting purposes, they

554

must wait until the bad debts are written off to claim a deduction for tax purposes. Therefore, initially when a company is recording anticipated bad debts as an expense, it gives rise to a deferred tax asset (originating difference). However, when the bad debts are realized and written off, the corresponding deferred tax asset is eliminated (reversing difference).

If we compare the income tax expense with the income tax liability during the period 1991–1993, the expense was higher during 1991 and 1993, whereas the liability was higher during 1992. Taken together for the three items, the deferred tax asset account decreased during 1991 and 1993 (reversing difference), while it increased during 1992 (originating difference). For instance, the tax liability will be lower (higher) than the accounting tax expense only when the bad debts written off during a year are greater (lower) than the bad debt expense. (Note that bad debts cannot be written off before recording the bad debt expense.) In summary, positive and negative numbers in the table reconciling the deferred tax expense indicate decreases and increases in deferred tax assets with respect to the three items.

Returning to bad debt expense, the company experienced originating differences in 1992 and reversing differences in 1991 and 1993. Consequently, the bad debt expense recorded by the company on its financial statements in 1992 was higher than the bad debts written off. In contrast, during 1991 and 1993, the bad debts written off were higher than the bad debts expense per books.

Second, let us turn our attention to the non-deductible accruals. The term "nondeductible" is somewhat of a misnomer. If they are truly "nondeductible," then they would be considered as permanent differences, and, therefore, will not affect deferred taxes. What Baldwin means by "nondeductible" is that these financial reporting expenses are not **currently** deductible for tax purposes. What might be these nondeductible expenses? Note that Baldwin has accrued for a number of expenses that have resulted in accrued liabilities (postretirement and postemployment expenses, supplementary retirement expenses and compensation). SFAS 106 and 112 requires companies to record postretirement and postemployment expenses using accrual accounting. However, deductions are allowed for tax purposes only when the liabilities are discharged by paying cash. Similarly, accrued liabilities for compensation might represent incentive bonus accrued for employees and management that are deductible when paid.

An examination of the components of the deferred tax expense suggests that, collectively, these "nondeductible" items resulted in the creation of a deferred tax asset (originating difference) during 1991 and 1992, and a reduction of the deferred tax asset (reversing difference) during 1993. This indicates that the financial reporting expenses were higher during 1991 and 1992, whereas the tax deduction was greater during 1993.

Third, with respect to inventory accounting, it appears that certain writedowns are not deductible immediately for tax purposes until "realized" through sale of inventory (and, consequent, lower profits). For instance, the IRS does not allow companies using the LIFO method (such as Baldwin Piano) to apply the lower of cost or market value rule for tax purposes. This might explain the deferred tax asset from financial reporting writedown of inventories. Regardless of whether one knows the IRS provision or not, the general intuition behind the lack of immediate deductibility is apparent.

It appears that during 1992 Baldwin wrote down certain inventories in its financial statements that were not deductible for tax purposes, resulting in the creation of a deferred tax asset (originating difference). In the other two years, the deferred tax asset is reduced since the effect of past financial statement writedowns were reflected in the tax statements through the subsequent sale of these items (reversing difference).

The final item deals with factory closing. Note that Baldwin does not report a deferred tax asset or liability for factory closing at the end of 1993. Given the magnitude of this item in 1991, it is unlikely to be a part of other deferred taxes at the end of 1993. Moreover, the typical chronological sequence of events would suggest that a company reports the accounting expense for factory closing (severance pay, write-off of property, plant, and equipment) as soon as it decides to close a factory. However, the tax deductibility occurs only when the severance pay is paid out in cash or the equipment is scrapped or sold. This suggests that the accounting expense for factory closing must have been reported first in the financial statements before allowed as a deduction for tax purposes (i.e., originally a deferred tax asset must have been created). Consequently, the $683,000 reported in 1991, which lowered the tax liability, must reflect the reversal of the timing difference that originated in a prior year.

C12-2. Sara Lee Corp.: Analysis of tax footnotes

Requirement 1:
Book journal entry for tax expense in 1994

DR Income tax expense	$155	
DR Deferred tax asset	222	
CR Income tax payable		$377

Requirement 2:
Sara Lee's pre-tax book income for 1994

Let X = Pre-tax book income (income before income tax)
$$\$136 = .35\,X$$
$$\$388.57 = X$$

Requirement 3:
Overall effective tax rate for 1994

$$\frac{\text{Income tax expense (per books)}}{\text{Pre-tax book income}} = \frac{\$155}{\$388.57} = 39.89\%$$

Requirement 4:
Taxable income pre-tax return in 1994

Let X = Taxable income per tax return
Income tax payable = Effective tax rate × X
$$\$377 = .3989X$$
$$\$945.10 = X$$
$$\underline{\$945.10}$$

C12-3. Sound Advice Inc. (KR): Analysis of tax footnotes

Requirement 1:
Journal entry for tax expense in 1993.

DR Income tax expense	$561,300	
DR Deferred income tax asset (net)	511,600	
CR Income taxes currently payable		$1,072,900

Requirement 2:
Taxable income for the year ended 6/30/93.
= $1,072,900/0.34 = $3,155,588

Requirement 3:
We first need to determine the dollar amount of income tax expense that was reported on Sound Advice's 1993 income statement. Let X equal this amount. Using the dollar amount of tax expense ($561,300) from the top schedule in footnote (5) given in the case and the 33.2% effective tax rate for the year, the following equation can be solved for the 1993 income tax expense:

$561,300 (current tax provision) = .332 X
X = $1,690,663 = pre-tax income reported on the 1993 income statement

The *tax effect* of "nondeductible expenses" are 1.5% of this amount or

1.5% × $1,690,663 = $25,360

To get the dollar amount of expenses that were nondeductible, we need to divide $25,360 by the statutory tax rate:

$25,360/0.34 =	$74,588
Less: Goodwill amortized in	
($122,509 - $98,059)	(24,450)
Other nondeductible expenses	$50,138

Other nondeductible expenses might included premiums paid or corporate executive life insurance policies where the company is the beneficiary and compensation expenses associated with certain employee stock options.

Requirement 4:
Book value of property and equipment for tax purposes.

Financial reporting book value of PP&E	$13,151,190
- Deferred tax liability due to accumulated depreciation divided by tax rate = $488,000/0.34	(1,435,294)
Book value of PP&E for tax purposes	$11,715,896

Requirement 5:
Relation between bad debt expense versus bad debts written off.

↓ (↑) DTA = decrease (increase) in deferred tax asset

Year	Calculation of Temporary Difference	Relation between expense per books and write-off per tax return
1993	$129,633/0.34 = $381,274 ↓ DTA	bad debt expense < bad debts written off
1992	$241,585/0.34 = $710,544 ↑ DTA	bad debt expense > bad debts written off
1991	$152,589/0.34 = $448,791 ↑ DTA	bad debt expense > bad debts written off

C12-4. Circuit City Stores Inc. (KR): Analysis of tax footnotes

Requirement 1:

Entry on 2/29/92:

DR Provision for income taxes	$45,900	
DR Net Deferred tax asset/liability	17,245	
CR Accrued income taxes		$63,145

Entry on 2/28/93:

DR Provision for income taxes	$65,000	
DR Net deferred tax asset/liability	19,478	
CR Accrued income taxes		$84,478

Entry on 2/28/94:

DR Provision for income taxes	$76,600	
DR Net deferred tax asset/liability	17,800	
CR Accrued income taxes		$94,400

Consistent with the terminology used by Circuit City, we have used the term provision for income taxes to indicate income tax expense and accrued income taxes to denote income tax liability.

Requirement 2:

Deferred Income Taxes

	DR
Balance as of 2/28/93	$87,588
Addition from journal entry for tax expense	17,800
Balance as of 2/28/94	$105,388

Accrued Income Taxes

	CR
Balance as of 2/28/93	$26,310
Addition from journal entry for tax expense	94,400
Cash paid (plug number)	(82,128)
Balance as of 2/28/94	$38,582

Requirement 3:

The revenue recognition footnote describes the accounting methods for recognizing revenues from sale of Circuit City's own extended warranty contracts and from sale of extended warranty contracts on behalf of unrelated third parties. It appears that the company recognizes the commission revenue for the third-party extended warranty plans *at the time of sale*. Since cash is usually received up front on the sale of extended warranty contracts, it appears that the revenue is included in the tax income statement also *at the time of sale*. Consequently, no deferred tax asset/liability would be created with respect to this source of revenue.

However, the company reports the warranty revenue from the sale of its own warranty contracts on a straight-line basis over the life of the contracts. The footnote further indicates that the revenue is "deferred" suggesting that the company has collected cash up front from its customers. Consequently, the company must have reported the revenue in its tax statement immediately upon cash collection. In essence, Circuit City Stores is reporting warranty revenue earlier in its tax statement (at the time of sale and cash collection) compared to its financial reporting income statement (over the life of the contract). This is likely to be the source of the deferred tax asset for deferred revenue.

If Circuit City Stores had reported the same revenue figures for warranty contracts both in its financial and tax income statements, then the deferred tax asset for deferred revenue would have not changed from 2/28/93 to 2/28/94. Since the deferred tax asset has increased by $16,760 ($99,364 - $82,604), it suggests that there were more originating differences during the year ended 2/28/94, i.e., the cash collected during this fiscal year was greater than the revenue recognized in the financial reporting income statement. Using the effective tax rate of 37%, for every dollar of cash received over and above the accrual accounting revenue, Circuit City would have added 37 cents to its deferred tax asset. If the deferred tax asset increased by $16,760, then it suggests that the cash collected was more than the accounting income by $45,297 (i.e., $16,760/0.37).

Requirement 4:
The formula for calculating the "earnings conservatism" ratio (EC) is given below:

$$= \frac{\text{Pre - tax book income}}{\text{Taxable income per tax return}}$$

Note that the information on pre-tax book income and taxable income are not directly provided in the case. However, the ratio can be estimated by dividing provision for income taxes by income tax liability. The numerator and the denominator of this ratio each differ from EC by a factor equal to the effective tax rate. Since this affects both the numerator and the denominator in a similar fashion, their effects cancel each other through division.

	For the years ended		
	2/28/94	**2/28/93**	**2/29/92**
Provision for income taxes	$76,600	$65,000	$45,900
Income tax liability	94,400	84,478	63,145
EC Ratio	**0.81**	**0.77**	**0.73**

In all three years, the ratio is well below 1.00, suggesting conservative financial reporting. However, one interesting trend is that this ratio has increased monotonically from 1992 to 1994. This might suggest that differences between the cash collected on the warranty contracts and the revenue recognized under the accrual accounting is gradually narrowing. This is consistent with a company reaching a steady-state maturity stage where the differences between cash collections and accrual revenues become smaller.

C12-5. UNC Inc. (KR): Interpreting tax footnotes and reconciling statutory and effective rates

Requirement 1:

	Tax Amount	**Tax Rate**
Tax expense at statutory rate of 34%	$3,703	34.00%
Amortization of cost in excess of net assets of acquired companies	1,076	9.88%
State taxes	927	8.51%
Change in the valuation allowance for deferred tax assets	(2,122)	-19.48%
Others (plug number)	(317)	-2.91%
Tax provision at actual rate	$3,267	30.00%

The expense at the statutory rate is calculated by multiplying the earnings before income taxes of $10,891 by 34%. The tax effects of amortization of goodwill (or cost in excess of net assets of acquired companies) and state taxes are given in the problem. The effect of change in the valuation allowance is calculated by subtracting the 1995 balance from its 1996 balance ($15,710 - $13,588). The tax provision at actual (or effective) rate is the income tax expense of $3,267. The "others" figure is a plug number.

The tax rate column is calculated by dividing the tax amount column values by the earnings before income taxes.

Requirement 2:

DR Income tax expense	$3,267	
DR Valuation allowance	2,122	
CR Income tax payable		$1,756
CR Deferred tax liability		2,000
CR Deferred tax asset		1,634
	$5,389	$5,390

The credit to the income tax liability represents the current portion of the income tax expense. The decrease in the deferred tax asset ($47,652 - $49,286) and the increase in the deferred tax liability ($12,957 - $10,957) are obtained from comparing the 1996 and 1995 balance sheet values. The one dollar difference between the total debit and total credit appears to be rounding error.

Requirement 3:
The decrease in the deferred tax asset for accounts receivable suggests that the bad debts written off during the year was greater than the provision for uncollectibles (or bad debt expense).

The deferred tax asset for inventories is due to additional costs inventoried for tax purposes and financial statement allowances. It appears that certain costs that are considered as product costs for tax purposes are considered as period costs for financial reporting purposes. In addition, it seems that certain writedown of inventories (financial statement allowances) are not allowed for tax purposes until the loss due to writedown of inventories is realized through the sale of inventories. Since certain costs are considered as product costs for tax purposes only, the expense for tax purposes is likely to be lower than that for the financial statement purposes when inventories are building up. In essence, these product costs are included in the inventory book values at the end of 1996 for tax purposes, whereas they have been expensed in the financial statements as part of operating expenses. Thus, the increase in the deferred tax asset for inventories is consistent with the inventory buildup indicated by the change in the balance sheet value from 1995 to 1996.
The deferred tax asset for employee benefits suggests that the company is using the accrual basis for expensing the cost of employee benefits in the

financial statements while using the cash basis for tax purposes. The decrease in the deferred tax asset for employee benefits suggests that UNC Inc. paid more of the employee benefits in cash when compared to the tax expense during 1996. Another possibility to consider is that, since the company has gone through significant restructuring, the reduction in the deferred tax asset might be indicative of the reduction in the liability for employee benefits from contract renegotiations. In fact, the income statement of the company reported a $6,000 credit from reduction in the employee benefit obligation (not provided in the problem).

The reduction in the deferred tax asset for accrual for costs of restructuring is consistent with the current payment for restructuring charges that were accrued in the GAAP income statement of the previous years. Alternatively, it might also indicate that the company had overprovided for restructuring charges in the past which are being reversed in the current year.

The deferred tax asset for accrual for disposal of discontinued operations was created to record the expected tax benefit from the loss on discontinued operations reported in the GAAP financial statements of the previous years. The reduction in this deferred tax asset suggests that a portion of the loss has been realized during the current year, thereby realizing the tax benefit.

Since the company reports a deferred tax liability for plant and equipment, it must mean that UNC Inc. is using a more accelerated depreciation for tax purposes compared to the financial reporting depreciation. However, the decrease in the deferred tax liability suggests that the 1996 depreciation expense for financial reporting purposes was higher than that for the tax purposes. Another explanation is that, since the company was involved in significant restructuring, it might have sold a portion of its depreciable assets, which would eliminate the corresponding deferred tax liability.

C12-6. Spiegel, Inc. (KR): Analysis of tax footnotes

Requirement 1:

12/31/1993

DR Income tax expense	$38,658	
DR Net deferred tax asset/liability	28,565	
CR Income tax payable		$67,223

12/31/1994

DR Income tax expense	$22,146	
CR Net deferred tax asset/liability		$10,640
CR Income tax payable		11,506

12/30/1995

DR Income tax refund receivable	$20,117	
CR Net deferred tax asset/liability		$13,791
CR Income tax benefit		6,326

Requirement 2:

	For the years ended		
	12/30/95	12/31/94	12/31/93
Statutory rate	35.0%	35.0%	35.0%
State income tax	6.5%	7.9%	6.7%
Amortization of goodwill	-11.9%	4.0%	2.3%
Change in statutory rate	0.0%	0.0%	0.3%
Others	10.5%	0.0%	0.0%
Effective tax rate	40.0%	46.9%	44.2%

Recall that the problem provides a table reconciling the difference between the expected tax expense based on the statutory rate versus the reported tax expense (the reconciliation table). The above table is constructed by dividing each item in the reconciliation table by earnings (losses) before income taxes of the corresponding year.

Note that since Spiegel reported a loss before income taxes during 1995, the company has an effective tax "credit" of 40%. In other words, for every dollar of pre-tax financial reporting loss, the governments (U.S. and state) are contributing 40 cents through refund of past tax payments.

The amortization of goodwill has an opposing effect on the effective tax of Spiegel in 1995 versus the other two years. In 1994 and 1993, Spiegel reported "earnings" before income taxes. In these years, the amortization of goodwill increased the effective rates by 4.0% and 2.3%, respectively. Since amortization of goodwill was a permanent difference for Spiegel, it is not allowed as a deduction for tax purposes. Consequently, although the financial reporting income is lower by the amount of goodwill amortization, the tax **liability** and tax **expense** are not correspondingly lower. This partially explains why the effective tax rates were higher than the statutory tax rate.

In contrast, Spiegel reported a "loss" before income taxes during 1995. In this year, although the financial reporting loss is higher by the amount of goodwill amortization, the tax **refund receivable** from the IRS and the tax **credit** in the income statement are not correspondingly higher. In other words, the effective tax credit for Spiegel is lowered by the nondeductible expense included in the financial reporting income statement. In summary, non-deductible expenses (or permanent differences) increase (decrease) the effective tax rate (credit) during income (loss) years.

Requirement 3:
In 1993, the income tax expense of Spiegel was higher by $260 due to the change in the statutory tax rate. Presumably, this was due to the effect of the increase in the statutory tax rate from 34% to 35%. Since the increase in the tax rate led to an increase in the income tax expense, it must mean that Spiegel had reported a net deferred tax **liability** at the end of 1992. Note that a one percentage point increase in the tax rate led to a $260 increase in the net deferred tax liability. This suggests that the net cumulative timing differences for Spiegel as of the end of 1992 were approximately $26,000 ($260/0.01), which would imply that the net deferred tax **liability** at the end of 1992 was approximately 34% of $26,000 or $8,840. The following table summarizes the calculation for the increase in the deferred tax liability using our assumptions:

Net deferred tax liability at the end of 1992 at 34%	$8,840
Net deferred tax liability at the end of 1992 at 35%	9,100
Increase in net deferred tax liability in 1993	$260

Note: we assume that Spiegel adjusted its deferred tax liability as of January 1, 1993.

Requirement 4:
First of all, let us review our effective tax rate calculations from the answer to Requirement 2. A fourth column is added to show the 3-year average for each of the components.

	For the years ended			
	12/30/95	12/31/94	12/31/93	Average
Statutory rate	35.0%	35.0%	35.0%	35.0%
State income tax	6.5%	7.9%	6.7%	7.0%
Amortization of goodwill	-11.9%	4.0%	2.3%	-1.9%
Change in statutory rate	0.0%	0.0%	0.3%	0.1%
Others	10.5%	0.0%	0.0%	3.5%
Effective tax rate	40.0%	46.9%	44.2%	43.7%

It may be tempting to look at the "average" column as a basis for calculating the future effective tax rate. For instance, the average of the past statutory tax rates may not be representative of what the future statutory tax rates are. The best approach is to consult a tax expert to find out what the next year's tax rate is. However, since the statutory tax rate had not changed during the period 1992-1996, we can use 35% as a starting point to forecast the next year's tax expense.

A similar approach (i.e., consulting a tax expert) is appropriate for calculating the effect of the state income taxes. Without additional information, we assume that the state income tax rate is 7%, being the average of the previous three years' rates.

Amortization of goodwill introduces an interesting issue. This item exhibits significant intertemporal volatility during the 3-year period. It is quite likely that the magnitude of goodwill amortization (and, therefore, its dollar effect on the income tax expense) was constant over the 3-year period. However, significant variations in the pre-tax income of Spiegel over this period results in differential "percentage" effects on the effective tax rate due to goodwill amortization. To see this, let us focus on the table that reconciles the difference between the expected tax expense based on the statutory rate versus the reported tax expense.

	For the years ended			
	12/30/95	**12/31/94**	**12/31/93**	**Average**
Tax expense (or benefit) at statutory rate	($5,532)	$16,536	$30,577	
State income tax	(1,027)	3,728	5,851	
Amortization of goodwill	1,885	1,882	1,970	$1,912
Change in statutory rate			260	
Others	(1,652)			
Income Tax Provision (Benefit)	($6,326)	$22,146	$38,658	

The tables shows that amortization of goodwill has had a very similar **dollar effect** on the income tax expense over the last years (the average being $1,912). Consequently, it may be more accurate to assume that the dollar effect of goodwill amortization will be around $1,900 in 1996 also.

Based on the above assumptions, the effective tax rate of Spiegel for 1996 is calculated as follows:

Forecasted income for 1996	$20,000		$80,000	
Tax at statutory rate of 35%	$7,000	35.0%	$28,000	35.0%
State income at 7%	1,400	7.0%	5,600	7.0%
Amortization of goodwill	1,900	9.5%	1,900	2.4%
Income tax expense	$10,300	51.5%	$35,500	44.4%

Note that the effective tax rate of Spiegel can be 44.4% or 51.5% depending on whether its pre-tax GAAP income will be $80,000 or $20,000. Since goodwill amortization is unlikely to vary with a change in the corporate financial performance, its effect on the tax rate is more pronounced when the pre-tax income or loss is smaller in magnitude.

Requirement 5:
While companies use the matching principle to estimate bad debt expense for financial reporting purposes, they must wait until the bad debts are written off to claim a deduction for tax purposes. Therefore, initially when a company is recording anticipated bad debts as an expense, it gives rise to a deferred tax asset (originating difference). However, when the bad debts are realized and written off, the corresponding deferred tax asset is eliminated (reversing difference). The decrease in the deferred tax asset for Allowance for doubtful accounts indicates that the bad debts written off during 1995 were higher than the bad debt expense.

The second item is the deferred tax asset for allowance for the gross profit on estimated future returns. Let us first recall Spiegel's revenue recognition policy:

> Revenue Recognition
> Sales made under installment accounts represent a substantial portion of net sales…The Company provides for returns at the time of sale based upon projected merchandise returns.

Although Spiegel uses installment contracts to sell inventory, it uses a point of sale method to recognize its revenue. This appears to be the case for both tax and financial reporting purposes. If Spiegel had used an installment method of accounting for tax purposes, then we would have seen a deferred tax liability for installment method of accounting. An important point can be made at this juncture on when installment method of accounting is *not* available for tax purposes. Under the current income tax law, companies cannot use the installment method to record gains on property held for sale in the ordinary course of business (e.g., inventory). For instance, if Spiegel sells an office building in exchange for an installment note receivable, then the gain on such a sale can be apportioned over the life of the note using the installment method.

The matching principle suggests that a company must be able to reasonably estimate all its sales returns if it records revenue at the point of sale. The deferred tax asset for allowance for the gross profit on estimated future returns suggests that although Spiegel is recording expected sales returns in its GAAP income statements, it is using a different method for tax purposes. While Spiegel is backing out the gross margin on expected sales returns in its GAAP income statement, it appears that such expected sales returns cannot be recorded for tax purposes. Consequently, the effect of sales returns is reported in the tax income statement in the year in which the sales returns actually take place.

The increase in the deferred tax asset for allowance for the gross profit on estimated future returns indicates that the reduction in the GAAP income due to expected sales returns was more than the lost gross profit from the actual sales returns that took place during 1995.

The third item is the deferred tax asset for reserve for distribution facility & store closings. In 1993, Spiegel recorded a restructuring charge of $39,000 in its GAAP income statement. However, it is allowed as an expense for tax purposes only when the expenditures are actually paid. The tax law in many instances disallows the use of "reserves" which are required under GAAP accounting for matching revenues and expenses.

The problem states that Spiegel added $2,400 to this reserve during 1995. However, we notice a decrease in the deferred tax asset for this item from 1994 to 1995. This suggests that the actual expenditures (paid in cash) on store closings were more than the $2,400 added to the reserve during the year.

The fourth item is the deferred tax liability for prepaid and deferred expenses. Companies are allowed to deduct prepaid expenses as a deduction for tax purposes in the year in which cash is paid. However, they are reported as an expense for GAAP purposes only in the period in which the company obtains the benefits from such expenses. It appears that Spiegel typically pays cash for certain expenses before they are expensed for GAAP purposes. This explains the existence of the deferred tax liability for prepaid and deferred expenses. The decrease in this deferred tax liability during 1995 suggests that the accrual expense for GAAP purposes was more than the cash paid (i.e., less of the timing difference remains at the end of the period compared to the beginning of the period).

The fifth item pertains to the deferred tax liability for gain on sale of accounts receivable. The footnotes indicate that during 1995 and 1994, the company recorded gains of $18,637 and $10,658, respectively, from the sale of its

567

installment accounts receivable. The existence of a deferred tax liability suggests that such gains are not reported in the tax statement in the years in which Spiegel "sells" its accounts receivable. It is possible that the tax laws do not recognize these transactions as "sales," and consequently, any income from the receivables is prorated over the duration of the installment contracts in computing taxable income.

The increase in the deferred tax liability suggests that the gain reported in the GAAP income statement is more than the income reported in the tax statement during 1995 (i.e., more timing difference remains at the end of the period compared to the beginning of the period).

The final item is the deferred tax liability for earned but unbilled finance charges. The revenue recognition footnote indicates that interest income on customer installment accounts receivable is recorded as income when earned. However, it appears that such interest income is reported in the tax statement only when the interest is "billed" to the customers. Thus, while "passage of time" appears to be the critical event for recording interest income in the GAAP books, the act of "billing the customer" is the critical event for tax purposes.

The increase in the deferred tax liability suggests that the interest income earned during the year was more than the interest billed to the customers (i.e., more timing difference remains at the end of the period compared to the beginning of the period).

Exercises

E13-1. Determining projected benefit obligation
(AICPA adapted)

The projected benefit obligation on 12/31/98 is computed as follows:

Projected benefit obligation, 1/1/98	$72,000
Service cost	18,000
Interest cost on beginning PBO (10% × $72,000)	7,200
Benefit payments	(15,000)
Pension benefit obligation 12/31/98	$82,200

E13-2. Pension liability on balance sheet
(AICPA adapted)

SFAS 87 requires that companies report a minimum pension liability. This amount is equal to the excess of the ABO over the fair value of plan assets ($4,300,000 - $3,450,000 = **$850,000**). This is the amount reported in the balance sheet.

E13-3. Determining prepaid pension cost
(AICPA adapted)

Funded status of the plan 12/31/98:	
Contributions	$1,000,000
Return on plan assets (10% × $1,000,000)	100,000
Less: Service costs + Interest costs	(620,000)
Amount of plan over funding	$ 480,000

E13-4. Determining employer's pension contribution
(AICPA adapted)

Since Webb fully funded its pension plan in 1995 and 1996, the beginning balance in the prepaid/accrued pension cost account is $0. T-account analysis shown below provides the required contribution.

Prepaid/Accrued Pension Cost

		$0	1/1/97 Balance
1997 Contribution	$50,000	75,000	1997 Pension expense
		90,000	1998 Pension expense
1998 Contribution	X		
		$15,000	Target balance 12/31/98

Amount of 1998 contribution would be $100,000 to provide the target balance in the accrued pension liability account.

E13-5. Required additional pension liability
(AICPA adapted)

The minimum liability is the excess of the accumulated benefit obligation (ABO) over the fair value of plan assets:

ABO on 9/30/98	$380,000
Fair value of plan assets on 9/30/98	(290,000)
Minimum liability	$90,000

The *additional liability* that must be recorded to produce the total minimum liability is $90,000 + $20,000 of prepaid pension cost = $110,000.

E13-6. Determining actual return on plan assets
(AICPA adapted)

The actual return on plan assets is equal to the beginning plan assets balance less the ending plan assets balance adjusted for contributions made to the plan and benefits paid to retirees during the period. Below is the formula for determining the actual return:

Actual return	=	(Ending plan assets	-	Beginning plan assets)	+	Benefits	-	Contributions
$150,000	=	($525,000	-	$350,000	) +	$85,000	-	$110,000

E13-7. Determining accrued pension liability on balance sheet
(AICPA adapted)

The accrued pension cost as of 12/31/98 is the excess of pension expense over the amounts funded in 1998, adjusted for the beginning debit balance in the prepaid pension cost account on 1/1/98. Pension expense for 1998 is:

Service cost	$19,000
Interest cost	38,000
Expected return on plan assets	(22,000)
Amortization of unrecognized prior service cost	52,000
Pension expense	$87,000

When pension expense is recorded, the off-setting credit is to the prepaid/accrued pension cost account. 1998 employer contributions ($40,000) are debited to the prepaid/accrued pension cost account and credited to cash, resulting in 12/31/98 accrued pension cost of $45,000:

Prepaid/Accrued Pension Cost

Beginning balance 1/1/98	$2,000	$87,000	Expense for 1998
Funding for 1998	40,000		
		$45,000	Ending balance 12/31/98

E13-8. Prepaid pension cost on balance sheet
(AICPA adapted)

The prepaid pension cost is the difference between pension costs funded and amounts expensed. Since the service cost for 1998 is fully funded, the prepaid pension cost is the difference between the funded portion and amortized portion of prior service costs determined as follows:

Funded portion of prior service costs	$114,400
Amortized portion of prior service costs	(83,400)
Prepaid pension costs	$31,000

E13-9. Prepaid pension cost on balance sheet
(AICPA adapted)

Prepaid pension cost is the amount of contribution less the amount of pension expense for the period. service costs of $150,000 are fully funded. Prior service costs amortized to expense for the year are $24,000, but $60,000 was contributed to fund prior service costs. Thus, the prepaid pension cost at 12/31/98 is computed as follows:

Prior service costs contribution	$60,000
Amortization of prior service costs	(24,000)
Prepaid pension costs on 12/31/98	$36,000

E13-10. Minimum pension liability
(AICPA adapted)

The first step is to find the minimum pension liability. This is the accumulated benefit obligation (ABO) less the fair market value (FMV) of the plan assets:

ABO	$103,000
FMV of plan assets	(78,000)
Minimum pension liability	$ 25,000

Next, we need to compute the prepaid/accrued pension cost balance as of 12/31/97.

Net pension expense for the period	$90,000
Employer's contributions	(70,000)
Accrued pension liability	$20,000

As shown, there is a $20,000 accrued pension liability. This amount is smaller than the minimum liability prior to recognizing the additional pension liability. The additional minimum pension liability is determined as follows:

Minimum pension liability	$25,000
Accrued pension liability already reported	(20,000)
Additional pension liability needed	$5,000

E13-11. Determining postretirement expense
(AICPA adapted)

Postretirement benefit cost is determined below:

Service cost	$240,000
Interest on APBO	40,000
Amortization of transition obligation ($200,000/20 years)	10,000
Postretirement benefit cost	$290,000

E13-12. Determining pension expense
(AICPA adapted)

Pension expense is calculated as follows:

Service cost	$160,000
Expected return on plan assets	(35,000)
Amortization of unrecognized prior service costs	5,000
Interest cost	50,000
Pension expense	$180,000

E13-13. Determining pension expense, actual and deferred return on plan assets

Requirement 1:

Determination of pension expense for Bostonian in 1998:

Service cost	$120,000
Interest on beginning PBO (10% × $2,500,000)	250,000
Expected return on plan assets (12% × $2,000,000)	(240,000)
Amortization of net pension asset at transition	(40,000)
Amortization of unrecognized actuarial loss	50,000
Pension expense for 1998	$140,000

Requirement 2:

Actual dollar return on plan assets for 1998:

Ending fair value of plan assets	$2,300,000
- Beginning fair value of plan assets	(2,000,000)
+Payments made to retirees	100,000
- Contributions made to plan during 1998	(80,000)
Actual dollar return on plan assets	$320,000

Requirement 3:

Dollar amount that is deferred in 1998:

Actual dollar return	$320,000
Expected return (12% × $2,000,000)	(240,000)
Dollar return deferred	$80,000

E13-14. Funded status reconciliation

Funded status reconciliation and solving for unrecognized net gain (loss).

Projected benefit obligation	($900,000)
Fair value of plan assets	307,500
Projected benefit obligation in excess of plan assets	(592,500)
Unrecognized prior service costs	190,000
Unamortized transition obligation	160,000
Unrecognized net (gain) loss	plug
Prepaid (accrued) pension cost	($112,500)

The amount needed to complete the funded status reconciliation is an unamortized net *loss* of $130,000.

E13-15. Determining postretirement (healthcare) benefits expense and obligation

Requirement 1:
Determining postretirement expense:

	($ millions)
Service cost	$35
Interest on beginning APBO (8% × $300)	24
Amortization of unrecognized transition obligation ($240/20 years)	12
Amortization of prior service cost credit ($45/15 years)	(3)
Net postretirement expense	$68

Requirement 2:
Determining 12/31/98 balance in accumulated postretirement benefit obligation account:

	($ millions)
Beginning balance 1/1/98	$300
Service cost	35
Interest on beginning APBO	24
Benefits paid to retirees	(64)
Accumulated postretirement benefit obligation, 12/31/98	$295

E13-16. Postretirement healthcare expenses and liability balance

Requirement 1:
Determination of postretirement health care expense for 1998:

Service cost		$20,000
Interest on accumulated benefit obligation (8% × $300,000)		24,000
Actual return on plan assets	($4,500)	
Less: Amount deferred	1,500	
Expected return on plan assets		(3,000)
Amortization of:		
Prior service cost credit		(5,000)
Cumulative unrecognized loss		7,000
Transition net loss		15,000
Postretirement expense		$58,000

Requirement 2:
Determination of benefits paid out:

Determine this from an analysis of changes in the fair value of plan assets:

Beginning fair value on 1/1/98	$30,000
+Contributions to the plan	12,000
+Actual return on plan assets	4,500
- Payments made to employees	(plug)
Ending fair value on 12/31/98	$40,000

Distributions to employees equal $6,500 to balance.

Requirement 3:
Balance of accumulated postretirement benefit obligation (APBO) at 12/31/98:

Beginning balance	$300,000
+Service cost	20,000
+Interest on beginning APBO balance	24,000
- Payments made to employees	(6,500)
Ending balance	$337,500

Problems

P13-1. Determining components of pension expense
(AICPA adapted)

Requirement 1:
Interest cost:

Beginning balance of PBO	$600,000
× Discount rate	× .08
= Interest cost	$48,000

Requirement 2:
Expected dollar return on plan assets:

Beginning balance of fair value of plan assets	$720,000
× Expected rate of return on plan assets	× .10
= Expected return on plan assets	$72,000

Requirement 3:
Actual return on plan assets:

Fair value of plan assets

1/1/98 balance	$720,000		
Contributions during the year	0	0	Pension benefits paid
Actual return on plan assets	X		
12/31/98 balance	$825,000		

Actual return on plan assets = $825,000 - $720,000 + $0 - $0 = $105,000

Requirement 4:
Balance in unrecognized prior pension gain account on 12/31/98:

Beginning balance on 1/1/98 (given)		$96,000
Amount of beginning gain recognized (amortized)		
Beginning balance	$96,000	
Corridor ($72,000 plan assets × 10%)	(72,000)	
Excess	24,000	
Average service life	÷ 12 yrs.	
Amount recognized		(2,000)
Deferred gain on plan assets for 1998:		
Actual return = $825,000 - $720,000 =	$105,000	
Expected return = 10% × $720,000 =	(72,000)	
Deferred gain in current year		33,000
Ending balance on 12/31/98		$127,000

Requirement 5:
Recognized prior service costs as a component of 1998 pension cost:

Unrecognized prior service cost (1/1/98)	$240,000
Average service life of employees	÷ 12
= Amortization of prior service costs	$20,000

Requirement 6:
Minimum amortization of unrecognized pension gain:

Step (1): Determine the "corridor" amount by taking 10% of the larger of PBO or the fair value of plan assets:

$720,000 × 10% = $72,000

Step (2): Calculate the difference between the value calculated in Step (1) and the unamortized prior pension gain:

$96,000 - $72,000 = $24,000

Step (3): Amortize the value obtained in Step (2) over the average service life of the employees:

$24,000/12 = $2,000 (minimum amortization)

P13-2. PBO, ABO and pension expense

Requirement 1:
Calculation of projected benefit obligation on January 1, 19X1:

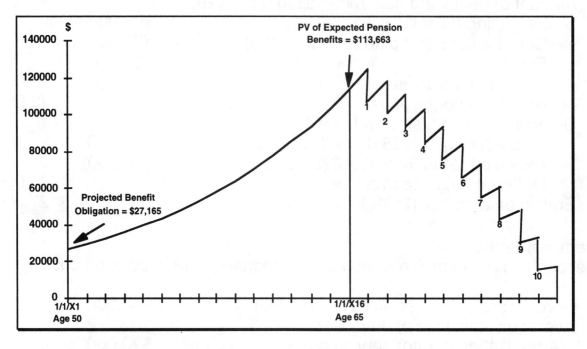

Annual pension benefits starting on 12/31/x16 and continuing for 10 years thereafter (11 years total = 76 - 65).

Years of service credit as of 1/1/X1: (10 yrs. × $250)	$2,500
Benefits tied to expected salary at retirement: (50% × $30,000)	15,000
Total annual pension benefit based on service credit earned up to 1/1/X1	$17,500

PV of expected pension benefits as of 1/1/X16 (date of *retirement*):

P_{OA} for 11 periods @ 10% × $17,500 = 6.495 × $17,500 =	$113,663

Projected benefit obligation on 1/1/X1 (date *plan adopted*):

PV of single amount for 15 periods @ 10% = 0.239 × $113,663 =	$27,165

578

Accumulated benefit obligation on actual salary level attained as of the date of computation (ignores future salary increase):

Benefits tied to actual salary as of 1/1/X1:
50% × $20,000 $10,000

Benefits tied to years of service credit as of 1/1/X1:
10 yrs. × $250   2,500

Total annual pension benefit based on service
credit and salary level as of 1/1/X1 $12,500

PV of expected pension benefits as of 1/1/X16 (date of retirement):

P_{OA} for 11 periods @ 10% × $12,500
= 6.495 × $12,500 = $81,188

Accumulated benefit obligation on 1/1/X1 (date of adoption):

PV of single amount for 15 periods @ 10%
= 0.239 x $81,188 = $19,403

Note: Projected benefit obligation > accumulated benefit obligation
          $27,165 $19,403

Requirement 2:
Calculation of projected benefit obligation on 1/1/X2:

Benefit based on years of service credit as of 1/1/X2:
11 yrs. × $250 $2,750

Benefits tied to expected salary at retirement:
50% × $30,000   15,000

Total annual pension benefit based on expected salary
and service credit earned up to 1/1/X2 $17,750

PV of expected pension benefits as of 1/1/X16:

P_{OA} for 11 periods @ 10% × $17,750
= 6.495 × $17,750 = $115,286

Projected benefit obligation on 1/1/X2:

PV of single amount for 14 periods @ 10%
= 0.263 × $115,286 = $30,320

Requirement 3:
Calculation of pension expense for 19X1:

Projected benefit obligation on 1/1/X2 =	$30,320
Projected benefit obligation on 1/1/X1 =	27,165
Difference = Service cost + Interest for 19X1	$3,155

Service cost component

P$_{OA}$ for 11 periods @ 10% × $250
= 6.495 × $250 = $1,624

PV of single amount for 14 periods @ 10% x $1,624
= 0.263 × $1,624=   + 428[*]

Interest component on PBO

10% × $27,165   + 2,717[*]

[*] Note: $428 + $2,717 ≠ $3,155 due to rounding error from using only three decimal places in PV calculations.

Return on plan assets
     Nothing invested as of the beginning of Year 1   0

Amortization of prior service cost
     $27,165/15 yrs. =   + 1,811

Amortization of actuarial gains/losses   0

Amortization of transition amount   0

     Total pension expense for 19X1 $4,956

P13-3. PBO, ABO and pension expense

Requirement 1:
With the entire amount of PBO funded on Jan. 1, 19X1, the return on plan assets (net of any deferral) reduces pension expense. The calculation of pension expense would be as follows for 19X1:

Service cost		$428
Interest on PBO 10% × $27,165		+ 2717
Return on plan assets Actual = 12% × $27,165 = Deferred = (12% - 10%) × $27,165 = Expected	$3,260 (543)	($2,717)
Amortization of prior service cost $27,165/15 yrs. =		+ 1,811
Amortization of actuarial gain/losses (None, since amount of deferred gain does not exceed the corridor)		0
Amortization of transition amount		0
Total pension expense 19X1		$2,239

Requirement 2:
Calculation of fair market value of plan assets on Dec. 31, 19X2:

Initial amount funded on Jan.1, 19X1	$27,165
Actual return on plan assets in 19X1 12% × $27,165	3,260
19X1 service costs funded on Dec. 31, 19X1	428
Fair market value of plan assets on Dec. 31, 19X1	$30,853
Actual return on plan assets in 19X2 10% × $30,853	3,085
19X2 service cost funded on Dec. 31, 1992[1]	724
Total pension assets on Dec. 31, 19X2	$34,662
Projected benefit obligation on Dec. 31, 19X2[2]	39,932
Net **underfunded** position on 12/31/X2	$5,270

581

[1] Pension expense for 19X2:

Service cost

P_{OA} for 11 periods @ 9% × $250

= 6.8052 × $250 = $1,701

PV of single amount for 13 periods @ 9%

= 0.3262 × $1,701 = **$555**

Interest on PBO at Jan.1, 19X2

9% x $36,153[a] 3,254

Actual return on plan assets

10% × $30,853 = (3,085)

Less: Amount deferred 0 ($3,085)

Amortization of prior service costs: $27,165/15 yrs. = + 1,811

Amortization of actuarial gains/losses 0

Amortization of transition amount 0

Total pension expense for 19X2 $2,535

Less: Amortization of prior service costs which were prefunded (1,811)

Amount of pension expense funded in 19X2 $724

[a] Calculation of PBO on Jan. 1, 19X2 based on 9% discount rate

Years of service credit earned as of 19X2: 11 yrs. × $250 $2,750

Benefits tied to expected salary at retirement: 50% × $30,000 15,000

Total annual pension benefit based on service credit earned up to 19X2 $17,750

PV of expected pension benefits as of 19X16:

P_{OA} for 11 periods @ 9% × $17,750 = 6.8052 × $17,150 = $120,792

PBO on 1/1/X2:

PV of single amount for 14 periods @ 9% = 0.2993 × $120,792 = $36,153

[2] Annual pension benefits starting on 12/31/X16 and continuing for 10 years thereafter (11 years total).

Years of service credit earned as of 12/31/X2: 12 yrs. × $250 $3,000

Benefits tied to expected salary at retirement: 50% × $30,000 15,000

Total annual pension benefit based on service credit earned up to 12/31/X2 $18,000

PV of expected pension benefits as of 1/1/X6 (date of retirement):

P_{OA} for 11 periods @ 9% × $18,000

= 6.805 × $18,000 = $122,490

Projected benefit obligation on 12/31/X2:

PV of single amount for 13 periods @ 9%

= 0.326 × $122,490 = $39,932

Calculation of Projected Benefit Obligation on December 31, 19X2: (9% Settlement Rate)

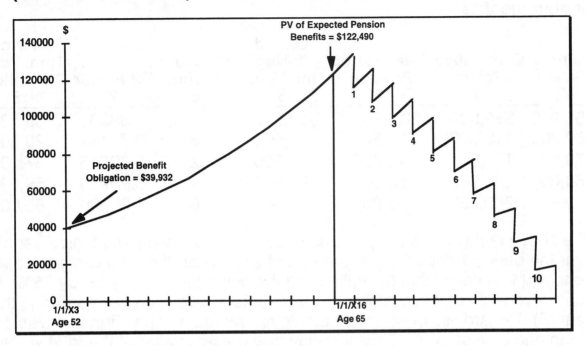

Explanation for Change in Funded Status:

The ABC Co. pension obligation was fully funded on December 31, 19X1 based on a 10% discount rate assumption (amount funded = $30,853 > PBO = $30,320). Despite the fact that the pension expense provision in 19X2 was fully funded, the pension fund is **under**funded by $5,270 on 12/31/X2 due to the fact that the discount rate (settlement rate) assumption used in computing the PBO for ABC Co. has declined from 10% to 9%. As the discount rate declines, the present value of the pension obligation increases.

P13-4. Effect of funding and discount rate assumption on pension expense

Requirement 1:

End of Year 1	Annual Salary 2	Cumulative Salary 3	Total Vested Pension 4	Vested During the Year 5	Discount Period 6	PV Factor 7	PV of Total Vested Pension 8
1998	$50,000	$50,000	$12,500	$12,500	4	0.68301	$8,538
1999	60,000	110,000	27,500	15,000	3	0.75131	20,661
2000	70,000	180,000	45,000	17,500	2	0.82645	37,190
2001	80,000	260,000	65,000	20,000	1	0.90909	59,091
2002	-	260,000	65,000	-	0	1.00000	65,000

The above table shows the present value of the total vested pension benefits over the period 1998–2002. At the end of each year, the total vested pension benefits (4) is calculated by multiplying the cumulative salary (3) by 25%. The year-to-year change in column (4) represents the pension vested during the year (5). Regardless of when the employee retires, the pension is payable only at the end of year 2002. Consequently, the present value of the total vested pension benefits is calculated by discounting the total vested pension amount for the discount period mentioned in column (6) using a discount rate of 10%.

Based on this information, the pension expense is calculated as follows:

Year	Vested During the Year	PV Factor	PV of Total Vested Pension	Change in the PV	Service Cost	Interest Cost
1998	$12,500	0.68301	$8,538	$8,538	$8,538	-
1999	15,000	0.75131	20,661	12,123	11,270	854
2000	17,500	0.82645	37,190	16,529	14,463	2,066
2001	20,000	0.90909	59,091	21,901	18,182	3,719
2002	-	1.00000	65,000	5,909	-	5,909
				$65,000	$52,452	$12,548

Conceptually, the annual pension expense for an unfunded plan is the change in the present value of the total vested pension benefit. The service cost is calculated by multiplying the amount vested during the year by the appropriate present value factor. The interest cost for a given year is calculated by multiplying the present value of the total vested pension benefit at the end of the previous year by the discount rate. Subject to rounding error, the sum of the service cost and the interest cost equals the change in the present value of the total vested pension benefits.

1998	DR	Pension expense	$8,538	
	CR	Pension liability		$8,538

1999	DR	Pension expense	$12,123	
	CR	Pension liability		$12,123

2000	DR	Pension expense	$16,529	
	CR	Pension liability		$16,529

2001	DR	Pension expense	$21,901	
	CR	Pension liability		$21,901

2002	DR	Pension expense	$5,909	
	CR	Pension liability		$5,909

	DR	Pension liability	$65,000	
	CR	Cash		$65,000

Requirement 2:

In this case, the pension expense will exactly equal the service cost:

Year	Service Cost	Interest Cost	Return on Plan Assets	Pension Expense
1998	$8,538	-	-	$8,538
1999	11,270	854	(854)	11,270
2000	14,463	2,066	(2,066)	14,463
2001	18,182	3,719	(3,719)	18,182
2002	-	5,909	(5,909)	-
Total	$52,452	$12,548	$(12,548)	$52,452

1998	DR	Pension expense	$8,538	
	CR	Cash		$8,538

1999	DR	Pension expense	$11,270	
	CR	Cash		$11,270

2000	DR	Pension expense	$14,463	
	CR	Cash		$14,463

2001	DR	Pension expense	$18,182	
	CR	Cash		$18,182

2002	DR	Pension expense	-	
	CR	Cash		-

Requirement 3:

Under the unfunded scenario, the pension expense is the sum of the service cost and interest cost, which equals $65,000 over the period 1998–2002. In the fully funded case, the pension expense equals only the service cost of $52,452. Note that in the fully funded case, the company is relinquishing the use of cash every period equal to the service cost. How much money could the company earn by investing the service cost in an investment that offers an annual rate of return of 10%?

Year	Annual Contributions	Investment Period	FV Factor	Future Value	Income Earned
1998	$8,538	4	1.46410	$12,500	$3,962
1999	11,270	3	1.33100	15,000	3,730
2000	14,463	2	1.21000	17,500	3,037
2001	18,182	1	1.10000	20,000	1,818
2002	-	0	1.00000	-	-
Total	$52,452			$65,000	$12,548

Consequently, in the unfunded case, if the company had invested the service cost, then it would have earned $12,548 over the period 1998-2002 assuming a rate of return of 10%. Therefore, under the unfunded option, the company's income will be higher because of the opportunity cost of being able to invest the cash saved from not funding the pension plan. This will be compensated by the higher pension expense.

Pension expense in the unfunded case	$65,000
- Income forgone by funding	(12,548)
Pension expense in the fully funded case	$52,452

Requirement 4:

	Discount Rate = 5%			Discount Rate = 10%			Discount Rate = 15%		
Year	Service Cost	Interest Cost	Total Expense	Service Cost	Interest Cost	Total Expense	Service Cost	Interest Cost	Total Expense
1998	$10,284	-	$10,284	$8,538	-	$8,538	$7,147	-	$7,147
1999	12,958	$514	13,472	11,270	$854	12,123	9,863	$1,072	10,935
2000	15,873	1,188	17,061	14,463	2,066	16,529	13,233	2,712	15,945
2001	19,047	2,041	21,088	18,182	3,719	21,901	17,391	5,104	22,495
2002	-	3,095	3,095	-	5,909	5,909	-	8,478	8,478
	$58,162	$6,838	$65,000	$52,452	$12,548	$65,000	$47,633	$17,367	$65,000

The following observations emerge from this comparison:

(1) Over the life of a company, the total pension expense is the same regardless of the assumed discount rate.

(2) However, the service cost is lower when the discount rate is higher, whereas the interest cost increases with the discount rate.

(3) Since interest cost represents the time value of money, more of the interest cost is recorded in later years when the discount rate is higher. This would result in a larger pension expense being recorded earlier when discount rates are lower.

P13-5. Determining effect of discount rate assumptions on pension expense and PBO

Note to the instructor: In order to minimize the effects of rounding errors, the solutions show all figures in dollars and cents.

First, let us focus on the case when the discount rate equals the rate of return on plan assets - 10%:

Requirement 1: Annual pension expense

Assumptions: Discount rate = 10% and Rate of return on plan assets = 10%

End of Year 1	Annual Salary 2	Cumulative Salary 3	Total Vested Pension 4	Vested During the Year 5	Discount Period 6	PV Factor 7	PV of Total Vested Pension 8
1998	$50,000	$50,000	$12,500	$12,500	4	0.68301	$8,537.63
1999	60,000	110,000	27,500	15,000	3	0.75131	20,661.03
2000	70,000	180,000	45,000	17,500	2	0.82645	37,190.25
2001	80,000	260,000	65,000	20,000	1	0.90909	59,090.85
2002	-	260,000	65,000	-	0	1.00000	65,000.00

Note that the PV of total vested pension represents the projected benefit obligation.

The following table summarizes the activities in the pension fund.

Pension Fund Investments and Earnings

	1998	1999	2000	2001	2002	Future Value
Contributions	$8,475.00	$847.50	$932.25	$1,025.48	$1,128.02	$12,408.25
Contributions		11,000.00	1,100.00	1,210.00	1,331.00	14,641.00
Contributions			15,000.00	1,500.00	1,650.00	18,150.00
Contributions				18,000.00	1,800.00	19,800.00
Year-end balance	$8,475.00	$20,322.50	$37,354.75	$59,090.23	$64,999.25	$64,999.25
Income earned	-	$847.50	$2,032.25	$3,735.48	$5,909.02	

The highlighted diagonal figures represent the inflow of cash from Magee Corp. The figures to the right of these numbers represent the future return earned by the pension fund from investing these cash flows at 10% per annum. Due to the compounding effect, the income from investment keeps increasing over time (as we move to the right). For instance, $8,475 in 1998 earns $847.50 (i.e., 10% of $8,475) during 1999, $932.25 [10% of ($8,475.00 + $847.50)] in 2000, and so on. The future value indicates the value to which each year's cash inflow will grow by investing at 10% through the end of 2002. Except for rounding errors, note that the future value of each year's cash inflow corresponds to the pension vested during the same year shown in the previous table.

The row titled "Year-end balance" provides the fair value of the plan assets at the end of each of the years. Of course, at the end of year 2002, the investments will be liquidated and the cash will be disbursed to the employee. The last row indicates the annual return on plan assets.

Based on the above information, we now calculate the pension expense as follows:

Year	Service Cost	Interest Cost	Return on Plan Assets	Pension Expense
1998	$8,537.67	-	-	$8,537.67
1999	11,269.72	$853.77	($847.50)	11,275.99
2000	14,462.81	2,066.12	(2,032.25)	14,496.68
2001	18,181.82	3,719.01	(3,735.48)	18,165.35
2002		5,909.09	(5,909.02)	0.07
				$52,475.75

Note: The figures for pension contributions were chosen such that the pension expense will approximate the service cost when the discount rate equals the rate of return on pension assets. Consequently, the balance in the pension fund at the end of the year 2002 ($64,999.25) approximates the pension liability of $65,000.

The funding status of the pension plan is provided below:

Requirement 2: Funded status under 10% discount rate

End of Year	1998	1999	2000	2001
Projected benefit obligation	$8,537.67	$20,661.16	$37,190.08	$59,090.91
- Fair value of plan assets	(8,475.00)	(20,322.50)	(37,354.75)	(59,090.23)
Net pension liability (asset)	$62.67	$338.66	($164.67)	$0.68

The balance in net pension liability (asset) can verified by preparing the T-account:

Pension Liability (Asset) at Year-End	1998	1999	2000	2001	2002
Beginning balance	-	$62.67	$338.66	($164.67)	$0.68
Pension expense	8,537.67	11,275.99	14,496.68	18,165.35	0.07
Cash received (paid)	(8,475.00)	(11,000.00)	(15,000.00)	(18,000.00)	(0.75)
Ending balance	$62.67	$338.66	($164.67)	$0.68	($0.00)

The tables are now reported under the other two scenarios regarding the discount rates.

Requirement 1: Annual pension expense

Assumptions: Discount rate = 8% and rate of return on plan assets = 10%

End of Year 1	Annual Salary 2	Cumulative Salary 3	Total Vested Pension 4	Vested During the Year 5	Discount Period 6	PV Factor 7	PV of Total Vested Pension 8
1998	$50,000	$50,000	$12,500	$12,500	4	0.73503	$9,187.87
1999	60,000	110,000	27,500	15,000	3	0.79383	21,830.39
2000	70,000	180,000	45,000	17,500	2	0.85734	38,580.25
2001	80,000	260,000	65,000	20,000	1	0.92593	60,185.19
2002	-	260,000	65,000	-	0	1.00000	65,000.00

Note that the pension fund investments and earnings will be identical under all the three scenarios. This is because the cash contributions to the pension fund and the rate of return earned by the pension fund are assumed to be the same regardless of the discount rate assumption. Consequently, the table showing the pension fund investments and earnings is not reported again.

Year	Service Cost	Interest Cost	Return on Plan Assets	Pension Expense
1998	$9,187.87	-	-	$9,187.87
1999	11,907.48	$735.03	($847.50)	11,795.01
2000	15,003.43	1,746.43	(2,032.25)	14,717.61
2001	18,518.52	3,086.42	(3,735.48)	17,869.46
2002		4,814.81	(5,909.02)	(1,094.21)
				$52,475.75

Requirement 2: Funded status under 8% discount rate

End of Year	1998	1999	2000	2001
Projected benefit obligation	$9,187.87	$21,830.39	$38,580.25	$60,185.19
- Fair value of plan assets	(8,475.00)	(20,322.50)	(37,354.75)	(59,090.23)
Net pension liability (asset)	$712.87	$1,507.89	$1,225.50	$1,094.96

Pension Liability (Asset) at Year-End	1998	1999	2000	2001	2002
Beginning balance	-	$712.87	$1,507.89	$1,225.50	$1,094.96
Pension expense	$9,187.87	11,795.01	14,717.61	17,869.46	(1,094.21)
Cash received (paid)	(8,475.00)	(11,000.00)	(15,000.00)	(18,000.00)	(0.75)
Ending balance	$712.87	$1,507.89	$1,225.50	$1,094.96	($0.00)

Requirement 1: Annual pension expense

Assumptions: Discount rate = 12% and rate of return on plan assets = 10%

End of Year 1	Annual Salary 2	Cumulative Salary 3	Total Vested Pension 4	Vested During the Year 5	Discount Period 6	PV Factor 7	PV of Total Vested Pension 8
1998	$50,000	$50,000	$12,500	$12,500	4	0.63552	$7,943.98
1999	60,000	110,000	27,500	15,000	3	0.71178	19,573.96
2000	70,000	180,000	45,000	17,500	2	0.79719	35,873.72
2001	80,000	260,000	65,000	20,000	1	0.89286	58,035.71
2002	-	260,000	65,000	-	0	1.00000	65,000.00

Year	Service Cost	Interest Cost	Return on Plan Assets	Pension Expense
1998	$7,943.98	-	-	$7,943.98
1999	10,676.70	$953.28	($847.50)	10,782.48
2000	13,950.89	2,348.87	(2,032.25)	14,267.52
2001	17,857.14	4,304.85	(3,735.48)	18,426.51
2002		6,964.29	(5,909.02)	1,055.26
				$52,475.75

Requirement 2: Funded status under 12% discount assumption

End of year	1998	1999	2000	2001
Projected benefit obligation	$7,943.98	$19,573.96	$35,873.72	$58,035.71
- Fair value of plan assets	(8,475.00)	(20,322.50)	(37,354.75)	(59,090.23)
Net pension liability (asset)	($531.02)	($748.54)	($1,481.03)	($1,054.51)

Pension Liability (Asset) at Year-End	1998	1999	2000	2001	2002
Beginning balance	-	($531.02)	($748.54)	($1,481.03)	($1,054.51)
Pension expense	$7,943.98	10,782.48	14,267.52	18,426.51	1,055.26
Cash received (paid)	(8,475.00)	(11,000.00)	(15,000.00)	(18,000.00)	(0.75)
Ending balance	($531.02)	($748.54)	($1,481.03)	($1,054.51)	($0.00)

Requirement 3:

The most (least) conservative approach for the purposes of income determination is when the discount rate is less (more) than the rate of return on the plan assets. Let us compare the pension under the three scenarios:

Pension Expense under Various Discount Rate Assumptions

Year	8%	10%	12%
1998	$9,187.87	$8,537.67	$7,943.98
1999	11,795.01	11,275.99	10,782.48
2000	14,717.61	14,496.68	14,267.52
2001	17,869.46	18,165.35	18,426.51
2002	(1,094.21)	0.07	1,055.26
	$52,475.75	$52,475.75	$52,475.75

In the first three years, the pension expense is the highest (lowest) when the discount rate is 8% (12%). However, in the last two years, the situation reverses. However, remarkably, the total expense over the 5-year period is the same regardless of the discount rate assumption. This is because the total expense is determined by only two things: (a) the rate of return earned by the pension plan assets and (b) the actual pension payments to be the employee.

591

(To illustrate this point, we have assumed that the contributions to the pension fund are unaffected by the discount rate assumption used for financial reporting purposes.) For instance, if the pension was completely unfunded, then the total pension expense will equal $65,000, the cash to be paid to the employee on retirement. If the pension is funded, then the total pension expense will equal the amount of periodic contributions sufficient to generate $65,000 at the end of year 2002. Of course, the sufficiency of the periodic contributions will be determined by the rate of return by the pension fund. The higher (lower) the rate of return, the smaller (greater) will be the periodic contributions. Since the periodic contributions and the rate of return on pension plan assets are fixed in the problem, the choice of the discount rate cannot affect the total pension expense. To see this, let us examine the total contributions to the pension fund:

	1998	1999	2000	2001	2002	Total
Contributions	$8,475.00	$11,000.00	$15,000.00	$18,000.00	$0.75	$52,475.75

The $0.75 during 2002 represents the shortfall in the pension fund at the end of 2002. Note that the total contributions to the pension fund equal the total pension expense regardless of the chosen discount rate. If the rate of return had been different, then the final shortfall would have been different, resulting in a different total expense for pensions.

However, one important point is that although the choice of the discount rate does not affect the total pension expense, It can lead to different allocations of the pension costs to different fiscal years. As discussed earlier, lower (higher) discount rates lead to more (less) conservative income figures.

P13-6. Components of pension liability and pension expense

Requirement 1:

Projected Benefit Obligation

	1999	2000	2001	2002
Beginning balance	$1,000,000	$1,200,000	$1,410,000	$1,631,000
+ Interest cost	100,000	120,000	141,000	163,100
+ Service cost	300,000	350,000	400,000	450,000
- Pension payments	(200,000)	(260,000)	(320,000)	(380,000)
Ending balance	$1,200,000	$1,410,000	$1,631,000	$1,864,100

Fair Value of Plan Assets

	1999	2000	2001	2002
Beginning balance	$1,000,000	$1,240,000	$1,488,000	$1,646,560
+ Actual return on plan assets	220,000	248,000	178,560	164,656
+ Contributions to pension fund	220,000	260,000	300,000	340,000
- Pension payments	(200,000)	(260,000)	(320,000)	(380,000)
Ending balance	$1,240,000	$1,488,000	$1,646,560	$1,771,216

In order to examine the changes in unrecognized gain, we have to calculate the net deferral and amortization over the period 1999–2002.

	1999	2000	2001	2002
Actual return on plan assets	$220,000	$248,000	$178,560	$164,656
- Expected return	(120,000)	(148,800)	(178,560)	(197,587)
Deferral of unrecognized gain/(loss)	$100,000	$99,200	$ -	($32,931)
Cumulative deferral (see calculation below)	$100,000	$199,200	$194,160	$158,279
Higher of PBO or fair value of plan assets	1,240,000	1,488,000	1,646,560	1,864,100
Cumulative deferral as a %	8.06%	13.39%	11.79%	8.49%
Cumulative deferral (see calculation below)	100,000	199,200	194,160	158,279
- 10% of the higher of PBO or fair value of plan assets	(124,000)	(148,800)	(164,656)	(186,410)
Deferral in excess of the threshold	-	50,400	29,504	-
Average remaining service period	10	10	10	10
Amortization of the deferred gain in the following year	-	5,040	2,950	-

Note that the deferral in excess of the threshold at the end of year 2000 (2001) is being amortized during 2001 (2002). At the end of 1999, the deferral amount is less than 10% of the higher of PBO and fair value of plan assets.

The balance in cumulative deferral is reconciled as follows:

Unrecognized Gain

	1999	2000	2001	2002
Beginning balance	-	$100,000	$199,200	$194,160
+ Excess of actual over expected return	$100,000	99,200	-	(32,931)
- Amortization of the deferral	-	-	(5,040)	(2,950)
Ending balance	$100,000	$199,200	$194,160	$158,279

Requirement 2:
The funded status of the plan is provided below:

End of Year	1999	2000	2001	2002
Projected benefit obligation	($1,200,000)	($1,410,000)	($1,631,000)	($1,864,100)
Fair value of plan assets	1,240,000	1,488,000	1,646,560	1,771,216
Fair value in excess of PBO	40,000	78,000	15,560	(92,884)
Unrecognized gain	(100,000)	(199,200)	(194,160)	(158,279)
Accrued pension liability	($60,000)	($121,200)	($178,600)	($251,163)

Requirement 3:

	1999	2000	2001	2002
Interest cost	$100,000	$120,000	$141,000	$163,100
Service cost	300,000	350,000	400,000	450,000
- Actual return on plan assets	(220,000)	(248,000)	(178,560)	(164,656)
+ Deferral of unexpected return	100,000	99,200	-	(32,931)
- Amortization of deferral	-	-	(5,040)	(2,950)
Pension expense	$280,000	$321,200	$357,400	$412,563

Requirement 4:

1999	**DR** Pension expense		$280,000	
	CR Accrued pension liability			$280,000
	DR Accrued pension liability		$220,000	
	CR Cash			$220,000
2000	**DR** Pension expense		$321,200	
	CR Accrued pension liability			$321,200
	DR Accrued pension liability		$260,000	
	CR Cash			$260,000
2001	**DR** Pension expense		$357,400	
	CR Accrued pension liability			$357,400
	DR Accrued pension liability		$300,000	
	CR Cash			$300,000

2002	**DR** Pension expense	$412,562	
	CR Accrued pension liability		$412,562
	DR Accrued pension liability	$340,000	
	CR Cash		$340,000

Accrued Pension Liability

	1999	2000	2001	2002
Beginning balance	-	$60,000	$121,200	$178,600
+ Pension expense	$280,000	321,200	357,400	412,562
- Contributions to pension fund	(220,000)	(260,000)	(300,000)	(340,000)
Ending balance	$60,000	$121,200	$178,600	$251,162

Note that the ending balances in the accrued pension liability are the same as those reported under the pension funding status reconciliations.

P13-7. Effect of actual vs. expected return on pension funding status and pension expense

Requirement 1:

Stable Economy

		Market Value of the Pension Assets		
End of year	**1998**	**1999**	**2000**	**2001**
Rate of return		10.00%	10.00%	10.00%
Plan assets	$100,000	$110,000	$121,000	$133,100
Income earned during the year		$10,000	$11,000	$12,100

Growth

		Market Value of the Pension Assets		
End of year	**1998**	**1999**	**2000**	**2001**
Rate of return		5.00%	10.00%	15.24%
Plan assets	$100,000	$105,000	$115,500	$133,102
Income earned during the year		$5,000	$10,500	$17,602

Decline

		Market Value of the Pension Assets		
End of year	**1998**	**1999**	**2000**	**2001**
Rate of return		15.00%	10.00%	5.22%
Plan assets	$100,000	$115,000	$126,500	$133,103
Income earned during the year		$15,000	$11,500	$6,603

Income earned for a year is calculated by multiplying the market value of plan assets at the end of the previous year by the rate of return of the current year. The year-end market value of plan assets is the sum of the market value of the plan assets at the end of the previous year plus the income earned during the year.

Regardless of the assumed state of the economy, the pension fund will have assets worth approximately $133,100 at the end of year 2001. This implies that the pension funds must have earned the same annualized rates of return over the 3-year period under all states of the economy. However, in a given year, the realized rate of return in one scenario may be different from those for the other scenarios. However, on average, the rates of return are the same, or, in other words, we expect the pension fund to earn a fixed annualized rate of return in the long run.

Requirement 2:

Stable Economy	1999	2000	2001	Total
Interest cost	$10,000	$11,000	$12,100	$33,100
- Return on plan assets	(10,000)	(11,000)	(12,100)	(33,100)
Pension expense	$ -	$ -	$ -	$ -

Note that there is no service cost since the company has canceled the pension plan as of December 31, 1998. Consequently, only interest cost and return on plan assets are relevant in this problem.

Under this scenario, the market value of the pension plan assets and the projected benefit obligation are identical at every point in time. This is because the realized rates of return (which determines the value of plan assets) equal the expected rates of return (which determines the PBO and the interest cost) in every period. In the other two scenarios, while the expected rate of return continues to be the same, the realized returns vary from year to year. Consequently, while the interest cost will be the same in all three scenarios, the return on plan assets will differ from year to year.

Growing Economy	1999	2000	2001	Total
Interest cost	$10,000	$11,000	$12,100	$33,100
- Return on plan assets	(5,000)	(10,500)	(17,602)	(33,102)
Pension expense	$5,000	$500	$(5,502)	$(2)

Declining Economy	1999	2000	2001	Total
Interest cost	$10,000	$11,000	$12,100	$33,100
- Return on plan assets	(15,000)	(11,500)	(6,603)	(33,103)
Pension expense	$(5,000)	$(500)	$5,497	$(3)

The total pension expense over the period 1999–2001 is the same figure regardless of the realized rates of return. This is because, as discussed in answer to Requirement 1, the annualized rates of return are the same under the three scenarios even though they differ from year to year. Consequently, depending on whether the realized return in a given year is greater or less than the expected return, the pension expense will be lower or higher.

Note: We will ignore the small difference between realized rates of return and the expected rate of return in the declining and growing economy scenarios. This is due to the fact that realized rates of return are rounded off to two decimal points, resulting in a small credit to the total pension expense (2 or 3 dollars). To simplify discussions, we will assume that the total expense is zero in all three scenarios.

Requirement 3:
Since there is no net amortization or deferral under the "Stable Economy" scenario, the calculations for pension expense are similar to those reported in Requirement 2.

Stable Economy	1999	2000	2001	Total
Interest cost	$10,000	$11,000	$12,100	$33,100
- Return on plan assets	(10,000)	(11,000)	(12,100)	(33,100)
Pension expense	$ -	$ -	$ -	$ -

The funded status of the pension plan is:

Stable Economy	1999	2000	2001
Projected benefit obligation	($110,000)	($121,000)	($133,100)
Fair value of plan assets	110,000	121,000	133,100
Accrued pension liability	$ -	$ -	$ -

However, under the other two scenarios, there will be net deferral of unrecognized gains or losses, and consequently, the calculations for pension expense will differ from those in Requirement 2.

Declining Economy	1999	2000	2001	Total
Interest cost	$10,000	$11,000	$12,100	$33,100
- Return on plan assets	(15,000)	(11,500)	(6,603)	(33,103)
Net amortization and deferral	5,000	500	(5,497)	3
Pension expense	$ -	$ -	$ -	$ -

Declining Economy	1999	2000	2001
Projected benefit obligation	($110,000)	($121,000)	($133,100)
Fair value of plan assets	115,000	126,500	133,103
Plan assets (-) PBO	5,000	5,500	3
Unrecognized gain	(5,000)	(5,500)	(3)
Accrued pension liability	$ -	$ -	$ -
Higher of PBO or fair value	$115,000	$126,500	$133,103
Unrecognized gain as a %	4.35%	4.35%	0.00%

Growing Economy	1999	2000	2001	Total
Interest cost	$10,000	$11,000	$12,100	$33,100
- Return on plan assets	(5,000)	(10,500)	(17,602)	(33,102)
Net amortization and deferral	(5,000)	(500)	5,502	2
Pension expense	$ -	$ -	$ -	$ -

Growing Economy	1999	2000	2001
Projected benefit obligation	($110,000)	($121,000)	($133,100)
Fair value of plan assets	105,000	115,500	133,102
Plan assets (-) PBO	(5,000)	5,500)	2
Unrecognized loss	5,000	5,500	(2)
Accrued pension liability	$ -	$ -	$ -
Higher of PBO or fair value	110,000	121,000	133,102
Unrecognized gain as a %	4.55%	4.55%	0.00%

Note: There is no need for amortizing the unrecognized gain or loss since it is well within the 10% threshold.

Requirement 4:
The answer to Requirement 2 shows that when net deferral and amortization of unrecognized loss or gain is ignored then pension expense may be highly volatile depending on the deviation of the realized rate of return and the expected rate of return in a given year. It is reasonable to argue that these deviations are typically beyond the control of either the pension fund manager or the management of the company that is offering the pension plan. Consequently, as long as the company has a sound estimate for the expected rate of return of the plan assets, ignoring the year-to-year difference between expected and realized rates of return provides meaningful estimates for the "true" pension cost. Even from a financial analyst's standpoint, the smoothing effects of net amortization and deferral are likely to improve his or her ability to forecast the future earnings.

P13-8. Components of OPEB and journal entries

Requirement 1:
```
DR  Cumulative effect of accounting change    $102,501
DR  Deferred tax asset                          52,804
    CR  Accumulated OPEB obligation                        $155,305
```

OPEB = Other Postretirement Employee Benefits (to distinguish from pensions)

Note: Alternatively, PNC Bank could have amortized the transition obligation on a straight-line basis over the *longer* of (a) the average remaining service period of active plan participants, or (b) 20 years.

Requirement 2:
```
DR  OPEB expense                              $18,923
    CR  Accumulated OPEB obligation                         $18,923
```

The components of the expense are (a) service cost of $5,483 and (b) interest cost of $13,440.

```
DR  Accumulated OPEB obligation               $5,528
    CR  Cash                                                 $5,528
```

Note: In manufacturing companies, a portion of the OPEB expense is likely to be added to work-in-process rather than immediately expensed. In that case, the journal entry is likely to be:

```
DR  Work-in-process                            XXX
DR  OPEB expense                                           XXX
    CR  Accumulated OPEB obligation                         XXX
```

Requirement 3:
```
DR  OPEB expense                              $5,528
    CR  Cash                                                 $5,528
```

Note: PNC Bank's OPEB expense is higher by more than 240% under SFAS 106.

Requirement 4:
All three components determine the interest cost. However, only the active employees and other active plan participants (to the extent it includes the dependents of active employees) influence the service cost.

P13-9. Amortization of actuarial gains (losses) and minimum pension liability

Requirement 1:

		Beginning of the Year					For the Year		End of the Year
Year (1)	Projected Benefit Obligation (2)	Fair Value of Pension Plan Assets (3)	Higher of (2) or (3) (4)	Corridor 10% of (4) (5)	Cumulative Unrecognized Gain (Loss) (6)	Excess of (6) over (5) (7)	Amortized Gain (loss) (8)	Excess Gain (loss) (9)	Cumulative Unrecognized Gain (Loss) (6) - (8) + (9)
2000	$450,000	$410,000	$450,000	$45,000	($70,000)	($25,000)	($5,000)	($60,000)	($125,000)
2001	570,000	500,000	570,000	57,000	(125,000)	(68,000)	(13,600)	(120,000)	(231,400)
2002	840,000	800,000	840,000	84,000	(231,400)	(147,400)	(29,480)	120,000	(81,920)
2003	1,000,000	1,100,000	1,100,000	110,000	(81,920)	-	-	175,000	93,080
2004	1,200,000	1,280,000	1,280,000	128,000	93,080	-	-	250,000	343,080
2005	1,450,000	1,310,000	1,450,000	145,000	343,080	198,080	39,616	80,000	383,464

Note that column (5) is unsigned in the sense that the magnitude of the cumulative unrecognized gain or loss should exceed the corridor before the amortization begins. Consequently, in calculating the excess of (6) over (5) [i.e., column (7)], column (5) is subtracted from column (6) when column (6) is positive. In contrast, column (5) is added to column (6) when column (6) is negative.

Column (8) shows how much of the cumulative unrecognized gain (loss) is amortized during a given year. amortization of gains decrease pension expense (year 2004), whereas amortization of losses increase pension expense (years 2000–2002).

Requirement 2:

End of Year	1999	2000	2001	2002	2003	2004
Projected benefit obligation	($450,000)	($570,000)	($840,000)	($1,000,000)	($1,200,000)	($1,450,000)
Fair value of plan assets	410,000	500,000	800,000	1,100,000	1,280,000	1,310,000
Excess of fair value over PBO	(40,000)	(70,000)	(40,000)	100,000	80,000	(140,000)
Unrecognized loss (gain)	70,000	125,000	231,400	81,920	(93,080)	(343,080)
Accrued pension asset (liability)	$30,000	$55,000	$191,400	$181,920	($13,080)	($483,080)

Requirement 3:

	Beginning of the year values			
Year **(1)**	**Projected Benefit Obligation (2)**	**Fair Value of Pension Plan Assets (3)**	**Accumulated Benefit Obligation (5)**	**Minimum Pension Liability (6)**
1999	$400,000	$390,000	$380,000	-
2000	450,000	410,000	427,500	$17,500
2001	570,000	500,000	541,500	41,500
2002	840,000	800,000	798,000	-
2003	1,000,000	1,100,000	950,000	-
2004	1,200,000	1,280,000	1,140,000	-
2005	1,450,000	1,310,000	1,377,500	67,500

First, we calculate the ABOs as 95% of the PBOs. The minimum pension liability is the excess of the ABO over the fair value of the pension assets.

End of Year

	1999	2000	2001	2002	2003	2004
Projected benefit obligation	($450,000)	($570,000)	($840,000)	($1,000,000)	($1,200,000)	($1,450,000)
Fair value of plan assets	410,000	500,000	800,000	1,100,000	1,280,000	1,310,000
Excess of fair value over PBO	(40,000)	(70,000)	(40,000)	100,000	80,000	(140,000)
Unrecognized loss (gain)	70,000	125,000	231,400	81,920	(93,080)	(343,080)
Adjustment to recognize minimum liability	(47,500)	(96,500)	-	-	-	-
Accrued pension asset (liability)	($17,500)	($41,500)	$191,400	$181,920	($13,080)	($483,080)

Note that the schedule for the funded status is based on end of year values. (The beginning of year values for 2000 in the previous table are the end of the year values for 1999 in the current table.)

The adjustment for minimum liability is required only during the first two years. The last year liability is already more than the minimum pension liability.

601

| 1999 | **DR** Intangible asset | $47,500 | |
| | **CR** Accrued pension liability | | $47,500 |

| 2000 | **DR** Intangible asset | $49,000 | |
| | **CR** Accrued pension liability | | $49,000 |

| 2001 | **DR** Accrued pension liability | $96,500 | |
| | **CR** Intangible asset | | $96,500 |

P13-10. Pension expense and funded status

Requirement 1:

For the Years Ended	1999	2000
Service cost	$125,000	$145,000
Interest cost	90,000	110,500
- Actual return on plan assets	(100,000)	(64,740)
+/- Deferral of unrecognized gain/loss	10,000	(53,950)
+ Amortization of prior service cost	-	11,000
Annual pension expense	$125,000	$147,810

Schedules showing the activities in the components that comprise the funded status are provided below:

Projected Benefit Obligation	1999	2000
Beginning of the year	$900,000	$1,105,000
Service cost	125,000	145,000
Interest cost	90,000	110,500
+ Prior service cost from plan enhancements	110,000	-
- Pension payments	(120,000)	(85,000)
End of the year	$1,105,000	$1,275,500

Fair Value of Plan Assets	1999	2000
Beginning of the year	$1,000,000	$1,079,000
Actual rate of return	100,000	64,740
+ Contributions to pension fund	99,000	123,000
- Pension payments	(120,000)	(85,000)
End of the year	$1,079,000	$1,181,740

Unrecognized Prior Service Cost	1999	2000
Beginning of the year	-	$110,000
+ Prior service cost from plan enhancements	$110,000	
- Amortization during the year	-	(11,000)
End of the year	$110,000	$ 99,000

Unrecognized Gain (Loss)

	1999	2000
Beginning of the year	-	$10,000
+ Actual returns in excess of expected returns	$10,000	(53,950)
End of the year	$10,000	($43,950)

Since the unrecognized gain at the end of 1999 is well within the corridor, it is not amortized during the year 2000.

Based on the above schedules, the funded status reconciliation is provided below:

As of 12/31	1998	1999	2000
Projected benefit obligation	($900,000)	($1,105,000)	($1,275,500)
(-) Fair value of plan assets	1,000,000	1,079,000	1,181,740
Fair value in excess of PBO	100,000	(26,000)	(93,760)
Unrecognized prior service cost		110,000	99,000
Unrecognized (gain) loss		(10,000)	43,950
Accrued pension asset (liability)	$100,000	$74,000	$49,190

Requirement 2:

1999	**DR** Pension expense	$125,000	
	CR Accrued pension asset		$125,000
	DR Accrued pension asset	$99,000	
	CR Cash		$99,000
2000	**DR** Pension expense	$147,810	
	CR Accrued pension asset		$147,810
	DR Accrued pension asset	$123,000	
	CR Cash		$123,000

Since the company is in the consulting business, it is assumed that all of the pension cost is expensed as a period cost.

Accrued Pension Asset

	1999	2000
Beginning of the year	$100,000	$74,000
- Pension expense for the year	(125,000)	(147,810)
+ Contributions to pension plan	99,000	123,000
End of the year	$74,000	$49,190

Requirement 3:

Recall the funded status reconciliation provided earlier:

As of 12/31	1998	1999	2000
Projected benefit obligation	($900,000)	($1,105,000)	($1,275,500)
- Fair value of plan assets	1,000,000	1,079,000	1,181,740
Fair value in excess of PBO	100,000	(26,000)	(93,760)
Unrecognized prior service cost		110,000	99,000
Unrecognized (gain) loss		(10,000)	43,950
Accrued pension asset (liability)	$100,000	$74,000	$49,190

At the end of 1998, the fair value of the pension plan assets is more than the projected benefit obligations. The situation reverses at the end of 1999 due to the retroactive enhancement of benefits. Thus, while the pension is over-funded at the end of 1998, it is slightly underfunded at the end of 1999 and 2000. However, for financial reporting purposes, the company continues to show accrued pension asset (i.e., "overfunded" plan).

The main item causing the difference between the two is from the unrecognized prior service costs. By retroactively enhancing the benefits, the economic balance sheet of the pension fund deteriorated immediately (i.e., fair value is less than the PBO). However, this economic obligation will be gradually recognized in the financial reporting balance sheet over a 10-year period by amortizing the enhanced benefits as part of the pension expense. consequently, until all of the enhanced benefits are reflected in the accrued pension liability, one might consider the difference between the economic obligation and the accrued pension asset as an off-balance-sheet liability.

P13-11. Solving for pension cost and funded status components

Requirement 1:

For the Years Ended	1999	2000
Service cost	$110,000	$130,000
Interest cost	44,000	54,720
- Actual return on plan assets	(55,000)	(71,400)
+/- Deferral of unrecognized gain/loss	-	11,900
+ Amortization of prior service cost	-	16,000
Annual pension cost	$ 99,000	$141,220

Calculations for 1999: Interest cost = $550,000 × 0.08; actual return on plan assets = $550,000 × 0.10. Since the actual return was equal to the expected return, there is no deferral during 1999.

Calculations for 2000: Interest cost = $684,000 × 0.08; actual return on plan assets = $595,000 × 0.12. Since the actual return was greater than the expected return by $11,900 [$71,400 - ($595,000 × 0.10)], the excess return results in an unrecognized gain during the year 2000 (which increases the pension cost).

Using the information on annual pension cost, we can break down the total pension cost between manufacturing and administrative employees:

Breakdown of the Annual Pension Cost	1999	2000
Manufacturing employees	$63,000	$85,000
Administrative employees (plug number)	36,000	56,220
Annual pension cost (from the above schedule)	$ 99,000	$141,220

Requirement 2:
Before we prepare the schedule for PBO, we have to calculate the change in the PBO from retroactive provision of benefits from plan enhancements. Recall that the answer to Requirement 1 indicates that the amortization of prior service cost was $16,000 during 2000 (the first year of amortization). The problem states that "the average remaining service period of employees expected to receive these retroactive benefits under the plan was 5 years." This must mean that the change in the PBO from plan enhancements was $80,000 (5 × $16,000).

Projected Benefit Obligation	1999	2000
Beginning of the year	$550,000	$684,000
Service cost	110,000	130,000
Interest cost	44,000	54,720
+ Prior service cost from plan enhancements	80,000	-
- Pension payments (plug number)	(100,000)	(100,000)
End of the year	$684,000	$768,720

Except for pension payments made during the years, we have all the other information. Consequently, the payouts from the pension plan to the employees are plug numbers.

Fair Value of Plan Assets	1999	2000
Beginning of the year	$550,000	$595,000
Actual rate of return	55,000	71,400
+ Contributions to pension fund (plug number)	90,000	120,000
- Pension payments (from the PBO schedule)	(100,000)	(100,000)
End of the year	$595,000	$686,400

In preparing the schedule for fair value of plan assets, we use the pension payments information from the PBO schedule with the plug number being the contributions made by the company to the pension plan.

The schedules for unrecognized prior service cost and unrecognized gain are straightforward.

Unrecognized Prior Service Cost	1999	2000
Beginning of the year	-	$80,000
+ Prior service cost from plan enhancements	$80,000	-
- Amortization during the year	-	(16,000)
End of the year	$80,000	$64,000

Unrecognized gain	1999	2000
Beginning of the year		-
+ Actual returns in excess of expected returns		$11,900
End of the year		$11,900

Requirement 3:

1999	**DR**	Work-in-process inventory	$63,000	
	DR	Pension expense	36,000	
		CR Accrued pension liability		$99,000
	DR	Accrued pension liability	$90,000	
		CR Cash		$90,000
2000	**DR**	Work-in-process inventory	$85,000	
	DR	Pension expense	56,220	
		CR Accrued pension liability		$141,220
	DR	Accrued pension liability	$120,000	
		CR Cash		$120,000

The year-end balances for the accrued pension liability can be compared with the schedule on the funded status as a check on our journal entries:

Accrued Pension Liability	1999	2000
Beginning of the year	-	$9,000
+ Pension cost for the year	$99,000	141,220
- Contributions to pension plan	(90,000)	(120,000)
End of the year	$9,000	$30,220

Funded Status Reconciliation

	December 31	
	1999	**2000**
Projected benefit obligation	$684,000	$768,720
Fair value of plan assets	(595,000)	686,400
Net unfunded obligation	89,000	82,320
- Unrecognized prior service costs	(80,000)	(64,000)
+ Unrecognized gain	-	11,900
Accrued pension obligation	$9,000	$ 30,220

P13-12. OPEB expense and journal entries

Requirement 1:

Service cost	$210,000
Interest cost	175,000
Amortization of transition obligation	100,000
OPEB expense	$485,000

Accumulated Benefit Obligation

Beginning of the year	$2,000,000
Service cost	210,000
Interest cost	175,000
- Benefit payments	(245,000)
End of the year	$2,140,000

Unrecognized Transition Obligation

Beginning of the year	$2,000,000
- Amortization during the year	(100,000)
End of the year	$1,900,000

Accumulated benefit obligation	$2,140,000
- Unrecognized transition obligation	(1,900,000)
Accrued OPEB obligation	$240,000

Requirement 2:

DR Accrued OPEB expense	$485,000	
CR Accrued OPEB obligation		$485,000

DR Accrued OPEB obligation	$245,000	
CR Cash		$245,000

Requirement 3:

Service cost	$210,000
Interest cost	175,000
OPEB expense	$385,000

Accumulated Benefit Obligation

Beginning of the year	$2,000,000
Service cost	210,000
Interest cost	175,000
- Benefit payments	(245,000)
End of the year	$2,140,000

Since there is no unrecognized transition obligation, the accumulated benefit obligation will equal the accrued OPEB liability.

DR Cumulative effects of accounting change	$1,300,000	
DR Deferred income taxes	700,000	
CR Accrued OPEB obligation		$2,000,000
DR Accrued OPEB expense	$385,000	
CR Accrued OPEB obligation		$385,000
DR Accrued OPEB Obligation	$245,000	
CR Cash		$245,000

If the transition amount is recognized immediately it appears below continuing operations "below the line" as an accounting change reduction in income. Whereas, if it is amortized as part of pension expense, it appears in continuing operations "above the line" and reduces income from operations $100,000 every year for the next twenty years. Thus, a number of firms that had a large enough retained earning balance to absorb the equity hit voluntarily chose to take the "big bath" when they initially adopted SFAS 106. For example, Deere and Company reduced net income by roughly one billion dollars, instantaneously eliminated approximately one billion of the two billion dollar retained earnings balance, and put one billion dollars of OPEB liabilities on their balance sheet in fiscal year 1993 when it adopted SFAS 106.

P13-13. Reconciling components of OPEB liability and journal entries

Requirement 1:

Accumulated Benefit Obligation

Beginning of the year	$17,028,000
Service cost	330,000
Interest cost	1,362,000
Unrecognized gains during the year (see below)	(122,000)
Benefit payments (plug number)	(975,000)
End of the year	$17,623,000

Unrecognized Net Gain

Beginning of the year	$3,494,000
Amortization of unrecognized gain	(119,000)
Additional unrecognized gains during the year (plug)	122,000
End of the year	$3,497,000

Unrecognized Transition Obligation

Beginning of the year	$15,272,000
Amortization of transition obligation	(898,000)
End of the year	$14,374,000

Since the OPEB plan is unfunded, the additional unrecognized gains during the year must be from the revaluation of the ABO from changes in assumptions. Consequently, $122,000 is subtracted from the ABO.

Requirement 2:

DR OPEB expense	$2,471,000	
CR Accrued OPEB liability		$2,471,000

DR Accrued OPEB liability	$975,000	
CR Cash		$975,000

If manufacturing employees were also eligible for OPEB, then a portion of $2,471,000 would have been debited to work-in-process.

Accrued OPEB Liability

Beginning of the year	$5,250,000
+ OPEB expense for the year	2,471,000
- Benefit payments	(975,000)
	$6,746,000

Requirement 3:
The expense would be the cash outflow of $975,000.

P13-14. Reconciling components of OPEB liability and journal entries

Requirement 1:

Accumulated Benefit Obligation

Beginning of the year	$1,161,346
Service cost	43,248
Interest cost	92,908
Unrecognized loss during the year (see below)	84,820
Benefit payments (plug number)	(63,022)
End of the year	$1,319,300

Unrecognized Net Loss

Beginning of the year	-
Unrecognized loss during the year (plug number)	$84,820
End of the year	$84,820

Unrecognized Transition Obligation

Beginning of the year	$1,161,346
Amortization of transition obligation	(58,067)
End of the year	$1,103,279

Requirement 2:

DR OPEB expense	$194,223	
CR Accrued OPEB liability		$194,223
DR Accrued OPEB liability	$63,022	
CR Cash		$63,022

Accrued OPEB liability

Beginning of the year	-
+ OPEB expense for the year	$194,223
- Benefit payments	(63,022)
End of the year	$131,201

Requirement 3:

It appears the company has changed the discount rate from the beginning to the end of the year. The assumed discount rate as of May 31, 1993, can be calculated by dividing the interest cost for the fiscal year 1994 by the ABO as of May 31, 1993 ($92,908/$1,161,346). The beginning-of-the-year discount rate was 8%. The footnote to the annual report indicates that the end-of-the-year discount rate was 7.5%. Holding everything else constant, when the discount rate decreases, the present value of future cash outflows will increase, and consequently, the ABO will be higher. The increase in the ABO from the unrecognized loss is consistent with this change in the assumption.

Other possible explanations for the unrecognized net loss include changes in assumptions regarding estimated life expectancy and/or changes in expected health care cost trend rates in the future.

Requirement 4:

	May 29, 1994
Accumulated benefit obligation	($1,319,300)
Unrecognized net loss from change in assumptions	84,820
Accrued OPEB liability	($1,234,480)

For the Year ended May 29	1994
Service cost	$43,248
Interest cost	92,908
Net periodic OPEB cost	$136,156

Accumulated benefit obligation	
Beginning of the year	$1,161,346
Service cost	43,248
Interest cost	92,908
Unrecognized loss during the year (see below)	84,820
Benefit payments (plug number)	(63,022)
End of the year	$1,319,300

Unrecognized Net Loss	
Beginning of the year	-
Unrecognized loss during the year (plug number)	$84,820
End of the year	$84,820

DR Cumulative effects of accounting change	$754,875	
DR Deferred income taxes	$406,471	
CR Accrued OPEB liability		$1,161,346
DR OPEB expense	$136,156	
CR Accrued OPEB liability		$136,156
DR Accrued OPEB liability	$63,022	
CR Cash		$63,022

Accrued OPEB Liability

At the time of initial adoption	$1,161,346
+ OPEB expense for the year	136,156
- Benefit payments	(63,022)
End of the year	$1,234,480

P13-15. OPEB reconciliation of funded status and expense components

Requirement 1:

Prior Service Cost from Plan Amendment	1996	1995	1994
Beginning of the year	$5,106	$5,629	$6,153
Amortization of prior service cost (plug)	(524)	(523)	(524)
End of the year	$4,582	$5,106	$5,629

First, let us begin with the reconciliation for prior service cost from plan amendment. Since there was no plan amendment after 1993, the year-to-year change in this item must be due to amortization. This enables us to break down the amortization of unrecognized assets into amortization of unrecognized prior service cost and amortization of unrecognized gain as follows:

	1996	1995	1994
Service cost	$675	$661	$785
Interest cost	1,138	1,336	1,144
Amortization of prior service cost	(524)	(523)	(524)
Amortization of unrecognized gain (plug)	(131)	(33)	(1)
Postretirement health benefit expense	$1,158	$1,441	$1,404

Solving for amortization of unrecognized gain enables us to complete the schedule for unrecognized net gain, the plug numbers being the year-to-year effect on ABO from change in assumptions.

Unrecognized Net Gain	1996	1995	1994
Beginning of the year	$2,038	$2,442	$61
Effect of change in assumptions (plug)	2,006	(371)	2,382
Amortization of unrecognized net gain	(131)	(33)	(1)
End of the year	$3,913	$2,038	$2,442

Now we can complete the schedule for ABO with the plug numbers being the benefit payments.

Accumulated Benefits Obligation	1996	1995	1994
Beginning of the year	$16,298	$14,803	$15,861
Service cost	675	661	785
Interest cost	1,138	1,336	1,144
Effect of change in assumptions	(2,006)	371	(2,382)
- Benefit payments (plug number)	(603)	(873)	(605)
End of the year	$15,502	$16,298	$14,803

Requirement 2:

| 1994 | **DR** OPEB expense | $1,404 | |
| | **CR** Accrued OPEB liability | | $1,404 |

| | **DR** Accrued OPEB liability | $605 | |
| | **CR** Cash | | $605 |

| 1995 | **DR** OPEB expense | $1,441 | |
| | **CR** Accrued OPEB liability | | $1,441 |

| | **DR** Accrued OPEB liability | $873 | |
| | **CR** Cash | | $873 |

| 1996 | **DR** OPEB expense | $1,158 | |
| | **CR** Accrued OPEB liability | | $1,158 |

| | **DR** Accrued OPEB liability | $603 | |
| | **CR** Cash | | $603 |

Accrued OPEB Liability	1996	1995	1994
Beginning of the year	$23,442	$22,874	$22,075
Postretirement health benefit expense	1,158	1,441	1,404
- Benefit payments	(603)	(873)	(605)
End of the year	$23,997	$23,442	$22,874

Requirement 3:

To answer this requirement, let us examine the schedule for ABO:

Accumulated Benefits Obligation	1996	1995	1994
Beginning of the year	$16,298	$14,803	$15,861
Service cost	675	661	785
Interest cost	1,138	1,336	1,144
Effect of change in assumptions	**(2,006)**	**371**	**(2,382)**
- Benefit payments (plug number)	(603)	(873)	(605)
End of the year	$15,502	$16,298	$14,803

The bolded numbers show the effect of changes in assumptions on the ABO. During 1994 and 1996, the changes in assumptions decreased the ABO, whereas they increased the ABO during 1995.

To better understand the reasons for the changes in ABO, let us focus on the assumptions made by the company:

End of Year	1996	1995	1994	1993
Discount rate	7.25%	7.25%	8.5%	7%
Health care cost trend rate (near-term)	8.5–10.0%	9.0–10.5%	11–12.5%	11–12.5%

From 1993 to 1994, the company had changed the discount rate from 7% to 8.5% without changing the assumption regarding the health care cost trend rate. With a higher discount rate, this should result in a decrease in ABO. Consistent with this, we find a decrease of $2,382 in ABO.

From 1995 to 1996, the company changed the range for the health care cost trend rate from 9–10.5% to 8.5–10%. Decreasing the cost trend rate will have a similar effect to increasing the discount rate. Consequently, as in 1994, the ABO decreased by $2,006 due to change in the health care cost trend rate.

However, from 1994 to 1995, the company had made two changes which affected the value of ABO in opposite directions. For instance, decreasing the discount rate from 8.25% to 7.25% would have increased the ABO. In contrast, decreasing the health care cost trend rate from 11–12.5% to 9–10.5% would have decreased the ABO. The two offsetting effects resulted in a small increase of $371 in ABO.

Cases
C13-1. AMR Corp.: Interpreting pension footnote disclosures

Requirement 1:
Determining the amount of cash contributed to the pension plan in 1993:

Prepaid pension cost increased from $347 to $398. This implies that funding exceeded pension expense for the period by $398 - $347 = $51 million.

Therefore, amount of cash paid into pension fund is $221 million as shown from the following journal entry.

		$ millions	
DR Pension expense (see given schedule)		$170	
DR Prepaid pension cost		51	
CR Cash			$221

Requirement 2:
Determining the amount of pension plan assets distributed to retirees in 1993:

Beginning fair value of plan assets	$2,928
+ Actual return on plan assets	638
+ Additional contributions	221
- Distributions to retirees	**(237) (plug)**
Ending fair value of plan assets	$3,550

Requirement 3:
The six components of pension cost as per SFAS No. 132 are as follows:

	$ millions
Service cost	$167.0
Interest cost	285.0
Expected return on plan assets (10.5% × $2,928)[1]	(307.0)
Amortization of unrecognized transition asset ($81 - $70)[2]	(11.0)
Recognized actuarial loss[3]	25.4
Prior service cost recognized (see below[4])	10.6
Pension cost	$170.0

---

[1] Fair value of plan assets on 12/31/92
[2] From funded status reconciliation
[3] Corridor = 10% of PBO on 12/31/92 = 10% × $3,368 = $337

[4] Unrecognized loss on 12/31/92	$845
Corridor (see above)	(337)
Cumulative loss in excess of corridor	$508
Average remaining service period	÷20 yrs.
Recognized loss	$25.4

Net amortization and deferral shown in footnote	$356 DR

Deferred gain on plan assets ($638 - $307)	331.0 DR
Recognized actuarial loss (see above)	25.4 DR
Prior service cost recognized **(plug figure)**	**10.6 DR**
Amortization of transition asset ($81 - $70)	(11.0) CR
Net amortization and deferral	$356.0

Requirement 4:
Determine the increase in the unrecognized net loss that AMR experienced as a result of the change in the discount rate from 9% to 7.5%. (Ignore any effects of the change in assumed rate of increase in compensation.)

	$ Millions	
Unrecognized net loss at beginning of year	$845.0	
+Increase due to change in interest rate	**468.4**	**(plug)**
- Deferred gain on plan assets in current year	(331.0)	(see part 3, footnote 4)
- Amortization of net loss	(25.4)	(see part 3, footnote 4)
Unrecognized net loss at end of year	$957.0	

Requirement 5:
Determine the amount of increase (decrease) in prior service costs as a result of amendments to the plan during the year.

	$ Millions	
Beginning PBO balance (given)	$3,368.0	
+Service cost	167.0	
+Interest on PBO	285.0	
+Change in interest rate assumption (see above)	468.4	
- Payments to retirees (see Requirement 2)	(237.0)	
- Decrease due to prior service cost amendment	**(47.4)**	**(plug)**
Ending balance – PBO (given)	$4,004.0	

C13-2. USX: Interpreting pension footnote disclosures

Requirement 1:
USX recorded a *credit* to pension expense of $228 million for its "main plan" and a $13 million charge for "other plans." This compares to charges (debits) to pension expense in 1985 of $31 million for "main plans" and $10 million for "other plans." The main explanation for the difference is the adoption of SFAS 87 which reduced total pension expense in 1986 by $275 million over what it would have been without the change. The main factors contributing to the reduction in pension expense were the expected return on plan assets that *reduced* pension expense by $948 million and the amortization of cumulative unrecognized actuarial gains and transition assets (excess of pension assets over PBO at date of plan adoption) which reduced pension expense by $80 million.

Requirement 2:
Actual % return on plan assets (In $ millions).

$$\frac{\$1,281}{\$8,707 *} = 14.71\%$$

*FMV of plan assets on 12/31/85

Requirement 3:
The deferred gain of $333 million represents the difference between the actual return on plan assets of $1,281 million in 1986 and the expected return obtained by taking the 11% *expected* long-term return on plan assets times the market value (or market-related asset value) of plan assets at the beginning of the year.

$8,707 FMV of plan assets on 12/31/85 $8,618 (plug figure — market-related asset value)
× 11%   × 11%
$958 [a] $948 (shown in footnote)

[a] This figure is $10 million more than amount reported for expected return in 1986.

Requirement 4:
USX was in an overfunded position of $588 million when SFAS 87 was adopted. Another indication is the unrecognized net *gain* from transition to the new pension standard in excess of net pension liability reported on the balance sheet which nets out to $588 million of assets in excess of PBO at 12/31/85 ($1,306 - $718).

Requirement 5:
Determination of cash payments to retirees:

FV of plan assets on 12/31/85	$8,707
+ Actual return on plan assets	1,281
+ Cash contributions to plan **	7
- Payments to retirees **(plug)**	(1,102)
FV of plan assets on 12/31/86	$8,893

** Decrease in accrued pension liability ($718 - $483) = $235
    Offsetting DR to current year's CR to pension exp. = (228)
    Additional DR from cash contribution to pension plan = $7

Requirement 6:

Factors that caused the PBO to increase from $8,119 million on December 31, 1985, to $8,658 million on December 31, 1986 (a $539 million increase) include the following:

	$ millions
Additional service cost benefits earned during the year	$80
Interest buildup because of passage of time 9% × $8,119 =	$720 ($730 based on calculation)
Reduction due to benefits paid to retirees (see schedule above*)	(1,102)
Adjustment due to change in int. rate	841 (plug)
change in PBO ($8,658-$8,119)	$539

Requirement 7:

The $483 million net pension liability that shows up on USX's balance sheet represents the cumulative difference between total pension expense recognized up through 12/31/86 and the amounts funded (cash contributed to pension fund trustee). Thus, through 1986 USX has recognized $483 million more in pension expense than has been funded in prior years.

C13-3. Atmos Energy Corp.: Interpreting pension footnote disclosures

Requirement 1:

Atmos Energy apparently *did not fund* its employee retirement plan in fiscal year 1992. This is evident from the decline in the prepaid pension cost of $347 in the funded status disclosure ($13,211 - $12,864). The pension expense journal entry was:

DR Net periodic pension cost		$347	
CR Prepaid pension cost			$347

Requirement 2:

The payout of plan assets to employees was apparently $4,257, computed as follows from information contained in the funded status disclosure:

Plan Assets at Fair Value

Beginning FY 1992 balance	$95,760		
Actual return on Plan assets (from expense computation)	12,534	$4,257	Distribution to employees (**plug**)
Ending FY 1992 balance	$104,037		

Requirement 3:

Components 3-6 of pension expense can be estimated as follows:

Component 3: Expected return on plan assets was approximately $8,618.

Our answer here is approximate since we do not have enough information to know whether Atmos computed the expected return using a 5-year moving average of plan assets or by using the beginning of year plan assets ($95,760). We will assume the latter approach. The expected long-term rate of return on assets was 9.0%. Multiplying this by the beginning plan assets at fair value ($95,760) yields an expected return of $8,618. Then:

Actual return for 1992	$12,534
Less: Expected return	(8,618)
Unrecognized gain deferred in 1992	$ 3,916

Component 4: Recognized gains and losses is zero for 1992.

At the beginning of fiscal year 1992, the PBO was $77,466 and the fair value of plan assets was $95,760. The corridor threshold is 10% of the larger of these, or $9,576, which exceeds the cumulative unrecognized gain of $4,463. Accordingly, there would be no amortization for this item in fiscal year 1992.

Component 5: Amortization of unrecognized transition asset is a credit of $217.

This figure is the decline in the unrecognized net asset amount during 1992 from $1,286 to $1,069, as disclosed in the funded status section of the footnote.

Component 6: Recognized prior service cost was apparently a debit of $282.

This number is "plugged," and is derived as follows:

Unrecognized gain deferred in 1992	$3,916	DR	(derived above)
Component 4:	0		(derived above)
Component 5:	(217)	CR	(derived above)
Component 6:	**282**	**DR**	**(plug figure)**
Net amortization and deferral	$3,981	DR	(from footnote)

Presumably, a plan "sweetener" was introduced in 1992 since the decline in unrecognized prior service cost ($94) is less than the amortization computed above ($282). The difference, $188, is the estimated amount of plan enhancements in 1992.

A side-by-side comparison of Atmos Energy Corporation's pre- and post-SFAS No. 132 net periodic pension cost disclosure for 1992 appears as follows:

	Pre-SFAS No. 132	SFAS No. 132 Format
Service cost	2,117	$2,117
Interest cost	6,783	6,783
Actual return on plan assets	(12,534)	
Net amortization and deferral	3,981	
Expected return on plan assets		(8,618)
Recognized gains or losses		0
Amortization of unrecognized transition asset		(217)
Recognized prior service cost		282
Net periodic pension cost	$347	$347

C13-4. GE: Interpreting OPEB footnote disclosures

Requirement 1:
The $829 million represents reductions in plan coverage subsequent to adopting SFAS 106. A number of firms reduced the benefits originally promised by retiree insurance plans shortly after implementing Statement 106.

One can only speculate about the reasons for the cutbacks:

a) Some suggest that corporate managers were unaware of the total cost of retiree benefit plans until compelled to compute the accrual cost by SFAS 106. Prior to Statement 106, expense was recorded on a "pay-as-you-go" basis, and many companies offering benefits had large numbers of young employees for whom no payments were yet necessary. Consequently, these people argue, firms were blissfully unaware of the true cost of the promised benefits.

This explanation makes many uncomfortable since it implies unsophisticated managerial behavior. On the other hand, the other remaining explanations do not reflect well on management either.

b) Another possibility is that once postretirement employee benefits were recorded in the financial statements, management began to worry about violations of loan and bond covenants. By reducing promised benefits, firms simultaneously reduced the threat of subsequent covenant violation.

This explanation is unconvincing. Many of the early adopters of SFAS 106 also immediately reduced promised benefits. The overwhelming majority of these 1991 and 1992 early adopters adopted SFAS 106 just as G.E. did—using the immediate recognition option. If these companies were suddenly worried about covenant violations, why didn't they adopt using the deferred recognition option?

c) The third explanation for introducing changes after adopting SFAS 106 relates specifically to those firms who used the immediate recognition option. Here, the potential motive is earning management.

The earnings management scenario is as follows. G.E. adopts SFAS No. 106 effective January 1, 1991. Doing so resulted in a pre-tax adjustment (decrease) in earnings of $2,710 million since G.E. opted for immediate recognition. This "hit" to earnings caused a decline in bottom line earnings of $1,667 million compared to 1990 earnings ($2,636 million of 1991 net income versus $4,303 million in 1990). While it is not clear how the market reacted to SFAS 106 induced earnings declines, one might hypothesize that it was the existence of an earnings decline—rather than the magnitude of the decline–that was "newsworthy." Thus, it is plausible that G.E. felt that whatever adverse market reaction might exist would be the same irrespective of whether the earnings decline was $1,667 or $3,667.

If this is indeed the way that the market reacts, then an earnings management scenario immediately ensues. Specifically, companies who were contemplating cutting back on postretirement plan benefits would have an incentive **not** to do so until after adopting SFAS 106. By not cutting back prior to 106 adoption, they would take a big "hit" when they did adopt SFAS 106. (But they would not be penalized by the size of the "hit" itself since the market was only presumably monitoring whether earnings were up or down.)

Requirement 2:
Immediately **after** adopting SFAS 106, companies could then cut back on previously promised benefits. Doing so generates an amount that will be amortized into *income* over future years as component 4d. In G.E.'s case, the total amount is $829 million. If we assume that the expected remaining service life of employees affected by the plan is 10 years (G.E. does not disclose the actual number), then G.E.'s income will be **increased** by $82.9 million per year over the next ten years through component 4d. Accordingly, the earnings management "plan" is clear. If the market does not penalize firms for the size of the one time "hit," then firms should strive to **maximize** the size of the "hit." Doing so maximizes the amount of the off-balance sheet unamortized amount that ensues once the postretirement cutback ($829 million in G.E.'s case) is effected. By maximizing this amount, companies have "locked into" an income increase in future years.

C13-5. Groupe Schneider (KR): Effect of postretirement benefits on company valuation

Caveat: The reason suggested in the article for the stock price drop may not necessarily be the "true" reason. The article is used merely to discuss a possible economic consequence of accounting disclosures rather than to illustrate either effective or ineffective handling of an administrative situation.

The article attributes the fall in the stock price to the possibility that Groupe Schneider failed to consider the economic obligation of Square D Co. for its retired employees when valuing the company for acquisition. If the article is correct, then Groupe Schneider might have "overpaid" for Square D. Co.'s stock.

An interesting issue is why might a company forget such an important economic obligation when valuing a potential acquisition candidate? The article states that "France's system of socialized health care creates a gulf between company operations in that country and in the United States. They are not used to doing what we do...." The point is that under the French system of socialized health care, the government apparently pays for the medical expenses of all French nationals. Consequently, French companies are not likely to offer post-retirement health-care benefits to their employees (obviously, the cost of the socialized health care must be borne by everybody through higher taxes). Thus, one possibility raised in the article is that Groupe Schneider did not consider the postretirement health-care benefits as a potential economic obligation since such a liability does not exist in France.

As discussed in the article, the situation might have been exacerbated by the fact that U.S. companies were using cash basis accounting prior to the adoption of SFAS No. 106. Consequently, the economic obligation for postretirement benefits was not included as part of liabilities of companies. Could this explain why Groupe Schneider might have "overpaid" for the acquisition? Even before the adoption of SFAS No. 106, companies were providing information on the cash outflows for postretirement benefits (similar to Square D's disclosures). Specifically, Square D had indicated the potential impact of SFAS No. 106 ("…change will result in significantly greater expense being recognized for these benefits…"). Consequently, any potential bidder should have been aware of this off-balance-sheet liability. However, as pointed out by Square D ("While the impact of this new standard has not been fully determined…"), there were uncertainties about the magnitude of the unreported liability.

Regardless of whether any liability is explicitly reported in a balance sheet, a potential acquirer is likely to have access to the internal records of the target company during takeover negotiations. Consequently, Groupe Schneider could have conducted its own actuarial valuation of this important liability.

In summary, the article raises three interesting issues regarding SFAS No. 106. First, it points to the cross-country differences in who is "paying" for health-care costs. Ignoring such differences might lead to real economic consequences such as inappropriate valuation. Second, did the capital market learn more about the value of the postretirement obligation based on the disclosures under the new accounting standard? Third, did the actual recognition of the liability on the balance sheet make any differences as opposed to merely disclosing the cash flows in the footnotes?

Another related issue is the reasons for reassigning Mr. Bommelaer. Is this because of a miscalculation of the Square D purchase price? While we might never know the "true" reasons, the articles reinforces how information both on and off the financial statements is relevant for evaluating the financial performance of a company.

A final issue the article discusses is "whether to account for the charge on the books of the French company or of Schneider North America, the U.S. subsidiary that includes Square D." Since the subsidiary's financial statements are consolidated with that of the parent company, the decision whether to show the adoption effect of SFAS No. 106 in the books of the parent or the subsidiary is irrelevant for external reporting purposes. However, since the company appears to be examining the two alternative accounting treatments, it must have some internal reporting issues. Maybe incentive compensation of the divisional managers is tied to accounting profits. Consequently, by taking the charge at the parent company level, the North American divisional managers may be insulated from the effects of the new accounting standard.

C13-6. United Technologies: Understanding postretirement footnote disclosures

Requirement 1:
The journal entry is:

DR Periodic postretirement benefit cost	$58	
CR Cash (plug number)		$46
CR Accrued postretirement benefit cost ($920 - $908)		$12

Requirement 2:
Reconciliation of APBO:

Accumulated Postretirement Benefit Obligation

		$1,030	12/31/92 Balance
Unrecognized net reduction		17	Service cost (1993)
of prior service costs	$222		
Reduction in APBO due to		65	Interest cost (1993)
payments of benefits (plug)	78		
		66[1]	Unrecognized net loss (portion attributable to APBO)
		$878	12/31/93 Balance

[1] Computed as follows:

Change in unrecognized net loss during 1993 ($73 - $4)		$69
Portion attributable to deferred gain or loss on asset returns		
Expected return ($118 × 8.5%)	$10	
Actual return (given)	7	
Deferred loss on assets		(3)
Deferred loss on APBO actuarial assumptions		$66

Requirement 3:
Reconciliation of plan assets at fair value:

Plan Assets at Fair Value

12/31/92 Balance	$118		
Actual return on plan assets	7	$78	Payment of benefits
Additions (see entry in Req. 1)	46		(from Req. 2)
Unexplained difference (given)	14		
12/31/93 Balance	$107		

C13-7. Chrysler Corporation (KR): OPEB expense and management incentive compensation

This problem illustrates the potential effects of mandatory changes in accounting methods on existing firm contracts. Prior to SFAS No. 106, companies typically used a cash basis method to report expenses for post-retirement medical payments to employees. However, SFAS No. 106 required companies to switch to an accrual basis method for reporting purposes. This impacted the income statement of companies in two ways. First, a move from a cash to the accrual basis increased the magnitude of the expense in most companies. Second, at the time of the switch from a cash to accrual basis, companies were left with a significant unrecorded liability. As per SFAS No. 106, this unrecorded liability can be brought into the books by taking a one-time hit to the income statement or by gradually amortizing it as a part of operating expenses over the following several years. Together, these two items decrease the current and future accounting income of most companies.

Since accounting earnings are used in various corporate contracts (e.g., bond contracts, credit agreements, compensation contracts, etc.), a change in the accounting measurement rules might negatively impact one or more of the parties to a pre-existing contract. In this problem, we focus on the potential impact of the SFAS No. 106 on the incentive compensation contract in Chrysler Corporation. Since the promulgation and the effects of this accounting standard were not fully anticipated, both Chrysler and its employees appear to have not considered the potential effects of this accounting standard when defining the accounting income to base the incentive awards.

When FASB required companies to change the accounting method, this would have had a significant impact on the incentive compensation potentially payable under the existing contract. The proxy statement suggests that by switching to an accrual basis accounting for postretirement benefits, the net income of the income would decrease by $240 million. If the existing contracts are left in place, then SFAS No. 106 will significantly reduce or even eliminate incentive compensation payable to its officers and senior executives.

The issue is why should Chrysler worry about paying "less" compensation to its employees. Wouldn't the company be better off? As pointed out by the company, its ability to hire and retain competent executives is dependent on paying them their "market" wages. Thus, while Chrysler may be better off in the short run if the existing incentive contract is unaltered, it might lead to significant personnel turnover at the executive ranks with the resultant adverse consequences.

A final issue deals with the question whether Chrysler is paying "too much" to its executives by failing to incorporate the "true" OPEB expense to calculate the incentive compensation. This is unlikely to be the case. One possibility is that if GAAP had all along required an accrual accounting approach for OPEB, then

Chrysler might have put a limit of, say, 10% on the amount that is transferred to the bonus pool rather than the currently specified 8%. In essence, the adjustment recommended by the management is to ensure that the existing system of incentive compensation does not become suboptimal.

Exercises
E14-1. Issuing common stock

Common stock–par value (600,000 shares issued × $3 par)	$1,800,000
Additional paid-in capital (600,000 shares × $4)	2,400,000
Stockholders' equity	$4,200,000

E14-2. Stockholders' equity
(AICPA adapted)

Because the shares are "retired" rather than "held in treasury," they are removed from the books of Peter Corporation. No gain or loss is recorded because the transaction involves owners, not "outsiders." The journal entry to record the repurchase is:

DR Common stock par (100,000 shares × $10)	$1,000,000	
DR Additional paid-in capital	800,000	
CR Cash		$1,800,000

The account balances after this entry are:

Common stock par (800,000 shares × $10)	$8,000,000
Additional paid-in capital	1,900,000
Retained earnings (unchanged)	1,300,000

E14-3. Entity and proprietary views

Requirement 1:
The bond will be recorded as a $10 million long-term liability with annual interest expense of $1.1 million (11% × $10 million) charged to the income statement. The preferred stock will be shown as a $1 million item on the balance sheet, after long-term debt but before stockholders' equity. The $75,000 annual payment to stockholders will be classified as a dividend (not an expense). The mandatory redemption feature of the preferred stock dictates its balance sheet classification in a "gray area" between liabilities and equities.

Requirement 2:

GAAP treats the bond as a transaction with "outsiders"—hence it is recorded as a liability and the interest payments are treated as an expense of the company. The preferred stock is viewed as a transaction with quasi-insiders—the financial instrument is classified (almost) as an equity and the dividend payments are not treated as an expense of the company.

E14-4. Various stock transactions
(AICPA adapted)

The capital transactions are described in the following schedule:

			Common Stock Accounts		
		Cash	Par	APIC	Treasury
1/5/98:	issued 100,000 shares at $5 each	$500,000	$500,000		
4/6/98:	issued 50,000 shares at $7 each	350,000	250,000	$100,000	
6/8/98:	issued 15,000 shares at $10 each	150,000	75,000	75,000	
7/28/98:	purchased 25,000 shares at $4 each	(100,000)			($100,000)
12/31/98:	sold 25,000 treasury shares at $8 each	200,000		100,000	100,000
	Balance at 12/31/98	$1,100,000	$825,000	$275,000	$0

E14-5. Return on common equity
(AICPA adapted)

	December 31	
	1997	1998
Common stock	$300,000	$400,000
Retained earnings	75,000	185,000
Common equity	$375,000	$585,000

Average common equity = ($375,000 + $585,000)/2 = $480,000

Return on common equity = (Net income - Preferred dividends)/average common equity

= ($120,000 - $10,000)/$480,000 = 23%

E14-6. How many shares?
(AICPA adapted)

The number of preferred shares issued can be found by dividing the balance in the preferred stock, par value account by the $15 per share par value:

$255,000/$15 = 17,000 shares issued

The number of common stock shares issued can be found by dividing the balance in the common stock account by the $5 per share stated value:

$300,000/$5 = 60,000 shares

assuming the shares were issued at this stated value.

E14-7. Stockholders' equity after a stock repurchase
(AICPA adapted)

		Par	APIC	Treasury	Retained Earnings
			Common Stock Accounts		
1/1/97:	Issued 200,000 $10 par stock at $15 per share	$2,000,000	$1,000,000		
	Net income for 1997–1999				$750,000
	Dividends for 1997–1999				(380,000)
1/5/99:	Purchased 12,000 shares at $12 for treasury			($144,000)	
12/31/99:	Sold 8,000 treasury shares at $8 each		(32,000)	96,000	
	Balance at 12/31/99	$2,000,000	$968,000	($48,000)	$370,000

Total shareholders' equity at 12/31/99 is $3,290,000.

E14-8. Stock dividends and retained earnings
(AICPA adapted)

The entry to record the stock dividend (900 shares × $8 = $7,200) is:

DR Dividend	$7,200	
CR Common stock, par		$4,500
Additional paid-in capital		2,700

The retained earnings balance on April 1, 1999, is:

Balance on 12/31/98	$73,000
Loss for quarter	(16,000)
Stock dividend	(7,200)
Balance on 4/1/99	$49,800

E14-9. Stock dividends and market prices
(AICPA adapted)

Two issues need to be resolved here: 1) how many shares of stock will be issued? and 2) what market price should be used?

The 5% common stock dividend is based on shares outstanding (not authorized shares), so 15,000 new shares (5% × 300,000 shares outstanding) will be issued. The market price used in the journal entry is the price at the distribution date—August 10, 1998. The entry to record the 5% stock dividend—15,000 shares at $32 per share is:

DR Dividend	$480,000	
CR Common stock, par		$375,000
Additional paid-in capital		105,000

Some students may prepare an entry at the declaration date (July 1, 1998) using the $30 share price. This approach would require a second entry at the distribution date to adjust the market price to $32 per share.

E14-10. Stockholders' equity after a stock split
(AICPA adapted)

The stockholders' equity accounts on June 30, 1998, after the split would show:

Common stock, par value $10; 200,000 shares authorized; 100,000 shares outstanding	$1,000,000
Additional paid-in capital	150,000
Retained earnings	1,350,000

E14-11. Employee stock options
(AICPA adapted)

Because the options have an exercise price equal to the stock's market price on the grant date, no compensation expense is recorded by Austin Company when the options are issued. In fact, the company makes no journal entry at that time, although a memorandum entry is made to note that options were granted.

On October 1, 1998 when the 500 options are exercised and stock is issued to the employee, Austin Company makes the following entry:

DR Cash	$2,500	
CR Common stock		$2,500

where $2,500 = ($35 - $30) × 500 shares.

Notice that no compensation expense is recorded when the options are exercised. When the employee sells the stock on December 2, 1998, there is no entry made on the books of Austin Company (unless Austin is the buyer, in which case a treasury stock purchase is recorded).

E14-12. Computing basic EPS
(AICPA adapted)

$$\text{Basic EPS} = \frac{(\text{Net income} - \text{Preferred dividends})}{\text{Weighted-Average common shares outstanding}}$$

10,000 common shares were issued and outstanding the full year, and another 2,000 shares were issued on July 1. So the weighted-average common shares outstanding is 10,000 + 2,000 × 1/2 year = 11,000 shares.

This means:

$$\text{Basic EPS} = \frac{\$10,000 - \$1,000}{11,000 \text{ shares}} = \$0.82 \text{ per share}$$

E14-13. Finding the number of shares for EPS
(AICPA adapted)

	Number of shares	Weight % of year	EPS Basic	EPS Diluted
Common shares outstanding 1/1/98	5,000,000	100%	5,000,000	5,000,000
Common shares issued 4/1/98	1,000,000	75%	750,000	750,000
Common shares issued 7/1/98	500,000	50%	250,000	250,000
Dilution from convertible debt	400,000	25%		100,000
Number of shares used in EPS computation			6,000,000	6,100,000

E14-14. Earnings per share
(AICPA adapted)

Requirements 1 and 2:

	EPS for 1998 Basic	EPS for 1998 Diluted
Common shares outstanding	90,000	90,000
Conversion of bonds		30,000
Conversion of preferred stock		20,000
Number of shares used in EPS computation	90,000	140,000
Net income as reported	$285,000	$285,000
After-tax interest on the bonds ($80,000 × .60)	$0	$48,000
Preferred dividends ($2.40 × 10,000 shares)	($24,000)	$0
Earnings used in EPS computation	$261,000	$333,000
Earnings per share	$2.90	$2.38

E14-15. Employee stock options
(AICPA adapted)

When the options are granted (July 18, 1998), Amos Corporation would record compensation expense equal to the excess of share market price over option exercise price at the grant date, multiplied by the number of options granted. That means Amos would record 1998 compensation expense of:

$(\$42 - \$30) \times 20,000$ options = \$240,000

No compensation expense is recorded in 1999 when the options are exercised.

E14-16. Incentives for stock repurchases

Requirements 1 and 2:

The answer to this question depends on when, during the year, shares are repurchased. The most straightforward calculation assumes shares are repurchased at the beginning of each year:

Target 1998 EPS = \$5.25 = \$10 million/shares

There must be 1,904,761 shares outstanding, so 95,239 shares must be repurchased at the beginning of 1998.

Target 1999 EPS = \$5.50 = \$10 million/shares

There must be 1,818,181 shares outstanding, so 86,580 shares must be repurchased at the beginning of 1999.

Requirement 3:

There are several reasons Keystone's management may want to maintain the company's record of earnings growth:

- Management compensation and loan agreements may be tied to specific earnings targets or growth levels;

- Maintain credibility with analysts and investors by delivering earnings consistent with management forecasts;

Student answers will vary.

E14-17. ESOPs

Requirement 1:

When Procter & Gamble's ESOP trust borrows money, the cash is used to buy preferred stock from the company. Consequently, the company makes two entries on its books—one to record the issuance of preferred stock, and a second entry to record the ESOP debt. Here are the entries made by Procter & Gamble for the \$1,000 borrowed by the trust in 1989:

DR Employee stock plan (deferred compensation)$1,000

    CR ESOP debt $1,000

DR Cash $1,000

    CR Preferred stock $1,000

Requirement 2:

The ESOP debt is guaranteed by Procter & Gamble, and debt principal and interest payments are funded by dividends on the preferred stock and/or other cash flows from the company to the trust. As a result, Procter & Gamble is obligated to send enough cash to the ESOP trust each year so that it can make the required debt payments. The amounts are $117 per year for the 1989 ESOP debt plus another $94 per year for the 1991 ESOP debt.

Requirement 3:

The company will record interest expense on the ESOP in the usual manner. In addition, Procter & Gamble will record compensation expense for any cash contribution in excess of preferred dividends needed to cover the required principal payments on the debt.

Problems
P14-1. Cash and stock dividends

Requirement 1:
Journal entries for the three dividend events are:

Preferred dividends: $10 per share $\times$ 50,000 shares.

DR Retained earnings	$500,000	
CR Cash		$500,000

Common stock cash dividend: $0.25 per share $\times$ 1,000,000 shares.

DR Retained earnings	$250,000	
CR Cash		$250,000

Stock dividend: Since the dividend is less than 25%, it is recorded at the market price of the company's stock. This means that retained earnings is reduced by $135 $\times$ 100,000 (i.e., 10% of 1,000,000) or $13,500,000, that common stock is credited for $600,000, and that additional paid-in capital is credited for $12,900,000 or ($135 - $6) $\times$ 100,000.

DR Retained earnings	$13,500,000	
CR Common stock		$600,000
CR Additional paid-in capital		12,900,000

Requirement 2:
The market value of the company's common stock at the time the stock dividend was declared is $135 $\times$ 1,000,000 (number of shares outstanding) which equals $135,000,000. After the stock dividend is paid, there are 1,100,000 common shares outstanding, but the market value of equity will be unchanged. As a result, the share price will fall from $135 to $122.73 ($135,000,000/1,100,000).

P14-2. Splits, dividends, and retained earnings

Requirement 1:
Both options allow the company to avoid violating the limit on cash dividend payments. With regard to option A, a stock split of 12 for 10 means investors exchange 10 shares of common stock for 12 shares of "new" common stock.

This option has **no** effect on the balance in the retained earnings account. All that would occur is that the par value of the stock would be reduced from $6 to $5 (i.e., 10/12 × $6), and additional shares would be issued to stockholders.

Option B also allows the company to avoid violating the limit on cash dividend payments. By increasing the size of the stock dividend from 20% to 30%, the company can use the par-value method rather than the market-value method of recording the dividend. Retained earnings would be reduced by the par-value of stock issued, or $1,980,000 (30% × 1,100,000 shares × $6 per share) but this will not violate the dividend constraint.

Requirement 2:
Stockholders prefer cash dividends and stock price appreciation to just more pieces of paper. All three of these options—20% stock dividend, a 12-for-10 stock split, and a 30% stock dividend—increase the number of shares held but don't add real value to the investment portfolio. The stock split, at least, doesn't reduce retained earnings, so it leaves open the possibility of higher cash dividend payments in the future. Otherwise, it is not clear that stockholders will have a strong preference for any of these options.

P14-3. Convertible debt
(AICPA adapted)

Requirement 1:
Journal entry to record the original issuance of the $10 million convertible bond at par:

DR Cash	$10,000,000	
CR Convertible bond payable		$10,000,000

Notice that this entry does not assign any value to the conversion option.

Requirement 2:
Interest expense on the bond would be computed and recorded in the usual manner using the effective-interest method described in Chapter 10. Since the bond was issued at par, its effective interest rate is its stated interest rate of 4%, so interest expense would be $400,000 (or $10 million × 4%).

Requirement 3:
When issued, each $1,000 bond certificate could be converted into 5 shares of common stock. After the three-for-one stock split, the conversion rate would be adjusted to 15 shares for each certificate. Since there are 10,000 certificates outstanding but only 40% are converted, there will be 60,000 new shares issued (10,000 certificates × 15 shares × 40%). The journal entry to

record the conversion (assuming all interest has been accrued to the conversion date) using the book value method is:

DR Convertible bond payable	$4,000,000	
CR Common stock, par		$ 600,000
CR Additional paid-in capital		3,400,000

Students may have used the market value-method described in Requirement 4.

Requirement 4:

The preceding entry used the book-value method to record the conversion— the issued stock was recorded at the book value of the debt retired. Had the market-value method been used, the following entry would have been made:

DR Convertible bond payable	$4,000,000	
DR Loss on debt conversion	1,400,000	
CR Common stock, par		$ 600,000
CR Additional paid-in capital		4,800,000

Notice that this entry records the stock at its market value ($90 per share) at the conversion date, a total of $5,400,000 for the 60,000 shares issued. This results in a loss on debt conversion being recorded. Managers avoid this accounting loss when the book-value method is used.

P14-4. EPS computations

Requirement 1:
Calculation of basic earnings per share:

$$\text{Basic earnings per share} = \frac{\text{Net income} - \text{Preferred dividends}}{\text{Weighted-average number of dividends of common shares}}$$

$$= \frac{\$1,700,000 - 200,000}{230,000*}$$

$$= \$6.52$$

*Calculation of weighted-average number of common shares:

Time Period	Shares Outstanding	% of the Year Outstanding	Weighted Average
1/1/98–6/30/98	200,000	50%	100,000
7/1/98–12/31/98	260,000	50%	130,000
		Total	230,000

637

Requirement 2:
Calculation of diluted earnings per share:

$$\frac{\text{Net income - Preferred dividends + Income effect of dilutive securities}}{\text{Weighted-average number of common shares + Shares for dilutive securities}}$$

$$= \frac{\$1,700,000 - 200,000 + 33,000^*}{230,000^{**} + 50,000^{***}}$$

$$= \$5.48$$

* ($500,000 × 0.10) × (1.0 - 0.34) = $33,000
** From Requirement 1 above.
*** ($500,000/1,000) × 100 = $50,000

Requirement 3:
Stock options, warrants, convertible preferred stock.

P14-5. Limits on dividends

Requirement 1:
Lenders restrict a subsidiary's ability to pay dividends to the parent corporation so that the subsidiary's cash flows are available to repay its debt. This reduces the lender's credit risk and lowers the interest rate charged the subsidiary. These restrictions are written into the subsidiary's loan agreement and may take the form of an explicit prohibition against dividend payments (as seems to be the case for three of the subsidiaries) or an implicit restriction tied to earnings (as is the case for General Chemical).

Requirement 2:
The parent company's dividend payout ratio was just over 7.05% (i.e., dividends of $3,176 divided by net income of $45,035).

Requirement 3:
At the end of the year, Tredegar Industries still had about $51,000 available for dividends, so the maximum dividend payment must have been this amount plus dividends paid for the year, or $54,176.

Requirement 4:
The year-end balance in retained earnings is $99,027 so the maximum legal dividend would be this amount plus dividends paid for the year, or $102,203, assuming the 1984 Revised Model Business Corporation Act does not apply.

Requirement 5:
The company declared dividends of $3,176 in 1996, far short of the amount it could have distributed.

P14-6. Stock options

Requirement 1:
Stock options are usually granted as part of a long-term incentive compensation program for employees and executives of the company. The vesting period serves as a way of retaining valued employees—they lose the rights to the stock options if they leave the company before the options are fully vested. Shortening the vesting period lessens the usefulness of stock options as an employee retention device. The term of the options—10 years, in this case—helps lengthen the decision horizons of employees and executives. With a 10-year term, employees know that they will be rewarded for actions taken today that show up on share prices 10 years from now. Shortening the term can also shorten decision horizons.

Requirement 2:
There were 4,131,000 options granted during 1996. If the exercise price was $2 below the market price at the grant date, the company would have been required to record compensation expense of $8,262,000 or $2 times the number of options granted.

Requirement 3:
Employees receiving the option grants would have been taxed on the $8,262,000 ($2 times number of options received) as additional compensation for the year. The cost depends on each employee's marginal tax rate, but a rate of 34% does not seem unreasonable.

Requirement 4:
The company would have recorded compensation expense equal to the number of options granted (4,131,000) in 1996 times the fair value of the options at the grant date ($21.07 from the footnote), or $87,040,170.

The journal entry would be:

DR Compensation expense	$87,040,170	
CR Outstanding stock option		$87,040,170

Requirement 5:
Reconciliation of 1996 net income:

Net income as reported	$851	million
Compensation expense (net of taxes at 34%)	(57)	million
Other adjustments for stock options	15	million
Pro forma net income	$809	million

The other adjustments are for changes in the fair value of previously outstanding stock options, and for options cancelled or lapsed during the year.

Note: The answers to Requirements 2 through 5 presume that the stock options were awarded for services rendered in the current or in past periods.

P14-7. Equity management

Requirement 1:

Calculations for earnings per share (EPS) and the debt-to-equity ratio are detailed in the following schedule:

| | Financing Alternatives | | |
	Issue Debt	Issue Preferred	Issue Common
Impact on basic EPS:			
Net income next year before financing alternatives	$10,000,000	$10,000,000	$10,000,000
After-tax interest on new debt ($8 million × 60%)	($4,800,000)	-	-
Preferred dividend	-	(6,000,000)	-
Net income used in EPS computation	$5,200,000	$4,000,000	$10,000,000
Common shares outstanding	10,000,000	10,000,000	10,000,000
New shares issued	-	-	1,000,000
Earnings used in EPS computation	$10,000,000	$10,000,000	$11,000,000
Basic earnings per share	**$0.52**	**$0.40**	**$0.91**
Impact on debt-to-equity ratio:			
Debt outstanding before financing alternatives	$425,000,000	$425,000,000	$425,000,000
New debt issued	100,000,000	-	-
	$525,000,000	$425,000,000	$425,000,000
Shareholders' equity before financing alternatives	$250,000,000	$250,000,000	$250,000,000
Preferred stock issued	-	100,000,000	-
Common stock issued	-	-	100,000,000
After-tax interest on debt	(4,800,000)	-	-
Preferred stock dividend	-	(6,000,000)	-
	$245,200,000	$344,000,000	$350,000,000
Debt-to-equity ratio	**2.14**	**1.24**	**1.21**

Requirement 2:

Considering only the effects of each alternative on EPS and the debt-to-equity ratio, issuing common stock would seem to be the best option. Financing the project with debt will violate the company's lending agreement because the debt-to-equity ratio rises above 2. Financing with preferred stock keeps the debt-to-equity ratio at a comfortable level, but EPS falls substantially.

P14-8. Stock repurchases and EPS

Requirement 1:
If the stock buyback had not occurred, an additional 1,237,000 shares would have been outstanding for ten months during 1995 (January through October) and 12 months during 1996. Thus, EPS would have been:

	1993	1994	1995	1996
			Year Ended October 31	
Earnings available for common	$2,376	$4,018	$8,458	$3,763
Average common shares outstanding (as reported)	4,752	5,023	3,383	3,330
Shares eliminated by stock purchase			1,031	1,237
Shares used in EPS computation	4,752	5,023	4,414	4,567
Earnings per share as reported	$0.50	$0.80	$2.50	$1.13
Earnings per share without share repurchase	**$0.50**	**$0.80**	**$1.92**	**$0.82**

Requirement 2:
After adjusting for the stock repurchase, it becomes clear that performance in 1996 has fallen back to 1994 levels.

Requirement 3:
Other reasons for the decline in average common shares include the elimination of dilutive securities (convertible debt, preferred stock, warrants and options) or a reduction in the dilution effect of these same securities.

P14-9. Earnings management

The following schedule shows the answers to Requirements 1 and 2:

	Earnings Available for Common	Restructuring Charges	Special Gains	Average Common Shares Outstanding	Earnings Per Share As Reported	Earnings Per Share Without Special Gains	Earnings Per Share Without Restructuring
1996	$7,280			1,655	$4.40	$4.40	$4.40
1995	6,573			1,685	3.90	3.90	3.90
1994	5,915	($1,189)		1,710	3.46	3.46	4.15
1993	4,424	(1,101)	$1,430	1,708	2.59	1.75	3.23
1992	4,305			1,715	2.51	2.51	2.51
1991	4,435			1,739	2.55	2.55	2.55
1990	4,303			1,778	2.42	2.42	2.42
1989	3,939			1,807	2.18	2.18	2.18
1988	3,386			1,801	1.88	1.88	1.88
1987	2,119	(1,027)	850	1,827	1.16	0.69	1.72
1986	2,492	(311)	50	1,819	1.37	1.34	1.54
1985	2,336	(447)	510	1,825	1.28	1.00	1.52

Requirement 3:

Several trends are evident from these data. First, some restructuring charges (as in 1994) occur in otherwise very good years. Others, as in 1993, are accompanied by special gains that dampen the impact of the restructuring charge. Still others, as in 1985 through 1987, are spread over multiple years and dampened by special gains. The net result is that GE has reported EPS increases in all but two of the years 1985 through 1996. Of course, the timing of both the restructuring charges and the special gains may just be coincidental.

Requirement 4:

Changes in accounting methods, changes in allowances and reserves such as bad debts, and changes in some expense items like R&D or maintenance can be used to manage reported earnings, the numerator in the EPS calculation. EPS can also be managed through stock buybacks that reduce the denominator of the EPS calculation. Notice that GE has reduced the average number of shares outstanding over the period covered by the problem. This reduction has contributed to the company's EPS increases.

Requirement 5:

On January 22, 1998, GE issued a press release announcing 1997 full-year results. The headline read: GE Reports Record 1997 Results; Earnings Per Share Up 14% to $2.50.... The company completed a two-for-one stock split on April 28, 1997, which clouds the comparison of 1997 per-share amounts with those of earlier years. The press release also indicated that the company recorded a $1.5 billion (after-tax) special gain in the fourth quarter of 1997, and restructuring charges of $1.5 billion (after-tax) during the year. The following table summarizes key elements of 1997 earnings:

($ in Millions Except Per-Share Amounts)	As Reported	Split Adjusted
Earnings as reported	$8,203	$8,203
Restructuring charges (after-tax)	($1,500)	($1,500)
Special gain (after-tax)	$1,500	$1,500
Average common shares outstanding	3,274	1,637
Earnings per share—basic	$2.50	$5.00
Earnings per share—diluted	$2.46	$4.92

P14-10. Stock buyback incentives

Requirement 1:

Hershey Food Corporation has issued dual class common stock to preserve family control of the company. Each share of common stock carries one vote, but each share of Class B common has 10 votes. There are about 75 million common shares outstanding (75 million votes) and 15 million Class B shares (150 million votes), so whoever controls the Class B stock also controls the company. Since voting rights usually have value, Class B common shares will have a higher market price than the company's regular common shares.

Requirement 2:

The average price per share the company received from common and Class B shares can be found by dividing the common stock book value balance by the number of shares outstanding at year end:

$$\$137,707/89,975 \text{ shares} = \$1.53 \text{ per share}$$

Requirement 3:

The average price per share the company paid for treasury stock can be found by dividing the treasury stock book value balance by the number of shares held in treasury at year end:

$$\$685,076/12,709 \text{ shares} = \$53.90$$

Requirement 4:

The company paid $500 million for 9,049,773 shares in 1995, or $55.25 per share. In 1993, the company paid $103.1 million for 2 million shares, or $51.55 per share.

Requirement 5:

The stock buyback appears to have been motivated by the cash needs of the Milton Hershey School, the company's majority (beneficial) stockholder through the Hershey Trust Company. Other reasons companies buy back stock are: to eliminate the investment of dissident stockholders; to concentrate ownership in "friendly" hands; to distribute cash to stockholders at capital gains' tax rates; and, perhaps, to manage reported earnings per share.

Requirement 6:

Based on the information provided, credit analysts may not react favorably to the company's 1995 stock buyback. The $500 million spent to purchase treasury stock wipes out the company's operating cash flow for the year, leaving nothing for reinvestment, debt reduction, or normal dividends.

P14-11. Preferred stock and credit analysis

Requirement 1:
Entry to record the issuance of preferred stock on January 1, 1996:

DR Cash	$1,646,000	
CR Preferred stock		$1,646,000

Requirement 2:
Entry to record 8% preferred dividends for 1996 and 1995:

1996:

DR Dividends	$210,000,000	
CR Cash		$210,000,000

($210,000,000 = $2,625,000 × 8%)

1995:

DR Dividends	$78,320,000	
CR Cash		$78,320,000

($78,320,000 = $979,000,000 × 8%)

Requirement 3:
The company would make entries identical to those in Requirement 2, except that Interest expense would be debited rather than dividends. The company would also receive a tax deduction for interest.

Requirement 4:
The interest coverage ratio calculations are shown in the following schedule:

	1996	1995
Interest expense on existing debt	$1,174.00	$877.00
Interest expense on debt from preferred	210.00	78.32
	$1,384.00	$955.32
Net income before interest and taxes	$1,178	$879
Interest coverage ratio as reported	1.00	1.01
Interest coverage ratio with debt from preferred	**0.85**	**0.92**

The long-term debt-to-equity ratio is:

	Long-Term Debt	Equity	Ratio
1996	$15,826	$9,498	1.67
1995	10,886	3,637	2.99

Requirement 5:
Lenders might restrict a company's ability to issue additional preferred stock when the stock carries a high dividend payment or mandatory redemption feature. In both cases, the cash flows dedicated to preferred stock payments would not be available for debt repayment, and this might increase the company's credit risk.

P14-12. Comprehensive EPS calculations

Requirement 1:
The preferred stock pays a 10% dividend ($500,000), so there must be $5 million of preferred stock outstanding. Since each share has a $100 par value, there must have been 50,000 shares issued (50,000 shares × $100 per share = $5 million). The preferred stock converts into 200,000 shares of common stock, so each $100 par value preferred share must convert into 4 shares of common.

Requirement 2:
The after-tax interest on the Series B debt was $300,000. Since this equals gross interest divided by one minus the 40% tax rate, gross interest must equal $500,000 (or $300,000/.60). Series B debt carries a 10% interest rate, so there must be $5 million outstanding ($5 million × 10% = $500,000 gross interest) or 5,000 certificates ($5 million/$1,000 per certificate). The debt converts into 200,000 shares of common stock, so each certificate must convert into 40 common shares (200,000 shares/5,000 certificates).

Requirement 3:
The after-tax interest on the $5 million of Series A debt was $240,000. Following the steps outlined in 2), gross interest must have been $400,000 (or $240,000/.60), so the interest rate must have been 8%. Series A debt converts into 250,000 shares of common stock at 50 shares per certificate.

Requirement 4:
Under the treasury stock method, the proceeds received from exercising stock options are used to buy back shares on the open market. In this case, $1 million of cash is generated when the options are exercised (50,000 options × $20 per share). Since the options add 33,334 shares to the EPS calculation, only 16,666 shares are repurchased, and the market price must be $60 per share ($1 million/16,666 shares).

Requirement 5:

One reason Series A debt carries a lower interest rate (8%) than Series B debt (10%) is that each $1,000 certificate converts into 50 shares of common stock instead of only 40 shares for the Series B certificates.

P14-13. Stockholders' equity
(AICPA adapted)

Requirement 1:

The company's statement of retained earnings appears below:

Trask Corp.
Statement of Retained Earnings
For the Year Ended December 31, 1998

Balance, December 31, 1997, as originally reported		$16,445,000
Less prior period adjustment from error		
understating depreciation	$350,000	
Less income tax effect	105,000	245,000
As restated		16,200,000
Net Income		2,400,000
Deduct dividends		
Cash dividend on preferred stock	300,000 [1]	
Dividend in kind on common stock	900,000 [2]	1,200,000
Balance, December 31, 1998		$17,400,000

Requirement 2:

The stockholders' equity section of Trask's balance sheet appears below:

Trask Corp.
Stockholders' Equity Section of Balance Sheet
December 31, 1998

Preferred stock, $100 par value, 6% cumulative; 150,000 shares authorized; 50,000 shares issued and outstanding	$5,000,000
Common stock, $2.50 par value; 4,000,000 shares authorized; 3,400,000 shares issued	8,500,000 [3]
Additional paid-in capital	16,675,000 [4]
Retained earnings	17,400,000
	47,575,000
Less common stock in treasury, 100,000 shares at cost	500,000
Total stockholders' equity	$47,075,000

Requirement 3:

The computation of book value per share appears below:

Trask Corp.
Computation of Book Value per Share of Common Stock
December 31, 1998

Total stockholders' equity	$47,075,000
Deduct allocation to preferred stock	5,000,000
Allocation to common stock	$42,075,000
Divided by number of common shares	
outstanding (3,400,000 - 100,000)	÷ 3,300,000
Book value per share of common stock	$12.75

Explanation of amounts:

[1] Preferred stock dividend

Par value of outstanding preferred shares	$500,000
Multiplied by dividend rate	× 06
Dividends paid on preferred stock	$300,000

[2] Dividend in kind on common stock

Fair market value of Harbor stock distributed	
(15,000 shares @ $60)	$900,000

[3] Number of common shares issued and outstanding

Number of common shares issued, 12/31/97	1,575,000
Less: Common shares retired	(25,000)
Number of common shares issued, 6/1/98	150,000
	1,700,000
Two-for-one stock split, 10/27/98	× 2
Number of common shares issued after stock split	$3,400,000
Less: Common shares held in treasury	100,000
Total number of common shares outstanding	$3,300,000
Amount of common shares issued	
Amount of common shares issued, 12/31/97	$7,875,000
Less: Common shares retired at par value	(125,000)
Amount of common shares issued, 6/1/98	750,000
Total amount of common shares issued	$8,500,000

[4] Amount of additional paid-in capital

Amount at 12/31/97 (1,575,000 @ $10)	$15,750,000
Less: Treasury stock retired [25,000 shares	
@ $5 ($10 cost–$5 par value)]	(125,000)
Amount received upon issuance of common	
shares, 6/1/98 (150,000 shares @ $7)	1,050,000
Total amount of additional paid-in capital	$16,675,000

P14-14. Valuing stock option grants

Requirement 1:
The risk-free rate chosen should match the duration of the options. The employees' plan has an expected life of only 1.5 years, but the long-term incentive plan has an expected life of 6 years. Accordingly, the company should use a short-term risk-free rate for the employees' plan and a moderate-term risk-free rate for the long-term incentive plan. From the annual report, we can see that the short-term interest rate (6.15%) was higher than the moderate-term rate (5.42%) when the options were valued by the company.

Requirement 2:
The following table gives the spreadsheet inputs and option values.

| | Option Plan | |
	Long-Term Incentive	Employees'
Stock price at grant date	$45.84	$56.25
Weighted-average exercise price	$45.84	$56.25
Expected life of option	6 years	1.5 years
Risk-free interest rate	5.42%	6.15%
Expected volatility of stock	39.00%	39.00%
Expected dividend yield	1.48%	1.21%
Option value from spreadsheet:	$18.58	$12.15
Option value as reported:	$18.47	$12.10

An expected life of 5.915 years for the long-term incentive plan, and 1.49 years for the employees' plan, produces option values equal to those reported by the company. Some rounding errors are to be expected.

Requirement 3:
The following table gives the spreadsheet option values for each combination of inputs.

| | Option Values | |
	Long-Term Incentive	Employees'
1. Expected dividend yield–low	$21.62	$12.81
2. Expected dividend yield–high	$12.74	$10.22
3. Expected volatility–low	$15.38	$9.64
4. Expected volatility–high	$21.65	$14.63
5. Risk-free interest rate–low	$18.17	$11.97
6. Risk-free interest rate–high	$18.99	$12.33
7. Expected life–low	$15.54	$6.76
8. Expected life–high	$20.79	$15.86
Option value computed in (2)	$18.58	$12.15
Option value reported by company	$18.47	$12.10

Requirement 4:
From the results in Requirement 3, the risk-free interest rate seems to have the smallest impact on option values. Dividend yield and expected volatility have the largest impact on the value of long-term incentive options. Expected life has the largest impact on the value of employees' plan options.

Requirement 5:
The maximum and minimum compensation expense for options granted in 1996 are:

	Options Granted	Option Value	Compensation Expense	After-Tax Expense
Long-term incentive plan				
Maximum option value from (3)	2,663,375	$21.65	$57,662,069	$34,597,241
Minimum option value from (3)	2,663,375	12.74	33,931,398	20,358,839
Option value as reported	2,663,375	18.47	49,192,536	29,515,522
Employees' plan				
Maximum option value from (3)	848,546	15.86	13,457,940	8,074,764
Minimum option value from (3)	848,546	6.76	5,736,171	3,441,703
Option value as reported	848,546	12.10	10,267,407	6,160,444

The after-tax expense (not required in the problem statement) is based on a 40% corporate income tax rate. The company reported net income of $63 million in 1996, and the annual report indicates that net income would have been only $40 million that year if compensation expense had been recorded following the guidelines of SFAS No. 123. The value of options granted during the year is only one component of the SFAS No. 123 expense.

P14-15. Stockholders' equity—ShopKo Stores, Inc.

Part A:

Requirement 1:
There are no shares of preferred stock outstanding (none have been issued), and the par value of preferred is $0.01 per share.

Requirement 2:
The journal entry to record the sale of 10,000 shares of preferred stock at $25 per share is:

DR Cash	$250,000	
CR Preferred stock		$100
CR Additional paid-in capital		249,900

Requirement 3:
The journal entry to record the $1.00 annual dividend on the 10,000 shares issued above is:

DR Dividends $10,000
      CR Cash $10,000

Requirement 4:
There were 32 million shares of common stock outstanding.

Requirement 5:
From the cash flow statement, we can see that no shares were issued during the year ended February 27, 1993. Shares were issued one year earlier as part of a $240,830 stock dividend.

Requirement 6:
The number of shares issued exceeds the number of shares outstanding when the company has repurchased its stock and holds the repurchased shares in the treasury account. Since ShopKo has 32 million shares of common stock issued and outstanding, we know it has no treasury shares.

Part B:

The schedule below shows the calculation using information from both the cash flow statement and the earnings statement.

	Common Shares Issued	Common Stock $0.01 Par Value	Additional Paid-In Capital	Retained Earnings	Total Stockholders' Equity
Balance at February 1990:	14,750,000	$147,500	$2,282,000	$226,069,000	$228,498,500
Net income for the year				45,080,000	45,080,000
Dividends paid				0	0
Common shares issued	-	0			0
Balance at February 23, 1991	14,750,000	$147,500	$2,282,000	$271,149,000	$237,578,500
Net income for the year				49,589,000	49,589,000
Stock dividends paid	17,250,000	172,500	240,657,500	(240,830,000)	0
Common shares issued	-	0			0
Balance at February 29, 1992	32,000,000	$320,000	$242,939,500	$79,908,000	$323,167,500
Net income for the year				50,059,000	50,059,000
Dividends paid				(14,080,000)	(14,080,000)
Common shares issued	-	0			0
Balance at February 27, 1993	32,000,000	$320,000	242,939,500	$115,887,000	$359,146,500

Cases

C14-1. A case study in political processes–Financial reporting for executive stock options

This is an interesting case that can be taught from several very different perspectives depending on the instructor's preference. First, there is the financial reporting theory issue of whether granting stock options to employees represents compensation expense. Second, there is the measurement accuracy issue. If options granted are an expense, is the technology for measuring the amount of the expense sufficiently accurate to warrant inclusion in the income statement? Third, there is the pervasive political dimension. What was really driving the opposition to the FASB? Were the motivations similar for members of Congress and corporate executives? Within the corporate executive group, were the motivations similar for high-tech Silicon Valley firms and established *Fortune 100* companies alike? What prompted the Big Six firms to side with the FASB's opponents? Fourth, the case can be addressed from an ethical perspective. Did all parties play fair? Finally, there is a pragmatic dimension. In light of what happened in this scenario, do students believe that the standard-setting environment will generate "good" GAAP?

Requirement 1:

Several different issues were apparently afoot in the preparer community. High-tech and start-up companies who opposed the FASB were undoubtedly concerned with the bottom-line effect of treating options granted as an expense. Would their stock prices suffer, thereby making it more expensive to raise equity capital in the future? Some instructors may want to introduce stock market efficiency here. Would institutional and other sophisticated investors be misled by the higher income arising from not charging options granted to expense?

What motivated executives of established companies who vociferously opposed the FASB is less clear. These companies had sufficient cash flow to pay competitive salaries. Furthermore, the prospective income statement "hit" was often trivial. To illustrate this, we list the income statement impact of treating options granted as compensation expense for a group of companies. These companies were cited in the *New York Times* articles (8/25/92 and 3/26/93) as opposing the board's stock option initiative.

Company	Adoption Method For SFAS 123	Income Decrease from Expensing Options	
		1996	1995
Anheuser Busch	Disclosure	0.6%	*
Citicorp	Measurement	N/A	N/A
Corning	Disclosure	N/A	N/A
General Electric	Measurement	N/A	N/A
General Mills	Disclosure	N/A	N/A
B.F. Goodrich	Disclosure	+0.1%	+0.2%
IBM	Disclosure	2.6%	2.3%
Pfizer	Disclosure	3.6%	0.9%
Philip Morris	Disclosure	N/A	N/A
Phillips Petroleum	Disclosure	N/A	N/A
PPG	Disclosure	N/A	N/A
Pacific Telesis	Measurement	N/A	N/A
Texas Instruments	Disclosure	36.5%	0.9%

N/A = either no effect or an immaterial effect
* = no disclosure

Except for Texas Instruments in 1996, notice that the income statement impact was either negligible or very small for all other firms. In light of this, what motivated the intense opposition?

One can conjecture that Senator Levin's "Stealth Compensation" initiative (partially) explains these large firms' opposition. Since the effect on their income was small, and since an altruistic defense of Silicon Valley's interests is probably not their highest priority, one might surmise that these executives believed that expensing the value of options granted would heighten compensation visibility. In turn, this would increase their vulnerability to shareholder (and general public) opposition to the level of executive compensation.

Instructors who wish to explore ethical issues in this setting could discuss how certain activist firms treated their compensation consultants. The New York Times story indicates that some firms threatened their compensation consultants who cooperated with the FASB's early 1992 study of the range of compensation estimates generated by then-existing technology. Obviously, firms can hire whom they please as consultants. But some people may object to the intimidation.

Requirement 2:
The Big Six accounting firms' position on the stock options issue is understandable since virtually all of their clients opposed the FASB's proposed treatment. Rather than antagonize their clients, the firms joined in the opposition. The February 17, 1993, letter quoted in the case indicates this

clearly. The position taken on the stock compensation issue was what prompted Walter Schuetze, then SEC Chief Accountant, to suggest that CPA firms may be behaving as "cheerleaders for their clients." (See Walter P. Schuetze, "A Mountain or a Molehill?" *Accounting Horizons* (March 1994), p. 74.)

Senator Levin's support for the FASB's approach is presumably the result of his opposition to what he believed to be excessive executive compensation. This attitude may be shaped by the fact that his state has many mature industries and experienced significant unemployment in the 1980s. Paying top managers high salaries and bonuses while thousands were being laid off created controversy in Michigan and elsewhere. Similarly, the two California senators were also representing the strong preferences of their constituency, dominated by high-tech, growth companies who were heavy users of options. What caused the large number of others to vote against the FASB in the sense of the Senate resolution can only be surmised. Obviously, those running for elective office are understandably responsive to potential supporters and contributors.

Requirement 3:
The FASB implicitly and explicitly used representational faithfulness as the cornerstone of its initiative. The Board contended that options had value on the grant date, could be measured reasonably accurately, and represented compensation expense. Consequently, representational faithfulness required that they be recognized in the financial statements, according to the Board.

Opponents disputed this, but their objections are open to different interpretations. For example, as quoted in the case, Senator Lieberman asserted that options cannot be valued when granted; he seems to be saying that their *ultimate* value can be known only at exercise. While true, this does *not* mean that they are valueless prior to exercise, as daily quoted prices for options in *The Wall Street Journal* testify.

Other opponents concede that options have value at the grant date but suggest that they cannot be measured accurately using available models. The reasons relate to the restrictions that exist in compensation option grants. Mr. Leisenring alluded to these complications in the quote at the beginning of the case. Indeed, these restrictions do lead to difficulties in applying options-pricing models in these settings.

C14-2. Tuesday Morning Corporation (CW): Shareholders' equity

Requirement 1:
The following schedule shows the computation of year-end balances:

	Common Shares Issued	Common Stock $0.01 Par Value	Additional Paid-In Capital	Retained Earnings	Treasury Stock Shares Held	Treasury Stock Carrying Value	Total Stockholders' Equity
Balance at the beginning of 1992	8,515,000	$85,150	$22,185,000	$32,775,000	-	$0	$55,045,150
Net income for the year				8,171,000			8,171,000
Dividends paid				0			0
Common stock issues for options	91,000	910	318,090				319,000
Common stock issued	195,000	1,950	2,417,050				2,419,000
Common shares retired	(160,000)	(1,600)	(1,388,400)				(1,390,000)
Balance at end of 1992	8,801,000	$86,410	$23,531,740	$40,946,000			$64,564,150

Requirement 2:
There were no shares of preferred stock issued and outstanding at the end of 1994, as shown on the balance sheet.

Requirement 3:
The par value of preferred stock is $1 per share, as shown on the balance sheet.

Requirement 4:
The journal entry to record the issuance of the preferred shares on March 1, 1995, is:

DR Cash	$2,500,000	
CR Preferred stock		$100,000
CR Additional paid-in capital		2,400,000

The journal entry to record the dividend declaration and payment on March 1, 1996, is:

DR Dividends	$250,000	
CR Dividends payable		$250,000

DR Dividends payable	$250,000	
CR Cash		$250,000

Or to record the *simultaneous* declaration and payment:

DR Dividends	$250,000	
CR Cash		$250,000

C14-3. RN Nabisco Group: Dividends and agency costs

This case describes a "partial spin-off" in which RJR Holdings is offering to sell 25% of its ownership interest in a subsidiary—the Nabisco Group—to the public. The plan is to create a market for Nabisco Group shares that is separate and distinct from the market for R.J. Reynolds Tobacco shares. The holding company would retain a 75% ownership position in Nabisco Group and have substantial influence over its financing, operating, and investment activities.

The board at Holdings has announced a 45% (of earnings) dividend payout rate for Nabisco Group shares. The board also says it reserves the right to change the dividend payout rate at any time, and that Nabisco Group is not required to pay dividends on its common shares. As a practical matter, this is the case for all public companies: there is no requirement to pay common dividends, and the dividend rate is generally set on a quarterly basis by the board of directors. These two language elements of the offering prospectus do not present any new agency problems for potential investors.

The second paragraph of the prospectus extract says that Nabisco Group dividends will be paid out of the lesser of (1) the Available Nabisco Dividend Amount (ANDA) and (2) funds of Holdings legally available therefor. The ANDA is similar to the amount that would be available for dividends if Nabisco were a separate Delaware company. Since most U.S. companies are incorporated in Delaware, no unusual problems surface from this portion of the passage. However, the second portion places an additional restriction on Nabisco dividend payments—funds must be available in Holdings.

We also learn in this paragraph that ANDA will be "increased or decreased" as appropriate income and expenses of Holdings are allocated to the Nabisco Group "on a substantially consistent basis." Now we have a potential agency problem!

To illustrate the nature of this agency problem, suppose Nabisco Group reports net income of $100 million. With the dividend payout set at 45%, this means that Nabisco investors should receive $45 million in dividends. But who are those investors? Under the proposed offering, Nabisco Group would be 25% owned by outside investors and 75% owned by Holdings. But the original buyout group, which includes management and board members, owns 49% of Holdings. According to the last paragraph of the prospectus extract, Holdings will let the Nabisco dividend "pass through" to owners of Reynolds stock. So, here is what will happen to the $45 million in dividends:

($ in millions)	Nabisco Stock		Reynolds Stock	
	Outsiders	Holdings	Outsiders	Buyout Group
Nabisco Group pays $45 million dividend:				
25% to outsiders with the remainder to Holdings	$11,250	$33,750		
Holdings "pass through" of its share:				
51% to outsiders with remainder to buyout group			$17,213	$16,538

The buyout group receives $16,538,000 as its share of the Nabisco Group dividend.

Now, suppose, instead, that Holdings decides to charge Nabisco Group a $45 million management fee and to dispense with the dividend payment. Earnings at Nabisco Group fall to $55 million (ignoring tax considerations), but $45 million cash is transferred to Holdings. And, let us suppose that Holdings now decides to declare a $45 million dividend on Reynolds stock. Here is what would happen:

($ in millions)	Nabisco Stock		Reynolds Stock	
	Outsiders	Holdings	Outsiders	Buyout Group
Nabisco Group pays $45 million management fee:	$0,000	$45,000		
Holdings pays $45 million dividend:				
51% to outsiders with remainder to buyout group			$22,950	$22,050

Now the buyout group receives $22,050,000 instead of just $16,538,000, and Nabisco outsiders get nothing. The buyout group, consisting of RJR Nabisco management and directors, can transfer wealth from outside Nabisco stockholders to Reynolds stockholders, including the buyout group itself.

Of course, the story is incomplete because actions of this sort would undoubtedly cause the price of Nabisco stock to fall. This would lower the value of Reynolds stock held by outsiders and the buyout group since Holdings owns 75% of Nabisco. This possibility should lessen the agency problem, but it may not eliminate the problem.

RJR Nabisco withdrew its Nabisco Group stock offering in late June 1993, after it became clear that there was little investor interest in the deal at the price ($17-$19 per share) RJR hoped to receive. Nabisco shares were finally sold to the public in 1995.

C14-4. Time Warner Inc.: Is it equity or debt?

Requirement 1:

All three preferred stock instruments have characteristics that resemble traditional debt financing: required payment of annual cash flow (called dividends here but interest when it is debt), and a scheduled redemption (or principal payment). In addition, two of the securities were issued solely for the purpose of transforming debt into preferred stock. Here are the details.

"PERCS": These securities were issued in August 1995 and replaced $385 million of the company's 4% subordinated notes. The subordinated notes have not been retired, but instead were placed in a "shell" subsidiary of the company, called PERCS. The cash flows from the company to PERCS for the 4% notes will be used to make the required cash distributions of 4% on the preferred stock. The preferred stock must be retired on December 31, 1997, for cash, or at the company's option, shares of stock in Hasbro. The company also has a call option that would permit early retirement of the preferred stock for cash or Hasbro stock. December 31, 1997, is also the day the 4% note is to be retired.

Preferred Trust Securities: These securities were issued in December 1995 and replace $592 million of the company's 8 7/8% subordinated debentures. The debt has not been retired, but instead was placed in a "shell" subsidiary of the company, called Preferred Trust Securities. The cash flows from the company to Preferred Trust Securities for the 8 7/8% debt will be used to make the required cash distributions of 8 7/8% on the preferred stock. The preferred stock must be redeemed for cash on December 31, 2025 (the retirement date for the debt), and the company has a call option that permits early redemption.

Series M Exchangeable Preferred: These securities were issued in April 1996 for cash in a private placement. Each preferred share carries a cumulative dividend requirement of 10 1/4% per year, payable in cash but pro-rated based on the cash distributions to the company from Time Warner Entertainment (TWE). The company is required to redeem the preferred stock for cash by July 1, 2016, with partial redemption beginning in 2012. If there is a reorganization of TWE, the company must either (1) exchange the Series M preferred for a Series L preferred, or (2) redeem the Series M preferred for cash. The Series L preferred has terms similar to the Series M except that (1) the company is required to pay dividends in kind (issuing most preferred shares) until June 30, 2006; (2) the Series L shares must be redeemed by 2011; and (3) the company has the option of exchanging the Series L shares for 10 1/4% senior debt.

All three instruments obligate the company to a series of predictable future cash outflows that closely resemble interest and principal repayments. Because the cash outflows cannot be avoided, most credit analysts will include them when assessing the credit risk of the company. Even though the cash flows are earmarked for dividends and preferred stock redemption, they will be treated similarly to interest and debt repayment for credit analysis purposes.

Requirement 2:
The following schedule treats all three preferred stock instruments as debt for purposes of calculating revised covenant levels:

	1996	1995
Long-term debt as reported at year end	$13,201	$9,907
Preferred stock reclassified as debt:		
PERCS	374	374
Preferred Trust Securities	575	575
Series M Exchangeable Preferred	1,700	-
	$15,850	$10,856
Common stockholders' equity at year end	$9,498	$3,637
Debt-to-equity/ratio	**1.67**	**2.98**
Net income before interest and taxes as reported	$1,178	$879
Interest expense as reported	$1,174	$877
Preferred dividends reclassified as interest:		
PERCS at 4% issued August 1995	$15	$5
Preferred Trust at 8 7/8% issued December 1995	$51	$4
Series M at 10 1/4% issued April 1996	$131	-
	$1,371	$886
Times-interest-earned ratio	**0.86**	**0.99**

Both covenants are violated at the end of 1996 (and 1995) if the preferred stock is treated like debt for loan purposes. Notice that the debt-to-equity covenant was violated in 1995 even without reclassification of the preferred stock.

Requirement 3:
The simple fix is to specify that debt, for purposes of the loan agreement, will include interest-bearing debt and preferred stock with mandatory redemption features. Similarly, interest, for purposes of the loan agreement, will include interest payments on debt plus dividend payments (accrued or paid) on preferred stock with mandatory redemption features.

Exercises
E15-1. Mark-to-market for trading and available-for-sale securities
(AICPA adapted)

Requirement 1:
Only the unrealized holding gains/losses from *trading* securities are recognized as income. Since the cost basis is the same on 12/31/97 and 12/31/98, the unrealized gain reported on the 1998 income statement would be the change in market values from 12/31/97 to 12/31/98 = $155,000 - $100,000 = $55,000.

Alternatively, the gain may be evaluated by examining the contra-asset market adjustment account's activity for 1997 and 1998:

1997: Cost $150,000 less Market $100,000 = $50,000 required *credit* to establish market adjustment account (debit to unrealized holding loss on income statement)

1998: Cost $150,000 less Market $155,000 = $5,000 required *debit* balance in market adjustment account

1998 Adjustment:

Current balance in market adjustment (end of 1997)	= $50,000	**CR**
Less: Required balance in market adjustment	= - 5,000	**DR**
Adjustment (debit market adjustment, credit		
unrealized gain on income statement)	($55,000)	Answer to Req. 1

Requirement 2:
Any gain or loss on Tyne's available-for-sale securities should be reported as a separate unrealized holding gain/loss in the statement of stockholders' equity. Since the cost basis is the same on 12/31/97 and 12/31/98, the net unrealized holding loss reported in the statement of stockholders' equity on 12/31/98 would be $150,000 - $130,000 = $20,000.

The net balance in the unrealized change in value for available-for-sale securities (owners' equity) may also be understood by reviewing the changes to the market adjustment account and the unrealized change in value for available-for-sale securities in owners' equity. The year-end balances of both of these accounts always reflect the difference between the aggregate historical cost of the available-for-sale securities and their aggregate market value.

1997: Cost $150,000 less Market $120,000 = $30,000 required <u>credit</u> to establish market adjustment account (debit to unrealized change in value of available-for-sale securities in owners' equity)

1998: Cost $150,000 less Market $130,000 = $20,000 required <u>credit</u> balance in market adjustment account and required debit balance in unrealized change in value of available-for-sale securities in owners' equity (answer to Requirement 2)

1998 Adjustment:

Current balance in market adjustment (end of 1997)	= $30,000	**CR**
Less: Required balance in market adjustment	= -20,000	**CR** Answer to
Adjustment (debit market adjustment, credit unrealized change in value of available-for-sale securities in owners' equity)	$10,000	Req. 2 **DR**

E15-2. Mark-to-market for available-for-sale securities
(AICPA adapted)

Rex should report a loss for the amount equal to the 12/31/97 market price of the securities less their cost.

Requirement 1:

Market value of securities on 12/31/97	$48,200
Less: cost of securities	(51,300)
Unrealized loss of available-for-sale securities	($3,100)

Requirement 2:
Computation of gain (loss) on sale of Company B stock:

Selling price of securities ($15 × 1,000 shares)	$15,000
Less: brokerage commissions and taxes	(1,500)
	$13,500
Less: cost of shares	(17,000)
Realized loss on sale	($3,500)

E15-3. Mark-to-market for trading securities

Requirement 1:
Aggregate cost of trading portfolio at 12/31/98 = $340,000
Aggregate market value of trading portfolio on 12/31/98 –

$340,000 cost + $8,000 unrealized gain - $52,000 unrealized loss =	296,000
Desired balance in market adjustment account =	$44,000 **CR**
Balance prior to adjustment	10,000 **CR**
Additional credit needed to market adjustment account	$34,000

Requirement 2:
<u>Journal Entry</u>:

DR Unrealized loss—trading securities	$34,000	
CR Market adjustment—trading securities		$34,000

E15-4. Equity method
(AICPA adapted)

Requirement 1:
Due to its investment in Otis, Harold has a new source of income and a new expense. The income results from the investee's net income. The expense is the amortization of the intangible asset (or goodwill) over ten years. Computations are shown below.

Otis' net income	$90,000
Harold's share in Otis	20%
Harold's equity in Otis' earnings	$18,000
Cost of investment in Otis	$400,000
Carrying value of Otis' net assets on 1/1/99	300,000
Intangible asset (Goodwill)	$100,000
(Amortized over 10 years)	
Amortization expense per year	$10,000
Income from equity investment	$18,000
Less: Amortization expense	(10,000)
Increase in Harold Corporation's income	**$8,000**

Requirement 2:

In addition to Otis' net income and amortization expense, Otis' payment of cash dividends will affect the balance in Harold's investment in Otis account. Otis paid $20,000 in cash dividends in 1999 so Harold would subtract its share (20%) from the balance in its investment account. The balance in investment in Otis is computed as follows:

Initial cost of investment in Otis	$400,000
Harold's share of Otis' net income	18,000
Amortization of intangible	(10,000)
Cash dividend	(4,000)
Balance in investment in Otis account on 12/31/99	**$404,000**

E15-5. Equity method
(AICPA adapted)

Requirement 1:
Amount Sage would report on 1998 income related to its investment in Adams.

First determine Sage's share of Adams' net income as shown below.

Computation of Income from Equity Investment

Cost of investment in Adams Corp.	$400,000
Adams net income	$120,000
Sage's share of Adams' common stock	40%
Sage's share of Adams' net income	$48,000

Next, we need to determine what portion of the excess of Sage's cost of book value of Adam's shares is attributable to depreciable assets, inventory, and implicit goodwill. The computations are as follows:

Cost of Sage's 40% interest in Adams	$400,000
Sage's share of Adam's net assets (40% of $900,000)	360,000
Excess of cost over book value of Adam's shares	40,000
Amount attributed to depreciable assets	
40% × $90,000 (excess of fair value over book value of Adams' depreciable assets)	(36,000)
Annual amortization = $36,000/18 yrs. = $2,000/yr.	
Amount attributable to inventory	
40% × $10,000 (excess of fair value over book value of Adams' inventory)	(4,000)
Excess attributed to implicit goodwill	$0

The amount that Sage would report on its 1998 income statement related to its investment in Adams can now be determined as follows:

Sage's equity in Adams' reported earnings	$48,000
Less: Amortization of excess attributed to depreciable assets	(2,000)
Amortization of excess attributed to inventory	(4,000)
Sage's net earnings from investment in Adams	$42,000

Requirement 2:
Balance in the investment in Adams account on December 31, 1998.

Sage's initial investment in Adams	$400,000
Equity in Adams' earnings net of amounts amortized	42,000
Less: Dividends received (40% of $20,000)	(8,000)
Balance in investment in Adams account on 12/31/98	$434,000

E15-6. Equity vs. cost method for long-term investments
(CMA adapted)

Requirement 1:
Net investment revenue reported by Boggs under the equity method is computed as follows:

Boggs' equity in Mattly's earnings	
30% × $300,000	$90,000
Goodwill amortization $200,000/20yrs.	(10,000)
Net investment revenue	$80,000

Note: Dividends received are not treated as investment income under the equity method because this would result in double counting the earnings of Mattly that were distributed. Dividends received are credited to the investment account under the equity method.

Requirement 2:
Under the cost method, the net investment revenue is simply Boggs' share of Mattly's dividend distribution = 30% × $100,000 = $30,000. There is no adjustment to this amount for goodwill write-off.

E15-7. Goodwill–purchase method
(AICPA adapted)

Cost of shares acquired		$620,000
Fair value of net assets acquired (without goodwill)		
Cash	$60,000	
Inventory	150,000	
Property and equipment	380,000	
Liabilities	(120,000)	470,000
Goodwill		$150,000

E15-8. Consolidated financial statements
(AICPA adapted)

Computation of consolidated retained earnings is shown below.

Beginning retained earnings (Pitt Company)	$500,000
Net income	200,000
Dividends	(50,000)
Ending retained earnings	**$650,000**

E15-9. Consolidated balance sheet
(CMA adapted)

After eliminations, the total dollar amount of consolidated assets would be as follows:

	Sea	Island	Eliminations	Consolidated
Other assets	$750,000	$320,000		$1,070,000
Investment in Island	187,500	- -	(187,000)	- -
Goodwill			37,500 [1]	37,500
Total assets	$937,500	$320,000		$1,107,500
Liabilities	($250,000)	($70,000)		($320,000)
Common stock	(450,000)	(200,000)	200,000	(450,000)
Minority interest			(100,000) [2]	(100,000)
Retained earnings	(237,500)	(50,000)	50,000	(237,500)
	($937,500)	($320,000)		($1,107,500)

[1] Purchase price less Sea's share of Island's net assets:
$187,500 - (60% × $250,000) = $187,500 - $150,000 = $37,500

[2] 40% × $250,000 = $100,000

The consolidated total assets will be $1,107,500 consisting of $750,000 of Sea Company assets other than the investment in Island Company, plus the $37,500 of goodwill originating from the purchase of Island's stock at a price above book value, and the Island Company's assets of $320,000.

E15-10. Transaction foreign exchange gain/loss
(AICPA adapted)

Requirement 1:
1998:

Year-end balance of receivable in dollars		
= $.19 × 250,000 francs	=	$47,500
September 1 balance of receivable in dollars		
= $.20 × 250,000 francs	=	50,000
Foreign exchange loss		$2,500

Requirement 2:

1999:

Dollar amount received on February 1, 1999

$\quad$ = \$.22 × 250,000 francs $\qquad$ = $\qquad$ \$55,000

12/31/98 balance of receivable in dollars

$\quad$ = \$.19 × 250,000 francs $\qquad$ = $\qquad$ 47,500

Foreign currency gain $\qquad$ \$7,500

E15-11. Mark-to-market for available-for-sale securities
(AICPA adapted)

Net unrealized losses on 12/31/98 (\$26,000 - \$4,000)	\$22,000
Amount reported in market adjustment account	(1,500)
Additional adjustment required	\$20,500

Entry:

DR Stockholders' equity–unrealized loss on
available-for-sale securities $\qquad$ \$20,500

$\quad$ **CR** Market adjustment–available-for-sale securities $\qquad$ \$20,500

E15-12. Mark-to-market for trading securities

Equity Security	Cost	1999 Market Value		Unrealized gain/(loss)
A	\$96,000	\$94,000	=	(\$2,000)
B	184,000	162,000	=	(22,000)
C	126,000	136,000	=	10,000
		Desired balance in allowance account		\$14,000 **CR**

Allowance to Adjust to Market

		\$18,000	Beginning balance (plug)
Change in current period to Mark-to-market	\$4,000		
		\$14,000	Ending (desired) balance

E15-13. Purchase vs. pooling
(CMA adapted)

Requirement 1:

Consolidated depreciation under the purchase method will be:

Depreciation recorded by Pushway for entire year	\$400,000
Depreciation recorded by Stroker for 1/2 year–from date when Pushway acquired Stroker (1/2 × \$100,000)	50,000
Depreciation on Stroker's assets written up as a result of the acquisition = \$200,000/10 yrs. × 1/2 yr. =	10,000
Total depreciation expense for consolidated entity	\$460,000

Requirement 2:
Consolidated depreciation under pooling method will be:

Note: Under the pooling method, operating results are combined as if the combination had occurred as of the beginning of the year. There is no write-up of the subsidiary's assets; therefore, depreciation expense for the consolidated entity is based on the depreciation recorded by each of the combining firms.

Depreciation recorded by Pushway for entire year	$400,000
Depreciation recorded by Stroker for entire year	100,000
Total depreciation expense for consolidated entity	$500,000

E15-14. Foreign currency translation
(AICPA adapted)

Since the local currency unit (LCU) is the subsidiary's functional currency, Ward Inc. must use the current rate method to translate the subsidiary's LCUs into U.S. dollars.

Under the current rate method, all expenses are translated at the weighted average rate of exchange for the year. LCU expenses total 400,000. Therefore, the dollar amount of these expenses included in the consolidated income statement would be:
$$400,000 \times .44 = \$176,000$$
where .44 is the average dollar equivalent of LCU for the year ended December 31, 1998.

E15-15. Transaction foreign exchange gain/loss
(AICPA adapted)

Lindy Corp. has engaged in a foreign currency *transaction*. The transaction is recorded on Lindy's books at its U.S. dollar equivalent and "marked-to-market" as the exchange rate changes. Any gains or losses go through income in the year that the change occurs.

On November 5, 1997, Lindy would make the following entry (not required):

DR Inventory	$42,950	
CR Accounts payable		$42,950

(To record the transaction at its U.S. dollar equivalent, i.e., 100,000 marks × .4295)

In preparing 1997 financial statements, the following adjusting entry would be made to reflect the year-end spot rate (not required):

DR Accounts payable $500
    CR Foreign exchange transaction gain $500
[To reflect the decrease in the dollar equivalent of the German mark payable: $(.4295 - .4245) \times 100,000 = \$500$.]

On January 15, 1998 Lindy would make the following entry (not required):

DR Accounts payable $42,450
DR Foreign exchange transaction loss 1,000
    CR Cash $43,450
(To record payment of the amount owed)

The $1,000 loss is measured as follows:

Dollar carrying value of payable at January 1, 1998 ($42,950 - $500)	$42,450
Dollar equivalent of settlement amount on January 15, 1998	43,450
Foreign exchange transaction loss	($1,000)

Thus, a $500 transaction gain would be recognized in 1997 and a $1,000 transaction loss would be recognized in 1998.

E15-16. Intercompany eliminations on consolidated statements
(AICPA adapted)

Requirement 1:
Determining intercompany profit in Scroll's ending inventory:

Step 1: Determine Pirn's gross profit on sales made to Scroll. Pirn's gross profit rate = $150,000/$500,000 = 30%

Step 2: Apply gross profit rate determined in Step 1 to the cost of units acquired from Pirn that are still in Scroll's ending inventory.

Total cost of goods acquired from Pirn[1]	$100,000
Less: Cost of goods sold acquired from Pirn (given)	(80,000)
Cost of goods in Scroll's ending inventory that were acquired from Pirn	$20,000
Pirn's gross profit rate	30%
Intercompany profit that should be eliminated from Scroll's inventory	$6,000

[1] Scroll's cost is the same as Pirn's sales to Scroll which is given in the problem.

Requirement 2:
Determining depreciation expense in Pirn's 1998 consolidated income statement:

Step 1: Determine book value of equipment that Pirn sold to Scroll:

Selling price of equipment (given)	$36,000
Gain on sale recorded by Pirn	(12,000)
Book value of equipment sold to Scroll	$24,000
Useful life of asset	÷ 4 yrs.
Annual depreciation based on Pirn's book value	$6,000
Depreciation recorded by Scroll ($36,000/4 yrs.)	9,000
Excess depreciation related to Pirn's profit on equipment sold to Scroll	$3,000

Step 2: Subtract excess depreciation from depreciation reported by Scroll:

Scroll's reported depreciation	$10,000
Less: Excess depreciation (see step 1)	3,000
Depreciation based on Pirn's book value	7,000
Depreciation recorded by Pirn	40,000
Consolidated depreciation for 1998	$47,000

E15-17. Intercompany eliminations–purchase vs. pooling
(AICPA adapted)

Requirement 1:
Determination of 1998 consolidated income under the purchase method:

Under the purchase method, consolidated net income is based on the combined operations of the parent and subsidiary *from the date of combination.* Thus, earnings of the subsidiary (Scott) prior to June 30, 1998, are *not* included in the consolidated earnings of Purl.

Step 1: Determine consolidated earnings before elimination of intercompany profit:

Purl's (the parent) earnings 1/1/98 to 6/30/98	$750,000
Purl's earnings from 6/30/98 to 12/31/98	825,000
Scott's (the subsidiary) earnings from 6/30/98 to 12/31/98	375,000
Consolidated earnings before elimination of intercompany profits	$1,950,000

Step 2: Eliminate intercompany profit on goods in Scott's ending inventory that were acquired from Purl:

Consolidated earnings *before* elimination of intercompany profit (see step 1)	$1,950,000
Less: Intercompany profit in Scott's ending inventory	(45,000)
Consolidated net income for 1998 under purchase method	$1,905,000

Requirement 2:
Consolidated net income under pooling of interests method:

Step 1: Under the pooling of interests method, consolidated net income is computed as if the combination had taken place at the *beginning* of the year.

Purl's earnings from 1/1/98 to 6/30/98	$750,000
Purl's earnings from 6/30/98 to 12/31/98	825,000
Scott's earnings from 1/1/98 to 6/30/98	225,000
Scott's earnings from 6/30/98 to 12/31/98	375,000
Consolidated earnings before elimination of intercompany profit	$2,175,000

Step 2: Eliminate intercompany profit in Scott's ending inventory	(45,000)
Consolidated net income under pooling method	$2,130,000

Problems
P15-1. Intercorporate investments–balance sheet

Requirement 1:

On January 1, 1998, Herb Corporation would have made the following entries on its books:

DR Cash	$425,000	
CR Common stock		$100,000
CR Other equity (paid-in capital)		325,000
DR Investment in Aside	$425,000	
CR Cash		$425,000

These entries then lead to the pre-consolidation trial balance shown below in columns (1) and (2). Since Aside Chemical was not a party to the transactions, its statement balances are the same as those reported at the start of the problem.

If we assume that the book value and fair market value of Aside's tangible net assets are equal ($300,000), the purchase premium is attributable to goodwill.

($ in thousands)	Herb	Aside	Eliminations	Consolidated
Investment in Aside	$425		① (300)	
			② (125)	
Goodwill			② 125	$125
Other assets	850	$400		1,250
	$1,275	$400		$1,375
Liabilities	$275	$100		$375
Common stock	300	100	① (100)	300
Other equity	700	200	① (200)	700
	$1,275	$400		$1,375

Requirement 2:

The journal entries for Req. 2 are identical to those shown above. The only difference is that the $425,000 investment represented only 80% of Aside's shares. The pre-consolidation trial balance is accordingly identical to that in

Req. 1. This question provides the instructor with an opportunity to introduce disclosure of minority interests.

($ in thousands)	Herb	Aside	Eliminations		Consolidated
Investment in Aside	$425		①	(240)	
			②	(185)	
Goodwill			②	185	$185
Other assets	850	$400			1,250
	$1,275	$400			$1,435
Liabilities	$275	$100			$375
Minority interest			③	60	60
Common stock	300	100	①	(80)	300
			③	(20)	
Other equity	700	200	①	(160)	700
			③	(40)	
	$1,275	$400			$1,435

Requirement 3:

The instructor might begin this segment by pointing out to the student two important similarities between the acquisition in Req. 1 and the acquisition in Req. 3.

a) In both Req. 1 and Req. 3, Herb issued 100,000 additional shares of stock and gained control of Aside.

b) In both Req. 1 and Req. 3, Aside's shareholders receive financial instruments with a value of $425,000. In Req. 1, the instrument is called cash and, in Req. 3, the instrument is Herb's common stock.

One can then help the students understand the difference in the accounting treatment between Req. 1 (purchase accounting) and Req. 3 (pooling of interests) by asking them to identify **what important condition differs between Req. 1 and Req. 3**. In other words, what is the economic factor that is used to justify the difference in accounting treatments?

The difference, of course, is what happens to the shareholders of Aside. In Req. 1, they "ride off into the sunset" never to be heard from again. In Req. 3, they become a part of the ownership group of the consolidated enterprise (presumably called "Herbside Chemical?"). The continuation of the owner of Aside in the consolidated group is the justification for the pooling method. Accounting views this as a "marriage" rather than an arm's-length transaction buyout. Importantly, no new basis of accounting arises and the *book values* of the pre-merger partners' net assets become the carrying amounts after consolidation. The acquisition journal entry is then:

```
DR Investment in aside              $300,000
    CR Common stock                           $100,000
    CR Other equity (paid-in capital)          200,000
```

($ in thousands)	Herb	Aside	Eliminations	Consolidated
Investment in Aside	$300		① (300)	
Other assets	850	$400		$1,250
	$1,150	$400		$1,250
Liabilities	$275	$100		$375
Common stock	300	100	① (100)	300
Other equity	575	200	① (200)	575
	$1,150	$400		$1,250

The simplicity of the example makes it easier for students to see the pooling rationale. The instructor might then extend the problem and explore the favorable income statement and ratio effects of pooling. Specifically, income is higher since there is no goodwill to amortize. Furthermore, both assets and equity are lower in poolings, thereby improving ratios like rate of return on assets and equity.

P15-2. Equity method

Requirement 1:
Investment income reported by Figland:

Figland's equity in Irene's earnings (40% × $600,000)	$240,000
Less:	
Amortization of excess paid over book value for inventory	(50,000)
Depreciable assets ($150,000/10 yrs.)	(15,000)
Goodwill ($200,000/40 yrs.)	(5,000)
Investment income for 1996	$170,000

Requirement 2:
Balance in investment in Irene Company on 12/31/96:

Cost of initial investment	$1,800,000
Investment income [see requirement (1)]	170,000
Less: Dividends received (40% × $325,000)	(130,000)
Balance in investment account on 12/31/96	$1,840,000

P15-3. Mark-to-market accounting

Requirement 1:
Under GAAP, trading securities are marked-to-market at each balance sheet date. The securities would appear on Giant Motors' balance sheet at $25 million.

Requirement 2:
Giant Motors' 1998 income statement is impacted in two ways as a result of its investment in Cooper Tire.

a) Giant Motors would recognize dividend income of $750,000 (i.e., $15,000,000 \times 0.05$).

b) In addition, Giant Motors would report an unrealized loss of $5,000,000 (before tax) because of the decline of the market value of the investment from $30 million to $25 million.

Requirement 3:
Under GAAP, available-for-sale securities are also marked-to-market at each balance sheet date. Thus, the securities would appear on Giant Motors' balance sheet at $25 million.

Requirement 4:
Giant Motors would still report the $750,000 of dividend income noted above, but the unrealized loss of $5,000,000 would not appear on its income statement. The unrealized gains/losses on available-for-sale securities would go directly to the stockholders' equity section of the balance sheet, bypassing the income statement in the process.

P15-4. Mark-to-market for trading securities

Requirement 1:
Journal entry for mark-to-market adjustment on 12/31/97:

Desired balance in market adjustment account

Cost	$80,000	
Market value on 12/31/97	85,000	$5,000 **DR**
Previous balance before adjustment		0
Required adjustment to market adjustment account		$5,000 **DR**

Entry:
DR Market adjustment—trading securities $5,000
       CR Unrealized gain on trading securities $5,000

Requirement 2:
Entry to record the sale of Company B common stock:

DR Cash	$14,000	
DR Market adjustment—trading securities[1]	2,500	
CR Trading securities–Co. B common		
stock (50% of $30,000)		$15,000
CR Realized gain on sale of trading securities		1,500

[1]Unrealized loss on Co. B common stock included in mark-to-market adjustment on 12/31/97 was determined as follows:

Cost of Co. B common stock	$30,000
Market value on 12/31/97	(25,000)
Unrealized loss included in 12/31/97 mark-to-market adjustment	5,000
Portion of Co. B shares being sold	50%
Market adjustment related to Co. B shares sold	$2,500

Requirement 3:
Mark-to-market adjustment of 12/31/98.

Desired balance in market adjustment account:

	Cost	12/31/98 Market	
Co. A Common	$50,000	$55,000	
Co. B Common	15,000	13,000	
Co. C Preferred	20,000	25,000	
	$85,000	$93,000	$8,000 **DR**

Previous balance after adjusting for Co. B stock sale on 6/30/97 ($5,000 **DR** + $2,500 **DR**)	7,500 **DR**
Required adjustment to market adjustment account	$500 **DR**

Entry:

DR Market adjustment—trading securities	$500	
CR Unrealized gain on trading securities		$500

Requirement 4:
Mark-to-market adjustment for 12/31/99.

Desired balance in market adjustment account:

	Cost	12/31/99 Market	
Co. A Common	$50,000	$58,000	
Co. B Common	15,000	10,000	
Co. C Preferred	20,000	18,000	
Co. D Warranty	10,000	12,000	
	$95,000	$98,000	$3,000 **DR**

Previous balance after 12/31/98 mark-to-market adjustment   8,000 **DR**
Required adjustment to market adjustment account $5,000 **CR**

Entry:

DR Unrealized loss on trading securities	$5,000	
CR Market adjustment—trading securities		$5,000

Requirement 5:
Required entry for Co. B common stock sale if considered an available-for-sale security:

DR Cash	$14,000	
DR Realized loss on sale of available-for-sale securities	1,000	
CR Available-for-sale Securities–Co. B common stock		$15,000

DR Market adjustment—available-for-sale securities[1]	$2,500	
CR Unrealized market gains/losses—stk. equity		$2,500

[1] Unrealized loss on Co. B common stock included in mark-to-market adjustment on 12/31/97 was determined as follows:

Cost of Co. B common	$30,000
Market value of 12/31/97	(25,000)
Unrealized loss included in 12/31/97 mark-to-market adjustment	5,000
Portion of Co. B shares being sold	50%
Market adjustment related to Co. B shares sold	$2,500

P15-5. Comprehensive intercorporate investments problem
(AICPA adapted)

Requirement 1:
Mark-to-market adjustment for available-for-sale securities on December 31, 1997:

Desired balance in Market Adjustment account

			Cost	12/31/97 Market Value	
Axe Corp.	1,000 sh. @ $40		$40,000	$42,000	
Purl Inc.	6,000 sh. @ $10		60,000	66,000	
Day Co.	2,000 sh. @ $27.50		55,000	40,000	
			$155,000	$148,000	$7,000 **CR**
	Previous balance in market adjustment account				-0-
	Required adjustment to market adjustment account				$7,000 **CR**

Journal Entry on 12/31/97:

DR Stockholders' equity–unrealized loss on
available-for-sale securities $7,000
    CR Market adjustment–available-for-sale securities $7,000

Requirement 2:
Entries to record realized gains of losses on Poe's sale of securities in 1998:

January 18–sale of 2,500 shares of Purl @ $13

DR Cash (2,500 sh. × $13) $32,500
    CR Available-for sale securities—Purl common
stock (2,500 × $10/sh. cost) $25,000
    CR Realized gain on sale of securities [2,500 × ($13 - $10)] 7,500

Entry to adjust market adjustment account for unrealized gain recorded on 12/31/97 related to the 2,500 shares of Purl being sold. (**Note:** An alternative solution would be to *not* make this adjustment to the market adjustment account at the time of sale. Rather, the adjustment could be made at the end of the year as part of the mark-to-market adjusting entry on the available-for-sale portfolio.)

DR Stockholders' equity—unrealized gain on
available-for-sale securities $2,500
    CR Market adjustment—available-for-sale securities
($11 market value - $10 cost) × 2,500 shares $2,500

June 1–Sale of 500 shares of Day Co. @ $21

DR Cash (500 sh. @ $21) $10,500
DR Realized loss on sale of securities   3,250
    CR Available-for-sale securities–Day common
         stock (500 sh. × $27.50/sh. cost) $13,750

Entry to adjust market adjustment account for unrealized loss recorded on 12/31/97 related to the 500 shares of Day Co. being sold.

DR Market adjustment–available-for-sale securities $3,750
    CR Stockholders' equity–unrealized loss on
         available-for-sale securities
         ($20 market value - $27.50 cost) × 500 shares $3,750

Requirement 3:
Entries to record receipt of dividends and equity method entries for Poe's investment in Scott Corp:

April 5–Dividends on Axe preferred stock

DR Cash ($1.20/sh. × 1,000 sh.) $1,200
    CR Dividend income $1,200

October 5–Dividends on Axe preferred stock

DR Cash ($1.20/sh. × 1,000 sh.) $1,200
    CR Dividend income $1,200

June 30–Dividend on Purl common stock

DR Cash ($1.00/sh. × 3,500 sh.) $3,500
    CR Dividend income $3,500

March 1, June 1, Sept. 1, and Dec. 1–Dividends on Scott Corp. stock

DR Cash ($.50/sh. × 100,000 sh.) $50,000
    CR Investment in Scott Corp. $50,000

Entry to record Poe's equity in Scott's earnings for 1998:

DR Investment in Scott Corp. (30% × $1,200,000) $360,000
    CR Investment income $360,000

Entry to record amortization of implicit goodwill arising from excess of Poe's cost of Scott stock ($1,700,000) over book value of Scott's stock held by Poe

678

($1,400,000). The $300,000 goodwill is being amortized over 40 years. ($300,000/40 yrs. = $7,500/yr.):

DR Investment income	$7,500	
CR Investment in Scott Corp.		$7,500

Requirement 4:
Mark-to-market adjustment for available-for-sale securities on December 31,1998. (**Note:** This solution assumes that the market adjustment account is adjusted at the time the shares are sold. An alternative solution would be to make no adjustment at the time of sale and adjust the market adjustment account at the end of the year for $18,250 rather than $17,000.):

Desired balance in market adjustment account

		Cost	12/31/97 Market Value	
Axe Corp.	1,000 sh. @ $40	$40,000	$56,000	= 1,000 @ $56
Purl Inc.	3,500 sh. @ $10	35,000	38,500	= 3,500 @ $11
Day Co.	1,500 sh. @ $27.50	41,250	33,000	= 1,500 @ $22
		$116,250	$127,500	= $11,250 **DR**

Previous balance in market adjustment account		
From 12/31/97 adjusting entry	$7,000 CR.	
From sale of Purl shares	2,500 CR.	
From sale of Day shares	3,750 DR.	5,750 **CR**
Required adjustment to market adjustment account		$17,000 **CR**

Journal Entry on 12/31/98:

DR Market adjustment–available-for-sale securities	$17,000	
CR Stockholders' equity–unrealized gain on available-for-sale securities		$17,000

P15-6. Intercorporate investments–Equity method

Requirement 1:
1998 Investment income:

$$= (\$25,000,000 \times 0.25) - (\$50,000,000/20 \text{ years})$$
$$= \$6,250,000 - \$2,500,000$$
$$= \$3,750,000$$

Big Time Motors' proportionate share of Cooper's net income (i.e., $25,000,000 × 0.25) is reduced by the amortization of the goodwill of $2,500,000. Since the net book value of Cooper's assets was $400 million when Big Motors purchased its interest, the total goodwill is $50 million = $150 million - $100 million ($400 × 0.25). Since the goodwill is being amortized over a 20-year period, the annual charge (reduction to investment income) is $2,500,000.

Investment in Cooper (1998 balance sheet):

= Acquisition Cost + Net Investment Income - Dividends
= $150,000,000   + $3,750,000   - ($15,000,000 × 0.25)
= $150,000,000   + $3,750,000   - $3,750,000
= $150,000,000.

Requirement 2:
Investment in Cooper on December 31, 1999, balance sheet:

The book value of Cooper at the time the additional investment was made is $400 million plus its 1998 net income of $25 million minus its 1998 dividends of $15 million, or $410 million. Since Big Time Motors paid $100 million for a 15% interest with a book value of $61.5 million (i.e., $410 million × 0.15), $38.5 million was paid for goodwill. Since this amount will be amortized over a 20-year period, the annual charge will be $1,925,000. This is in addition to the $2,500,000 annual charge for the goodwill related to the initial purchase of Cooper's stock by Big Time Motors in 1998.

Calculation of Big Time's equity in loss of Cooper for 1999:

	($ in 000)
Cooper's reported loss	($40,000)
Big Time's equity (25% + 15%) in Cooper	40%
	(16,000)
Less: Amortization of goodwill from 1998 purchase	(2,500)
Less: Amortization of goodwill from 1999 purchase	(1,925)
Big Time's equity method loss adjusted for goodwill amortization	($20,425)

Balance of Big Time Motors investment in Cooper Tire on December 31, 1999:

Cost of initial investment on 1/1/98	$150,000
+Equity in Cooper's 1998 income (.25 × $25,000)	6,250
- Amortization of implicit goodwill ($50,000/20 yrs.)	(2,500)
+Dividends received from Cooper in 1998 (.25 × $15,000)	(3,750)
+Cost of additional investment on 1/1/99	100,000
- Equity in Cooper's loss for 1999 (.40 × $40,000)	(16,000)
- Amortization of goodwill from 1998 purchase	(2,500)
- Amortization of goodwill from 1999 purchase	(1,925)
- Dividends received in 1999 (.40 × $18,000)	(7,200)
December 31, 1999 balance of investment in Cooper's account	$222,375

P15-7. Business combination–purchase vs. pooling
(CFA Exam)

Requirement 1:
Aspen Pharmaceuticals–pooling method
Pro forma balance sheet at December 31, 1998

Aspen Pharmaceuticals **Balance Sheet** **December 31, 1998** **($ millions)**	
Assets	
Current assets ($4,500 + $1,000)	$5,500
Property, plant, and equipment ($5,000 + $200)	5,200
Total assets	$10,700
Liabilities and stockholders' equity:	
Current liabilities ($3,500 + $300)	$3,800
Long-term debt ($1,000 + $300)	1,300
Deferred taxes ($1,000 + $0)	1,000
Stockholders' equity ($4,000 + $600)	4,600
Total liabilities and equity	$10,700
Book value per share equals $4.18 ($4,600/1.1 billion shares)	

Aspen Pharmaceuticals—pooling method
Pro forma 1999 income statement

Aspen Pharmaceuticals
Income Statement
Year Ended December 31
($ millions except per-share data)

	1999
Sales ($10,500 + $3,360)	$13,860
Cost of goods sold ($2,500 + $2,880)	(5,380)
Marketing and administration ($2,700 + $110)	(2,810)
Depreciation ($200 + $20)	(220)
Interest ($100 + $20)	(120)
Research ($1,000 + $0)	(1,000)
Pre-tax income	4,330
Income tax expense ($1,200 + $130)	(1,330)
Net income	$3,000

Earnings per share equals $2.73 ($3,000/1.1 billion shares)

Requirement 2:
Aspen Pharmaceuticals—purchase method
Pro forma balance sheet at December 31, 1998

Aspen Pharmaceuticals
Balance Sheet
December 31, 1998
($ millions)

Assets	
Current assets	$5,500
Property, plant, and equipment	6,200
Goodwill	1,400
Total assets	$13,100
Liabilities and Stockholders' Equity:	
Current liabilities	$3,800
Long-term debt	4,300
Deferred taxes	1,000
Stockholders' equity	4,000
Total liabilities and equity	$13,100

Book value per share equals $4.00 ($4,000/1.0 billion shares)

Aspen Pharmaceuticals–purchase method
Pro forma 1999 income statement

Aspen Pharmaceuticals Income Statement Year Ended December 31 ($ millions except per-share data)	
	1999
Sales	$13,860
Cost of goods sold	(5,380)
Marketing and administration	(2,810)
Depreciation	(320)
Interest	(420)
Research	(1,000)
Amortization of new goodwill	(70)
Pre-tax income	3,860
Income tax expense	(1,170)
Net income	$2,690

Earnings per share equals $2.69 ($2,690/1.0 billion shares).

Note that the estimate of taxes under pooling is the composite amount $1,330 ($1,200 + $130). Under purchase accounting, the best estimate is the composite amount less $160 [40% times the sum of depreciation ($100) and interest ($300)]. Goodwill is not tax-deductible except in certain circumstances.

Requirement 3:
Reasons Aspen would likely prefer to use a share-for-share exchange and pooling of interests accounting:

1) Pooling of interest makes the transaction tax-free to PSI shareholders; otherwise, Aspen might have to pay more for PSI.

2) Pooling eliminates the need to create goodwill. Goodwill amortization would reduce reported earning in the years following the merger.

3) Carrying assets at historical cost avoids any possible write-up of fixed assets, which would increase depreciation (reducing reported earnings) in future years.

4) Pooling sets up an opportunity to recognize gains when PSI assets are subsequently sold, because they are carried at their (original) historical cost rather than being written up to fair market value at the time of the merger.

5) Use of common stock does not require a cash outlay or debt financing. With no incremental debt financing, there will be no additional interest expense.

6) Earnings per share will be higher under pooling than under purchase accounting.

7) Book value per share will be higher under pooling than under the purchase method.

8) Pooling consolidates earnings for the entire year regardless of when during the year the merger actually occurs. Thus, acquiring firms with poor earnings can increase their earning through pooling.

9) Aspen's ratios will look better under pooling than under purchase accounting. Return on assets (ROA) will be higher and debt ratios will be lower.

Requirement 4:
Criticisms of pooling of interest accounting from the analyst's point of view:

1) Assets (and liabilities acquired) are not stated at fair value and are usually understated.

2) The understatement of assets leads to an understatement of capital in the business and leads to an overstatement of return on investment (ROI or ROA) and return on equity (ROE).

3) As these understated assets are disposed of, gains are overstated.

4) The comparability of financial statements of firms using pooling of interest with financial statements of firms using the purchase method is lessened.

5) Historical-cost depreciation of the understated assets produces an understatement of expenses and an overstatement of income; so does the absence of goodwill amortization.

6) Prior years' financial statements are restated, so the historical record of firm performance is rewritten.

7) Pooling of interest was originally intended to account for mergers of equal-size firms. In this case, Aspen is a much larger company than the firm, PSI, it is acquiring.

P15-8. Business acquisitions and ratio analysis
(CFA Exam)

Requirement 1:
The purchase method of accounting for acquisitions combines two different companies without restating prior data and creates a discontinuity, which distorts growth rates and other trends. Without additional data, the analyst does not know whether changes in growth rates or in ratios are caused by changes in the ongoing business or by combining the companies. Because the postmerger ratios of Company B are not strictly comparable with the premerger ratios of Company B, using trend data can lead to misleading conclusions.

Requirement 2:
Company B's original assets are carried at historical cost, whereas each acquisition's assets are carried at fair market value as of the date acquired. This results in mixing historical costs and market values in combined accounts. Because AutoParts Heaven's assets are all carried at historical cost, comparing the ratios of Company B with those of AutoParts Heaven is difficult.

Requirement 3:
Under the pooling method, the financial statements of the acquirer and the company acquired are combined *without adjustment*, and *prior financial statements are restated*. Under the purchase method, financial statements are combined effective only at the acquisition date (*no restatement*), and assets and liabilities are recorded at *fair value at the acquisition date*. These purchase method adjustments also affect postacquisition reported earnings.

(a) **Gross profit margin percentage** (gross profit/sales) is lower using the purchase method. Because inventories are written up to fair market value under the purchase method, subsequent period cost of goods sold is higher during a period of rising prices. Sales are the same under both methods.

(b) **Long-term ratio of debt to equity** is lower using the purchase method. Equity is higher under the purchase method (except in the rare case when the purchase price is below the stated equity of the acquired firm) than under the pooling method. This is caused by recording the fair value of the stock issued (rather the acquiree's book value) under the purchase method. Under the purchase method, acquired debt is recorded based on current interest rates. Under pooling, acquired debt is carried forward at historical cost.

685

(c) **Pre-tax earnings** are lower using the purchase method. Under the purchase method, pre-tax earnings are lower because of factors such as higher cost of goods sold [see (a)], higher depreciation expense resulting from writing up property to its fair value, and goodwill amortization.

P15-9. Translation effect on ratios
(CFA Exam)

Remeasurement is the process under which local currency results are translated into the functional currency. SFAS 52 requires translation using the *temporal method.* Under the temporal method, nonmonetary assets and liabilities (mainly inventories and property) are translated using *historical exchange rates.* These rates are also used to translate cost of goods sold and depreciation expense. Using FIFO inventory accounting results in a lag in recognizing exchange rate changes.

(1) **Gross profit margin percentage** (gross profit/sales) is higher after remeasurement. With the local currency appreciating, sales (translated at the weighted average exchange rate) will rise (in functional currency) more rapidly than cost of goods sold. Thus, gross profits will generally increase after remeasurement.

(2) **Operating profit margin** (operating profit/sales) is higher after remeasurement. In addition to the reason given in (1) above, depreciation expense is lower. Depreciation is lower because property (and, therefore, depreciation) remains at historical exchange rates. With an appreciating local currency, depreciation expense will rise more slowly than sales.

(3) **Net profit margin** (net income/sales) may be higher or lower after remeasurement. Transaction gains and losses included in reported income under the temporal method may offset the effects discussed in (1) and (2). The actual effect depends on the asset and liability composition of the particular company and exchange rate changes.

P15-10. Business acquisitions and ratio analysis

1) Immediately following the investment in C Corp., ABD's own balance sheet would be the following: ($ in millions):

Equity Method	ABD Inc.
Assets:	
Cash	$200
Accounts receivable	0
Inventory	300
Current assets	500
Investment	350
Plant and equipment, net	0
Total assets	$850
Liabilities and shareholders' equity	
Accounts payable	$250
Long-term debt	0
Total liabilities	$250
Common stock ($1 par per share)	350
Additional paid-in capital	150
Retained earnings	100
Total liabilities and shareholders' equity	$850

(It should be noted that this balance sheet would never be *reported* to the public in the United States because consolidation is required under these circumstances.)

2) The eliminating entry that would be required to accomplish the consolidation would be the following: ($ in millions)

DR Common stock	$200	
DR Retained earnings	150	
CR Investment		$350

The consolidated balance sheet would look like the following:

Purchase Method:	**ABD Inc.**
Assets	
Cash	$200
Accounts receivable	600
Inventory	300
Current assets	$1,100
Plant and equipment, net	800
Total assets	$1,900
Liabilities and shareholders' equity	
Accounts payable	$250
Long-term debt	1,050
Total liabilities	$1,300
Common stock ($1 par per share)	350
Additional paid-in capital	150
Retained earnings	100
Total liabilities and shareholders' equity	$1,900

The equity method views the transaction as an investment in securities, while the consolidation method views the transaction as an acquisition of a *bundle* of assets and liabilities. For example, ABD acquired accounts receivable, plant and equipment, and long-term debt when it acquired C Corp. Any ratio involving balance sheet information would be affected, including the current ratio, the debt-to-equity ratio, the return on assets, etc.

3) This modification would increase both C's assets and liabilities by $5,000 without changing the book value of the company. Therefore, the answer to part 1 wouldn't change at all! However, the answer to part 2 *would* change because consolidation portrays the bundle of assets and liabilities. The consolidated plant and equipment would be $5,800 and the consolidated long-term debt would be $6,050. The equity method provides no information about the structure of assets and liabilities which underlie the investments. For this reason, firms sometimes structure their operations so as to qualify for the equity method. For example, if two firms form a joint venture (each holding 50% of the venture's stock), then they will each get to recognize 50% of the venture's income without having to recognize the venture's assets and liabilities (other than the 50% book value in investments).

4) We cannot allow C's receivable and ABD's payable to coexist in the consolidated balance sheet, because it would appear that the entity (ABD, Consolidated) owed *itself* some money! Therefore, an additional eliminating entry would be required.

DR Accounts payable	$20	
CR Accounts receivable		$20

5) The equity method (parent company) accounting for this situation would require that the investment in part 1 be $400 (rather than $350) and that the additional paid-in capital be $200 (rather than $150). But to know how the consolidated statement will look, we must determine why ABD was willing to pay $50 over C's book value in the acquisition. If C had an undervalued asset that could be specifically identified (e.g., a patent that C had developed or a piece of property that was worth more than its depreciated value), then that asset will appear in the consolidated statements. If the "premium" was due to C's additional future earnings power that cannot be tied to specifically identifiable assets, then the premium is recognized as an asset called goodwill. The required entries and resulting balance sheets are given below for (1) the case where plant and equipment had been undervalued and (2) the case where the premium is due to goodwill.

($ in millions)

Case (1)		Case (2)	
DR Common stock	$200	**DR** Common stock	$200
DR Retained earnings	150	**DR** Retained earnings	150
DR Plant and equipment	50	**DR** Goodwill	50
CR Investment	$400	**CR** Investment	$400

ABD Inc.		ABD Inc.	
Assets		Assets	
Cash	$200	Cash	$200
Accounts receivable	600	Accounts receivable	600
Inventory	300	Inventory	300
Current assets	1,100	Current assets	1,100
Plant and equipment, net	850	Plant and equipment, net	800
Total	$1,950	Goodwill	50
		Total	$1,950

Liabilities and shareholders' equity		Liabilities and shareholders' equity	
Accounts payable	$250	Accounts payable	$250
Long-term debt	1,050	Long-term debt	1,050
Total liabilities	$1,300	Total liabilities	$1,300
Common stock ($1 par)	350	Common stock ($1 par)	350
Additional paid-in capital	200	Additional paid-in capital	200
Retained earnings	100	Retained earnings	100
Total	$1,950	Total	$1,950

The consolidated income statements in subsequent periods would have to recognize the additional depreciation (in case 1) or the amortization of goodwill (in case 2).

6) The new information has two implications. First, ABD paid the same price for only 80% of C Corp., so the amount paid for goodwill would increase (assuming that all the premium is attributable to goodwill). The value would now be $400–80% (C's book value), or $120, rather than $50 in part 5. Further, ABD now owns an 80% claim on C's assets and liabilities, while another group of shareholders holds the remaining 20%. The consolidation process brings in 100% of C's assets and liabilities (because an 80% shareholder controls all of the assets and liabilities) and recognizes a claim called *minority interest in net assets of consolidated subsidiaries*. This amount is not a liability (because it is a shareholder-type claim), but it is not a claim by ABD's shareholders. Therefore, it is placed between liabilities and shareholders' equity in the consolidated balance sheet and has a value equal to 20% of the book value of C Corp.

Here is the entry required to consolidate:

DR Common stock	$200	
DR Retained earnings	150	
DR Goodwill	120	
CR Investment		$400
CR Minority interest in net assets		70

The balance sheet would look like: ($ in millions)

Purchase Method: **ABD Inc.**

Assets
Cash	$200
Accounts receivable	600
Inventory	300
Current assets	$1,100
Plant and equipment, net	800
Goodwill	120
Total assets	$2,020

Liabilities and shareholders' equity
Accounts payable	$250
Long-term debt	1,050
Total liabilities	$1,300
Minority interest in net assets	70
Common stock ($1 par per share)	250
Additional paid-in capital	200
Retained earnings	100
Total liabilities and shareholders' equity	$2,020

7. If ABD had exchanged its shares directly for those of C Corp., it would use the pooling-of-interests method of accounting for the acquisition. In this method, the book values of the assets, liabilities and retained earnings are

simply added together (intercompany receivables and payables are eliminated.) The contributed capital is also added together, though there may be some movement between the components of contributed capital—common stock and additional paid-in-capital.

Pooling-of-Interests Method:	ABD Inc.
Assets	
Cash	$200
Accounts receivable	600
Inventory	300
Current assets	$1,100
Plant and equipment, net	800
Total assets	$1,900
Liabilities & shareholders' equity:	
Accounts payable	$250
Long-term debt	1,050
Total liabilities	$1,300
Common stock ($1 par per share)	350
Retained earnings	250
Total liabilities and shareholders' equity	$1,900

Note that there is no recognition of the premium paid over C's book value, so there is no write-up of assets or recognition of depreciation. Therefore, there would be no additional depreciation or amortization against income in future years. In effect, when the acquisition premium is paid for in the form of stock, it does not show up in the financial reports [as a comparison of parts (5) and (7) confirms].

Cases
C15-1. The Seagram Company Ltd.: Equity method

Requirement 1:
Footnote 1 to Seagram's 1988 Annual Report indicates that Seagram owns 22.9% of the outstanding common stock of Du Pont, which provides it with effective economic control over the net assets of Du Pont. In addition, Seagram has the right to designate 25% of Du Pont's board of directors and Du Pont has two seats on Seagram's board. This mutual board representation further indicates a significant economic relation between the two firms, providing additional justification for use of the equity method.

Requirement 2:
Seagram's recording of Du Pont's dividends as dividend income ($179.48 million before tax and $165.37 after tax) is consistent with the use of the equity method. Normally, dividends received under the equity method are credited to the investment account, not to dividend income. But this treatment assumes that the investor company is picking up its share of the *total earnings* of the investee in the current period as investment income. In Seagram's case, it is only reporting its share of the *unremitted* (or undistributed) earnings of Du Pont. Since dividend income reported on Seagram's income statement represents its share of Du Pont's distributed *(remitted)* earnings for the year, the two numbers combined ($179.48 million of dividends before tax plus $211.21 million of Seagram's share of Du Pont's *unremitted* earnings less interest and other amortizations) equals Seagram's share of Du Pont's total earnings for 1988 (less amortizations, which are described in Req. 3). This is exactly the amount that should be reported under the equity method. Seagram is simply reporting its share of Du Pont's earnings in two parts: (1) that part received in the form of dividends of $179.48 million (before tax) which represents an actual cash inflow to Seagram; and (2) that portion which was *not distributed* in the current period ($211.21 million) which increases Seagram's accrual basis net income but does not affect Seagram's cash flows in the current period.

Requirement 3:
The amount of the excess of Seagram's investment cost over the book value of Du Pont's stock which was amortized to Seagram's earnings in the current period is determined as follows:

	$ Millions
Du Pont's 1987 net income (See Note 1)	$1,786
Seagram's equity interest	22.9%
Seagram's interest in Du Pont's earnings before amortizations	$408.99
Minus: Before-tax amount of Du Pont's earnings reported in	
Seagram's 1988 income statement $179.48 + $217.99 [1] =	-397.47
Amounts amortized to Seagram's equity in Du Pont's earnings	$11.52 [2]

Requirement 4:
Reconciliation of beginning and ending investment account balances:

	$ Millions
Investment in Du Pont stock 1/31/87 (see B/S)	$3,329.73
Add: Seagram's equity in Du Pont earnings (22.9% × $1,786)	408.99
Less: Dividend received from Du Pont (before tax)	(179.48)
Less: Amounts amortized against Seagram's equity in Du Pont's earnings (see item 3 above)	(11.52)
Less: Interest (net of tax) allocated against Du Pont's earnings	(6.78)
Add: Additional investment made in Du Pont's stock in 1987 (plug)	46.52
Investment in Du Pont stock on 1/31/88 (given)	$3,587.46

Requirement 5:
Return on Seagram's wine and spirits operation:

$$\text{ROA} = \frac{\text{Net income (after tax)} + \text{Interest (1- T) from wine and spirits}}{\text{Avg. assets exclusive of Du Pont investment}}$$

$$= \frac{\$144.52 + \$80.40\,(1-.30)^*}{\$3,756.37^{**}} = \frac{\$200.8}{\$3,756.37} = \underline{5.34\%}$$

$$* \frac{\text{Income tax expense}}{\text{Income before taxes}} = \frac{\$60.8}{\$205.3} = 30\%$$

		($ millions)
** Assets exclusive of Du Pont investment on 1/31/87		
$6,886.46 - $3,329.73	=	$3,556.73
Assets exclusive of Du Pont investment on 1/31/88		
$7,543.47 - $3,587.46	=	$3,956.01
		$7,512.74
		÷ 2
Avg. assets–wine and spirits operations		$3,756.37

---

[1] $211.21 reported on income statement + $6.78 interest (net of tax benefit) charged against unremitted earnings of Du Pont.

[2] $11.52 for excess depreciation and other amortizations charged to unremitted earnings.

Return on Seagram's investment in Du Pont

$$= \frac{\text{Seagram's share of Du Pont earnings (less taxes on dividends \& amort.)}}{\text{Avg. book value of Seagram's investment in Du Pont}}$$

$$= \frac{\$408.99 - \$14.114 - \$11.52}{(\$3,329.73 + \$3,587.46)/2}$$

$$= \frac{\$383.36}{\$3,458.60} = \underline{11.08\%}\ ^3$$

[3]Alternative ROA if adjustment for taxes on entire earnings of Du Pont: $408.99 x (1 - .20) - $11.52 / $3458.60 = $315.67 / $3458.60 = 9.12%. NOTE: Because of 80% dividend exclusion rule of U.S. Tax Code, Seagrams only needs to accrue taxes on 20% of its share of Du Pont's earnings.

C15-2. Tyler Corporation: Business acquisitions and analysis of sales growth

Requirement 1:
When an acquisition is accounted for as a purchase, time-series comparability in the basic financial statements is impaired. Since Thurston was acquired on April 6, 1979, its revenues and expenses are included in the income statement only from that date forward. 1978 results are for a three-division company, while 1979 results include the original three divisions plus nine months of Thurston's sales and expenses.

To achieve comparability in these instances, one must look to the pro forma figures in the footnote. These numbers are prepared as if Thurston were acquired on the earliest date for which comparative figures are provided, here January 1, 1978. Comparing sales growth of all *four* divisions between 1978 and 1979 reveals an increase of $60,279,000 or 12.6%.

The instructor might point out that the minimum GAAP pro forma disclosures are so limited (i.e., sales, net income and EPS) that reconstruction of fully-comparable, complete financial statements is not possible. Because of this, time-series analyses of ratios and trends for companies who have acquired others using the purchase method are frequently so non comparable as to be misleading.

Requirement 2:
Under pooling of interests accounting, the 1978 and 1979 income statements would have included Thurston's results for each of the years. Accordingly, the income statements would be more comparable. However, the acquired company's *book value* (not its fair value) is reflected on the balance sheet. Hence, there are also considerable (but different) problems for statement readers when poolings occur.

Requirement 3:
One can only conjecture here. Perhaps Tyler was trying to redirect attention away from the fact that net income grew by only 1.7%. This question provides a classroom opportunity to discuss how firms can use financial information to alter or influence statement readers' perceptions.

C15-3. City Holding Company: Mark-to-market accounting for available-for-sale securities

Requirement 1:
Before-tax unrealized holding gain on available-for-sale securities in 1995:

12/31/95		Desired balance in Market
Fair value	Cost	Adjustment account
$143,649,000	$142,990,000	$659,000 **DR**

12/31/94		
Fair value	Cost	
$82,777,000	$87,529,000	4,752,000 **CR**

Unrealized holding gain in 1995 (required
adjustment to market adjustment account) $5,411,000

Requirement 2:
Deferred tax liability related to this unrealized gain in 1995—see deferred tax footnote:

Deferred tax *asset* on unrealized loss on available-for-sale securities 12/31/94	$1,890,000
Deferred tax *liability* on unrealized gain on available-for-sale securities 12/31/95	264,000
Net change (credit) to deferred taxes in 1995	$2,154,000

Requirement 3:
Entry to record unrealized gain (net of tax effects) on the available-for-sale securities:

DR Market adjustment–available-for-sale $5,411,000
  CR Deferred tax liability on available-for-sale securities $2,154,000
  CR Unrealized gain on available-for-sale securities (S.E.)   3,257,000

Requirement 4:

Entry to record sales of available-for-sale securities in 1995:

DR Cash (from investment section of cash flow statement)	$55,185,000	
DR Realized loss on sales of available-for-sale securities	101,000	
CR Realized gain on available-for-sale securities		$103,000
CR Available-for-sale securities (cost basis)		55,183,000

Requirement 5:

Explain the year-to-year change from 12/31/94 to 12/31/95 in the cost basis of the available-for-sale securities.

Beginning balance 12/31/94 (from footnote schedule)			$87,529,000
+ Cost of securities purchased (from cash flow statement)			52,617,000
+ Fair value of securities transferred from held-to-maturity to available-for-sale in 1995= Cost	$69,389,000		
(from Note 4–Investments) + Unrealized gain	242,000	69,631,000	
- Cost basis of available-for-sale securities sold in 1995			
Proceeds from sales of available-for-sale securities (from cash flow statement)		55,185,000	
Proceeds from maturities and calls of available-for-sale securities (from cash flow statement)		11,331,000	
- Net gain on sales and calls of securities in 1995 (from Note 4–Investments and cash flow statement)		(2,000)	
			66,514,000
			143,263,000
Ending balance 12/31/95 (from footnote schedule)			142,990,000
Unaccounted-for difference			$273,000

C15-4. Acquisitive Inc.: Purchase vs. pooling

Requirement 1:
Prepare the pro forma balance sheets for the merged firm:

	Acquisitive, Inc. Pro Forma Post-Combination Balance Sheet Purchase Accounting		
	Acquisitive, Pre-Merger	Merger Adjustments	Acquisitive Post-Merger
Cash	$117	$150[1]	$267
Noncash assets	22,083	4,875[2]	31,558
		4,000[3]	
		600[4]	
Total	$22,000		$31,825
Liabilities	$11,800	4,825[5]	$16,625
Common stock, $2.50 par value	750	150[6]	900
Paid-in capital in excess of par value	650	4,650[7]	5,300
Retained earnings	9,000		9,000
Total	$22,200		$31,825

[1] The recorded value of Target's cash.

[2] The recorded value of Target's noncash assets.

[3] The estimated value of Target's unrecorded patents.

[4] The estimated value of goodwill implicit in the merger. Target's total fair value, based on the trading price of Acquisitive's shares, is $4.8 billion (60 shares of Acquisitive stock, at a price per share of $80, times 1 million Target shares). Assuming that, with the exception of the unrecorded patents, Target's identifiable assets and liabilities are recorded at the approximated fair values, goodwill implicit in the combination is equal to the total fair value of Target ($4.8 billion) less (1) the recorded value of Target's net identifiable assets ($200 million) and (2) the estimated value of Target's unrecorded patents ($4 billion).

[5] The recorded value of Target's liabilities.

[6] The par value of Acquisitive shares issued to effect the combination (60 shares of $2.50 par value stock times 1 million shares of Target stock).

[7] The difference between Target's total fair value ($4.8 billion) and the par value of Acquisitive's stock to be issued in the merger ($150 million).

Acquisitive, Inc.
Pro Forma Post-Combination Balance Sheet
Pooling of Interests Accounting

	Acquisitive, Pre-Merger	Merger Adjustments	Acquisitive Post-Merger
Cash	$117	$150 [1]	$267
Noncash assets	22,083	4,875 [2]	26,958
Total	$22,000		$27,225
Liabilities	$11,800	4,825 [3]	$16,625
Common stock, $2.50 par value	750	150 [4]	900
Paid-in capital in excess of par value	650	(23) [5]	627
Retained earnings	9,000	73 [6]	9,073
Total	$22,200		$27,225

[1] The recorded value of Target's cash.
[2] The recorded value of Target's noncash assets.
[3] The recorded value of Target's liabilities.
[4] The par value of Acquisitive shares issued to effect the combination (60 shares of $2.50 par value stock times 1 million shares of Target stock).
[5] Total par value of shares issued by Acquisitive ($150 million) exceeds Target's total paid-in capital ($127 million). According to paragraph 53 of APB Opinion No. 16, this $23 million excess is first used to reduce Acquisitive's existing paid-in capital in excess of par and, if necessary, is then used to reduce retained earnings of the combined firm. Because Acquisitive's paid-in capital in excess of par value is sufficient to absorb this excess, no adjustment to retained earnings is required.
[6] The recorded amount of Target's retained earnings.

Acquisitive, Inc.
Comparative Balance Sheets—Pre-Merger,
Pro Forma Purchase, Pro Forma Pooling of Interests

	Pre-Merger	Pro Forma Purchase	Pro Forma Pooling of Interests
Cash	$117	$267	$267
Noncash assets	22,083	31,558	26,958
Total	$22,000	$31,825	$27,225
Liabilities	$11,800	$16,625	$16,625
Common stock, $2.50 par value	750	900	900
Paid-in capital in excess of par value	650	5,300	627
Retained earnings	9,000	9,000	9,073
Total	$22,200	$31,825	$27,225

Requirement 2:
Why is the combination accounted for as a pooling of interests?

Acquisitive's insistence on accounting for the business combination as a pooling of interests apparently has to do with the unrecorded patents, valued at approximately $4 billion, and the $600 million goodwill implicit in the merger. If the business combination is accounted for as a purchase, these values would be capitalized and, based on an estimated economic life of eight years for the patents and an assumed amortization period of five years for the goodwill, would result in annual amortization of $620 million or $1.72 per share (based on 360 million outstanding shares). The "bottom-line" impact would be reduced by the tax effects of the patent amortization. However, because goodwill amortization is not currently deductible for tax purposes, the goodwill amortization would flow directly to the bottom line. (Note that a goodwill amortization period is not specified in the case because students are to infer the existence of goodwill without the "hint" that might be provided by a statement regarding goodwill amortization.)

If, on the other hand, the business combination is accounted for as a pooling of interests, the patents and goodwill would not be recorded and would result in no dilution of the combined firm's earnings in future periods.

Requirement 3:
Is Acquisitive's management's insistence on accounting for the combination as a pooling of interests rational or irrational? Provide circumstances for each case.

The real issue underlying the assignment question is, what motivates Acquisitive's management to avoid the amortization that would result from capitalizing the unrecorded patents and goodwill? Does it relate to management's belief that the stock market would react negatively to the amortization drag on earnings? If so, is this a rational belief in light of the lack of any differential cash flow effects of the two methods? If this is the basis for management's insistence, and if the market tends to "see through" accounting treatment differences, then is management's position rational?

Certainly, the tax status of a business combination (i.e., taxable versus tax-deferred or tax-free) has cash flow implications and is usually a critical factor in negotiating and structuring a business combination. However, the tax status is based on criteria contained in the tax law rather than criteria contained in APB Opinion No. 16. Accordingly, a combination's tax status is unaffected by the accounting method used for a particular business combination. Therefore, the classification of a combination as a pooling of interests vis-a-vis a purchase should have no effect on a combined company's income tax cash flows.

An alternative reason for Acquisitive management's insistence on use of the pooling of interest method might relate to the existence of management incentive contracts which tie management compensation in some way to reported company earnings. If such contracts exist, how would they be affected by the business combination, especially with respect to the issue of the differential effects of purchase and pooling treatment? For example, would management bonuses be affected by patent/goodwill amortization resulting from use of the purchase method to account for the combination? Or, are the contracts structured so that such "accounting" differences do not affect compensation?

Requirement 4:
Can the merger of Acquisitive and Target be accounted for as a pooling of interests?

In its discussion of the validity of the pooling of interests concept, APB Opinion No. 16 notes that:

> "A business combination effected by issuing common stock is different from a purchase in that no corporate assets are disbursed to stockholders and the net assets of the issuing corporation are enlarged by the net assets of the corporation whose stockholders accept common stock of the combined corporation. There is no newly invested capital nor have owners withdrawn assets from the group since the stock of a corporation is not one of its assets. Accordingly, the net assets of the constituents remain intact but combined; the stockholder groups remain intact but combined. Aggregate income is not changed since the total resources are not changed. Consequently, the historical costs and earnings of the separate corporations are appropriately combined. In a business combination effected by exchanging stock, groups of stockholders combine their resources, talents, and risks to form a new entity to carry on in combination the previous businesses and to continue their earnings streams. The sharing of risks by the constituent stockholder groups is an important element in a business combination effected by exchanging stock. By pooling equity interests, each group continues to maintain risk elements of its former investment and they mutually exchange risks and benefits."
> (Paragraph 28)

The facts and circumstances of the case indicate that the major exception to the above discussion related to the special dividend paid by Target to its shareholders—the owners of Target have withdrawn assets from the corporation. If the stock-for-stock business combination proceeds, the dividend could be viewed as an attempt to get cash to the owners of Target in the combination. From a slightly different perspective, the stock exchange, in combination with the dividend, could be viewed as a sale of shares by the

Target shareholders for cash and stock: Each share of Target stock was exchanged for $100 cash and 60 shares of Acquisitive stock. From either perspective, the dividend appears to violate the strict economic substance of a pooling of interests as a uniting of the ownership interests of the two companies.

With respect to the specific pooling criteria contained in paragraphs 45 through 48 of APB Opinion No. 16, two of the 12 criteria appear to be in question. The first is an "attributes of the combining companies" criterion:

> "Each of the combining companies is autonomous and has not been a subsidiary or division of another corporation within two years before the plan of combination is initiated." (Paragraph 46.a)

Martin Johnson controls Target through MJ, Inc., a personal holding company. Does the fact that Target is a subsidiary of MJ, Inc., violate this criterion?

This issue was dealt with by the AICPA staff in Accounting Interpretation No. 28 of APB Opinion No. 16. According to this interpretation, if the personal holding company is a convenience established for federal income tax purposes and the subsidiary is operated by the owners as if the personal holding company did not exist, then the personal holding company may be disregarded and the subsidiary considered autonomous for purposes of applying paragraph 46.a of APB opinion No. 16. The facts and circumstances of the case, while not conclusive, indicate that Johnson operates Target as if MJ, Inc., did not exist, in which case, the Paragraph 46.a criterion is not violated.

The more critical potential violation has to do with the special $100 dividend which Target declared and paid after Acquisitive's initial offer. One of the criteria relating to the manner of combining interests is as follows:

> "None of the combining companies changes the equity interest of the voting common stock in contemplation of effecting the combination either within two years before the plan of combination is initiated or between the dates the combination is initiated and consummated; changes in contemplation of effecting the combination may include distributions to stockholders and additional issuances, exchanges, and retirements of securities." (Paragraph 47.c)

APB Opinion No. 16 elaborates on this criterion with the following discussion:

> "Distributions to stockholders which are no greater than normal dividends are not changes for this condition. Normality of dividends is determined in relation to earnings during the period and to the previous dividend policy and record. Dividend distributions on stock of a combining company that are equivalent to normal dividends on

the stock to be issued in exchange in the combination are considered normal for this condition." (Paragraph 47)

Did Target pay the special dividend within the two-year period specified in the criterion? The facts and circumstances of the case indicate that the special dividend was declared and paid approximately one year ago. This means that the special dividend's impact on this criterion must be examined unless the plan of combination is not initiated for at least another year (see APB Opinion No. 16, paragraph 46, for a definition of "initiation date").

Was the dividend paid "in contemplation of effecting the combination"? The usual interpretation is that a larger-than-normal dividend paid within the specified two-year period is assumed to have been paid in contemplation of effecting the business combination. This interpretation is corroborated by the facts and circumstances which suggest that the dividend would not have been paid had Acquisitive not approached Target with the merger proposal.

Was the dividend larger than a "normal dividend"? The facts and circumstances are intentionally vague on this issue and do not indicate whether, if ever, Target has paid dividends in the past. However, a $100 million "special" dividend paid by a company which, after the dividend, has a retained earnings balance of $73 million would likely be viewed by most as "large." Target has the burden of proof to show by comparisons to its current earnings and its past dividend policy and record that such a dividend is not "large" for purposes of the Paragraph 47.c criterion.

In summary, it is the opinion of the authors that this dividend violates the Paragraph 47.c criterion.

Requirement 5:
If you concluded in answer to Question 4 that the combination could not be accounted for as a pooling of interests, could anything be done by either of the companies to remedy the violation(s) and allow the combination to be accounted for as a pooling of interests?

Authoritative literature does not deal with this issue. In the opinion of the authors, the violation could be "cured" by having Target's shareholders repay the dividend (perhaps with interest), so that equity interests are as if they had not been changed.

C15-5. Air Products: Joint ventures and off-balance-sheet effects

Requirement 1:
The primary reason that companies enter into joint ventures is because different companies have expertise in different areas. If a particular project requires expertise that is beyond the capability of one company to undertake

independently, it makes sense to seek out another company that has that expertise. This is undoubtedly the primary explanation for joint ventures.

Having said this, it is also true that if the joint venture is **exactly** 50:50, then–under GAAP rules–neither joint venturer needs to consolidate the venture since control is defined as *more than* 50% ownership. These joint ventures are often highly leveraged. This causes some to suggest that the frequency of 50:50 joint ventures may be partly attributable to the fact that the venture's assets and debt are off *both* venturers' balance sheets, thereby improving ratios like return on assets and debt-to-equity.

Requirement 2:
All of the following computations depend upon estimates and assumptions. As a consequence, one must understand that the "adjusted" ratios are undoubtedly computed with error.

Return on assets ratio:

We begin by computing the return on assets ratio "conventionally," that is:

$$\frac{\text{Net income} + \text{interest expense} \times (1 - \text{tax rate})}{\text{Total assets}}$$

Specifically:

$$\frac{\$416 + \$83.9}{\$6,522} = .0766$$

[Note: $83.9 = $129 (interest expense) times (1 - .35)]

But the conventional denominator–assets–excludes the assets of the joint ventures. The instructions say to assume that Air Products' proportionate ownership in the equity affiliates averaged 40%. This is probably reasonable since its share of 1996 income–as given in the footnote–was $101 million divided by total equity affiliates' income of $226 million, or 44.7%. The total assets of the equity affiliates at the end of fiscal 1996 were:

Current assets	$751	million
Noncurrent assets	3,164	million
	$3,915	million

40% of $3,915 is $1,566 million. This is the estimated amount of assets that would have appeared on Air Products' balance sheet had it undertaken its share of the venture individually. But the balance sheet shows an account investment in net assets of and advance to equity affiliates with a $759 million balance. So, to approximate the additional assets that would have been on Air Products' balance sheet, we do the following:

Estimated proportionate share of
   equity affiliates' assets $1,566
   Amount already on balance sheet   (759)
   Incremental asset adjustment $807

Using this estimate, the adjusted return on assets ratio becomes:

$$\frac{\$416 + \$83.9}{\$6,522 + \$807} = .0682$$

After adjustment, the ratio declines from .0766 to .0682, or a drop of approximately 11%. This is clearly an approximation since we are <u>not</u> provided with the amount of interest expense of the equity affiliates that is included in the income figure of Air Products. Consequently, it is not possible to adjust for this equity affiliate interest in the interest expense adjustment in the numerator.

Debt-to-equity ratio:

The conventionally computed debt-to-equity ratio is:

$$\frac{\$1,739}{\$2,574} = .676$$

The footnote discloses that the noncurrent liabilities of the equity affiliates totaled $2,129. But how much of this was long-term debt? We have no way of knowing for sure. If the affiliates are in businesses that are similar to Air Products', one might assume that the industry commonality translates into financial statement commonality. Using this logic, the ratio of long-term debt to total noncurrent liabilities on Air Products' balance sheet at September 30, 1996, was:

$$\frac{\$1,739}{\$2,685} = .648$$

[Note: $2,685 is $1,739 + $364 + $582]

(Of course, if the affiliates' businesses are different from Air Products', the .648 figure potentially introduces error into the analysis.)

If we multiply the .648 by the $2,129 total noncurrent liabilities of equity affiliates, we get $1,379.6. The estimated additional long-term debt amount if Air Products had undertaken its share of the venture individually is shown below:

Total noncurrent liabilities of equity affiliates	$2,129
Air Products' ratio of long-term debt to total noncurrent liabilities	×.648
Estimated equity affiliates' long-term debt	$1,379.6
Estimated Air Products' portion	× .40
Estimated additional long-term debt	$551.8

The adjusted debt-to-equity ratio would then be:

$$\frac{\$1,739 + \$551.8}{\$2,574} = .89$$

The debt-to-equity ratio unadjusted was .676. Adjusted, it is .89. This is a deterioration of 31.7%.

C15-6. Texaco and Exxon: Functional currency choices

This is a subtle case that students will probably find challenging. Answering the questions posed in the case requires a general understanding of foreign currency markets as well as insights regarding financial reporting strategies.

Requirement 1:
The key point here is that when the U.S. dollar is strengthening, and a company has an exposed net liability position, it then will experience foreign currency *gains*. Exxon reports that had it chosen the dollar as the functional currency, it would have reported higher income over the period 1980-1982. We can infer this from annual report note 2 which tells us that "the effect of implementing... [the current rate approach] was to decrease net income for 1980, 1981, and 1982 by $300 million ($.34 per share), $741 million ($.86 per share), and $130 million ($.15 per share), respectively."

The relatively higher exposed net liability position under the temporal method immediately follows. Here is why. The current rate method almost always has an exposed net asset position since *all* assets and *all* liabilities are considered to be exposed under this approach. Net liability exposures exist only for firms with negative equity. (Exxon, of course, had positive equity.) If the temporal method had had a *higher* net asset exposure, then abandoning the temporal method should have led to higher reported income, not lower, with a strengthening U.S. dollar.

Requirement 2:
When changes in exchange rates cause a subsidiary's activities to have a readily determinable actual or potential impact on U.S. dollar cash flows, then the subsidiary's functional currency should be the U.S. dollar. Straightforward examples are overseas marketing subsidiaries (these impact U.S. dollar *inflows*) or production subsidiaries (these impact dollar *outflows*). While subsidiaries that "are relatively self-contained and integrated within a particular country or economic environment" should generally choose the local currency as the functional currency (SFAS No. 52, para. 80), there are exceptions. One important exception is where "sales prices for the foreign entity's products are primarily responsive on a short-term basis to changes in exchange rates" (SFAS No. 52, para. 42). This price responsiveness clearly exists in the multinational oil industry since petroleum pricing was (and still is) based in U.S. dollars. The only scenario that is consistent with the numbers in the disclosure is that Exxon had a net liability exposure under the temporal method.

Why then did Exxon (and a few others like Mobil) choose the local currency as the functional currency for most of their subsidiaries? One possible reason is that the logic underlying SFAS No. 52 is subtle and perhaps not widely understood. As examples, Phillips Petroleum has an error of fact in its description of the foreign currency remeasurement process in its 1982 annual report (see Phillips Petroleum's 1982 Annual Report, p. 44).

However, it is unlikely that Exxon's choice was based upon a lack of understanding of SFAS No. 52. Instead, it seems more likely that Exxon was using the flexibility in GAAP to improve the appearance of its financial results. Choosing the foreign currency as the functional currency would accomplish this result for the following reasons:

1) The switch to the foreign currency as the functional currency lowers its net liability exposure (see the answer to Requirement 1, above).

2) Indeed, Exxon would have a net asset exposure under the current rate method. If the dollar did fall–as was being forecast in early 1983–then translation gains would result and would go directly to owners' equity. (By contrast, under the temporal method, losses would have probably resulted and, worse yet, would have been run directly through the income statement.)

Thus, Exxon's reporting choice may have been motivated by a desire to improve future periods' income. Students may be led astray by the fact that the functional currency choice lowered *past* periods' income. But notice that the 1982 "hit" was trivial since it lowered reported income by only about 3% [i.e., $130 million ($4,186 + $130)].

Collaborative Case

C15-7. The Tribune Company: Financial statement effects of consolidating vs. not consolidating a subsidiary

Requirement 1:
The Tribune Company's decision not to consolidate QUNO is consistent with a strict literal interpretation of the rules for when a subsidiary must be consolidated. The operative language from ARB 51 paragraph 2 (reaffirmed in SFAS 94, paragraph 13) reads:

> "The usual condition for a controlling financial interest is ownership of a majority voting interest, and, therefore, as a general rule ownership by one company, directly or indirectly, of over fifty percent of the outstanding voting shares of another company is a condition pointing toward consolidation."

The existing standard equates "control" with "majority voting interest." But this aspect of GAAP is currently being re-examined by the FASB. To illustrate why, consider the following: If Tribune Company owned 49% of the voting shares of QUNO and each of the other shareholders owned 1% or less, it is clear that *real* control rests with Tribune Company because of the diffused "outside" interest. Despite this, since 49% does not represent a strict majority, current GAAP guidelines do not require consolidation. Some observers suggest that since effective control can exist even without majority ownership of voting shares, consolidation should be required under such circumstances.

However, the facts of this case raise at least three additional issues regarding what constitutes control. First, Tribune Company holds QUNO's $138.8 million subordinated debenture which is convertible *at the option of Tribune Company* into 11.7 million voting shares of QUNO. Conversion would accordingly give the Company 20.5 million shares which represent 69.5% of all QUNO voting shares. Since the Tribune Company has the option (at least through December 27, 1997–the call date of the debenture) to become the majority shareholder, it is not unreasonable to argue that effective control also exists at the 1993 statement date.

Second, Tribune Company also owns 4.2 million nonvoting common shares. The fact that Tribune Company owns 59% of QUNO's total of 22 million outstanding common shares in conjunction with the likelihood that the ownership of the remaining nine million common shares is highly diffused further underscores the existence of real control by Tribune Company, despite its "minority" voting position.

Finally, Note 2 in Exhibit 3 indicates that the Company has "take or pay" contracts with QUNO extending through 2007. While "take or pay" contracts are often viewed as mechanisms for locking in production capacity "off balance sheet," they can also be viewed as a type of *guarantee* to the supplier. Do such guarantees convey additional incidents of control to the guarantor? If so, then the case for consolidation is even stronger.

Requirement 2:
We can only conjecture about reasons why Tribune Company would have structured the IPO to give itself minority voting ownership and the option to deconsolidate. The most obvious explanation relates to the improvement that results from having a highly leveraged subsidiary "off-balance-sheet." The pro forma disclosure from the 1992 Annual Report (see Exhibit 1) reveals the following:

	As Reported in 1992 Financials	Pro Forma Deconsolidated 1992 Amounts
Long-term debt-to-equity ratio	.922	.637
Long-term debt-to-total-capital ratio	.306	.240

Thus, the improvement from deconsolidation, especially in the debt-to-equity ratio, is significant. This is the same type of ratio improvement that motivates firms to form joint ventures; neither of the 50:50 ventures are required to consolidate the venture since neither owns a majority interest. Similar off-balance motivations led to pre-SFAS 94 nonconsolidation of finance, leasing, and real-estate subsidiaries that were deemed to be in radically different lines of business than the parent.

In a narrative section of the 1993 Annual Report titled "Answers to Investors' Questions" (pp. 5–6), Tribune Company discusses its recent acquisitions as well as its contemplated acquisition strategy. One question and answer is particularly illuminating:

> **What is Tribune's financial capability to continue making acquisitions and investments at the level we have seen recently?** As we have stated in our dialogue with shareholders and the investment community, we intend to supplement our revenue stream by acquisitions in high-growth businesses. Tribune is a strong cash generator. At the end of 1993, our debt position was at about $535 million, *about half of what it was three years ago* (emphasis supplied). Our debt-to-total-capital ratio is slightly more than 30%. As a result, our current credit and commercial paper ratings are strong. We have sufficient flexibility to finance further acquisitions.

If the company believes that credit markets naively monitor statement ratios and are oblivious to off-balance-sheet considerations, then a strong incentive to deconsolidate exists. Similarly, if the company is constrained by covenant restrictions (an unlikely scenario in this instance), deconsolidation is again attractive.

Requirement 3:

Using the pro forma deconsolidation disclosure from the 1992 Annual Report in conjunction with the 1993 Annual Report, the following two-year comparison emerges:

	(1) 1992 Numbers As Reported in 1993 Annual Report	(2) 1992 Numbers under Pro Forma Deconsolidation	(3) 1993 Numbers as Reported in 1993 Annual Report
Long-term debt-to-equity ratio	.922	.637	.490 $\left\{ \dfrac{\$510.8 + \$25.8}{\$1,095.6} \right.$
Long-term debt-to-total-capital-ratio	.306	.240	.212 $\left\{ \dfrac{\$510.8 + \$25.8}{\$2,536.4} \right.$
Pre-tax return on assets	.102	.117	.141

The absence of retroactive restatement of the 1992 figures in the 1993 Annual Report makes the year-to-year "improvement" arising from deconsolidation (column 1 versus column 3) more extreme than the retroactively restated year-to-year change (column 2 versus column 3).

This failure to retroactively restate the 1992 numbers on a comparable (deconsolidated) basis is probably not a violation of GAAP, although it is admittedly a gray area. APB Opinion 20 ("Accounting Changes," July 1971) defined a change in a reporting entity as follows (para. 12):

> "One special type of change in accounting principle results in financial statements which, in effect, are those of a different reporting entity. This type is limited mainly to (a) presenting consolidated or combined statements in place of statements of individual companies, (b) *changing specific subsidiaries comprising the group of companies for which consolidated financial statements are presented,* and (c) changing the companies included in combined financial statements. A different group of companies comprise the reporting entity after each change. A business combination accounted for by the pooling of interests method also results in a different reporting entity." (Emphasis added)

Alternative (b) seemingly captures the situation in the QUNO deconsolidation.

After defining what is meant by a change in a reporting entity, the APB then required the following disclosure for such changes (para. 34):

> "The Board concludes that accounting changes which result in financial statements of a different reporting entity (paragraph 12) should be reported by **restating the financial statements of all prior periods** presented in order to show financial information for the new reporting entity for all periods." (Emphasis supplied)

Following these disclosure guidelines raises the possibility that retroactive restatement of the 1992 numbers in the 1993 Annual Report might have been warranted when QUNO was deconsolidated.

However, the SEC staff does not interpret APB 20 in this manner. In the *Division of Corporation Finance Training Manual* (July, 1992), the following statement appears (p. 9):

> "The mere disposition of a subsidiary (that does not qualify as discontinued operations) [sic] either by sale or otherwise is not a change in reporting entity."

Disposing of a portion of a previously consolidated subsidiary would not *itself* necessitate restatement according to the SEC's interpretation of APB 20. Only if QUNO constituted a discontinued operation pursuant to paragraph 13 of APB 30 would retroactive restatement be required, in the view of the SEC staff. But since Tribune Company continued to own 49% of QUNO's voting shares, QUNO does not qualify as a discontinued operation. Consequently, retroactive restatement would seemingly not be required under SEC guidelines.

A slightly different perspective is presented in the 1989 *Deloitte & Touche Professors' Handbook* (pp. 24–12):

"If a parent sells a controlling interest in its subsidiary but still retains an investment of 20% or more, that remaining investment should be reflected in the balance sheet at the end of the period as a single line item, using the equity method; the subsequent results of operations should also be recast on a one-line basis .... In prior periods' comparative financial statements the subsidiary may be deconsolidated and restated using the equity method presentation; however those prior-period statements may also be left unchanged, and footnote disclosure given as to the later deconsolidation."

Thus, existing GAAP disclosure requirements on this topic are subject to differing interpretations.

Exercises
E16-1. Determining cash flows from operations

Using the indirect method, cash flow from operations is computed below:

Net income		$280,000
Add:		
Equity in investee loss	$20,000	
Decrease in prepaid expenses	7,000	
Depreciation expense	13,000	
Increase in salaries payable	8,000	
		48,000
Subtract:		
Amortization of premium on bonds payable	(10,000)	
Increase in inventory	(21,000)	
Increase in accounts receivable	(15,000)	
Decrease in accounts payable	(2,000)	
		(48,000)
Cash flow from operations		**$280,000**

E16-2. Determining cash flows from operations
(AICPA adapted)

Lino's net cash from operating activities is calculated below:

Net income	$150,000
Increase in accounts receivable[1]	(5,800)
Decrease in prepaid rent	4,200
Increase in accounts payable	3,000
Cash flow from operations	**$151,400**

[1]The increase in accounts receivable is net of the allowance for doubtful accounts:

Beginning accounts receivable	$23,000
Less: Beginning allowance for doubtful accounts	(800)
Beginning net accounts receivable	$22,200
Ending accounts receivable	$29,000
Less: Ending allowance for doubtful accounts	(1,000)
Ending net accounts receivable	$28,000
Increase in net accounts receivable:	
Ending net accounts receivable	$28,000
Beginning net accounts receivable	(22,200)
Increase in net accounts receivable	$5,800

E16-3. Cash flows from operations
(AICPA adapted)

Requirement 1:
Calculate accrual basis net income for December:

Sales revenue		$350,000
Cost of goods sold (70% of sales)		(245,000)
Gross profit (30% of sales)		105,000
Selling, general, and administrative expenses		
Fixed portion =	$35,000	
Variable portion = 15% × $350,000 =	52,500	(87,500)
Net income (accrual basis)		**$17,500**

Requirement 2:
Adjust accrual basis income to obtain cash flows from operations:

Accrual basis net income	$17,500
- Increase in gross trade accounts receivable	(10,500)
- Increase in inventory	(5,000)
+ Charge for uncollectible accounts (1% × $350,000)	3,500
+ Depreciation expense included in S, G&A	20,000
Cash flows from operating activities	**$25,500**

E16-4. Analysis of changes in balance sheet accounts
(AICPA adapted)

Requirement 1:
Determining depreciation on machinery for 1999:

Step 1: Determine the amount of accumulated depreciation on equipment sold during 1999:

Cost of machine sold (given)	$40,000
Less: Accumulated depreciation	?
Book value of equipment sold	?
Less: Cash received from sale	26,000
Loss on sale (given)	$4,000

Working backwards, the book value of equipment sold is $30,000 and the accumulated depreciation is $10,000.

Step 2: Analyze the accumulated depreciation account to determine the amount credited to this account when depreciation expense was recorded for the year:

Accumulated Depreciation

		$102,000	Beginning balance
Accumulated depreciation on equipment sold (see above)	$10,000	?	Depreciation expense for the year
		$120,000	Ending balance

From the T-account analysis, we can determine that depreciation expense for the year is $28,000.

Requirement 2:
To determine machinery purchases, the solutions approach is to set up a T-account for machinery and solve for the missing debit for equipment purchases:

Machinery

Beginning balance	$250,000			
Purchases	?	$40,000	Cost of equipment sold
Ending balance	$320,000			

The T-account can by analyzed to determine that 1999 machinery purchases totaled $110,000.

E16-5. Cash flows from investing and financing activities
(AICPA adapted)

Requirement 1:
Net cash flows from operating activities are computed as follows:

Net income	$300,000
+ Depreciation	52,000
- Gain on sale of equipment	(5,000)
Cash flows from operating activities	**$347,000**

Requirement 2:
Below is the computation for cash flow from investing activities:

Sale of equipment[1]	$18,000
Purchase of equipment[2]	(20,000)
Cash outflow from investing activities	**($2,000)**

[1] Computation of cash from sale of equipment:

Cost of equipment	$25,000
Accumulated depreciation	(12,000)
Book value of equipment sold	13,000
Gain on sale of equipment	5,000
Amount of cash received in exchange for equipment	$18,000

[2] Computation of cash paid for equipment:

Cost of new equipment	$50,000
Less: amount paid with note payable	(30,000)
Cash paid for equipment	$20,000

E16-6. Cash flows from investing and financing activities
(AICPA adapted)

Requirement 1:
Cash flow from investing activities:

Sale of equipment	$10,000
Purchase of A.S., Inc., bonds	(180,000)
Net cash used in investing activities	($170,000)

Requirement 2:
Cash flow from financing activities:

Dividends paid	($38,000)
Proceeds from sale of treasury stock	75,000
Net cash provided by financing activities	$37,000

E16-7. Cash flows from investing activities
(AICPA adapted)

Purchase of stock in Maybel	($26,000)
Sale of investment in Rate Motors	35,000
Purchase of 4-year certificate of deposit	(50,000)
Net cash used in investing activities	**($41,000)**

E16-8. Cash flows from investing and financing activities
(AICPA adapted)

Requirement 1:
Cash flows from investing activities:

Sale of investment	$500,000
Purchase of equipment	(125,000)
Purchase of real estate	(550,000)
Net cash used in investing activities	**($175,000)**

Requirement 2:
Cash flows from financing activities:

Dividends paid	($600,000)
Issue of common stock	250,000
Bank loan for real estate purchase	550,000
Paid toward bank loan	(450,000)
Net cash used in financing activities	**($250,000)**

E16-9. Determining operating cash flows
(AICPA adapted)

Net Income	$150,000
Increase in investment in Videogold, Inc.	(5,500)
Increase in deferred income tax liability	1,800
Decrease in premium on bonds payable	(1,400)
Net cash provided by operating activities	**$144,900**

E16-10. Determining operating, investing, and financing cash flows
(AICPA adapted)

Requirement 1:
Net cash provided by operating activities:

Net income	$790,000
Gain on sale of long-term investment	(35,000)
Increase in inventory	(80,000)
Depreciation expense	250,000
Decrease in accounts payable and accrued liabilities	(5,000)
Net cash provided by operating activities	**$920,000**

Requirement 2:
Net cash used in investing activities:

Purchase of short-term investments	($300,000)
Sale of long-term investments	135,000
Sale of plant assets	350,000
Purchase of plant assets (see T-account which follows)	(1,190,000)
Net cash used in investing activities	**($1,005,000)**

Plant Assets

Cost of equipment acquired	$110,000	$600,000	Cost of building sold
Cost of plant assets purchased	X		
Net increase	$700,000		

$110,000 + X - $600,000 = $700,000
X = $1,190,000

Requirement 3:
Net cash provided by financing activities:

Payment of dividends ($500,000 - $160,000)	($340,000)
Issuance of short-term debt	325,000
Issuance of common stock (10,000 × $22)	220,000
Net cash provided by financing activities	**$205,000**

Check: (Not required)	
Cash provided by operating activities	$920,000
Cash used in investing activities	(1,005,000)
Cash provided by financing activities	205,000
Increase in cash and cash equivalents	$120,000

Problems

P16-1. Determining cash provided (used) by operating, investing and financing activities
(AICPA adapted)

Requirement 1:

Cash flows provided by operating activities:

Net Income		$690,000
Increase in inventory	($80,000)	
Increase in accounts payable	105,000	
Gain on sale of investment[1]	(35,000)	
Goodwill amortization[2]	10,000	
Depreciation expense[3]	250,000	
		$250,000
Cash flows from operations		**$940,000**

[1] Gain on sale of investment is determined as follows:

Proceeds from sale of investments (given)	$135,000
Less: Book value of investment sold	
($300,000 - $200,000)	(100,000)
Gain on sale of investment	$35,000

[2] Goodwill amortized is equal to change in the goodwill account for the year = $100,000 - $90,000 = $10,000

[3] Depreciation expense recorded in year 2000 is determined from an analysis of the accumulated depreciation T-account.

Accumulated Depreciation

		$450,000	Beginning balance
Accumulated depreciation		X	Depreciation expense for year
on equipment sold*	$250,000		
		$450,000	Ending balance

*Cost of equipment sold =	$400,000
Less: Carrying value	(150,000)
Accumulated depreciation	$250,000

Solving for depreciation expense amount X in T-account
$450,000 + X - $250,000 = $450,000
X = $250,000 = Depreciation expense for year 2000

Requirement 2:
Cash flows used in investing activities:

Sale of equipment	$150,000
Sale of long-term investment	135,000
Purchase of plant assets [4]	(1,100,000)
Purchase of short-term investments	(300,000)
Cash outflows from investing activities	**($1,115,000)**

[4] Cash payments for plant assets is obtained from an analysis of the plant assets T-account:

Plant Assets

Beginning balance	$1,000,000	$400,000	Cost of equipment sold
Purchase of additional assets	X		
Ending balance	$1,700,000		

Solve for X:
$1,000,000 + X - $400,000 = $1,700,000
X = $1,100,000 = Purchase of plant assets

Requirement 3:
Cash flows provided by financing activities:

Dividends paid	($240,000)
Sale of common stock[5]	220,000
Short-term debt	325,000
Cash flows from financing activities	**$305,000**

[5] 10,000 shares @ $22/sh. = $220,000

Proof: (Not required)

Cash from operating activities	$940,000
Cash used for investing activities	(1,115,000)
Cash from financing activities	305,000
Net increase in cash	$130,000

P16-2. Comparing direct and indirect methods of determining cash flows from operations
(CMA adapted)

Requirement 1:
The statement of cash flows for Spoke Company, for the year ended May 31, 1998, using the direct method is presented below:

Spoke Company Statement of Cash Flows For the Year Ended May 31, 1998		
Cash Flows from Operating Activities:		
Cash received from customers[1]		$1,235,250
Cash paid		
to suppliers[2]	$664,000	
to employees[3]	276,850	
for other expenses[4]	10,150	
for interest[5]	73,000	
for income taxes[6]	43,000	1,067,000
Net cash provided by operating activities		$168,250
Cash Flows from Investing Activities:		
Purchase of plant assets		(40,000)
Cash Flows from Financing Activities:		
Cash received from common stock issue	$40,000	
Cash paid		
for dividends	115,000	
to retire bonds payable	30,000	
Net cash used for financing activities		(105,000)
Net increase in cash		23,250
Cash, May 31, 1997		20,000
Cash, May 31, 1998		$43,250
Note 1: Schedule of noncash investing and financing activities.		
Issuance of common stock for plant assets		$50,000

Supporting calculations:

[1] Collections from customers:

Sales	$1,255,250
Less: Increase in accounts receivable	20,000
Cash collected from customers	$1,235,250

[2] Cash paid to suppliers:

Cost of merchandise sold	$712,000
Less: Decrease in merchandise inventory	40,000
Increase in accounts payable	8,000
Cash paid to suppliers	$664,000

[3] Cash paid to employees:

Salary expense	$252,100
Add: Decrease in salaries payable	24,750
Cash paid to employees	$276,850

[4] Cash paid for other expenses:

Other expense	$8,150
Add: Increase in prepaid expenses	2,000
Cash paid for other expenses	$10,150

[5] Cash paid for interest:

Interest expense	$75,000
Less: Increase in interest payable	2,000
Cash paid for interest	$73,000

[6] Cash paid for income taxes:

Income tax expense (given)	$43,000

Requirement 2:

The calculation of the cash flow from operating activities for Spoke Company, for the year ended May 31, 1998, using the indirect method, follows:

Spoke Company		
Statement of Cash Flows		
For the Year Ended May 31, 1998		
Cash Flows from Operating Activities:		
Net income		$140,000
Adjustments to reconcile net income to cash		
Provided from operations:		
Depreciation expense	$25,000	
Decrease in merchandise inventory	40,000	
Increases in:		
Accounts payable	8,000	
Interest payable	2,000	
Accounts receivable	(20,000)	
Prepaid expenses	(2,000)	
Decrease in salaries payable	(24,750)	28,250
Net cash provided by operating activities		$168,250

Requirement 3:
Both the direct method and the indirect method for reporting cash flows from operating activities are acceptable in preparing a statement of cash flows according to SFAS 95; however, the FASB encourages the use of the direct method. Under the direct method, the statement of cash flows reports the major classes of cash receipts and cash disbursements and discloses more information; this may be the statement's principal advantage. Under the indirect method, net income on the accrual basis is adjusted to the cash basis by adding or deducting noncash items included in net income, thereby providing a useful link between the statement of cash flows and the income statement and balance sheet.

P16-3. Determining amounts reported on statement of cash flows
(AICPA adapted)

Requirement 1:
Cash collections from customers can be determined by examining the accounts receivable T-account, shown below:

Accounts Receivable			
Beginning balance	$24,000		
Sales	155,000	X	Cash collections
Ending balance	$34,000		

We can find the amount of cash collections from customers by solving for X.

$24,000 + $155,000 - X = $34,000; X = $24,000 + $155,000 - $34,000; X = $145,000

Cash collections from customers would appear in cash flows from operating activities as $145,000.

Requirement 2:
Cash payments for purchase of property, plant, and equipment are calculated as follows:

Property, Plant, & Equipment			
Beginning balance	$247,000	$40,000	Sale of equipment
Acquired from bond refinancing	20,000		
Cash purchases	X		
Ending balance	$277,000		

Solving for X: $247,000 + $20,000 + X - $40,000 = $277,000; X = $50,000

Purchases of PP&E would be classified as cash flows from investing activities.

Requirement 3:
Proceeds from sale of equipment can be found by first looking at the accumulated depreciation account:

Accumulated	Depreciation		
	$167,000	Beginning balance	
	33,000	Depreciation expense	
Depreciation on equipment sold X			
	$178,000	Ending balance	

By solving for X , we can find the depreciation on the equipment that was sold.

$167,000 + $33,000 - X = $178,000; $167,000 + $33,000 - $178,000 = X
X = $22,000

Since we know the accumulated depreciation on the equipment sold, we can determine its carrying value or book value as follows:

Cost of equipment	$40,000
Accumulated depreciation on equipment	(22,000)
Carrying value of equipment sold	$18,000

Now that we know the carrying value of the equipment that was sold, we can determine the proceeds from sale of equipment.

Carrying value (book value) of equipment sold	$18,000
Gain on sale of equipment	13,000
Proceeds from sale of equipment	$31,000

This amount would be classified as cash flows from investing activities.

Requirement 4:
To find dividends paid, we need to first determine dividends declared by analyzing retained earnings:

Retained	Earnings		
	$91,000	Beginning balance	
	28,000	Net income	
Dividends declared X			
	$104,000	Ending balance	

Solving for X, we get:
$91,000 + $28,000 - X = $104,000
X = $91,000 + $28,000 - $104,000
X = $15,000 = dividends declared

The amount of cash dividends paid can be determined by T-account analysis of dividends payable:

Dividends Payable

		$5,000	Beginning balance
		15,000	Dividends declared
Cash dividends paid	X		
		$8,000	Ending balance

Solving for X, we get:

X = $5,000 + $15,000 - $8,000

X = $12,000 = Cash dividends paid

$12,000 should be reported on the statement of cash flows as a financing activity.

Requirement 5:

Redemption of bonds payable can be found by using the bonds payable T-account:

Bonds Payable

		$46,000	Beginning balance
		20,000	Bonds issued in 1998
Redemption of bonds	X		
		$49,000	Ending balance

Solve for X:

$46,000 + $20,000 - X = $49,000; $46,000 + $20,000 - $49,000 = X

X = $17,000

Redemption of bonds payable is $17,000 reported under cash flows from financing activities.

P16-4. Determining amounts reported on statement of cash flows
(AICPA adapted)

Requirement 1:
Cash collections from customers can be determined by examining the accounts receivable T-account below:

Accounts Receivable			
Beginning balance	$30,000		
Sales	538,800		
		X	Cash collections
Ending balance	$33,000		

We can find cash collections from customers by solving for X.

$30,000 + $538,800 - X = $33,000; $30,000 + $538,800 - $33,000 = X
X = $535,800

Cash collections from customers are $535,800.

Requirement 2:
To solve for cash paid for goods sold, we must first determine how much was purchased. We can do this by first looking at the inventory account to determine total purchases for the period:

Inventory			
Beginning balance	$47,000		
Purchases	X		
		$250,000	Cost of goods sold
Ending balance	$31,000		

To find purchases, solve for X.

$47,000 + X - $250,000 = $31,000
X = $250,000 + $31,000 - $47,000
X = $234,000

Next, to find out how much cash was paid on accounts payable, we plug the purchases number into the accounts payable T-account and solve for cash payments on account:

Accounts Payable			
		$17,500	Beginning balance
		234,000	Purchases
Cash paid	X		
		$25,000	Ending balance

Again, we can solve for X.

$17,500 + $234,000 - X = $25,000
X = $17,500 + $234,000 - $25,000
X = $226,500

Cash paid for goods to be sold is $226,500.

Requirement 3:
We can determine cash paid for interest as follows:

Interest expense (1998)	$4,300
Less: Amortization of bond discount in 1998	(500)
Cash paid for interest	$3,800

Requirement 4:
Cash paid for income taxes:

Income Taxes Payable			
		$27,100	Beginning balance
		20,400	Income tax expense
Income taxes paid	X		
		$21,000	Ending balance

Solving for X:
$27,100 + $20,400 - X = $21,000
X = $27,100 + $20,400 - $21,000
X = $26,500

Next, we must take into account deferred income taxes.

Ending balance	$5,300
Beginning balance	(4,600)
Change in deferred income taxes payable	$700

Income taxes paid	$26,500
Change in deferred income taxes	(700)
Cash paid for income taxes	$25,800

Requirement 5:
Cash paid for selling expenses:

One third of the depreciation expense has been allocated to selling expenses. This is a noncash expense and should be subtracted from selling expenses to find the answer.

Selling expenses	$141,500
Depreciation allocated to selling[1]	(500)
Cash paid for selling expenses	$141,000

[1] Depreciation expense calculated:

Ending balance in accumulated depreciation	$16,500
Beginning balance in accumulated depreciation	(15,000)
Depreciation expense for 1998	$1,500

One third allocated to selling expense	$1,500/3 =	$500

P16-5. Preparation and analysis of cash flow statement

Requirement 1:
Statement of cash flows under indirect method:

Global Trading Company
Statement of Cash Flows
For the Year Ended December 31, 1996

Cash flow from operations	
Net loss for the year	($279,500)
+ Depreciation expense	50,000
+ Goodwill written off	70,000
+ Decrease in net accounts receivable	240,000
+ Decrease in inventory	170,000
+ Decrease in prepaid insurance	20,000
+ Increase in accounts payable	78,000
+ Increase in salaries payable	6,000
Cash flow from operations	**$354,500**
Cash flow from financing activities	
Repayment of bank loan	($307,500)
Dividends paid[1]	(35,000)
Cash flow from financing activities	**($342,500)**
Net increase in cash	**$12,000**

---

[1] **Calculation of dividends**

Beginning retained earnings	$320,000
- Net loss for the year	(279,500)
- Ending retained earnings	(5,500)
= Dividends paid	$35,000

Requirement 2:
Assessment of financial performance of Global:

- Net loss for the year is an indication of poor operating performance.

- Positive cash flow may be misleading since cash flow does not do a good job of matching revenues and expenses.

- Goodwill written off is from an acquisition made last year indicating that the potential benefits from the acquisition have been exhausted.

- Decrease in accounts receivable coupled with a decrease in inventory is an indication of decreasing demand. A mere change in the collection policy cannot explain the reduction in inventory.

- Increase in accounts payable could indicate that the company is not paying off its suppliers because of the constraint on bank loan.

- The repayment of the bank loan probably is not voluntary but enforced by the debt covenants.

- Payment of dividends when the company is incurring substantial losses is not a sign of prudent financial management and drains the cash reserves of the company.

- Ratio of accumulated depreciation to property, plant, and equipment of 0.9 (last year was 0.8) implies that, on average, the life of the fixed assets is one year and the company needs to invest in these assets immediately.

Requirement 3:

Determination of bad debts written off can be obtained from T-account analysis of the allowance for doubtful accounts:

Allowance for Doubtful Accounts

		$30,000	Beginning balance
		55,000	Bad debt expense
Accounts written off	X		
		$20,000	Ending balance

Solve for X:

+ $55,000 - X = $20,000

X = $65,000 = accounts written off in 1996.

Determination of credit sales for the year can be obtained from T-account analysis of accounts receivable:

Accounts Receivable

Beginning balance	$300,000		
		$65,000	Bad debts written off (see preceding page)
Sales on account	X	1,250,000	Collections on account
Ending balance	$50,000		

Solve for X:

$300,000 + X - $65,000 - $1,250,000 = $50,000

X = $1,065,000 = sales on account.

Requirement 4:

Effect of omission of inventory purchase:

Income Statement

No effect. (Purchases are understated, and ending inventory is understated by equal amounts. Thus, net effect on income is zero.)

Statement of Cash Flows

No effect. (Purchase was on account for credit.)

Balance Sheet

The balance sheet balances, but the year-end amounts for both accounts payable and inventory are understated by $35,000.

P16-6. Preparation of cash flow statement and balance sheet

Requirement 1:
Statement of cash flows under the direct method:

JKI Advertising Agencies Statement of Cash Flows for the Year Ended 12/31/98 Direct Method	
Operating Activities:	
Cash collected from clients	$215,000
Rent collected	50,000
Salaries paid	(130,000)
Cash paid for insurance	(12,000)
Cash paid for interest	(9,000)
Cash paid for customer lawsuit	(32,000)
Cash paid for taxes	(31,000)
Cash flows from operations	**$51,000**
Investing Activities:	
Proceeds from sale of land	$150,000
Purchase of office equipment	(20,000)
Cash flows from investing activities	**$130,000**
Financing Activities:	
Borrowing from TownBank	$50,000
Repayment of building loan	(85,000)
Issuance of capital stock	35,000
Dividends declared & paid	(18,000)
Cash flow from financing activities	**($18,000)**
Increase in cash for the year	**$163,000**

Requirement 2:
December 31, 1997 balance sheet

The figures for the 12/31/97 balance sheet can be attained by T-account analysis of the relevant accounts:

Accounts Receivable

Balance as of 12/31/97	X		
Advertising revenue	$250,000	$215,000	Cash collected from clients
Balance as of 12/31/98	$80,000		

Solve for X:
$80,000 = X + $250,000 - $215,000
X = $45,000

Prepaid Insurance

Balance as of 12/31/97	X		
Cash paid for insurance	$12,000	$12,000	Insurance expense
Balance as of 12/31/98	$3,000		

Solve for X:
$3,000 = X + $12,000 - $12,000
X = $3,000

Land

Balance as of 12/31/97	X		
		$150,000	Sale of land (cash received = book value)
Balance as of 12/31/98	$0		

Solve for X:
$0 = X - $150,000
X = $150,000

Accumulated Depreciation–Building

	X	Balance as of 12/31/97
	$20,000	Depreciation expense - building
	$380,000	Balance as of 12/31/98

Solve for X:
X = $380,000 - $20,000
X = $360,000

Office Equipment

Balance as of 12/31/97	X	
Purchase of office equipment	$20,000	
Balance as of 12/31/98	$80,000	

Solve for X:
X = $80,000 - $20,000
X = $60,000

Accumulated Depreciation–Office Equipment

	X	Balance as of 12/31/97
	$8,000	Depreciation expense–office equipment
	$39,000	Balance as of 12/31/98

Solve for X:
X = $39,000 - $8,000
X = $31,000

Salaries Payable

		X	Balance as of 12/31/97
Salaries paid	$130,000	$126,000	Salaries expense
		$7,000	Balance as of 12/31/98

Solve for X:
X = $130,000 - $126,000 + $7,000
X = $11,000

Interest Payable

		X	Balance as of 12/31/97
Cash paid for interest	$9,000	$10,000	Interest expense
		$3,500	Balance as of 12/31/98

Solve for X:
X + $10,000 - $9,000 = $3,500
X = $2,500

Liability for Customer Lawsuit

		X	Balance as of 12/31/97
Cash paid for customer lawsuit	$32,000		
		$0	Balance as of 12/31/98

Solve for X:
X - $32,000 = 0
X = $32,000

Rent Received in Advance

		X	Balance as of 12/31/97
Rent revenue	$36,000	$50,000	Rent collected
		$14,000	Balance as of 12/31/98

Solve for X:
X = $50,000 - $36,000 - $14,000
X = $0

Bonus Payable

		X	Balance as of 12/31/97
		$25,200	Employee incentive bonus
		$25,200	Balance as of 12/31/98

Solve for X:
X + $25,200 = $25,200
X = $0

Taxes Payable

		X	Balance as of 12/31/97
Cash paid for taxes	$31,000	$33,920	Income tax expense
		$2,920	Balance as of 12/31/98

Solve for X:
$2,920 = X + $33,920 - $31,000
X = $0

Borrowing from TownBank

		X	Balance as of 12/31/97
		$50,000	Borrowing from TownBank
		$50,000	Balance as of 12/31/98

Solve for X:
X + $50,000 = $50,000
X = $0

Building Loan

		X	Balance as of 12/31/97
Repayment of building loan	$85,000		
		$35,000	Balance as of 12/31/98

Solve for X:
$35,000 = X - $85,000
X = $120,000

Capital Stock

	X	Balance as of 12/31/97
	$35,000	Issuance of capital stock
	$135,000	Balance as of 12/31/98

Solve for X:

$135,000 = X + $35,000

X = $100,000

Retained Earnings

		X	Balance as of 12/31/97
Dividends declared & paid	$18,000	$50,880	Net income
		$264,380	Balance as of 12/31/98

Solve for X:

$264,380 = X + $50,880 - $18,000

X = $231,500

JKI Advertising Agencies
Balance Sheet as of 12/31/97

	1997
Cash	$30,000
Accounts receivable	45,000
Prepaid insurance	3,000
Land	150,000
Building	600,000
Less: Accumulated depreciation	(360,000)
Office equipment	60,000
Less: Accumulated depreciation	(31,000)
Total assets	**$497,000**
Salaries payable	$11,000
Interest payable	2,500
Liability for customer lawsuit	32,000
Rent received in advance	
Bonus payable	
Taxes payable	
Borrowing from TownBank	
Building loan	120,000
Capital stock	100,000
Retained earnings	231,500
Total of liabilities and equities	**$497,000**

Requirement 3:
Operating section of cash flow statement under indirect approach:

JKI Advertising Agencies Statement of Cash Flows for the Year Ended 12/31/98	
Net income	$50,880
+ Depreciation expense–building	20,000
+ Depreciation expense–office equipment	8,000
- Increase in accounts receivable	(35,000)
- Decrease in salaries payable	(4,000)
+ Increase in interest payable	1,000
- Decrease in liability for customer lawsuit	(32,000)
+ Increase in rent received in advance	14,000
+ Increase in bonus payable	25,200
+ Increase in taxes payable	2,920
Cash flow from operations	**$51,000**

Requirement 4:
Evaluation of statements:

a) Depreciation is a noncash charge, and therefore, by adding depreciation to net income we, in effect, eliminate this noncash item from the net income figure.

b) Note that while depreciation expense is subtracted in determining net income, the cost of long-lived assets is not subtracted from the cash flow from operations. Consequently, net income over the entire life of a company would be equal to the sum of cash flow from operations and cash flow from investing.

Requirement 5:
Effect of revised bonus formula on operating cash flows:

Cash flow from operations for the year 1998 would remain unchanged since this is merely an accrual entry (i.e., liability increases and retained earnings decreases). However, when the incentive bonus is paid in cash, say, in 1999, it will show up as operating outflow.

The operating section of the cash flow statement under the indirect approach demonstrates the main point. The three italicized items change when the incentive bonus is increased from 20% to 25%. However, because this is an accrual entry, the net effect of these three on the cash flow from operations is zero. Since the net income is different and since it is the beginning point for calculating the cash flow from operations, it might be tempting to say that the cash flow from operations will be lower.

JKI Advertising Agencies	
Statement of Cash Flows for the Year Ended 12/31/98	
Net income (see below)	*$47,100*
+ Depreciation expense–building	20,000
+ Depreciation expense–office equipment	8,000
- Increase in accounts receivable	(35,000)
- Decrease in salaries payable	(4,000)
+ Increase in interest payable	1,000
- Decrease in liability for customer lawsuit	(32,000)
+ Increase in rent received in advance	14,000
+ *Increase in bonus payable (see below)*	*31,500*
+ *Increase in taxes payable (see below)*	*400*
Cash flow from operations	**$51,000**

Supporting computations for revised cash flow statement:

Revised bonus expense (.25 × $126,000) =	$31,500
Previous bonus expense	25,200
Before-tax increase in bonus expense	$6,300
Times (1 - .4)	.6
After-tax decrease to net income	$3,780
Previous net income	50,880
Revised net income	$47,100

T-account to support change in taxes payable:

Taxes Payable

		0	Balance as of 12/31/97
Cash paid for taxes	$31,000	$31,400	Income tax expense
		$400	Balance as of 12/31/98

Revised tax expense:

Before-tax increase in bonus expense	$6,300
Times tax savings	.4
Decrease in income tax expense	$2,520
Previous income tax expense	33,920
Revised income tax expense	$31,400

P16-7. Reconciliation of changes in balance sheet accounts with amounts reported in cash flows statement

Requirement 1:
Reconciling changes in accounts receivable reported on the cash flow statement with change in receivables shown on the balance sheet:

Briggs & Stratton Corp.

For Briggs & Stratton, the decrease in receivables of $2,384,000 reported in the 1994 cash flow statement is equal to the change in the *net* receivables as reported in the balance sheet ($122,597,000 - $124,981,000).

Ramsay Health Care, Inc.

Here, the decrease in receivables of $3,677,000 from the balance sheet (i.e., $23,019,000–$26,696,000) is different from the **increase** in the patient accounts receivables of $2,169,000 reported in the cash flow statement.

Learning Objective

The purpose of this exercise is to present the two different reporting practices commonly adopted by companies and illustrate how both approaches lead to same cash flow numbers.

Requirement 2:
Explanation of different reporting practices with respect to receivables:

It is instructive to discuss initially the mechanics of converting sales or service revenue to cash collected from customers. We reconstruct the T-accounts of Ramsay Health Care to figure out the cash collected from customers. Although one can arbitrarily choose any sales number to get the intuition, let us pick the actual 1994 revenue of $137,002,000 (not provided in the problem).

Allowance for Doubtful Accounts			
		$4,955,000	Beginning balance
		5,846,000	Provision for bad debts
Bad debts written off	X		
		$3,925,000	Ending balance

Solve for X:
$4,955,000 + $5,846,000 - X = $3,925,000
X = $6,876,000

Patient Accounts Receivable

Beginning balance	$31,651,000		
Revenue	137,002,000	$6,876,000	Bad debts written off (from previous page)
		X	Cash collected
Ending balance	$26,944,000		

Solve for X:

$31,651,000 + $137,002,000 - $6,876,000 - X = $26,944,000

X = $134,833,000

The figure for cash collected can be determined using either one of the two reporting practices. For instance, if Ramsay had followed Briggs & Stratton's reporting practice, the adjustment for change in receivables would be as follows:

Ramsay Health Care, Inc., and Subsidiaries

Using Briggs & Stratton's Reporting Strategy	
Revenue	$137,002,000
- Provision for doubtful accounts	(5,846,000)
+ Decrease in **Net** A/R	3,677,000
Cash collected from customers	$134,833,000

Obviously, revenue less the provision for doubtful accounts is already reflected in the net income figure. It is important to understand that the net accounts receivable balance (gross A/R minus allowance for doubtful accounts) is affected by revenue as well as provision for doubtful accounts. Consequently, to figure out the cash collected from customers, we should jointly consider revenue, provision for doubtful accounts and change in receivables. The intuition behind the above table can be clarified by examining the reporting practice adopted by Ramsay Health Care, which follows.

Ramsay Health Care, Inc. and Subsidiaries

Revenue		$137,002,000
- Provision for doubtful accounts		(5,846,000)
Adjustments to reconcile net income to cash flows		
+ Provision for doubtful accounts		5,846,000
+ Decrease in **gross** A/R*	$4,707,000	
- Bad debts written off*	(6,876,000)	
- Decrease in patient accounts receivable		(2,169,000)
Cash collected from customers		$134,833,000

Note: The two * items were not separately reported by Ramsay Health Care. Instead, it reported the sum of the two items, i.e., ($2,169,000) = $4,707,000 - $6,876,000

Under this reporting practice, firms first add back the provision for doubtful accounts which, in essence, eliminates the noncash accrual expense. The remainder of the adjustments (revenue (+) decrease in gross accounts receivable (-) bad debts written off) represent all the items in the T-account for patient accounts receivable (i.e., gross accounts receivable) expect cash collected from customers which is being solved.

Another way to provide the intuition is to focus on the two possible reasons for decrease (in this example) in accounts receivable, i.e., (1) cash collections and (2) bad debts written off. By adding the decrease in **gross** accounts receivable, we attribute the entire decrease to cash collections. However, by subtracting the bad debts written off, we adjust for any decreases in accounts receivable that merely represent bad debts.

P16-8. Preparation of cash flow statement–indirect method
(AICPA adapted)

Cash flow for 1998 using the indirect method:

Bergen Corporation Statement of Cash Flows For the Year Ended December 31, 1998	
Operating Activities:	
Net income	$253,000
Adjustments for noncash items:	
+Depreciation	149,000
- Amortization of bond premium	(2,000)
+Increase in deferred income taxes payable	15,000
- Gain on sale of securities	(20,000)
- Gain on sale of equipment	(5,000)
- Increase in accounts receivable, net	(90,000)
- Increase in inventories	(115,000)
- Decrease in accounts payable and accrued expenses	(63,000)
Net cash flow provided by operations	122,000
Investing Activities:	
Sale of securities	95,000
Sale of equipment	33,000
Purchase of equipment	(392,000)
Net cash outflow from investing activities	(264,000)
Financing Activities:	
Proceeds from long-term note payable	450,000
Cash dividends	(30,000)
Payment of tax assessment from prior period	(20,000)
Payment under capital lease	(25,000)
Net cash flow provided by financing activities	375,000
Net increase in cash	233,000
Beginning balance in cash	308,000
Ending balance in cash	$541,000

P16-9. Preparing an income statement from statement of cash flows and comparative balance sheets

---

Kang-Iyer Financial Consultants
Statement of Cash Flows for the Year Ended 12/31/98

Cash Flow from Operations:

Cash collected from customers	$250,000
Cash paid to employees	(70,000)
Cash paid for interest	(50,000)
Cash flow from operations	**$130,000**

Cash Flow from Investing:

Land purchased	($200,000)
Building acquired	(500,000)
Cash flow from investing	**($700,000)**

Cash Flow from Financing:

Dividends paid	($15,000)
Additional borrowings from village bank	500,000
Proceeds from share issue (capital contributions)	45,000
Cash flow from financing	**$530,000**

Change in cash	**($40,000)**
Beginning cash balance	**70,000**
Ending cash balance	**$30,000**

Kang-Iyer Financial Consultants
Income Statement for the Year Ended 12/31/98

Consulting revenue		$356,500
Less: Expenses		
Depreciation—building	$10,000	
Salaries expense	150,000	
Interest expense	65,000	
Bad debts expense	48,000	
Rent expense	30,000	303,000
Net income		$53,500

Accounts Receivable

Beginning balance	$15,000		
Consulting revenue	X	$41,500	Bad debts written off
		250,000	Cash collected
Ending balance	$80,000		

Solve for X:
$80,000 = $15,000 + X - $41,500 - $250,000
X = $356,500

Allowance for Doubtful Accounts

		$1,500	Beginning balance
Bad debts written off $41,500			
		X	**Provision for doubtful accounts**
		$8,000	Ending balance

Solve for X:
$8,000 = $1,500 + X - $41,500
X = $48,000

Salaries Payable

		$20,000	Beginning balance
Cash paid	$70,000		
		X	**Salaries expense**
		$100,000	Ending balance

Solve for X:
$100,000 = $20,000 + X - $70,000
X = $150,000

Interest Payable

		$5,000	Beginning balance
Cash paid	$50,000		
		X	**Interest expense**
		$20,000	Ending balance

Solve for X:
$20,000 = $5,000 + X - $50,000
X = $65,000

Prepaid Rent

Beginning balance	$30,000		
		X	**Rent expense**
Cash paid	0		
Ending balance	$0		

Solve for X:

$0 = $30,000 + $0 - X

X = $30,000

Accumulated Depreciation–Building

	$0	Beginning balance
	X	**Depreciation expense**
	$10,000	Ending balance

Solve for X:

$10,000 = $0 + X

X = $10,000

P16-10. Determining components of cash flow statement
(AICPA adapted)

Requirements 1–3:
Cash provided by operating, investing, and financing activities:

Best Corporation
Statement of Cash Flows
For the Year Ended December 31, 1999

Cash Flow from Operating Activities:

Net income		$700,000
Add (Subtract):		
Depreciation expense	$130,000	
Increase in accounts receivable	(280,000)	
Increase in inventory	(290,000)	
Increase in accounts payable	390,000	
Increase in accrued expenses	170,000	
Loss on sale of fixtures	10,000	
Cash provided by operating activities		**830,000**
Cash Flow from Investing Activities:		
Sale of fixtures	20,000	
Purchase of fixtures	(630,000)	
Cash used in investing activities		**(610,000)**
Cash Flow from Financing Activities:		
Issuance of common stock	125,000	
Cash paid for dividends[1]	(85,000)	
Cash provided by financing activities		**40,000**
Net change in cash balance		**$260,000**

---

[1] Dividends declared	$125,000
– Increase in dividends payable	(40,000)
Cash dividends paid	$85,000

Fair market value of Best Corporation's common stock.

The debit to retained earnings for the fair market value of the stock dividend can be found by an analysis of the retained earnings T-account:

Retained Earnings

		$330,000	Beginning balance
Dividends declared	$125,000	700,000	Net income
Stock dividend	X		
		$630,000	Ending balance

Solve for X:
$630,000 = $330,000 + $700,000 - $125,000 - X
X = $275,000 = fair market value of stock dividend

On a per-share basis, Best's common stock has a value of

$275,000/20,000 shares = $13.75

P16-11. Analysis of statement of cash flows

Requirement 1:
Statement of cash flows for the year ended 12-31-1998:

Cavalier Toy Stores Statement of Cash Flows For the Year Ended December 31, 1998		
Cash Flow from Operating Activities:		
Net loss		($250,000)
Add:		
Depreciation expense	$75,000	
Decrease in accounts receivable	405,000	
Decrease in prepaid insurance	30,000	
Decrease in inventory	500,000	
Increase in salaries payable	20,000	
Increase in accounts payable	188,000	1,218,000
Less:		
Decrease in interest payable		(8,000)
Cash flow from operating activities		**$960,000**
Cash Flow from Investing Activities:		
Purchase of building		(900,000)
Cash flow from investing activities		**($900,000)**
Cash Flow from Financing Activities:		
Loan from Thrifty Bank		140,000
Dividends		(300,000)
Decrease in dividends payable		(50,000)
Cash paid for dividends		($350,000)
Cash flow from financing activities		**($210,000)**
Net change in cash balance		**($150,000)**

Requirement 2:
(a) Bad debts written off during the year:

Beginning balance in allowance for doubtful accounts	$30,000
Add: Bad debt expense	100,000
Less: Ending balance in allowance for doubtful accounts	(10,000)
Bad debts written off during the year	$120,000

(b) Cash collected from customers:

Beginning balance in accounts receivable	$525,000
Add: Credit sales	1,500,000
Less: Bad debts written off	(120,000)
Less: Ending balance in accounts receivable	(100,000)
Cash collected from customers	$1,805,000

(c) Purchases made during the year:

Beginning inventory	$550,000
Add: Purchases	?
Less: Ending inventory	(50,000)
Cost of goods sold	1,200,000
Purchases	$700,000

(d) Cash paid to the suppliers for purchases of inventory:

Beginning balance in accounts payable	$64,000
Purchases	700,000
Less: Ending balance in accounts payable	(252,000)
Cash paid for inventory purchases	$512,000

(e) Cash paid for insurance:

Beginning balance in prepaid insurance	$35,000
Add: Cash paid for insurance	?
Less: Ending balance in prepaid insurance	(5,000)
Insurance expense	30,000
Cash paid for insurance	$0

Requirement 3:
Thrifty Bank should be concerned about renewing the loan or increasing the credit limit for the following reasons:

(a) Depletion of accounts receivable and inventory and increase in accounts payable to boost cash flow from operations–this cannot be done every year to increase cash flow from operations.

(b) Use of working capital (accounts receivable and inventory and increase in accounts payable) to finance building–a nonproductive asset

(c) Very large dividend in a loss year.

(d) Decreasing gross margins (from letter) from competitive pressures.

(e) Net loss.

P16-12. Preparation of cash flow statement
(AICPA adapted)

Farrell Corporation
Statement of Cash Flows
For the Year Ended December 31, 1998

Operating Activities:

Net income		$141,000
Add (Deduct):		
Depreciation	$53,000	
Amortization of goodwill	4,000	
Loss on sale of equipment	5,000	
Equity in net income of Hall, Inc.	(13,000)	
Increase in deferred income tax payable	11,000	
Decrease in accounts receivable	10,000	
Increase in inventories	(118,000)	
Increase in accounts payable and accrued expenses	41,000	(7,000)
Net cash provided by operating activities		**134,000**

Investing Activities:

Sale of equipment	19,000	
Purchase of equipment	(63,000)	
Net cash provided from investing activities		**(44,000)**

Financing Activities:

Sale of common stock	23,000	
Sale of treasury stock	25,000	
Cash dividends paid	(43,000)	
Net cash provided by financing activities		**5,000**

Simultaneous Financing and Investing Activity Not Affecting Cash:

Purchase of land with long-term note	$150,000	

Net increase in cash		**$95,000**
Beginning balance in cash account		**180,000**
Ending balance in cash account		**$275,000**

P16-13. Statement of cash flows—indirect method
(AICPA adapted)

Omega Corporation
Statement of Cash Flows
For the Year Ended December 31, 1996

Cash Flow from Operating Activities:

Net income		$360,000
Adjustments to reconcile net income to cash provided by operating activities:		
Depreciation[1]	$150,000	
Gain on sale of equipment[2]	(5,000)	
Undistributed earnings of Belle Co.[3]	(30,000)	
Changes in assets and liabilities:		
Decrease in accounts receivable	40,000	
Increase in inventories	(135,000)	
Increase in accounts payable	60,000	
Decrease in income taxes payable	(20,000)	60,000
Net cash provided by operating activities		**420,000**

Cash Flows from Investing Activities:

Proceeds from sale of equipment	40,000	
Loan to Chase Co.	(300,000)	
Principal payment of loan receivable	30,000	
Net cash used in investing activities		**(230,000)**

Cash Flows from Financing Activities:

Dividends paid	(90,000)	
Net cash used in financing activities		**(90,000)**

Net increase in cash	**$100,000**
Cash at beginning of year	**700,000**
Cash at end of year	**$800,000**

---

[1] Depreciation

Net increase in accumulated depreciation for the year ended December 31, 1996		$125,000
Accumulated depreciation on equipment sold:		
Cost	$60,000	
Carrying value	35,000	25,000
Depreciation for 1996		$150,000

[2] Gain on sale of equipment

Proceeds	$40,000
Carrying value	35,000
Gain	$5,000

[3] Undistributed earnings of Belle Co.

Belle's net income for 1996	$120,000
Omega's ownership	25%
Undistributed earnings of Belle Co.	$30,000

Cases

C16-1. Q-Mart Retail Stores, Inc. (KR): Analysis of statement of cash flow

Requirement 1:

Q-Mart Retail Stores, Inc.
Statement of Cash Flows for the Year Ended 12/31/98

Cash Flow from Operating Activities:	
Net income	$81,250
+ Depreciation expense–building	25,000
+ Depreciation expense–computer	35,000
- Increase in net accounts receivable	(361,000)
- Increase in inventory	(275,000)
- Increase in prepaid insurance	(20,000)
- Decrease in salaries payable	(32,000)
- Decrease in accounts payable	(5,000)
+ Increase in income tax currently payable	7,000
Cash flow from operations	**($544,750)**
Cash Flow from Investing Activities:	
Additions to building	($250,000)
Purchase of computer equipment	(140,000)
Cash flow from investing activities	**($390,000)**
Cash Flow from Financing Activities:	
Borrowing from Upstate Bank	$200,000
Proceeds from stock issuance	390,000
Dividends paid	(40,000)
Cash flow from financing activities	**$550,000**
Change in cash balance	**(384,750)**
+ Beginning cash balance	504,750
Ending cash balance	**$120,000**

Calculation of dividends:	
Beginning balance of retained earnings	$341,750
Add: Net income	81,250
Less: Ending balance of retained earnings	-383,000
Dividends paid	$40,000

Requirement 2:
Bad debts written off = beginning balance of allowance for doubtful accounts + bad debts expense - ending balance of allowance for doubtful accounts

= $11,000 + $50,000 - $50,000

= $11,000

Requirement 3:
Cash collected = beginning balance of accounts receivable + sales - bad debts written off (from above) - ending balance in accounts receivable

= $100,000 + $1,500,000 - $11,000 - $500,000

= $1,089,000

Requirement 4:
Purchases of inventory = ending balance of inventory + cost of goods sold - beginning balance of inventory

= $350,000 + $1,050,000 - $75,000

= $1,325,000

Requirement 5:
Cash paid = beginning balance of accounts payable + purchases (from above) - ending balance of accounts payable

= $17,000 + $1,325,000 - $12,000

= $1,330,000

Requirement 6:
Cash flow from operations is the main reason for the decline. The increase in accounts receivable is a good signal if it is commensurate with growth in sales. On the other hand, it could suggest collection problems as well as inadequate provision for doubtful accounts. There is also an increase in inventory. This could be positive news if the buildup is in anticipation of demand. Again, this could be negative if the obsolete items have not been written down. The investment in property, plant, and equipment is financed by loan and equity.

Additional information required:

- What is the sales increase over last year?
- By how much have the purchases increased over the last year?
- Why haven't the suppliers extended credit with the rise in purchases?
- What is the change in net income over last year?

Requirement 7:
If the sales had been stopped, the net income would be lowered, and, therefore, the cash flow from operations would decline ultimately. What is necessary is to reduce the average collection period for accounts receivable and speed up the collection process.

Requirement 8:
Depreciation is a noncash item and is added back to the net income. Therefore, even if higher depreciation had been provided, the amount that is added to the net income would have been originally subtracted from revenues to determine net income and, consequently, would not affect the cash flow.

Requirement 9:
Matching is an important feature of accrual accounting that is lacking in the cash flow statements. However, accruals are subject to greater managerial discretion. See answer to "reasons for decline" as an example of jointly analyzing the two statements.

C16-2. Tuesday Morning Corporation (CW): Analysis of cash flow statement

Requirement 1:
None of its 1994 sales were made on credit (i.e., they were 100% in cash). This is because sales in the income statement of $190,081 is exactly the same as cash received from customers in the cash flow statement.

Requirement 2:
Tuesday Morning paid $0 in cash for income taxes in 1994. The operating cash flow section of the cash flow statement reveals that the firm received a cash refund of $1,911.

Requirement 3:
Tuesday Morning reported $198 of interest income in its 1994 income statement, all of which was received in cash in 1994 (see the operating cash flow section of the cash flow statement).

Requirement 4:
Cash flow provided by operating activities using the indirect method:

Net earnings (loss)	$2,651
Adjustments to reconcile net earnings (loss) to net cash provided by (used in) operating activities	
Depreciation and amortization	3,862
Deferred income taxes	313
Loss on sale of fixed assets	12
Changes in operating assets and liabilities:	
Income taxes receivable	2,133
Inventories	6,736
Prepaid expenses	(683)
Other current assets	597
Other assets	(251)
Accounts payable	(2,943)
Accrued expenses	(1,359)
Income taxes payable	988
Total adjustments	9,405
Net cash provided by (used in) operating activities	$12,056

C16-3. Comptronix Corporation (KR): Comprehensive statement of cash flows

Requirement 1:

Comptronix Corporation
Statement of Cash Flows for the Year Ended 12/31/93

Operating Activities:

Net loss		($11,403)
+ Dividend in kind		162
+ Depreciation		8,330
+ Loss on write-off of machinery & equipment		227
+ Non-cash portion of settlement with Exicom		1,775
+ Bad debt expense		238
+ Decrease in gross accounts receivable		13,782
- Bad debts written off		(315)
+ Decrease in income tax receivable		6,731
+ Decrease in inventory		22,459
- Increase in prepaid expenses		(835)
- Decrease in trade accounts payable		(22,725)
- Decrease in accrued payroll		(1,259)
+ Increase in accrued interest		33
- Decrease in other payables		(19)
- Decrease in accrued settlement	($2,432)	
- Decrease in long-term accrued settlement	(1,500)	(3,932)
- Increase in deferred financing costs	(413)	
+ Increase in owners' equity for these costs	400	(13)
Cash flow from operations		**$13,236**
Investing Activities:		
Purchase of property, plant, and equipment		(1,085)
Cash flow from investing activities		**($1,085)**

(continued)

Financing Activities:

Increase in preferred stock	$1,937	
- Dividend in kind	(162)	
- Noncash settlement with Exicom	(1,775)	-
Repayment of principal on IDR bonds		($320)
Retired revolving line of credit		(19,973)
Retired equipment line of credit		(15,762)
Borrowing on new revolving line of credit		21,006
Borrowing on new equipment line of credit		6,000
Repayment of notes secured by equipment		(3,982)
1993 bank loan secured by real property		
(i) Borrowing	3,000	
(ii) Repayment	(1,500)	1,500
1993 equipment loan at 9%		
(i) Borrowing	200	
(ii) Repayment	(97)	103
Increase in common stock + paid-in capital	526	
- Non-cash stock for financing charges	(400)	126
Cash flow from financing activities		**($11,302)**
Change in cash		**849**
Beginning cash balance		**48**
Ending cash balance		**$897**

Details of selected T-accounts:

Accumulated Depreciation

		$18,630	Beginning balance
		8,330	Depreciation expense
Acc. dep. of asset written off	$633		
		$26,327	Ending balance

Property, Plant and Equipment

Beginning balance	$55,574		
		$860[1]	Original cost of asset written off
Purchase of PP&E	1,085		
Ending balance	$55,799		

[1] BV of asset written off $227
+ Acc dep. of asset written off 633
= Original cost of asset written off $860

Allowance for Doubtful Accounts

		$608	Beginning balance
		238	Bad debt expense
Bad debts written off	$315		
		$531	Ending balance

Accounts Receivable

Beginning balance	$32,803		
Sales revenue	184,137	$315	Bad debts written off
		197,604	Cash collected
Ending balance	$19,021		

Requirement 2:

Comptronix Corporation
Statement of Cash Flows for the Year Ended 12/31/93
Operating Section under the Direct Method

Cash collected from customers:

Sales revenue	$184,137	
+ Decrease in gross accounts receivable	13,782	
- Bad debts written off	(315)	$197,604

Cash paid to suppliers:

Cost of sales	(181,010)	
+ Depreciation	8,330	
+ Decrease in inventory	22,459	
- Decrease in trade accounts payable	(22,725)	(172,946)

Cash paid for marketing, etc., expenses:

Marketing, general & admin. expenses	(7,227)	
+ Bad debt expense	238	
- Increase in prepaid expenses	(835)	
- Decrease in accrued payroll	(1,259)	(9,083)

Cash paid for interest:

Interest expense	(5,417)	
+ Increase in accrued interest	33	(5,384)

Interest income on income tax refund		1,048

Cash paid for Exicom settlement:

Settlement with Exicom	(1,837)	
+ Noncash portion of settlement with Exicom	1,775	(62)

Cash paid for other expenses:

Other expenses	(935)	
+ Loss on write-off of machinery & equipment	227	
- Decrease in other payables	(19)	
- Increase in deferred financing costs	(413)	
+ Increase in owners' equity for these costs	400	(740)

Income tax refund received		6,731

Cash paid for accrued settlement costs:

- Decrease in accrued settlement	(2,432)	
- Decrease in long-term accrued settlement	(1,500)	(3,932)

Cash flow from operations		**$13,236**

C16-4. MGM Grand, Inc. (KR): Comprehensive statement of cash flows

Requirement 1:

MGM Grand, Inc. Statement of Cash Flows For the Year Ended 12/31/93	
Cash Flows from Operating Activities:	
Net loss	($117,586)
+ Depreciation expense	8,018
+ Aircraft carrying value adjustment	68,948
+ Loss on sale of property, plant & equip.	
(book value $2,501–cash received $684)	1,817
- Increase in net accounts receivable	(29,869)
- Increase in prepaid expenses	(10,536)
- Increase in inventories	(12,508)
+ Decrease in pre-opening costs	10,677
- Increase in other operating assets	(5,485)
+ Increase in accounts payable	9,859
+ Increase in accrued salaries & wages	7,249
+ Increase in accrued interest on LT debt	43
+ Increase in other accrued liabilities	23,758
+ Increase in deferred revenue	10,784
Cash flow from operations	**($34,831)**
Cash Flows from Investing Activities:	
Sale of property, plant & equipment	684
Purchase of PP&E and cost of building	(480,054)
+ Increase in construction payables[1]	64,548 (415,506)
Cash flow from investment activities	**(414,822)**
Cash Flow from Financing Activities:	
Repayment of principal in capital lease	(1,564)
Additional borrowing (laundry loan)	10,000
Issuance of additional common stock	72,559
Cash flow from financing activities	**80,995**
Total change in cash	**(368,658)**
Cash at 12/31/92	**579,963**
Cash at 12/31/93	**$211,305**

[1] Alternatively, this could be shown as a financing activity cash inflow.

Note on significant non-cash transaction: The Company entered into a capital lease agreement and recorded an asset and a corresponding liability for $16,987.

Property, Plant and Equipment

Beginning balance	$471,506		
New capital lease	16,987	$14,751	Cost of asset sold (net book value $2,501 + Acc. dep. $12,250)
Other new additions	X		
Ending balance	$953,796		

Solve for X:
$$\$953,796 = \$471,506 + \$16,987 + X - \$14,751$$
$$X = \underline{\$480,054}$$

Accumulated Depreciation

		$21,796	Beginning balance
Acc. depr. of asset sold	X	8,018	Depreciation expense
		68,948	Carrying value adjustment
		$86,512	Ending balance

Solve for X:
$$\$86,512 = \$21,796 + \$8,018 + \$68,948 - X$$
$$X = \underline{\$12,250}$$

Capital Lease Obligation (including current maturities)

		$451	Beginning balance
Repayment of principal	X	16,987	New capital lease
		$15,874	Ending balance

Solve for X:
$$\$15,874 = \$451 + \$16,987 - X$$
$$X = \underline{\$1,564}$$

```
┌─────────────────────────────────────────────────────────────────┐
│                MGM Grand, Inc.–Alternative Approach               │
│                    Statement of Cash Flows                        │
│                 For the Year Ended 12/31/93                        │
├─────────────────────────────────────────────────────────────────┤
```

Cash Flows from Operating Activities:

Net loss		($117,586)
+ Depreciation expense		8,018
+ Aircraft carrying value adjustment		68,948
+ Loss on sale of property, plant & equip.		
(Book value $2,501 - Cash received $684)		1,817
+ Bad debt expense		*3,855*
- Increase in gross accounts receivable	*($33,071)*	
- Bad debts written off	*(653)*	(33,724)
- Increase in prepaid expenses		(10,536)
- Increase in inventories		(12,508)
+ Decrease in pre-opening costs		10,677
- Increase in other operating assets		(5,485)
+ Increase in accounts payable		9,859
+ Increase in accrued salaries & wages		7,249
+ Increase in accrued interest on LT debt		43
+ Increase in other accrued liabilities		23,758
+ Increase in deferred revenue		10,784
Cash flow from operations		**(34,831)**

Cash Flows from Investing Activities:

Sale of property, plant & equipment		684
Purchase of PP&E and cost of building	(480,054)	
+ Increase in construction payables	64,548	(415,506)
Cash flow from investment activities		**(414,822)**

Cash Flow from Financing Activities:

Repayment of principal in capital lease		(1,564)
Additional borrowing (laundry loan)		10,000
Issuance of additional common stock		72,559
Cash flow from financing activities		**80,995**

Total change in cash		**(368,658)**
Cash at 12/31/92		**579,963**
Cash at 12/31/93		**$211,305**

Under the alternative approach, we are merely breaking down the change in net accounts receivable into three components which are italicized. This is done in order to convert the indirect statement to a direct statement. Of course, this step can be omitted.

Gross Accounts Receivable

Beginning balance	$2,178	$653	Bad debts written off
Revenue	57,800	X	Cash collected
Ending balance	$35,249		

Solve for X:
$35,249 = $2,178 + $57,800 - $653 - X
X = $24,076

Allowance for Doubtful Accounts

		$1,531	Beginning balance
Bad debts written off	X	3,855	Bad debt expense
		$4,733	Ending balance

Solve for X:
$4,733 = $1,531 + $3,855 - X
X = $653

Note: These T-accounts may be useful when preparing the direct cash flow statements. Note that we have to consider the change in deferred revenue to calculate the "correct" amount of cash collected from customers.

Requirement 2:

MGM Grand, Inc.
Direct Method

Cash Flow from Operations
Cash collected from customers:

Total revenue	$57,800	
- Increase in gross A/R	(33,071)	
- Bad debts written off	(653)	
+Increase in deferred revenue	10,784	$34,860

Cash paid for direct operating expense (approx.):

Direct operating expense (casino + ... + airline)	(39,262)	
- Increase in prepaid expenses	(10,536)	
- Increase in inventories	(12,508)	
- Increase in other operating assets	(5,485)	
+Increase in accounts payable	9,859	
+Increase in accrued salaries & wages	7,249	
+Increase in other accrued liabilities	23,758	(26,925)

Cash paid for SG&A expenses:

SG&A expenses	(19,679)	
+Bad debt expense	3,855	(15,824)

Cash paid for hotel pre-opening expenses:

Hotel pre-opening expenses	(45,130)	
+Decrease in pre-opening costs	10,677	(34,453)

Interest income		12,231

Cash paid for interest expense:

Interest expense	(6,596)	
+ Increase in accrued interest on LT debt	43	(6,553)

Cash received from other non-operating items:

Other, net	16	
+Loss on sale of PP&E	1,817	1,833

Cash flow from operations		**($34,831)**

Note: The direct approach obviously requires assumptions regarding which operating assets and liabilities pertain to which revenue and expense items.

C16-5. Sound Advice, Inc. (KR): Preparation and analysis of the cash flow statement

Requirement 1:
Notes:

1) Since the company did not declare or pay any cash or stock dividends during the year, the change in the retained earnings of $1,127,664 must be the net income for the year.

2) The T-accounts for property and equipment and accumulated depreciation are prepared to solve for the new acquisitions of property and equipment during the year.

Accumulated Depreciation

		$6,822,553	Balance as of 6/30/92
Acc. dep. of scrapped asset	$57,107	2,265,735	Depreciation expense (given)
		$9,031,181	Balance as of 6/30/93

Property and Equipment

Balance as of 6/30/92	$20,637,912		
New acquisitions	1,608,943	$64,484	Orig. cost of the scrapped asset
			($57,107 + $7,377)
Balance as of 6/30/93	$22,182,371		

First by crediting the accumulated depreciation T-account with the depreciation expense for the year, we find that the accumulated depreciation on the scrapped asset must have been $57,107 (the plug number). Since the book value of the scrapped asset was $7,377, the original cost of the asset must have been $64,484 ($57,107 + $7,377). This amount would have been credited to the property and equipment T-account. The resulting plug number of $1,608,943 must be the cost of new property and equipment acquired during the year.

3) The change in the accumulated amortization of $24,450 must represent the non-cash amortization expense for the year.

4) The words "deferred credits" suggest that the liability account other liabilities & deferred credits must be a operating liability rather than a financial liability.

5) To calculate the financing cash flows from long-term debt, it is useful to focus on the total long-term rather than split them into current and long-term portions.

Long-Term Debt:	6/30/93	6/30/92	Borrowing	Repayments
Term loan	$3,420,000	-	$3,600,000	($180,000)
Mortgage note	534,475	555,455		(20,980)
Total	$3,954,475	$555,455	$3,600,000	($200,980)
- Current installments	(681,716)	(21,348)		
Long-term debt (less) current installments	$3,272,759	$534,107		

6) Although revolving credit agreements appear as a current liability, they are a financing liability. Consequently, they will be reflected in the financing section of the cash flow statement.

```
┌─────────────────────────────────────────────────────────────────┐
│                      Sound Advice, Inc.                           │
│                  Statement of Cash Flows                          │
│                 For the Year Ended 6/30/1993                      │
├─────────────────────────────────────────────────────────────────┤
```

Operating Activities:

Net income for the year	$1,127,664
+ Amortization of goodwill	24,450
+ Depreciation expense	2,265,735
+ Loss on disposition of equipment	7,377
Decrease in net receivables	1,540,275
Decrease in inventories	815,162
Decrease in prepaid expenses	254,183
Decrease in income tax receivable	1,500,482
Increase in deferred tax asset	(511,600)
Decrease in pre-opening costs	506,721
Increase in accounts payable	3,102,873
Increase in accrued liabilities	768,144
Increase in other liabilities & deferred credits	763,872
Cash flow from operations	**$12,165,338**

Investing Activities:

Purchase of property and equipment	($1,608,943)
Cash flow from investing activities	**($1,608,943)**

Financing Activities:

Issuance of new shares	8,998
Borrowing on term loan	3,600,000
Repayment of term loan	(180,000)
Repayment of mortgage note	(20,980)
Repayments under revolving credit agreement	(13,933,009)
Cash flow from financing activities	**($10,524,991)**

Change in cash	**$31,404**
Cash balance as of 6/30/92	**19,481**
Cash balance as of 6/30/93	**$50,885**

Requirement 2:

Caveat: The analysis is handicapped by the limited amount of information available in the problem. The learning objective of this assignment is to enable the students to evaluate the cash flow statement rather than perform a comprehensive analysis of the financial performance of Sound Advice, Inc. The cash flow from operations (CFO) of Sound Advice, Inc., is almost 11 times more than the net income of the company. Given the Wall Street adage that "Cash Flow is King and Earnings Don't Matter," does this mean that the financial performance of Sound Advice is really 11 times better than that indicated by its net income? Let us examine the sources of the high CFO to see whether Sound Advice can sustain this level of cash flows in the future.

First of all, the company's receivables decreased by more than $1.5 million. Roughly, the company collected that much more cash than the revenue booked in the accrual accounting income statement. This might be good news if the company has improved its collection efforts. Even so, this is unlikely to happen year after year if a company is growing, i.e., collecting more cash than the accrual revenue. Consequently, this is likely to be a temporary phenomenon.

A second source of the higher cash flow is the drop in the level of inventory. One possibility is that the drop is due to an unexpected sale at the end of the year. However, this is unlikely since the company experienced a drop in the receivables also, i.e., if there were unexpectedly large sales at the end of the year, we might expect the accounts receivable to go up. More importantly, inventory level provides a signal about future demand, i.e., companies are likely to build up (decrease) inventories when they expect a surge (fall) in demand. Therefore, another possibility is that the company saved some cash in the current year by buying less inventory, but it might generate less cash during the next year by selling less inventory. In any case, it is unlikely that inventory levels can continue to decrease when companies are growing. In fact, in the following year, the company built up almost $10 million of inventory which resulted in a negative CFO. The main message here is that neither cash flows nor accounting income by itself can tell the whole story. A joint examination of the two is likely to be constructive.

A third factor is the increase in accounts payable by more than $3 million. More credit from suppliers is not necessarily a bad sign, i.e., suppliers are unlikely to extend credit when they believe their customers have impending financial difficulties. However, an increase in accounts payable usually happens when there is a buildup in the inventory level. Consequently, one should examine why Sound Advice's accounts payable are increasing when its inventory level is falling. One possibility is that the company was "forced" to pay off its revolving credit under the current agreement (see financing cash flow). This might have delayed the payment to the suppliers.

A fourth item is the cash received from the decrease in the income tax refund receivable. When is it likely for a company to have an asset called income tax refund receivable? There are two possibilities. First, the company paid more taxes during a year when compared to what it owed the IRS based on its actual taxable income, i.e., the actual income was less than the anticipated income. A second possibility is that the company incurred a net loss in the recent past, and, using the loss carryback provision, the company is expecting to receive a tax refund. Either scenario suggests that the company has encountered difficulties in the recent past. In fact, Sound Advice incurred a net loss of almost $2.5 million during the fiscal year 1992.

Similar comments can be made on other operating assets and liabilities.

The fact that the company borrowed a term loan of $3.6 million is a positive signal. First of all, the company has convinced a creditor to lend it money. Secondly, the loan is a long-term one, and therefore, a substantial portion of the principal payments are unlikely to be due in the near term. The company has paid back about 5% of the term over a 4-month period. On an annual basis, this translates into 15% of the loan, i.e., the company has the potential to use the term loan to finance a part of its working capital needs over the next several years.

Collaborative Learning Case

C16-6. Best Buy Co., Inc. (KR): Analysis of financial performance from the cash flow statement and other information

Caveat: Due to limited information available in the problem, our analysis cannot provide a complete picture of the financial performance of the company over the 3-year period. The learning objective for this problem is to enable the student to examine the items that cause net income to be different from the cash flow numbers.

Requirement 1:
Comparison of earnings and operating cash flows:

The company's net income has consistently declined over the 3-year period, from almost $60 million during the fiscal year 1995 to less than $2 million during 1997. In contrast, the cash flow from operations (CFO) was the highest during 1996 at almost $100 million. During 1995 and 1997, operations were a drain on the company's cash flows. If accrual accounting results in better matching of revenues and expenses, then the company's performance has deteriorated over the 3-year period. However, how might an analyst interpret the company's CFO which did not change in the same direction as the net income?

Recall that when operating assets increase (or decrease), they are a drain on (or they increase) the operating cash flows. The opposite is true for the operating liabilities. An examination of the operating section of the cash flow statements suggests that Best Buy had been building up inventories and receivables during 1995 and 1996, and had been liquidating its inventories and receivables during 1997. An important task is for the analyst to understand whether these trends signify positive or negative news about the company.

To understand the buildup in inventories, let us focus on the statistics on new store openings:

	1997	1996	1995	1994
Number of stores at the end of year	272	251	204	151
Number of new stores opened during the year	21	47	53	

When retail companies, such as Best Buy, expand by acquiring or building new stores, then they experience a sudden demand for new working capital. This is clearly communicated by Best Buy in its annual report.

> Each new store requires approximately $3 million of working capital, depending on the size of the store, for merchandise inventory (net of vendor financing), leasehold improvements, fixtures and equipment.

Note that the words "net of vendor financing" suggests that the $3 million is for the investment in inventory and other assets minus the credit extended by the suppliers through accounts payable.

It is quite likely that these new stores will not have reached their expected annual revenue projections during the first year of operations. Consequently, the increase in working capital will result in a drain on the operating cash flows during the years of rapid expansion until the new stores reach their projected annual sales targets.

Requirement 2:
Analysis of working capital needs:

Let us try to calculate the expected increase in the working capital during each of the three years due to new store openings:

	1997	1996	1995
Need for working capital per new store	$3,000	$3,000	$3,000
Number of new stores opened during the year	21	47	53
Total working capital needed for the new stores	$63,000	$141,000	$159,000

Now, let us compare these figures with the actual change in the working capital during the same period:

Change in Working Capital

For the fiscal years ended	03/01/97	03/02/96	02/25/95
Receivables	($41,857)	$36,998	$31,496
Merchandise inventories	(69,083)	293,465	269,727
Income taxes and prepaid expenses	(8,174)	16,273	5,929
Accounts payable	186,050	(278,515)	(106,920)
Other current liabilities	(4,788)	(50,599)	(46,117)
Deferred revenue and other liabilities	27,262	(12,994)	(19,723)
Net increase in working capital	**$89,410**	**$4,628**	**$134,392**

Note that each of the figures in the above table is taken from the **operating section** of the statement of cash flows. However, their signs have been reversed since working capital is defined as current assets (minus) current liabilities. Consequently, increases in assets and liabilities have the positive and negative signs, respectively. The opposite is true for the decreases.

Given the explosive growth during 1995 (adding 53 new stores), it is not surprising that Best Buy's working capital increased by more than $130 million. In fact, it is less than the $159 million that was expected based on the working capital requirements of the new stores. Consequently, an analyst is unlikely to be concerned about the negative CFO during 1995 since it is consistent with what might be expected based on the growth experienced by Best Buy. However, an analyst must carefully follow up to examine how well the new stores are doing.

Requirement 3:
Analysis of year-to-year changes in inventory and how these changes were financed:

During 1996, although the company added another 47 stores, its working capital increased only about $5 million compared to the expected increase of more than $140 million. This is because there is a substantial difference in how the growth in inventory was financed between the two years.

	1996	1995
Increase in merchandise inventories	$293,465	$269,727
Increase in accounts payable	278,515	106,920
% of increase in inventory financed by accounts payable	95%	40%

While only about 40% of the increase in inventory was financed through supplier credit in 1995, almost the entire growth in inventory was financed by the suppliers during 1996. One big question is whether this type of financing is

770

sustainable in the long run. The answer to this becomes apparent when we examine the cash flows for 1997.

The fiscal year 1997 was obviously a challenging year for Best Buy. As discussed before, the company's profit during this year was the lowest in recent history. The operating cash flows indicate that the company has taken substantial efforts to improve its financial position by reducing its inventory level by almost $70 million. While this may be an indication of improved inventory management, it is also consistent with a fall in future demand, and, therefore, the company is buying less inventory. In addition, as discussed above, the company had to pay off its creditors (almost $190 million), and, therefore, the smaller than expected growth in the 1996 working capital level was not sustainable.

Accounts receivable follow a pattern similar to that of inventory. During 1995 and 1996, the company had been building up its receivables, which is consistent with growth in sales. However, the company was liquidating its receivables during 1997. Was this because the company changed its collection policy? Was it because the growth in sales is decreasing? In essence, this is an important item for the analyst to follow up with the company.

In addition to investment in inventory, pre-opening costs are also a significant drain on the working capital of the company.

	1997	1996	1995
Pre-opening costs per store	$300	$300	$300
Number of new stores opened during the year	21	47	53
Total pre-opening costs per year	$6,300	$14,100	$15,900

Based on the number of new stores opened, these costs ranged from $6.3 million in 1997 to almost $16 million in 1995. One would expect these one-time costs as a necessary investment in business expansion. This must be kept in mind when evaluating the negative operating cash flows during the growth years.

Requirement 4:
Insights from the investing and financing sections of the cash flow statement:

The investing cash flows suggest that the company has substantially decreased its capital expenditures during 1997 to less than $90 million from around $120 million in the previous two years. Once again, this may be an indication of downsizing by the company.

Finally, let us focus on the financing cash flows. The most important issue is how the business expansion was financed. In addition to using supplier credit, the company raised $230 million during 1995 by issuing convertible preferred securities. Since opening new stores requires a "permanent" increase in the working capital, it is optimal for the company to use a long-term financing source, such as preferred stock, to fund the business expansion.

The following are selected excerpts from the management discussion and analysis section of the 1997 fiscal year 10-K report of the company. The management discusses many of the issues that were brought out in our analysis of the cash flows of Best Buy.

In fiscal 1997, the Company curtailed the pace of expansion to a level that could be reasonably supported by internally generated funds. The rapid pace of growth and store openings in the two previous years was funded with funds generated from the public securities and bank debt markets. The funds from a securities offering in November 1994 and the Company's bank-financed master lease facility provided the majority of the financing to rapidly open stores and increase distribution capacity. *Due to the reduced profits available to support a high level of store growth, the Company substantially reduced the number of new store openings in fiscal 1997. (Emphasis added.)*

Cash flow from operations in fiscal 1997, before changes in working capital, was impacted by the decline in earnings. After adjusting for the $25 million in noncash inventory charges, cash flow from operations, before working capital changes, was $94 million, compared to $104 million in fiscal 1996 and $97 million in fiscal 1995. Changes in the components of working capital, after adjusting for markdown reserves, *included a $44 million decrease in inventories in fiscal 1997, despite the addition of 21 new stores, due to improved inventory management.* Inventories increased $293 million in fiscal 1996 and $270 million in fiscal 1995 due to the higher levels of business expansion in those years. Working capital financing provided by accounts payable and financing arrangements was reduced by $152 million in fiscal 1997 and increased by $291 million and $178 million in fiscal 1996 and 1995, respectively, reflecting the change in activity levels at each of the respective year ends.

Cash used in investing activities was $20 million in fiscal 1997, compared to $159 million in fiscal 1996 and $192 million in fiscal 1995. *Due to the slower rate of growth in fiscal 1997, capital spending was $88 million, compared to approximately $120 million in each of the two previous years...* Management expects that capital spending and investment in property development will decline further in fiscal 1998 as the number of store openings is reduced.

Management believes that, as a result of lower levels of investment in property development and improvement in inventory management resulting in faster inventory turns, the Company's working capital borrowing requirements will be lower in fiscal 1998 than in fiscal 1997. The ability of the Company to meet the covenants required by its credit facilities is dependent upon future operating results. While there can be no assurance that the Company will be able to achieve the required performance necessary to remain in compliance, management believes that sufficient alternative sources of working capital financing are available to support the Company's planned operations for fiscal 1998.

Exercises
E17-1. Why do financial reporting rules differ?

One important determinant of a country's reporting standards arises from regulators' actions and the demands of external statement users.

In jurisdictions where capital is raised from a broad range of outside investors–as is the case in the United States and Canada–these users require detailed and informative disclosures in order to make effective investment decisions. Their demand for information helps ensure passage of disclosure laws and the development of reporting standards which provide the necessary information.

But in countries where much of the capital needed by firms is raised privately–say, from banks or from related companies in the *keiretsu*–public disclosure rules are less important. The primary capital providers have direct contact with those firms which are raising capital as well as the power to request detailed information regarding the firms' financial strengths and prospects. In these situations, the demand for informative public disclosures is lessened, and reporting standards are frequently weak.

E17-2. Overcoming reporting diversity

Uniform reporting standards would improve comparability to some extent in certain circumstances. Two examples will serve to illustrate the point. Capital lease accounting is not used in Japan. But insofar as long-term, non-cancelable leases that transfer property rights to the lessee exist in Japan, then comparisons between United States and Japanese firms would be hampered. Uniform lease capitalization rules would enhance comparability here. A second example is The Netherlands where variable costing is allowed for inventory accounting. Again, comparisons between Dutch firms using variable costing and other firms in countries which require absorption costing would be impeded. A uniform standard might help here.

But, uniform international reporting rules cannot overcome all obstacles. U.S.-type equity method accounting rules when applied to Japanese interlocking *keiretsu* investments–as discussed in the text–are an example. The philosophy underlying reporting rules like equity method accounting–i.e., 20% or greater ownership conveys some degree of control–do not apply in Japan. To generalize, other examples of a lack of conformity between the objective of specific reporting rules and institutional arrangements in certain countries undoubtedly exist. Uniform rules will not enhance comparability in such instances.

E17-3. Alternative return measures

Requirement 1:
Spanish GAAP ROA = 112,608/3,109,222 = .0362 or 3.62%

Requirement 2:
U.S. GAAP ROA = 125,069/(3,109,222 - 126,552)

= 125,069/2,982,670

= .0419 or 4.19%

Requirement 3:
There is no "better" ROA. The appropriate ROA measure to use is based on the following issues: (1) which ROA better reflects the firm's economic performance, and (2) which ROA allows users of the financial report to compare Telefonica de Espana, S.A. to other firms of interest.

As stated in the chapter, some countries' accounting standards are not intended to measure and report economic reality. Instead, the accounting standards are tied to the tax laws or other statutory reporting requirements of the country. In some cases, countries have not expended the resources necessary to develop a comprehensive set of accounting standards. For example, Spanish GAAP does not address the accounting for capital versus revenue expenditures. Firms reporting in accordance with U.S. GAAP would be required to capitalize the cost of overhauling machinery if the overhaul increased the efficiency of the asset, i.e., changed the economic performance of the assets. Firms reporting in accordance with Spanish GAAP could either capitalize or expense the cost of the overhaul. The lack of guidance could result in accounting data that do not reflect underlying economic circumstances.

It is important to note that Spanish GAAP has less stringent disclosure requirements than U.S. GAAP. Telefonica, when reporting in accordance with Spanish GAAP, would not have to disclose financial information that analysts typically use to adjust earnings and asset figures before calculating a firm's ROA, e.g., nonoperating or nonrecurring items.

E17-4. Current cost accounting

Requirement 1:

Highrate Company
Current Cost Income Statement
For the Year Ended 1998

Sales		$20,000
Cost of sales ($8,000 × 1.25)		10,000
Gross margin		10,000
Depreciation ($2,000 + $1,000)	$3,000	
Other operating expenses	8,000	11,000
Net income (loss)		($1,000)

Requirement 2:

Which income figure is more useful depends upon two sets of factors: 1) the procedures used to generate the current cost numbers, and 2) the specific type of analysis that is being undertaken by the user.

Some people find current costing to be attractive conceptually. But in real-world settings, this conceptual appeal might not be realized. One reason is the reliability of the company's estimates of current cost. That is, is the measurement error large? Can accurate measures of the replacement cost of inventories and fixed assets be made? For inventories, the answer is frequently "yes" since purchases are usually continuous and the latest purchase price provides an estimate of replacement cost. For fixed assets, the reasonableness of the replacement cost estimate depends upon the availability of detailed price indices by specific asset category for things like buildings and readily available market price information for production equipment (e.g., "Redbook" values, "Bluebook" values, etc.). In certain industries, such data are available. To cite one example, in the airline industry, the *Avmark Newsletter* provides information on recent sales of used aircraft broken down by specific model and other specifications. Another procedure issue is how frequently firms revalue their assets. For example, revaluation is permitted in the United Kingdom. But once a firm has revalued its assets, there is no requirement that new revaluations must be made at specified intervals. Consequently, the current cost data being used may be several years old, i.e., not "current" at all! In countries like Mexico where current cost adjustments are required by Mexican GAAP, this is obviously not a problem.

The specific type of analysis being undertaken by the user is also an important determinant of usefulness. In the previous paragraph, some of the pitfalls of current costing were outlined. But the deficiencies of historical cost numbers for analytical use can be even worse. Chapter 9 (pp. 452–456.) has an extensive discussion of the problems that arise when analysts use historical cost numbers to undertake time-series analyses for an individual firm. Other problems arise when historical cost numbers are used in cross-sectional comparisons.

To summarize, which approach is more useful depends upon specific circumstances.

E17-5. General price-level accounting
(AICPA adapted)

General price-level depreciation expense for 1998 is $7,900, computed as follows:

Date Acquired	(a) Historical Cost Depreciation	(b) Adjustment Factor	(c) General Price Level Depreciation (a) × (b)
1996	$3,000	150/100	$4,500
1997	2,000	150/125	2,400
1998	1,000	150/150	1,000
			$7,900

E17-6. Distinguishing between monetary and nonmonetary items

The nonmonetary items are:
(3) Minority interest (sometimes called noncontrolling interest)
(6) Equity investment in unconsolidated subsidiaries
(7) Obligations under warranties
(8) Accumulated depreciation of equipment

Minority interest is nonmonetary since it is comprised of:
Minority ownership % × (Assets - Liabilities).

Since many of the underlying assets and liabilities are nonmonetary, the net minority interest is nonmonetary.

Equity investment in unconsolidated subsidiaries is nonmonetary for the same reason minority interest is nonmonetary. It represents an ownership % times net assets, many of which are nonmonetary.

Obligations under warranties are nonmonetary since these liabilities will be settled through use of nonmonetary assets and labor services.

Accumulated depreciation of equipment is nonmonetary since the equipment itself is nonmonetary.

E17-7. General price-level accounting
(AICPA adapted)

The investment and long-term debt are both monetary items and would be shown at their historical cost balance sheet amounts, i.e., a debit balance of $60,000 and a credit balance of $80,000, respectively. The land would be shown on a general price-level accounting balance sheet amount of:

$$\$120,000 \times \frac{110}{100} = \$132,000$$

E17-8. Attitude of U.S. companies toward IASC standards

Requirement 1:
If foreign issuers of securities in the United States were allowed to use IASC standards rather than reconciling to U.S. GAAP in Form 20-F, controversy would undoubtedly ensue.

Some of the controversy would arise because there are differences between IASC and U.S. standards. But whether these differences would make the "playing field" unlevel is not clear. Those who argue that the more "lenient" IASC standards would put U.S. firms at a disadvantage contend one or more of the following:

a) Disclosures will be too cryptic to allow knowledgeable analysts to reconcile IASC standards to U.S. GAAP, thereby leading to noncomparability in evaluating U.S. versus foreign issuers.

b) Some less knowledgeable investors will be oblivious to the reporting differences and will judge foreign issuers who use IASC standards more favorably than their underlying economic performance warrants.

c) Foreign issuers with excellent prospects won't "signal" their extraordinary potential in some way–say, by voluntarily supplying the more stringent U.S. GAAP data to allow meaningful comparisons and "showcase" their more favorable prospects.

On the other hand, consistent with the discussion solution to E17-2, it is not clear whether a single, uniform set of standards can adequately capture the subtle institutional and national differences that cause foreign firms' operating environments and prospects to diverge from their U.S. competitors. In this view, since no single set of standards could ever completely reflect these differences, using different standards for foreign issuers might be no worse than the noncomparability that arises under the Form 20-F reconciliation.

Requirement 2:

It is unclear how U.S. managers will respond as the SEC debates whether to allow foreign issuers to use IASC standards. Some may oppose the proposal on "uneven playing field" arguments while others–for reasons discussed below–may privately hope the SEC allows IASC rules.

If the SEC does allow foreign issuers to use IASC standards, the position of top managers of U.S. companies becomes more predictable. Since IASC standards allow more latitude, many U.S. managers might prefer them to the more "stringent" U.S. rules and actually lobby for permission to use the IASC standards domestically instead of U.S. GAAP. In the ensuing political debate, the avowed rationale would be to "re-level the playing field." The issue of contracting advantages arising from the more lenient rules would–of course–go unmentioned.

Problems
P17-1. Capital sources and disclosure differences

Requirement 1:
In Equityland, the primary users of the financial reports are the shareholders who buy and sell stock on the public stock exchanges. In Debtland, the primary users of the financial reports are the creditors who provide capital to Debtland companies.

Requirement 2:
Both types of users are interested in assessing the profitability of firms. Shareholders are concerned about profitability because they have dividend expectations. In addition, shareholders are concerned about a firm's growth and growth potential because growth will have an impact on the firm's market appreciation. Creditors are concerned about profitability because profitability is linked to long-term cash flows and creditors want to assess firms' abilities to cover interest payments. In addition, creditors are concerned with liquidity. A firm's liquidity is useful in assessing its ability to pay back its debts.

Requirement 3:

Equityland	Debtland
ROE	ROE
ROA	ROA
EPS	Times interest earned
Current ratio	Debt-to-equity ratio
	Current ratio

Requirement 4:
The disclosure environments of Equityland and Debtland might be quite different. Firms in Equityland would be expected to provide more public disclosures of financial and nonfinancial information simply because individual investors are not privy to company records. Firms in Equityland may provide more information about their financial position and operating performance via footnotes to the financial statements. In addition, Equityland firms may meet with financial analysts and other intermediaries to disseminate information. A demand for additional financial information exists in Debtland but firms often won't publicly disclose the information. Public disclosures are not essential in

780

these settings since creditors have the power to examine company records that shareholders typically cannot access.

P17-2. Overcoming reporting diversity

Requirement 1:
The footnote states that the reduction in the carrying value of certain assets represents the write-down of certain planning and development costs. U.S. GAAP does not allow planning and development costs to be capitalized. They must be expensed in the period incurred and reported as part of operating expenses. On the other hand, if the assets were legitimately included in property, plant, and equipment, the reduction in the carrying value may reflect an impairment of an asset. According to FASB No. 121, a loss on the impairment of a long-term asset should be reported as part of income from continuing operations, generally in the other expenses and losses section. The loss should not be reported as an extraordinary item.

Requirement 2:
Summary financial information, e.g., net income, total assets, stockholders' equity, is a function of the accounting methods a firm employs in preparing its financial statements. Thus, one must exercise caution in comparing summary statistics across international firms because firms will be reporting in accordance with different sets of accounting standards. U.S. GAAP is more restrictive in its accounting method choices relative to other domestic GAAPs. However, even within U.S. GAAP, firms have discretion in selecting accounting methods. Thus, data services that provide only summary financial information are limited in their usefulness.

Requirement 3:

Income (loss) as originally reported		($1,282)
Add: Tax reimbursements		8
		($1,274)
Less:		
Estimated expenses associated with contingent liabilities	$111	
Costs related to financial restructuring	406	
Reduction in carrying value of certain assets	1,206	
		($1,723)
Revised continuing income (loss)		($2,997)

In general, there is limited information to determine the proper classification of the items Euro Disney classified as exceptional items. For example, consider the gain reported due to payable forgiveness. In accordance with FASB

Statement No. 114, if Euro Disney's pre-restructure carrying amount of the debt exceeds the total future cash flows related to the restructured debt, then Euro Disney would report an extraordinary gain on the debt restructuring. However, if the total future cash flow after restructuring exceeds the total pre-restructuring carrying amount of Euro Disney's debt, no gain would be reported. Income (loss) from continuing operations is an important calculation for the users of financial statements. The measure is considered to represent the firm's sustainable earnings, i.e., earnings that will persist in the future. Expected earnings are used to estimate future cash flows, which are relevant in valuing a firm's stock. Users of financial statements must realize that income (loss) from continuing operations reported on the income statement can vary depending upon the GAAP employed.

P17-3. Overcoming reporting diversity

Requirement 1:
The text identifies four approaches to bringing about uniformity to foreign issuers' financial reporting.

a) Dual reporting

b) Reconciliations

c) Adopting an alternative set of standards

d) Reporting in accordance with an internationally acceptable set of accounting standards.

Requirement 2:
Yizheng Chemical Fibre Company has chosen to provide dual reporting (more than one set of financial statements) as well as use an internationally acceptable set of accounting standards.

Requirement 3:

a) Turnover is another word for sales.

b) The operating section of the IASC profit and loss statement is highly condensed. The PRC accounting profit and loss statement provides more details (although still quite limited) and, thus, would be considered more useful in assessing the performance of Yizheng Chemical Fibre Company.

c) The differences in accounting method choices available under IASC relative to those available under PRC accounting standards causes the difference in operating profit. For example, differences in valuing inventory, valuing investments, calculating depreciation, accounting for leases and pensions, etc., all have an impact on operating income.

d) The profit figure used depends upon several factors. First, users may choose one profit figure over another because they are more familiar with one set of accounting standards over the other and, as a result, are better able to interpret the information. Second, if the profit figure is being used to compare Yizheng's performance to another firm, the user will pick the profit figure calculated by the standards that correspond more closely to the accounting standards employed by the other firm. Based on information disclosed in the footnotes, the user might have to adjust the income statement numbers to account for any differences in the accounting method choices of the firms. Finally, if the financial report user believes that one set of standards better measures the economic performance of Yizheng, the profit figure calculated from those standards will be used.

In general, users of financial reports must be cognizant of the fact that the informativeness of the financial statements is a function of the accounting standards used to construct them. Some sets of accounting standards allow firms much more discretion in their choice of accounting methods (e.g., Swiss GAAP, Italian GAAP). In addition, some standards do not require as many financial disclosures (e.g., Norwegian GAAP, Finnish GAAP). Thus, firms preparing financial reports in accordance with one set of standards may generate a more "loose" set of financial information than firms following alternative sets of accounting standards. Analysts might, therefore, prefer to perform the analysis using the "tighter" GAAP measures since they presumably provide better interfirm comparability.

P17-4. Current cost ratio effects

Requirement 1:
The option to revalue assets provides management with additional accounting discretion. If management systematically revalues assets and is consistent in its measurement of revaluation, there is minimal concern about the consistency of accounting numbers over time, i.e., the ability to compare firm's accounting numbers from one period to the next. However, if management does not systematically undertake revaluations, or changes the methods by which it estimates revaluations, then the comparability of accounting information is compromised.

The revaluation of assets can also cause difficulties when making interfirm comparisons. The revaluation of assets is often based on an estimate of market value rather than the objective measure of market value provided by an arm's-length exchange of assets. The users of financial statements must be aware that firms have different methods of measuring the revaluation of fixed assets.

Requirement 2:
Note: The assessment of a ratio improving or weakening is made in very general terms. Assessing the consequences of changes in ratios is firm-specific.

a) Total shareholders' equity to total assets would increase: Ratio improved. (Note: The ratio would be unaffected for an all-equity firm.)

b) Long term debt to assets would decrease: Ratio improved.

c) There would be no effect on the current ratio.

d) Return on assets would decrease: Ratio weakened.

P17-5. Overcoming reporting diversity

Requirement 1:
United Kingdom GAAP ROE = 1,835/1,369 = 1.34 or 134%

United States GAAP ROE = 800/4,735 = .169 (rounded) or 16.9%

Requirement 2:
According to U.S. GAAP, the amortization of goodwill is reported as an operating expense on the income statement. The expense reduces net income that results in a decrease in earnings per share. The write-off of goodwill at the time of purchase affects ROE of the current period via the denominator of the ROE calculation. Stockholders' equity will be reduced by an amount equal to the purchase price of the goodwill. Since the denominator is decreasing and the numerator, net income, is not affected by the goodwill write-off, ROE will be higher in the period of the write-off. As far as the impact on future periods' ROE, the difference in stockholders' equity due to the write-off will ultimately be eliminated; the amortization expense systematically reduces stockholders' equity via net income. However, since net income measured in accordance with U.K. GAAP will be higher relative to U.S. GAAP net income, U.K. GAAP ROE will also be higher than U.S. GAAP ROE until the point in time that the goodwill is fully amortized.

Requirement 3:
One could argue that the U.K. GAAP ROE is a better measure of economic performance because net income is not garbled with a cost allocation estimate, i.e., goodwill amortization. However, since stockholders' equity is reduced by the goodwill write-offs, the ROE may be overstated. ROE calculated under U.S. GAAP may not measure "true" economic performance either. Managers' have discretion in choosing amortization periods which influences net income and, consequently, ROE. It isn't the case that one ROE better reflects economic performance. Rather, the appropriate ROE should be based on the comparisons being made; SmithKline Beecham to a U.K. firm that

wrote off goodwill or SmithKline Beecham to a U.S. firm or U.K. firm that capitalized goodwill.

P17-6. Overcoming reporting diversity

Requirement 1:
ROE = 81,257/778,364 = .1044 or 10.44%

Requirement 2:

Revised Shareholders' Equity:	
Fixed assets at current value	$858,000
Less: Fixed assets at cost	692,913
Addition due to revaluation	165,087
Add: Shareholders' equity at historical cost	778,364
Shareholders' equity restated	$943,451
Revised Net Income:	
Net income as reported	81,257
Less: Additional depreciation expense	12,106
Net income restated	$69,151

Revised ROE = 69,151/943,451 = .073 or 7.3%

Requirement 3:
The ROE in Requirement 1 is probably more relevant in comparing Stork's performance to the performance of an industrial firm domiciled in the United States. However, even though U.S. GAAP requires historical cost accounting for its fixed assets, there may be other accounting method differences between Dutch GAAP and U.S. GAAP. Thus, while the ROE in Requirement 1 is more relevant than the restated ROE, it still might need to be adjusted to be comparable.

Requirement 4:
While ROE in Requirement 2 may be more relevant in comparing Stork's performance to the performance of an Australian firm, there probably are differences between Australian GAAP and Dutch GAAP. Differences in the accounting method choices available under Dutch GAAP relative to the accounting method choices available under Australian GAAP would make the ROE in Req. 2 noncomparable unless further adjustments are made to Stork's net income and stockholders' equity to bring them in line with Australian GAAP.

In some instances, accounting standards might seem similar when, in fact, the standards are quite different. For example, in 1997, U.S. accounting standard setters issued a standard on segment reporting, as did the International Accounting Standards Committee. On the surface a user might think that the two standards would generate similar financial information. However, due to the differences in the way the standards define a business segment, a firm could end up reporting very different segment data depending upon whether it followed U.S. GAAP or the IASC standard.

P17-7. Overcoming reporting diversity

The conceptual framework of U.S. GAAP defines expenses as the use or outflows of assets during a period from delivering or producing goods, rendering services, or carrying out the activities that constitute the entity's normal business operations. Since none of the special items disclosed in the footnote appear to be incurred in conjunction with Electrolux's normal business activities, they should be reclassified as nonoperating gains or losses if Electrolux is preparing U.S. GAAP financial statements. Specifically, the following reclassifications should be made:

Special item	Income Statement Presentation
Capital gains on sales of real estate	Other income section
Losses on sales of operations	Discontinued operations–net of taxes
Capital gains on sale of shares in Email Ltd.	Other income section

By reporting these special items as operating expenses, Electrolux increased operating expenses by seven million Swedish Kroners and buried the 325 million Kroner loss from discontinued operations in the body of the income statement.

P17-8. GAAP differences

Requirement 1:

a) Generally, if inventory levels are increasing, Novo Nordisk's earnings would be lower under Danish GAAP relative to U.S. GAAP because of the expensing of direct labor and production overhead costs. This issue is discussed in Chapter 8. However, if inventory levels decreased, Novo Nordisk's Danish GAAP net income would be higher than its net income measured in accordance with U.S. GAAP.

b) Danish GAAP earnings would be higher than U.S. GAAP earnings since amortization expense is not recorded on intangible assets.

c) Dividends have no effect on earnings.

d) Danish GAAP earnings would be lower than U.S. GAAP earnings since construction interest is expensed rather than capitalized.

Requirement 2:

a) Inventory would have a higher carrying value under U.S. GAAP relative to Danish GAAP. Thus current assets, total assets, and stockholders' equity would all be larger under U.S. GAAP.

b) Since intangible assets are being amortized under U.S. GAAP, U.S. GAAP would result in a lower carrying value for intangible assets and, in the aggregate, lower total assets. Because income would be lower, stockholders' equity would also be lower.

c) Dividends declared are recorded as a liability in the declaration period under U.S. GAAP. Thus, Novo's current liabilities would increase if Novo prepared a U.S. GAAP balance sheet.

d) Under U.S. GAAP, Novo would have to capitalize construction interest. This would result in larger fixed asset and stockholders' equity balances.

P17-9. GAAP differences

Requirement 1:
One difference is the order of the accounts. In the United States, firms list assets in descending order of liquidity—most liquid to least liquid. Remy lists its long-term assets first and its current assets towards the bottom of the balance sheet. Another difference is in the reporting of prepaid and deferred charges. Remy reports them as a separate line item in a non-classified category of assets. In the United States, prepaid assets are usually classified as current and deferred charges can be either long-term or current. Remy does not report accounts receivable separately from notes receivable nor does Remy report them at their net realizable value. There is just one category for investments. It is not clear if the investments are long-term or short-term.

At the time Remy's balance sheet was prepared, French GAAP did not require firms to estimate bad debts and set up an allowance for doubtful accounts. French GAAP was linked to tax reporting which did not allow a deduction for bad debts unless the firm owing the accounts receivable was in bankruptcy or receivership. Thus, the asset valuations reported on the balance sheet were dependent on the tax rules in effect.

In addition to the differences in accounting methods across alternative sets of GAAP, there can be substantial differences in GAAP disclosure requirements. Some GAAPs require extensive disclosures to be part of the published financial report (e.g., U.S. GAAP). Other GAAPs do not require as many financial disclosures (e.g., German GAAP). Firms can voluntarily provide financial disclosures to supplement those required by the GAAP employed and, thus, the variation in disclosure practices across GAAPs generally is less of a concern than the variations in accounting methods.

In summary, firms can voluntarily improve their financial reporting by increasing their financial disclosures and/or preparing their financial reports in accordance with a more stringent set of accounting standards, i.e., standards that restrict a firm's choice of accounting methods. Strong firms can "signal" their strength by choosing more stringent standards.

Requirement 2:

Intangible fixed assets would include the value of Remy's brand names. Given the nature of Remy's business, brand names are critical to Remy's economic success.

Requirement 3:

U.S. GAAP requires the cost of purchased brand names or trademarks to be capitalized and amortized over their estimated useful lives. Costs related to internally generated brand names and trademarks must be expensed in the period incurred. In adjusting Remy's statements, reasonable estimates of amortization expense would need to be calculated and deducted from net income for the current period. Under U.S. GAAP, the cost of brand names would be amortized over the brand name's estimated useful life using the straight-line method. Accumulated amortization, i.e., the sum of the amortization expense since the brand names were acquired, would be subtracted from the carrying value of the intangible fixed assets and from retained earnings. As a consequence, total assets and stockholders' equity would be decreased for the accumulated amortization.

Cases

C17-1. Tyler Corporation (II): Adjusting reported trend data

Requirement 1:

For illustrative purposes, we will assume that the adjustment procedure was applied to quarterly data. Notice that Tyler adjusted income statement items to *year-end* purchasing power so each quarter's sales were adjusted as follows:

Quarter	Price-index adjustment factor
1st	$\dfrac{\text{12/31/79 CPI}}{\text{1st Qtr '79 Ave CPI}}$
2nd	$\dfrac{\text{12/31/79 CPI}}{\text{2nd Qtr '79 Ave CPI}}$
3rd	$\dfrac{\text{12/31/79 CPI}}{\text{3rd Qtr '79 Ave CPI}}$
4th	$\dfrac{\text{12/31/79 CPI}}{\text{4th Qtr '79 Ave CPI}}$

Reported sales for each quarter would be multiplied by the appropriate adjustment factor to convert nominal dollars into 12/31/79 year-end purchasing power. The sum of these four quarterly adjustments equals $546,992,000. The inflation adjustment increased sales by ($546,992 - $519,242)/$519,242, or 5.3%. If sales and inflation occurred evenly over the year, the adjustment should have been the 13.3% CPI increase divided by 2. The 5.3% is lower than this, thereby implying that sales in the second half of the year were higher and/or the inflation rate was uneven.

Requirement 2:

The $458,952,000 number was derived using a procedure similar to that illustrated above. For example, the first quarter adjustment would be:

$$\text{Reported 1st Qtr 1978 Nominal sales \$s} \times \frac{\text{12/31/79 CPI}}{\text{1st Qtr '78 Ave CPI}}$$

Repeating this procedure for each quarter expresses 1978 sales in year-end 1979 dollars, thereby facilitating evaluation of period-to-period *real* sales growth. It would require $458,952,000 at December 31, 1979, to have the same purchasing power, on average, as $390,873,000 (reported 1978 nominal sales in C15-2) did at mid-year 1978.

Requirement 3:

The 5-year summary helps answer this question.

($546,992 - $458,952)/$458,952 = 19.2%.

Notice that this is sales growth after factoring out overall inflation; however, this does not adjust for the acquisition of Thurston.

Requirement 4:

It is easy to adjust for both inflation and the acquisition simultaneously. The key is to apply the inflation adjustment factors to the pro-forma sales data given in C15-2, rather than to the income statement data themselves.

We saw in Requirement 1 that the inflation adjustment factor for 1979 was 5.3%. The factor for 1978 is:

($458,952 - $390,873)/$390,873, or 17.4%.

The simultaneous adjustment approach proceeds as follows:

	Pro Forma Sales No.	Adjustment Factor	Adjusted Sales
1979	$540,327,000	1.053	$568,964,330
1978	$480,048,000	1.174	$563,576,350
Increase			$ 5,387,980

Adjusting for both the acquisition and inflation results in a year-to-year computed increase of $5,387,980, which is less than a 1% change in real sales.

790

C17-2. Tyler Corporation (III): Borrowing strategies under inflationary conditions

The Credit Commitments footnote shows that gross long-term debt increased by $46,633,000 during 1979 (i.e., $78,561,000 - $32,928,000) which is only slightly greater than the approximately $45,500,000 cash purchase price for Thurston. This is consistent with Tyler's disclosure that "long-term debt has been the primary vehicle for financing the acquisition of each of the four operating units." However, more than 100% of the debt increase is attributable to **floating-rate** debt ($43,000,000 at 106% of prime and $4,150,000 at prime).

Tyler stated that shareholders benefited from inflation because the debt was repaid "with dollars having less purchasing power." But floating rate debt is designed to negate this wealth transfer between lenders and borrowers since interest payments increase in response to inflation. Thus, it is unclear how Tyler intended to benefit shareholders by financing the Thurston acquisition with floating rate debt.

It might be worthwhile pointing out to students that the direction of the wealth transfer can't be known with certainty *ex ante* even with fixed rate debt. Lenders are not oblivious to inflation and a quoted fixed interest rate of, say, 9% might be comprised of a desired "real" return of 5% plus anticipated inflation of 4%. Borrowers benefit from inflation only if the *ex post* realized inflation rate over the duration of the loan turns out to be higher than the anticipated 4% inflation factor built into the interest rate. If realized inflation is only 2%, then the lender (who earned an unexpectedly large return) benefits at the expense of the borrower.

C17-3. Tyler Corporation (IV): Inflation's effect on GAAP ratios

Requirement 1:
The instructor may wish to mention that the 11-year period covered in the ad represented the most sustained and significant level of inflation in the United States since the Korean War.

Under GAAP accounting rules, inflation injects a two-fold upward bias on reported ROE–both a "favorable" numerator effect and a "favorable" denominator effect.

The numerator effect is usually most pronounced for capital-intensive firms, that is, those with high proportions of long-lived assets as a percentage of total assets. This effect is attributable to historical cost reporting for the assets and consequent "underdepreciation" (in comparison to current value) on the income statement. This makes income "too high" and (*ceteris paribus*) overstates ROE. Other numerator overstatements include, as examples, LIFO dipping, and various inflation-induced debt "games" (e.g., debt-for-debt swaps) discussed in Chapter 10.

Since assets exceed liabilities for virtually all going concerns, the GAAP failure to adjust assets **understates** the denominator when prices are rising, especially for capital-intensive firms. During inflation, GAAP historical cost accounting for fixed rate debt overstates liabilities' real burden (and, thus, overstates the denominator). But since assets exceed liabilities for most firms, the asset effect dominates. (Of course, for firms with significant amounts of floating rate debt–like Tyler–there is a reduced denominator effect from inflation since the book value and market value of floating rate debt should be roughly equal.)

The ad shows that GAAP ROE has averaged close to 20% over the 11-year period. Over the period covered by the ads, GAAP ROE would have been overstated each year in comparison to inflation-adjusted ROE. Since the effect of inflation is cumulative, this means that inflation-adjusted ROE was falling over the period covered by the ad.

Requirement 2:
Inflation-adjusted ROE was falling for the overwhelming majority of *Fortune* 500 companies over this period, not just Tyler. But the disparity between GAAP ROE and inflation-adjusted ROE was not the same across *Fortune* 500 firms. Firms with a higher proportion of long-lived assets as a percent of total assets will have a relatively higher overstatement in ROE under GAAP. Thus, the validity of the comparison between Tyler's ROE over the period and the median of the *Fortune* 500 depends upon the relative capital intensity of Tyler in comparison to the average of the other 499.

C17-4. Robinson Company: General price level and current cost adjustments

Requirement 1:

Robinson Company
Statement of Historical Cost/Constant Dollar Income
Year Ended December 31, 1998

Sales revenues	$\left(\$8,600 \times \dfrac{200}{190}\right)$		$9,053
Cost of goods sold	$\left(\$4,000 \times \dfrac{200}{178}\right)$	$4,494	
Depreciation	$\left(\$1,000 \times \dfrac{200}{100}\right)$	2,000	
			6,494
Historical cost/constant dollar income from continuing operations			2,559
Loss on net monetary items			820#
Total historical cost/constant dollar income			$1,739

#Calculation of Loss on Net Monetary Items

	Historical $s	Restatement Ratio	Constant $s December 31, 1998
Net monetary assets, Jan. 1, 1998	$5,000	$\dfrac{200}{180}$	$5,556
Increase in net monetary assets: From sales revenues	8,600	$\dfrac{200}{190}$	9,053
Decrease in net monetary assets: To pay dividends	(3,600)	$\dfrac{200}{190}$	(3,789)
Net monetary assets in 12/31/98 dollars			10,820
Net monetary assets in historical dollars, 12/31/98	$10,000		(10,000)
Loss on net monetary items			$820

Robinson Company
Historical Cost/Constant Dollar Statement of Financial Position
December 31, 1998

<u>Assets</u>   <u>Equity</u>

Cash $10,000

Inventory $\left(\$4,000 \times \dfrac{200}{178}\right)$ 4,494

Fixed asset $\left(\$10,000 \times \dfrac{200}{100}\right)$ 20,000

Less: Accum. dep. $\left(\$6,000 \times \dfrac{200}{100}\right)$ (12,000)

                                                    $\underline{\$8,000}$ Owners' Equity $\underline{22,494}$[@]
                                                    $\underline{\$22,494}$ $\underline{\$22,494}$

[@]<u>Direct Calculation of Owners' Equity</u>

January 1, 1998 Owners' equity in 1/1/98
    constant dollars:

Cash $5,000

Inventory $\left(\$8,000 \times \dfrac{180}{178}\right)$ 8,090

Fixed asset $\left([\$10,000 - \$5,000] \times \dfrac{180}{100}\right)$ $\underline{9,000}$

                                                                  22,090

Adjustment factor to roll-forward
    to 12/31/98 $s $\left(\dfrac{200}{180}\right)$ $\times \underline{1.1111}$

January 1, 1998 Owners' equity in
    12/31/98 constant dollars   = 24,544

Plus: 1998 Constant dollar income   1,739

Minus: 1998 Dividend $\left(\$3,600 \times \dfrac{200}{190}\right)$ $\underline{(3,789)}$

                                                                  $\underline{\$22,494}$

Requirement 2:

Robinson Company
Statement of Current Cost Income
Year Ended December 31, 1998

Sales revenues		$8,600
Current cost of goods sold ($875 × 5)	$4,375	
Current cost depreciation ($7,000/5)	1,400	
		5,775
Current cost income from continuing operations		$2,825

Robinson Company
Current Cost Statement of Financial Position
December 31, 1998

Assets			Equity	
Cash		$10,000		
Inventory ($890 × 5)		4,450		
Fixed asset	$14,000*			
Less: Accumulated depreciation	(8,400)	5,600	Owners' Equity	$20,050[&]
		$20,050		$20,050

*Computation of fixed asset and depreciation

January 1, 1998 replacement cost of an identical fixed asset	$7,000
Imputed value of 5-year-old asset if it were new: $7,000 × 2 =	$14,000
Accumulated depreciation: ($14,000/10) × 6 years =	($8,400)

[&]Direct Calculation of Owners' Equity

1/1/98 Current cost balance (Cash, $5,000; + Inventory, $8,100; + Fixed asset, $7,000)	$20,100
Plus: Current cost income from continuing operations	2,825
Increases in inventory current costs (holding gains):	
10 units @ ($875 - $810) =	650
5 units @ ($890 - $875) =	$75
	$725
Less: Dividend	(3,600)
December 31, 1998 Owners' equity balance	$20,050

Whether the $2,825 current cost income figure represents the payout that would facilitate maintenance of physical capital is open to some question in this specific setting.

Notice that Robinson Company did not immediately reinvest the sales proceeds. Because the replacement cost of the five units of inventory has increased still further since the time of sale (i.e., $890 vs. $875), a shortfall may exist. This underscores the fact that the standard physical capital maintenance computation assumes virtually immediate reinvestment of sales proceeds into nonmonetary assets.

On the other hand, the $2,825 figure may be overly conservative. The problem states that Robinson sets prices in order to earn a target return of 20% on *original cost*. A hidden assumption of the physical capital maintenance approach is that output prices adjust virtually instantaneously to changes in input costs. This is clearly not the case when a company utilizes historical cost pricing. Obviously, the prevalence of historical cost pricing in actual practice is unknown. In the absence of tax effects, however, it may be possible for Robinson to maintain physical capital with a payout in excess of $2,825 provided that the company can continue to earn a 20% return on the actual future asset costs it incurs.

Finally, the technological change issue complicates matters. The $2,825 income figure assumes eventual replacement of the identical assets currently employed. Since the technologically improved asset is more expensive, the reported current cost number does not incorporate potential replacement with improvement assets. SFAS No. 33 specified, however, that depreciation should reflect the current cost of the *existing* assets (unless the net amount of cash expected to be recoverable from the use or sale of the asset–i.e., the "recoverable amount"–is lower).

C17-5. Japan Finance Ministry: Differences in reporting philosophies

Requirement 1:
The financial reporting philosophy implicit to the Japan Finance Ministry announcement appears to be based on "social/economic engineering." That is, *financial reporting rules* are being used in an attempt to achieve specific economic and social objectives. These objectives are two-fold: 1) to prop up Japanese share prices, and 2) to allay fears about the health of Japanese banks. In the United States, these types of goals are usually pursued through the use of fiscal and monetary policy and through passage of laws, tax reform, investment tax credits, etc. Financial reporting itself is rarely used this way in the United States. The dominant goal in the U.S. reporting philosophy is to "tell-it-like-it-is" in order to facilitate efficient resource allocation. There have been one or two notable exceptions, however. Many believe that SFAS No. 15 ("Troubled Debt Restructurings" issued in June 1977), deliberately avoided recognizing the full extent of bank credit losses and, thus, was similar in

philosophy to the Finance Ministry approach. SFAS No. 123 ("Accounting for Stock-Based Compensation" issued in October 1995) is another example; here, political pressures caused the FASB to abandon *measurement* of the estimated value of stock options issued to employees and settle for footnote *disclosures.*

Requirement 2:
The negative financial data that banks would be permitted to withhold related to loan losses and reserves. Apparently, the announcement meant that realistic loan loss reserves would not be imposed on banks, nor would the Finance Ministry require that bad loans be written off.

Requirement 3:
Answering this question takes us out of the realm of financial reporting and forces us to forecast human behavior. One might argue that the Japan Finance Ministry approach could have exacerbated the problem. Here's how.

Suppose that, prior to August 19, 1992, the consensus in the financial community was that 30% of the loans on the books of Japanese banks were in jeopardy. Further assume that financial decision-makers widely believed that their consensus estimate was fairly common knowledge and known to the Finance Ministry. In this setting, the Finance Ministry announcement could have been interpreted as a signal that the real loss percentage exceeded the 30% consensus estimate. Accordingly, rather than restoring confidence, the announcement could have heightened fears regarding the true extent of the losses that were apparently too large to be "safely" revealed.

C17-6. Daimler-Benz (KR): Understanding foreign financial statements

Requirement 1:
During 1991 and 1992, German GAAP income was lower than U.S. GAAP income due to provisions, reserves, and valuation differences (or hidden reserves). Since U.S. GAAP does not allow hidden reserves, Daimler-Benz was adding to its hidden reserve during the two years by increasing its expenses. This suggests that the two years were probably "good" earnings years, and, consequently, Daimler-Benz was "saving" some of its income for future years when the company might not be doing so well. In fact, 1993 appears to be a year of "bad" earnings. The pre-tax German GAAP income of Daimler-Benz was higher by DM 4,262 million due to using the hidden reserves to absorb current year losses. (See 1993 item "Changes in appropriated retained earnings...") Thus, by creating additional expenses during "good" earnings years, such as 1991 and 1992 for Daimler-Benz, German companies are able to bolster their earnings during "bad" earnings years such as 1993.

The following excerpt from the 20-F filing explains how Daimler-Benz had created the hidden reserves:

> The adjustments to stockholders' equity of DM 5,770 and DM 9,931 would have reduced other provisions at December 31, 1993 and 1992 by DM 4,883 and DM 8,105, respectively. The remainder of the adjustments would have increased property, plant, and equipment, inventories and other receivables under U.S. GAAP.

"Other provisions" appears to indicate that a substantial majority of the hidden reserve was the result of creating various accrued liabilities. However, some of the hidden reserves were created through extra depreciation expense and conservative valuation of inventories.

From a net worth standpoint, the German approach to creating hidden reserves has resulted in conservative financial reporting. At the end of 1993 and 1992, the company added about DM 5.77 billion and DM 9.93 billion, respectively, to its retained earnings to eliminate the hidden reserves. Consequently, over the prior years, the company must have recorded more expenses than required based on realistic business expectations. However, from an income statement standpoint, while the German approach results in smoother income figures, it is not always more conservative than the U.S. approach. This is because the creation and the depletion of the hidden reserve is very much at the discretion of management. For instance, while the hidden reserves approach led to lower German income during 1991 and 1992, it led to a higher income number in 1993 under German GAAP.

Requirement 2:
Daimler-Benz essentially uses the completed contract method even when the U.S. GAAP would require the percentage of completion method. Consequently, the question we are answering is whether the completed contract method is more or less conservative than the percentage of completion method. While both methods immediately report all expected losses, the completed contract method reports gains only after the contracts are completed. Consequently, the completed contract method (German GAAP) is more conservative than the percentage of completion method (U.S. GAAP).

This is obvious from the additions made to the retained earnings at the end of 1993 and 1992 (DM 207 million and DM 131 million, respectively). However, the adjustments to the net income figures provide a different picture. For instance, in contrast to 1993, Daimler-Benz reported higher income in 1991 and 1992 by using the completed contract approach. This might be because the gross profits of long-term contracts *completed* during 1991 and 1992 were greater than the gross profits on the work *performed* during the same period. Note that the work on some of the long-term contracts completed during 1991 and 1992 would have been performed in the prior years. In 1993, it appears that the gross profits on the work performed was greater than the gross profits on the completed contracts.

Requirement 3:

Under German GAAP, goodwill need not be amortized to the income statement. Instead, it can be written-off directly to retained earnings without flowing through the income statement as an expense. The reconciliation of the retained earnings suggests that this is what Daimler-Benz must have done in its German GAAP financial statements. Since such direct write-offs are not allowed under U.S. GAAP, goodwill must be added back to the retained earnings. From the income standpoint, since goodwill must be amortized as an expense under U.S. GAAP, the income statement reconciliation shows a reduction from German GAAP income to arrive at the U.S. GAAP income. However, regardless of the amortization rules, the net book value of the goodwill can be never be negative (at the worst, it can be zero). Consequently, although the retained earnings are lower under German GAAP due to the direct write-off, the net income is higher due to omitting the goodwill amortization expense.

Requirement 4:

Under U.S. GAAP, any gain on sale of discontinued operations is postponed until the gain is actually realized. In contrast, under German accounting, it appears that both gains and losses from discontinued operations can be recognized when the contract to sell is signed. It appears that the contract to sell AEG KABEL was signed during 1991, but the actual cash from the sale was realized only during 1992. Since the sale resulted in a gain, U.S. GAAP rules do not allow Daimler-Benz to recognize this gain until 1992. Consequently, the gain on sale is subtracted from the 1991 German income and added to the 1992 German income to bring the income statements into conformity with U.S. GAAP.

An interesting point is that the amount subtracted from the 1991 income (DM 490 million) is different from the amount added to the 1992 income (DM 337 million). Daimler-Benz provides the following explanation for this disparity:

> In addition, applying the differing accounting principles between German and U.S. GAAP **results in differing book values** of the underlying businesses. As a result, the German and U.S. GAAP accounting gain or loss on a business disposition may be different.

To illustrate, the net book value under German GAAP is likely to be lower due to existence of the hidden reserves. Consequently, the gain on sale reported under the German GAAP (DM 490 million) is higher than the gain on sale under the U.S. GAAP (DM 337 million). When Daimler-Benz eliminated the hidden reserves, the net book value of the discontinued operations must have gone up.

Requirement 5:
German GAAP allows companies to use the entry age method for pension cost as defined in the German tax code. However, U.S. GAAP requires companies to use the projected unit credit method.

For OPEB, U.S. GAAP has required the use of the accrual method since the early 1990s. However, it appears that Daimler-Benz uses cash basis accounting under German GAAP. Note that the income statement reconciliation shows the cumulative effects of adopting SFAS No. 106 as an adjustment to the German GAAP net income.

Overall, it appears that the German accounting methods for pension and OPEB result in a less conservative book value for net worth. At the end of 1993 and 1992, Daimler-Benz subtracted DM 1.82 billion and DM 1.21 billion, respectively, from its German GAAP retained earnings to arrive at the U.S. GAAP numbers.

Requirement 6:
Under U.S. GAAP, both gains and losses from derivative instruments to hedge anticipated or future transactions are marked to market, i.e., the unrealized gains and losses flow through the income statement. In contrast, under German GAAP, it appears that while the German Commercial Code requires a provision for unrealized losses on such instruments, unrealized gains are not recorded until they are realized. (Note that this is an example of how the commercial law in Germany drives the financial reporting standards.) Consequently, this results in more conservative financial reports under German GAAP. Consistent with this, we find that Daimler-Benz added DM 381 million (DM 580 million) at the end of 1992 (1991) to its German GAAP retained earnings to conform to the U.S. GAAP requirements.

Requirement 7:
If Daimler-Benz were using the equity method, then consolidation of Deutsche Aerospace Airbus would have had no impact on the net income of Daimler-Benz. This is because Daimler-Benz' share of Deutsche Aerospace Airbus' net income will have been included under the equity method. While consolidation will change the components of the income statement, the bottom line will be unaffected. Therefore, it appears that Daimler-Benz was using the cost basis approach to report the investment in the equity securities of Deutsche Aerospace Airbus.

C17-7. British Petroleum: Understanding non-U.S. financial statements

Requirement 1:
a) Group statements are what are called *consolidated* statements in the United States. The United Kingdom rules which govern when subsidiaries must be consolidated are more stringent than U.S. rules. In both the United States and the United Kingdom, consolidation is required when the parent

exerts **control** over the subsidiary; control is defined in the United States as more than a 50% ownership of voting stock. More than 50% ownership of voting stock indicates control under U.K. GAAP, too. But in the United Kingdom, control can exist even in situations where less than 50% of voting stock is owned. Examples include 1) where the parent has the right to appoint or remove board members entitled to exercise a majority of the voting rights, 2) where the parent owns convertible debt or options that allow it to gain control, and 3) other, more technical, conditions.

b) *Stocks* is inventories

Debtors is accounts receivable

Creditors is accounts payable and other accrued short- as well as long-term liabilities

Capital and reserves is owners' equity

Called-up share capital is common stock par or stated value

Share premium account is paid-in-capital in excess of par or stated value

Reserves is retained earnings (and, potentially, other special items like revaluation surplus)

c) *Turnover* is sales revenue

Exceptional items are material items that merit separate disclosure. They are shown pre-tax and are, thus, roughly equivalent to U.S. "above the line" special or unusual items. However, U.K. accounting differentiates between *non-operating* exceptional items (profits or losses on disposals of fixed assets or an entire operation, and reorganization costs) and all other exceptional items. Non-operating exceptional items are shown below a line labeled "operating profit." U.S.-type extraordinary items that are shown net of tax are virtually prohibited in the United Kingdom.

Investments in associated undertaking is investments where the investor exerts significant influence (defined as 20% or more ownership). These are accounted for using the equity method.

Requirement 2:

a) *Stock holding gains* are the realized inventory holding gains that were discussed in both Chapters 8 and 17. LIFO is not allowed in the United Kingdom so these gains flow through to the bottom line under historical cost inventory accounting when prices are rising.

Adding-back realized inventory holding gains to replacement cost income—as BP does—results in a traditional historical cost income number. Again, this is discussed in both Chapters 8 and 17.

Energy costs are easily observable by consumers. The costs of heating their homes or apartments as well as fueling their cars are important budget outflows. This makes oil companies politically vulnerable if consumers seek a "scapegoat" for rising energy expenditures. BP has used this disclosure format for stock holding gains for many years. One conjecture is that it hopes that informed statement readers will not confuse high historical cost profits with "price-gouging." Separating holding gains makes it easier to see its real, sustainable margin.

b) These are examples of exceptional items discussed in Requirement 1.c., above. Both would be considered "above-the-line" items in U.S. GAAP disclosure and, thus, be shown pre-tax. They are also shown pre-tax in the BP statement. However, both are considered nonoperating exceptional items and are, thus, shown below the line labeled replacement cost operating profit.

c) U.S. balance sheets list assets in descending order of liquidity, starting with cash. Many European balance sheets begin with fixed assets. The BP balance sheet format is:

Assets - Liabilities = Equity.

What "balances" is that the computed gross equity number (£12,795 at December 31, 1996) is then reconciled to the detailed equity components.

The BP balance sheet computes working capital–i.e., current assets minus current liabilities–which is £135 at December 31, 1996. This number is not highlighted and must be computed by readers of U.S. balance sheets.

d) The format differences here are numerous. In U.S. statements, interest received and paid, as well as dividends received are classified as operating cash flows. In the U.K. statement, these are in a separate section labeled "Servicing of finance and returns on investments." To some observers, the U.K. classification seems better. These items are included in the operating cash flow section in U.S. reports and many believe that:

1) interest and dividends received are really better classified as investing cash inflow, and

2) interest paid should be treated as a financing cash flow.

Since interest and dividends received do not need to be separately disclosed in U.S. reports, this alleged "misclassification" cannot be adjusted, and the U.K. approach would be preferred by some.

The BP breakdown of what is termed "Investing Cash Flows" in a U.S. statement is also slightly more detailed. Capital expenditures and asset sales are reported separately from acquisitions and dispositions of entire businesses. These are usually reported together in a single section in U.S. statements.

Most of the other differences are minor. For example, taxes paid are shown separately on the face of BP's cash flow statement while taxes paid are usually disclosed in a footnote in U.S. reports.

Requirement 3:

a) This appears to be the holding company which has legal ownership of the various operating subsidiaries and entities.

b) Since the holding company is not an operating entity, income and cash flow statement disclosures would not be particularly informative.

c) The £2,411 balance in the investments account consists primarily of the carrying amount of BP's investment in its operating subsidiaries, probably accounted for on the equity basis.

The £5,114 balance in the debtors account is comprised primarily of advances made by the holding company to the operating subsidiaries.

The equivalence of the amounts of called-up share capital and share premium account in the "parent" and "group" columns exists because the holding company owns the operating subsidiaries. Hence, the group share capital plus share premium must be identical to that of the parent.

d) Often in other (continental) European countries, separate parent data are also provided for the income statement. There is no clearly apparent economic reason for providing separate parent data unless the parent—which is a separate legal entity—has its own operating activities. However, these balance sheet disclosures are required in all cases by the European Economic Community (now called the European Union) in the Seventh Company Law Directive on consolidated accounts, which was adopted in 1983.

e) Differentiating between group and parent statements provides an opportunity for harmonization even in countries where book-tax conformity is required. Here's how. The book-tax conformity could be satisfied using the parent statements while the group accounts could use reporting rules that are different from the tax rules. Harmonization could proceed without disrupting conformity between book and tax accounting since the conformity would exist on the parent's books.